Great Britain and Ireland

John Szponarski

D1824448

Absolute Press

First published in Great Britain
in 2001 jointly by:

Absolute Press
Scarborough House
29 James Street West
Bath BA1 2BT
Phone 44 (0) 1225 316013
Fax 44 (0) 1225 445836
E-mail
info@absolutepress.demon.co.uk
Website
www.absolutepress.demon.co.uk

Gay Times Books
an imprint of Millivres Ltd
part of
Millivres Prowler Group
Worldwide House
116-134 Bayham Street
London NW1 0BA
Website
www.gaytimes.co.uk

Copyright ©
Absolute Press / Gay Times Books

A catalogue record of this book is
available from the British Library

ISBN 1 899791 58 2

Printed and bound in Italy by
Lego Print

Every effort has been made to
ensure that the facts in this book
are accurate and up-to-date.
It is still recommended that
travellers obtain advice and
information from airlines,
switchboards, etc. about
current travel and accommodation
requirements and from clubs and
venues to ensure that details have
not changed since this book
went to print. The author and
publishers cannot accept any
responsibility for inconvenience,
injury or loss resulting from the
information herein.

Contents

Gay Times	5
The author	6
Foreword	7

1

Essentials	9
Getting there	11
Getting about	11
Getting by	13
Getting settled	14
Getting help	16
Getting in touch	20
Getting out	21
Getting a taste	25
Getting news	26
Getting to know	27

2

Scene	33
You and the law	35
Sexual activity	35
Drugs	36
Pubs and clubs	37
Accommodation	38
Saunas	39
Cruising grounds	40
Using this guide	41

3

England	43
including	
Birmingham	51
Blackpool	65
Brighton and Hove	90
Liverpool	148
London	156
Manchester	258

4

Scotland	331
including	
Edinburgh	336
Glasgow	348

5

Wales	357
including	
Cardiff	360

6

Ireland	369
including	
Belfast	372
Dublin	379

Notes

Gay Times

The most trusted name in gay publishing. At last, guides for the independent holidaymaker that are thoroughly researched and regularly updated, by lesbians and gay men who know each destination as well as you know your home town. Each book will detail and demystify the local scene and explore the lifestyle, attractions and history that frame it.

Co-publishers Absolute Press are responsible for the gay biography imprint, *Outlines*, and the most groundbreaking gay guide of recent times, *The Ultimate Gay Guide*. This series will grow to include guide books to the key destinations across the world. It sets a new standard of excellence in gay travel guide publishing.

The author

John Szponarski has lived and travelled across Britain and Ireland for much of his life. In this time he has visited, stayed at and been barred from many a gay venue. He is never far from his notebook and a dry towel and this guide is the result of years of dedicated (but more to the point, pleasurable) research. Already the published author of *The Ultimate Gay Guide*, the most groundbreaking gay guide of recent times, John is now keen to put his mark upon this new series of Gay Times travel guides. And so we have this opening chapter, Great Britain and Ireland, the most rigorously researched and up-to-date gay guide available. John lives in Manchester where, to his dismay, and despite his celebrity, he still cannot land reduced door admissions or free drinks. He is a consulting editor for the Gay Times series of travel guides.

Acknowledgments
My heartfelt appreciation, as always, goes to my friend Matt Inwood at Absolute Press, who never fails to amaze me with the ease with which he is able to turn my scribbled notes and appalling grammar into something that resembles 'proper' English. Thanks also to the publisher, Jon Croft and the managing director of Millivres-Prowler Group, Simon Topham, for having faith in this project.
Finally, with gritted teeth, I thank my closest and dearest friends, in particular David, Paul and Martin, who quite often chose to go out on the piss rather than help.

Foreword

Attitudes towards gays and lesbians are changing, which can only be a good thing. Not more than a generation ago there was so much stigma about being gay that only a course of electrotherapy and a good seeing to by the right woman (or man) could ever put you on the straight and narrow. But now? Hey, it's a new century. Being gay is as accepted as the colour of your skin. The bigots still exist, but they are in the minority. Ignorance still persists, but there is much more education. Equality finally looms on the horizon. Look around and you will see that times are changing. This environment makes Britain and Ireland as refreshing a place as anywhere in the world. The variety of scenes, the different customs and cultures and the way in which these countries have embraced rather than merely tolerated their gay community makes for a unique experience. Enjoy your visit.

Essentials

1

Getting there

Routes into Great Britain and Ireland

By air from North America: direct flights to London Heathrow, London Gatwick, London Stanstead, Birmingham, Manchester, Glasgow, Dublin, Shannon and Belfast. **From Australasia**: direct on stop flights to Heathrow. Flights via places such as Singapore or Hong Kong (often with free stop overs available) can be found to most of the other large airports. **From Europe**: direct flights to major airports mentioned above, as well as a large number of regional airports including, Newcastle, Edinburgh, Bristol, Cardiff, Cork, Galway and Sligo. **By sea from Europe**: ferry connections (with cars) sailing from Belgium, Denmark, France, Germany, Netherlands, Norway, Spain and Sweden to major ports including Dover, Hull, Harwich, Portsmouth, Newcastle, Lerwick, Rosslare and Plymouth. **By rail from Europe**: direct Channel Tunnel Rail Link on the Eurostar, which runs frequently between Paris, Brussels, Lille and London. Plans for direct links to Glasgow and Manchester have so far come to nothing. Even more frequent Eurotunnel shuttles carry vehicles too.

Required paperwork

Most European nationals (except those from the former Eastern Bloc) need only a passport to enter Britain and Ireland, as do citizens from USA, Canada, Australia and New Zealand (as long as they stay no longer than six months). Visas are needed for all other nationalities.

Customs

Adults (over 17 years old) entering Britain from another EU country do not have to declare excisable goods such as alcohol, cigarettes and perfume, provided that they have already had the duty paid on them in another European country and they are for personal use. Duty-free goods are subject to the following limits: 200 cigarettes or 100 cigarillos or 50 cigars or 250 grams (8.82 ounces) tobacco; two litres of still table wine plus either one litre of spirits or strong liqueurs (over 22 per cent alcohol by volume) or 2 litres fortified wine (under 22 per cent abv), sparkling wine or other liqueurs; 60 millilitres of perfume; 250 millilitres of toilet water; other goods to the value of £145 for non-commercial use. The import of meat, meat products, fruit, plants, flowers and protected animals is restricted or forbidden.

For travellers entering Ireland the limits are similar to the British entry requirements as set out above, with the main difference being the importing of other goods for non-commercial use: in Ireland it is up to the value of £34 per person (and of this allowance you may import only 12 litres of beer).

Getting about

By air

Distances inside Britain and Ireland are comparatively modest, and the usual airport delays slow you down, making planes not much quicker overall than, say, trains. So it is only worth going by air over the longest routes or over the Irish Sea – between London, Newcastle, Edinburgh, Glasgow, the Scottish outer islands, Dublin and Belfast. There are shuttle flights between many of these destinations, with hourly departures during peak times.

By train

The British invented railways, and the rail network is still remarkable, allowing you to travel (in theory) from Penzance to Wick and from Holyhead to Dover. It was never the most efficient of services, but it worked. Since the railways were privatized in the 1990s though, standards have plummeted, with passengers soon taking delays, cancellations, muddle and appalling conditions as the norm. The different train operating companies offer a mind-numbing selection of fares, passes and railcards, but there is little consistency. All the same, train travel at its best (which can still be encountered) is supremely comfortable, swift and safe. You can get details from **National Rail Enquiries** on 08457 484950 or make online bookings at www.trainline.com for most longer journeys. In Ireland the situation is the reverse. The railway system is old-fashioned, efficient and reliable, but not very extensive (especially in the west and north). For travel information and timetables phone (01) 836 6222 or visit the website at www.cie.ie. Eurail passes can be used both here and in the UK.

By bus

'Bus' in Britain generally means a short-haul vehicle with frequent stops. These local services are comparatively cheap, if sometimes a little scruffy. In big cities such as London, the bus is often faster and more convenient than the underground, while in remoter areas it is often the only form of public transport available. Sad, then, that so many urban bus stations are filthy, run-down and unpleasant places.

By coach

Longer-haul buses are termed 'coaches'. There is a far-reaching network of coach services, with over 1,200 destinations including the Republic of Ireland. The best-known companies, **National Express** and **Bus Eireann**, offer a bargain travel pass for tourists. For National Express enquiries phone 0990 808080 or visit the site at www.gobycoach.com. For Bus Eireann enquiries phone (01) 8366111 or visit www.buseireann.ie.

By car

The roads can get staggeringly crowded, especially in big cities (average vehicle speed in gridlocked London is around three miles per hour) and on the main arterial or orbital roads such as the M1 and M25. So don't bother to drive in London or between major centres – the parking restrictions alone could ruin your holiday. Car travel does give you independence though, and allows you to reach remote places fairly quickly. Renting a car in the UK or Ireland is expensive, as is fuel.

By taxi

There are two main types of taxi service in the UK – black cabs and minicabs. You can hail London's famous **black cabs** in the street, and find others at railway stations, airports or designated taxi ranks. They're also used in most other major UK cities and despite being known as 'black' they confusingly come in all colours of the rainbow! Make sure the car is properly marked to show that the driver is licensed and council-regulated. Black cabs are expensive, so if you are taking anything other than short journeys negotiate a fare beforehand. Drivers expect tips of around 10 per cent. **Minicabs (or private hire cabs)** must be booked in advance, which is normally done over the phone. They will generally be cheaper than a black cab. Most minicabs will only seat four (whereas you can get five in a black cab) although large minibuses are sometimes available. The phone numbers of minicab firms can often be found by payphones in pubs and clubs. Never take an unbooked ride in a minicab, however, as the driver may not be insured. There are currently plans to overhaul the system of pre-booking minicabs, due to the number of 'rogue drivers' trawling the major cities purporting to be minicab drivers.

On foot

This is a serious form of travel for the tourist in big cities – especially London. Distances within the capital are much shorter than people (and the Underground map) would have you believe. Paddington Station, for example, is less than 30 minutes' stroll from Oxford Street.

By bicycle

At last, cyclists are being taken seriously. A national network of cycle paths was opened by the British organization SusTrans (Sustainable Transport Systems) in 2001, and it is hoped that the overall length will be doubled within a few years to 20,000 miles. The bicycle is still the fastest option in London – though a dangerous one – and can be a very pleasant and cheap way of touring country lanes and National Parks. Bikes can be rented in most towns and cities (visit www.sustrans.org.uk for further information).

Getting by

Costs

Britain and Ireland are among the most expensive places in the world. About £30 per day is the bare minimum for eating, accommodation and travel by public transport. If you stay at hotels, rent a car and eat at restaurants, this figure can be swiftly doubled. Obviously, outside London and other major cities things are slightly easier.

Currency

The UK has retained its pound sterling (£), a decimal currency that is made up of 100 pence (p). There are notes for £5, £10, £20 and £50, and coins for 1p, 2p, 5p, 10p, 50p, £1 and £2. While Britain has kept resolutely out of the European Monetary System with its euro coinage, Ireland has been happy to join. As a result the Irish pound or 'punt' (IR£) now has a slightly different value, fluctuating with exchange rates. Towards the end of 2001 the punt will be completely phased out to be replaced with the Euro.

Banks and bureaux de change

The best course is to exchange your money before you leave home. If your forget, avoid if possible the exchange kiosks at airports, which often give poor deals. Banks are a better bet – most are open Monday to Friday from 0930 to 1630, and some high street branches operate on Saturday mornings as well.

Credit cards and traveller's cheques

The major credit cards are accepted in most places except the smaller or more remote establishments, and are safer than carrying cash. It is also advisable to take a certain proportion of your money in travellers' cheques, which can be cashed at almost any bank.

VAT

When leaving the UK or Irish Republic non EEC visitors get a refund of the value added tax (VAT). The VAT rate in Great Britain is set at 17.5 per cent and is added on to most purchases, including hotel and restuarant bills. Refunds are available at shops partaking in the Retail Export Scheme. To receive back the tax, ask for the paperwork from the particpating retailer who must fill out the form on the spot. Present this form, along with the goods purchased, to the customs officers at the airport or ferry terminal. Some stores charge a fee for processing your refund. In the Irish Republic, VAT currently accounts for a hefty 21 per cent of the purchase price of many goods and 12.5 per cent of those that fall outside the luxury category. Apart from clothing, most items of interest to visitors, right down to ordinary toilet soap, are rated at 21 per cent. Most crafts outlets and department stores operate a system called Cashback, which enables US and Canadian visitors to collect VAT rebates in the currency of their choice at Dublin Airport on departure. Otherwise, refunds can be claimed from individual stores after returning home. As with Britain, forms for the refunds must be picked up at the time of purchase, and be stamped by customs before leaving Ireland. Most major stores deduct VAT at the time of sale if goods are to be shipped overseas; however, there is a shipping charge.

Getting settled

Accommodation

Standards of accommodation vary greatly throughout the UK, from the fabulous to the downright grotty, and, of course, every conceivable type in between. Fortunately, the majority of gay and gay-friendly accommodation is above average. There are some though that would benefit from an extensive course in basic hotel management. Generally, you get what you pay for. **Tourist information centres** should be able to suppy you with a list of places to stay in the area. Some will be able to organise bookings and reservations for you, usually for a fee. It is always best to book well in advance of your visit, especially during the high season. If you don't then larger towns and cities should still have available accommodation to offer. Prices can vary greatly, depending on the type of accommodation, its location, facilities and the duration of your stay. It can be worth your while haggling for extra facilities or cheaper prices.

Differences

The variety of accommodation on offer is staggering. At the top end of the scale stands the incomparable country house hotel. Usually set in rolling acres of parkland, boasting resplendent architecture, and replete with vast log fires, four-poster beds and billiard rooms, they are a visitor's dream of the grand rural style. At the cheaper end there are camping sites (of which there are thousands) and youth hostels, which are often not as basic as you might expect. In between these two extremes there is a bewildering array of options – romantic farmhouses; traditional bed and breakfasts; lively pubs and, of course, the modern chain hotels where you know exactly what to expect, from the identical rooms to the muzak in the lifts. (For information on British and Irish camping and caravanning sites visit **www.handbooks.co.uk**. For information on youth hostels visit **www.yha.co.uk** for both England and Wales; **www.syha.org.uk** for Scotland; and **www.iol.ie/~discover/hostel.htm** for Ireland.)

Much of the gay and gay-friendly accommodation listed herein is of the **bed and breakfast** or **guest-house** variety. This category covers an enormous range, from the simple and sometimes severe seaside lodgings to the larger sub-hotels with en-suite bathrooms and bars. The 'bed and breakfast' (or B & B) is a great institution in Britain and Ireland, and if you strike lucky you will have a warm welcome and cosy accommodation – all at a reasonable tariff. The more archaic of these still list hot and cold water, metered electricity and colour TVs as bonuses! They are in the minority and these are pretty much standard throughout British accommodation. If you are 'walking in off the street' it is acceptable procedure to view the room before booking. Most hotels should not object to this either.

Farmhouse accommodation is a sub genre of the good old B & B culture, one that has grown in popularity both with tourists who love to sample rural life and with the farmers who are glad of the extra income. Most farmhouses, however, tend to be in villages or off the beaten track so a car is essential to reach them.

An increasing number of **pubs** and **inns** now welcome overnight guests and some provide a service that is comparable to a three-star hotel. Note the word 'some' – they are the exception!

For those who aim to stay in one place for more than few days there is a wide selection of **rooms, flats, houses, cottages** and even **caravans** that can be rented by the week or even month. These self-catering places give you freedom and independence and usually work out far cheaper than standard forms of accommodation – usually, but not always. Remember to calculate any additional costs before settling on this kind of accommodation. There are also **holiday cottages** available, in wonderful locations – notably those belonging to the **National Trust** or the **Landmark Trust**.

Tips   Be prepared. Get a list of your requirements together and interrogate the receptionist or proprietor and get them to assure you that they can offer exactly what you require. Smokers should check that their habit will be catered for when they arrive. Some, especially private-owned guesthouses are non-smoking establishments. Find out if breakfast is included: if you have difficulty getting out of bed much before midday this will not benefit you – therefore, ask for a discount that rules out breakfast.

Enquire about check-in and check-out times – if check-out is early ask if you can leave you luggage in the hotel until you are ready to leave. Is the accommodation licensed (many are not)? Are you able to get ice and glasses for the vodka you have successfully smuggled in? Find out. You'll probably be surprised at the flexibility of most places.

Probably the most important information you can glean prior to booking is the establishment's cancellation policy. Usually three days notice should entitle you to a full refund of all deposits paid. There are, however, some establishments that require longer notice and only if they are successful in re-letting your room will you get your money back. Establish your rights before you confirm anything. Once you have made your booking you will be required to pay your deposit. This is usually for the amount of the first night's stay or it could be as much as 50 per cent of the total expected bill. Paying this by credit card is prudent – you will have more chance of promptly getting your money back should you need to cancel.

If you are looking to experience the gay scene when you visit then ask about its proximity to your chosen accommodation (paying more for accommodation in the area of your choice may be wiser than opting for cheaper accommodation out of town, and having the expense and trauma of travelling). Obviously, distances to sightseeing and transport stations should also have a bearing on your choice. Ask for information on transport services, including numbers for reputable private taxi firms.

Finally, always ask for the cheapest rate available. This applies particularly to the larger group hotels, many which work on the principle that all available rooms should be let even, if it means cutting their room rate to the bare minimum. Many large hotels are not able to offer reduced rates on the day of stay and only the published rack rate (room-only rate) can be charged. Pre-booking a day in advance though, through a central reservation office or the reservations office at the hotel, can save you masses. Be hard, be ruthless but, overall – be extremely polite whilst pleading a little poverty.

Getting help

Medical services

Britain and Ireland are – contrary to headlines – very healthy countries, with excellent health services, clean water and dependable hygiene standards. EU citizens get most medical treatment free, as do nationals and residents of many other countries with reciprocal health care agreements. Others have to pay (except, of course, for emergency care) – so be sure to check your exact entitlement and ensure that you have sufficient insurance before you leave home. No vaccinations or other kinds of immunisation are needed. It is a good idea to get health insurance cover before you come, or check to see that your existing health insurance covers you whilst on holiday. Also advisable are policies that cover lost baggage or the canceling of travel arrangements.

Police

Fortunately, British police officers (by and large) really do live up to their reputation of being reliable and helpful – all without the use of firearms. You are able to approach them for any information on law and order. If a member of the public makes a complaint to the police they are duty-bound to investigate further. They are also veritable tourist information centres.

Disabled access

Facilities for the disabled feature on the reform agendas of many local councils and establishments across Britain and Ireland. Things are improving, across a wide range of services, and disabled visitors can now benefit from improvements to transport and all manner of public buildings from museums to night clubs. Gay pubs and clubs are part of this growing trend. Legislation coming into place in 2004, as part of the 1995 Disability Discrimination Act, aims to enforce that the majority of public access buildings are disabled-friendly by that time.

For disabled visitors to London, an essential bit of kit to lay your hands on is the book Access in London (Quiller Press, £7.99) or, alternatively, the **London Tourist Board** (020 7932 2000) pamphlet, London For All. For information on arts venues throughout Britain with disabled facilities phone **Local Resource Arts Line** (0207 388 2227). **Central Holiday Care Service** (01293 734 535) can offer advice on holiday bookings and suitably equipped hotels. **RADAR** is the Royal Association for Disability and Rehabilitation (0207 250 3222) and they can offer you advice and information relating to most disabled matters.

Embassies and consulates

Make sure that you have the address and telephone number of your own national embassy or consulate handy. You should only need it in the case of an extreme emergency. The following is a list of embassies located in London and Dublin. For regional embassies, contact the tourist information centre of the town into which you are arriving to find you nearest representative.

(London)

Afghanistan 31 Princes Gate SW7 1QQ (020 7589 8891)

Albania 59 Eccleston Square SW1 (020 7976 5295)

Algeria 54 Holland Park W11 (020 7221 7800)

Angola 98 Park Lane W1 (020 7495 1752)

Argentina 53 Hans Place SW1 (020 7584 6494)

Australia Australia House, Strand WC2 (020 7379 4334)

Austria 18 Belgrave Mews West SW1X 8HU (020 7235 3731)

Bahrain 98 Gloucester Road SW7 4AU (020 7370 5132)

Belgium 103 Eaton Square SW1 (020 7235 5422)

Bolivia 106 Eaton Square SW1 (020 7235 4255)

Brazil 32 Green Street W1 (020 7499 0877)

Bulgaria 186 Queen's Gate SW7 (020 7584 9400)

Burma 19a Charles Street W1 (020 7499 8841)

Cameroon 84 Holland Park W11 3SB (020 7727 0771)

Canada 38 Grosvenor Street W1 (020 7258 6356)

Chile 12 Devonshire Street W1N 2DS (020 7580 1023)

China 49-51 Portland Place W1 (020 7636 8845)

Colombia Flat 3a, 3 Hans Crescent SW1X 0LR (020 7589 9177)

Costa Rica 36 Upper Brook Street W1 (020 7495 3985)

Cote d'Ivoire 2 Upper Belgrave Street SW1 (020 7235 6991)

Cuba 167 High Holborn WC1 (020 7240 2488)

Czech Republic 26 Kensington Palace Gardens W8 (020 7243 1115)

Denmark 55 Sloane Street SW1X 9SR (020 7333 0200)

Ecuador Flat 3b, 3 Hans Crescent SW1X 0LN (020 7584 1367)

Egypt 26 South Street W1 (020 7499 2401)

Estonia 16 Hyde Park Gate SW7 (020 7589 3428)

Ethiopia 17 Prince's Gate SW7 (020 7589 7212)

Fiji 34 Hyde Park Gate SW7 (020 7584 3661)

Finland 38 Chesham Place SW1 (020 7235 9531)

France 58 Knightsbridge SW1X 7JT (020 7235 8080)

Gabon 27 Elvaston Place SW7 (020 7823 9986)

Germany 21-23 Belgrave Square SW1 (020 7235 5033)

Greece 1a Holland Park W11 (020 7229 3850)

Guatemala 13 Fawcett Street SW10 (020 7351 3042)

Honduras 115 Gloucester Place W1 (020 7486 4880)

Hungary 35 Eaton Place SW1 (020 7235 2664)

Iceland 1 Eaton Terrace SW1W 8E (020 7730 5131)

India India House, Aldwych WC2 (020 7836 8484)

Indonesia 38 Grosvenor Square W1 (020 7499 7661)

Iran 27 Princes Gate SW7 (020 7584 8101)

Ireland 17 Grosvenor Place SW1X 7HR (020 7235 2171)

Israel 2 Palace Green W8 (020 7957 9500)

Italy 38 Eaton Place SW1 (020 7235 9371)

Japan 101 Piccadilly W1 (020 7465 6500)

Jordan 6 Upper Phillimore Gardens (020 7937 3685)

Kazakhstan 5 Kensington Palace Gardens W8 (020 7229 8027)

Kenya 45 Portland Place W1 (020 7636 2371)

Korea (South) 4 Palace Gate W8 5NF (020 7581 3330)

Kuwait 46 Queen's Gate SW7 (020 7589 4533)

Latvia 45 Nottingham Place W1 (020 7312 0040)

Lebanon 21 Kensington Palace Gardens W8 (020 7229 7265)

Liberia 2 Pembridge Gate W2 (020 7221 1036)

Lithuania 17 Essex Villas W8 (020 7938 2481)

Luxembourg 27 Wilton Crescent SW1X 8S (020 7235 6961)

Mexico 8 Halkin Street SW1 (020 7235 6393)

Monaco 4 Cromwell Place SW7 (020 7225 2679)

Mongolia 7 Kensington Court W8 (020 7937 0150)

Morocco 97-99 Praed Street W2 (020 7724 0719)

Mozambique 21 Fitzroy Square W1 (020 7383 3800)

Nepal 12a Kensington Palace Gardens W8 (020 7229 1594)

Netherlands 38 Hyde Park Gate SW7 5DP (020 7584 5040)

Nicaragua 8 Gloucester Road SW7 4PP (020 7584 4365)

Norway 25 Belgrave Square SW1 (020 7235 7151)

Oman 44a Montpelier Square SW7 (020 7225 0001)

Pakistan 35 Lowndes Square SW1X 9JN (020 7235 2044)

Panama 48 Park Street W1 (020 7493 4646)

Paraguay Braemar Lodge Cornwall Gardens SW7 (020 7937 6629

Peru 52 Sloane Street SW1 (020 7235 6867)

Philippines 9a Palace Green W8 (020 7937 1600)

Poland 73 New Cavendish Street W1 (020 7580 0476)

Portugal Silver City House 62 Brompton Road SW3 (020 7581 8722)

Qatar 1 South Audley Street W1 (020 7493 2200)

Romania 4 Palace Green, Kensington W8 (020 7937 9667)

Russia 5 Kensington Palace Gardens W8 (020 7229 8027)

El Salvador 5 Great James Street WC1 (020 7430 2141)

Saudi Arabia 32 Charles Street W1 (020 7917 3000)

Senegal 11 Phillimore Gardens W8 (020 7937 0925)

Slovenia Cavendish Court, 11-15 Wigmore Street W1 (020 7495 7775)

South Africa Trafalgar Square WC2N 5DP (020 7930 4488)

Spain 24 Belgrave Square SW1 (020 7235 5555)

Sudan 3 Cleveland Row, St James's W1 (020 7839 8080)

Sweden 11 Montagu Place W1H 2AL (020 7917 6413)

Switzerland 16-18 Montagu Place W1H 2BQ (020 7723 0701)

Syria 8 Belgrave Square SW1 (020 7245 9012)

Tajikstan 5 Kensington Palace Gardens W8 (020 7229 8027)

Thailand 29-30 Queen's Gate SW7 5JB (020 7589 0173)

Tunisia 29 Princes Gate SW7 (020 7584 8117)

Turkey 43 Belgrave Square SW1X 8PA (020 7235 5252)

Ukraine Kensington Park Road W11 (020 7727 6312)

United Arab Emirates 48 Prince's Gate SW7 (020 7589 3434)

United States 24-32 Grosvenor Square W1A 2LH (020 7499 9000)

Uruguay 140 Brompton Road SW3 (020 7584 8192)

Venezuela 1 Cromwell Road SW7 5JB (020 7584 4206)

Vietnam 12-14 Victoria Road W8 (020 7937 1912)

Yemen 57 Cromwell Road SW7 2ED (020 7584 6607)

Zaire 26 Chesham Place SW1X 8HG (020 72356137)

(Dublin)	**America** 42 Elgin Road D4 (01 668 8777)
	Australia 15 Ailesbury Court, 93 Ailesbury Road D2 (01 269 4577)
	Belgium Shrewsbury Road D4 (01 269 2082)
	Britain 29 Merrion Road D2 (01 269 5211)
	Canada 65 St Stephens Green D2 (01 478 1988)
	Denmark 121 St Stephens Green D2 (01 475 6404)
	France 36 Ailesbury Road D4 (01 269 4777)
	Germany 31 Trimleston Avenue, Booterstown (01 269 3011)
	Israel Carrisbrook House, 122 Pembroke Road D4 (01 668 0303)
	Italy 63 Northumberland Road D4 (01 660 1744)
	Japan 22 Ailesbury Road D4 (01 269 4244)
	Netherlands 160 Merrion Road D4 (01 269 3444)
	Norway 69 St Stephens Green D2 (01 478 3133)
	Portugal Knocksinna House, Knocksinna, Foxrock D18 (01 289 4416)
	Spain 17a Merlyn Park D4 (01 269 1640)
	Sweden Sun Alliance House, Dawson Street D2 (01 671 11640)
	Switzerland Ailesbury Road D4 (01 269 2515)

Getting in touch

Using the phone

Telephones in Britain and Ireland are relatively cheap and extremely efficient. There are public telephones in most pubs and hotels, scattered through towns and in some surprisingly remote places – though the rise of the mobile has brought threats of a run-down of this service. Most machines accept coins and credit cards. You can also purchase phone cards, with various amounts of credit (and from various suppliers), which you can use at boxes and kiosks marked with the phonecard sign. You can purchase phonecards at post offices, newsagents and most major supermarket chains.

Important numbers

Emergency Britain: 999 and Ireland: 999 or 112
Operators (local) Britain: 100 and Ireland: 10
Operators (international) 155 for Britain / 144 for Ireland
Directory enquiries Britain: 192 and Ireland: 1190
Country code Britain 44 Ireland 353
International access codes Britain and Ireland: 00

So, to dial the USA from either country you need to dial 001, followed by the number minus the initial zero. Likewise for Australia, the code would be 0061. It should be noted that all numbers in this book are given as the national numbers. Phoning a Dublin number from London is an international call so you would need to dial 00353 first, followed by the number (minus the initial zero). The only exception to this is that Northern Ireland can be reached from Southern Ireland by using 08 instead of 0044.

Postal services The British invented the modern postal service, so you'd expect an efficient system. Towns have main and sub-post offices, and many villages (though, sadly, a decreasing number) have combined shops and post offices. These offer a number of functions, notably receiving letters and parcels for dispatch, and keeping poste restante mail. Stamps can also be purchased in many shops, and mail can be posted in the characteristic red boxes, or green boxes if you are in the Republic of Ireland.

Internet Although they are not yet numerous, it is becoming increasingly easy to find internet cafés in most large towns. There is a selection of regional cafés listed in this book, which is by no means exhaustive. The larger hotels and public libraries also offer internet services.

Getting out

There are many festivals and events that you can either spectate at or take part in throughout the year. Some of the outdoor events are held to ransom by the changeable weather. Whilst the following list is by no means exhaustive it does feature many of the internationally renowned annual events. Many cities throughout the UK now host their own Pride event. They help to boost funds for the local gay community and highlight the gay scene. Opposition from the local council and residents is par for the course and cancellations and restrictions do happen. London and Manchester are the best-established. Both attract attendances reaching well over the million mark. Manchester Gayfest is the largest of these events, running the entire length of the August Bank Holiday weekend and 2002 plans are underway to combine the event with the Commonwealth Games, running the events concurrently turning Gayfest into 21 fun-filled days. The dates given for these Pride events are at the mercy of much council red tape and all are subject to change.

Annual events and festivals

January 1 Hogmanay: the Scottish New Year festivities
25 Burns Night : celebration of the Scots' greatest poet
London International Boat Show at Earl's Court, London
February Chinese New Year: main celebration in Soho, London
Jorvik Festival, York: Viking jamboree
March Grand National: great steeplechase event at Aintree, Liverpool
Crufts Dog Show, NEC Birmingham
(17) St Patrick's Day (Ireland's patron saint)
Oxford & Cambridge Boat Race on River Thames, London
April Irish Grand National, Fairyhouse, Meath
London Marathon: from Greenwich to Buckingham Palace
(23) St George's Day (English patron saint)
(23) Shakespeare's birthday (theatre season begins at Stratford)
World Irish Dance Championships

May Chelsea Flower Show, London

Bath International Music Festival

FA Cup Final: the high point of the English football season

International Highland Games, Blair Atholl, Scotland

June Derby Week: horse-racing festival at Epsom, Surrey

Trooping the Colour: Queen's birthday parade, Whitehall, London

All England Lawn Tennis Championships, Wimbledon

Beaumaris Festival, Wales

Glasgow International Jazz Festival

Royal Highland Show, Edinburgh, Scotland

Grosvenor House Art and Antique Fair, London

July Royal Welsh Show, Builth Wells

Galway Arts Festival, Ireland

Cowes Week: grand yachting gathering , Isle of Wight

Cambridge Folk Festival

August Fleadh Cheoil Nah Eireann: big but informal Irish music festival

The Proms (mostly Albert Hall, London)

Royal National Eisteddfod: traditional Welsh arts gathering, Llangollen

Edinburgh International Festival

Brecon Jazz Festival, Wales

Notting Hill Carnival: Caribbean carnival, London

Beatles Festival, Liverpool

September Blackpool Illuminations: Five miles of stunning lights

Royal Highland Gathering: Braemar, Scotland

International Festival of Light Opera, Waterford, Ireland

October Dublin Theatre Festival, Ireland

Britten Festival, Aldeburgh, Suffolk

Cheltenham Literature Festival, Gloucestershire

Wexford Opera Festival, Ireland

November 5 Guy Fawkes Night, England: bonfires ands fireworks

London Film Festival

Belfast International Festival

Lord Mayor's Procession and Show, London

December Christmas Tree Lights, Trafalgar Square, London

Regional Pride events

May Birmingham Gay Pride

June Dublin Gay Pride

Glasgow Gay pride (Glasgay)

London Gay Pride (Mardi-Gras)

July Blackpool Gay Pride

Portsmouth Gay Pride

Newcastle Gay pride

Leicester Gay Pride
Leeds Gay Pride
Nottingham Gay pride
August Belfast Gay Pride
Peterborough Gay Pride
Bournemouth Gay Pride
Brighton Gay Pride
Manchester Gay Pride (Gayfest)
Bristol Gay Pride
September Cardiff Gay Pride

Entertainment

You will never be short of things to do in Britain and Ireland. The diversity of culture and entertainment is as rich as anywhere else in the world. Indeed, it's a comletely separate guidebook. Each major city (London, Birmingham, Manchester, Glasgow, Edinburgh, etc.) have individual What's On-style magazines, available from all newsagents with detailed listings of exhibitions, arts programmes, museums, theatres and cinemas. An essential bit of kit for visitors to London is a copy of the well-established Time Out magazine, which is the most extensive guide there is to the hundreds of different events happening in the city each night. Many of the broadsheet newspapers also offer extensive listings of entertainments across the country, particularly the weekend papers, some of which come with specific 'what's on' supplements.

Museums and art galleries throughout the UK usually offer free admission and the majority are exceptionally good. You can expect to pay at some of the smaller specialist galleries that are more often than not privately owned. Many of these are well worth a visit, assuming the subject matter interests you, and the admission is nominal providing essential funds to upkeep the project.

Shopping

The giant department store of Harrods in London always used to boast that it could obtain anything you wanted from anywhere in the world. These days there are plenty of other emporia which could claim the same. London, Edinburgh and Dublin are home to a host of shops (Debenhams, John Lewis, Selfridges et al), offering everything from the most glamorous fashion labels to an astonishing range of everyday household items. There are monster bookshops and record stores, as well as excellent specialist foodshops. Many of these can be found in the bigger towns as well, as, of course, can the ever-present supermarkets, which are often sited on the outskirts with plentiful parking.

Britain (and England especially) is also a splendid hunting ground for antiques and second-hand curios. The large cities have their auction rooms and open-air markets, while smaller towns – in quainter areas such as the Cotswolds – are rarely without their antiquarian bookseller. Craft shops are also booming, specialising in local products. In Ireland, look out for lace in County Kerry, linen in County Donegal and glass in

Waterford. In the Scottish Highlands you will find splendid tweed, shortbread and knitwear. Wales is famous for its pottery and wooden carvings.

Climate

Nowhere in Britain or Ireland is very far from the sea. The great mass of water (warmed by the Gulf Stream) rules the climate, making temperatures moderate and slow to alter, and making the atmosphere generally moist. This combination of mildness and dampness somehow symbolizes the British character, but it produces weather which is by and large gentle, with few dramatic swings.

The shifts from summer to winter and back again are almost imperceptible, and extreme conditions are rare. In England, Wales, most of Scotland and Ireland the thermometer seldom falls much below freezing point – or rises much above 30C. Mountainous areas, however, such as the Cairngorms in Scotland, can become impenetrable with heavy snow in the depths of winter. Rainfall is highest on the western coasts, especially of Ireland and the Scottish Highlands, while the east coasts are drier but cooler.

When is the best time to visit? Midsummer (July and August) are generally hottest and driest, but the most busy and expensive (that is when Britons go on holiday). Much better is late spring, the fields are at their lushest and early flowers and blossom are out. Go to the Scottish Highlands in spring and you will avoid the infuriating attentions of the midge population. Autumn (fall) is also a magical period in almost any region, especially one with deciduous woodlands to gawp at.

Public holidays

January 1 New Year's Day 2 (Scotland only)

March 17 St Patrick's Day (Irish Republic only)

March/April Good Friday

Easter Monday

May (first Monday) May Day (UK only)

(last Monday) Late Spring Holiday (UK only)

June (first Monday) June Holiday (Irish Republic only)

July 12 (Northern Ireland only)

August (first Monday) August Holiday (Scotland / Irish Republic only)

(last Monday) Bank Holiday (UK only)

October (last Monday) October Holiday (Irish Republic only)

December 25 Christmas Day

26 Boxing Day / St Stephen's Day

Opening hours

Offices usually open Monday to Friday from 0900 until 1700. Shops often open until 1730 with many open on Saturdays, and an increasing number (especially supermarkets and high street shops) open on Sundays too. In small towns, shops may have one early closing day (usually Wednesday). Banks usually open Monday to Friday from 0930 to

1630 (some in larger towns open on Saturday mornings also) – except, of course, on bank holidays. Museums' opening times vary considerably: major museums and galleries are open every day of the week, while minor ones have very limited hours.

Getting a taste

Food

British food is seen to be emerging from the Dark Ages. A Michelin star is no longer a mind-boggling rarity, and the finest of British and Irish restaurants can bear comparison with anything mainland Europe has to offer. There is, too, the burgeoning pride in 'gastro-pubs' – traditional hostelries offering exciting and high-quality meals. But the rise of these wonderful institutions should not mask the fact that a large proportion of everyday food is depressingly dire. The divide between good and bad has actually widened, and at the (very broad) bottom are the tacky fast-food outlets, the abysmal theme pubs and the kebab vans which infest every town. Many ordinary Britons still view food as a boring necessity, and spend on average less than 20 per cent of their income on it (in France and Italy, it's nearly 35 per cent).

Let's look on the bright side, however. Today you are far more likely to find a decent meal in a pub or restaurant than was the case 20 years ago. There are pretty good sandwiches available just about everywhere, from the local Marks and Spencer's to the buffet on the intercity train. Most towns now boast their own delicatessen or health-food shop, and the standard and range of fruit and vegetables have vastly improved. Chain-owned coffee shops and bars (usually designed on American or continental lines, with appropriate menus) offer excellent quality and reasonably priced meals and beverages, as do many of the ethnic establishments – from the longstanding Indian, Chinese and Italian ones to the more recent Mexican, Thai and North African.

Traditional British and Irish fare has undergone a pleasing revival. To the unfailing regional standards of fish and chips, Cornish pasties, roast beef, Yorkshire pudding, Irish stew, haggis, cloutie dumpling and laver bread have been added (or restored) an imaginative range of old and adapted dishes. They make use of local produce, including the wonderful and growing range of local cheeses.

Drink

And then there are the pubs. Beer is one of the glories of both Britain and Ireland, and a far cry from the insipid fizz produced in Australia and the USA for example. Naturally foaming and best served at room temperature, it is a magnificent drink, and can be found in many varieties brewed by companies giant and tiny, up and down the land. Alas, so can the chemically dead, artificially bubbly stuff which pulls in the brewers' real profits. This will be dispensed from little taps on the bar: look out for the longer handpumps which denote a 'real' beer. Ireland's tipple is stout, a much darker and richer brew. The conventionally accepted king of these is Guinness, which can be found on tap virtually everywhere. There is a carefully-cultivated aura of mystery about this product, which insists that it tastes best in Ireland. In fact, this is marketing hype. Draught Guinness tastes much the same anywhere, and is generally a grave disappointment, being served far too cold and fizzy, and lacking in magic. It's far better from the bottle (not chilled), or – if you're very lucky – from the few remaining handpumps in the Republic. Whisky (spelled 'whiskey' in Ireland) is one of Britain's imperishable gifts to the world. Scotland is recognized as the spirit's true home, and no visit there is complete without a tour round at least one of the traditional single-malt distilleries, complete with their copper pot stills (the main centres are Speyside and the island of Islay). Irish whiskey is a subtly different drink – smoother and lighter, but no less satisfying.

Getting news

Newspapers

The national daily newspapers form an important part of British and Irish life. At the top end are the worthy broadsheets, such as The Times, the Irish Times, the Scotsman, the Guardian and the Daily Telegraph, while at the bottom are the tabloids (Sun, Mirror, Star), which have few words and plenty of gossip and pictures. In between, come the middle-brow papers, notably the Mail and the Express. Some are stridently right-wing in tone, and most waver between Conservative and Labour. Only two – the Guardian and the Independent – lean consistently to the liberal left of centre. A handful of newsagents will stock foreign papers, particularly in the tourist centres of major towns and cities.

Magazines

Newsagents' shelves groan beneath the weight of magazines, covering every conceivable hobby or interest from needlepoint to satire (Private Eye stands almost alone here) and from computers to pornography. Many agents stock international titles and some stock foreign titles too.

Gay press

Both Britain and Ireland are well served by literature aimed specifically at gays and lesbians. First and foremost there is Gay Times and its sister publication Diva (lesbian monthly), which are published monthly and are widely available through the majority of newsagents. There are also other glossy monthlies, such as Attitude, Axiom, Dublin Life (good gay section), Scotsgay (bi-monthly) and Fluid. The American gay magazine Advocate can be picked up from many newsagents too. The free magazine and paper market changes rapidly. These are distributed mainly through pubs and clubs and the availability of titles depends on the region you are in. The main nationals are currently Boyz, Pink Paper, NOW, and the humorous and irreverent DNA (all UK); Scene Out (Scotland); and Gay Community News (Ireland). The main regionals are QX (London), G-Scene (Brighton), Zone (West Midlands), G-News (UK, fortnightly) and Out (Manchester).

Television

There are two state-run channels operated by the BBC (Ireland's state service is RTE), plus three independent channels – ITV, Channel 4 and Channel 5. These, however, are just the traditional end of the market, with the older ones providing remarkably high-quality reportage, features and entertainment. Since the 1980s, however, they have come under increasing pressure from the monstrous cable and satellite-beamed networks, SkyTV and their ilk. Suddenly, there is a massive choice of programmes – though the vast majority of it is garbage. BBC, ITV, Channel 4, and many other channels besides, are now offering their own digital spin-off channels which offer services dedicated to news, film, sports and classic repeats.

Britain, at least, is fairly liberal when it comes to gay-specific television, and, to a lesser extent, lesbian-specific. The BBC has tried a number of magazine program formats aimed specifically at the gay market – the latest incarnation being 'That Gay Show' on its digital channel BBC Choice (which, it must be said, is an improvement on the rest). Channel 4 commissioned the original Queer as Folk, which has been a worldwide hit, and has recently been re-made (and toned down) for the American market. Much of the programming, not least the soap operas, have regular gay characters and there are notable gay entertainers fronting chat shows and entertainment programmes – Graham Norton, Michael Barrymore and Dale Winton among Britain and Ireland's best-known, the latter hosting Britain's weekly National Lottery programme for the last couple of years.

Radio

The BBC also runs five national radio stations, from pop-pushing Radio One through classical music on Radio Three to sports fodder on Radio Five, where standards are still remarkably high. The challenge here comes from the burgeoning commercial radio sector, and, less so, from the proliferation of local radio stations.

Getting to know

People

A Conservative politician leapt to unsavoury fame in 2001 by voicing the fear that the British were becoming 'a mongrel race'. This would be the dreadful result, he said, of multi-culturalism. His remarks showed astounding ignorance of both the present and the past (not to mention dogs). The fact is that the people of the British Isles are already mongrels – a bewildering mixture of races and tribes and creeds and customs.

It would be impossible for anyone to claim descent from a completely pure line of anything. How could they, in a land where the original inhabitants of England live in Wales and Scotland, having driven the natives of those places off to Ireland? Or where neolithic farmers gave way to Celts, who in turn gave way to Romans, Angles, Saxons, Danes and Normans, to say nothing of 20th-century settlers from the Caribbean and the Indian subcontinent?

All the same, strong hints of the old national stereotypes can be found in most regions. You will still encounter the garrulous and charming Dubliner, the cockney geezer, the gruff Yorkshireman, the rubicund

Somerset countryman and the dour Highland Scot. You will certainly be struck by the polite, sometimes constipated, reserve of the middle class English person, and by the stifling grip of the class divide.

There are definite signs, however, that things are loosening up. Slowly, Britons have taken on board the more relaxed attitudes fostered in the 1960s. They dress more daringly, they eat more adventurously and they even allow their emotions to spill out in public more readily. The most recent proof of this was at the tragic death of the Princess of Wales. In 1997, an hysterical outburst of national grief which took everyone by surprise.

At bottom, the British and Irish are proud of being different. They cherish their separation from continental Europe, and the fact that they have not been invaded for 900 years. This confident pride has helped them to develop a sense of individuality and apartness. No nations in the world are so sceptical of their leaders and institutions, and yet so reluctant to change them. None are so solemn in appearance and yet so blessed with a sense of humour and appreciation of the absurd.

Regional differences

The UK and Ireland contain a bewitching variety of landscapes within a pretty small package – everything from bleak moorlands and forbidding mountain ranges to lush meadows and rolling downs. But the overriding influence is the fact that they are islands. The sea is never more than 100 miles away from anywhere, and thus the coastlines are enormously long, with a bewildering range of bays, estuaries and inlets.

The most crowded and built-up part of England is centred on London. It is also the flattest. To the south lie the lush fields of Kent and Sussex, while to the north-east are the barely rippling vistas of East Anglia and the featureless fens. Central England is also a flat region – though Northamptonshire and Lincolnshire contain some of the most gently lovely (and neglected) scenery in the land.

England

As you get further from London, the landscape grows wilder. Westward are the bare and dramatic expanses of Salisbury Plain, Dartmoor and Exmoor. Go northward, through the fertile and picturesque 'heart' of the Cotswolds and Warwickshire, and you reach Derbyshire's Peak District, the Yorkshire Dales and moors, and the rugged hills of Northumbria. This is wonderful walking country, outshone only by the Lake District, one of the most beautiful places in the world (and the setting for England's highest point, Scafell Pike, which is a modest 978 metres above sea level).

Wales

Wales is generally thought of as a land of mountains, and certainly the Snowdonia National Park in the north contains some celebrated peaks including the great Snowdon itself (1,085 metres high). The less taxing, but no less enchanting, Brecon Beacons in the south form another National Park. However, Wales has many other marvels to offer which include moorland, intimate little valleys, fast-flowing rivers and dramatic waterfalls. Its chief glory is its coastline, from the vast and lonely beaches of the south-west to the spectacular sea cliffs of Holy Island in the north.

Scotland

Scotland splits fairly naturally into two parts – the Lowlands, and the Highlands and Islands. The latter make up the wildest, least-populated and perhaps most awe-inspiring region in the whole of Britain. This area begins in the windtorn islands of Orkney and Shetland, only a few degrees outside the Arctic Circle, and stretches down through gloriously unspoilt glens and mountain ranges to the geological fault known as the Great Glen, setting for a string of lochs (lakes). The Grampian Mountains also rise in this region, the tallest of them being Ben Nevis (1,344 metres). To the west is the entrancing scenery of the hundreds of islands – notably Skye and Mull. The Lowlands have a very different character and atmosphere. Here are the fertile farmlands, busy fishing villages and sophisticated cities, including of course Edinburgh and Glasgow. But there are hills and lochs here too. Loch Lomond is the most romantic of all Scotland's lakes, and the heathery uplands of the Cheviots and Trossachs have plenty of charm.

Ireland

Ireland may simply be described as a flat land with hills and mountains around the coast. This bald account conveys nothing of the island's beguiling mystery, or of the staggering variety of scenery, but it is a start. The flat centre is mostly green farmland, punctuated with bogs and pretty lakes and drained by the mighty River Shannon which flows from Lough Ree to Limerick. The more affluent and industrial areas lie to the east of the Shannon, most importantly the major cities of Belfast and Dublin. The west of Ireland contains the most magnificent landscape, including a series of coastal mountain ranges stretching from Donegal through Mayo and Connemara to Kerry, which boasts the highest spot in all of Britain and Ireland – Carrauntoohill at 1,041 metres. The west coast also features a host of superb cliffs, islands and inlets, while the gentler south coast contains the fine natural harbours of Cork and Waterford.

History

On the face of it, Great Britain and Ireland are not in a very promising spot. They are simply small islands on the north-west edge of Europe, backed by the grim Atlantic and well away from the cheery Mediterranean sun. Yet they have had an astounding history, and can boast a massive influence on world affairs.

Go back 4,000 years and England, Wales, Scotland and Ireland were not nations at all, but weak groupings of tribes, easy prey for a succession of invaders from Europe – Celtic, Roman, Scandinavian and Anglo-Saxon. They all left their racial and cultural marks, from mysterious stone circles and straight Roman roads to Christianity and the first rudiments of the English language.

The last to arrive were the Normans, who won a pivotal victory at Hastings in 1066 and then battered their way northwards from the south coast, eventually landing in Ireland a century later. Since then – and this is where British and Irish history are unique in Europe – the islands have never been conquered again.

The Normans, in their stern but effective manner, imposed some order on the chaos. They refined the Anglo-Saxon form of government, beefed up the collection of taxes, and founded the English class system by creating a ruling elite of French-speakers. They built mighty castles as barracks and command centres, though these did not interrupt a dismal catalogue of civil wars, rebellions and royal murders.

The trouble was that English rulers were usually distracted by external battles. Richard I spent most of his reign from 1189 fighting in the futile Crusades in Palestine or in France. France, indeed, was the main focus of attention for the monarchy, as successive kings of the Plantagenet dynasty tried and failed to capture the French throne with a series of costly wars (including the so-called The Hundred Years' War of 1337 to 1453).

Slowly, however, the shapes of the nation states began to emerge from this bloody fog. The very first Irish parliament met in 1264, and the first English parliament to include a 'Commons' (representatives other than noblemen) convened a year later. Scotland was a strong and stable country from the 1200s on – powerful enough to push back the advancing English, thanks to heroic victories by William Wallace and Robert the Bruce. Wales, after a glorious period under King Llewellyn the Last, succumbed to English muscle in 1277.

Yet another civil clash – the 'Wars of the Roses' – split England from the 1450s. The eventual victor in 1485, Henry Tudor, ushered in an age which was to change Britain's status in the world forever. King Henry VII (as he became) brought peace, while his son Henry VIII brought a momentous break with the religious authority of Rome which meant that, despite the efforts of his eldest daughter Mary, England turned her back on Catholicism for good.

The greatest of all English monarchs, Elizabeth I, focused national feeling as never before between 1558 and 1603. She outfaced treason at home and threats from Catholic enemies abroad, and presided over an astounding era in both the arts (Shakespeare, Marlowe, Tallis) and world exploration (Drake, Raleigh, Frobisher).

After Elizabeth's death, the English and Scottish crowns were united under the Stuarts, but national cohesion soon disintegrated. Religious strife, coupled with growing demands for power by parliament, rattled the arrogant new rulers and in 1642 England descended once more into civil war. The victorious Parliamentary side chopped off King Charles I's head, and a brief republican period began, under the gloomy Oliver Cromwell.

The monarchy was cheerfully restored by Charles II in 1660, and by the end of the17th century, the Protestant religion had taken a firm hold of Great Britain. The political binding of England, Wales and Scotland was made permanent by the Act of Union in 1707. Ireland was the only nation which had stuck to its Catholic traditions, though the English policy of bullying and immigration was swiftly increasing the Protestant community.

Having been ruled successively by monarchs of French, Welsh, Scots and Dutch descent, the British, in 1714, opted for a German dynasty. George I of Hanover spoke no English, and left practical affairs to his politicians under Robert Walpole (the first-ever prime minister). Thus, the power and influence of parliament continued to grow – as did Britain's stature in the world.

The foundations were being laid for a vast empire, with crucial victories in India and Canada, and pioneering settlements in Australia and New Zealand. The loss of the American colonies in 1782 was humiliating but not fatal, and prestige was soon restored by the role of British troops and leaders in the final defeat of France and Napoleon in 1815.

Meanwhile, Britain's engineers and scientists were spearheading the drive into a mechanized Age of Industry. Canals, foundries, cotton mills and steam railways transformed the landscape and the economy, and turned the country into an international giant of commerce. When Victoria became queen in 1837, Britain was the world's major player.

Industrial expansion brought huge problems too – dislocation of the working class, inadequate housing, disease and a vast gulf between rich and poor. Governments struggled to overcome these, and to compete with growing commercial rivals, notably Germany and the USA. The death of Victoria in 1901, followed by the horror of the First World War (1914-18), spelt the start of a long decline.

Yet what Winston Churchill termed the country's 'finest hour' was still to come in the Second World War (1939-45). When the German armies conquered France in 1940, Britain stood virtually alone against Nazi power in Europe. Grim determination, coupled with luck and the decisive entry of the USA into the war brought victory in the end, but at a shocking cost.

The post-war Labour government introduced radical social and economic changes, with the birth of the Welfare State and the nationalization of key industries. The British Empire was now in its final throes, as former colonies became independent. A striking symbol of Britain's declining importance in world affairs was provided by the disastrous attempt to occupy the Suez Canal zone – and the humiliating climb-down – in 1956.

Ireland had stayed neutral during the war. Rebellion against British rule in 1916, followed by civil war, had delayed the establishment of Home Rule (originally sanctioned in 1914), and it was not until 1949 that Eire was recognized officially as an independent republic. This left Northern Ireland alone as still part of the United Kingdom, a source of prolonged and violent unrest following a resurgence of 'The Troubles' in 1969.

During the second half of the 20th century, Britain made two significant moves to strengthen ties with the European mainland. One was the digging of a tunnel rail link beneath the English Channel. The other was the joining (along with Ireland) of the EEC, later the European Union, in 1973. After four thousand years of trying, full integration with Europe now seems a distinct possibility.

Scene

2

Scene

2

You and the law

Equality may be drawing nearer, but there are still incongruities between the law as it stands for straights and the law as it is for gays. I feel a great pride in the fact that gay men are now considered equal to their straight counterparts. Yet, society can still be ignorant, bigoted and discriminating. You can fornicate in saunas, cruise in bars and kiss in Old Compton Street, but veer away from the gay clubs and villages and attitudes can be very different, and public shows of affection – the simple gesture of holding hands – can draw scathing looks and prejudiced remarks. Change is a slow process. Integration will one day deflate the protective bubbles in which so many gay communities exist. Until then, Britain and Ireland have scenes that are both accepting and liberating and increasing in size, and a patronage that is growing in number and becoming more expressive.

Age of consent   Thankfully, the age of consent in Britain has now been addressed and balanced to offer homosexuals equality with heterosexuals. Since January 2001 the consenting age has been 16. It was, since 1994, previously 18. Prior to that, a medieval 21! Homosexuality was legalised in 1967. In The Republic of Ireland it has been fixed at 17 for many years.

Discrimination   Whereas the age of consent has now been brought into proportion in Britain, there are still areas of discrimination that remain, most notably the infamous Section 28. This archaic piece of British law (though in actual fact only part of British law since 1988) was brought into practice by Margaret Thatcher in response to tabloid newspaper articles that claimed 'loony left' councils were spending taxpayers' money on gay and lesbian groups. Section 28 sought to prohibit the promotion or encouragement of homosexuality through publications or campaigns or in schools. Whilst no local authority has yet been prosecuted for breach of the clause, it has been invoked more than 30 times to prevent projects from going ahead. Many see the abolition of Section 28 as a symbolic measure against intolerance, but, as yet, the government of England and Wales has still not repealed the law. It looks extremely likely that they will though, and that Scottish government will follow suit. Ireland, in contrast, has a government that invests in gay and lesbian projects, and the leading gay paper, Gay Community News, is actually state-funded.

Sexual activity

Public places   Cruising for sex in a public place is illegal. Although you won't be imprisoned, you may be charged with importuning. Sex in saunas is also illegal. It is, however, widely accepted as part of the gay scene. Police raids are practically non-existent and, indeed, will only occur if drug dealing or prostitution is thought to be taking place on the premises.

Having sex in a public place (like a park), even at night, where the chance of someone happening upon you is slim, is illegal. If you are 'caught in the act' you will more than likely be charged with a public disorder offence, most probably gross indecency. When cruising, and ultimately copping off with someone, always find somewhere where you will have the time to adjust your clothing if you fear being sprung. The police cannot satisfactorily press charges if they only 'suspect' what you have been up to – they will actually need some evidence, such as seeing you in the act or, an admission from you (you should never offer such and admission, no matter how indisposed you were, until you have seen a solicitor). If you should be arrested, duty solicitors are free at the police station and it is your right to have access to them.

Finally, the police in the UK and Ireland are, on the whole, much like their stereotypical image, friendly and approachable. They will not, however, respond well to verbal abuse or smart-arse comments, and they can make life difficult for you. Know your rights, but be polite – you will probably want their help someday.

Inequality

There still exist some blatant inequalities between gay and straight practice. Group sex or 'sex parties', for instance. In the straight world it is quite acceptable for a group of men and women to indulge in this practice, even openly advertising on the internet for 'swingers' to join in a group session. If the same scenario involved a group of gay men getting together for a good Saturday night session in the privacy of someone's home, the police could legitimately arrest everyone on the premises and charge them with a breach of the sexual offences act.

Gay sex in saunas used to be quite a contentious issue too. Today it's a well-known staple of the gay sauna scene and in some cases a local police authority will welcome the opening of a sauna, particularly in a well-known cruising area. This 'rather we have it hidden away' school of thought is acceptable to a point. But sexual acts within these establishments are still a transgression of law. Why not, therefore, abolish the statute 'you are breaking the law'? This 'nanny state' mentality is not, of course, limited to the gay community. The illegal act of prostitution on the streets is offensive to the residents of well-known red light areas and yet governments, despite their liberal veneer, will not address the matter and legalise brothels.

Drugs

Prohibition

Drugs are still a sore point of law. Whilst many, including politicians and senior public figures, are calling for the legalisation of some drugs (most notably cannabis) there still seems to be stoic resistance on the part of governments past and present to make any radical decisions. There is a thriving culture of recreational drug use in these countries. Many feel that the war against drugs is one that governments can no longer control. More drugs than ever before are being imported into Britain. The argument goes that governments could legalise the use, and control the supply of certain drugs and concentrate their efforts on driving the culture out from the underground. Money could be put towards educating people in the use, misuse and abuse of drugs instead of plundering more millions towards prevention and prohibition measures which are so signally failing.

Drug culture

The future may yet bring about change. For now though, the use, possession and supply of most drugs remains illegal – all can lead to arrest and possible fines or imprisonment. Police are trying to curb drug taking within the dance and club culture. Crackdowns have included spot searches on people waiting in club queues and raids upon clubs (although these are not too frequent). Such raids are always strategically planned (as a result of ongoing surveillance or tip-offs) and they usually turn up trumps (so be warned). Poppers, however, are quite acceptable and there are usually no problems in carrying and using them in most gay venues. Visitors from the States, where nitrates are illegal, seem to be in awe of this acceptance, much the same as we view the permissive and widespread use of cannabis in the Netherlands. Ecstasy tabs are easily available in most big cities, and you can get hold of them within some venues too. Again, the use, possession and supply of ecstasy is prohibited. The quality of ecstasy in the UK is dubious – nothing at all like it was back in the early 90s – and so be extremely careful of accepting anything from anyone. The bottom line is that Britain and Ireland both claim to be cracking down on drugs, but both have a dance and club culture of which drug-taking is an intrinsic part. Be careful.

Alcohol

The most commonly abused yet accepted drug of them all is alcohol. Pubs and clubs are a firm part of Britain and Ireland's culture, and alcohol is intrinsic to that scene. It is also widely available from off-licences, supermarkets and other stores. You must be over 18 years of age to purchase alcohol. Certain city by-laws prohibit the consumption of alcohol in open places. Conventional licensing hours across Britain and Ireland usually see pubs stop serving alcohol at 2300, Monday to Staurday and 2230 on Sunday. There are exceptions to this rule. A late-night licence can be applied for by an establishment if there is late-night entertainment or if food is being served, and some city centres have a more relaxed attitude to late night drinking. Some cities, for instance, often give bars with their own DJ or those located around a night club an extension, in keeping with club hours. Clubs, for the most part, often have drinks licences well into the early hours. The British government is currently reviewing licensing laws with a view to new legislation in a couple of years' time. At the heart of the changes are plans to scrap the 2300 closing rule and to allow later opening where it is appropriate. This should mean that tourist areas and city centres will have outlets staying open and serving alcohol until much later.

Pubs and clubs

Over the past five years or so, the gay club and pub scene has gone through some remarkable changes. Gone are the locked doors with the sliding shutter, hidden away down some dubious side-street, far from the town centre. They have been replaced with some of the trendiest bars in the country that make the straights green with envy. So much so in fact, that it has, to an extent, become the victim of its own success.

Bent straights

Now the straights are clamouring to be seen in the trendy gay pubs and clubs around the country. If they are seen in a gay venue they declare it's because it is trendy, not because they are looking for a bit of how's your father! The downside to all of this 'integration' is the fact that trying to pick someone up in a bar becomes a teensy bit more difficult if you are not sure whether your 'dreamboat' is straight or gay. The straight patronage of gay bars may worry a potential gay clientele. There are though, some 100 per cent heteros who prefer going to gay bars because they know that they will enjoy themselves more than they might in attitude-filled straight bars. Approaching these people has never been a problem – they know the score and are aware that they may be chatted up and most will inform you right away that they are not gay.

Night names

A practice that most pubs and clubs have recently adopted is the naming of each and every night. It can sometimes serve as a pretty useful description of what to expect once inside. The majority though, fall wide of the mark and most are just cheap play-on-words monikers. 'Disco Inferno', for instance, is a night that hard house clubbers should perhaps give a wide berth. 'Saturday Night Beaver', on the other hand, is one that could baffle many a lesbian – slightly non-descript, yet highly evocative. I hope that the listings that follow demystify this genre of pub and club culture. Incidentally, there is a gay London club that the name 'Charlie and The Snow Queen' could serve quite aptly! Hmm, now, where could that be I wonder?

Dress code

Another recent practice that incenses many are venues insisting on some sort of dress code. This is archaic stereotyping. It seems to incorrectly assume that if you do not dress the way that promoters want you to dress, then the club night will be brought into some sort of disrepute. The wearing of trainers, T-shirt and tracksuit bottoms may be the choice of clubwear for some people, yet if a promoter thinks that spangly, sparkly tops are nice and sexy (pass the sick bucket) the motion is carried and everyone who falls outside the code will be excluded. The result? You get a club with a stereotyped crowd. Some promoters are fighting against this and there are still a wealth of different nights and places to explore; it's just a shame that it has become so prevalent across a scene that should be knocking boundaries down.

Accommodation

Choosing accommodation is obviously one of the most important decisions you will have to make, either planning or during your travels. If you are looking for gay-owned or specifically gay-friendly accommodation then your choices are already severely limited. That doesn't mean that you're going to be disappointed though. As Britain and Ireland have become more accepting, more liberal and laid-back, accommodation has become more integrated and more specialist businesses have been set up seizing the opportunities that exist and serving the needs of an increasing gay tourist industry. Good quality gay accommodation is there for the taking and this guide will direct you to such places in nearly all of the major cities throughout Britain and Ireland.

Defining accommodation

The establishments listed in this guide are foremost either gay-run and/or -owned. Failing that, they are either gay-friendly and catering without prejudice, or corporate hotels with a policy of non-discrimination towards gays and lesbians. It is actually quite rare, particularly in major cities throughout the UK, to find any form of discrimination from hotel proprietors – rare, but not extinct! This makes life so much easier, particularly in busy towns and cities with a healthy gay scene, saving on unnecessary travelling.

Saunas

Over the last few years the gay sauna scene has become increasingly more popular and acceptable than in the past. Local government and police authorities see the gay sauna as a way of getting gay cruising off the streets and into an environment where the activity can cause no offence to the general public.

Breaking the stereotype

If you have never been to a gay sauna before then I have only one piece of advice for you – go now. Don't for one moment think that it will be the ill-conceived stereotype of the mature male leering and letching at you – it's not. Of course, that is not to say that they will not be there, they will, but so too will a very good mixture of other types. Married men looking for a bit on the side, the (supposed) straight lad, afraid of being seen in the gay pubs and clubs and a whole medley in between. You will not have to take part in group sex. You are free to do your own thing and usually there's the opportunity for most sorts of 'things'(!). There's always clean bath towels to cover your modesty and condoms and lube will always be available at the reception desk or situated somewhere near to the rest rooms. Just go and enjoy yourself! Indeed, perhaps the hardest part about going to a sauna is actually finding the place. More often than not they are hidden away in a back street somewhere. It is nearly always advisable to phone beforehand to get some detailed directions from staff at the venue.

Membership

One final note regarding membership. The majority of saunas are members-only establishments and the first time that you go, you will be required to join. The joining fee will always be very modest – £5 at the very most. You will be asked to give your name and address – usually a name and postal district will suffice. Sauna operatives are aware of the need to preserve members' anonymity, so don't worry about having to complete a three-page application form and sitting down to the Spanish Inquisition – 'John Jones from London' may well suffice. If you do have any qualms about giving your details explain this to the staff who more often than not will offer a compromise.

Cruising grounds

In 1967, the decriminalisation of homosexuality meant that gay and bisexual men no longer had the need to frequent cruising areas in order to have sex or to meet other like-minded males. Then came the upsurge in gay pubs and clubs, particularly in towns and cities, and the need to resort to cottages and cruising grounds should have become quite unnecessary. This, however, has not been the case. Cruising grounds have become even more popular and widespread, much to the annoyance of the police force whose armoury of 'embarrassment factor' has diminished considerably. There is little, if any, stigma felt by the men who do go cruising. They look upon it as yet another outlet for picking up other men just for sex' sake.

Many men choose cruising as a viable way of meeting other men, whether for casual sex or in the hope that they will meet a prospective long-term partner (although this option is highly unlikely). Cruising can be exciting as well as dangerous, and this excitement is one of the reasons that many men are drawn back time and again. Being an opportunistic recreation, you will never know who might turn up. There may be occasions when there is no one that takes your fancy. On another occasion, you may be spoilt for choice!

You and the law Soliciting for sex (paid or otherwise) and having sex in a public place is illegal. The police have a duty to investigate all complaints from the public, which will consequently result in regular patrols of the cruising area, and men convicted of 'victimless' public sex offences may have their name included in the sex offenders register, along with paedophiles. It is best to avoid any unwelcome visits by the police by curtailing your activities to areas where the public will not 'happen upon you'.

Policing The policing of cruising grounds is (apparently) 'low priority'. This does not alter the fact that the police do make arrests and are usually helped with an admission from the defendant. It is not illegal to be walking through a park, or any other area for that matter, late at night, despite the fact that the area might be a well-known cruising ground. It is well known that undercover policemen patrol cruising areas, although this is becoming rare. If you choose to have sex in an exhibitionistic way, then the chances of you being caught (with your trousers down, so to speak) are greatly increased. It is always best to go to a spot where there are absolutely no onlookers, and where the risk of you being caught is reduced. One method being adopted across cruising grounds to alert cruisers to the presence of police patrols is for their fellow cruisers to beep their car horns twice. Don't rely on this pulling you out of a pickle though. If you are unfortunate enough to be caught by the police there are three golden rules that you should adhere to: firstly, admit nothing –

no matter what the police say they have seen or what they might accuse you of; secondly, say nothing – even though they may try to get you to lose your temper by name-calling; and thirdly, if arrested, always (without fail) ask for a solicitor to represent you at the station.

Contentious

The activity of cruising is an extremely contentious issue, not only with the straight community, but also with some members of the gay community. The latter, however, do seem to be more tolerant of the activity, believing that 'lifestyle choice' should not be dictated or morally judged by anyone for any reason. That said, you should have the decency to respect other people's feelings. You do not need to provoke hostile reaction by openly engaging in 'mutual affection' when there is the slightest possibility that any member of the public could chance upon you. At some of the more 'open' cruising areas (such as parks) I'd recommend you pick up and take away to a more secluded area. There are also some wholly inappropriate places for cruising – why would people want to carry out such activity in a cemetry?

Be careful

Finally, it is well worth remembering that cruising, by its very nature, may well be dangerous. You must always be on your guard, be particularly aware of your surroundings and remember, above all else, that if you feel you are in danger, you probably are. Never carry cash or valuables with you, You should also never carry weapons (even as a self-defence measure) – these will be near-impossible to explain away to the police if you are apprehended. Whilst the idea of cruising with friends might appeal, it is not really practical. It will more than likely scare away potential interest (no sane single man would approach a pack of interested men) and it will certainly curtail your chances of success. I would advise though, that you let someone know where you are going before you leave for a ground. Attacks on gays are rare. In cruising grounds, more so. Do not assume, though, that cruising grounds are safe or that they will deter straights or disapproving parties. Have your wits about you. Get out at the first sign of trouble and phone any local gay switchboard if you are after advice on how to report or deal with attacks or threats. Switchboards can even report the incident to the police on your behalf.

Using this guide

I have tried to convey as much information in the most basic way possible. No unnecessary symbols, nothing partisan – just facts and honest opinion. These listings are the most complete ever published. You can substantiate this for yourself. If you have any further information or corrections – or any free tickets or membership passes(!) – please contact me at **gaytimes@absolutepress.demon.co.uk**.

Proprietors' note

A note to venue proprietors: help me out! Some of you are notoriously difficult to get information out of! If your venue or establishment has not been included or lacks relevant information, then please contact me in order that any amendments can be made for subsequent editions.

Newcomers

If you're new to the country or have never been to a gay venue before and are wary about going in alone, contact your nearest switchboard to find out details of 'Icebreakers' groups for men or 'Stepping Stones' groups for women. You can then experience the gay scene with someone who is in exactly the same situation as yourself. Age has never been an issue in gay establishments – young and old mix extremely well in most venues. If you think you're 'past that sort of thing' then think again – you are missing out on an awful lot: the scene has never been so vibrant.

Definitions

I have listed the standard opening hours of establishments under the **Open** fields in this book. This field follows the description for each listed venue/night. These hours are forever at the mercy of promoters changing their minds, late licenses being sought or cancelled, and you should always check prior to any specific visit, that the night and/or venue you are travelling to is (a) running; and (b) running to the same hours as listed. The gay scene is probably the fastest shifting scene there is: things change! I have also indicated the **Price** range you can expect to pay. For London and Glasgow, where establishments fall close to **Tube** stations, I have listed the nearest available station. The accommodation listings retain the price field, which here relates to the price you can expect to pay as a couple sharing a double/twin room (with en-suite facilities, if available), booking high season. These usually constitute the most expensive rooms available. I have indicated where the price relates to a different type of accommodation. In most cases there are standard rooms available at a lower cost and nearly all establishments offer a reduced rate for midweek stays. Ask!

It is always worth mentioning this travel guide as the source for your enquiry. Some establishments expressed an interest in offering a reduction to readers of this guide. Details of accommodation have been provided by the guest-house or hotel proprietors themselves. As stated already, these accommodation listings are limited to establishments that are gay-run, gay-owned or exclusively gay and, failing these criteria, only when the venue is known to be genuinely gay-friendly. And finally, to cruising. Grounds are not advertised. They are difficult to detail and sometimes difficult to find. I've tried to do both. Again, I request that you e-mail me with your additions, retractions and amendments: **gaytimes@absolutepress.demon.co.uk**. There are a few grounds that are inappropriate for cruising. The listing of such unsuitable places is by no means a condonation. I try to recommend alternative nearby grounds, clubs, bars or saunas.

Disclaimer

I am obliged to inform you that 'soliciting for sex' whether paid for, or otherwise, is illegal. The publishers, contributors and myself cannot be held responsible for any action whatsoever brought against you or any acquaintance of yours, nor can we be held responsible for any incident caused to you or any acquaintance of yours from any use of the listings.

England

England

3

Think of England and you think of London.
But England is a different world. London
alone cannot convey the thousands of years
of heritage inherited by this amazing country.
If you want to sample the 'real England' you will
have to move away from the capital. The towns
and cities that make up England are as equally
rich in history and culture, and each principality
is unique in its own way. Take Manchester and
Liverpool for example. Neighbours, separated
by less than fifty miles, yet the accent of the
locals, their fierce loyalty to their city and their
customs and 'ways' could not be more different.
Likewise, through the rest of the country, each
county, town and city embracing their own culture and eccentric ways, but willing to share
them with anyone who takes an interest.

To understand the English would take a lifetime
and much more, but, as Sir William Harcourt
once observed, 'You may not witness history
in the making, but you will certainly absorb the
spirit of the land with a stop at the local tavern.'

Amersham Cruising grounds

A413
A picnic site on the north side of the A413 dual carriageway, west of Amersham. This site is not one of the busiest places but it's well worth a look if you are passing. Evenings offer a nice shady place to hang around.

Arundel Cruising grounds

Whiteways Picnic Area
This place is just outside the town, on the junction of the A29 and A284. There is a large wooded area with action happening throughout the day and into the evenings. There are toilet facilities where you are able to pick up and take away. Police at this site can be a problem so be warned; be discreet.

Aylesbury Pubs

The Saracen's Head
5 Rickfords Hill, Aylesbury HP20 2RT Phone 01296 421 528
The only gay bar in Aylesbury and as such it has to cater for the wide range of tastes of the community. So, you have the pool table, the comfy seating, the stripper (last Sunday of the month) quiz nights, disco and so on. They also serve cask-conditioned ales, food at lunchtimes, and during the summer – the beer garden opens up. Find it in the town centre opposite Safeway supermarket. **Open** Monday-Saturday 1100-2300. Sunday 1100-2230

Aylsford Cruising grounds

Cobtree Manor Country Park
This is a park just off the M20 (J6), near the Travis Perkins depot. You can park up at night and join the cruising that goes on in the nearby woods. Police are known to patrol the area.

Barnsley Pubs

Baker Street
46 Sheffield Road, Barnsley S70 Phone 01226 280 258
I suppose we have to be thankful for small mercies! Throughout the week Baker Street is a mixed gay and straight bar. Tuesdays and Thursdays however, are published as the official gay nights. Why they do not simply identify themselves as a gay-friendly bar through the whole week is beyond me. Anyway, like I said – small mercies, and it is – of course – better than nothing. Expect cabaret and disco on both nights. **Open** Tuesday 1900-2300. Thursday 1900-0000

Saunas

Greenhouse Health Club

56 Sheffield Road, Barnsley S70 1HS Phone 01226 731 305
E-mail info@gay-sauna.com Web www.gay-sauna.com
Another arm from the Greenhouse group of saunas. Smaller than their sister venues in Luton and Darlaston although more than filling a niche in this gay venueless part of the world. Well laid out over three floors, with stairs either end of the venue which means you can quite comfortably cruise around to your heart's content. 'Bears Night' is every second Saturday of the month, however, this is not an exclusive night and you will certainly not be excluded admission if you are not big and bulky. The venue is quite easy to find. If you should have any problems – give the venue a call and they will be only too pleased to help. **Open** Monday-Friday 1100-2300. Saturday 1100-2200. Sunday 1200-2300 **Price** £9 plus £1 annual membership

Barnstaple Cruising grounds

North Devon Link Road: A39

The rest area on the North Devon link road between Barnstaple and Bideford. This area was quite popular until a couple of guys got busted a few years ago in a police raid. The area is slowly coming back into prominence, although the police still look into the toilets during the early evening every now and again. The evening trade is still unsure and a visit is recommended if you are passing, but it's probably not worth making a special trip for.

Basildon Club nights

Colors @ The Kingswood Rooms

Southernhay, Basildon SS14 1DQ Phone 01268 242 031
Colors is a bi-weekly gay club space in the Kingswood function rooms. On Wednesday, apart from the disco, expect to see 'Alternative Cabaret' which may sound like some up-and-coming cutting edge event but in fact is a general free-for-all on the stage – including karaoke, stand-up and whatever else people dream up! An excellent night out in a town where the next nearest gay venue is about twelve miles away. Friday is like anywhere else – full to the rafters with a predominantly young crowd of boys and girls packed like sardines onto the dance floor. Manager Steve, who incidentally used to run Colors at Romford before its closure, is battling to get investment from the proprietors of The Kingswood Rooms in order to get the venue refurbished. Once done, he plans to open up the venue as a gay space every night of the week. Until then, be thankful that such a venue exists. For resident gays in the Basildon area there is a monthly police surgery every first Friday of the month. Phone the above number for further details. As a footnote, there are plans to organise a monthly women-only night. Keep an eye on the gay press for more information on this. **Open** Wednesday and Friday 2000-0200 **Price** £2 Wednesday. £2-4 Saturday

Bath

The famous Roman Baths are the best-preserved Roman remains to be found anywhere in England and they are the centrepiece of this beautiful, historic city. The springs originate in the eastern Mendips, collecting mineral salts along the way and surface again in Bath. In the early 18th century, these waters were believed to have special healing powers and people would travel across land and sea to cleanse and bathe in them. Adjoining the Roman Baths are the Pump Rooms where the famous waters can be observed whilst you drink the most civilised cup of tea that the city has to offer. Bath has a history that goes back well over 2,000 years. The city was named Aquae Sulis (literally: the waters of Sul – the pre-Roman Celtic goddess who presided over the hot springs) and this was changed to Bath during the Dark Ages. The stunning sandstone buildings of Bath – not least Bath Abbey, The Circus and The Royal Crescent – are jaw-droppingly beautiful; no other place in Britain is as architecturally rich. There is, however, little else for the gay visitor: only one gay pub serves the whole city (albeit very well), so it may be worth pencilling in a trip up the road to nearby Bristol for a fuller flavour of what the south-west of England has to offer.

Getting in touch

Bath is a small city with a huge tourist industry. Consequently, the **Tourist Office** (01225 477 101) gets extremely busy during the summer months, and it may be wise to get here either first thing in the morning or later in the evening. The office is in the city's centre at Abbey Chambers. Bristol's **Gay Switchboard** (0117 942 0842) serves Bath too and is open Monday to Friday from 2000 to 2200. **Gay Men's Health Project** is a Bath-based advice line for men (01225 833 900) and the West branch of **Terrence Higgins Trust** (01225 444 347) is also based here.

Pubs

The Tap   19 St James' Parade, Bath BA1 1UL Phone 01225 404 344
Formerly known as The Bath Tap – now just The Tap – this is the only exclusively gay venue in Bath. Bright and modern, it occupies three floors with a small late-licensed basement night club, which opens over the weekend only. The ground floor is the main bar area – minimalist, wooden floor and so on, whilst the top floor is a smart and comfortable lounge bar. **Open** Monday-Wednesday 1200-2300. Thursday-Saturday 1200-0200. Sunday 1200-2230 **Price** £1.50-2.50, Friday-Saturday after 2230

Accommodation

Kennard Hotel   11 Henrietta Street, Bath BA2 6LL Phone 01225 310 472
Fax 01225 460 054 E-mail info@kennard.co.uk Web www.kennard.co.uk
The Kennard is a delightful and luxurious Georgian townhouse built in 1794 as a lodging house for Bath's grand era of prosperity. Now, after

loving and considerate restoration it still reflects that period of graceful living. The gorgeous bedrooms come complete with en-suite facilities, welcome tray, satellite television, direct dial telephone and hairdryer. Breakfast, included in the price, is served in the garden-style breakfast room. Self-serve juice and cereal whilst your breakfast is being freshly prepared. **Price** £84-95 **Number of rooms** 13, all en-suite

Cruising grounds

**M4 J18 /
A46 Rest Area**

Head towards Bath. Two to three hundred metres on the right, there is a rest area and car park with toilet block and adjoining woods. It is best to park in the car park and walk across the road to follow the path through the trees. Follow the well-trodden trails to enter the woodland and main cruising ground. This has been a hot action spot for years. Action throughout the day, hotting up from 2000 onwards, especially during the summer months. If you are dubious about going to the woods on your first visit, the car park itself may hold some surprises!

**Sydney
Gardens**

(Sydney Road, BA2) Sydney Gardens is surrounded by the A36 so it is easy enough to drive around the gardens until you find a suitable place to park up. There are two main areas of activity in the gardens; first, the area between the railway cuttings and the canal towpath which runs the entire length of the garden. This area usually gets busy later on in the evening. Secondly, and probably the more obvious, is the toilet facility on Sydney Place side. This is busy throughout the day though be warned – police do patrol through the park quite regularly so it may be best to pick up and take away to a more secluded space.

Beaconsfield Cruising grounds

Jordans

Leave the M40 (J2) at the Beaconsfield exit and go north to the A40. Turn right towards Gerrards Cross and take the first left to Jordans. Between here and the railway there are several parking places and a public footpath crossing the road into woodland on both sides. This site is busy every evening with car drivers going home from work, and at all times during the weekend. Weekday evenings can often be hit-and-miss. Note: care should be taken as this place is used by genuine dog walkers.

Bedford Pubs

**The Barley
Mow**

72 St Loyes Street, Bedford MK40 1EZ Phone 01234 359 355
A traditionally styled gay bar for all ages and sexes. Chesterfield seating dominates the main room, making it more of a drink and chat type of venue rather than the cruise and/or dance kind of place. Karaoke is held twice a week on Wednesday and Sunday. Bedford isn't that well served with gay venues and so most of the town's gays will probably frequent this place at some time during the week. **Open** Monday-Saturday 1100-2300. Sunday 1100-2230

Clarence Hotel   13 St Johns Street, Bedford MK42 0AH Phone 01234 352 781
The Clarence Hotel is a predominantly gay venue. Each weekend they put on a disco (Friday) and some sort of cabaret (Saturday). On the last Friday of the month, it runs the TUF night (Transsexual, Uniform, Fetish), running from 2100 onwards. The Clarence is a pub with a club atmosphere, being both cruisy and social. TVs are especially welcome, as are well-behaved straights (usually friends of gays). En-suite accommodation is also available for around £35-40 per couple. **Open** Monday-Saturday 1100-2300. Sunday 1100-2230

Club nights

QT @ The Club   125 Midland Road, Bedford MK40 1DE Phone 01234 350 374
This is a weekly gay night for the lesbians, gays and bisexuals of Bedford and the surrounding areas. It's something akin to a school disco but to be honest it's a welcome alternative to the small Bedford scene. There is no set music policy, it could be anything from chart hits to '70s retro. Nor is there a dress code – you are welcome to wear anything that you feel comfortable in. People and ages are spread across the twenties to forties spectrum, from students to disco dollies, all rubbing shoulders in this attitude-free environment. If you are local and planning to come here quite often it may be wise to become a member (you'll need to bring two passport photographs with you). If you don't fancy the membership you can expect to pay £4 for guest admission. **Open** Friday 2200-0200 **Price** £2.50 members / £4 guests

Biggin Hill Cruising grounds

**Keston
Picnic Area**   This is located in a picnic car park approximately one mile on from the main terminal of Biggin Hill Airport, heading towards Bromley. This area has both its good days and its bad. The action takes place in a couple of secluded corners of the wood behind the cottage. If you are going to use this ground then beware of genuine picnickers, especially on warm days.

Birmingham

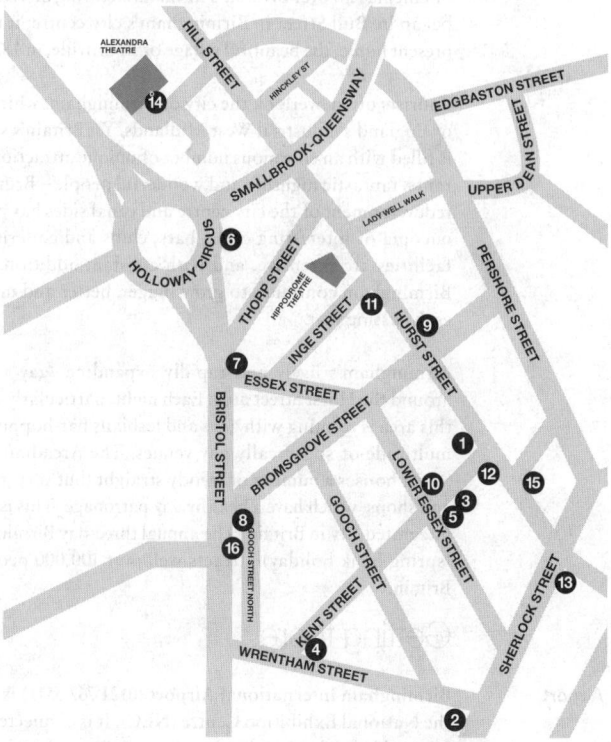

Map key

1 Angel's Café Bar	**9** Missing
2 Boots Bar	**10** The Nightingale
3 DV8	**11** Partners
4 The Fountain Inn	**12** Route 2
5 The Fox	**13** Telstar
6 The Jester	**14** Victoria Theatre Bar
7 Kudos Café Bar	**15** The Village
8 Looking Glass Sauna	**16** The Wellington Hotel

Birmingham is Britain's second city and is home to about one million people. Thirty other places around the world (and even a crater on the moon) share the name Birmingham – but there is nowhere quite like the real thing. It has more parks than any other European city, more miles of canal than Venice and Europe's largest public library. It is officially Britain's cleanest large city. It was at the heart of the industrial revolution and its pioneering history has given us the spinning jenny, electroplating, celluloid and the pnumatic tyre. Oxygen was discovered here and the first medical X-ray was taken here too. The first Odeon cinema was set up in the Perry Barr suburb of the city in 1930, spawning a chain of cinemas all over Britain. The manufacturing of Cadbury's chocolate began in Bull Street in Birmingham's city centre; it then moved to its present home, the beautiful village of Bournville, in 1879.

Tourists often overlook the city of Birmingham, which sits at the heart of England's industrial West Midlands. Yet Britain's second largest city is filled with an enormous number of unique attractions, superb restaurants, fantastic nightlife and wonderful people – Brummies. A massive redevelopment of the city centre and canal sides has given rise to a cornucopia of interesting cafés, bars, clubs and galleries. The shopping facilities are extensive, and with constant additional improvements, Birmingham continues to grow bigger, better and more exciting with each passing year.

Birmingham's lively and rapidly expanding gay village is situated around the Hurst Street area. Each night, particularly over the weekend, this area is teeming with gays and lesbians bar-hopping in and out of a multitude of specifically gay venues. The Arcadian Centre on Hurst Street houses a number of trendy straight (but very gay-friendly) bars and shops, which have a healthy gay patronage. This is perhaps the most integrated city in Britain. The annual three-day Birmingham Pride event (spring bank holiday) attracts well over 100,000 people from all over Britain.

Getting there

Airport

Birmingham International Airport (0121 767 5511) is directly opposite the National Exhibition Centre (NEC). It is connected to **Birmingham International Station** that has direct trains to London as well as **New Street** station. There are also a number of national coach services that operate from here and direct bus connections to the city centre. A black cab to the city centre will cost about £15, but ask for an estimate first.

Trains

Most trains into the city arrive at **Birmingham New Street** station (0121 654 4243), one of the busiest railway stations within Britain. Services to most parts of Britain operate from here. The remainder use **Moor Street** and **Snow Hill** stations. The **Lost Property and Left Luggage** office is just outside the glass doors at the main station entrance. You can phone (0121 654 4286) Monday to Saturday between 0645 and 2145 and Sunday between 1100 and 1845. Another handy number for your transportation needs in Birmingham is the **Centro** hotline (0121 200 2700). Centro are responsible for promoting and developing public tranport services throughout the West Midlands.

Coaches

Digbeth Coach Station in the city centre is a nationwide hub for **National Express** coaches (0990 80 80 80). There are links to all over Britain from here. The National Express office is open Monday to Saturday from 0715 to 1900 and Sunday from 0815 to 1700.

Getting about

Metro

The first line of the new metro system is now open (0121 254 7272). Its trams run from Snow Hill in the city centre out to Wolverhampton to the north. Metro are now in the process of phasing out ticket machines on the stations and introducing conductors on the route. If the ticket machine on the station you board is not working then try the machine on the other platform. If still unsuccessful, you will have to purchase a ticket when you alight the tram.

Buses

The main bus station is also located at Digbeth Street (0121 622 4373). There is a luggage storage facility here (£1-3). The main service provider is **Travel West Midlands**, but there are also several private companies who offer competitive fares. The bus map is extensive and you'd need many years of intensive study to be able to work out what was going on. The website, however should help sort out your journey (www.travel-wm.co.uk) or you could try phoning **Travel Line** (0870 608 2608) or the Centro hotline (0121 200 2700).

Taxis

As you would expect with such a major city, Birmingham is served by fleets of taxis. There are ranks outside all major entrance points into the city and there's also a choice of many private firms.

Tourist information

The **Visitor Centre** (0121 605 7777) is situated in Victoria Square in the city centre. There is also a **Visitors Bureau** at 130 Colmore Row (0121 693 6300) and an additional one at City Arcade, Union Street (0121 643 2514). From any of these offices you are able to sort out hotel bookings and pick up maps, guides and other tourist information essentials.

Bureaux de change

American Express (0121 644 5533) at Bank House, 8 Cherry Street, is open Monday to Friday from 0830 to 1730 and Saturday from 0900 to 1700. There is also the main post office at 1 Pinfold Street, Victoria Square with a facility that is open Monday to Friday from 0830 to 1730 and Saturday from 0830 to 1800. Many high street banks lie within and off the centre too.

Getting help

Police, hospital and pharmacy

Birmingham's main **Police Station** (0121 626 5000) is situated at Lloyd House, Colmore Circus, Queensway. **Birmingham University Hospital** (0121 432 3232) at Oak Tree Lane, Selly Oak is the main hospital that serves the city, although there are several others. The police station holds a list of late-night chemists.

Getting in touch

Internet

There is not yet a flurry of cafés opened up in Birmingham's centre. It will just be a matter of time though. **The Internet Centre** is at 8 Fletchers Walk, Paradise Circus and there is also a good café at **The Pallasades** shopping centre, just before the escalators which lead down to the New Street station concourse.

GLBT Helplines Birmingham **Switchboard** (0121 622 6589) is the lesbian and gay switchboard for the city. The lines are open between 1900 and 2200 every night of the year. If lesbians wish to speak to a member of the same sex then they can phone 0121 773 5310 every Wednesday between the hours of 1930 and 2130. You can write with your questions or concerns to PO Box 3626, Birmingham B5 4LG.

Pubs

Angel's
Café Bar

127-131 Hurst Street, Birmingham B5 6SE Phone 0121 622 4880
E-mail info@angels-birmingham.co.uk
Web www.angels-birmingham.co.uk
By day Angels is at the hub of Birmingham's gay scene with people meeting up and enjoying either lunch, a snack or a cappuccino (food served up 'til 2100). Sunday lunch is available at £6.50 for three courses and you will be hard pressed to find a better venue to enjoy it in. By night the pace and the music speeds up, but such is the size of the venue that you can always find a quiet corner to chat with friends. Weekend nights get really lively and full to capacity. Tip: free coach to Subway City from here on Thursday and Saturday evenings. **Open** Monday-Saturday 1200-2300. Sunday 1200-2230

Boots Bar

77 Wrentham Street, Birmingham B1 Phone 0121 622 1414
If you have ever been to the cruise bars in Amsterdam then you will know exactly what to expect here. If you have never been then expect a dark, cruisy and very sexy atmosphere as the punters are only here for two things – the beer and the pulling (and I'm not talking pints). This is a man's bar – no drag or suits, leather, uniform, skins, combats and so forth in evidence. You're OK with jeans and T-shirts and even the scally wear of shirts over trousers. In fact, anything horny. Boots is split into three areas – the basement which is a very, very dark room (I've said too much as it is), the ground floor bar and the upstairs club. Sundays (free admission) has the well-populated 'Blackout' session and if you don't know what that means then this is not the place for you. Note: the Monday and Tuesday opening hours are limited in order to comply with our archaic licensing laws; if you are in the area then pop in for a quick pint but don't expect it to be as busy as the rest of the week. 'The Barracks' accommodation facility is sadly no longer in operation. **Open** Monday-Tuesday 1100-1300, Wednesday-Saturday 2000-0200. Sunday 1500-2300 **Price** £2-4 Wednesday-Saturday

The Fountain
Inn

102 Wrentham Street, Birmingham B5 6QL Phone 0121 622 1452
E-mail fountainpub@yahoo.co.uk
Birmingham's premier leather, uniform and denim gay bar. Predominantly men-only, with real ale and cask-conditioned beer. Hotel accommodation available too (enquire at venue). The Fountain hosts one bear's night (every third Friday) and two (MSC) leather nights per

month. This is a social group for men who have an interest in leather, rubber, uniforms and skinheads, meeting on the first Friday and third Sunday of every month. Happy hours from Monday-Friday between 1700 and 2000 when selected drinks are on offer. Ask! Beer Garden is open in the summer and there's regular strip fests throughout the week. **Open** Monday-Friday 1700-2300. Saturday 1300-2300. Sunday 1300-2230

John Ronald Reuel Tolkien, author of The Hobbit and The Lord of the Rings, spent his childhood in Sarehole, Birmingham. This tiny village is said to have been the model for the Shire, home of Bilbo in the book The Hobbit. Sarehole attracts many thousands of visitors every year, but they come to see the Mill, rather than learn of the Tolkien legend. Sarehole Mill is the only surviving watermill in Birmingham. It dates back to the 16th century, and for most of its life it was used to grind corn. It was later used to make flour, sharpen tools, roll metals and make buttons and ceased operation in 1919. Tolkien is said to have based two of the characters of Lord in the Rings on the father-and-son millers that were in occupancy at the turn of the 20th century. He described the son in his book as 'the White Ogre'.

The Fox   17 Lower Essex Street, Birmingham B5 6SN Phone **0121 622 1210**
An old-fashioned traditional gay pub catering predominantly for the women of of Birmingham. During the week it is intimate and cosy but come the weekend, the place livens up and gains that party atmosphere. As you might expect, all ages and types come in here at some time or other and either stay or move on to the other venues in the village. **Open** Monday-Sunday 1900-2300

The Jester   Horsefair, Holloway Circus, Birmingham B1 1EG Phone **0121 643 0155**
Situated on Holloway Circus at the very top of Hurst Street you will find what is probably Birmingham's longest-running gay bar. Set in the basement you will find a social, cruisy atmosphere helped along by the circular bar taking up most of the room. It is a community-style pub, with lots of regulars (which to an outsider may seem to be a bit cliquey but in reality this is not the case). Popular with the older (over 25 and out of nappies) male although some of the younger guys and tourists will pub-hop through here whilst 'doing the scene'. A new management team has recently taken over and has introduced a stage as well as removing part of the seating area giving you more room to cruise, dance and mingle around. The décor has also changed to a smart and trendy blue and silver, going against the grain of the traditional nicotine colour. From Thursday to Sunday there is a drag DJ playing the camp and disco tunes, but apart from that there is no regular cabaret or karaoke – not for the present anyhow. **Open** Monday-Saturday 1200-2300. Sunday 1200-2230

Kudos Café Bar   28 Horsefair, Birmingham B1 1DD Phone **0121 666 6806**
E-mail **birmingham@kudosgroup.com** Web **www.kudosgroup.com**
On the outskirts of the gay village (Horsefair – behind the Hippodrome) Kudos, the London gay group of Crush fame café-bars, have opened up a new venue here in Birmingham. The centre full-length

plate glass window is adorned with a huge 'Q' (for Queer, Queen or perhaps even Qudos) lets you know you have arrived. Once inside you are affronted by a huge open-plan room and a very long bar, plus the compulsory feature of all 'Q' venues, the video wall – that's it! Oh, there is also a spiral staircase that will lead you to a smaller lounge bar. Regular entertainment throughout the week, with Monday being the Crush Bar (as opposed to the traditional Thursday). You know the deal: featured artist on the screen equals two-for-one drinks at the bar. Tuesday sees all drinks at £1 when the red light flashes (you are not restricted to how many you order either – so well worth waiting for the light before you offer to 'get them in'). Wednesday is Camp Night. Thursday is Britpop, pop and trash... blah, blah. On Friday you can get to hear some decent music with top DJs on rotation and there's bar staff shenanigans with 'Debbie Dallas Does'. Saturday is a continuation of Friday's themes although there are plans for regular monthly parties also. Sunday is Kudos' attempt to get the Brummie girls in for a night called Ultragirl, showcasing all the girlie popsters on the video wall. Tip: get in well before 2300 over the weekends and save yourself £3. **Open** Monday-Tuesday 1700-0100. Wednesday-Saturday 1700-0200. Sunday 1200-2230 **Price** £2-3, weekends after 2300

Missing

48 Bromsgrove Street, (Corner of Hurst Street), Birmingham
Phone 0121 622 3951
A friendly all-type / all-age (though mostly young) Mediterranean-style bar in blues and greys – that is except for the imposing stage which is like a giant freedom flag! The stage is utilised throughout the week: karaoke on a Thursday hosted by Lady B (one of the most popular events in the midweek Birmingham calendar) and Play Your Cards Right shenanigans on Monday, once again hosted by Lady B (and also very popular). The weekends see the place full as the disco glitterball goes into overdrive with the very able DJ Mal. Missing tends to get some real top notch cabaret acts onto its pride stage so it is always worth checking out the gay press to see who will be gracing the stage during the week. Sunday is packed. Why? Well, that is when they have their camp party day, starting with drag cabaret and including camp classics and stripper – again hosted by Lady B (does she ever get a day off?). Sunday lunch is available in the restaurant upstairs for £8.50. **Open** Monday-Wednesday 1200-2300. Thursday-Saturday 1200-0000. Sunday 1200-2230

Partners Bar

27-35 Hurst Street, Birmingham B5 4BD Phone 0121 622 4710
E-mail partners.bar@virgin.net Web www.welcome.to/partners
Situated next to The Hippodrome is Partners, a popular gay cabaret bar in the centre of the village. Established over many years it has become a firm favourite with a mixed gay and lesbian clientele. This '60s feel, relatively small cellar bar has one large L-shaped bar and a well-used pink stage – very camp. A reputation for fun and friendliness and a place where anything goes, any given night of the week. Even the staff are well known for their fun antics on any night when the stage can be occupied and an impromptu show held. There is also a pool table along with gaming machines to keep you occupied whilst waiting for that bit of stuff to

come in. Happy hour is from 1700-2030 Monday-Thursday (and all day Wednesday) to get you in the party spirit early. Open Monday-Thursday 1400-2300. Friday-Saturday 1300-2300. Sunday 1400-2230

Route 2

139-147 Hurst Street, Birmingham B5 6JD Phone 0121 622 3366
'Best Venue' winners of Midland Zone reader awards confirms that this venue is something really special. Late night drinking every night of the week from Monday with its Pink Pound extravaganza with most drinks being only £1. Tuesday is pretty much the same, only an influx of students (this being student night) gives you a choice from ten of the best drinks, also for £1. From Thursday, the venue gets more of a clubby vibe – admission prices start to kick in and the earlier you arrive means the less you have to pay on the door; before 2100 is free and before 2300 is cheap; after this you will be paying around £3. Friday nights is 'Flesh': a stripper night and disco. Saturday is cabaret with some pretty good acts and disco. Sunday is … well, fuck all really, just a chance to relax in this cool, continental-style bar-come-club-come-good-time-place. Open Monday-Saturday 1900-0200. Sunday 1900-2230 Price £1.50-3, after 2300, Thursday-Saturday

Telstar

116 Sherlock Street (corner of Hurst Street), Birmingham B5 6NB
Phone 0121 693 5042
Only just changed its name. What was formerly The White Swan and a cosy and traditional gay bar in the centre of Birmingham's gay village is now a completely refurbished bar with a brand new bright and modern image. Wednesday evenings are the domain of karaoke and every weekend they host their own disco nights. The White Swan used to be a totally attitude-free place that accommodated a large crowd who went through here on their way to the clubs or simply used it as a meeting-up place. There's no reason why that crowd shouldn't give this place their patronage too. Open Monday-Saturday 1200-2300. Sunday 1200-2230

Victoria Theatre Bar

48 John Bright Street, Birmingham B1 1BN Phone 0121 633 9439
Gay-run and gay-friendly mixed venue, billed as Birmingham's oldest gay bar. Situated next door to The Alexandra Theatre. Their restaurant is now open and licensed 'til midnight. Friday night is karaoke night with cheap drink offers. There's also a restaurant offering pre- and post-theatre meals. Open Monday-Saturday 1200-2300

Birmingham boasts the largest road junction in Europe. The Gravelly Hill Interchange has so many underpasses, overpasses, and inter-twined roads that it has been nicknamed Spaghetti Junction.

The Village

152 Hurst Street, Birmingham B5 6RY Phone 0121 622 4742
Exclusively gay venue in the heart of the gay village. There is nothing pretentious about this place. If you want a good drink in cosy surroundings at the right price with gay people (predominantly male-orientated) then this is where you go. Limited accommodation available too, where advance booking is required (see accommodation listing). Open Monday-Saturday 1200-2300. Sunday 1200-1500 / 1930-2230

The Wellington Hotel	72 Bristol Street, Birmingham B5 7AH Phone 0121 622 2592

The Wellington is a mock Tudor-style building incorporating PK's Bar. There are regular Tuesday night line-dancing goings on with The Midland Mavericks. There are two bars on one level, including a lounge with an upstairs function room which opens only on weekends and at major events (like Pride). There's karaoke on a Friday and Saturday, with the addition of cabaret on a Saturday as well. Popular venue for Sunday lunch as they offer five courses for around £6.99 which means that it is advisable to book or otherwise face a wait for a table. The Wellington also offers standard room accommodation (five, none-en-suite) from around £30 for a double room (credit cards not accepted). **Open** Monday-Friday 1600-2300. Saturday 1200-2300. Sunday 1200-2230

Clubs

3

DV8 — 16 Kent Street, Birmingham B5 6RD Phone 0121 6666 366

A new late-licensed gay club which opened its doors to the lucky people of Birmingham in June 2001, just as this guide was going to press. This place is surely going to be a cracker. Built more or less from scratch, from what was formerly an indoor car park and storage area, it consists of three bars and two dance areas. On the top floor there is a laid-back, comfortable lounge-bar-come-chill-out area, with views down to the main club. The focus at DV8 will be on the music and dancing although I'm sure the cruising and boozing will soon follow. At the moment the music policy is camp and cheesy on a Thursday with classic house and dance the rest of the week. With two distinct dance areas there will be a choice of musical styles to more or less suit everybody. DV8 is situated opposite giant club complex The Nightingale, but I doubt very much that they will suffer any loss of trade – on the contrary, with Birmingham's gay village finally sorting itself out with some choice venues, it seems that it will undoubtebly become the city of choice for weekend clubbers. **Open** Thursday-Saturday 2200-0400. Sunday 2200-0200 **Price** £1-5

The Nightingale — Essex House, Kent Street, Birmingham B5 6RD
Phone 0121 622 1718 E-mail enquiries@nightingaleclub.co.uk
Web www.nightingaleclub.co.uk

The Nightingale is a massive club complex with five bars, two discos, restaurant/café-bar and games room, spread out over three floors and with a capacity for around 1,800-plus homos. The ground floor disco radiates an award-winning state-of-the-art lighting rig and an industri-al-style viewing gantry giving you a bird's eye-view of all the talent on the dance floor. The winding staircase will take you to the first floor where you will find a multi-atmosphere extravaganza, containing the very plush Ma Smith lounge, a comfortable and quieter café-bar, pool and gaming area and finally a first class restaurant serving everything from light snacks to a three course candlelit dinner. On the top floor (The Attic) is the second disco boasting once again superb sound and light facilities. The Nightingale is at the very hub of Birmingham's gay scene and it comes as no surprise that it is absolutely crammed week in and week out. One warning though, it is primarily for the disco queens (G-A-Y-stylee) If you like a harder edge to your music you will have to venture up to The Attic on a Saturday (Dance Federation) or a little out of your way to The Subway (see listing). If, however, you don't fancy trolling off to the other side of town, then The Nightingale will more than satisfy your dancing (and cruising) needs. It is worth mentioning that The Nightingale is a members' club although guests are now allowed in at the manager's discretion, without having to have a signatory. At the time of writing a new night was due to start: 'Ultimate Karma' taking place every second Friday of the month. This will be an Asian dance night (in The Attic – use separate entrance) similar to London's Club Kali. **Open** Tuesday-Wednesday 2200-0230.Friday 2100-0330. Saturday 2100-0400. Sunday 2100-0000 **Price** £1-2 midweek and £3-5 at weekends

Subway City   27 Water Street, Old Snow Hill, Birmingham B3 1HL Phone 0121 233 0310   **3**
E-mail info@subwaycityclub.com Web www.subwaycityclub.com
Situated under the arches at the top of Water Street close to Snow Hill railway station is Subway City, voted club of the year by readers of Midland Zone and Boyz on a regular basis, and not surprisingly – the two floors contain five bars, two dancefloors, a café and an indoor beer garden. Subway is no longer a members' club and neither is it strictly a gay club, except for Thursday and Saturday. At other times it is hired out to various promoters (some of whom – such as 'Oi!' and 2Klub's 'Sweat' – may operate a gay night, so it is wise to keep an eye on the gay press for details). The club has a capacity for around 1,200 peeps and has a kind of underground feel to it. The main room is cavernous with lots of secluded areas for you to... well, you know... and the second room is smaller (and lower – ouch!) but ideal for chilling and taking time out. Thursday is the gay 69'ers consisting of strippers and cheap drinks (from 69p, hence the name). For a midweek session this night is extremely busy. The music policy is different in each room (commercial house / chart). Saturday is, of course, the night when the stops are pulled out: the main room plays hard and commercial house and the extraordinarily busy Pink Room takes you back a couple of decades playing '70s and '80s retro. The first Saturday of the month is the well-established Blue Night – open 'til 0600 with many of the country's top DJs playing for your pleasure: names such as Little Miss Natalie (Paradise) and Ken

Ferguson. This is always a busy session and I'd recommend you get here early and gain cheap drinks (before 2300) and admission (half-price before 2200 and escalating every half hour thereafter). Tip: Get to Angels Café Bar (see separate listing) and take advantage of the free coach to Subway every Thursday and Saturday. **Open** Thursday 2200-0300. Saturday 2200-0400 (or 2100-0600 Blue, every first Saturday) **Price** £1-3 Thursday, £2-10 Saturday

Club nights

Decades Music Bar

43-47 Bartholemew Street, Dale End, Birmingham Phone 0121 248 1970
The nearest thing Birmingham has to a gay all-nighter; it's a shame there aren't more. The admission is nominal and the music is ace (assuming you've had enough of chart and camp) as the policy is house (hard, funky and vocal) from Thursday to Saturday, with a garage vibe on Sunday. To get in on Saturday (the only exclusively gay night) you will need a flyer, available after closing hours from the distributors outside The Nightingale, Subway and DV8 (you might also find them in some bars in the area). These flyers allow you some sort of discount on your admission but first and foremost they are proof of your status as a steaming big pufftah – a neccessity for admission. There is no dress code on Thursday to Saturday – even trackies and trainers are acceptable (big plus-points to Decades). Sundays though are a return to the smart frock department (boo!). Saturday is described as 'The Breakfast Bender – a party for the twatted generation' an apt description, so go and enjoy. By the way, remember to use the entrance at the rear of the club – not the main entrance. **Open** Thursday-Saturday 0200-0600. Sunday 1500-2230 **Price** £2-3

Oi! Club @ Subway City

27 Water Street, Old Snow Hill, Birmingham B3 1HL Phone 0161 273 2074 or 07956 808 142 E-mail info@oiclub.co.uk
Web www.oiclub.co.uk
Oi! What you fuckin' lookin' at? Erm.. once a month Subway City becomes home to this dead 'ard gay night where 'Steps' are not your twee little pop outfit, but the things you walk up to get to the cruise zone and 'Camp' is the word that comes after 'Boot'. Skinheads either adjust the collars on their Ben Sherman's or hoist up their bleached jeans to emphasise their crotch. The lad in the trackie bottoms and Nike vest looks at you – you return the glance – he turns away grinning slyly to himself. Oi! is hard! The music is hard! And the people..? They are the ones that you pass in the street and wonder if, and then pray that you will see them in this club over the weekend. Oi! Club is a fantasy that comes to life! Based in the confines of Subway City it is at the very opposite of the homo spectrum to G-A-Y. Unfortunately, once a month here is not enough (every first Friday), however, you can continue the sexperience on the second and fourth Saturday of the month down in Liverpool (The Escape: see listing) where the sexual atmosphere buzzes in a very different way to Subway. Tip: if you know the dance movements to Steps' hits give this place a miss! **Open** First Friday of the month 2200-0300 **Price** £6-8

| Sweat @ | 27 Water Street, Old Snow Hill, Birmingham B3 1HL |
| Subway City | Phone 07866 370 423 E-mail sweat@2klub.com Web www.2klub.com |

A relatively new Friday monthly night at one of Birmingham's best clubs brought to you by the 2Klub crew. Sweat by name and sweat by nature – the funkiest tribal house, the hottest hard house and the horniest nu-nrg sounds. Nearly ten hours of sheer pleasure gives you your 'fix' to see you through 'til the next event. The music policy for Sweat is to build the atmosphere on the main floor from funky but hard US-style house through to cutting-edge UK/Euro hard house and nu-nrg. They deliberately say 'cutting-edge' to emphasise the fact that they don't play tunes which have been over-played for months elsewhere. Any club can do that. They have deliberately 'acquired' DJs who have access to, or are creating, new sounds, aiming to provide clubbers with an interesting musical experience, different from anything in most other clubs. The year 2001, they predict, will be the one in which 'funky' is going to become more popular. Hear where things are heading in the Funky Room where they play funky US house throughout the night for those who like something a little more relaxed and sexy. The organisers are not just counting on the talents of resident DJs: the likes of Eddie Halliwell combining the hardest of hard house with superb scratching to re-mix tunes (live!) plus Adam Moore (Sherbet / 2Klub) and Chris G (a relative but talented newcomer to the DJing scene). They are also drafting in hordes of the big names such as Jon The Dentist (Infamous), Steve Thomas (Trade), Fergie (Sundisential) and EJ Doubell (FIST). Even though 2Klub and Sweat is a monthly gay night, sexuality is not an issue; what matters is your attitude and that you get a buzz from you and other people having a really great, happy night out. Remember to get here well before the opening time or else you will be queueing for half the night. If you can (and to more or less guarantee entry), try to buy your tickets from Ticketmaster or other ticket outlets. Tip: obtain free membership online which will give you a discount on admission. **Open** Friday 2130-0600 Last Friday of the month **Price** £6-8

Saunas

| Looking Glass | Unit 5: Kent House, Gooch Street North, Birmingham B5 |
| Sauna | Phone 0121 666 7529 |

The Looking Glass is situated slap-bang in the middle of the village, off Wrentham Street. Parking is difficult during the day because the facility car park fills up quickly, which leaves you the option of finding a parking meter on Gooch Street North or parking in the NCP. This is a spotless sauna and you sometimes feel a little guilty depositing your fluids! But never mind, that's what the place is for. The usual sauna facilities are here: Jacuzzi, steam room and sauna cabin, although they are far from being the most spacious, which is not a problem if you are squeezing up to someone you like – if the 'someone you like' moves away quite sharpish it might mean that he thinks you're a pig (so stop hassling him!) He may, however, be encouraging you to follow him to one of the five individual rest rooms or to the communal rest area for a group sesh. Being so close to all the bars and clubs means that this venue can get quite busy after the venues close – particularly over the weekend (all-nighters), but as with all saunas it is quite impossible to say when the busy times are. One thing to note is that on your first visit you will be expected to pay a £2 membership fee in addition to the £9 entrance. If you can prove you are a tourist you will normally be able to gain entry without paying the membership. Also, for visitors to the area, remember there is a Gooch Street and a Gooch Street North. You want the latter – do not make the mistake of trolling up and down the wrong one. **Open** Monday-Thursday 1200-2300. Friday-Saturday 1200-0600. Sunday 1300-2300 **Price** £9 (£5 concession)

Birmingham's Centenary Square is made up of more than half a million individual bricks – all hand-laid! It also accommodates one of the largest fountains in Europe (nicknamed 'The Floozie in the Jacuzzi') with a flow of 3,000 gallons per minute.

3

Spartan Health Club

127 George Road, Erdington, Birmingham B23 7SH
Phone 0121 382 3345
Occupying a three-storey building, the Spartan Health Club is a friendly, welcoming establishment with an intimate capacity for only fifty people. The ground floor provides all the wet area facilities whilst the upstairs houses the rest rooms and video lounges. Because of its location it does tend to attract the gay or bi man looking for relief outside of their own area. Smoking is not allowed anywhere in the building except for an area set aside in reception. Directions to the sauna are quite straightforward; it is approximately two minutes from Spaghetti Junction. Exit Junction 6 off the M6 (North to South) and take the first left at the island which should bring you out on Slade Road. The third left is George Road, opposite Brookvale Reservoir. Admission after 1800 lets you in for only £8. **Open** Monday-Saturday 1200-2300. Sunday 1300-2200 **Price** £8-10

Accommodation

Sebastian House

266 Monument Road, Edgbaston, Birmingham B16 8XF
Phone 0121 455 9459 Fax 0121 454 7307
Built in the late 18th-century Sebastian House is a Grade Two-listed building, retaining much of the charm and character of a Georgian house. With seven rooms – most en-suite and a delightful four-poster bed room (£65). All rooms have direct dial telephone and welcome tray. It's situated about a ten minute taxi ride from the gay village it won't take you long to get home of a night. Reservations can be made by cheque or credit as one night's deposit, although Access and Visa credit card bookings incur an additional 4 per cent charge. Cancellations are accepted 48 hours before you are due to take up your room; after this period a one night room let is levied. Continental breakfast is included in the price but an additional surcharge of £3.50 is payable if you require a full English breakfast. **Price** £55 en-suite double room **Number of rooms** 7, all en-suite

The Sheiling Guest House	1267 Stratford Road, Hall Green, Birmingham B28 9AJ

The Sheiling Guest House

1267 Stratford Road, Hall Green, Birmingham B28 9AJ

Phone 0121 777 6139

An elegant and stylish guest-house set within its own well-maintained gardens. Facilities include private parking, large comfortable TV lounge and spacious conservatory dining room with sun terrace. Rooms include hospitality trays with hairdryers and ironing facilities on request. It is worth bearing in mind that Hall Green is not near the gay scene and it will cost about £5 in a taxi to get to and from the venues. **Price** £45 **Number of rooms** 6, only 1 en-suite

The Village

152 Hurst Street, Birmingham B5 6RY

Phone 0121 622 4742 Fax 0121 622 4679

Bright, comfortable and clean accommodation in the rooms above this popular gay bar. All rooms come with TV and welcome tray. **Price** £45 double room **Number of rooms** 6, all en-suite

Cruising grounds

A426

Exit Junction 6 off the M42 or the roundabout at Stonebridge on the A45 and follow the sign onto the A426 heading towards Brownhills or Lichfield. Don't worry, you won't be going up that far. The lay-by you are after is on the opposite carriageway which is quite visible as you drive up. Once spotted, take the next exit and do a U-turn. Park up in the lay-by (if you can) and walk to the end by the fence. Walk through the woods following the disused railway line until you get to the bridge. This is it.

Cannon Hill Park

(Edgbaston) Just off the B4217 Edgbaston Road. Action both in the toilets and the wooded area towards the back. The park is behind the Police Training College – so watch out!

Coleshill (A446 / M6 Junction)

(Solihull) Outdoor action in the woodland located next to the lay-by on the northbound A446 road, immediately south of its junction with the M6 Motorway. Action can be found at most times during the week. Caution advised in this location but nothing too much to worry about.

Highbury Park

(Kings Heath) Not much is known about this site, but it's still worth a mention. The action (apparently) takes place in the bushes just beneath Highbury House.

Kennedy Gardens

(Colmore Circus) Situated close to Colmore Circus. Not much information regarding this area: more would be appreciated.

Sandwell Valley

(Sandwell Valley Park) Cited as one of the best cruising grounds in Birmingham but this is up to you to decide for yourself. Take Junction 1 off the M5 heading towards Birmingham. As soon as you pass the football ground, take the first left (before the BP garage) and follow this lane all the way to the bottom of the hill. There are two car parks here, the one nearest to the cemetery is considered to be the best but this does get quite busy and so the other will also suffice. It does get visited at times by the police and it has also been known for undercover police to patrol the area.

Retail & Other

Clone Zone

Arcadian Centre, 84 Hurst Street, Birmingham Phone 0121 666 6640
Gay men's sex shop with outlets in most major cities throughout the UK. Sells practically everything you could possibly need from [those kind of] magazines and books to condoms and lube. They will also be able to inform you of any events going on in the city and supply the tickets you need to gain admittance. All the free gay press and club flyers are available here and it is always worth asking the pleasant staff if there are any specialist events going on that will suit your area of interest. **Open** Monday-Wednesday 1030-1800. Thursday-Saturday 1030-2200. Sunday 1300-1900

Funky Crop Shop

86 Hurst Street, Birmingham B5 4TD Phone 0121 622 2302
Sister salon to the Funky Crop Shop in Manchester now firmly established in their new shop next door to Missing and Clone Zone. Like the Manchester salon, you are invited to pop in here to collect the gay press and flyers to nearly all the gay events happening in Birmingham. **Open** Monday-Saturday 1000-1800. Thursday 'til late, by appointment only **Price** £10 dry cut

Brindley Twist Tafft and James Solicitors

Aspect Court, 4 Temple Row, Birmingham B2 5HG
Phone 0121 609 4625 E-mail graham@bttj.com Web www.bttj.com
A practice that employs over fifty staff with specialist gay and lesbian lawyers. There is also a no win – no fee service available. Office also in Coventry. **Open** Monday-Friday 0900-1715

Blackburn Club nights

C'est La Vie

11-15 Market Street, Blackburn BB2 2DE Phone 01254 691 877
Long running weekly gay night in this usually young straight venue. Now in it's fourth year it still provides a welcome outlet for the local gay boys and girls of Blackburn and surrounding areas. The admission policy is a little confusing, increasing it's charges half-hourly until 2200 with the final entry at 2230, so it is wise to get here as early as you can. There is an adequate free buffet provided on the gallery upstairs. This is put out on opening so it gives you more incentive to arrive early, otherwise all you are left with is the dried-up salad and fag-end garnish. Music is rather mainstream, although this does tend to suit the mixed boy and girl crowd, who probably need the respite to come down from a hectic weekend. This is quite a good night out, offering opportunity to meet new people, although I wouldn't personally travel a great distance to come here. **Open** Sunday 2100-0000 **Price** £2-4

Blackpool

Back in the latter part of the 18th century, Blackpool was a quiet resort town catering for a small number of well-to-do holiday-makers. The introduction of the railways in 1840 and electric street lighting in 1879 saw the resort's popularity extend to the working classes of the north, who poured into the town in their droves. Today, it is no different. Blackpool caters wholeheartedly for those same working classes and has an atmosphere that is unique within Britain. Today, more than eight million tourists flock to Blackpool every year to visit a town that is cheap, tacky and gaudy. Strangely enough though, this is not to knock Blackpool; on the contrary, it's why the place is so successful and well-loved. This is a town where glare, excess and fun go hand-in-hand – a land of deckchaired beaches, 'kiss-me-quick' hats and bags of winkles and cockles. The sea-front stretch of road that links north pier to south pier is known as The Golden Mile and hosts a fascinating array of attractions and businesses from amusement arcades, Louis Tussauds Waxworks (the poor relation to Madame Tussauds in London), Ripley's 'Believe it or Not' and all manner of souvenir shops where brazen displays of tack and tat pack the shelves. The famous national cuisine – fish and chips – can be found in abundance here, every shop claiming to serve the best that you've ever tasted. September to November sees Blackpool showing off its lightbulbs – five miles of them to be exact – commemorating Blackpool's claim as the first town to have electricity. Better known as 'Blackpool Illuminations', this time of year constitutes the high season for hoteliers and getting a room can be pricey (replacement bulbs are also hard to come by). Blackpool is innocent and honest fun and is the undisputed king of saucey postcard, kitsch-embracing British seaside life.

The main gay spot is Talbot Road, home to the majority of the town's gay bars and the one-and-only gay club, Flamingo's. Here you will find swarms of gay tourists hopping from bar to bar, drinking down the ale and drinking in the atmosphere. During the summer months everyone seems to end up at The Flying Handbag at the top of Talbot Road where the drag DJs, cheap beer and constant rounds of strippers help create a hedonistic and jovial atmosphere where inhibitions collapse just as freely as the legs of the soused patrons.

Getting in touch

You can find the **Tourist Information Office** (01253 621 623) at 1 Clifton Street, where gay-friendly staff can provide you with all the information you require. They are open Monday to Friday from 0900 to 1700 and Saturday to Sunday from 1000 to 1600. There are additional offices which share the same hours: one is on the promenade by the tower, the other smaller branch, is across from the Pleasure Beach at 87 Coronation Street. Useful numbers you may require whilst in Blackpool include **Gay and Lesbian Switchboard** (01253 621 834) which is open

Monday to Thursday from 1930 to 2130; **Body Positive** (01253 292 803) for health advice and information and **Connect** (01253 751 047), a centre for young persons' health and information.

Pubs

Basils On The Strand

9 The Strand, Blackpool FY1 1NX Phone 01253 294 109
E-mail basils@ukonline.co.uk Web www.in-the-pink.com
A popular choice for a mixed age group throughout the week. A first floor bar and dance-floor with a busy karaoke night on Mondays. The rest of the week is disco with additional bits thrown in like cheap drinks on a Thursday and cabaret at midnight on a Friday. Up the spiral staircase is a large relaxing seating area and pool table. **Open** Monday-Saturday 1230-2430. Sunday 1230-0000

Churchill's

83 Topping Street, Blackpool FY1 3AF Phone 01253 622 036
The gay-friendly Churchill's, situated opposite the famous 'Winter Gardens' is a small traditional-styled pub – very cosy, with a great friendly atmosphere. From Wednesday through to Sunday you can expect to be entertained by the resident drag Vicki Le Plume. **Open** Monday-Saturday 1030-2300. Sunday 1200-2230

The Flying Handbag

170-176 Talbot Road, Blackpool FY1 3AZ Phone 01253 625 522
E-mail admin@itp.uk.com Web www.in-the-pink.com
This is without doubt the busiest gay bar in Blackpool, particularly over the weekend and, of course, on a Sunday afternoon (stripper). Most nights there is something going on – usually in the form of drag DJ Chris D'Bray hurling insults to anyone who dares cross her path! An ideal final resting place before you hit Flamingo's (next door). Talking of which, there is now an entrance to the club via Flying Handbag which will enable you to get in for free on a Tuesday, Wednesday and Thursday if you are in the bar. Using the club's main entrance on these nights will cost you about £2. The bar will close down at 2300 (2230 Sunday) while the punters either make their way out of the venue or into the club (via the bar); it then re-opens as part of the club. **Open** Monday-Saturday 1100-2300. Sunday 1100-2230

Hello Dollies (formerly The Cow Bar)

74 Cookson Street, Blackpool FY1 3DR Phone 01253 621 274
Don't be misled by the outward appearance of this bar which may, to some, seem like an old traditional pub containing bar billiards, the local prozzy and an ample supply of milk stout. Make your way through the doors and you will find camp heaven, which for Blackpool, as with being continuously drunk, is a necessity. The former purple and yellow puke-inducing interior has now been totally refurbished into a bright gold and cream modern gay venue. Plenty of room to chat and mingle, or if the groove gets you, plenty of room to get up and dance – yeah baby! There is also a games room, but watch out for the pisshead practising his darts – ouch! Cheap drinks a-plenty, and I mean cheap, at prices that Londoners have never seen in their lives. Try and catch the happy hours every day from 1200-2100 and get Boddingtons bitter for

£1.37 a pint or lager for £1.47. **Open** Monday-Saturday 1200-2300. Sunday 1200-2230

Lucy's Bar

9-11 Talbot Road, Blackpool FY1 1LB Phone 01253 293 204
This bar has a reputation for being 'just' a girl's bar, which is quite untrue. Although the girls do tend to use Lucy's bar above any other in Blackpool, it does in fact offer a warm welcome to all members of the gay community, particularly TVs and TSs (and their admirers). The basement bar is situated on Talbot Square (underneath Rumours Fun Pub). There is one long bar, a pool table (always busy) and a small dance floor. Cheap drinks are a regular feature, as are the live DJs and cabaret. During the summer season, the bar is heaving and there seems to be a constant 'party' atmosphere (must be the sea air). Lucy's bar is well known by all in Blackpool. It is one of the oldest gay bars in the country having opened over thirty years ago. (Lucy herself died over five years ago – the woman behind the bar is Linda … not Lucy.) **Open** Monday-Thursday 2100-0200. Friday-Saturday 2000-0200 Sunday 2000-2230

Mardi Gras

114 Talbot Road, Blackpool Phone 01253 296 262
One of the rare Blackpool gay venues that is not owned by Basil Newby's 'In The Pink' Company. The Mardi Gras is a large basement cabaret bar with DJ box, well-used stage and dance floor. This is one of the best venues in Blackpool for drink promos (about £1.50 a pint) available from Monday to Wednesday, 1200 to 2100, all day Thursday and Friday to Saturday between the hours of 1200 and 1900. **Open** Monday-Saturday 1200-0200. Sunday 1200-0030 **Price** £2, Friday after 2200 and Saturday after 2000

Blackpool is a city of big boasts: The Pleasure Beach is the second most popular fun fair in Europe and takes up a massive 40 acres (second only to that place in Paris). Blackpool Tower is 518 feet and 9 inches tall, to the top of the flagpole (well, it all counts!). Blackpool has more hotel beds available than the whole of Portugal. There are nearly 40,000 theatre seats available throughout Blackpool every night. And, of the 800 donkeys working on Britain's beaches, 228 are licensed to work on Blackpool beach alone.

Pepe's

94 Talbot Road, Blackpool FY1 1LR Phone 01253 626 691
E-mail **pepes@ukonline.co.uk** Web **www.in-the-pink.com**
Pepe's is a narrow basement bar near the top of Talbot Road. Recently refurbished, it has lost the dark, dull interior in favour of a more modern open-plan style. It is still very much favoured by the raunchy denim and leather crowd as well as the disco girls and boys bar-hopping their way up the road on their way to the club. Some sort of entertainment happens each and every night, from strippers (Tuesday) to cabaret (Friday), with DJ and cheap drinks at most other times. **Open** Monday 1200-0100. Tuesday 1200-0200. Wednesday-Thursday 1200-0100. Friday-Saturday 1200-0200. Sunday 1200-0000

Clubs

Flamingo's
174-176 Talbot Road, Blackpool FY1 3AZ Phone 01253 624 901
E-mail admin@in-the-pink.com Web www.in-the-pink.com
Blackpool's only gay club (established 1980) and the flagship in the Basil Newby empire, which also includes Funny Girls, Pepe's and Basils, to name but a few. During the week only the downstairs main dance arena is open, but come the weekend, the whole complex opens up, giving you a choice of music style to dance your socks off to. On Tuesday, Wednesday and Thursday it is free entry to the club via the adjoining door at Flying Handbag. After 2300 you will have to use the main club entrance which on a Thursday (Ascension) admission is £2. On a Sunday the club has started a 'Tea dance' (this may or may not carry on through the year so phone for up-to-date info). Admission is free before 2100 and costs £2 after and there's loads of cheap drinks on offer. The good thing about this place is that as it's the only gay club, pretty much everyone tends to end up here (which does save time trawling the bars in the hunt for cock!). **Open** Monday-Saturday 2200-0200. Sunday 1700-0000 **Price** £2-5

Funny Girls
1-9 Queen Street, Blackpool FY1 1NL Phone 01253 624 901
E-mail funnygirls@ukonline.co.uk Web www.itp.uk.com
Funny Girls is a burlesque-style cabaret showbar for a mixed gay and straight audience, and usually the straights far outweigh the gays! Even so, it is a night designed for the latter. Betty Legs Diamond and her troupe of she-boys put on a sharp, slick show that would not look out of place in the West End – well, not quite, but it is an evening of sheer campery and the crowds love it. You can choose between either standing, seating or seating with waitress service (all of which carries an appropriate price). Usually, most places are pre-booked (phone the booking office Monday to Friday, 0900-1700 on the number above), however, if the place is not fully booked you may be able to pay on the door for standing room, or seating if there are any vacancies (Fridays and Saturdays usually see the place full). If you do have time to spare in Blackpool and are not on the hunt then this may be an entertaining alternative to the bars. The show finishes at 2330 (bar closes at 2300) so there is always plenty of time to get to the club. **Open** Monday-Saturday 1900-2330. Sunday 1900-2300 **Price** £3.50-5 standing; £7.50-10 seating; £10-15 seating with waitress service

Club nights

Fussy Pussy @
Flamingo's
Talbot Road, Blackpool FY1 2BN Phone 0161 288 2727
E-mail fussy@vanillagirls.co.uk Web www.vanillagirls.co.uk
Another excellent Fussy Pussy night out for a mixed (mainly) girl and gay boy crowd on the main floor of this fab venue. This is usually a themed party night giving you the chance to dress up in all your fancy dress gear depending on the theme (see website for this month's theme). Past parties have included Demons and Angels, Wild Wild West and

Doctors and Nurses. Although this night is hosted by the girls at Vanilla (Manchester) it carries the same ethos of girls and boys playing together in a high spirited holiday atmosphere. Meet up at Flying Handbag (see listing). **Open** Friday 2200-0200 Every third Friday of the month **Price** £4

Saunas

Acquasauna 25-27 Springfield Road, Blackpool FY1 1QW Phone 01253 294 610
E-mail info@acquasaunas.co.uk Web www.acquasaunas.co.uk
A new addition to this long-running sauna (formerly GS Sauna) is The Castle Crypt – a themed room with stocks and sling, etc. It also has the usual sauna facilities of sauna, steam room, Jacuzzi and individual rest rooms. Admission from Sunday through to midnight on a Thursday has been reduced to £5. All other times remain at the standard £10. Membership is available and necessary for entry although this £3 fee has been suspended for the Blackpool venue for the whole of 2001. Just pay your £5-10 admission and play. The other Acquasauna is in Carlisle. **Open** Monday-Thursday 1200-0000. Friday-Saturday 1200-0700. Sunday 1200-2200 **Price** £5-10

The Honeycombe 99 Egerton Road, Blackpool FY1 2NN Phone 01253 752 211
Located about two minutes from Trades Hotel this is the second sauna to cater for Blackpool's gay and bi male crowd. The low admission price ensures that the sauna is pretty much always busy and it gets cheaper still if you are resident at any of their sister Keyline hotels (Trades, Mardi Gras or The Highlands), to a paltry £3 plus the £5 initial membership (which is mandatory). Even so, this is cheap for a sauna (and a good sauna at that). Even better, this admission also entitles you to two hot or cold drinks. All the usual sauna facilities are here including a dungeon room in the basement, communal rest room upstairs and about five individual porno rooms (rest rooms with porno vids playing). The Honeycombe is pretty much an afternoon and late evening sauna; last entry is at 2100 so if there is no-one in that twists your melon by this time – you may as well go home. **Open** Monday-Sunday 1200-2330 **Price** £5, plus £5 annual membership

Accommodation

Abbeyville 39 High Street, Blackpool FY1 2BN Phone 01253 752 072
Member of BAGS (Blackpool Accommodation for Gays). A very friendly and relaxed establishment.**Price** £30 **Number of rooms** 7, none en-suite

Amalfi Hotel 19-21 Eaves Street, Blackpool FY1 2NH Phone 01253 622 971
Established for more than 13 years, The Amalfi is a well-established, comfortable and homely guest-house, catering mainly for gay women and their male gay guests. Member of BAGS. All rooms are either ground floor or first floor. **Price** £30-40 **Number of rooms** 8, en-suite available

Arendale Hotel   23 Gynn Avenue, Blackpool FY1 2LD
Phone 01253 351 044 Fax 01253 318 433
Straight-owned but extremely gay-friendly. It is worth pointing out that there are no double beds here, only twins. **Price** £38 **Number of rooms** 7, 5 en-suite

Astoria Guest House   50 Park Road, Blackpool FY1 Phone 01253 622 377 F 01253 291 321
E-mail astoria@ic24.net Web www.gay-hotels.com/astoria
Gay-owned and -run guest-house about five minutes' walk from all gay venues. Member of BAGS.

The illuminations run six miles along the sea front from Starr Gate to Bispham. The 2000 illuminations were staged at an estimated cost of £2.4 million! Of that, £2.2 million came from the council tax contributions of the locals. That means that the average Blackpool household contributes £48.84 towards the illumination fund. The lights and equipment are valued at £10 million and over 72 miles of electric cable are used every year. The 2000 Illuminations were switched on by Irish boy band Westlife. Previous light-switchers have been Sir Matt Busby (1968), Red Rum – the race horse! (1977), Shirley Bassey (1994), The Bee Gees (1995), The Muppets (1979), Jayne Mansfield (1959) and George Formby (1953)

The Athol Hotel   3 Mount Street, Blackpool FY1 2DQ Phone 01253 624 918
Licensed bar open 'til late. Free off road secure parking for ten cars. Two minutes to gay bars. **Price** £44 **Number of rooms** 11, none en-suite

The Baricia   40-42 Egerton Road, Blackpool FY1 2NW Phone 01253 623 130
Three-diamond English Tourist Board hotel with a warm, gay-friendly atmosphere. Men and women couples made welcome. All rooms en-suite with special weekly and weekend rates from £17 per person per night. **Price** £35 **Number of rooms** 12, all en-suite

The Belvedere Hotel   77 Dickson Road, Blackpool FY1 2BX Phone 01253 624 733
E-mail belvhotel@btinternet.com Web www.gay-hotels.com/belvedere
A small, immaculate hotel offering quality en-suite accommodation. Ideally situated in the north shore district of Blackpool, just a few minutes walk from the scene. Member of BAGS. All rooms have hairdryer, tea/coffee-making facilities. Special rates available for longer stays. **Price** £30 **Number of rooms** 7, all en-suite

The Birdcage   27 Cocker Street, Blackpool FY1 3BZ Phone 01253 620 988
Formerly known as Dudley House Hotel. Member of BAGS. All en-suite rooms are themed – bordello, Egyptian, gothic, Chinese, Hollywood, astrological, dungeon, royal, Victorian. Licensed bar. **Price** £35 **Number of rooms** 10, 7 en-suite

Casablanca Hotel   20 Bairstow Street, Blackpool FY1 5BN Phone 01253 620 380
Affordable gay accommodation, about a ten minute walk from the Talbot Road gay venues. There is no price difference on en-suite and

standard rooms; it is a matter of first come, first served. The hotel is licensed and will keep the bar open late if there is demand. Breakfast is included in the price. **Price** £30 **Number of rooms** 10, 7 en-suite

Chaucer House   59 High Street, Blackpool FY1 2BN Phone 01253 299 099
Exclusively gay bed and breakfast open all year. Established for over eight years. Close to the scene and station.

Coastings   62 Coronation Street, Blackpool FY1 4PD Phone 01253 623 269
Hotel   Gay-owned and -run and a member of BAGS. Five minutes from all gay bars and club. Late bar available. **Price** £35 **Number of rooms** 13, most en-suite

Colin's Hotel   9-11 Cocker Street, Blackpool FY1 1SF Phone 01253 620 541
In my opinion this is one of the best hotels to stay at in Blackpool – nothing too fancy, in fact, it's quite basic, but it's cheap, central and extremely hospitable. Not only that, but on Sunday evening there is a buffet laid on in the bar lounge where all the residents get together after a night on the town. Colin's Hotel was one of the original gay hostels that adopted the 'room to roam' concept. You know the score – leave your door open if you want gentleman callers to pay you a midnight visit or keep it closed (with a chair wedged under the handle) if you don't. Perfect. This is pretty much always fully booked over the weekend, so either book early or call for cancellations. **Price** £30 **Number of rooms** 26, 2 en-suite

Corniche Hotel   60 Charnley Road, Blackpool FY1 4PF Phone 01253 291 330
Mixed gay and straight hotel and a member of BAGS. The Corniche organises themed weekends every now and again such as bears weekends, leather and rubber weekends and so on. If you are interested, ask to have your name put on the mailing list. **Price** £44 **Number of rooms** 19, all en-suite

The Cove   9 Banks Street, Blackpool FY1 1RN Phone 01253 621 438
E-mail thecove1@btinternet.com Web www.cove.freeserve.co.uk
All rooms en-suite and newly refurbished, TV, mini fridges, tea/coffee-making facilities in all rooms. Twenty yards to the promenade, and an easy five minute walk to all gay venues. Men and women welcome. **Price** £36 **Number of rooms** 6, all en-suite

Back in 1993, when Blackpool was trying to gain a coveted blue flag for effluent treatment, it was rumoured that Blackpool's famous donkeys would be forced to wear nappies, in order to catch the animals' droppings. The blue flag requires that beaches be spotless and sea water clear.

The Edenfield   17 Cocker Street, Blackpool FY1 2BY
Phone 01253 624 009 Fax 01253 625 568
Evening meal available on request. Close to sea front and a matter of minutes to the gay scene. Late, late bar. **Price** £30-35 **Number of rooms** 11, 6 en-suite

Edgeley
Guest House
7 Kent Road, Blackpool Phone 01253 624 712
Gay-owned and -run comfortable guest-house in central Blackpool and about a ten minute walk to the gay scene. **Price** £30 **Number of rooms** 4, none en-suite

Fairhaven Hotel
42 Dickson Road, Blackpool FY1 2AJ Phone 01253 624 497
Gay-friendly hotel very close to all the gay venues. Licensed bar now in operation. Evening meal available at an additional cost. Some rooms can accommodate up to five people although the rates are charged on a per person basis (approximately £10 in the week and £15 at weekends) **Price** £20-30 **Number of rooms** 14, none en-suite

The Glencor
Hotel
39 Lord Street, Blackpool FY1 2BD Phone 01253 622 920
Fax 01253 291 857 E-mail info@glencorhotelblackpool.co.uk
Web www.glencorhotelblackpool.co.uk
Ideally situated in the North Shore area of Blackpool, just a few minutes walk from the Tower, Winter Gardens and close to all the local amenities including the gay pubs and clubs. **Price** £36 **Number of rooms** 10, all en-suite

Glenroy Hotel
10 Trafalgar Road, Blackpool FY1 6AW Phone 01253 344 607
Both men and women are welcome in this clean, comfortable and hospitable hotel. Hairdryers in all rooms. Men and women welcome. Tea/coffee-making facilities. Licensed bar. Forty yards to the promenade. **Price** £45 **Number of rooms** 10, all en-suite

Granby Lodge
Hotel
15 Lord Street, Blackpool FY1 2AZ Phone 01253 627 842
Granby Lodge is a small and friendly hotel, ideally situated for either a relaxing or fun-packed holiday break. Only a few minutes walk from the railway station, north pier and scene. Tariff includes full English breakfast or a veggie alternative. There is also a free car park. **Price** £40-50 **Number of rooms** 9, most en-suite

Heatherdale
Lodge
2 Pleasant Street, Blackpool FY1 2JA Phone 01253 626 268
Heatherdale Lodge is a gay Christian guest-house. A friendly atmosphere prevails as guests generally share an interest in the spiritual side of life – although it is not necessary to have religious beliefs to stay here. Situated at the north end of Lord Street, it's a five minute walk to the town centre and railway station. There is a choice of standard or en-suite rooms with own shower and toilet. **Price** £30 **Number of rooms** 6, en-suite available

The Hertford
Hotel
18 Lord Street, Blackpool FY1 2BD Phone 01253 292 931
E-mail ceges@dircon.co.uk Web www.ceges.dircon.co.uk
The Hertford is a small, friendly place with a licensed bar, close to all major attractions of the resort. On-street parking and large local car parks available nearby. Pets can be accommodated by prior arrangement. The Hertford has been inspected by The English Tourism Council and has been awarded three diamonds, two years running. **Price** £38 **Number of rooms** 10, 4 en-suite

Highbank
Guest-House
46 Banks Street, Blackpool FY1 2BE Phone 01253 294 797
E-mail hotel@highbank-hotel.co.uk Web www.highbank-hotel.co.uk
The Highbank is a clean, comfortable and friendly guest-house.
Although no rooms are fully en-suite, good quality toilet and shower
facilities are provided. The Highbank is situated near the north pier and
the main railway station and is just a couple of minutes' walk to the
town centre, the tower and theatres. Plenty of car parking space available (which is quite remarkable in Blackpool). All rooms face 'the front'
so you can lean out of your window and encourage complete strangers
to come up and give you one! **Price** £25-35 **Number of rooms** 7, none en-
suite

The Highlands
46-54 High Street, Blackpool FY1 2BN
Phone 01253 752 264 Fax 01253 294 598
E-mail highlands@gayhotel.net Web www.gayhotel.net
Although not 100 per cent gay, The Highlands is gay-owned and welcomes both male and female gay visitors. A 32-bedroom hotel – including 18 en-suite and 14 standard rooms – conveniently situated for
nightlife, town centre, beach, shops and shows. The Highlands takes the
overflow of visitors from the group's other hotels (Trades and Mardi
Gras). The hotel is licensed to residents and has a pool table. **Price** £45
Number of rooms 32, 18 rooms en-suite

Hotel Zeus
37 General Street, Blackpool FY1 1SG Phone 01253 297 197
Newly refurbished for the up-coming season and only two minutes from
the scene. Catering for gay men and women, along with their straight
friends. Tea/coffee-making facilities in all rooms and licensed bar available. **Price** £33 **Number of rooms** 7, 5 en-suite

Kingsmead
Guest-House
58 Lord Street, Blackpool FY1 2BJ
Phone 01253 624 496 Fax 0870 055 3984
E-mail Kingsmead@redhotant.co.uk Web www.kingsmeadgg.co.uk
Situated in the north shore area of Blackpool and five minutes from the
scene. Member of BAGS. **Price** £30 **Number of rooms** 12, all en-suite

Lexham Hotel
14 Banks Street, Blackpool FY1 1RN Phone 01253 627 158
Mixed gay and straight hotel. Very friendly and discreet atmosphere.
Situated about five minutes from the gay scene and town centre. Free car
parking (limited – requires pre-booking). Direct dial phone and tea/cof-
fee-making facilities in all rooms. **Price** £50-55 **Number of rooms** 18, all
en-suite

The Lonsdale
Hotel
25 Cocker Street, Blackpool FY1 2BZ
Phone 01253 621 628 E-mail stephen@lonsdalehotel.freeserve.co.uk
Web www.lonsdalehotel.freeserve.co.uk
An Edwardian-styled guest-house only two minutes from the beach and
scene. The rooms are tastefully decorated and all have private en-suite
facilities with WC, wash hand-basin and shower. The Lonsdale is not
licensed but you are welcome to bring your own drink. Ice and glasses
are provided by the hotel. **Price** £34-40 **Number of rooms** 7, all en-suite

Lowen Guest-House
19 Carshalton Road, North Shore, Blackpool FY1 2NR
Phone 01253 626 608
Member of BAGS. Extremely gay-friendly guest-house, with straight friends also welcome. Gay-owned and -run. **Price** £30 **Number of rooms** 5, 1 en-suite

Mardi Gras
41-43 Lord Street, Blackpool FY1 2BD Phone 01253 751 087 Fax 01253 294 598 E-mail mardigras@gayhotel.net Web www.gayhotel.net
Sister hotel to Trades Hotel and The Highlands. A predominantly gay clientele. Reduced admission to The Honeycombe sauna is available to residents. **Price** £30-35 **Number of rooms** 21, all en-suite

Miracles Hotel
46 Dickson Road, Blackpool FY1 2AJ
Phone 01253 622 810 E-mail hotel.enquiry@ntworld.com
Web www.btinternet.com/~miracles.hotel
Although gay-owned and -run this is not an exclusively gay hotel, although I'm sure the welcome here will be a lot more hospitable than a straight-run hotel. Situated only two minutes from Blackpool North railway station, so you are only a few minutes away from all the local night life. The local tram and bus stops are just around the corner, making it easy to get to other parts of the town. **Price** £30 **Number of rooms** 10, 7 en-suite

The Mount Hotel
30 Exchange Street, Blackpool FY1 2BD Phone 01253 625 659
Gay-owned and -run hotel, particularly welcoming a lesbian clientele. **Price** £30 **Number of rooms** 12, none en-suite

Nevada
23 Lord Street, Blackpool FY1 2BD
Phone 01253 290 700 Fax 01253 622 749
E-mail nevada@gaybeds.co.uk Web www.gaybeds.co.uk
A member of BAGS, situated within walking distance of all gay venues. Most rooms are en-suite, all have TV, coffee/tea-making facilities and central heating. The hotel has a licensed bar and a comfortable TV lounge. The price quoted is for a one night stay for two persons; this can be reduced to £25 for more than one night. Comfortable and economical. **Price** £30 **Number of rooms** 13, most en-suite

The Newholme Hotel
77 Lords Street, Blackpool FY1 2DG Phone 01253 625 059
Part of JR Leisure, incorporating The Silverdale Hotel. **Price** £30 **Number of rooms** 12, 4 en-suite

The Primrose House Hotel
16 Lord Street, Blackpool FY1 2BD Phone 01253 622 488
Men-only licensed guest-house right in the heart of Blackpool's gay scene. Clean, friendly and comfortable. Member of BAGS. **Price** £45 **Number of rooms** 10, all en-suite

Raffles Hotel
73-75 Hornby Road, Blackpool FY1 4QJ Phone 01253 294 713
Clean, quality en-suite rooms and English Tourist Board recommended (three diamonds). Parking available. **Price** £46 **Number of rooms** 17, all en-suite

Renaissance   268 Central Drive, Blackpool FY1 5JB Phone 01253 400 160
Guest-House   E-mail lynda@renaissance2.demon.co.uk
This home-from-home guest-house caters particularly for (and is extremely popular with) the transgendered community. The Renaissance is a very friendly place with a very open attitude. Guests are made to feel at home with very few restrictions. Linda chairs the TV/TS social group that meets twice a month. You are welcome to phone for any further information that you may require. **Price** £40 **Number of rooms** 8, none en-suite

Sandolin   117 High Street, Blackpool FY1 2DW Phone 01253 752 908
Guest-House   Gay-owned and -run guest-house and member of BAGS. **Price** £25 **Number of rooms** 6, 1 en-suite

Sandylands   47 Banks Street, Blackpool FY1 2BH
Guest-House   Phone 01253 294 670 Fax 0870 284 9893
Sandylands Guest-House is a quieter hotel suited to the over forties, senior citizens or families with children over the age of eight years. Situated just one minute from the seafront, close to the town centre, shops, Tower and all main attractions. Open from March to October, it offers bed and breakfast and evening dinner (optional). Most of the food is home-made, and special needs can be catered for provided they are notified in advance. They also offer a variety of price packages to suit your needs. Special discounts are given the longer the stay. **Price** £25 **Number of rooms** 8, en-suite available

Every year, for the last 50 years, a convoy of over 80 black Hackney taxis ferries handicapped children to Blackpool Pleasure Beach. It's a heart-warming sight and if you're in town, there's no missing this happy parade, as the taxis are bedecked with balloons and ribbons and most of the drivers wear fancy dress.

The   26 Shaftesbury Avenue, Blackpool FY2 9QH
Shaftesbury   Phone 01253 352 453 E-mail karen-edda@the-shaftesbury.fsnet.co.uk
Hotel   Web www.gay-hotels.com/shaftesbury
Gay-owned and -run, welcoming a mixed clientele – mostly gay and mostly women. Small dogs can be accommodated by prior arrangement. Vegetarians catered for. **Price** £35-40 **Number of rooms** 10

Sheron House   21 Gynn Avenue, Blackpool FY1 2LD Phone 01253 354 614
E-mail sheronhouse@amserve.net Web www.gay-hotels.com/sheron
An English Tourism Council (three diamonds) guest-house situated in a quiet area of the resort in the north shore area adjacent to Queen's Promenade (no comments please!). Only one street back from the promenade, it's handy for town, clubs (a ten minute eager walk there and a twenty minute stagger back!) and the whole of the Fylde Coast with trams and buses leaving either end of the avenue, along the promenade and also on the street behind. The accommodation comprises six de-luxe en-suite rooms, all with tea/coffee-making facilities and hair dryers and each decorated to a very high standard. Each room is individually

named after the southern lakes in the nearby beautiful Lakeland. A hearty breakfast is included in the price and, as an extra, superb evening meals can be provided. The facilities of the house include a comfortable and restful lounge with TV, games, cards, chess and so on and a comprehensive supply of local information and guides. Tip: book early for bank holidays and illuminations. **Price** £40 per room **Number of rooms** 6, all en-suite

Silverdale Hotel   21 Lord Street, Blackpool FY1 2BD Phone 01253 626 904
Part of JR Leisure, incorporating The Newholme Hotel. **Price** £40 **Number of rooms** 17, 4 en-suite

Starlight Hotel   46 Dickson Road, Blackpool FY1 Phone 01253 622 810
Gay-owned and -run hotel and a member of BAGS. Late bar available. **Price** £35 **Number of rooms** 12, most en-suite

Sunnyside Hotel   16 Charles Street, Blackpool FY1 3HD Phone 01253 622 983
Gay-owned and -run homely styled guest-house established since 1988. All rooms are spotlessly clean. Member of BAGS (proprietor is actually a committee member). Lesbians and gay men equally welcome. Although the room rates reflect the price for a single night, The Sunnyside offers reduced rates for longer stays. Charles Street is within walking distance of all the gay venues in Blackpool, and less than a minute away from Flamingo's. Excellent. **Price** £32 **Number of rooms** 7, 5 en-suite

Thorncliffe Hotel   63 Dickson Road, Blackpool FY1 2BX Phone 01253 622 508
Gay-owned and -run hotel with licensed bar, TV, tea/coffee-making facilities. Close to pubs, clubs and station. **Price** £32 **Number of rooms** 10, all en-suite

Trades Hotel   51-55 Lord Street, Blackpool FY1 2BJ Phone 01253 294 812
Fax 01253 294 598 E-mail trades@gayhotel.net Web www.gayhotel.net
A well-known, and long-established gay hotel which is decidedly cruisy with the 'room to roam' concept. Late bar over the weekends to guests and residents of their sister hotels, Mardi Gras and Highlands. Reduced admission to Honeycombe Sauna for residents. **Price** £35-50 **Number of rooms** 34, most en-suite

Tremadoc Hotel   127-129 Dickson Road, Blackpool FY1 2EU Phone 01253 624 001
E-mail tom@tremadoc.com Web www.tremadoc.com
Gay-owned and -run and very, very hospitable and friendly. **Price** £32 **Number of rooms** 10, 2 en-suite

Warwick Holiday Flats   39 Banks Street, Blackpool FY1 2AR Phone 01253 623 787
E-mail holiday@warwickflats.co.uk Web www.warwickflats.co.uk
Situated very close to the town centre, railway station and the scene. All apartments are comfortably furnished and totally private. Facilities include a fully equipped kitchen with microwave, fridge and all the necessary cooking utensils. You will need to bring your own towels, tea

towels and toilet requisites. There is one apartment that can accommodate up to four people. **Price** £30 **Number of rooms** 5, 4 en-suite

Welcome Hotel 33 General Street, Blackpool FY1 1SG Phone 01253 294 631
A new, fully licensed, totally refurbished hotel for the gay community. Men and women are both welcome and there are family rooms available for those with children. Credit cards accepted. **Price** £35

Willowfield 51 Banks Street, Blackpool FY1 2BE Phone 01253 623 406
Guest-House The Willowfield is a delightful guest-house catering for gay men, women and their families. Occupying a favourable position close to the beach, and only 200 yards from the station and Talbot Road. Full breakfast served between 0900 and 0930 only with vegetarians catered for (please express your requirements on arrival). Member of BAGS. **Price** £25-30 **Number of rooms** 6, none en-suite

The Woodleigh 11 Yates Street, North Shore, Blackpool FY1 2DE Phone 01253 624 997
E-mail woodleigh-hotel@talk21.com Web www.woodleigh-hotel.co.uk
A friendly gay-owned hotel practically in the centre of the gay village. This is a small but comfortable, quality hotel, with every effort made to make guests' stays as pleasurable as possible, with friendly personal service at all times. Evening meals can be arranged at an additional cost. **Price** £30 **Number of rooms** 8, none en-suite

Cruising grounds

Middle Walk (North Pier) When the clubs close and it's too early to go back to your hotel you have two choices. Either go the sauna (all-nighter weekends) or take your chances at this cruising ground. Slightly north from the North Pier is the war memorial obelisk. Follow the path that runs behind the Metropol hotel and just keep walking for about half a mile until you come to the action. Alternatively, take the scenic route past the Metropol and follow the beach around for about half a mile until you come to a side entrance allowing you access underneath the prom. It sounds complicated but it isn't. Always very busy during the summer season and quite a regular pick-up place for the locals off-season.

St Annes Road The sand dunes near 'Starr Gate', opposite Pontins Holiday's chalets and frequented during the summer months. The area used covers the car park and toilet facility on Clifton Drive North and ends at Starr Hills by the old people's home. Not usually as busy as Middle Walk but it does offer a viable alternative. This area is mainly used by the gay-curious 'straight' lads who find Middle Walk a little too heavy for them.

Retail

Clone Zone 3 The Strand, Blackpool FY1 1NX Phone 01253 294 850
E-mail info@clonezone.co.uk Web www.clonezone.co.uk
For poppers, magazines, videos (shortly to stock R18), clubwear, CDs and practically everything else to keep your bedside drawer fully

stocked. There is also a Clone Zone kiosk in Flamingo's. **Open** Monday-Saturday 1100-1800. Sunday 1200-1700

Bolton Pubs

Bar Random

150 Crook Street, Bolton BL3 6AS Phone 07941 249 042
E-mail **martinfurber@hotmail.com** Web **www.barrandom.co.uk**
What was once the straight Academy Bar is now the latest men-only gay bar to open in Bolton. Decked out in stainless steel and very, very black, leaving you in no doubt that this is undoubtedly a cruisy venue. The atmosphere is friendly and light-hearted and whether you come in here, alone or with a group of friends, you are absolutely sure to enjoy yourself. Music policy is varied depending on the night, however, more often than not it is happy handbag and gay anthems. Thursday is The Supper Club: a very busy night with free entry and a hot-dog supper served at 2330. Sunday also tends to be very busy (last admission is at 2230), staying open 'til late, usually with a stripper waving his bits around. Bar Random is not a very large venue, able to cope with only 200 or so and filling up quite quickly, but this just adds to the intimacy. **Open** Wednesday 2000-0100. Thursday-Saturday 2000-0200. Sunday 1900-2230 **Price** £2-3 after 2300, Friday and Saturday

The Church Hotel

174 Crook Street, Bolton BL3 6AS Phone 01204 521 856
Situated opposite the railway station, this is a very friendly, mixed gay bar, comprising two rooms: the lounge bar and the disco bar where all the entertainment happens. Regular cheap drink promotions and extended happy hours a feature. Thursdays are karaoke, Fridays and Saturdays are a popular mainstream disco and Sundays are cabaret. There is also a separate pool room. **Open** Wednesday 1600-2300. Thursday-Saturday 1600-0200. Sunday 1600-2430 **Price** £2.50 after 2300, Friday and Saturday

The Star

11 Bow Street, Bolton BL1 2EQ Phone 01204 361 113
Traditionally styled intimate gay bar with a separate disco room opening up from Thursday onwards and providing the mixed gay crowd of all ages with somewhere to go if they don't want to venture further afield. On a Sunday they stage a karaoke show in addition to the disco and on Wednesday there are games such as Bingo and cardz(zzzzz). This may not obviously suit everybody but you do tend to get a friendly local community vibe in here. **Open** Monday-Wednesday 1700-2300. Thursday-Saturday 1300-2300. Sunday 1200-2230

Bournemouth

The town of Bournemouth is relatively young, dating only from the early 19th century. Yet ever since this time it has been attracting tourists by the score, and today it is as popular as ever. The town originated in 1810 when retired army officer Lewis Tregonwell decided to build a house on this pretty stretch of the Dorset coast. He planted pine trees in the deep valleys, known as 'chines', that are still characteristic of the area today. At the time the scent of pine trees was said to be able to relieve the symptoms of tuberculosis. Thus, people began to visit the area in an attempt to improve their health. As a result the town grew quickly around Tregonwell's estate, and by the beginning of the 20th century over 50,000 people had settled here. As the threat of tuberculosis began to fade by the late 19th century the town became less of a convalescent resort for sick people, yet still attracted visitors, as the new era saw the Victorians indulging their passions for seaside resorts. It flourished into one of Britain's most popular resorts. Today, the area is a well-known retirement spot, boasting fantastic coastline with long stretches of clean golden sands and perfect waters.

Bournemouth has a small, but thriving, gay scene, adequate for the area and more than enough for the visitor. Bournemouth presents its first ever Pride event in 2001 (visit www.pridebournemouth.com for details). The gay area is based around The Triangle at Westcliffe, about a five-minute walk from West Cliff promenade.

Getting in touch

You can find the **Tourist Information Office** (0906 802 0234) at Westover Road and you can pick up free, small street-planner maps when you arrive with your queries. Gay-specific information, help and support is offered by **Dorset Lesbian and Gay Switchboard** (01202 318 822) which operates between the hours of 1930 and 2230 throughout the week. **Body Positive** (01202 297 386) and the **HIV and AIDS Helpline** (01202 311 166) offer health advice and support. You can also contact the lesbian and gay police liason officer (01202 257 478) or attend the regular police liason surgeries at **Over The Rainbow** café bar. Finally **WLID** (01202 470 981), which stands for 'It's A Woman's Life In Dorset', is an excellent resource for lesbians (and bi-sexual women) to get to know each other.

Pubs

The Branksome Arms 152-154 Commercial Road, Bournemouth BH2 5LU
Phone 01202 552 544 E-mail info@thebranksomearms.com
Web www.thebranksomearms.com
The Branksome Arms is a very friendly Victorian gay pub in the heart of Bournemouth's main gay area – The Triangle. Entertainment of some sort is provided each and every Tuesday, Thursday and Sunday: cabaret, disco, quiz and so on. At all other times it is a social venue with the emphasis being on drinking and chatting. No thumping loud music which suits the older patrons of the bar. **Open** Monday-Saturday 1200-2300. Sunday 1200-2230

Bakers Arms 77 Commercial Road, Bournemouth BH2 5RT Phone 01202 555 506
Very popular mixed gay venue with a cosy traditional feel about the place, attracting all ages from spring chickens to old crows. Excellent

reputation for lunchtime food (1200-1500) which draws folk in and makes for quite a mixed crowd, which is no bad thing. Karaoke takes place three times a week on Wednesday, Saturday and Sunday. **Open** Monday-Saturday 1100-2300. Sunday 1200-2230

Dorothy's Café Bar
111 Commercial Road, The Triangle, Bournemouth BH2 5RT
Phone 01202 315 615 E-mail info@dorothyscafebar.com
Web www.dorothyscafebar.com
Situated within The Triangle, Dorothy's Café Bar is one of those ideal places to meet your mates in Bournemouth. This high-profile location is just right for either the party animal starting out on a wild night on the town or for those just wanting a stylish night out in attractive surroundings. You can pop in for a drink (Dorothy's is fully licensed) or just coffee and cake. The menu ranges from huge combo starters to winter warmers and mega desserts. Set out on two floors Dorothy's seats 60 people comfortably and has both high-profile seating and quiet corners for those out on a first date or just wanting a quiet night out. Other features include a state-of-the-art sound system and three TV screens. **Open** Monday-Saturday 0900-2300. Sunday 0900-2230

The Queens Hall Hotel
14 Queens Road, Westbourne, Bournemouth BH2 6BE
Phone 01202 764 416
This is Bournemouth's oldest gay pub. It's extremely busy and is a ten minute or so walk from the town centre. It is also the home of H2O sauna which has its own discreet entrance around the back (see separate listing). The large expanse of the ground floor contains pool room and two bar areas – the first is the large main bar and the second middle bar houses the dance area that comes to life with a varied mix of people and ages over the weekends. Catch the male stripper each and every Sunday evening! **Open** Monday-Saturday 1200-2300. Sunday 1200-2230

The X-Change Wine Bar
4 The Triangle, Bournemouth BH2 5RY Phone 01202 294 321
A lively community-based wine bar catering for a majority lesbian, gay, TV and gay-friendly straight crowd. The X-Change is a young venue, both very friendly and welcoming. The long bar leads to the stage at the far end and everywhere in between there is ample comfortable seating and standing room. On bank holidays all the stops are pulled out and it's just one non-stop party. Cheap drinks, themed weekends, cabaret and everything else that goes with having a good time. **Open** Monday-Saturday 1830-0100. Sunday 1830-2230

Clubs

Bolts @ The Opera House
570 Christchurch Road, Bournemouth BH1 4BH Phone 01202 399 922
Bournemouth's superclub for the masses – the 2,000 capacity Opera House goes gay each and every bank holiday Sunday throughout the year. Times and admission vary from event to event so it is prudent to check the press or contact the venue prior to attending. As the name suggests, this is a converted former theatre with the ornate trappings and décor of a Victorian era that suits us queens, princesses and maids right

down to the ground. The Opera House is synonymous with quality clubbing and has been going strong now for well over 16 years. The likes of Judge Jules guest regularly at the Friday night 'Slinky' club event held every week. But hang on! We don't have to wait for the bank holiday to enjoy this club. In fact, on a Saturday at least a third of the punters here probably bat for our side anyway. So, if hard house and garage is your bag then here is a quick run down on what to expect throughout the week; Wednesday is 'Disco Bonanza', a very young and straight-ish night (£2-3; 2130-0200). Thursday is student cheap drink night 'Hot'n' Horny' (£2-3; 2030-0200), with party house in the main room and an eclectic mix in the other. Friday is the aforementioned 'Slinky', pumping house in the main (Slinky) room and garage in the (Switch) room (£7-9; 2100-0300). Saturday is 'Curious': house anthems in the main room and shitty retro in the other (£4-8; 2100-0300). Dress policy is smart-casual or clubwear, particularly on 'Slinky' and due to a backward Dorset by-law there is no admission to the club (any club) after 0030. **Open** Bank Holiday Sunday 2100-0300 **Price** £6-8

Triangle Club   29 The Triangle, Bournemouth BH2 5SE Phone 01202 297 607
E-mail info@trianglenightclub.com Web www.trianglenightclub.com
The Triangle Club, with a capacity of around 600, is now into its fif-teenth successful year. The top lounge bar has now been completely refurbished with air conditioning installed. The basement disco bar is lively and friendly and plays a selection of handbag and current dance classics. The atmosphere in general is dance-orientated, with plenty of room to cruise and be cruised. A weekly Friday night venue for Bournemouth Leather: 2130-2300. **Open** Tuesday-Thursday 2130-0200. Friday-Saturday 2130-0300 **Price** £2-4

Saunas

H2O Sauna   Queen's Hall Hotel, 14 Queen's Road, Westbourne, Bournemouth BH2 6BE Phone 01202 764 416
The entrance to this sauna, which is incorporated on the first and sec-ond floor of the Queen's Hotel, is discreet and situated around the back of this popular gay pub. Spread out over two levels, the first houses the café and snack bar, a 100-capacity locker room, a video lounge, two sauna cabins, a steam room, a Jacuzzi and a multi-purpose gym. On the top floor there is a stand up solarium cabin, a communal rest room and about ten individual rest rooms. No membership is required: just turn up and play! **Open** Monday-Sunday 1200-2300 and later **Price** £10

The Spa Sauna   121 Poole Road, Westbourne, Bournemouth BH4 9BG
Phone 01202 757 591
Established in 1994 as a gay sauna and still going strong. No member-ship is required, just pay and play (as they say). The Spa isn't the biggest in the world but does offer a friendly, welcoming, no-attitude play space for all. The ground floor is the TV lounge and complimentary drinks area, whilst the downstairs houses the wet area. If you plan on returning to this venue within the same week (Monday-Sunday) you can gain

admission for only £7 if you can tell them the day on which you visited and your locker number (the lad at reception will tell you what to do). **Open** Monday-Saturday 1200-2000. Sunday 1400-1900 **Price** £9

Accommodation

The Bondi Hotel   43 St Michael's Road, Bournemouth BH2 5DP Phone 01202 554 893
E-mail **colin&malcolm@bondihotel.freeserve.co.uk**
Small, clean and comfortable lodgings situated a mere couple of minutes from the gay scene. Along with the main hotel, there is also a fully equipped self-catering apartment available down the road. This comprises two double bedrooms (able to sleep four), kitchen and lounge, plus a video, hi-fi and extra bits and pieces that are not usually standard in a hotel. The rate for this apartment is £60 per night. Phone the Bondi for more information. **Price** £40 **Number of rooms** 6, 4 en-suite

The Chine
Beach Hotel   14 Studland Road, Alum Chine, Bournemouth BH4 8JA
Phone 01202 767 015 Fax 01202 763 670
The Chine Beach is a comfortable homely (very) gay-friendly hotel, about a twenty minute walk to the gay quarter (£4 taxi). Beyond the sunny patios, the wooded gardens lead via steps to the beautiful Alum Chine where the beach is just two minutes away. Many of the rooms have beautiful sea and Chine views. There is ample parking at the hotel. The attractive bar lounge is comfortably furnished with leather Chesterfields, and the bar has a good selection of beers, wines and spirits. Bar snacks, sandwiches and tea and coffee are available to order during the day. French windows open from the bar area onto the patio overlooking the Chine where you can enjoy drinks in a peaceful, attractively furnished setting. En-suite bathroom and shower room, colour TV (28-inch screen sets in some of the deluxe rooms), hairdryer, radio, alarm clock and tea/coffee-making facilities are standard features in the rooms. Unfortunately, TV/TS cannot be accommodated. The owner apologised profusely. Better to know and avoid it than turn up and be disappointed, I suppose. **Price** £50 **Number of rooms** 24, all en-suite

The Claremont   89 St Michaels Road, Bournemouth BH2 5DR Phone 01202 316 668
Comfortable accommodation; about a two minute walk to all gay venues. **Price** £50 **Number of rooms** 15, 4 en-suite

The Creffield   7 Cambridge Road, Bournemouth BH2 6AE Phone 01202 317 900
Well-established (nine years), exclusively gay guest-house accommodating both men and women. Two of the rooms have sexy four-poster beds (£65); ideal for those romantic weekends away from home. Tariff includes full English breakfast served in the delightful conservatory. Two minutes from the gay scene and a ten minute drive to Studland (gay beach). Roger is a very hospitable host who is more than happy to help you plan your itinerary in Bournemouth. Stays in excess of seven days will receive a 10 per cent discount. **Price £55 Number of rooms** 9, all rooms en-suite

The Hedley   125 West Hill Road, Bournemouth BH2 5PH Phone 01202 317 168
E-mail **hedley.hotel@tinyworld.co.uk**
Comfortable, small licensed hotel just a couple of minutes from the prom. All rooms include TV, tea/coffee-making and ironing facilities. Triple rooms and special midweek rates are also available. **Price £36-48 Number of rooms** 11, all en-suite

The Orchard   15 Alumdale Road, Bournemouth BH4 8HX
Phone 01202 767 767 E-mail **mail@gayhotelbournemouth.com**
Web **www.gayhotelbournemouth.com**
The Orchard is an exclusively gay and lesbian, fully-licensed bed and breakfast hotel situated on the edge of Alum Chine, a beautiful wooded valley that leads to the sea. It has ten bedrooms, all furnished to a high standard. The beach is just a three-to-four minutes walk away through the trees at Alum Chine, whilst the gay pub, The Queens Hall and the restaurants, shops and gay sauna at Westbourne (The Spa) are ten minutes away by foot. The ferry for the naturist beach at Studland is a five minute car journey away or you can get a bus from the top of the road. If you are looking for a comfortable yet unpretentious place to stay in Bournemouth then The Orchard is for you. They will certainly do everything they can to make your visit a happy and memorable one. **Price £32-43 double room Number of rooms** 10, 5 en-suite; 5 with shared facilities

Westover
Gardens Hotel   5-7 Westover Road, Bournemouth BH1 2BY
Phone 01202 556 380 Fax 01202 299 686 E-mail **west.gdns@faxvia.net**
One of Bournemouth's most central gay-friendly hotels, within easy walking distance of all bars and clubs. En-suite rooms are available and

3

the hotel has a bar too. Ask about their midweek discounts. **Price** £36
Number of rooms 6, all en-suite

Wrenwood
Hotel

11 Florence Road, Bournemouth BH5 1HH
Phone 01202 395 086 Fax 01202 396 511
E-mail peter@wrenwood.co.uk Web www.wrenwood.co.uk
A delightfully friendly and hospitable hotel, ideally situated, only 400
yards from the prom and half that to The Opera House (home of Bolts –
see separate listing). All rooms are en-suite and have TV and tea/coffee-
making facilities. Late or early breakfasts can be arranged and ironing
facilities are available. Bank holiday weekends carry a supplement and a
minimum three-day stay. Evening meals can also be provided at an additional charge. **Price** £45-49 **Number of rooms** 14, all en-suite

Cruising grounds

The Gardens
(Queens
Gardens)

Access from Queens Road (just down from the Queens Hall Hotel gay
pub). Less activity over the last few years due to the radical pruning of
shrubs in the area, and also substantiated reports of physical attacks.

Meyrick Park

(Central Drive) Near the Town Hall in the centre of the town there are
two car parks: the first on the left is all gay and mainly young. The toilets have been demolished so now the action is in the woods and after
dark. I am led to believe that the car park to aim for is the one opposite
the bowling green. The second car park on the left is hard to find. Look
for a white single chain and post fence on the right; the hidden entrance
to the car park is fifty yards on the left. Not much gay action as yet,
although married couples occasionally seek single males here. There is
some action in the car park adjoining the golf course after dark. Both
car parks are about a quarter of a mile apart.

Studland /
Shell Bay

(Isle of Purbeck) This beach is reported to be one of the very best. Very
cruisy at the back of the nudist section, with plenty of action in the
dunes and woods. The area is patrolled by National Trust wardens (easily spotted – they're the ones with walkie-talkies). The wardens can be a
hassle though, even to those who are genuinely into sun worship.
Approach from the north by ferry (best on foot or bike because of the
queue for cars), or south, from Corfe Castle and Studland Village. Park
on the road where most cars are at the halfway point and walk along an
obvious path through to the beach (about one mile). At the last moment,
veer off to the left for about 200 metres. Now you can start exploring.
This area is always busy especially at around teatime before everyone
goes home.

Moors Valley
Country Park

Find this place on the A31, between Ringwood and Ferndown. Turn left
at the roundabout, sign-posted Country Park. The toilets and car park
are in use 24 hours a day but it's best in the evening after dark, 'til
approximately 0200. This area is also frequented by a few married couples looking for action with single males. Plenty of warning of cars
approaching the car park.

Retail

Dorothy's
Internet Café

20 St Michaels Road, Bournemouth BH2 5DX
Phone 01202 298 256 E-mail info@dorothysinternetcafe.com
Web www.dorothysinternetcafe.com
An internet café on the outskirt of the gay quarter and a sister venue to
Dorothy's Café Bar on Commercial Road (see separate listing). **Open**
Monday-Sunday 0900-2300 **Price** £2 per hour

Bracknell Cruising grounds

Englemere
Pond

A nature reserve. This place has an extensive wooded area and is used in
the afternoons, but mainly in the evening. The afternoon tends to have
an awful lot of people (not a lot of awful people!) walking their dogs, so
do not presume anything. The car park seems to be the starting point
with encouragement coming from others to follow them.

Bradford

Bradford has an Anglo-Saxon name that means the 'Broad Ford'.
Throughout the Middle Ages Bradford was, like Leeds, an important
woollen and textile centre but the town did not really begin to grow until
the 19th century. Bradford's industrial growth attracted labour from all
over Europe and the British Empire and Bradford is still famed as a cultural melting pot with people of Irish, German, Italian, Eastern
European, West Indian and Asian descent. Most of Bradford's famous
buildings are Victorian, but one of Bradford's oldest buildings is its 15th
century cathedral in Church Bank; a large church which reflects
Bradford's size and status in medieval times. The imposing Victorian
Mill in Saltaire, designed by Titus Salt in the mid-18th century, contains
Europe's largest collection of works of the Bradford-born artist David
Hockney. Into the more modern era, there is the impressive National
Museum of Film and Photography that opened in 1983. It claims to be
the home of the world's biggest lens, the smallest camera and the first
ever photographic likeness. It also boasts Britain's biggest cinema
screen. Bradford is renowned for being the 'curry capital' of the UK – a
title deeply contested by Birmingham and Leicester, which are also
home to large Asian and ethnic communities. Even so, they say you can
probably get a better curry here in Bradford than you can throughout
many parts of India!

The gay scene here in Bradford is small, compared to its neighbour over
in nearby Leeds and although it serves the community very well it does
seem to be stuck in a late-'80s time warp. Travelling over to Leeds is par
for the course for most of Bradford's gays, where the scene is much
healthier and livelier.

Getting in touch

Bradford **Tourist Information Centre** (01274 753 678) is at City Hall on Centenary Square and is open Monday to Saturday from 0930 to 1730 and Sunday (during April to October only) from 0930 to 1730. If you require any help or advice relating to the gay scene you can phone the **Bradford Lesbian and Gay Switchboard** (0845 345 2449) on Tuesday, Thursday, Friday and Saturday between 1930 and 2130.

Pubs

The Sun Hotel 124 Sunbridge Road, Bradford BD1 2ND Phone 01274 737 722
This is cited to be the city's oldest gay pub. It's about 100 yards from their sister venue, the S29 club (see listing) as well as being right next door to Rimmers Sauna. There's loads going on throughout the week at this very popular establishment. Monday through to Wednesday is either cheap drinks, quiz night or singles night. From Thursday onwards a resident DJ gets you in the mood to go across to the S29 club by playing cheesy and camp hits. Last Friday of the month the Bears UK crew meet up in the bar (phone beforehand in case the dates change). There's also limited accommodation on offer above the pub. **Open** Monday-Saturday 1200-2300. Sunday 1200-2230

Clubs

Club Kaleidoscope Salem Street, Bradford BD1 4QH
Phone 01274 775 434 (day) 01274 200 020 (evening)
One of the newest club nights for gays, lesbians and the transgendered in Bradford. A very nice venue, all black and chrome and right in the heart of the city centre (near Forster Square Station). Admission increases after 2300 on all nights so it is wise to get here early to save a few quid. Music policy is varied, starting off light with the charty commercial stuff progressing rapidly to a harder uplifting house style. Dress code is smart and casual – trainers may be a problem if they are not clean and smart. At the time of writing the Sunday night had not yet started, so admission prices are not yet agreed upon, although it should be around the £3 mark. **Open** Friday-Saturday 2200-0400. Sunday 2100-0100 **Price** £3-5

S29 Club 29 Sackville Street, Bradford BD1 2AJ Phone 01274 740 644
What was formerly known as the Sackville Lounge and the S29 club is now, after extensive refurbishment, collectively known as the S29 Club. Both floors have been combined to make one super club. The venue is still a modern establishment, catering to a predominantly young mixed gay, bi and lesbian crowd. Downstairs the music is cheesy and charty whilst upstairs it's got harder with uplifting dance and commercial house. Some things haven't changed; the huge video screens provide opportunity for the voyeurs amongst you who want to watch what's going on – or even catch your boyf' snogging someone else on the way to

the toilet (hey! trust me it happened). S29 is the sister club to The Sun Hotel (see listing) – the pre-club meeting place before you trawl through here. Food is available from the in-house cafe open the same hours as the club. Thursday is the night for bargain beer hunters – £1 admission and all drinks are £1.50. Find the venue off Westgate (A6181). **Open** Wednesday-Sunday 2100-0300 **Price** Thursday £1. Friday-Saturday £3-5. Sunday £1

Saunas

Rimmers Sauna   122 Sunbridge Road, Bradford BD1 2ND Phone 01274 775 177
Bradford's only gay sauna with full facilities – sauna, Jacuzzi, crash room with video, video lounge, VIP room with Jacuzzi, and so on. This venue used to be at Simes Street, above the Bombay Restaurant, but has now successfully moved into the gay quarter. **Open** Monday-Sunday 1200-2200 **Price** £10

Accommodation

The Sun Hotel   124 Sunbridge Road, Bradford BD1 2ND Phone 01274 737 722
Only a few rooms, but clean and comfortable ones at that. The Sun Hotel is the city's oldest gay pub, and the accommodation is based above. With Rimmers Sauna situated exactly next door you could have all your needs catered for without having to walk more than a few feet! All rooms have tea/coffee-making facilities and offer concessions to S29 club. Continental breakfast is the only extra included in the price. **Price** £32.50 **Number of rooms** 3

Cruising grounds

Lister Park   I don't have much information for this ground, so the exact location in the park is not known. The rather cruisy Rimmers Sauna might provide a more appropriate nearby venue for your activities.

Manningham Park   The area by the bowling green is popular during the day (especially during the summer months). Here you will have an excuse for sitting around at least. When you start to admire the pensioners playing bowls, you have been sitting there for far too long... it's time to move on.

Bradford-on-Avon Accommodation

Leigh House

Leigh Road West, Bradford-on-Avon BA15 2RB
Phone 01225 867 835 E-mail leigh.house@virgin.net
Web http://business.virgin.net/leigh.house
A spacious 16th-century farmhouse granted by Queen Elizabeth I to her favourite, Robert Dudley, Earl of Leicester. This peaceful country guesthouse is set in large grounds on the outskirts of historic Bradford-on-Avon, eight miles from Bath. All bedrooms have bathrooms or showers en-suite, are centrally heated and comfortably furnished. There is also a former bakehouse that has been tastefully converted into a self-contained cottage for use on a self-catering basis. It consists of a sitting room with open log fireplace, sofa bed, a double and a treble bedroom, bathroom and kitchen. The cottage can sleep up to seven (two people per week: £206). Leigh House is a good base for exploring Bath, Bristol, Cheddar, Glastonbury, Longleat and Stonehenge and many nearby National Trust properties. **Price** £52

Braunton Cruising grounds

Braunton Burrows

Before you reach for your map... this one is in north Devon, not far from Barnstaple. Only used during the summer time. Take the road from Braunton to Croyd and follow the signs to 'The Burrows'. Park in the

Sandy Lane car park and then follow the well-beaten path to the beach. Go past the large dune with the flagpole on the top and keep going in a straight line. When you get to the beach, instead of going on to it, turn left. Walk along the path at the top of the dunes for 300-400 yards and then turn back into the burrows. Lots of cruising with all ages of guys popping up out of the long grass. There are wardens, but the area is so large that they are not much of a threat. If you pick your spot correctly you will have plenty of warning. I believe this location is open between April and October only. Mind you, it's worth waiting half of the year for, as the action is always there.

O
Outlines

Quality gay biography
David Hockney

www.absolutepress.demon.co.uk

O
Outlines

Quality gay biography
k. d. lang

www.absolutepress.demon.co.uk

O
Outlines

Quality gay biography
Bessie Smith

www.absolutepress.demon.co.uk

Brighton and Hove

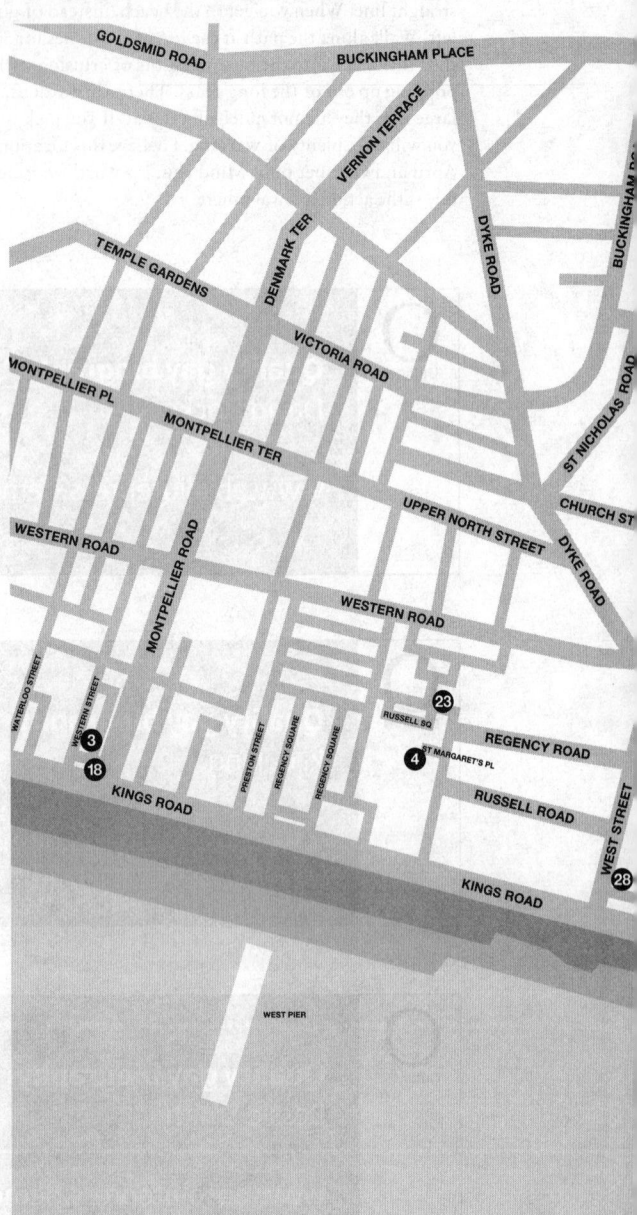

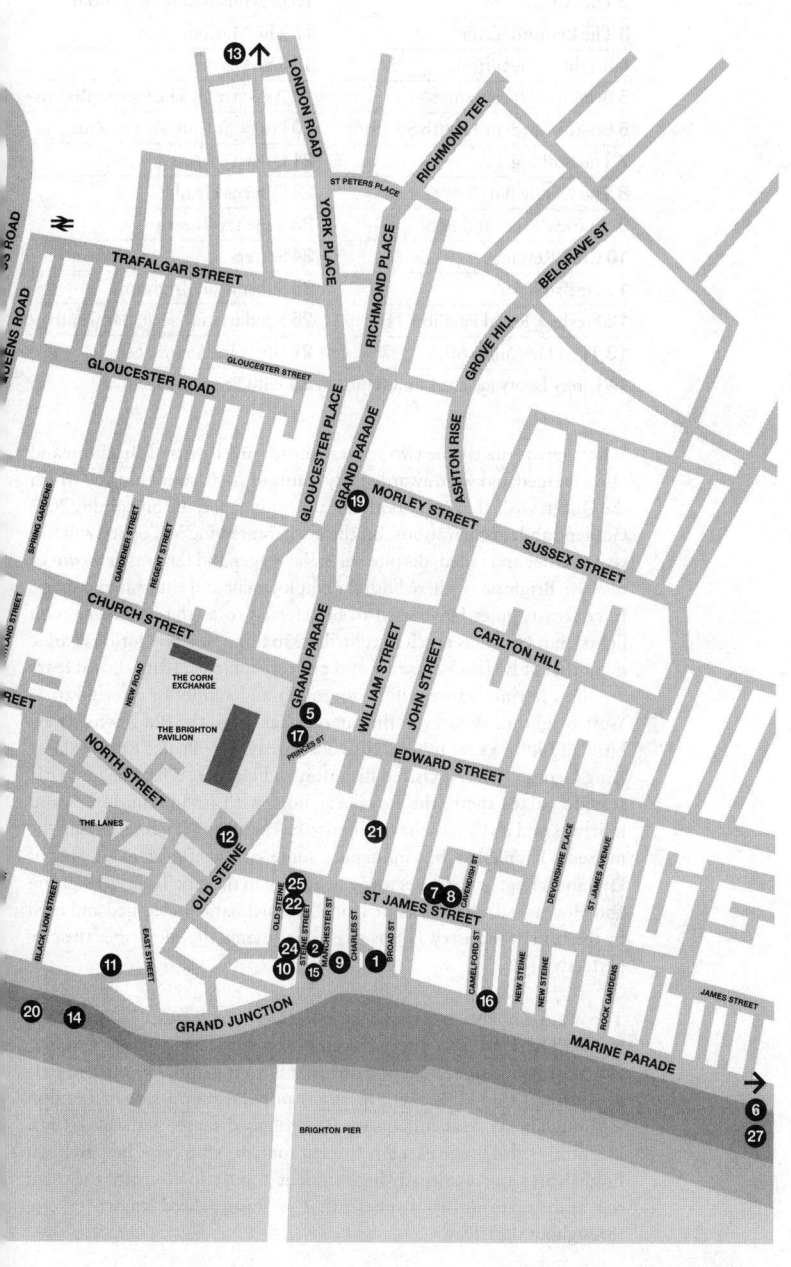

Map key

1 The Amsterdam Bar / Sauna	**15** Kruze Bar and Lizard Lounge
2 The Aquarium	**16** Legends Bar/Schwartz Bar
3 The Bedford Tavern	**17** The Marlborough
4 Bright 'n' Beautiful	**18** The Oriental
5 Brighton Oasis Sauna	**19** Popstarz @ The Ocean Rooms
6 Bristol Gardens Health Spa (off)	**20** Pussycat Club @ The Zap
7 The Bulldog Tavern	**21** Queen's Arms
8 The Candy Bar	**22** Queens Head
9 Charles Street and Pool	**23** Regency Tavern
10 Club Revenge	**24** Secrets
11 Dr Brighton's	**25** Substation Brighton
12 Fresh @ Royal Pavilion Tavern	**26** Sunday Sundae @ Bar Centro
13 The Harlequin (off)	**27** Unit One Sauna (off)
14 Kinky Booty @ The Honeyclub	**28** Wild Fruit @ Paradox

What were formerly the two separate bordering towns of Brighton and Hove merged and were awarded city status in 2000, something by which the Queen wished to mark both the millennium and the on-coming 2002 Golden Jubilee celebrations. Brighton attempted the feat on its own five years earlier and failed, despite being the bigger and far brassier town of the two. Brighton is where both the employment and entertainment lies. In contrast, quiet Hove used to be referred to as the 'cemetery with lights', but Hove has much to contribute to this new city: glorious parks, magnificent Regency terraces and a spectacular sea front. Local fears are that, in time, Hove will be forgotten and simply be referred to as West Brighton. Whatever, this merger has given the old towns a new buzz and it looks set to revitalise both areas. The Prince Regent (later King George IV) first visited Brighton and Hove in 1783. His fantastic seaside palace there, the Royal Pavilion, with its Indian domes and minarets and its Chinese-style interior has become a landmark not to be missed. Thanks to his influence, some of the finest examples of England's Regency architecture can be seen in the city. Today's Brighton and Hove is indeed a 'Pleasure Dome' – a nickname welcomed and used by the tourist industry. For us gays, it is a name that describes the city perfectly.

The main gay area is Kemptown, referred to as 'Camp Town' by the locals. There are many gay businesses occupying St James's Street, which runs through this area, one that is young and vibrant and that also contains possibly the largest gay population outside of London (although many Mancunians would strongly disagree with this claim). Brighton is also home to many foreign students who come here to learn English and join an already high student population to paint the town red and create an atmosphere that is unsurpassed anywhere else throughout the UK.

Getting there

Airport

The nearest airport is **London Gatwick**. Many London-to-Brighton trains stop here and there are also direct coach services. Services from London to Brighton are frequent, about six per hour, with a comfortable journey time of around 75 minutes. All London to Brighton trains stop at Gatwick.

Trains

Brighton mainline station is situated at the end of Queen's Road, about a ten minute walk from the sea front or town centre. There are services to other parts of the country from here, including, of course, London, which is the base from which you will be able to access many more destinations.

Coaches

National Express coaches stop at **Pool Valley**, situated opposite Brighton (Palace) Pier. Tickets for all National Express coaches are purchased from **One Stop Travel** (01273 700 406) on Old Steine. This office is open Monday to Saturday from 0830 to 1745 and Sunday from 1100 to 1630.

Getting about

Buses

The **Brighton and Hove Bus Company** (01273 886200) run an intensive network of local bus routes, serving the conurbation of Brighton and Hove from Shoreham through to Newhaven as well as longer-distance routes to Eastbourne, Lewes and Tunbridge Wells.

Taxis

Brighton is served by **Streamline** (01273 747474). The fares are quite reasonable. (By the way, if you puke up in the back of a taxi it will cost you £50.) Taxis are ranked outside the railway station and at Pool Valley by the National Express coach station. Also, Brighton, like London, is not a car-friendly city. Parking on the street is near-impossible and you will probably be confronted by 'resident-only' parking schemes or a confusing voucher system (vouchers are purchased in newsagents or shops displaying the green 'V' sign). There are eleven multi-storey car parks throughout Brighton but these fill up quickly.

Tourist information

The main **Tourist Information Office** (01273 292 599) is situated at 10 Bartholomew Square. From here you can get loads of information such as free What's On guides, maps, promotional leaflets to nearby historical sights and details of all sightseeing tours. They will also be able to arrange accommodation for you (a nominal fee of around £1 per adult, plus 10 per cent booking fee). The office is open Monday to Friday from 0900 to 1700 and Saturday and Sunday from 1000. During the summer months the office operates longer opening hours.

Bureaux de change

American Express (01273 321 342) is on 82 North Street and is open each day from 0900 to 1730. The high street banks are situated on and around North Street, between West Street and Old Steine.

Getting help

Police, hospital and pharmacy
The local police station (01273 606 744) is on John Street, which runs on from George Street, at the beginning of St James's Street. **The Royal Sussex County Hospital** (01273 696 955) is on Eastern Road, close to St James's Street and parallel to Marine Parade. Two of the later-opening hours chemists are **Ashton's** (01273 325 020) on Dyke Road and **Weston's** (01273 605 354) on Coombe Terrace, Lewes Road. Both open Monday through to Sunday from 0900 to 2200.

Getting in touch

Internet
Cybar is at 9-12 Middle Street and is a trendy restaurant and bar with internet access that costs about £2.50 per half-hour. **PC Corner Cybercafe** at 218 Portland Road is in what was the old Hove district. Access here is also around the £2.50 per half-hour mark.

GLBT Helplines
The **Lesbian and Gay Switchboard** (01273 204 050) serves the community and can help you with any problems or information you might require. It is open daily from 1700 to 2300. The **HIV and AIDS Helpline** (01202 311 166) is also available.

Pubs

The Amsterdam Bar
11-12 Marine Parade, Brighton BN2 1TL Phone 01273 688 825
E-mail enquiries@amsterdam.uk.com Web www.amsterdam.uk.com
A cocktail of nearly everything you need when visiting Brighton – bar, sauna and hotel. The bar area, considered to be the biggest gay bar in Brighton, is bright and modern incorporating two bars and an expansive sea view terrace practically begging you to spend the complete day there just getting wasted. The top class hotel (see separate listing) has many rooms based around themes Egyptian, Thai, Roman and the like. I asked if one of the rooms had a squatter's flat theme but there was a rolling of the eyes and complete silence – which I took to be a no! Residents also have 24-hour access to the bar. As if this wasn't enough there is a also a gay sauna on the premises (see separate listing) which is open to non-residents, consisting of all the usual facilities including those oh-so-necessary rest rooms. If you are not resident here you can join in the late night fun on the beach as it has become, through no specific intent, an unofficial cruising ground (as if such a thing exists). Simply make your way on to the beach opposite the hotel, and hang around looking horny... erm... I mean, pretty! **Open** Monday-Saturday 1100-2300. Sunday 1200-2230

The Aquarium
6 Steine Street, Brighton BN2 1TE Phone 01273 605 525
A cosy, intimate traditional pub with a very cruisy atmosphere. An exclusively gay crowd regularly bar-hop through the venue taking advantage of the many 'happy hours' and drink promos. **Open** Monday-Saturday 1100-2300. Sunday 1100-2230

The Bedford Tavern

30 Western Street, Brighton BN1 2PG Phone 01273 739 495 / 739 465
E-mail info@bedfordtavern.com Web www.bedfordtavern.com
The Bedford Tavern, just off the seafront on the borders of Brighton and Hove, is a charming 200 year-old pub, similar to a traditional country pub but in the heart of town! It boasts a wealth of original features such as exposed beams, open fires and 'resident ghost' (cue dramatic horror film scream). A straight-friendly, intimate pub where gays and straights get on well together (60/40 – gay/straight). The cosy, friendly ambience of the pub coupled with it's attitude-free and cosmopolitan environment has proved itself to be popular with all sections of the community (including TVs and trannies). The Bedford hosts monthly themed party nights, which are usually a good excuse to dress up (fancy dress optional) and have a party. Lovers of cask-conditioned ales can also whet their whistles here with the likes of Harvey's Best, Bombardier and Old Speckled Hen in addition to a guest beer. As is also traditional in country pubs there is a separate restaurant – Mariners Kitchen – specialising in fish and seafood as well as organic meats and veggie dishes, different from the rest because the food is cooked in front of your very eyes. There are no more than 18 covers, which means that it fills up quickly and so a reservation must be made. Tip: book well ahead for the popular Sunday lunch, at less than a tenner it's not surprising that it gets booked up pretty damn quick. **Open** Monday-Saturday 1100-2300. Sunday 1200-2230

The Bulldog Tavern

31 St James's Street, Brighton BN2 Phone 01273 684 097
Spread over two floors. The main bar is an olde-worlde-stylee-pubee, popular predominantly with Brighton's (over 25) men, although women and TVs/TSs are welcome. The modern upstairs disco room, open on a Saturday night only, hosts a popular retro disco club night. Sunday is cheap drinks all day (the all day-long happy hour) with additional happy hours throughout the week from 1500-1900. The Bulldog is a kind of local's local – heads turn as a stranger walks through the door, making it quite obvious that this is going to be a rather cruisy kind of joint. Sitting around the bar you will find many of Brighton's local character's and it doesn't take much to get them to tell tales of old or gossip about the latest happenings – a pint will usually suffice. **Open** Monday-Saturday 1100-0000. Sunday 1200-2230

The Candy Bar

33 St James's Street, Brighton BN2 1RF Phone 01273 622 424
E-mail info@candy-bar.co.uk Web www.candy-bar.co.uk
Blatantly exposing itself on the corner of St James's Street is a welcome and long-awaited addition to the Brighton lesbian scene – and it's not a dive either. On the contrary, The Candy Bar is a stylised, spacious haven for the girls, kitted out in cool lilac, beech and chrome. Girls pose in the huge windows like a dyke version of Amsterdam's Walletjes, sipping coffee or drinking fruit smoothies. In the evening the music gets turned up, the lights get turned down and the party begins. **Open** Monday-Sunday 1100-2300

Charles Street and Pool

8 Marine Parade, Brighton BN2 1TA Phone 01273-624 091
E-mail info@poolclub.co.uk Web www.poolclub.co.uk
Brighton's newest bar and club combo with Charles Street being the bar and Pool the (small) nightclub. Charles Street is trendy, bright and modern. The layout is good with plenty of room to circulate and to lose the moose that's giving you the eye. A generally young crowd has made this their own in the evenings, although during the day everyone seems to come through the doors, either for a coffee or a bite to eat. The upstairs Pool nightclub has never really taken off but salvation was to come to the rescue as 'Crash' (see London listing) takes over the venue once a month (£3-4; usually every second Thursday, but phone for dates or see the gay press) as well as 'Wet Pussy' from The Candy Bar (every third Thursday of the month). And lastly, London's Coco-Latte crew are now in here every Sunday from 2100 to 0100 (phone or check the flyers in the bar for details of what this new club night holds in store). It may be wise to phone Pool to ensure that these events are still running. Note: winter season sees opening times reduced. **Open** Monday-Saturday 1000-2300. Sunday 1000-2230 (Charles Street) 2200-0200 (Pool) **Price** £2-4

Dr Brighton's

16-17 Kings Road, Brighton BN1 1NE Phone 01273 328 765
Dr Brighton's is a popular pre-club meeting bar for most of Brighton's one-nighter and regular club nights – including Kinky Booty, Revenge and Popstarz. It is not exclusively gay but you just wouldn't guess! A recent facelift smartened the place up a bit – the furniture was re-arranged to accommodate the new pool table and the posters on the

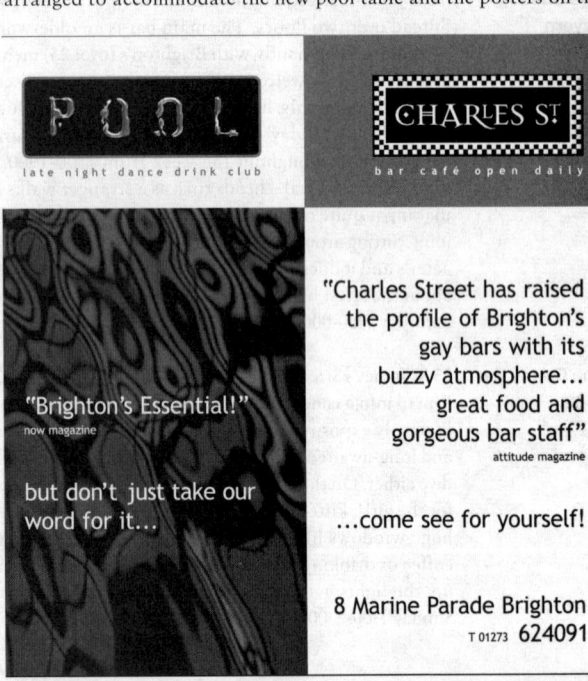

walls were discarded to accommodate real pictures. The old fashioned décor has been spruced up with greens and creams and the venue still retains the welcoming charm that visitors and locals have come to enjoy. A seafront position ensures you can ogle the passing rollerblading totty whilst necking a few pints at the same time. **Open** Monday-Saturday 1100-2300. Sunday 1100-2230

The Harlequin   43 Providence Place, Brighton BN1 4GE Phone 01273 620 630
E-mail **harlequin.brighton@talk21.com** Web **www.run.to/harlequin**
The Harly', behind Woolworths, is a gay bar which caters for a mix of people from TVs/TSs to students and from a young, up-for-it crowd to the coffin dodgers. This bar has changed names and ownership several times over the past few years (remember Marilyns?). It has now settled down with a formula of entertainment and disco throughout the week. It's a large, tiered, open-plan room with a stage-cum-dance floor and plenty of seating space. The beginning of the week caters mainly for the karaoke queens and students. From Thursday, the Harly takes on more of a disco vibe with the addition of some drag cabaret on Friday and Saturday. Tip: you can get a pass from The Queens Arms, giving you free admission. **Open** Monday-Saturday 1900-0200. **Price** Monday-Thursday £2 after 2300. Friday-Saturday £3-5 after 2200

Kruze Bar and   7 Marine Parade, Brighton BN2 1TA Phone 01273 608 133
Lizard Lounge   Another new café-bar to join the St James's street family. Kruze is a meeting, eating and socialising place; very bright and very art deco-ish with a strong Miami feel to it. Straight couples mix seamlessly with the predominant gay crowd and it works extremely well. The upstairs lounge bar (Lizard Lounge) is comfortable and plush. An ideal setting for sipping those cocktails whilst chatting with your friends. In the evenings the music does get a little louder but not to the extent where you have to shout to make yourself heard. Ideal. **Open** Monday-Saturday 1030-2300. Sunday 1030-2230

Legends Bar /   The New Europe Hotel, 31-32 Marine Parade, Brighton BN2 1TR
Schwartz Bar   Phone 01273 624 462 E-mail **info@neweuropehotel.co.uk**
Web **www.neweuropehotel.co.uk**
Part of the long-established New Europe Hotel complex, conveniently situated on the seafront in the heart of Kemptown. It contains two bars catering for two totally different tastes. Legends Bar, is a stylish café-bar open throughout the day serving drinks, tea, coffee and snacks to Brighton's gay visitors and locals. In the evenings you can gawp at strippers (Monday) get cheap drinks (Tuesday) or take part in a very camp party (Sunday). In contrast, there is the Schwartz Bar. To gain admission to this basement dress code bar (Friday and Saturday, 2200-0200) you will have to adhere to the strict dress code of rubber, uniform, leather or denim – strictly no trainers (and be willing to pay £2 for the privilege). Once inside though, you will be able to dance, play pool or cruise this famous subterranean Man-Fest. For details of The New Europe Hotel see the separate listing. **Open** Monday-Saturday 1200-2300. Sunday 1200-2230 **Price** £2, Schwartz Bar, weekends only

The Marlborough

4 Princes Street, Brighton BN2 1RD Phone 01273 570 028

The Marlborough is a very friendly, mixed gay venue comprising two bar rooms, the first being the (quieter) theatre bar (wood-panelled with leather upholstery) – popular with the students, more mature gays and theatre goers – and the main bar which is a mixed gay space – usually loud and atmospheric. The Marlborough does not tout itself as a women's venue as such, but it does have a high number of women customers (of all ages), particularly over the weekend. Don't think that lads are not made welcome, though. Quite the contrary – they are. There is absolutely no attitude here whatsoever, from either the punters or the picture-perfect staff! If you are going to Popstarz here in Brighton then this will be the bar that you will most likely be meeting up in (first and third Wednesday of the month, and you can get your Q-Jump tickets here as well). Above the bar is a fully working 50 seat theatre, used once a month for the Freakshow Comedy Club (regular dates in G-Scene and gay press) as well as independent productions (gay and straight). There was a recent independent bar survey in Brighton (one of those mystery shopper-type things) and The Marlborough gained a staggering 84 per cent with a by-note of 'this would be one bar that we would certainly revisit!' I couldn't disagree, except that I would have given them a higher percentage. Tip: if you're visiting on a Sunday you should stop and try lunch for £5.25. **Open** Monday-Friday 1100-2300. Saturday 1200-2300. Sunday 1200-2230

The Oriental

5-6 Montpelier Road, Brighton BN1 2LQ Phone 01273 728 808

Mixed gay, straight-friendly and TV/TS bar situated at the 'other side of town' (a few blocks past West Pier). The Oriental is a compact and well-established lively venue with karaoke on a Tuesday, a music hall-style drunken sing-a-long on a Friday and cabaret on a Sunday. Some may say it is in dire need of refurbishment. However, I think if smartened up, The Oriental would lose it's atmosphere and just become another gay bar. **Open** Monday-Thursday 1700-2300. Friday-Saturday 1200-2300. Sunday 1200-2230

Queen's Arms

7 George Street, Brighton BN2 1RH Phone 01273 696 873

At the beginning of St James's Street is the Queen's Arms, easily spotted by even the most shortsighted of people because of the huge rainbow flags proudly waving in the sea breeze. A cabaret and entertainment bar for gay boys and girls and the foolhardy straights that wander in off the street take one look in disbelief and wander out again. The well-used stage plays host to more than the average amount of karaoke and a stream of well-known and not-so-well-known cabaret artists. Take Betty Swollocks for example – hostess extraordinare (if that doesn't put you off drink and drugs, then nothing will). There's camp entertainment every single night of the week and an ever-changing roster of events; this is a good place to get tanked up and have a laugh. Tip: get here on a Sunday and grab the free sarnies at 1900. **Open** Monday-Saturday 1200-2300. Sunday 1200-2230

Queens Head   10 Steine Street, Brighton BN2 1TE Phone 01273 602 939
This is a true community venue with shed-loads of stuff going on for the
benefit of Brighton's gays and lesbians. This place welcomes everyone,
whether you're into frocks, leather, denim, feathers, whatever, and as a
general rule, it works really well. There is no regular entertainment
schedule as such, bar a cabaret show during the week. Additionally there
are off-the-cuff events such as disco and karaoke. The Queens under-
went a complete programme of reburbishment in the spring of 2001 and
the venue now boasts two new distinct areas – a comfortable lounge bar
and a modern and rather cool bar space which leads off it. There's also a
popular Sunday lunch available from 1200-1600. The Queens is situated
off St James's Street and it tends to attract a predominantly local crowd.
Open Monday-Saturday 1200-2300. Sunday 1200-2230

Regency   32-34 Russell Square, Brighton BN1 2EF Phone 01273 325 652
Tavern   A very camp but mixed gay and straight bar in London's namesake. A
very friendly atmosphere and a good choice of cask-conditioned ales
adds to the enjoyment of whiling away the hours. Popular venue for bar
food and in particular the value for money Sunday lunch which has been
described as '...busy, quite similar to the first day of a Harrods sale'.
Open Monday-Saturday 1100-2300. Sunday 1100-2230

The Sanctuary   51-55 Brunswick Street East, Hove BN3 1AU Phone 01273 770 002
E-mail sue@thesanctuarycafe.co.uk Web www.thesanctuarycafe.co.uk
Sanctuary is foremost a funky, flavoursome and another word beginning
with 'F' café-bar. It's gay-owned and -run, and more than warrants an
inclusion here in the pubs section as it is also licensed to sell beer, plus
the regular café fare of cappuccinos, fruit smoothies, teas and so on.
Winner of the 'Juicy Guide 2000' award for Brighton and Hove's best
café and a worthy winner at that. The café provides vegetarian and
vegan dishes, fish on Fridays, sumptuous snacks, scrumptious cakes,
specialist teas and coffees and even organic alcohol. Regular exhibitions
on display, community notice board, newspapers and free magazines –
it's a safe gay friendly space where all are welcome and Brighton's gay
community tends to flock here. The Cella', situated in the basement
plays host to regular performance nights such as Rainbow Chorus
(Brighton's gay choir) as well as alternative quality gay entertainment
and private parties. It may be in Hove but remember, Hove is only walking distance from all the gay bars in Kemptown. That word beginning
with 'F'...? Fabulous! **Open** Monday-Sunday 0900-2300

Star of   32 Brunswick Street West, Hove BN3 1EL Phone 01273 771 355
Brunswick   The Star is not an exclusively gay venue but it is extremely gay-friendly,
both in the bar and in the basement club (VATS – open Monday to
Saturday, 2000 to 0100). Entrance to the club can be gained through the
bar, entitling you to a discount on the admission charge. Otherwise,
access to the club is from the street after 2300 with an admission charge
of £4. The traditionally styled bar is just that – a traditional bar with no
karaoke, no camp drag hostesses and no pretension. It has a complete
age range from 18 years to 80, real ale and the '...I remember when this

was all just green fields' regulars. The small club is more suited to the younger generation looking for a convenient place for a late night drink, including those that like to dabble! Very raw and very... interesting. **Open** Monday-Friday 1700-2300. Friday-Saturday 1200-2300. Sunday 1200-2230 **Price** £4, after 2300

Clubs

Club Revenge   32-34 Old Steine, Brighton BN1 1EL Phone 01273 606 064
E-mail info@revenge.co.uk Web www.revenge.co.uk
Every year it seems that this club wins Boyz' weekend club of the year, and quite rightly so – two levels, two bars, two dancefloors and packed at the weekend to the proverbial rafters with a typical G-A-Y crowd. During the week it has some of the best entertainment in the town – from strippers on a Monday (Mantrap) with the DJ playing house and dance trax through to Friday (Lollipop) when Pooh La May and side-kick Betty Blojob assaults the crowd and plays tracks from three decades – '90s on level one and '70s and '80s on level two. The size and scope of the venue gives plenty of opportunity to cruise and be cruised. **Open** Monday-Thursday 2230-0200. Friday-Saturday 2200-0200. **Price** £1-3 / £3-6.50

Secrets   25 Steine Street, Brighton BN2 1TE Phone 01273 609 672
Long-running popular gay club (mostly men) with lots of entertainment going on at various times throughout the week. **Open** Monday-Saturday 2100-0200 **Price** £2-3

Club nights

Fresh @ Royal   Royal Pavilion Tavern, 7-8 Castle Square, Brighton BN1 1FX
Pavilion Tavern   Phone 01273 827 641
Long-running predominantly lesbian night in the club above The Royal Pavilion Tavern. Musically the tried and tested '70s shit is still played and due to some protestations it can also include some commercial house. But the girls still come! and no surprise really as the club choice in Brighton for the dykes is 'take it or leave it'. Still, the chance of getting slaughtered with late night drinking holds some precedent and old habits die hard. Meet up at The Marlborough beforehand and give it a try – it just might be up your street. During the day this pub is another well and truly mixed (more straight than gay) cheap beer watering hole – watch out for those splinters! **Open** Friday 2200-0200

Kinky Booty @   214 King's Road Arches, Brighton BN1 1NB Phone 01273 202 807 (club)
The Honeyclub   E-mail kinky@wildfruit.co.uk Web www.wildfruit.co.uk
Kinky Booty is fast becoming Brighton's most fashionable Friday night out. Based within the confines of The Honeyclub which bills itself as Brighton's leading independent club, resulting in a perfect mixture: Honeyclub is chic, glamourous and camp and Kinky is smart and club-by. Remember though, before you part with your hard-earned cash, it is not strictly a gay club night. The mix of gays to straights is about fifty-

fifty at best, totalling a regular attendance of around 600 people, but the atmosphere (because of the mix) is top notch. Resident DJs on rotation include Adam-H, Dan, Pete Hayward and Simon Barr who are all joined by special guests including Princess Julia and Farley Jackmaster Funk. In addition to the main funked-up dance floor there is also the luxurious 'Queens Lounge' hosted by the drunken slag Miss Dolly Rocket. It is worth pointing out that the the door is 'manned', by a ferocious drag queen who will increase the admission if she thinks you are not quite dressed for the occasion or increase it to a prohibitive amount if you are part of a group of lads who look like they've wandered off the wrong bus. You are able to try out The Honeyclub during the summer days when it doubles up as a seafront café-bar. Tip: if you are keen to get in, purchase a discounted Q-Jump ticket from Dr Brighton's. **Open** Friday 2230-0400 **Price** £7-8

Popstarz @ The Ocean Rooms 1-2 Morley Street, Brighton BN2 2RA Phone 07956 549 246
E-mail info@popstarz.co.uk Web www.popstarz.co.uk

Still rebelling against the gay stereotype, Simon Hobart and the Popstarz crew have taken their successful London club to the south shore for a monthly cheap piss-up party. The same formula of indie, rock and alternative dance in room one and disco-dolly dancing in room two. Meet up at The Marlborough and get your discounted Q-Jumps and be ready to join the crowds of gay studenty-type indie lovers getting ready for a good old-fashioned sesh. With an atmosphere reminiscent of a student union bar it is definitely not to everyone's taste. Formerly taking place on the first Wednesday of the month at The Honeyclub it has now gone bi-monthly and moved to the recently refurbished Ocean Rooms. This venue seems to be a suitable choice for the event but academic as the cheap booze takes over your sense of reality and you could in fact be anywhere. Tip: don't wear Prada – vomit tends to stain! **Open** 2200-0200, every first and third Wednesday of the month **Price** £3-4

Pussycat Club @ The Zap 189-192 Kings Road Arches, Brighton BN1 1BN Phone 01273 202 407
E-mail info@pussycatclub.net Web www.pussycatclub.net

Meet up at Dr Brighton's or Charles Street prior to embarking on this fab Friday nighter. Be warned that it is not an exclusively gay night – the mix is about 30 per cent homo and the rest straight – but for those of you who like an open music policy of uplifting house/garage or techno/trance this night will suit you down to the ground. Rave reviews from the likes of DJ Magazine and Ministry Magazine have gushed that '... popular ain't the word for this night... great, fantastic' and '...fast becoming an essential mixed/gay night.' It's hard to argue – The Zap has all the renown of The Ministry of Sound as an excellent clubbing venue. It may be intimate with a capacity of around 550 but the high ceilings, close contact and DJ 'in the Gods' give an atmosphere of the mosh pit (kind of) at an open air concert. To prove the kudos of the place, past guest DJs have included Tall Paul, Boy George, Brandon Block, Sonique and Judge Jules – name-dropping but a few. The Zap Club is situated on the Brighton sea front between The Palace Pier and The West Pier – directly opposite The Old Ship Hotel. To get in, remember that dress is everything – the policy is glam and glitz. Clubwear will suffice but be careful of those oh-so-naughty trainers. The doormen here have a reputation for being utter arseholes and won't hesitate to turn you away if you don't pass muster, so be warned. Finally, since it's Friday, you will have to decide whether to go here or to Kinky Booty (see separate listing) – now what would Brian Boitano do? **Open** Friday 2200-0400 **Price** £7-10

Sunday Sundae @ Bar Centro 2-6 Ship Street, Brighton BN1 1AD Phone 01273 327 083
E-mail **sundae@wildfruit.co.uk** Web **www.wildfruit.co.uk**
Before Sunday Sundae there was just 'Songs of Praise' and 'Antiques Roadshow' on the telly or a quick early evening wank in the cottage on the beach. In fact, ever since Brighton's first gay and lesbian tea dance opened in 1999 at Bar Centro, Sundays have never been the same since (although the quick early evening wank in a different location still stands second best). With resident DJs Pete Haywood and friends playing classic house and NY disco mixed along with vocal club anthems to a fun-loving and (extremely) varied crowd of around 400 peeps it seems that Sunday's will never be the same again. Tip: with the archaic UK Sunday licensing laws it is wise to work out your Sunday drink and dance schedule well before you start to cram in all those gin and tonics, ensuring that you get the best out of this traditionally dull day. **Open** Sunday 1800-2230 (extra one hour on bank holidays) **Price** £1-3

Wildfruit @ Paradox 78 West Street, Brighton BN1 1AL Phone 01273 327 083
E-mail **info@wildfruit.co.uk** Web **www.wildfruit.co.uk**
This long-running (eight years) monthly themed event is billed as 'The South's Biggest Gay and Lesbian Party!' and it would be extremely hard to find anyone to disagree with it. A huge 1,500 capacity venue on two levels which is always full, accommodating both gay boys and girls. A balcony overlooks the dance floor enabling you to cruise around the joint without looking like a complete slut. There's four bars, a restaurant and a state-of-the-art computerised light and laser system. It is recommended that you arrive early, otherwise you'll be queueing for ages. The dress code is anything smart goes, from outrageous to really outrageous. Previous themes have been 'Doctors and Nurses', 'Festive Fruit' (Christmas), and 'Roman Orgy' to mention just a few and nearly all make the effort. Dressing up enables you to legitimately queue-jump. For the date and theme of each month's party phone the number above, read the press or visit the website. Sadly, at the time of going to press, the Birmingham Wildfruit night, formerly held at Eros, had just bit the bullet. **Open** First Monday of the month 2200-0200 **Price** £5-6

Saunas

The Amsterdam Sauna 11-12 Marine Parade, Brighton BN2 1TL Phone 01273 688 825
E-mail **enquiries@amsterdam.uk.com** Web **www.amsterdam.uk.com**
An absolutely spotless sauna on the premises of The Amsterdam with sauna cabin, steam room and rest rooms. There is also a fair amount of seating space dotted around to sit back and enjoy a cup of coffee. It's a bit too compact for my tastes but I can't be too critical as at just £6 you

certainly get your money's worth. As I mentioned on the Amsterdam Bar listing, the beach and prom opposite the hotel has become quite cruisy of late and if you can't afford the few quid to get in here then hang around the front, look cheap and you could get lucky. **Open** Monday-Thursday 1400-0400. Friday-Saturday 1400-0600. Sunday 1400-0400 **Price** £6 (half-price to residents)

Bright 'n' Beautiful

9 St Margarets Place, Brighton BN12FD Phone 01273 328 330
Located in a small cul-de-sac behind the Metropol Hotel (the entrance being next to the NCP hotel car park) the sauna utilises two floors. The ground floor is the wet area whilst the upper floor is completely dedicated to relaxation in any of the ten or so individual rest rooms. Since the opening of Brighton Oasis and The Amsterdam it seems that this little sauna has suffered in the way of migrated trade but it still retains a loyal following. **Open** Monday-Saturday 1200-2200. Sunday 1200-2000 **Price** £9 or £7 after 1800

Brighton Oasis Sauna

75-76 Grand Parade, Brighton BN2 2JA T 01273 689 966
E-mail enquiries@oasissauna.com Web www.oasissauna.com
A nice clean and bright gay sauna with all the usual facilities. The ground floor houses reception, coffee shop (smoking is allowed in a designated area of the coffee shop only – it is not allowed in any other part of the venue), eight rest rooms and has also been designated a family room – and a big one at that! In the basement is a 28-foot heated swimming pool (with inflatables), two sauna cabins (one of which can hold over thirty people and will, of course, be subtly lit. There is a steam room and whirlpool down here as well. This is the sister venue to The Denmark Oasis sauna in Hove. **Open** Monday-Thursday 1200-2230. Friday 1200-0400. Saturday 1200-0600. Sunday 1200-0000 **Price** £7-11

Bristol Gardens Health Spa

24-26 Bristol Gardens, Brighton BN2 5JR Phone 01273 698 904
E-mail bghs@dircon.co.uk Web www.bghs.co.uk
I'm listing this sauna just to clarify the position of whether or not it is a gay sauna. I contacted Bristol Gardens and asked specifically 'would gay activity be tolerated?' and the reply was 'No! not at all!' Bristol Gardens is listed in some magazines as a gay-friendly sauna – which it is, although that's like saying Woolworths is a gay-friendly store. Although, should you start blowing someone off over the pick 'n' mix I'm sure you would be asked to leave – pronto. Brighton now has more than its fair share of gay saunas so you are quite able to find one that caters for your needs. However, if you like risk-taking and have the twelve quid to spare... well, the rest rooms upstairs are not there for nothing are they? **Open** Monday-Sunday 1200-2230 **Price** £12

The Denmark Oasis

84-86 Denmark Villas, Hove BN3 3TJ Phone 01273 723 733
The layout of The Denmark consists of a series of corridors with soft lighting throughout (very flattering). There's a coffee shop (incorporating a TV room), a changing area with large spacious lockers and opposite the showers is the steam room, which usually has eucalyptus essence pumped into the steam. The T-shaped sauna cabin is the next facility

down the corridor, then the rest area and massage room (£20 per hour). Down another corridor are the private rest rooms, each with a Hollywood Diva nameplate on the door in case you get lost and at the end is the Jacuzzi room. **Open** Monday-Sunday 1200-2200 **Price** £11

Unit One Sauna St Margarets Flats, High Street, Rottingdean, Brighton BN2 7HA
Phone 01273 307 253

Probably the longest-established gay sauna in the country – 33 years in the same location (do you know one older?). One large level which seems to encompass lots of little rooms – ideal for cruising round without it looking like you've got 'I'm gagging for it' tattooed on your forehead. Facilities include the usual sauna cabin, steam room (albeit with a shower inside) and a swimming pool. Eight individual rest rooms, TV lounge and a non-smoking area by the swimming pool. Situated about three miles east from Brighton town centre, not too far from Telscombe Beach. **Open** Monday-Sunday 1100-2200 **Price** £11

Accommodation

Alpha Lodge Hotel 19 New Steine, Brighton BN2 1PD
Phone 01273 609 632 Fax 01273 690 264
E-mail alphalodge@cwcom.net Web www.alpha-lodge.net

Brighton's longest established (since 1980) exclusively gay hotel is a Grade Two-listed building situated in a pleasant Regency square, overlooking the Victorian Palace Pier. The Steine Room Suite consists of a

Turkish bath, a rest area with an open fire and a colour TV, a shower area, hair dryer, toilet facilities and individual lockers for your valuables. Towels and wraps are provided, and the whole facility is free to residents on Wednesdays, Fridays and Saturdays for one and a half hours in the early evening. The Alpha has ten rooms, all of which are available as singles, but five are double-bedded, each with their own private shower. The remainder, with single beds, are both with and without private showers. All the rooms have colour TVs, radios, intercoms and hot drinks facilities, and individually controlled central heating. There are no petty restrictions and everything is geared to make your stay comfortable and relaxing. A map of gay Brighton, a privilege card to gain entry into the gay clubs and welcoming drink on arrival are all provided as part of the basic charge for the room. Visa, Access, American Express, Solo and Switch accepted. Phone Derrick or Cathal if you require further information. **Price** £44 – 60 **Number of rooms** 10, all available as single; 5 with double beds

The Amsterdam Hotel
11-12 Marine Parade, Brighton BN2 1TL Phone 01273 688 825
E-mail enquiries@amsterdam.uk.com Web www.amsterdam.uk.com
The Amsterdam is one of the biggest hotels in town – that's if you don't count The Grand (but that doesn't count 'cos it's not gay). All the rooms are en-suite and you can choose between sea view rooms (most expensive), side rooms (less expensive) or back rooms (cheaper) or spend £6 and stay in the sauna (which you may as well do because you'll probably spend most of your time in there anyway, or am I being too presumptuous?). If you do decide to stay in the hotel you'll be in the heart of the gay village, have access to a 24-hour bar and be treated like a king (or queen). Breakfast is charged as an extra and available at Charles Street Café so you can't come down in your dressing gown and mules – you'll have to get dressed. The rooms are clean and comfortable and contain everything you could possibly require. You can also choose from a selection of themed rooms: Roman, Thai or Egyptian – that sort of thing. Very nice and you can't get better (not counting The Grand). **Price** £85, double deluxe with sea view **Number of rooms** 24, all en-suite

Avalon
7 Upper Rock Gardens, Brighton BN2 1QE Phone 01273 692 344
E-mail avalonguesthse@talk21.com
Grade two listed, The Avalon is well situated just two minutes from the sea front and just off St James's Street. All bedrooms are clean and comfortable and fully en-suite. Other facilities include TV radio alarm, tea and coffee courtesy tray and most rooms are equipped with CD players and fridges. **Price** £44 **Number of rooms** 8

Bannings Guest-House
14 Upper Rock Gardens, Brighton BN2 1QE Phone 01273 681 403
E-mail info@bannings.co.uk Web www.bannings.co.uk
Bannings is conveniently situated just off St James's Street and close to all that this gay village has to offer. All of the bedrooms are either en-suite or with showers and all are equipped with colour televisions, radio alarm clocks and tea/coffee-making facilities. Ironing and hair drying facilities are available upon request. **Price** £42-48 **Number of rooms** 6,

some with shower facility

Benyon House 24 St Georges Terrace, Brighton BN2 1JJ Phone 01273 681 014
Benyon House is located at the far end of St Jame's Street this is a small, quiet bed and breakfast. All rooms are en-suite with a shower and wash hand basin, with tea/coffee-making facilities in each room too. **Price £44 Number of rooms 6**

Brighton Royal Hotel 76 Grand Parade, Brighton BN2 2JA Phone 01273 604 182
Fully licensed, very gay-friendly hotel on the edge of the gay village, ideally situated above the Brighton Oasis Sauna (see listing). Rooms are semi-en-suite, which means that although there are wash facilities in the rooms the WC facilities are shared. Women are also made very welcome. **Price £60 Number of rooms 10**, semi-en-suite

Brighton's famous gay village area, Kemptown, houses the offices of a number of direct-action campaign groups, notably Justice?. Justice? is a collective formed in the mid-1990s in opposition to the Criminal Justice Bill. They are famous for squatting in a number of municipal buildings throughout the town to highlight the scandal of empty buildings not being used, either to house homeless people, or for socially beneficial community functions.

Catnaps Guest House 21 Atlingworth Street, Brighton BN2 1PL
Phone 01273 685 193 Fax 01273 628 739
This is a very gay-friendly guest-house, well located about half-way down off St James's Street. All rooms have tea/coffee-making facilities and there are also reduced midweek rates available. **Price £50 Number of rooms 10**, all en-suite

Courtlands Hotel 23-27 The Drive, Hove BN3 3JW Phone 01273 731 055
Fax 01273 328 295 E-mail reservations@courtlandshotel.com
Web www.courtlandshotel.com
The Courtlands is Hove's premier hotel. It's gay-friendly and situated in the centre of Hove on a wide arboreal avenue leading to the sea front. This three-star hotel offers traditional hospitality and modern facilities and is within minutes of Brighton's busy conference and commercial centre, and only a short drive to the beautiful South Downs and the

Sussex countryside. Amongst the facilities on offer are a heated indoor swimming pool and excellent in-house dining at the Dolphin Restaurant. There are also executive rooms and a private car park. **Price** £75-90 **Number of Rooms** 67, all en-suite

Cowards
Guest-House

12 Upper Rock Gardens, Brighton BN2 1QE Phone 01273 692 677
Small, exclusively gay men-only guest-house in the centre of the gay village. Late breakfasts accommodated for. All rooms are fully en-suite or with showers and wash-basin. Tea/coffee-making facilities in the room. **Price** £55 **Number of rooms** 8

Craven Court
Hotel

2 Atlingworth Street, Brighton BN2 1PL
Phone 01273 607 710 Fax 01273 628 739
Exclusively gay hotel with most rooms having en-suite facilities. **Price** £45 **Number of rooms** 12

Four Seasons
Hotel

3 Upper Rock Gardens, Brighton BN2 1QE Phone 01273 673 574
E-mail joehalpenny@compuserve.com
The Four Seasons used to be a women-only guest-house. Now under new ownership, the tradition of welcoming women is maintained but the doors are now open to men as well. Situated within easy walking distance of St James's Street the rooms are comfortable and all have showers, TV, tea/coffee-making facilities. What is not provided is the traditional cooked English breakfast – there is an ample continental breakfast though. There is also a family room available, easily accommodating three people in a double and a single bed (approximately £75). **Price** £65, double en-suite **Number of rooms** 7, most en-suite

George IV
Guest-House

24 Regency Square, Brighton BN1 2FJ Phone 01273 321 196
Only five minutes from the gay village and near-opposite the west pier, this five-storey regency hotel offers comfortable accommodation. All rooms are en-suite and have TV, tea/coffee-making facilities and direct dial phone. **Price** £50 double room **Number of rooms** 8, all en-suite

Gullivers Hotel

10 New Steine, Brighton BN2 1PB
Phone 01273 695 415 Fax 01273 622 663 E-mail GulliversH@aol.com
AA-rated, QQQ and RAC-acclaimed. A Regency guest-house in a Brighton sea front square. English or vegetarian breakfast served in the dining room, or a continental breakfast served in the privacy and comfort of your own room. All rooms have hospitality tray, TV, direct dial phone with en-suite available. Women are made very welcome. **Price** £52 per double room **Number of rooms** 8, all en-suite

Hotel Nineteen

19 Broad Street, Brighton BN2 1TJ Phone 01273 675 529
Fax 01273 675 531 E-mail hotel.nineteen@brighton19.fsnet.co.uk
Web www.hotelnineteen.co.uk
A new modern minimalist hotel near Brighton sea front but also within the St James's area. Merging the best informal hospitality with vivid modern artworks and offering guests an experience with a difference. King rooms have illuminated glass bricked beds which radiate a soft

glow and all rooms have mirrored white shower rooms or bath-and-shower rooms. **Price** £95-125 **Number of rooms** 7, all en-suite

Hotel Pelirocco   10 Regency Square, Brighton BN12FG Phone 01273 327 055
Fax 01273 733 845 E-mail info@hotelpelirocco.co.uk
Web www.hotelpelirocco.com

Hotel Pelirocco is situated on Regency Square on the sea front in the centre of Brighton. It is very close to Brighton's vibrant shopping areas, within spitting distance of the conference centre and a stagger away from the bars, clubs and restaurants. It will tickle the tastebuds of pleasure seekers on the hunt for something new. There are 18 different bedrooms created by noted artists, maverick musicians, cult fashion labels and inspired individuals: Jamie Reid's 'Magic Room' , 'Hysteric Glamour', ' Absolut Love', ' Betty's Boudoir' and others all with a wacky or sexy theme ! And what do you do when you stay in a hotel like this eh? Have sex of course. In fact it is quite hard not to – even if you're by yourself. Room service will bring you all that you need – even a cucumber for use as a dildo – whatever is your bent. Excellent! There is one thing to note though; weekend bookings must take in at least two nights – weekdays are offered at a reduced rate. Tip: book early. **Price** £65-105 **Number of rooms** 18

Hudsons   22 Devonshire Place, Brighton BN2 1QA Phone 01273 683 642
Fax 01273 696 088 E-mail hudsons@brighton.co.uk
Web www.brighton.co.uk/hotels/hudsons

Hudsons is a fabulous little guest-house welcoming gay men and women. Designer-converted from an early 19th-century gentleman's townhouse to offer clean, comfortable rooms – some fully en-suite – some shower-only and all with TV, coffee and tea trays and direct dial phones. Some have sofas. Upon arrival they welcome you with a cup of tea (or a glass of sherry) and a map and guide to the bars, clubs, restaurants and tourist attractions of Brighton, all of which are a very short walk away. Hudsons is the only exclusively gay hotel inspected and approved by the Tourist Office. You can be sure that though the prices are modest, the standards are very high. Non-smokers can take advantage of either of the two exclusive no-smoking rooms that are available. **Price** £60 **Number of rooms** 9, most en-suite

| **Montpelier Hall Hotel** | 17 Montpelier Terrace, Brighton BN1 3DF |

Montpelier Hall Hotel
17 Montpelier Terrace, Brighton BN1 3DF
Phone 01273 203 599 Fax 01273 706 030
A fabulous Grade Two-listed Regency villa in the centre of Brighton (it is in fact the last late Regency Italianate Villa left in Brighton and of significant architecural interest). Montpelier Hall is set in 250 feet of private grounds. Spacious rooms overlook the spectacular walled garden. Relax in the grand drawing room, dine in the period dining room or wander around the garden with a cup of Earl Grey. All rooms have TV, tea/coffee-making facilities and the hotel has its own private car park. Throughout the summer they host barbeques in the garden each weekend (which are also open to non-residents, although you will have to book by 1600 on the day). The hotel is within easy walking distance to most of Brighton's gay scene venues. **Price** £48, double room **Number of rooms 8**, none en-suite

New Europe Hotel
31-32 Marine Parade, Brighton BN2 1TR
Phone 01273 624 462 E-mail enquiries@neweuropehotel.co.uk
Web www.neweuropehotel.co.uk
The New Europe Hotel is a privately owned, friendly gay hotel (women also welcome) opposite Brighton beach and with panoramic views of the famous palace pier. The hotel is situated in the heart of Kemptown with its fascinating narrow streets full of interesting shops and bars. Within easy walking distance are local amenities including The Brighton Centre, The Royal Pavilion, theatres, The Lanes and shopping centre. All the rooms are centrally heated with en-suite shower rooms, colour TV and phone, with many having sea views (the sea view rooms do not carry a premium and are let on a first come, first served basis). There are no parking facilities at the hotel, although the staff will advise you on the best place to park. All rooms are en-suite and a late bar is open 'til 0500 for residents. (See the listings for Legends Bar and Schwartz Bar also.) **Price** £60 (weekend rate) **Number of rooms 30**

Not a lot of people know that prior to the merger in 2000 that united the separate towns of Brighton and Hove as one city, Hove, with a population of some 60,000 people, was the largest town in the United Kingdom without a McDonalds restaurant. How ever did they cope?

Portland House Hotel
55-56 Regency Square, Brighton BN1 2FF
Phone 01273 820 464 Fax 01273 746 036 E-mail portlandhh@aol.com
Web www.portlandhousehotel.co.uk
This gay-run hotel is a Grade Two listed Regency building situated in Brighton's premier sea front square, adjacent to conference halls and close to all main attractions and amenities. All the rooms are individually styled, with en-suite facilities, colour TV, direct dial phone and radio/alarm clock. Tea/coffee making facilities, hairdryers, and iron are all available as complimentary extras on request. Out of the 24 rooms, twelve have sea views of the historic West Pier. The hotel has a lift to all floors and Regency Square has its own underground car park. **Price** £50-85 **Number of rooms 24**, all en-suite

3

Prince Regent

29 Regency Square, Brighton BN1 2FH
Phone 01273 329 962 E-mail princeregent@ukonline.co.uk
Web www.princeregenthotel.co.uk
The Prince Regent is a quality gay-friendly hotel standing at the top of Regency Square, overlooking the lawns down to the sea. It is a Regency mid-terrace mansion with 20 bedrooms, decorated with individual character including many mirrors and fine chandeliers. All rooms have purpose-built en-suite facilities, phone, TV, hospitality tray and some have a mini bar. There's also a ground floor room with a whirlpool bath. For that special occasion the hotel has two 19th-century four-poster beds. Or, there's a magnificent balcony room – with a kingsize tester bed – that offers a panoramic seaview (£150). Dinner, though not available in the hotel, may be sampled in one of at least 30 restaurants in the street adjoining Regency Square, with a variety of tastes and prices to suit most guests. **Price** £85-150 **Number of rooms** 20, all en-suite

Shalimar Hotel

23 Broad Street, Brighton BN2 1TJ
Phone 01273 605 316 E-mail shalimar@dircon.co.uk
Very gay-friendly guest-house off the front end of St James's Street. En-suite and non-smoking rooms available. **Price** £50 **Number of rooms** 6, 3 full en-suite, 3 with shower

The White House Hotel

6 Bedford Street, Brighton BN2 1AN Phone 01273 626 266
A beautiful Regency house only 200 yards from the sea front and five minutes from the pubs and clubs. All double and twin rooms are en-suite with TV and hospitality trays. For the more decadent amongst you there is also a room with a four-poster bed or a selection of themed rooms to choose from. **Price** £50 **Number of rooms** 9, all en-suite except single

Cruising grounds

Dukes Mound

The bushes situated by the Marina at the end of Madeira Drive. You need to make your way to the bushes on the sand banks near to the official nudist beach. Lots of action at all times during the year but, like most places, the summer months more so. Late evenings are the best. The daytime hours, especially around teatime, can be worthwhile too. Since the opening of The Amsterdam (see listing) the beach front outside the hotel has also doubled up as a little bit of a cruising ground – makes for quite a nice circuit really! It is worth noting that the nudist beach is also situated in front of Dukes Mound which is good and convenient for a spot of daytime cruising and voyeuristic opportunity. Isn't Brighton wonderful?

Hove Sea Front

It's not hard to find the Queen Victoria statue on Hove promenade. Nor is it hard to find some willing bit of man-meat around the prom and beach front within her gaze. What is hard though... wait for it... is finding a bit of privacy. You've not much option but to pick up and take away. Where to though? In the day it's practically impossible, particularly during the summer with families around. The evenings however, are a completely different kettle of fish. Whilst most civil folk are tucked up watching Cilla in their B&Bs you can quite safely creep down to the beach, find a nook and partake in a bit of sand-wrestling!

Retail & Other

Cardome 2000   47a St James's Street, Brighton BN2 1RJ Phone 01273 692 916
Gift shop selling adult cards, gay magazines, books, aromas and novelty items. **Open** Monday-Saturday 1030-1800.

Clone Zone   32 St James's Street, Brighton BN2 1RF Phone 01273 626 442
E-mail info@clonezone.co.uk Web www.clonezone.co.uk
Gay men's sex shop with outlets in most major cities throughout the UK. Sells practically everything you could possibly need from (those kind of) magazines and books to condoms and lube. They will also be able to inform you of any events going on in the city and supply the tickets you need to gain admittance. All the free gay press and club flyers are available here and it is always worth asking the staff if there are any specialist events going on that will suit your area of interest. **Open** Monday-Thursday 1100-1900. Friday-Saturday 1100-2100. Sunday 1200-1800

Galeria Travel   2 George Street, Brighton BN2 1RH Phone 0870 220 1705/6
E-mail galeria.travel@virgin.net Web www.galeriatravel.com
Conveniently situated off St James's Street, Galeria Travel are specialists in all gay and lesbian sunshine travel destinations as well as arranging city breaks to most European gay destinations. **Open** Monday-Friday 1100-1730. Saturday 1100-1400

Madison Travel   118 Western Road, Hove BN3 1DB Phone 01273 202 532
E-mail enquiries@madisontravel.co.uk Web www.madisontravel.co.uk
Madison Travel have been serving the gay community and arranging holidays for over 14 years. Their staff have over 30 years experience in dealing with the most demanding travel arrangements. Membership of the Association of British Travel Agents (ABTA) means they are fully bonded so your money is completely safe with them. Having recently joined the Worldchoice Consortium enables them to offer a full range of holidays at the most competitive cost. Find them on the border of Brighton and Hove. **Open** Monday-Saturday 1000-1730

Out! Brighton   4 & 7 Dorset Street, Brighton BN2 1WA Phone 01273 623 356
E-mail info@out-brighton.co.uk Web www.out-brighton.co.uk
Out! Brighton opened in 1994. Predominantly a lesbian and gay bookshop, it also stocks magazines, videos, cards, T-shirts, leather, rubber, lubes and toys. You are welcome to browse through the books and other merchandise in a relaxed and friendly atmosphere and you will find the helpful staff ready to attend to any queries you might have. Unlike the chain bookstores, lesbian and gay books are the specialism of Out! Brighton: you will not encounter homophobia or sneers here. Tip: use it – or lose it. **Open** Monday-Thursday 1000-1800. Friday-Saturday 1000-1900. Sunday 1100-1700

Perforations

21 Preston Street, Brighton BN1 2HN Phone 01273 326577
E-mail piercing@perforations.co.uk Web www.perforations.co.uk
Gay-friendly piercing and branding studio off Kings Road. Very friendly and helpful. As a rough price guide all facial piercings with ring are about £15. For those of you who want to enhance your piercings take a look at the Wildcat listing. **Open** Monday-Sunday 1200-1730

The Pink Pamper

74 St James's Street, Brighton BN2 1PA Phone 01273 608 060
E-mail info@thepinkpamper.co.uk Web www.thepinkpamper.co.uk
If you aim to go swanning up and down Brighton beach it is fortunate for you that The Pink Pamper offers a complete back and chest waxing service to give you that fresh smooth model-like appearance. Of course, the men aren't left out either. Eyes, hair, nails, facials, hair and bikini line are all taken care of at this swish, trendy and very pink men and women's beauty and hair salon. There is also an incorporated coffee shop where you can pick up the gay press and flyers to most of Brighton's events. A cut and blow for the girls is around £17.50 and for the boys it will cost £14.50. **Open** Monday-Wednesday 0900-1800. Thursday-Friday 0900-2100. Saturday 0900-1800

Scene 22

129 St James's Street, Brighton BN1 3AA Phone 01273 626 682
Sitauted above the former Zanzibar, Scene 22 is a combined coffee bar and sex shop. An odd combination perhaps, but it's a nice opportunity to check what's on the shelves whilst sipping your café latté. Scene 22 is a pro-community place and offers two internet-ready terminals – free of charge! In return, contributions to the charity box are appreciated. Cards, videos, magazines, fetish wear and the free gay press and flyers are available here. **Open** Monday–Saturday 1030-1800. Sunday 1230-1730

Tattooing at Gunpoint

3 Victoria Terrace, Hove BN3 2WB Phone 01273 206 226
Gay-friendly tattooist. The kind of place where you can have 'all you can eat, for free' tattooed above your pubic region. **Open** Tuesday-Saturday 1100-1800

Wildcat Collection

16 Preston Street, Brighton BN1 2HN Phone 01273 323 758
E-mail info@wildcat.co.uk Web www.wildcat.co.uk
If you have your nipples pierced – or come to that – any other parts of your body, then you really must pop in here to see what can replace those

BRIGHTONS ONLY GAY SHOP AND COFFEE BAR
129 St James Street, Brighton. Tel 01273 626682

boring ringy things. Imagine having your nipple shielded by a disc of metal slightly elevated with a hole from which the nipple protrudes ..hmmm ..or how's about a spider's web... nice.... Well, aside from these two suggestions there are simply racks of alternatives for you to choose from in addition to funky mainstream jewellery like earrings, belly button adornments and so on. In fact if you have 'something' that can have 'something' attached to it there is no doubt that you can find it here. **Open** Monday-Saturday 1000-1800

Bristol

Bristol used to be England's second city. It was a thriving trade centre with an industry that attracted wealth and reputation. To its discredit, the 18th century saw Bristol dirty its hands in the transatlantic slave trade – it is a past which the city still has difficulty accepting today. The famous Victorian engineer Brunel has left his mark on the city, most notably in the forms of The Clifton Suspension Bridge and the terminus for the Great Western Railway – the old station at Temple Meads. Bristol has a rich maritime heritage, some of the country's finest Georgian architecture and acres of beautiful parkland and estates. Today it is still a major city – a centre for media and the arts and a growing reputation as the clubbing capital outside of London. Bristol is the young and slovenly sister to the less fashionable, but well-to-do Bath. More often than not these city names appear in the same sentence, since only a twenty-minute stretch of road separates them. Bath, however, does not share Bristol's eclecticism or atmosphere, nor its night life, nor its gay scene. If the Bristol gay scene does not quite appeal to your tastes then fear not; this student-based city has a rather relaxed and tolerant attitude and a straight scene, particularly across the dance clubs, that is integrated and welcoming.

Getting in touch

The **Tourist Office** (0117 926 0767) is situated at St Nicholas Church on St Nicholas Street. They can book theatre tickets and accommodation (subject to a booking fee) and they offer a wide selection of tourist guides and maps. They are open daily from 0930 to 1730. Useful gay-specific phone numbers you may require whilst in Bristol include **Gay Switchboard** (0117 942 0842) which is open Monday to Friday from 2000 to 2200; **Southwest Gay Switchboard** (01392 422 016) which is open Monday from 1930 to 2200; **Terrence Higgins Trust** (0117 955 1000), formerly the Aled Richards Trust, and **Victim Support** (0117 963 1114).

Pubs

The Elephant   20 St Nicholas Street, Bristol BS1 1UB Phone 0117 925 2820
Established as a public house since 1787(making it one of the oldest pubs in the UK), it has recently been renovated, turning what was once a dingy little bar into a bright, modern social space for all the gay commu-

nity. It's become a particular favourite with the girls. Sunday is exceptionally busy when the weekly cabaret and party atmosphere draws in the crowds. For those of you who like to see oiled-up man flesh, then make sure you are here for the last Friday of the month when the male stripper bares all for the sake of art. Well, it's actually for the sake of 50 quid, but who's counting? Open Monday-Saturday 1200-2300. Sunday 1200-2230

The Griffin

41 Colston Street, Bristol BS1 5AP Phone 0117 930 0444
E-mail info@the-griffin-pub.co.uk Web www.the-griffin-pub.co.uk
The Griffin is unashamedly Bristol's only mature gay venue, catering for gay men around 30-plus who, along with their admirers, enjoy the company of bear and leather types. Recently refurbished, the pub is on two levels. The ground floor has a Victorian theme, classy but still invitingly seedy. Upstairs, is the dark and interesting, horny cruise bar known quite aptly as The Twilight Zone (Friday-Sunday; from 2000). It's safe and lots of fun. The opening hours mentioned below are only a guide. The Griffin does hold a late licence for each night and will usually gauge the closing time on the evening, so if the bar is busy and playful then expect a late night. What's striking is the total lack of any kind of attitude – bar staff are happy to serve and punters are never content to be wallflowers. All combined, it marks this pub out as quite an enjoyable place to just be yourself. Open Monday-Saturday 1200-2300. Sunday 1200-0000

The Old Castle Green

44 Gloucester Lane, Bristol BS2 0DP Phone 0117 955 0925
A medium-sized pub, just off West Street in the Old Market and only ten minutes' walk from the centre of Bristol. This is the nearest gay venue to Club Wynns and as such tends to be the meeting-up place prior to a night of clubbing. The Green is a rather laid-back, no-attitude kind of place, more for the social butterfly rather than the disco bunny and as such does not have a packed calendar of events to entice you in. It does, however, have friendliness and charm and everyone, no matter what their age or sexuality, is made to feel welcome. They do host their own disco (Tutti Frutti) once a month on the third Saturday which for a pub running a free night cannot be faulted. Wednesday evening hosts the long-running Curry Night, which for £4.99 gets you a curry and a pint. Sunday lunches are also available (two courses for £4.99) although these do have to be booked. Open Monday-Wednesday 1200-1430/1700-2300 Thursday-Friday 1100-2300. Saturday 1900-2300. Sunday 1200-2230

The Pineapple

37 St Georges Road, Bristol BS1 5UU Phone 0117 907 1162
The Pineapple is a typical friendly gay pub, full of fun and energy. Men, women and TVs are all welcome. There's a varied music policy, from camp to hard house. Sky TV and happy hour is from 1700 to 2000 every day. The perfect place to come and relax after work. Excellent beer prices. Open Monday-Saturday 1200-2300. Sunday 1200-2230

Queenshilling

9 Frogmore Street, Bristol BS1 5NA Phone 0117 926 4342
E-mail mail@queenshilling.com Web www.queenshilling.com
The recently refurbished Shilling tends to attract the younger crowd of gay boys and bender babes, being one of the most popular venues for

Bristol's student community. This large, 350-capacity and extremely live-ly venue has some sort of entertainment each and every night. Monday is CRAP (Chart, Retro And Pop – not shitty!). Tuesday is a cheap drinks night. Thursday is another cheap drinks night, this time pandering to the large student population (£2 admission after 2200, although an NUS card will get you in for free). Weekends are full-on discos and it's pretty much guaranteed that the place will be packed, so an early arrival is advised. **Open** Monday-Saturday 2000-0200. Sunday 2000-2230 **Price** Sunday-Wednesday; £2-3 after 2200. Thursday; £2 after 2100/2200 Friday-Saturday; £2 after 2100 and £3 after 2200

Clubs

Castro's

72-73 Old Market Street, Bristol BS2 0EJ Phone 0117 922 0774
Castro's is a members-only club although you will be allowed entry as a guest. However, if you wish to return after your first visit (which I'm sure you will as the music rocks) you will be 'encouraged' to join (£10). This is no bad thing as you will get sizeable discounts off your admis-sion. On a Saturday there is a breakfast club running from close 'til at least midday on a Sunday (gulp!) There is a condition though – you have to be in the club on a Saturday night. If you do choose to go elsewhere then you will not be admitted to the breakfast club. Admission to this is a mere £2. On the first and third Saturday the club opens up through to 0800 and the admission is reduced to £5 on the first and £7 on the third. There is no dress code for Castro's (very sensible) as the emphasis is on enjoying the music, the company and just being a party animal. The mix of people is slightly more straight than gay – fifty-fifty at a stretch, and this gives you a slight uneasy feeling in the pit of your stomach. There are three floors playing commercial to hard house with a sprinkling of trance. The chill-out room on the first floor gives you opportunity to relax a little and give you a welcome break from the hectic, fast-paced mayhem in the main dance arenas. If you are absolutely sick of the camp shite being pumped out in the majority of places then this place may well tide you over. **Open** Thursday 2000-0200. Friday-Saturday 2200-0600(first and third Saturdays 2200-0800) **Price** £3-9 Friday-Saturday; £4 Sunday

Winn's Club

23-25 West Street, Old Market, Bristol BS2 0DG Phone 0117 941 4024
E-mail winns@winnsclub.com Web www.winnsclub.com
Winn's is a large, exclusively gay club with a capacity for around 350. It consists of a large main arena with appropriate sized dancefloor and two bars. Several adjoining 'back rooms' form chill-out and cruise areas and a third bar (which used to be the vault in this former bank). There is also a café-bar in the basement. The late licence that this club holds and the cheap admission and drinks ensure the venue is always busy with a young up-for-it crowd of no-nonsense party-goers. The music policy stretches a little further away from the screaming camp and incorporates a harder edge, commercial house sound that the boys (and significant number of girls) seem to love. **Open** Thursday 2200-0300. Friday-Saturday 2100-0400 **Price** Thursday £1. Friday £2-5. Saturday £4-6

Club nights

Spank!

Different venues, Bristol Phone 09094 644 113

Spank! Is a monthly fetish party that has been running for over nine years, and operates on the first Saturday of the month, at a central Bristol location. Phone for venue details or you'll need to enquire at Religion (see retail listing). The usual rooms layout are as follows; room one is where resident DJs unleash a sonic riot of hard house and trance, guaranteed to make you sweat. If you prefer to sit this one out, feast your eyes on the erotic video wall with fetish overlays from SawDid Visuals. Room two is an area of an altogether different nature. Think medical trolley, PVC recliners, cages and whipping bench and you'll be on the right track. Dress code is as strict as ever, with a policy of rubber, leather, PVC, bondage, fantasy, uniforms, lingerie, etc. being enforced by the Perv Police. A leather jacket is not enough, nor is a little lycra frock (if you do not meet the dress code you will not be allowed entrance into the club, and will be asked to go home, change and return to enter the real world of fetish!). The cloakroom is staffed all night, so your coats and bags will be kept safe until it is time to return to the real world. There is also a strict code of fetish etiquette, which means 'Look, but don't touch unless invited.' For Spank! advance tickets at £7.50, visit Religion at 128 Cheltenham Road, Bristol, or pay £10 on the door. Nothing to wear? Go visit Religion for a full range of fetish clothing and accessories. Religion will also be able to help with enquiries regarding Spank! if you have trouble getting through on the above number. **Open** First Saturday of the month **Price** £7.50-10

Saunas

Cottage Health Club

19 West Street, Old Market, Bristol BS2 DDF
Phone 0117 903 0622 E-mail chclub@aol.com

Membership is absolutely vital to gain entry to this gay and bisexual sauna, however, no details are kept on computer except your initials and date of birth. When you turn up at the door on your first visit you will be expected to show some positive proof of identity, with your name and address. This is just to prove you are who you say you are; no details are recorded. You will then be issued with your membership card. The Cottage is a deceptively large building, utilising all four floors and the facilities are laid out as follows: on the ground floor you have the TV lounge, new steam room and showers. The first floor houses the sauna cabin and toilets. The third floor is the 'interesting' floor, with about 15 individual rest rooms and a communal video lounge. The fourth floor, in the attic, houses the communal rest areas. During the week, like all places, it can be rather hit-and-miss. The weekends, though, are notoriously busy, hence the all-night opening hours. Even Sundays, throughout the daytime, are immensely popular. **Open** Monday-Thursday 1600-0000. Friday-Saturday 1300-0800. Sunday 1300-2300 **Price** £10 plus £4 annual membership

Accommodation

Maison George 10 Greville Road, Southville, Bristol BS3 1LL Phone 0117 963 9416
Gay-owned and -run affordable accommodation for a mixed gay and straight clientele about one mile from the gay scene. Full English or vegetarian breakfast included in the price. All rooms with TV and welcome tray. **Price £40 Number of rooms** 5, none en-suite

---

There is a phenomenom in Bristol that has baffled experts and had locals at their wits' end for more than 30 years. The source of this mystery is a humming noise that is heard mostly at night. The problem is that no one knows what causes the noise, although there have been plenty of theories – from water pipes to air conditioning, factory fans to radar defence systems, and even creatures from another planet! Experts have visited the homes of sufferers to try and find out what is causing the hum but have failed to come up with a plausable explanation. Unlike other background noises that are constant and therefore blocked out by the ears, this noise comes and goes, so sufferers never quite get used to it. It adds up to countless sleepless nights and even the onset of madness for a few of the tortured locals. Indeed, one resident, J. Hall, committed suicide after the hum drove him crazy. Hmmm, I wonder....

Woodstock 534 Bath Road, Brislington, Bristol BS4 3JZ
Phone 0117 987 1613 E-mail woodstock@yahoo.co.uk
A private guest-house situated on the A4, one mile out of Bristol on the main Bath Road. Woodstock (the original name) is a late 1800s Victorian house with a homely atmosphere and pleasant, relaxing gardens. A full no-smoking policy applies throughout the house. English Tourist Board rating of three diamonds. Most major credit cards accepted. **Price £45 Number of rooms** 4, all en-suite (separate toilet facilities)

Cruising grounds

Bristol Downs Bristol's infamous cruising ground. Situated on the promenade close to the observatory, under the suspension bridge on Clifton Downs. Mixed age range catering for all tastes and mostly attitude-free although care does need to be taken. You are strongly advised not to use the cruising ground before 2000. Police patrols after that time will be extremely limited. The Cottage Sauna in Bristol's Old Market (see listing) would be the most viable alternative to using this place. You can get all that you require without any risk whatsoever. (Particularly popular with married or bisexual men.)

Retail

Clone Zone 45 Colston Street BS Bristol Phone 0117 929 7666
The newest branch of the infamous gay sex shop chain, selling those R18 videos as well as the other bits and bobs necessary for spicing up

our love lives.

Religion

128 Cheltenham Road, Bristol BS6 5RW
Phone 0117 904 2239 / 0117 907 4194

Religion specialises in rubber, leather, PVC and corsets, filling a niche in the West for clothes both classic and curious. Stockists of Liz Lewitt, Catwalk Collection, Prohibition, Invincible, Dane, Surrender, Vince Ray and Honour, plus Ritual, Underground and Fantasy shoes. A highly skilled workshop team supply the shop with new designs weekly and can repair or alter garments brought in by customers. Complete commission design and garment construction service is available in leather, latex, PVC, lycra, silk and chiffon. This service is for new and regular clients as well as for the television and film industries. The friendly and approachable staff ensure complete discretion for the shy customer or those with unusual commission needs. They also cater for more specialist customers, as they make 80 per cent of the stock themselves. The shop holds a full range of fetish basics and they have a bargain rail which is regularly replenished for the first-time fetishist. The shop also has costume hire service available and features one-off collections from British and European designers on a regular basis. **Open** Thursday-Sunday 1100-1800

Bury Saunas

Nero's Roman Spa

Whitelegge Street, Bury BL8 Phone 0161 764 2576
E-mail info@neros.co.uk Web www.neros.co.uk

Nero's is situated about ten miles from Manchester city centre. It occupies two floors of what was once an old warehouse, and is regarded as one of the best saunas in the north-west. The ground floor comprises the wet area, lovely large Jacuzzi, large steam room (easily accommodating 30), sauna cabin, plenty of seating and a huge cold plunge pool. The upstairs consists of the café (value-for-money home-cooked food), comfortable TV lounge (smoking) and separate seating areas leading to the dark rooms. There are about ten individual rest rooms, all with lockable doors and dimmer switches, a small but nevertheless ample cinema room and the infamous 'maze' – a darkened series of corridors leading to a communal room in the centre. Nero's is well known as a clean and very friendly sauna – serving the needs of all gay and bi men where city centre Manchester may be too close to home. It also benefits from the nearby motorway links giving a huge catchment area from Yorkshire to Liverpool and beyond. Sundays do tend to have a reputation for being the busiest day, particularly from 1300-1900, however, most days can provide an ample supply of men of all ages. Immortalised on film last year as the location for the 'sauna scene' in Channel 4's Queer As Folk. Recommended. **Open** 1200-0000 (late closing on a Saturday) **Price** £10 (membership required)

Cambridge

More than three million visitors come to Cambridge every year; either to enjoy the delights and traditions of the historic city itself, or to use it as a base for exploring some of the gentlest and finest unspoilt country-side in England. The famous university is composed of around 35 or so smaller colleges. It doesn't take a genius to work out that the student population is quite high. You would have thought that this high concentration of young guns would enable Cambridge to have a decent-sized gay scene. This is sadly not the case. A small scene exists in the bars and clubs on Market Hill, that becomes the focus of street credibility and the source of youth culture in this fine city. Whether gay or straight, you'll be able to mix in and be accepted.

Getting in touch

The **Visitor Centre** (01223 322 640) on Wheeler Street, behind the Guildhall, is jam-packed with information leaflets, flyers, maps and guides, and most of these are free to take away. **Cambridge Gay and Lesbian Switchboard** (01223 246 031) is available for all general or specific gay enquiries. If your call is lesbian-specific then you may prefer phoning the **Cambridge Lesbian Line** (01223 246113) each Friday between 1800 and 2200. **Cambridge AIDS Helpline** (freephone 0800 697697) is open Tuesday to Wednesday from 1930 to 2200 and Saturday from 1200 to 1400.

Pubs

The Five Bells 126-128 Newmarket Road, Cambridge CB5 8HE Phone 01223 314 019
Very friendly mixed gay pub with occasional discos and pool competitions. Comprising two basic bar areas, one with background music, the other much louder. Every three months they hold a Fantasy Fair Fetish party organised by The Leather Rose Society (ticket only – phone 0705 027 4545) who provide their wonderful dungeon equipment. Go along, dress to impress and be ready for fun! Dress code is fetish dress (PVC, leather, rubber, military, Victorian, etc.) and bring your toys (human or otherwise). During the summer the beer garden opens up – a haven for the non-smokers! **Open** Monday-Saturday 1900-2300. Sunday 1200-2230

The Town and Gown   Northampton Street, Pound Hill, Cambridge CB3 0AE

Phone 01223 353 791

Well-established gay pub with regular promotions and events and cabaret over the weekend. Comprises two bars and a separate pool room and lots of cosy corners. This is more of a local than a clubby bar space but it does offer opportunities to meet new friends. **Open** Monday-Tuesday 1900-2300. Wednesday-Saturday 1200-1400/1900-2300. Sunday 1200-2230

Club nights

Dot Cottons @ The Junction   Clifton Road, Cambridge CB1 4GX Phone 01223 511 511

E-mail info@junction.co.uk Web www.junction.co.uk

A five minute taxi ride from Cambridge town centre will bring you to the park-and-ride car park, home of arts centre The Junction. The Dot Cotton Club is The Junction's longest-running mixed gay and straight club night with a capacity of just over 1,000. Each 'Dot' features regular DJs Chris G and Lee plus guests playing a complete pot-pourri of musical styles, guaranteed to satisfy pretty much everyone. There is always a top live PA (check out their website for up-to-date info). This venue is always busy, always loud and always a great night out. There is no pretentious dress code so you can wear anything you like. By the way, students can gain admission on the door for £4 (on production of the necessary NUS card). **Open** 2200-0300 last Saturday of the month **Price** £7-8

Cruising grounds

Jesus Green   Jesus Green, the big park behind the college, has to be one of the most fervent spots in the country for summer daytime cruising. During the daytime you should take your pick-ups elsewhere – indeed, this is perhaps the wisest course of action at all times. However, after dark there is cruising throughout the park and action can be found amongst the bushes, as well as the retaining wall behind the public swimming pool. Lots (and lots) of students and college-aged tourists from all over Europe.

Lammas Land   As you pass Lammas Land on your left, and the road swings to your right, there is a small road which runs down sharp-left (there is another straight ahead) down to a car park that serves as a recreation area. A wooded path runs from the back left-hand corner of the car park. Take this path; walk for approximately 30 metres and you will come to a raised part of the wood on your left. This is a very popular cruising spot with plenty of cover. Best times here are lunch-times and going home time. After dark, the action shifts across the river. Take the small footbridge near the front end of the car park and then turn left. Action can be found amongst the trees ahead of you, backing onto another bit of the river. During the summer months this place can be going to 0200 or even later. The cottage near the car park is open only during the summer but should be avoided if there are families about. It does tend to see some action during late evening.

Canterbury Pubs

Bar 11 | 11-12 Burgate, Canterbury CT1 2HG Phone 01227 478 707
Canterbury and the surrounding areas aren't exactly hives of gay life so it comes as a nice surprise when you happen on a venue that actively encourages gays and their lifestyle. Bar 11 is one such place. It's trendy and chilled and everyone mixes well in this young vibrant café-bar. Wednesday and Sunday evenings are the gayest nights where the music gets cranked up a bit louder than normal and the familiar 'gay party' atmosphere takes over the bar. During the day tourists and families saunter through to grab a bite to eat ('til 2030) and come the evening, the lights dim, the candles are lit and the well dressed and stylish take their places, order flambouyant cocktails and prepare themselves for a night on the town. **Open** Monday-Saturday 1100-2300. Sunday 1100-2230

Carlisle Saunas

Acquasauna | Atlas House, Nelson Street, Carlisle CA2 5ND Phone 01228 533 28
E-mail info@acquasaunas.co.uk Web www.acquasaunas.co.uk
This is Cumbria's only gay sauna and it is a welcome addition to an otherwise sparse scene. Facilities include a sauna cabin, a large steam room and a spa. There is also a lounge, cinema cabins and a coffee shop. If you get in between 1400 and 1600 you will get the benefit of having half-price entry or if you visit twice in the same week you can get in on Sunday for free. The venue is situated only three miles from the M6. Membership is available and necessary for entry. The standard membership charge is £3 per year, for admission to any of the Acquasauna chain of venues. Alternatively, various stages of membership can be purchased from £75, entitling you to £5 admission in any venue, to £250 for free admission to any venue for twelve months. **Open** Monday-Sunday 1200-2200 **Price** £9

Chatham Clubs

Secrets | 12b New Road, Chatham ME4 4QR Phone 01634 832 433
Secrets is the only gay club in Chatham and operates a strict members only policy. Non-members can join on the night or be signed in as a guest. The venue itself is on one level and is extremely lively, friendly and fun. Clientele consists of a healthy mix of 90 per cent gay men and women with the remainder being straight (but gay-friendly). The admission charges tend to be rather steep after 2100 which encourages people to get here early or pay through the nose. Thursday is the weekly strip fest (members only) and Sunday is the karaoke session. **Open** Tuesday 2000-late. Thursday 2000-0200. Friday-Saturday 2000-0200. Sunday 1900-1200 **Price** £2-6

Cruising grounds

Cobham Woods Take the A2 from London. About 30 miles out (between Gravesend and Chatham) look for the sign to Thong (there is also a sign for 'Hotel'). As you come off the motorway take the very narrow road on the right (controlled by traffic lights) which effectively takes you over the top of the A2. Follow the winding lane. Car parking is at the end. Action is found in the woods and on the other side (it will make sense when you get there). Always reliable action.

Great Lines Wooded area overlooking the shopping centre with outdoor action during the daytime and early evening. Very busy during the summer.

Victoria Gardens A small park, used for take-aways. I would advise caution at this site. No other information available, unfortunately.

Chelmsford Pubs

The Army and Navy 138 Parkway, Chelmsford CM2 7PU Phone 01245 354 155
It is only predominantly gay on two nights of the week – Wednesday and Sunday, although it is of course gay-friendly during the rest of the week. This large venue is not the place to go if you are after a quiet evening sat around a table chatting to mates. To start with, there are only three or so

tables and, secondly, apart from a couple of two-seater settees, there are only three or so stools or chairs in the whole place. The DJ-led music is loud, fun pop and on a Wednesday there is always some sort of cabaret or stripper. Another pub (not listed) that seems to embrace the pink pound is The Wig and Mirkin on Moulsham Street. It too shows it's gay-friendly colours on a Wednesday by promoting this as a gay night. **Open** Wednesday 2000-2300. Sunday 2000-2230

Cheltenham Pubs

Bar Icon

20 High Street, Cheltenham GL50 1DZ
Phone **01242 260 706** E-mail **Bar_icon@yahoo.com**
Bar Icon is a large venue spread over three floors (although the top floor is not open at present). The ground floor contains the main bar and dancefloor and the basement houses another dancefloor and DJ booth. This is now the only full time gay venue in Cheltenham. **Open** Tuesday-Thursday 2200-0200. Friday-Saturday 2100-0200. Sunday 2100-0100. **Price** £2-3, Saturday and £4 Sunday

Chester

The city of Chester is well over 2,000 years old and is encircled by a medieval city wall that is breached by seven gates. One of these gates, Northgate, was rebuilt in 1808 to house the city's gaol, 30 feet below ground. The bridge outside that gate is nicknamed 'The Bridge of Sighs': it carried the soon-to-be-executed convicts from the gaol to the chapel for their last mass. Walking along the top of the walls is free of charge and from up there you will be able to take in the fantastic Cheshire countryside which lies on the other side. Chester Cathedral is no less awe-inspiring. It dates back to 1092 and has had several facelifts over the centuries. The most distinctive medieval feature of the city is The Rows. These are two-tier walkways with a continuous line of balconies and with a staggering array of shops at street and first-floor levels. The city also boasts the largest Roman amphitheatre ever uncovered in Britain.

Getting in touch

There are two tourist information centres in the city. They are located at the **Town Hall** (01244 402 111) and **Chester Visitor and Craft Centre**, Vicars Lane (01244 351609). They can both help plan your visit and you can pck up free maps and tour details to exploring The Walls. No specific gay and lesbian switchboard serves Chester directly. If you should need to contact a gay switchboard your best bet is to call the **Lesbian and Gay Foundation** at Manchester (0161 235 8000) which is open seven days a week between 1600 and 2200.

Pubs

The Amsterdam Bar

The Amsterdam, 1 Boughton, Chester CH3 5AA Phone 01244 313 608
This is the most popular bar in Chester, and considering there are only two gay bars in the city you've no reason for doubting the foundations of such a claim. A large open-plan room with a raised dance floor and DJ area gives the punter some scope to cruise around and mingle. There's late opening from Wednesday onwards and this draws in the young and lively crowds (boys and girls) and creates a party atmosphere. This is influenced by drag DJs such as Pussy Galore and friends, and the monthly stripper. The Amsterdam fills to almost-bursting point on Friday and Saturday nights when Alchemy and Rush host their gay club nights. **Open** Monday-Tuesday 1900-2300. Wednesday-Saturday 1900-0200. Sunday 1900-2230

Liverpool Arms

79 Northgate Street, Chester CH1 2HQ Phone 01244 310232
E-mail **info@liverpool-arms.co.uk** Web **www.liverpool-arms.co.uk**
Being situated underneath Chester Walls makes the Liverpool Arms the ideal venue for a spot of welcome relief in between cruising (see The Walls listing). Consisting of two rooms, the larger one being loud and busy, the second, more relaxed. Weekday evenings tend to be rather quiet and unless you are part of a group you may feel a little left out of it. **Open** Monday-Saturday 1200-2300. Sunday 1200-2230

Clubs

FAB @ Alchemy

20-24 City Road, Chester CH1 3AE Phone 01244 314 794
Before gay club Rush opened its doors, FAB was the only club night available to the Chester gay community. Since then the cake has been divided into two and obviously the punter quota has diminished. Despite this, it still manages to hold its own and for a city with limited gay outlets it does a pretty good job. This normally straight venue is on one basement level with a quieter room for chatting and chilling. The music is progressive, starting with chart and disco and moving through to a heavier dance set. A good mix of ages and although there are more men, the girls do have a healthy presence. The usual pre-club venue is The Amsterdam, more or less around the corner, although some die-hards show their loyalty by trekking to The Liverpool Arms. At the time of going to press rumours are that the building is due to be demolished! **Open** Friday 2200-0200 **Price** £4-5

Rush @ Love Street

Love Street, Chester CH1 1QY Phone 01244 340 754
Rush is the name of the bi-weekly gay night held in this normally straight club in Chester. The game is a gay get-together of like-minded souls after meeting up at either The Amsterdam or The Liverpool Arms. Chester isn't served that well in the form of gay clubbing – if you don't like charty camp à la G-A-Y then the only alternative is to go to the straight venues for the harder stuff. Love Street is a better-than-average two bar, one large level, 500-capacity venue and full marks for introduc-

ing some sort of choice for the Chester gays and gals. UV lighting pre-vails here, which obviously goes towards making even the palest moose look glam – but try not to scream too loud when you wake up in the morning when you realise just 'what' you have brought home! The Wednesday night mayhem also comprises some kind of drag cabaret with Leena and Nancy, whilst Saturday is a full-on happy-clappy housey disco with the drag girls doing a turn about 0100. DJ Steph 'Spin-a Disc' is in control of the decks on both nights providing the tunes that will satisfy nearly everyone. Tuesdays here are not openly advertised as a gay night but the '70s retro 'Pop Machine' night attracts more than its fair share of benders. Membership is available at reception for reduced and privileged admission. Also, for those of you with an interest in the diverse and perverse, there's the monthly Roissy Workshop every first Thursday of the month (£10; 2100-0200; no admission after 2300). The local fetish emporium Nice 'n' Naughty (see listing) is always in atten-dance with their stall and helpful advice on the latest additions for your toy box. In addition, the venue provides an outstanding free hot buffet just after midnight; hot dogs or pizza and, of course, chips with dips. Where else can one indulge in a chip buttie in such historic surround-ings? **Open** Tuesday, Wednesday and Saturday, 2200-0200 **Price** £3.50-£4

Chester is one of the few remaining places in Britain that still retains the services of a town crier. He appears in summer time at midday and can also be seen at other times of day or year, striding around the city's streets in full red regalia, right down to the famous tricorn hat. As is the custom, he arrives, rings his bell and performs his official function, which has remained the same over the passing of centuries: to make public proclamations of city news.

Cruising grounds

Broxton Picnic Area

Located on the junction of the A41 (to Whitchurch) and the A534 between Whitchurch and Chester. The easiest and most straightforward route is to get to the end of the M56 (Ellesmere Port) and then follow the A41 to Whitchurch. The area itself is a picnic area / lorry park with toi-lets that stay open all night. Adjoining the picnic area is a small wood where most of the action takes place. Alternatively, it is not unknown for people to take a stroll around the lorry park or to use one of the many darkened corners around the car park (you are able to see quite clearly if anyone is approaching but they cannot see you). Remember not to park your car in the lorry spaces. Weekdays are popular between 2100 and 0100; weekends between 2100 and 0300. Police activity is reported to be rare but not unknown.

Chester Railway Station

This is a warning to stress that the toilets at Chester station are really a no-go area. A video camera is in operation 24 hours of the day monitor-ing the use of the toilet and the railway police are quite avid in their quest to catch gays 'at it'.

The Walls

There are several entrances to The Walls of Chester. Each entrance can be a good, viable and lucrative point to pick up, although in these cases you will not be too sure who will be around. Therefore, on your first visit it is advisable to make your way to Upper Northgate Street (opposite The Liverpool Arms) and enter The Walls from this side. There are two entrances here, one on either side of the road, it doesn't matter which one you use because you wil be turning right. Keep walking for about 100 yards until you come to a complete right-angled turn, walk for about a further 30 yards or so and you will soon spot a collection of young men taking a moonlit stroll around this subtly lit area. There is a wooden flight of stairs leading down to a secluded, wooded area. Once you are familiar with this layout you will be able to park your car in the adjoining car park and be able to pop in and out as you please. Friday and Sunday evenings seem to be the busiest times, however, I'm sure that you will be able to find something to take your fancy most nights.

Chesterfield Pubs

The Old Feathers

26 Lordsmill Street, Chesterfield S41 7RW Phone 01246 232 018
This is a very camp establishment; loads of drag queens, TVs, TSs (and admirers), with cabaret and entertaining the punters high on the agenda. Recently refurbished, the old horseshoe-shape bar has gone and they have opted for a Miami style art deco look with loads of black and silver. Regular events through the week include cabaret on a Sunday, stripper every Wednesday and a staff review show each Saturday. There is always a good, friendly atmosphere and a predominantly young crowd intent on enjoyment: in this place it would be exceedingly hard not to enjoy yourself. **Open** Wednesday-Saturday 1900-2300. Sunday 1900-2230

Club nights

Time

Church Walk, Stephenson Place, Chesterfield S40 1XL
Phone 01246 203 463
A small but perfectly formed basement club that has been running a successful gay night every Wednesday for the past seven years. A strict door policy ensures a majority gay and gay-friendly audience. Two bars and lots of red leather alcove seating dominate the venue giving you the opportunity to rest your weary old bones. Music is dance-orientated but not too hard or trancey, more of an uplifting house style. Three quid for three hours of dancing is not all that steep and there are always plenty of cheap drink offers available (usually £1.50) to get you quickly tanked up. Get here early to make the most of it. **Open** Wednesday 1100-0200 **Price** £3

Chichester Pubs

The Bush Inn

16 The Hornet, Chichester PO19 4JG Phone 01243 782 939
The Bush Inn is a well-established gay pub and has been for well over 19 years in the city centre at the eastern end of the shopping centre.

Recently refurbished to make one large open-plan room. They host a camp, charty disco each Wednesday, Friday and Saturday with karaoke once a month. Popular with the whole of the gay community: gay, bi, lesbian, TV and TS. **Open** Monday-Saturday 1100-2300. Sunday 1200-2230

Colchester Pubs

Fox and Hounds

Bentley Road, Little Bromley, Colchester CO11 2PL Phone 01206 397 415
Although the pub is set in a rural location situated off the A120, five miles out of Colchester, it is very far from having a rural attitude, making it an ideal out-of-town experience without you being bored stiff. This is a gay bar and due to the lack of gay venues in this area, it does attract a crowd that goes right across the spectrum. Pretty quiet at the beginning of the week where the venue is more of a social meeting hole, but come the weekend the late licence entices everyone out of the woodwork to a good, old, happy-clappy disco. You can also get a value-formoney traditional roast dinner on Sundays between 1200 and 1500. **Open** Wednesday 1900-0000. Thursday 2000-0000. Friday-Saturday 2000-0200. Sunday 1200-1500/2000-2300. **Price** £2.50 after 2115, Friday and Saturday

Coventry Pubs

Rainbows

88 Short Street, Parkside, Coventry CV1 2LW Phone 024 7655 1738
This is Coventry's one and only gay venue, catering for a mixed gay clientele with a welcome to their straight family and friends, all fetishes, transvestites and transsexuals. Very friendly and sociable venue on two levels: the ground floor is the bar and chill-out area and upstairs is the nightclub and bar (which is open from 2130, Thursday onwards). The summer months see the opening of the courtyard garden with loads of seating for those hot summer nights. Recently voted into third place in 'The Midlands Best Gay Bar' Awards (Zone Magazine). Monthly group meetings in the upstairs bar for Mesmen, Coventry Friend, and The Police Liaison Group. **Open** Monday-Wednesday 1900-2300. Thursday 1900-0200. Friday-Saturday 1200-0200. Sunday 1200-1500/1900-2230 **Price** £1-3, Thursday and Saturday

Clubs

Solitaire Club

Station Square, Coventry CV1 2GT Phone 07939 914 841
Quite an integrated venue, with lots of gays and straights coming together, particularly over the weekend for the excellent clubbing music. During the week it offers karaoke on a Monday and strippers on a Thursday. There's cheap drinks galore most nights and the admission is nominal, except when live gigs are hosted over the weekend where the charge reflects the PA. Situated next door to Coventry railway station. **Open** Monday-Sunday 2100-0200 **Price** £2-6

Crewe Pubs

The Park   42 Wistaston Road, Crewe CW2 7RE Phone 01270 662 677
Social and intimate, true gay bar near to the centre of Crewe comprising
three bars on two levels. The top level is used only as a meeting space for
gay groups and for special occasions. The venue itself is a melting pot
for the Cheshire gay community including a fair proportion of bisexuals, TVs/TSs and no-attitude friendly straights. The entrance bar area is
not unlike your living room (that is if you have a load of drunks around
your house every night) meaning that it's cosy and friendly with pool
table and dart board. On a Friday they put on their staff revue: 'Cabaret
Showtime' and Saturday sees cabaret on the events programme again. A
stripper is booked for every other Wednesday and to make the evening
even more like a house party, a free buffet is laid on. **Open** Monday-
Saturday 1930-2330. Sunday 1230-2300

Croydon Pubs

The Bird of   291 Sydenham Road, Croydon CR0 Phone 020 8864 1469
Pride   E-mail info@skinnersarms.co.uk Web www.skinnersarms.co.uk
The Bird of Pride (off Wellesley Road) is a cosy, elegant traditional gay
bar in the heart of Croydon. Having undergone a major refurbishment
in 2000, they are now in the process of doubling the size, and building a
large extension and conservatory in order to offer cabaret, games room,
large screen, food and loads more. There's regular pub-like activities
such as quizzes (Tuesday), camp bingo (Thursday) and a regular Sunday
jackpot draw (often reaching between £300 and £400). There's always
something going on and it's a great friendly place to meet people or
bring your friends. See also The Skinners Arms listing (London, SE5).
Open Monday-Saturday 1200-2300. Sunday 1200-2230 **Tube** West
Croydon

The Goose and   128 Wellesley Road, Croydon CR0 2AH Phone 020 8689 3473
Carrot   Formerly known as The Horse and Jockey this is a typical pub/club over
two floors, the basement being a dance area which was formerly known
as The Pink Parrot Club, now returning back as an extension of the
upstairs bar. Upstairs the atmosphere is more relaxed and social. Plenty
of entertainment to keep you amused, particularly from Thursday
onwards when there is a disco and cabaret laid on. The G & C is a very
friendly establishment that actively welcomes TVs and TSs. **Open**
Monday-Thursday 1600-2300. Friday 1600-0130. Saturday 1300-0130.
Sunday 1300-2330 **Price** £4 Friday and Saturday after 2300

Cruising grounds

Addington Hills   (Oaks Road) Addington Hills – where the A212 Coombe Road intersects
with A212 Coombe Lane – is a large heavily wooded park on the A212 in
Croydon. There are two active areas here and both are by the car parks

at different ends of the park. The first is off Shirley Hills Road by the car park just inside the park -this is the area near to Addington Golf Course. Dense woodland and trail paths offer a significant amount of cover. The second area is off Oaks Road / A212 junction where there are two public toilets – on either side of the road (near enough) and a car park. This may be the more popular area of the two but what's to stop you trying them both out?

Darlaston Saunas

Greenhouse Health Club

Willenhall Road, Darlaston WS10 8JG Phone **0121 568 6126**
E-mail info@gay-sauna.com Web www.gay-sauna.com
This is one top-notch sauna which ranks alongside Chariots 1 in London (more welcoming – but less passing trade). It's easily accessible from the M6 (Junction 9/10 off the M6 to Darlaston – phone if you get lost) from all parts of the north-west and the West Midlands and beyond. The facilities are superb, particularly the swimming pool with a 'hidden' room behind the ornamental waterfall. The layout ensures you get lost and you somehow keep finding yourself at some point on the grand stairway, but after a few hours you begin to gain your bearings. There are just so many rooms to explore and some you just find by accident – particularly the room off the room with the big cage maze in it. The dark rooms seem to take up the top floor on both sides of the building (the only complaint I have is that they are 'too' dark, which means that punters stand by the doorways looking to see who is going in leaving the areas rather empty. The addition of some sort of subdued lighting would not go amiss). That aside, this is a fabulous place that, as I said, must be the best outside London. I actually remember the old Greenhouse in Darlaston. That was also a favourite of many a sauna dweller and this new venue has retained the cruisy feel of the old place. Within the grounds there are now a number of double-bedded cabins (en-suite accommodation) available to rent for £25 per night and that includes a light breakfast. Unfortunately there is no discount to the sauna. Every third Saturday of the month is (not exclusively though) for bears and cubs with the inclusion of a free buffet. Tip: do not chew gum or they'll shout at you. **Open** Monday-Thursday 1000-0200. Friday 1000-0600. Saturday 1000-0800. Sunday 1200-0200 **Price** £10

Dartmouth Cruising grounds

Slapton Beach   Gay at far-left. Cross the small cliff at the end for the private beach. All ages and plenty of action in the caves. Further information required for this listing.

Derby Pubs

Curzons   23-25 Curzon Street, Derby DE1 1LH Phone 01332 363 739
Curzons is the sister venue to Freddies Bar. The club itself is a fair-sized venue on two levels catering for the gay community, so you will get all types and all ages going in. Quite a cruisy venue, with loads of dark nooks and crannies to explore. Mainstream disco with a welcome late licence 'til 0400 from Thursday onwards. Sunday at the club is quite a party atmosphere with a stripper and staff revue show. At around 2330 a free supper is put out for those of you with the munchies. **Open** Monday-Wednesday 2200-0200. Thursday-Saturday 2200-0400. Sunday 2100-2430 **Price** £2, Friday and £3, Saturday

Freddies Bar   101 Curzon Street, Derby DE1 1LH Phone 01332 204 290
Freddies Bar is the feeder bar to its sister venue, Curzons. A bright continental-styled bar on one large level divided by stages into three different areas. The music is loud, to get you in the mood for a night on the town. All ages and types including a fair few TVs and TSs, who seem to be more prominent on Mondays and Tuesdays. Again, like Curzons, this can be a cruisy type of venue. Occasional cabaret and entertainment is staged, although the concentration is more on the music, drinking and just having a jolly good time. **Open** Monday-Saturday 1900-2300. Sunday 1900-2230

Green Lane Gallery   130 Green Lane, Derby DE1 1RY Phone 01332 368 652.
A traditionally styled bar catering for the gay and lesbian community. **Open** Monday-Thursday 1900-2300. Friday-Saturday 1300-2300. Sunday 1300-2230

The Vine   22 Ford Street, Derby DE1 1EE Phone 01332 200 266
New ownership of this popular bar means lots of new ideas to make this traditional venue even better. Lots of girls tend to use this place and more men are required to balance things out a little bit. Late hours throughout the week including a drag DJ spinning the camp tunes from Friday onwards to get you in the party mood quite quickly. On Monday they put on a camp bingo session from 2100 and a quiz night on Thursday, also at 2100. The disco room now houses the new pool table available at all times, although the disco does not run until the weekend. **Open** Monday-Saturday 1900-0100. Sunday 1900-2330 **Price** £1 after 2230, Friday-Saturday

Doncaster Pubs

The Vine   2 Kelham Street, Balby, Doncaster DN1 3RE Phone 01302 364 096
After the closure of Feeling Fruity @ The Warehouse and subsequently
Paradise @ Eden this is now the only gay venue in Doncaster. A traditional styled venue albeit with a welcome late license, it obviously gets
rather busy at all times but particularly over the weekend where a nominal cover charge comes into effect at around 2200 – make sure you are in
before this time to avoid paying. Lots going on through the week such as
karaoke, bingo, drag DJs, disco over the weekend and cabaret now and
again. **Open** 2000-0200 Monday-Saturday. 2000-2230 **Price** £3 after
2200, Friday-Saturday

Dorchester Cruising grounds

A35 Stinsford   On the A35 near Stinsford (heading away from Dorchester towards
lay-by   Puddletown) there is a lay-by with toilets on your left. You may experience difficulty turning right if you are heading towards Dorchester.
Most of the action takes place outside the cubicles or in the woods
behind the lay-by.

Dover Cruising grounds

Sea front   The sea front toilets, situated about halfway between the eastern and
western docks, are closed at dusk. You may, however, be able to pick up a
bit of trade (usually truckers) by hanging around the benches and shelters.

Eastbourne Pubs

The Hartington   89 Cavendish Place, Eastbourne BN21 3RR Phone 01323 643 151
This is now the only gay venue in Eastbourne, with Brighton being the
nearest city for a proper homo night out. The Hartington is a one-level
venue with a separate club room that opens on Wednesdays for karaoke
and over the weekend for disco goings-on. As the only gay venue it sees a

mixed variety of punters coming through the door – all ages, all tastes, men and women, boys and girls. **Open** Monday-Thursday 1200-2300. Friday-Saturday 1200-0100. Sunday 1200-2300

Accommodation

Ambleside Private Hotel

24 Elms Avenue, Eastbourne BN21 3DN Phone 01323 724 991

A small owner-run hotel, central to all main attractions and services in an attractive Victorian Avenue close to the sea front, theatres, pubs and clubs. The rooms are comfortable with TV, central heating and own keys. **Price** £40 **Number of Rooms** 8, 5 en-suite

Cruising grounds

Open-air theatre

Make your way to the open-air theatre and along the road above it. Police patrols take place, but it is very dark – so go with a pal. Further information required for this site.

Exeter Pubs

Northbridge Inn

11 St David's Hill, Exeter EX4 3RJ Phone 01392 252 535

A small, provincial gay venue that caters for the entire cross-section of the gay community. Nothing much in the way of weekly entertainment except for a dubious quiz night on a Wednesday evening. **Open** Monday-Saturday 1200-2300. Sunday 1200-2230

The Queens Vaults

8 Gandy Street, Exeter EX4 3LS Phone 01392 426 416

The Queens Vaults is a massive underground venue (hence the name) catering for a mixed gay and no-attitude straight crowd. There is no doubt about it: in Exeter, this is almost certainly the place in which you will end up (particularly if you are a young hip, happening dude). Music is constantly playing, courtesy of the free jukebox and there are regular drinks promotions. There is no regular scheduled entertainment, except for the busy karaoke on a Tuesday and Sunday evening. At the time of writing a late licence has been applied for, which will make the Vaults the only late-licence gay pub in Exeter (and further good news is that they will never charge you admission!). **Open** Monday-Saturday 1200-2300. Sunday 1900-2230

Clubs

Kaz Bar @ Bart's Tavern

53 Bartholomew Street West, Exeter EX4 3AJ Phone 01392 275 623

The Kaz Bar (formerly known as Liberty's) is the upstairs club at the straight Bart's Tavern and is exclusively gay on Friday and Saturday evenings. In addition to this there is a women's only night on the first Tuesday of the month – 'Women Take Liberty's' and a men-only session on the second Tuesday of the month (both 2100-0200 – £2). New faces are always welcome and more details can be obtained by contacting the venue. The bar staff are friendly and accommodating (and noticeably good). Complete age range and types on gay nights. Remember to get here early if you wish to avoid paying the high admission. **Open** Friday and Saturday 2100-0200 **Price** £2-5

Club nights

Boxes on Tuesday

Boxes Nightclub, 37-39 Commercial Road, The Quay, Exeter EX2 4AE
Phone 01392 259 292 E-mail info@wbb.org.co.uk
Web www.visitweb.com/wbb
Commercial Road is along Exeter's famous Quayside. This building space comprises three clubs in total: The Warehouse, Boogies and Boxes. Boxes, which has its own separate entrance, turns gay every Tuesday night. The rest of the time you'll find straights and gays brushing shoulders (and possibly other anatomical parts) with each other in any and all of these three gay-friendly venues. However, it's Tuesday nights at Boxes that's the specific gay night for your Exeter diary. This night has been running here under different names for more than 18 years, making it one of the longest-running discos for gays in the area. For more than three years, the night has been co-promoted by DJ Alan Quick, who has widened the music policy to playing the best of today mixed in with some favourite club classics. Boxes is a friendly young club that has recently undergone many alterations, including a new sound system, lighting and dance floor. There is a good atmosphere and regular patrons attend from across the south-west and from further afield. During the rest of the week Boxes throws up various events that may be of interest, with an admission price levied at about £3 and opening hours usually running from 2100 to 0100 (early close even on Saturdays). There's always cheap drink promos to take advantage of though, which somewhat make up for the curtailed clubbing hours. Perhaps the best other night is on a Friday where commercial dance and house tunes are played in one room and indie in the other. **Open** Tuesday 2100-0100 **Price** £4

Cruising grounds

Halden Hill

At the top of Halden Hill. The road between the A380 and A38: there are two car parks where cruising occurs. There is plenty of woodland cover available. Caution advised: police surveillance has been reported and is probably on-going at regular intervals.

Gloucester Club nights

Hysteria @ Crackers Nightclub

Bruton Way, Gloucester GL1 1DG Phone 01452 300 289
A busy gay club night each week at this normally straight venue. Ideally placed – underneath the NCP car park, opposite the railway station and in front of the bus station – so getting to and from the venue should be relatively simple. Crackers is one large open-plan venue (capacity for 240) with a small staged area and a mixed music policy including commercial dance which gets progressively harder as the night goes on.

Membership is not necessary although it is in place to distinguish the regular gay folk from the people who wander in here innocent of it all.
Open Monday 2200-0200 **Price** £4 first visit; £2.50 thereafter

Gravesend Cruising grounds

Pepper Hill

A cruisy park: the A2 at Pepper Hill. Known locally as the 'Gravesend Lighthouse' because cars drive all around this service area at night. The toilets are now pretty much well blown but there are woods behind, and a lot of guys in their cars. It is wise to stand out of your cars, smoking, drinking coffee or simply taking a stroll!

Great Yarmouth Pubs

Kings Wine Bar

42 King Street, Great Yarmouth NR30 2PN Phone 01493 855 374
A mixed gay and straight venue that has had an extensive facelift. Disco on Friday and Saturday with regular drink promotions and karaoke session each Sunday from 2100. Coffee and snacks available during the day.
Open Monday-Saturday 1100-0000. Sunday 1800-2330

The Recruiting Sergeant

33 Alma Road, Great Yarmouth NR30 3HB Phone 01493 332 888
Popular with Norfolk's lesbian community and a bar-hop necessity for the boys. Free pool on Friday nights and sing-along drunken sessions on Friday and Sunday. **Open** Monday-Saturday 1200-2300. Sunday 1200-2230

Clubs

Oxygen

63 North Quay, Great Yarmouth NR30 1JB
Phone 01493 332 783 E-mail enquiries@oxygennightclub.co.uk
Web www.oxygennightclub.co.uk
Oxygen may be a small venue for a club (capacity about 200) but this just adds to the atmosphere and you tend to feel like a (welcome) guest at a private house party. Most nights cater for the masses with the inevitable karaoke (Wednesday and Sunday) and happy handbag and '70s the rest of the week. Well, until Saturday that is when Shine, a night of commercial house and trance, attracts a younger and keener crowd than the rest of the week. For those looking for a (wait for it...) quiet corner, there is the Headliners Bar – small and upmarket but incredibly comfortable and intimate. Ladies should enquire about a new women-only night due to be starting on the last Thursday of the month some time later on in the year. **Open** Wednesday, Friday & Saturday 2100-0200. Thursday & Sunday 2000-0200 **Price** £2-4, Friday & Saturday

Accommodation

M-Jays

37 Camperdown, Great Yarmouth NR3 3JB Phone 01493 843 882
Quality and cleanliness assured at Great Yarmouth's newest lesbian and gay guest-house. Walking distance to the club and pubs and close to the

sea front. Full and generous English breakfast included in the price.
Price £30-35 **Number of Rooms** 3, all en-suite

Guildford Pubs

The Elm Tree   13 Stoke Fields, Guildford GU1 4LS Phone 01483 440 006
E-mail info@theelmtree.co.uk Web www.theelmtree.co.uk
This is the venue that Guildford and the surrounding area has been waiting for and finally it's here – the first 100 per cent gay pub. The Elm Tree
is a young and lively mixed gay venue with loads of stuff going on
throughout the week. There is a stripper on Wednesdays, karaoke on
Thursdays and a happy-clappy disco, that spills over into the beer garden, on Fridays and Saturdays. **Open** Monday-Friday 1700-2300.
Saturday 1200-2300. Sunday 1200-2230

Cruising grounds

Hindhead   The A3, ten miles south of Guildford and north of Hindhead village.
Common   Here there is a large picnic area (café and toilets). Truckers use this place
as an overnight stop. During the day, there are genuine dog walkers using
the area, so be careful not to presume anything.

Hastings Cruising grounds

Barnets Wood   Take the A21, heading for Hastings and just before Tonbridge you'll find
Picnic Site   Barnets Wood Picnic Site. There's activity in the toilets and woods
throughout the day. Closes early but I'm led to believe that the action
carries on in the lay-by.

Bathing Pool   Check out the area called the 'Bathing Pool' (locals will know it). This
area is mostly active at night, though the Marina toilets are busy both
throughout the day and night. There are occasional police patrols in this
area, so be careful.

Haydock Cruising grounds

A580 East   Not so much a cruising ground, more of an ideal spot to take a rest from
Lancs. Road   driving. This part of the East Lancashire Road consists of a series of lay-
(Just off the M6)   bys. The idea is that you park your car (leaving the sidelights on) and
another car will pull up behind (or in front) of you. A couple of these
lay-bys have shrubbery by the side of them where action will take place.
It is well worth spending a couple of hours here on an evening, even if
it's just for a change of scenery. The best times are at weekends after
2300 and probably until 0300. Weekdays are quiet, although if you hang
out long enough something will come along. So, the next time you fancy
a break from driving....

Hayton Cruising grounds

Hayton Castle

From the M6/North/J43 take the A69 towards Newcastle. You will be directed towards a picnic area situated on a lay-by between Carlisle and Brampton. It is busy most of the day (though not all will be there for the same reason as you, so be careful). However the best times to go are between 1700 and 0100 weekdays and 2100 and 0300 weekends. The site is used by lorry drivers (mostly weekdays) who will use this area instead of the motorway service lorry park(!). The toilets here are open 24 hours. Most of the action takes place around the wooded area in addition to the quite lanes nearby. Police activity is frequent. It is an area well known to them and they can be quite intimidating if you let them.

Hereford Pubs

The Saracen's Head

1 St Martins Street, Hereford HR2 7RD Phone 01432 275 480
Hereford is really too small to have its own gay bar so this weekend space in the back bar of the normally straight pub is welcome and appreciated. The back bar also contains the pool table, games and the free gay press. Also, once a month on the first Saturday they host a gay party night called Bedlam. **Open** Every other Saturday, 2000-2300

Club Impulse @ The Jailhouse

Gaol Street, Hereford HR1 2HU Phone 01432 383 158
Formerly held at Doc's Nightclub it has now moved to The Jailhouse – a scruffy (but nice) basement club usually home to much live gigging. Profits from this popular monthly night go back into helping Hereford's gay community. Pre-club meeting place is The Saracens Head (see separate listing). Club Impulse is an exclusive gay night organised by the gay men's health project and all the gay community are welcome in addition to TVs/TSs and gay-friendly straight guests. The atmosphere is friendly and welcoming; especially to newcomers to Hereford's gay scene and someone will be on hand to help you with any questions or concerns that you may have. In addition to Gay Men's Health Project there is also Hereford and Worcester Switchboard available for advice on any gay matters. Phone them at any time on 01432 275 700 (answer phone at unmanned times). Alternatively, you can write to PO Box 178, Hereford, HR4 0XU. There is also a drop-in centre at 27a St Owens Street, Hereford (phone 0374 977 817) where you can collect the free gay press and have a coffee and a chat (very friendly). **Open** third Thursday of the month, 2200-0200 **Price** £2

Hounslow Pubs

The Queen's Arms

223 Hanworth Road, Hounslow TW3 3UA Phone 020 8230 1505
E-mail info@thequeensarms.com Web www.thequeensarms.com
Exclusive gay and lesbian venue. Sundays tend to get a large lesbian following. Karaoke on Monday (busy) and Disco each night from Friday

through to Sunday. Saturday also sees some sort of cabaret getting on stage at around 2200. **Open** Monday-Saturday 1200-2300. Sunday 1200-2230 **Tube** Hounslow Central (ten minutes)

Huddersfield Pubs

The Greyhound Hotel
16 Manchester Road, Huddersfield HD1 3HJ Phone 01484 420 742
The only exclusively gay bar in Huddersfield. Entertainment consists of karaoke on a Wednesday and strippers on Tuesday, Thursday and Sunday. The Greyhound is a traditional kind of bar: one large room with a couple of alcoves for privacy. **Open** Monday-Saturday 1900-2330. Sunday 1900-2300

Lily Lincoln's
64-66 John William Street (entrance on Northumberland Street), Huddersfield HD1 1EH Phone 01484 533 588
The sign by the door exclaims that you are entering a gay space. Straight punters are made welcome as well – but only if they behave themselves. This is the newest venue in Huddersfield, a town whose gay scene previously revolved around The Greyhound. Lily Lincoln's has been warmly received by the community and their late licence goes a long way to attracting late-night revellers in this somewhat dull city. Entertainment comprises of karaoke on a Wednesday and a drag DJ and cabaret over the weekend, when the massive dance floor is put to good use. Sunday is the strip-fest for males and females – but only the female stripper shows her bits, on the last Sunday of the month. **Open** Wednesday 1900-2330. Thursday-Saturday 1900-0200. Sunday 1900-2330 **Price** £2 after 2230, Friday-Saturday

Cruising grounds

Greenhead Park
Around the war memorial most evenings and nights. Some more information for this site would be appreciated.

Hull

East Yorkshire, in the north-east of England, was, until recently, called Humberside. Up until 1974, the county of Yorkshire was the largest county in England and was divided into three areas – North, West and East Ridings (the word riding is derived from the Old English word 'thriding', meaning third). In 1974 Yorkshire was divided into North, West and South Yorkshire and Humberside. Then Humberside became East Yorkshire. Officially known as Kingston-upon-Hull, Hull – as it is better known – is a city and port situated at the junction of the Hull and Humber rivers. It is linked to the south bank of the estuary by a bridge completed in 1981. The growth of Hull as a sea port was closely linked with the whaling and fishing industries and you can get some insight into its maritime history by visiting the Maritime Museum, in Queen Victoria Square.

Getting in touch

The **Tourist Information Office** (01482 223 559) can be found at 1 Paragon Street. There is a dedicated **Lesbian Line** (01482 214 331) run by lesbians, offering communication, information and a befriending service, which operates Monday from 1900 to 2100. There is no specific gay switchboard serving Hull, but you can try the nearby **Leeds Switchboard** (0113 245 3588) for help and advice. It opens daily from 1930 to 2200.

Pubs

The Polar Bear
229 Spring Bank, Hull HU3 1LR Phone 01482 323 959
The Polar Bear is an old traditionally styled, mixed gay and straight venue which is extremely popular with the local lesbians. The front bar is used as a meeting place prior to going to the Silhouette Club over the weekend, and discounted tickets to this event are available from behind the bar (when they are available). Though in need of refurbishment, The Polar Bear is an extremely friendly and social place, where gay and straight mix together comfortably. Pool, darts and gay press are also available. **Open** Monday-Friday 1600-2300. Saturday 1200-2300. Sunday 1200-2230

The Vauxhall Tavern
1 Hessle Road, Hull HU3 2AA Phone 01482 320 340
What used to be a cruisy men's bar is now a comfortable 'homely' traditional bar lounge. There's two rooms: the main bar is the general meeting space with an abundance of nick-nack ornaments and flowers. The second, a smaller lounge, still has the pool table and tends to be the space for the local girls. Beer garden opens up during the summer. **Open** Monday-Saturday 1100-2300. Sunday 1200- 2230

Clubs

Silhouette Club
29 Park Street, Hull HU2 8RR Phone 01482 227 173
Established as a gay venue for over 20 years The Silhouette is the main gay club space in Hull and the surrounding area. Open three nights of the week only (at the moment) with these nights bringing together a decidedly mixed clientele – except Friday, when the punters are predominantly gay – but this integration just adds to the overall atmosphere of the place. Wednesday is 'Lollipop' a retro night of '70s and '80s camp and kitsch. Friday is one of the region's best gay nights with great music and atmosphere. Saturday – Indie night – sees the venue entirely full with a young, mixed gay and studenty crowd. Silhouette is a large one-floor venue, comprising a main disco stage and dance area, with a smaller chill-out lounge bar with music videos, which is ideal for a sneaky, well-earned breather from your dance-floor efforts. There are pre-club meet-ups at either the Polar Bear or The Vauxhall. For reduced admission, and loads of other loyalty bonuses, apply for one of Silhouette Club's free 'privilege cards'. **Open** Wednesday 2200-0200. Friday-Saturday 2200-0300 Price £2-5

Saunas

Blue Corner Sauna

43 High Street, Hull HU1 1PT Phone 01482 620 775

Hull's first sauna, exclusively for gay and bisexual men opened its doors in December '98 and has gone on to be extremely successful. It occupies two levels in a picturesque old warehouse, refurbished to a high standard. The stylish café area, split into two to accommodate the smokers and non-smokers is situated with the vantage point of being able to see all the comings and goings of the wet area. On the ground you have the sauna, Jacuzzi, showers, sun bed and coffee shop. On the first floor there are two changing areas, five individual rest rooms, video room, TV lounge and communal rest area. **Open** Monday-Thursday 1200-2200. Friday-Saturday 1200-0400. Sunday 1300-2000 **Price** £12 first visit; £9 after

Kings Lynn Pubs

Hob In The Well

Littleport Street, Kings Lynn PE30 1PP Phone 07710 538 431
E-mail hobwell@aol.com Web www.hobinthewell.co.uk
A straight-friendly, traditional and intimate riverside pub built onto the historic wall of Kings Lynn. A sociable local bar with cheap drinks and a friendly welcoming atmosphere. There are two bar rooms. The first is the main bar where the social niceties take place and the second smaller room is where the dancing and partying happens. The Hob is the only gay bar in the area and short of trekking off to Norwich or Peterborough it will have to do. **Open** Thursday-Saturday 2030-2300. Sunday 2030-2230

Kingston upon Thames Clubs

Reflex

184 London Road, Kingston upon Thames KT2 6QW
Phone 020 8549 9911 E-mail info@reflexnightclub.com
Web www.reflexnightclub.com
A fully air-conditioned, friendly, attitude-free gay club located just outside the centre of Kingston that has been recently refurbished. Happy uplifting sounds from resident DJs Steve Lush and Miss Annabelle. It is only a gay club over the weekend. The rest of the week sees different events organised by various promoters. A good local venue with many top name cabaret artists showing off over the weekend. **Open** Friday-Saturday 2200-0300 **Price** £3-5

Lancaster Pubs

The Albert Inn

84 King Street, Lancaster LA1 1RJ Phone 01524 650 75
The only gay pub in the city, catering for just about anybody and everybody who comes through the doors. Over the weekend a disco is put on

with drag DJs. Accommodation is offered in the rooms above the pub (£20 per couple without breakfast; £32 with breakfast) **Open** Monday-Tuesday 1800-2300. Wednesday 1600-2300. Thursday 1400-2300. Friday-Saturday 1200-2300. Sunday 1200-2230

The Navigation Penny Street, Bridge Wharf, Lancaster LA1 1XN Phone 01524 849 484
E-mail info@partycruises.co.uk Web www.partycruises.co.uk
Located in the city centre off Thurnham Street car park, this is a friend-ly, gay-run, continental-style wine bar with canal-side gardens, world beer bar and large conservatory. Not the place for the disco dolly but ideal for a relaxing day and evening in a friendly and welcoming envi-ronment. Checkout Oscar the Macaw and the camper-than-camp toilets (cherubs and chandeliers? Please!). There is also a jolly interesting menu with a good veggie selection. During the summer it is open throughout the day (September to March evenings only) and boat trips can be arranged for you and your friends. **Open** Monday-Saturday 1100-2300. Sunday 1100-2230 (April-September)

Cruising grounds

Caton Village East of Lancaster on the A683 (Junction 34 on the M6). Just outside Caton Village there are two picnic areas (one either side). This is an iso-lated and usually quite safe area. Most popular after 2100. The abun-dance of service areas on this stretch of the M6 makes this area a bril-liant circuit during the week. The lack of truckers (if that's your bag) over the weekend somewhat minimises the availability of trade. However, if you do have the spare you won't be disappointed.

Leeds

Leeds is the second largest metropolitan district in Britain, extending 15 miles from east to west, and 13 miles from north to south. It sits midway between Edinburgh and London, quite literally at the heart of Great Britain. Leeds is a buzzing, multi-cultural city, that has spawned numer-ous household names. The famous Marks and Spencer department store began life as the Penny Bazaar that Michael Marks first opened in Leeds Market. The makers of the board game Monopoly, Waddington's, was founded here. Thomas Chippendale first made fur-niture in this city. And Europe's largest clothing factory was controlled in Leeds by Burton's founding father, Montague Burton, a name syn-onymous with every British high street. The gay scene here is now in a state of extensive growth; welcome news to a scene that had become rather staid over recent years. The newest bar to seduce Leeds is Fibre, and the proprietors are already underway with plans to build a huge, 1,000-capacity club called Mission, across the road from Fibre, within eight of the railway arches. Other gay businesses are casting their eyes over the remaining arches and there seems a real chance that Leeds could soon have its own gay village, similar to Manchester, developing here.

Getting in touch

Leeds tourist information office, known as **Gateway Yorkshire**, is situated within the main railway station on City Square (0113 242 5242) and is open Monday to Saturday from 0930 to 1800. Leeds' Lesbian and Gay Switchboard (0845 345 2449) is open Tuesday, Thursday, Friday and Saturday between the hours of 1930 and 2130. Leeds' **Lesbian Line** (01132 453 588) runs Tuesdays only between 1930 and 2130.

Pubs

Bar Fibre 168 Lower Briggate, Leeds LS1 6LY Phone 08701 200 888
E-mail info@barfibre.com Web www.barfibre.com
This is an extremely cool café-bar and just what Leeds needed to kick-start an ageing and extremely dull gay scene. The chrome exterior and the floor-to-ceiling windows proudly convey the simplistic and minimalist ethos behind this interior. Catering for the younger, designer drink crowd it has quickly established itself as a pre-club venue for the gays and straights and also as a late-night drinking hole for the skinflints who can't afford the admission into The Queen's Court pub. The good news is that there are never any admission charges. On Monday and Tuesday there is only background music playing. From Wednesday onwards there is a DJ playing uplifting house – there is never camp charty music played (hallelujah!) Breaking news is that Bar Fibre will be opening a club in Leeds later on in the year. **Open** Monday-Wednesday 1100-0000. Thursday 1100-0100. Friday-Saturday 1100-0200. Sunday 1200-2300

The New Penny 57-59 Call Lane, Leeds LS1 7BT Phone 0113 243 8055
Leeds' longest-established gay-owned and -run pub. A cruisy and social atmosphere with a mixed gay and straight clientele. Thursday night at this venue is very busy because of the regular male stripper. Wednesday is karaoke and there is occasional cabaret put on over the weekend. At the time of writing the New Penny had applied for a late licence so the opening hours may be extended in the near future. **Open** Monday-Saturday 1200-2300. Sunday 1400-2230

Poptastic @ Swinegate, Leeds LS1 4AG Phone 07074 248 247
The Cockpit E-mail info@poptastic.co.uk Web www.poptastic.co.uk
Leeds is a special location for Poptastic as The Cockpit venue gives them the opportunity to have three rooms of top tunes, which means that for the price of one and a half pints, you get a good night of either cheesy and chart pop in The Kitsch Bitch Lounge, indie and alternative in The Indie Playground or happy house and handbag in The Clubber's Kitchen. Or all three if you really want. **Open** Thursday 2300-0230 **Price** £2.50-£3.50

Queen's Court Lower Briggate, Leeds LS1 6NA Phone 0113 233 9691
Following a massive re-fit The Queen's Court re-opened to an eager gay public back in May, and no-one was let down. Everything within the old

bar was gutted. It has now become a super-stylish gay venue. As The QC is a Grade Two-listed building there was not much that could be done to the exterior and courtyard of the building but the clever use of light in the form of floods and projectors (which beam the logo onto the frontage), ensures that no-one is likely to stray past and miss this place. Inside the ground-floor bar, modular seating has been added to provide a café-style layout facilitating the service of food during the day. This can easily be removed to provide standing and dancing space during the evening. And it's the evening when the lighting dims and the downstairs bar becomes a stylish meeting and drinking venue. Minimalist décor and the projected lights on the wall-cum-canvas helps to create ever-changing moods and atmospheres. Upstairs, the club has been totally re-designed – the dance floor is now at least three times larger and little pockets of seating and chill-out space have been created as an escape from the main hullabaloo. There's an abundant use of metal and resin which creates an industrial, hard-edged feel and this works a lot better than the comfortable lounge atmosphere of the previous club. The club is open every night except Sunday and provides a wide range of music from hard house (Saturday) to retro and chart (Monday – 'The Pink Pounder'). Wednesday is student night with coaches laid on to transport our learned beer-swilling friends to and from all the surrounding areas. (for more info on this phone the venue direct). Tip: get here well before 2300 to avoid paying admission on Friday and Saturday. **Open** Monday-Thursday 1000-0200. Friday-Saturday 1000-0400. Sunday 1000-0000 **Price** Monday £1. Friday-Saturday £5-6

Saunas

Plastic Ivy

33 Leeds Road, Dewsbury, Leeds WF12 7BB Phone 01924 455 600
This sauna is not strictly in Leeds, but in Dewsbury, although finding the place is really straightforward from Leeds. Just bear off the Dewsbury ring road onto Leeds Road and look for the number 33. There is no outside sign displaying that this is a gay sauna. Facilities are small and compact; namely, just a steam room, Jacuzzi, sauna and rest rooms. There is also a long dark corridor with video screens constantly showing porno films. Early birds can get reduced admission (£6) if they arrive at the sauna between 1200 and 1300. The same deal applies to those arriving late, between 2100 and 2200. **Open** Wednesday-Monday 1200-2300 **Price** £12 first visit and £10 after

**Spartan
Mantalk**

72 Bayswater Road, Harehills, Leeds L58 5NW Phone 0113 248 7757
This small and compact sauna is a fair distance away from the main gay areas of Lower Briggate. Basic facilities include sauna, steam room, Jacuzzi, video lounge and TV lounge. There are about four individual rest rooms and one communal rest room. Spartan Mantalk is set within a highly residential area, so be careful where you park. **Open** Monday-Sunday, 24 hours. **Price** £10

Leicester

Leicester is a city with a long and varied past, one that is very much ingrained into the fabric of its buildings and the character of its businesses and people. More than that though, it is a city of diversity, a mixture of colours and races, offering citizens and visitors alike the benefits of a cosmopolitan environment. The city centre has been renovated, streets have been pedestrianised and many buildings restored. In 1990, Leicester became Britain's first Environment City, in recognition of the efforts it was making towards restoration, recycling, and sustainable development. Two years later at the United Nations' Earth Summit, this initiative was praised as one of the top twelve local environmental initiatives throughout the world. Leicester's history goes back to the Iron Age. The original inhabitants, the Corieltauvi tribe, gave their name to the settlement of the conquering Romans, Ratae Corieltauvorum, which prospered as a trading centre on the Fosse Way. Evidence of the Roman past can still be found today. There are numerous mosaics gathered in the Jewry Wall Museum, itself built alongside a Roman wall and baths.

Getting in touch

Leicester's main **Tourist Information Office** is at 7-9 Every Street, Town Hall Square (0116 299 8888). It is open Monday to Saturday frm 0900 to 1830. **The Lesbian and Gay Switchboard** (0116 255 0667) is open Thursday and Friday from 1900 to 2100.

Pubs

Bossa

110 Granby Street, Leicester LE1 1DL Phone 0116 233 4544

Very friendly, small and compact café-bar catering for a mixed gay and straight trendy crowd. Very good selection of continental beers, cocktails and spirits. Wednesday is a half price cocktail night (£1.75) and happy hours run throughout the week from 1700 to 2300 (Sunday to Tuesday) and 1700 to 2000 (Thursday to Saturday). A good place for cheap snacks and toasties (£1) and nachos and salsa dip (£2.50). You can find Bossa situated in the city centre close to the railway station. **Open** Monday-Saturday 1100-2300. Sunday 1500-2230

Dolly's Dover Castle

34 Dover Street, Leicester LE1 6PT Phone 0116 222 8826

One of the most popular and friendly places in Leicester for a mixed gay crowd and their straight friends. Recently refurbished, you enter through a traditionally styled bar that leads up to a modern trendy cocktail bar area. There is a well-used beer garden open at all times, even when it's raining. Entertainment through the week starts on a Monday with karaoke hosted by drag DJ Rusty. Tuesdays and Wednesdays are dedicated to drink promos and socialising. On Thursday local radio DJ Mark Christian hosts Radio Replay (chart disco) and on Friday it's progressive disco, from camp chart to a harder house style. Saturdays and Sundays are just non-stop entertainment and the place is usually rammed. They are in the process of fitting web cams within the premises, in order that punters will be able to check how busy it is on certain nights before leaving their home! Recommended. **Open** Monday-Thursday 1200-0000. Friday-Saturday 1200-0200. Sunday 1200-0000 **Price** £1 Saturday, 1830-2230 only

Hartley's   64 Belgrave Gate, Leicester LE1 3GQ Phone **0116 233 1009**

A mixed gay and straight venue on two floors that caters for a young club crowd. There's a disco on every night (except Tuesday) and a New DJ Showcase on Monday (phone the bar if you want to take part in this unusual and innovative night). On Tuesdays there's Cinema Night where you can watch films with a beer and good company and Wednesday is Student Night with cheap drinks (although it should be said that the drinks prices here are cheap most nights). Thursday is a night for house and techno music fiends and similarly Friday and Saturday is a good progressive blend of more funky house and techno. Sunday is a night for chilling or entering into the weekly party spirit. There is a dress code to the club of no sportswear – but anything else should get you in. **Open** Monday-Tuesday 2000-2300. Wednesday-Saturday 2000-0200. Sunday 2000-0200 **Price** £2 after 2300, Friday and Saturday

Monroes   27 Burleys Way, Leicester LE1 3BE Phone **0116 262 3384**

Popular lesbian and gay bar with a late licence. Formerly known as The Pineapple. Monroes is a large L-shaped room split into three different areas: the bar, sofa lounge and the main disco space at the back. Entertainment during the week is limited, except for disco from Wednesday onwards and a stripper on the last Sunday of the month. All ages and types use the bar, making it a friendly, sociable and welcoming place to be. Despite the late opening hours there is no admission charge at any time – a refreshing change to some money grabbing supposedly gay venues. Food is also available both afternoons and evenings. **Open** Monday-Saturday 1100-1500 / 2000-0200. Sunday 1200-1600 / 2000-0000

The Q-Bar   15 Wellington Street, Leicester LE1 6HH Phone **0116 254 1750**

This café-bar is part of the Leicester Lesbian, Gay and Bisexual Centre. The Q-Bar provides a quiet place for people to have a drink, a bite to eat and a friendly chat. If you are new to the area, this is the place to go to find out what is going on. Once a month they have their social for les-bian, gay and bisexual people from ethnic minority communities. For more info on this night phone Sonny on 0116 254 1747 or 0378 268 532. **Open** Monday-Tuesday 1200-1400. Wednesday-Friday 1200-1400 / 1800-2130. Saturday 1100-1800

Quebec   96 Belgrave Gate, Leicester Phone **0116 2513 8110**

A stylish gay bar with a touch of the continental about it – it's even got three internet booths for your use. Due to its close proximity to the Haymarket and Phoenix Theatre it does tend to attract a lot of actors and celebrities (does Adam Rickett count?). Every last Friday of the month is Asian night 'RANG' (2200-0200) which is the only one of its kind outside London. This is an extremely popular night organised by

Trade (Leicester's men's health charity) with people coming in from as far as London. The music is a good mix of Western and Asian tunes. Normally, the bar is a drinking and chilling venue until the weekend when the DJ provides a stormer of a set and gets the crowd up on the floor. Free admission for late night drinking (which is almost unheard of). **Open** Monday-Saturday 1200-0200. Sunday 1200-0000

Clubs

Leicester Place   24 Dryden Street, Leicester LE1 3QE Phone 0116 251 0785
Leicester Place is the name of the venue that incorporates a bar and a club. The bar was formerly known as The Crown and the club was and still is known as Streetlife. A bit confusing perhaps, but all you need to know is that both now lie as one under this roof. The venue is not exclusively gay. On a Wednesday the cheap admission and drink offers entice the students in which makes for a 60/40 mix in favour of the straights. The music policy on Wednesday is commercial chart rather than anything too taxing. Fridays and Saturdays see the gay quota rising sharply. The music on Friday is more retro to current day and gets a bit harder towards the end of the evening. On Saturday the music is more uplifting house with a little bit of trance thrown in for good measure. The club is long and narrow with a recently added balcony with its own bar that serves as a chill-out and chatting space. The design of the club has been maintained to resemble a street scene, with the bar cunningly disguised as an off-licence. **Open** Wednesday 2030-0200. Friday 2030-0230. Saturday 2030-0300 **Price** Wednesday £2.50 after 2300. Friday £1.50 before 2300 and £2.50 after. Saturday £4.50 before 2200 and £6 after

Club nights

Bam Bu Da   Carey's Close, Leicester LE1 5NS Phone 0116 262 6969
Not strictly a gay night but an evening where people of all persuasions (gay and straight) get together for a superb dance night. Music policy can best be described as disco house – nothing too heavy, but not the usual, boring camp and chart sounds. Bam Bu Da is situated above Po Na Na and is a stylish new venue with a heavy Moroccan influence. The club's capacity is around 330 and the success of this attitude-free night usually makes for a strict door policy of one-in-one-out come 2330 (so get there early or risk disappointment). There is no dress code but there is a door policy that expects the right attitude: if you can't get along with each other you are certainly not welcome here. **Open** Friday 2230-0200 each fortnight **Price** £5-7

SLAG @ Soho   41 Halford Street, Leicester LE1 1TR Phone 0116 222 6891
SLAG @ Soho (Straight, Lesbian And Gay) is, as the name suggests, a mixed smart dress night for those with no attitude. The club is on three floors, with loads of little nooks and crannies to explore during the night. There's even a downstairs cinema. The night plays hard house to trance with a (little) bit of soul and funk along the way. There are also hosts that ensure you make the most of your night in the venue. Soho is

normally a straight club and if it takes your fancy there are some excellent straight dance nights such as the housey affair Peruvia on Saturday (2130-0730; £8 for NUS or before 2300 and £10 after). **Open** Friday 2200-0600 **Price** £6-8

Saunas

Eros Sauna

38 Narborough Road, Leicester LE3 0BQ Phone 0702 118 7197

This is more of a gay venue than a sauna. A fabulous place over four floors with just about everything your depraved little mind can think of (including whips, chains and manacles in the dungeon room). What makes this place stand out from the rest is the provision of free vodka (on optic) to pep up your orange juice or whatever. They also provide free beer on a Tuesday (usually Red Stripe) at no extra charge (between 1900-2330). Their attitude to their customers is quite refreshing: they want to provide as much value for money as possible in addition to making the venue a safe gay space to do exactly what you want in. The building occupies four floors comprising the following facilities: steam room, mini gym and chilled-out seating area on the ground floor. On the lower ground floor there is the well-equipped dungeon room, complete with cobwebs, chains and what-not. The first floor houses the sauna cabin, the bubble room (this is a camp little room with mirror ball and glittery wallpaper and a bubble blowing machine that gives you a little tingle when the bubbles pop on your skin) which leads through to the communal darkroom and video lounge. On the top floor there are the individual rest rooms and video cinema. Besides all this there are regular themed party nights. Highly recommended. **Open** Sunday-Thursday 1200-0000. Friday 1200-0200. Saturday 1200-very late **Price** £10, first visit and £8 after

John Carey Merrick, otherwise known as The Elephant Man, was born at 50 Lee Street in Leicester, in 1862. He developed tumors on his face just before his second birthday. His condition quickly worsened as bulbous, cauliflower-like growths grew from his head and body. Later, he would travel the world starring in 'freak shows', for which the famous pseudonym was created. His tragic life ended in 1890, from asphyxiation.

Sauna 31

31 New Bond Street, Leicester LE1 4RQ Phone 0116 251 6710

This sauna used to be one of those places that wasn't advertised and unless you knew of its existence it was impossible to find. Subsequently it became quite run down. Now, it has been taken over by a new proprietor and plans are afoot to promote and fully refurbish the place (at present it looks like the last time it was decorated was in the 1950s, however, these things do take time and investment). Having said that though, it is still a gay sauna (which is better than nothing) and with an advertising programme under way it will not be too long before this place will be able to afford newer and better facilities. It is discreetly located in the middle of town, at the rear of The Shires Shopping Centre. Look out for the number 31 on the building and then make your way up to the first floor. **Open** Monday-Thursday 1100-2100. Friday-Saturday 1100-0000.

Sunday 1100-1900 **Price** £7.50

Accommodation

Friends Guesthouse

50 Narborough Road South, Leicester LE3 2FN Phone 0702 118 7199
Comfortable and affordable accommodation offered by those nice people who own Eros Sauna. Single rooms at £20, include a monster full English breakfast. **Price** £40 **Number of Rooms** 5, 1 en-suite

---

Lincoln Pubs

Angels

78 Canwick Road, Lincoln LN5 8EX Phone 01522 567 686
Angels is the only gay venue in the complete county of Lincolnshire (nearest city being Nottingham about 40 minutes drive away) and as such is extremely busy most nights. Despite this, the owners do not rest on their laurels and put big-time effort into making each night enjoyable and entertaining for their punters. Entertainment throughout the week varies from karaoke on Monday (very busy) to quiz and game night on a Tuesday – sounds boring but it isn't, the top prizes ensure a healthy audience and the drag hostess intercedes with mucho bitchiness. Wednesday is perhaps the quietest night; background music gives you the opportunity to chill and prepare for the weekend. Thursday is another busy karaoke session. Friday is the first disco of the week with 'Tutti Frutti' a compilation of all that was wrong (musically-speaking) with the '70s through to the '90s. Saturday is the main night with drag DJs at the reins and you can expect the venue to be absolutely crammed, so early entry is advised. Angels has just been renovated into a gothic-style venue – lots of wood and churchy stuff – very nice, if you like that sort of thing. Every second Wednesday of the month is women-only – a welcome night just for the girls called 'Ruby's' (no admission charges, except when a stripper is performing and then only a nominal charge). This night has all-female bar staff, door staff and DJ. It has only been running for about three months but already has proven quite a hit. Finally, membership is available at the venue for a paltry £5 per year and this will entitle you to loads of concessions including reduced admission. **Open** Monday-Wednesday 2000-2300. Thursday-Saturday 2000-0100. Sunday 1900-2230 **Price** £1-3, Friday-Saturday

Liverpool

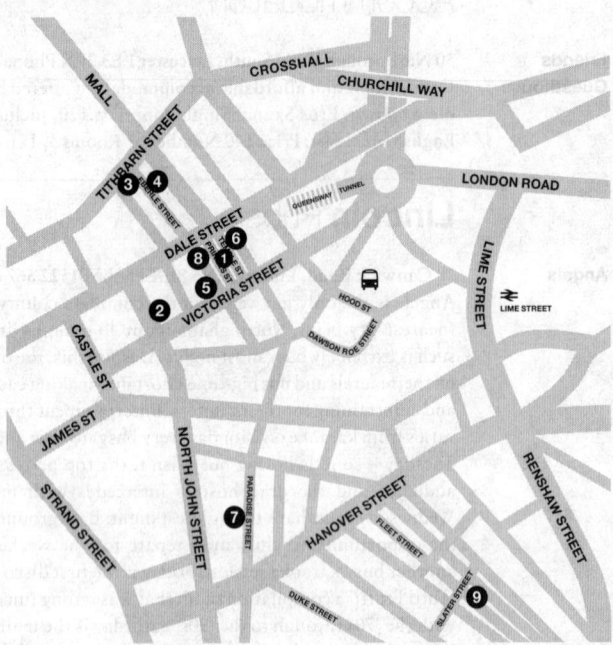

Map key

1 Curzon Club	**6** Masquerade Bar
2 Fussy Pussy @ Zero	**7** Oi! Club/Poptastic @ The Escape
3 G-Bar	**8** Pacos Bar
4 Garlands	**9** Society
5 Lisbon	

Located on the north-west coast of England, this region has a great variety of places to visit and a wide range of places to stay. There's easy access by rail, road, sea or air and local transport and motorway networks make getting around the region simple too. Liverpool, at the heart of Merseyside, is one of a handful of truly world-famous cities, with a reputation around the globe, particularly for The Beatles, its football club and the outstanding architecture. At present the city is bidding to be the European Capital of Culture in 2008, and music is very much part of that culture – classical at the Philharmonic, contemporary in venues such as the Cavern, the Picket and the Lomax and dance at Cream. The Liverpool Playhouse is Liverpoool's famous theatre which has just been restored to its former glory. Innovative theatre is staged at the Everyman, whilst ballet, opera and musicals can be seen at the largest regional theatre in Britain, the Empire. The city's galleries house more collections of national significance than any other area of Britain outside of London. There's something to suit all tastes from the classic collection at the Walker Art Gallery to the ultra-modern Tate Liverpool and both have a frequently changing programme of exhibitions featuring national and international artists. The fascinating work of the museum and gallery conservators can be seen at the award-winning Conservation Centre, recently voted European Museum of the Year. Liverpool is a truly multi-cultural city, and in celebration of the city being home to the oldest established Chinese community in Europe, a spectacular new arch has recently been erected in Chinatown by workers from Liverpool's sister city, Shanghai. Some of the north-west of England's best Chinese restuarants can be found throughout the city.

For such a large and vibrant city the gay scene is relatively modest and seems to lack the vibrancy and energy of other comparable cities, such as Birmingham or Manchester. Liverpool does not have a 'gay village' as such and what is noticeably missing is that feeling of a community atmosphere. Nevertheless, what is available is good and may well be more than enough for the visitor.

Getting there

Airport

Visitors arriving into Liverpool via air will land at **Liverpool John Lennon Airport** (0151 486 8877). The airport is approximately eight miles south of the city centre. Although comparatively small, visitors will find the airport modern and functional. Scheduled international flights also operate through **Manchester International Airport**, 30 miles from Liverpool.

Trains

Liverpool's main station is **Lime Street** (**National Rail Enquiries** 08457 484 950) with **Moorfields**, **James Street** and **Central** stations serving mainly as transfer points to local **Merseyrail** trains. Left luggage facilities are available at Lime Street (0151 702 2477). For more information on public transport, phone the **Mersey Travel** hotline on 0151 236 7676.

Coaches and buses

National Express coaches stop at **Norton Street** coach station. Other buses stop at the **Queen Square** and **Paradise Street** stations.

Getting about

Taxis

Most of Liverpool is served by **Mersey Cabs** (0151 298 2222), the largest taxi operator outside of London.

Tourist information

The **Merseyside Welcome Centre** is located in the Clayton Square Shopping Centre. Pick up the visitor guide to Liverpool and Merseyside (£1) which contains a comprehensive list of the sights in the county and a map of the city. A smaller tourist information office is at **Atlantic Pavilion** on the Albert Dock (0151 708 8854).

Bureaux de change

American Express (0151 708 6673) at 54 Lord Street has facilities that are open Monday to Friday from 0900 to 1730 and Saturday from 0900 to 1700. You can also change money at the main **Post Office** at 33

Whitechapel. There is also a branch in the **Lyceum** building on Bold Street. Both branches open Monday to Friday from 0900 to 1730 and Saturday from 0900 to 1900.

Getting help

Police, hospital and pharmacy

The main police station is at Canning Place (0151709 6010). **Royal Liverpool Hospital** (0151 706 2000) and **Arrowe Park Hospital**, Wirral (0151 678 5111) both have accident and emergency departments. There are no 24-hour pharmacies but the late-opening of **Mass Chemists** on London Road should be able to cope with most demands. It is open daily from 0600 to 2300.

Getting in touch

Internet

Café **Internet** at 28 North John Street is open Monday to Saturday from 1000 to 1700. There is also **Planet Electra** at 36 London Road, between Lime Street and the National Express coach station, open Monday to Wednesday from 1000 to 1730, Thursday from 1000 to 1930 and Friday to Saturday from 1000 to 1800.

GLBT Helplines

Liverpool Gay Switchboard (0151 705 9552) has lines that are open daily from 1900 to 2200. The **AIDS Helpline** (0151 709 9000) is open Monday to Wednesday and Friday from 1900 to 2100.

Pubs

Curzon Club

8 Temple Lane, Liverpool L2 Phone 0151 236 5160
Long-established, large gay pub and club venue, with three bars and two dance floors. Busy most evenings with a young gay crowd, as it is the only gay bar with a late licence. The upstairs club is only open on Friday and Saturday evenings. Regular male strip night is on a Monday and there's a disco over the weekend. Admission prices come into effect from 2100 most nights, except Thursday, so expect to pay in the region of £1-2 Monday to Friday, £3 on a Saturday before 2300 and £4 after. **Open** Monday-Saturday 1200-0200 **Price** £1-2, Monday-Wednesday. £2-4, Friday -Saturday

Lisbon

35 Victoria Street, Liverpool L1 6BG Phone 0151 231 6831
Another basement bar catering for a very mixed crowd of gays, gay-friendly straights and TVs. This bar is quaintly old-fashioned, retaining the Victorian charm that is conducive to the building itself and does not pretend to be anything other than a good, wholesome, friendly pub. During the day the regulars (mostly of advancing years) take their regular places at the bar ready to put the world to rights. The evenings see a somewhat younger crowd pop in, particularly on Sundays and Tuesdays when a disco is laid on and on Thursdays for the karaoke. A good, no-nonsense branded doubles bar is always in operation at £2 with happy hours running from Sunday to Thursday between 1700 and 2000. **Open** Monday-Saturday 1200-2300. Sunday 1700-2230

Masquerade   10 Cumberland Street, Liverpool L1 6BU
Bar   Phone 0151 236 7786 E-mail masquerade.bar@virgin.net
Masquerades is a basement bar with two bars and always something
going on to keep you entertained during the evening à la karaoke, disco
sort of thing. On Thursday Masquerade seems to be the choice for the
Liverpool girls who descend on the venue from 2100 onwards. The interi-
or of this venue has no windows and you tend to get a strange feeling of
time loss, particularly on a Sunday – a very busy day – when they stage
their all-day party with a succession of drag queens taking to the mike.
Open Monday-Saturday 1100-2300. Sunday 1100-2230

---

*Behind Princess Landing Stage at Liverpool's Pier Head, is the Titanic
Memorial. It was intended to commemorate the engineers and firemen
lost in the Titanic disaster of 1912, but, to avoid upsetting the passengers boarding the liners, it was simply, and more obliquely, dedicated to
'The Heroes of the Engine Room'. The inscription reads, 'In honour of
all heroes of the marine engine room. This memorial was erected by
international subscription MCMXVI'.*

Paco's Bar   25 Stanley Street, Liverpool L1 6AA Phone 0151 236 9737
Situated off Dale Street (A57), Pacos is a small, sociable and intimate
bar on two levels. The basement bar area is open all week and can best
be described as cruisy, dark and very friendly – as is the Scouse way.
Expect to hear karaoke on a Monday and Thursday and a DJ over the
weekend. The upstairs bar is open only on Friday and Saturday
evenings; it's a brighter lounge area where you can just sit and relax, but
with all that malarky going on below – why bother? Paco's is notably the
oldest gay bar in Liverpool (established for over 30 years and still under
the same ownership). Excellent and cheap happy hour from 1800 to
2000 with really (no, I mean really) cheap drinks (double spirit for
£1.40!). Paco's is not everyone's idea of an ideal gay venue. It's not smart
and it does not have millions to spend, but, realistically, trappings and
furnishings do not make a good bar – friendliness and the right attitude
do, and it's for that reason alone that I like this place. **Open** Monday-
Saturday 1200-2300. Sunday 1200-2230

Clubs

G-Bar   1-7 Eberle Street, Liverpool L2 2AG
Phone 0151 236 9338 E-mail info@g-bar.com Web www.g-bar.com
G-Bar is a gay venue and hosts events for the gay community: monthly
themed nights and weekly camp entertainments. It is a very friendly and
popular venue and even the doormen have gained recognition for being
helpful. Wednesdays and Thursdays offer camp classics from the drag
DJs. Friday sees all three rooms open up with a good recipe of uplifting
house, trance and pop. Also on Friday nights is the first of two Breakfast
Clubs: a popular, mixed gay and straight dance club open from 0100 'til
0500 (£5). On Saturday the venue gets the same musical treatment as on
Friday, only this time the women of Liverpool are catered for with their
own space in the basement from 2130 to 0200. The second and final

Breakfast Club of the week runs afterwards from 0300-0800 (£5) and sees the venue get totally hard with a combination of trance, uplifting and hard house. Remember, on Saturday the venue closes at 0200 and re-opens again at 0300 for the Breakfast Club (see also the listing for sister venue Society) **Open** Wednesday-Saturday 2200-0200. Sunday 2100-0000 **Price** Breakfast Club £5

Garlands

8-10 Eberle Street, Liverpool L2 2AG Phone **0151 236 3307**

There's no doubt that gay clubbers will be venturing into this place during your visit to Liverpool. It's only gay on Fridays and Saturdays, (having said that it's more of a mixed gay/straight affair on the Friday and is predominantly gay on a Saturday). On the Friday, only the downstairs part of the venue is open, playing harder house and uplifting music from top name guest DJs (such as Fergie and Jon Pleased Wimmin) in the main room and complemented with trashy retro in the smaller adjoining room. On Saturdays the whole complex is open. Upstairs in the main room you get vocal house with the '70s and '80s malarky in the back bar (this is piped up from the retro room downstairs). Downstairs, the main room plays harder house and the retro room plays the aforementioned '70s and '80s stuff. There is a dress code policy in operation: smart, casual or clubwear (why, I don't know, because once inside shirts and tops are discarded to reveal gym-pumped bodies and beer bellies). For those of you who have difficulty sleeping after a night on the tiles, there is the Saturday night / Sunday morning breakfast club across the road at G-Bar (see listing). Finally, plans are being drawn up to open the club on a Sunday with a Retro Disco (what else?). Admission will be in the region of £3 and will be predominantly gay-orientated. Opening hours will be announced at a later date – phone the venue for more information on developments. **Open** Friday 2200-0300. Saturday 2200-0400 **Price** £6, Friday. £10, Saturday

---

Liverpool is renowned for its outstanding architecture. It is second only to London for the amount of historically listed buildings and boasts more Georgian buildings than Bath.

Society

47 Fleet Street, Liverpool L1 4AR Phone **0151 258 1230**

E-mail **info@society-liverpool.com** Web **www.society-liverpool.com**

This is Liverpool's newest club, open since September 2000. There are a couple of nights midweek which offer a 'different' night out, such as 'Ish' (very studenty, probably because of the cheap admission – £3-5; 2230-0300 – and lots of cheap drink offers). There is also The Old Skool Society on a Friday where you will hear a fusion of disco, old skool and pop (£5; 2230-0300). However, it is Saturday when the homos come out in force clutching their lightsticks, and the club takes on a New York warehouse party vibe. The music policy is house/vocals and funky disco. The punters dress to impress (have to, to get through the door) with fashion ranging from Westwood to Hollywood. The club has a capacity for 800 over the two floors and capacity is usually attained quite early on in the evening – so get here early. And when the doors close you can roll into the Breakfast Club at G-Bar (same owners – see G-Bar listing for details). **Open** Thursday-Friday 2230-0300. Saturday 2230-0400 **Price** £3-5 Thursday-Friday. £10 Saturday

Club nights

Fussy Pussy
@ Zero

11-15 North John Street, Liverpool L2 5QY Phone 0151 237 2921
E-mail **fussy@vanillagirls.co.uk** Web **www.vanillagirls.co.uk**
A new highlight in the monthly calendar for the girls of Liverpool and the surrounding areas as they get together for the hedonistic fun of infamous lesbian club night Fussy Pussy. Girls and their male friends (about an 80/20 mix of girls to boys) pile onto the dance floor for the excellent clubbing and disco sounds as belted out by top lesbian DJ Sara Furey (Manto / Breakfast Club / Classix / Paradise Factory). The venue is ideally placed, near Moorfields railway station and just off Dale Street close to G-Bar and Garlands. There is no pre-club meeting space since the venue opens at 2130 with two-for-one drink offers, eliminating the need to get tanked up elsewhere! The girls of Liverpool have never really had a club night to call their own, although the basement at G-Bar provides a women-only space each Saturday night. This dedicated and high-profile night is sure to bring more girls out of the closet. As with all Fussy Pussy nights, the age range is decidedly mixed. From October 2001, the dates for this top event will be rigidly fixed to the first Saturday of every month; until then phone the venue or checkout the website for details of which Saturday in the month to set aside. Finally, each Fussy-Pussy event in Liverpool promises at least 100 selected drinks available on a 'buy-one-get-one-free' basis, which should save you megabucks. Recommended! **Open** Every first Saturday 2130-0230 **Price** £3

Oi! Club @
The Escape

41-45 Paradise Street, Liverpool L1 3BP
Phone 0161 273 2074 / 07956 808 142
E-mail **info@oiclub.co.uk** Web **www.oiclub.co.uk**
Another two nights per month for this infamous, horny, men-only club night. If you're used to getting turned away from gay venues that don't allow you to wear trainers and trackies, Rockports, sportswear, etc. then come here. You will be welcomed with open arms. It really is about time most clubs got to grips with reality and allowed people to wear what they want (reality check: tight-fitting lycra and club wear is not gay uniform: it does not appeal to everyone). Oi! is a club that started for men who like men, free of attitude and camp kitsch. Men who you would normally pass on the street and secretly wonder whether they swing this way or that (and hope it was this way): they're here! DJ Psyche and Lord K play bouncy hard house and Dassos and Cereal Killer play retro. At the time of going to press, this club night has temporarily closed down for a while; it may well re-open at a later date. (See the other Oi! listings at Manchester, London and Birmingham.) **Open** Every second and fourth Saturday of the month, 2200-0400 **Price** £5-7

Poptastic @
The Escape

41-45 Paradise Street, Liverpool L1 3BY Phone 07074 248 247
E-mail **info@poptastic.co.uk** Web **www.poptastic.co.uk**
Packed with top indie tunes and trashy pop, Liverpool's version of

Poptastic is yet another fun night out for happenin' homos, lusty lesbos and daring don't-knows! Full of fresh-faced funksters, the top, tackiest night of the week brings you the world's most copied copping-off invention, 'ShagTags'. Oh yes, if it should interest you – cheap beer too! **Open** Friday 2230-0230 **Price** £2.50-3.50

Saunas

The Dolphin Sauna

129 Mount Road, Wallasey, Liverpool L45 9JS Phone 0151 630 1516

A long way out of Liverpool's town centre, this sauna occupies a former shop premise that is still part of a small row of shops within a cul-de-sac. The place is very clean and hospitable, although whenever I visit the age range always seem to be on the older side. The limited available space is utilised to its fullest extent but this means there is no room to cruise around or escape any unwanted passes. The ground floor comprises a smart snack bar which leads through to the changing facilities. Upstairs is the wet area and TV lounge. As far as gay saunas go this does serve its purpose. However, you may find yourself better off travelling across to Manchester where the sauna scene is a lot more popular with a wider age range. **Open** Monday-Sunday 1400-2130 **Price** £9

Accommodation

Feathers Hotel

119-125 Mount Pleasant, Liverpool L3 5TF Phone 0151 709 9655

Fax 0151 709 3838 E-mail feathershotel@feathers.uk.com

Web www.feathers.uk.com

Feathers Hotel (part of the Feathers group) is a gay-friendly hotel close to the city. Adjacent to both cathedrals and only a few minutes' walk from all the shops, clubs, restaurants, bars, and the mainline Lime Street Railway Station and central Bus Station. The room rate quoted below is for a double room with en-suite; however, there are standard rooms available, as well as more expensive deluxe suites and it is wise to phone the hotel in order to get a rate to suit your budget. They will also be able to arrange full board to include an evening meal. The lack of gay establishments offering accommodation in Liverpool leaves you with very little choice. Here though, the room prices are reasonable and the facilities and service are well above average. **Price** £65 per double room **Number of rooms** 75, all en-suite

Parkfield Manor Hotel

34 Parkfield Road, Liverpool L17 8UJ

Phone 0151 726 9229 Fax 0151 283 1800

Parkfield Manor Hotel was built by Mr A. Thomas, a Liverpool merchant in the early 1800's in the fashionable area of Sefton Park. It was a luxury private house for the Thomas Family and managed to survive the blitz of the Second World War, when a bomb landed in the rear garden. The hotel is within easy walking distance of Sefton Park where the landscaped lakes and grottoes provide the chance for a breath of fresh air and a relaxing stroll through the park. It is also not that far from the gay bars in Liverpool centre (about £6 by taxi). The Parkfield is not exclusively gay, though it is gay-owned and -run. **Price** £45 per double room

Number of Rooms 14, 8 en-suite

Cruising grounds

Crosby Marine   Located at the end of South Road. The cottage is quite busy at lunch times and early evenings. If it feels safer, try the Marine Gardens or Crescent Gardens next to the cottage – an area, that also gets quite busy.

Eleanor Rigby is still in Liverpool. She can be found sitting on a bench in Stanley Street, only a stone's throw away from Mathew Street. She was sculpted in 1982 by the pop singer, Tommy Steele, as a tribute to The Beatles. Inside the bronze sculpture are a four-leaf clover (representing Nature), a page of the Bible (representing Spiritual Matters), a football sock (representing Leisure), Dandy and Beano comic books (representing Comedy), and four sonnets (representing Romance). A plaque next to the monument dedicates it 'To All The Lonely People'. The name Eleanor is taken from that of Eleanor Bron – the actress, while Rigby is taken from a Bristol shop front which Paul McCartney saw whilst visiting the city.

Otterspool   As you leave Albert Dock, turn right and keep going straight for as long as you can. Go past the Festival Park on your right, and past another park. You will then soon come to a sign that says 'Otterspool'. This place consists of a series of car parks (around six in all) with virtually no lighting whatsoever. The main ones of interest to you are car parks '3' and '4'. From here you can walk into the park and bushes where you'll find lots of activity. After car park '4' there is car park '5' (obviously); however, this one is set back and can easily be missed if you are just driving past. You'll find more action here. Popular times to go are between 2300 and 0200 in the week, and 2300 and 0300 on weekends. Police patrols happen now and again; they will move you on. It is best to move along before being told to and to return a little later on. The 'Dead End' sign at the far end of the road is in fact a barrier in the middle of the road and can quite easily be passed if you drive on the pavement. You can U-turn and re-enter this way. (Remember, driving on the pavement is illegal; it may be best to re-enter the way you came in.) Despite being well out of the town centre, this area can get extremely busy. The presence of parkland makes this place ideal and if your first visit is not successful then rest assured that another will almost certainly be fruitful.

London

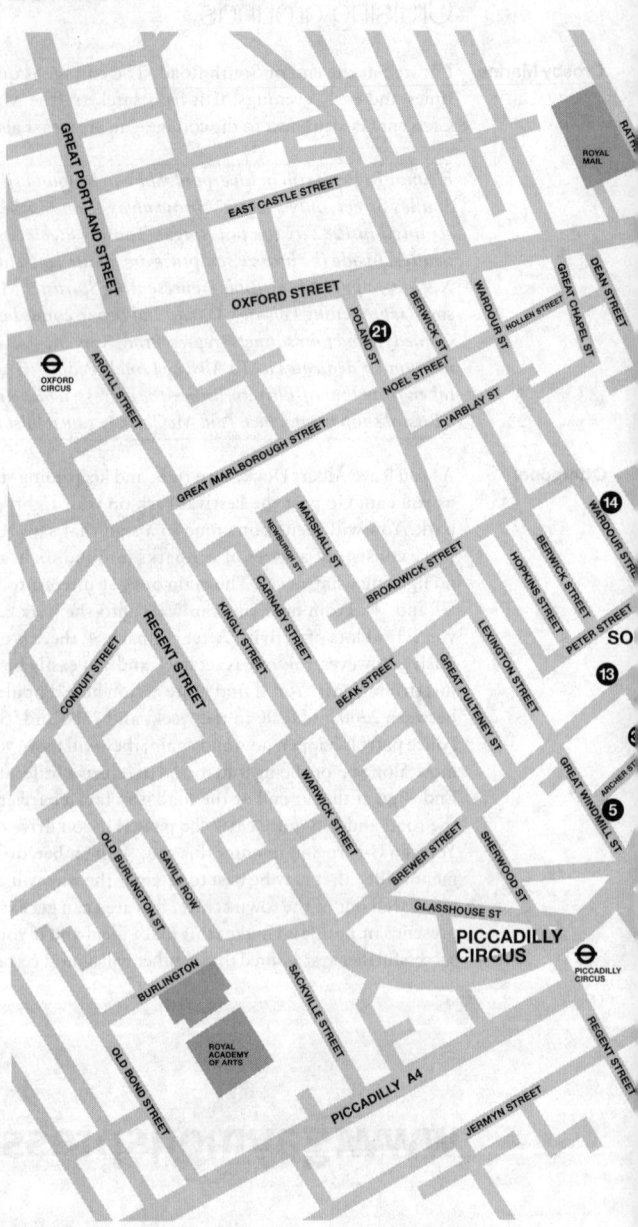

GREAT PORTLAND STREET

EAST CASTLE STREET

OXFORD STREET

DEAN STREET

GREAT CHAPEL ST

HOLLEN STREET

WARDOUR ST

BERWICK ST

POLAND ST

21

NOEL STREET

D'ARBLAY ST

OXFORD
CIRCUS

ARGYLL STREET

GREAT MARLBOROUGH STREET

MARSHALL ST

MEDBURN ST

CARNABY STREET

KINGLY STREET

BROADWICK STREET

REGENT STREET

CONDUIT STREET

BEAK STREET

GREAT PULTENEY ST

LEXINGTON STREET

HOPKINS STREET

BERWICK STREET

WARDOUR STR

14

PETER STREET

SO

13

WARWICK STREET

GREAT WINDMILL ST

ARCHER ST

5

OLD BURLINGTON ST

SAVILE ROW

BREWER STREET

SHERWOOD ST

GLASSHOUSE ST

**PICCADILLY
CIRCUS**

PICCADILLY
CIRCUS

BURLINGTON

ROYAL
ACADEMY
OF ARTS

SACKVILLE STREET

OLD BOND STREET

REGENT STREET

PICCADILLY A4

JERMYN STREET

ROYAL
MAIL

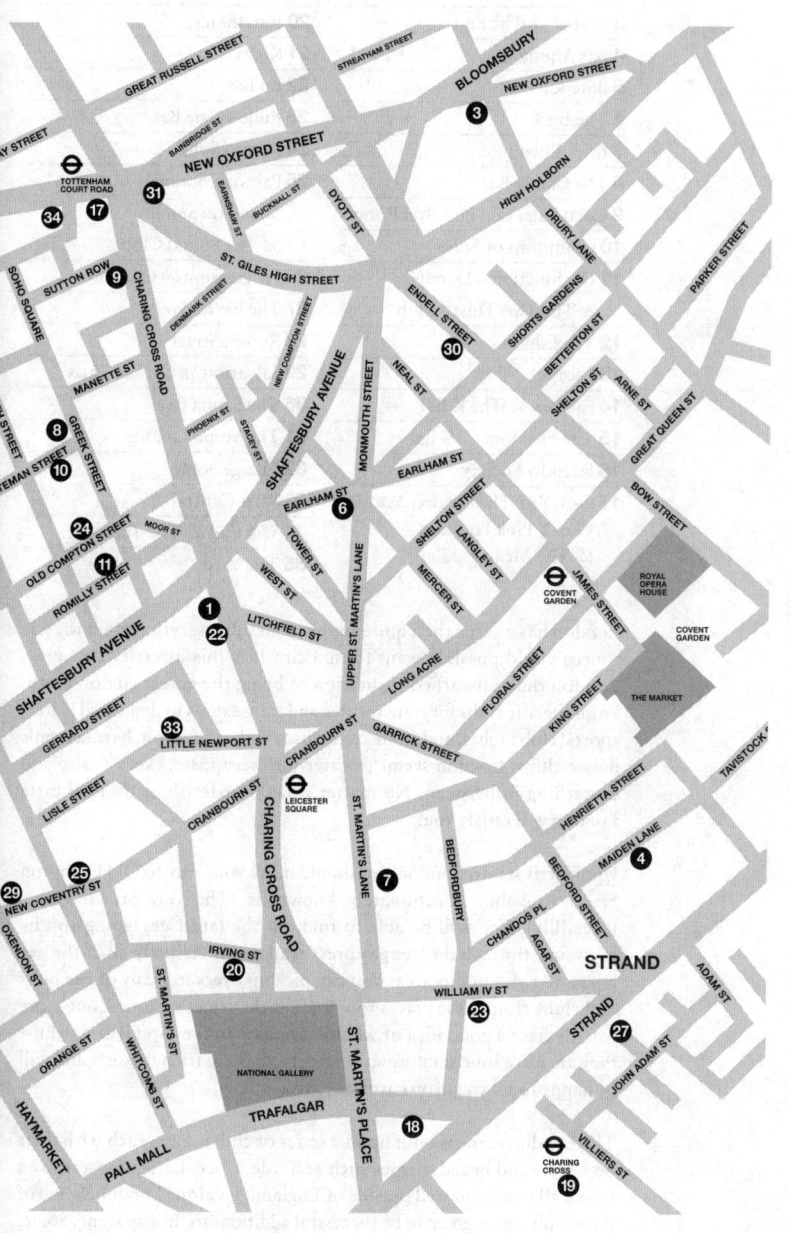

3

See overleaf for key

Map key

1 79 CXR
2 Admiral Duncan
3 Atelier @ The End
4 Bar Aquda
5 Barcode
6 The Box
7 Brief Encounter
8 The Candy Bar
9 Coco Latte @ The Velvet Rooms
10 Comptons of Soho
11 Dysfunctional Dandy @ The Two Thirty Club
12 The Edge
13 Escape
14 Factory @ The K Bar
15 The Freedom Café Bar
16 Friendly Society
17 G-A-Y @ The London Astoria / G-A-Y Pink Pounder @ The Mean Fiddler
18 Halfway to Heaven
19 Heaven
20 Jonathan's
21 Kings Arms
22 Ku Bar
23 Kudos Café Bar
24 Manto Soho
25 Paradise Sound / Sound on Sunday @ The Sound Club
26 Progression @ CC Club
27 The Retro Bar
28 Rupert Street
29 Salvation @ Café de Paris
30 The Sauna Bar
31 The Vespa Lounge
32 Village Soho
33 West Central
34 Wig Out @ The Tube
35 The Yard

London has a scene that, quite simply, contains everything that the gay tourist could possibly want from a city. It is this diversity that gives London the well-earned reputation of being the gayest city on earth. From specific clubs for transvestites and transexuals to dedicated watersports' club nights, and from camp disco clubs to full-on, hard-as-nails dance clubs, London seems to cater for every taste, every desire and everything in between. No matter what your fetish or musical taste London will satisfy you!

Upon arrival into London you should make your way to Old Compton Street in Soho, affectionately known as 'The Gay Street' (tube: Piccadilly). You will be able to find out the latest gay goings-on by browsing through the free gay press available at virtually all of the gay bars and cafés in this area. You can pick up flyers to many of the pubs and clubs from these places too. Staff at the street's Clone Zone store usually have a good idea of what is going on in the capital and, whilst they are not a tourist information centre, they are friendly sorts and will be happy to fill you in on current events.

The London scene is built upon a series of club nights, each with their own style and brand; names such as Trade, Coco-Latte, Popstarz and Crash all now echo well outside of England, let alone London. Some of these club nights go on to be successful additions to the gay scene. Some, however, don't last the course; they run for a couple of months and then resign themselves to the increasing high pile of failed attempts. But, no matter, despite a gay scene that is already bloated and that already offers so much, another promoter is always ready to come along with a night that promises to be 'the best' in London. This, of course, all makes for more choice, but it also means that the gay pie is being sliced thinner and thinner with increasing regularity. The punter will ultimately decide the longevity of these club nights but it seems that there will always be more than enough for the city's spread of gays and lesbians. Thus, attempting to map out a gay scene that is forever changing and enlarging is an arduous task. Visitors to London are advised to phone the venue direct before making a long journey.

Whilst Soho and Piccadilly serve as the hub of London's scene and encompass the majority of gay bars and clubs, there are several other areas that enjoy their own little village. Earl's Court is one such place, which is enjoying a revitalised growth of gay retail and leisure venues. Vauxhall is another area to explore, particularly for those interested in the leather and dress code scene such as The Fringe and Dukes. Farringdon also boasts some of the capital's best gay venues – the world-famous Turnmills (for club nights such as Trade and One Nation) and Chariots Sauna. The London scene is spread out and diverse: explore it.

Whilst travelling around our grand metropolis, be very aware of pick-pockets and con-artists. Oxford Street is a well-known hotspot, as is Covent Garden and any other well-populated tourist centre. Bag snatching is also on the increase and the police have special undercover squads, continually on the lookout for thieves. The current trend of back-satchel-wearing gives the opportunist thief chance to steal your belongings without you realising. If you have to use these bags then ensure that they are well-secured. Entry into some gay venues may require you and your belongings to be searched. This search is performed in the name of 'security', but it's as likely that they're checking to make sure you are not taking your own alchohol into the venue. London is not an especially dangerous or criminal city, but do keep your wits about you.

Drugs are a big problem in some venues and sporadic police raids on queues of customers waiting to get into a popular venue are not unheard of. In many of the top dance clubs too, there will be undercover police posing as punters. Buying, selling and concealing drugs in these environments carries extreme risks. Be warned!

London, like any other major city, cannot be explored fully in a couple of days and, if time is not on your side, there is always the old tour bus as a last resort that will enable you a quick snapshot of London's highlights as well as an opportunity to sit down. Most tour buses start their journey from either Marble Arch or outside Victoria Tube station. Reservations are not normally required and, due to immense competition, the charges are pretty reasonable (about £10). If you are around for longer then, as the breadth of the listings that follow indicates, there is lots to see and do. London will not disappoint you!

Getting there

Airport

Heathrow Airport in Hounslow, Middlesex (020 8759 4321) is the world's busiest international airport with planes landing approximately every single minute. The best way to get into London from Heathrow is either via the underground (Piccadilly Line, about 45 minutes) or by hopping aboard the **Heathrow Express** which travels between Heathrow and Paddington every 15 minutes between 0500 and 2340. **Gatwick Airport** in West Sussex (01293 535 353) is London's second airport. From here you can catch the **Gatwick Express** train to Victoria Station. They leave every 15 minutes between 0500 and 0000, and approximately every 30 minutes between 0000 and 0500 (08457 484 950 for more information). **National Express** coaches run between Gatwick and Victoria from 0500 to 2020 and prices are in the region of £15 for a return ticket. It should be noted that Heathrow is not close to the city of London and Gatwick is even further. Both airports have 24-hour restaurants, visitor centres and bureaux de change.

Trains

Seven main railway stations run into and out of London. **Euston** serves Bangor, Birmingham, Carlisle, Chester, Coventry, Glasgow, Holyhead, Inverness, Liverpool, Llandudno, Manchester, Perth, Preston and Shrewsbury. **Kings Cross** serves Aberdeen, Bradford, Cambridge, Dundee, Durham, Edinburgh, Glasgow, Inverness, King's Lynn, Leeds, Newcastle, Perth and York. **Liverpool Street** serves Colchester, Ipswich and Norwich. **Paddington** serves Bath, Bristol, Cardiff, Exeter, Gloucester, Newton Abbot, Oxford, Penzance, Plymouth and Swansea. **St Pancras** serves Derby, Leicester, Nottingham, Sheffield. **Victoria** serves Brighton, Canterbury, Dover and Hastings. **Waterloo** is for the Eurostar Trains to Paris and the continent as well as serving Hampton Court, Penzance, Portsmouth, Salisbury and Southampton.

Docklands Light Railway (DLR) is London's newest transport system. It connects the developments of the old docks with the city of London. The tube's zoning system applies to the DLR network too and these DLR lines appear on all up-to-date tube maps. DLR fares cost the same as tube fares and all standard travelcards are valid on these services. The red line runs north-south connecting with the tube at Bow Church and Stratford. The green line runs west-east to merge with the red line and extends five miles to the east. The N50 night buses serve the Docklands area late at night. (020 7918 4000 with any DLR enquiries.)

Coaches

The main **National Express** coach station, with services to all locations in the UK, is located in **Victoria** on Buckingham Palace Road. This is the hub of Britain's coach network and is easily accessible from the Victoria tube station (the coach station is well signposted from here). As London is so accessible by coach to all locations in the UK it may be worth taking a coach trip to any destination just to explore a little further afield. For example, Brighton is only an hour away by train and 90 minutes away by coach.

Getting about

Buses

The famous London red buses run from about 0600 to 0000 every day. After that the service is reduced to night buses (marked by the letter 'N'), but these run on selected routes only. By day, unless you want to sample the cramped and stuffy interior of a bus, you will be better off taking the tube or walking.

The Underground

Otherwise known as the tube. With about 275 stations spread over eleven lines, the tube is probably the quickest and most convenient way of travelling around London, except perhaps during the hectic 'rush hours' of 0800 to 0930 and 1630 to 1800. Small, but invaluable, 'journey planner' maps are available at all stations. London is divided into zones and your tube fare will depend on the number of zones you wish to travel through. Tickets can be purchased from either the ticket window or from ticket machines at each station (these machines are at present being modernised with touch-screen features and credit card facilities). This ticket allows you to go through the automatic gates – keep this ticket with you, as you will need it for the gates at your destination station. All fares must be purchased before boarding the tube. The majority of 'last trains' leave central London stations between 0000 and 2430 and service resumes at around 0600. This gap is partially bridged by the aforementioned night bus services. It is worth bearing in mind that most underground stations feature long, steep escalators and staircases. To avoid being pushed out of the way by irate commuters remember to stand to the right and walk on the left.

The Tube map is easy to follow. Each of the eleven tube lines are colour-coded. Here's a list of the tube lines and the destinations that they link. **Bakerloo Line** (brown): runs from Elephant and Castle to Queens Park and Harrow and Wealdstone (with rail connections to Watford), with links to Waterloo, Oxford Circus, Baker Street and Paddington. **Central Line** (red): runs from Ealing Broadway to Epping and Hainault, with links to Notting Hill Gate, Bond Street, Oxford Circus, St Pauls and Liverpool Street. **Circle Line** (yellow): runs in a continuous loop around inner London, with links to Victoria, Paddington, Baker Street, Kings Cross and Liverpool Street. **District Line** (green): runs from Upminster to Richmond, Ealing Broadway and Wimbledon, with links to Tower Hill, Westminster, Victoria, Earl's Court, Hammersmith and Kew Gardens. **East London Line** (orange): runs from Shoreditch to New Cross and New Cross Gate, with links to Whitechapel and Rotherhithe. **Hammersmith and City Line** (pink): runs from Hammersmith to Whitechapel, with links to Paddington, Baker Street, Kings Cross and Liverpool Street. **Jubilee Line** (silver): runs from Charing Cross to Stanmore and from Charing Cross to the Docklands, with links to Green Park, Bond Street and Baker Street. **Metropolitan Line** (purple): runs from Aldgate to Amersham and Watford, with links to Liverpool Street, Kings Cross, Baker Street and Harrow on the Hill. **Northern Line** (black): runs from Morden to Edgeware and High Barnet City Section, with links to Clapham, London Bridge, Moorgate, Kings Cross and Euston, Central Section, with links to Waterloo, Leicester Square and Euston. **Piccadilly Line** (dark blue): runs from Heathrow Airport to Cockfosters, with links to Earl's Court, Knightsbridge, Green Park, Piccadilly, Leicester Square, Covent Garden and Kings Cross. **Victoria Line** (light blue): runs from Brixton to Walthamstow, with links to Oxford Circus, Euston and Kings Cross.

Taxis

Our famous black London cabs are by far the best in the world. In order to gain a Hackney Carriage licence, 'cabbies' must sit a rigorous examination called 'The Knowledge' to demonstrate that they know the city's streets by heart and will be able to take customers to their destination via the quickest route. A taxi is available for hire if the yellow light on the bulkhead of the cab is lit. Fares are metered within London, with additional charges for extra passengers and baggage. A ten per cent tip is expected. If you should have cause to complain: inform the driver of the reason for your discontent, obtain a receipt for the journey, make a note of the driver's badge number (which will be on display) and then phone 020 7230 1631 and this office will deal with and register your complaint.

Tourist information

There are many of these offices dotted about London. You can find information centres at most of the major railway and underground stations (Kings Cross, Liverpool Street, Oxford Circus, Piccadilly, St James's Park, Hammersmith for example) and all of these carry information about public transport systems. There are some main general information offices. Victoria Station forecourt, SW1 is open daily from 0800 to 1900 and offers an accommodation service that carries a hefty £5 booking fee. They also have shed-loads of free tourist information on where to go, what to see and so forth. **The British Travel Centre** at 12 Regent Street (020 8846 9000) is run by the British Tourist Authority and is ideal for tourists with destinations to get to outside of London. There are usually long queues here so if you require their services get here early (Monday to Friday; 0900 to 1830 and Saturday to Sunday 1000 to 1600). **The City of London Information Centre** (020 7606 3030) specialises in information about the city of London but staff here will also be able to answer questions about wider parts of London (open daily from 0930 to 1700). **The Greenwich Tourist Information Office** at 48 Greenwich Church Street (020 8858 6376) will be able to provide you with information on sights in Greenwich and its surrounding areas (open daily from 1000 to 1700).

Bureaux de change

There are currency exchange offices at all the major airports and railway stations. **American Express**, high street banks, major tour operators such as **Thomas Cook**, and larger post offices also offer currency exchange services. Your passport is usually required as identification if you wish to cash traveller's cheques. Be wary about currency exchange bureaux within the major tourist areas, such as Piccadilly. They may not charge a commission but their exchange rates aren't usually the best. Get your money exchanged before you hit the city.

Getting help

Police, hospital and pharmacy   There are police stations in every district of London, including the police headquarters, **New Scotland Yard**, at Broadway SW1 (020 7230 1212). **Release**, 388 Old Street, London EC1 is a company offering free, confidential legal advice and referrals to anyone who has been arrested (020 7729 9904, or the out of office hours number 020 7603 8654, for advice). **London Gay Switchboard** (020 7837 7324) also offers advice with such matters. In an emergency you can be treated free of charge within the accident and emergency ward of a hospital. The following hospitals have 24-hour walk-in casualty departments: **Royal London Hospital**, Whitechapel Road E1 (020 7377 7000); **Royal Free Hospital**, Pond Street NW3 (020 7794 0500); **Charing Cross Hospital** Fulham Palace Road (entrance is on St Dunstan's Road) W6 (020 8846 1234); **St Thomas' Hospital**, Lambeth Palace Road SE1 (020 7928 9292); **University College Hospital**, Gower Street (entrance on Grafton Way) WC1 (020 7387 9300). There is also an emergency dental ward at **Eastman Dental Hospital**. Phone for location, emergency treatment and open-hours (020 7915 1000). **The Dental Emergency Care Service** (020 7955 2186) is open from Monday to Friday between 0845 and 1530 and will refer callers to either a private or an NHS dental surgery that is open. Every police station keeps a list of emergency doctors and chemists in its area. There are also listings of all chemists throughout London in the Yellow Pages phonebook under 'chemists'. You can find these Yellow Pages in telephone kiosks. **Bliss Chemist** at Marble Arch (020 7723 6116) is open daily from 0900 to 0000.

Lost property   If you are intending to make an insurance claim, you must report the loss to the police for your claim to be valid, remembering to get an incident report number for the loss to be traced. Report lost or stolen passports to both the police and your local embassy (see Essentials section for a full list). If you have lost property on the London Transport system (buses) contact the **Lost Property Office** at 200 Baker Street, Marylebone, London NW1 (020 7486 2496 for recorded information). For property lost on the underground, fill in a lost property form at any Underground station (you have to wait three days before submitting this form). If you have lost your property in a London Black Hackney Carriage (taxi) contact **Taxi Lost Property** at 15 Penton Street, Islington, London N1 (020 7833 0996).

Getting in touch

Internet   There are plenty of internet cafés dotted across London. These days, there's not many of London's main streets that you can walk down without stumbling upon one, so if you're desperate to mail or surf then you shouldn't have too far to venture. Away from the centre, as with the majority of towns and cities, internet cafés are still something of a novelty. It won't be difficult, however, to find a library or other public building with adequate internet facilities (you'll be unlikely to get that accompanying cappuccino though). There are several internet café chains with various branches across London. Whilst they hardly represent the lion-share of this large and growing market they should suffice as a quick reference to a few of the places that you can drop into to check and send your mail. **Easy Everything** cafés claim to have more available PCs than any other café chain, and competitive prices to boot. They stay open 24 hours a day. You can find Easy Everything branches at 12 Wilton Road, Victoria SW1; Tottenham Court Road W1; Trafalgar Square W1; and 456-459 The Strand WC2. There's also **Nethouse**, who have branches at 138 Marylebone Road NW1 and 193a Holloway Road N7. They too are open 24 hours. **Internet Exchange** are another growing chain with two branches: one along Queensway W2 and one at The Trocadero Centre in Picadilly W1V. And finally **Cybergate**, who have outlets at 117 Euston Road NW1 and 3 Leigh Street WC1H.

GLB Helplines

London has the only gay switchboard in the country that is open 24 hours a day, 365 days of the year (020 7837 7324). This line is always very busy, but keep trying. This number is the only one you need for information regarding all sorts of gay, lesbian and transgender groups across London. They will be able to give you referral numbers to Bisexual Helpline, Lesbian Line, Jewish Helpline, Black Helpline, Irish helpline, TV/TS Helpline and many more. Make a note of this number!

Pubs

79 CXR

79 Charing Cross Road, London WC2H 0NE Phone 020 7734 0769
This extremely busy bar is spaced out over two floors and is jam-packed most nights with some of the best looking guys in London. The lighting is on its lowest setting, so everyone looks good! A fun, party atmosphere through to the early hours and one of the places to be after the local pubs close. A resident DJ pumps up the volume from Thursday through to Saturday. Both floors can be pretty cruisy; indeed, the first floor balcony enables you to select your 'victim' before descending to make your move. During the day there are tables and chairs on the street which give you a good opportunity to just sit, relax and watch the world go by. Happy hours are from 2000 'til 2200 every day. Very nice. **Open** Monday-Thursday 1300-0200. Friday-Saturday 1300-0300. Sunday 1300-2230 **Price** £2, after 2230 **Tube** Leicester Square

---

If you find yourself in Soho, look out for the blue plaque above Café Italia in Frith Street where in 1926 John Logie Baird first demonstrated the wonder of television to an unsuspecting world.

Admiral Duncan

54 Old Compton Street, Soho, London W1V Phone 020 7437 5300
The Admiral Duncan has been a mixed gay, homely venue in the heart of the gay village for over two years. A busy place at weekends that offers great value for money. Friendly staff, good atmosphere, brilliant jukebox and an excellent range of traditional beers (which are sometimes hard to obtain in gay establishments around Soho). The venue itself consists of one open-plan room, which opens out onto the street in the summer.

The Admiral welcomes all gay and straight walks of life with TVs/CDs more than welcome. **Open** Monday-Saturday 1100-2300. Sunday 1200-2230 **Tube** Piccadilly / Leicester Square / Tottenham Court Road

---

On Friday 30 April 1999, a bomb, concealed in a sports bag left at the bar, ripped through the Admiral Duncan pub. The effect of the explosion within such a confined space was devastating. It killed three people and more than 70 others suffered extensive burns and serious wounds; there were several amputees among them. David Copeland was arrested on 1 May and charged with three counts of murder. He admitted responsibility for the bomb and also the explosions on 17 April in Brixton (a south London neighbourhood with a large black population) and 24 April in Brick Lane (an east London neighbourhood with a large Bangladeshi population). David James Copeland, now known as The Soho Bomber, is currently serving six life sentences for three nailbomb attacks on the capital's black and gay communities. One year later, the reserved yet consistent chime of the bell of St Annes's Church in Soho, signalled the start of the poignant first remembrance of the victims of The Admiral Duncan bombing. In the nearby church gardens, three cherry trees were planted in memory of Andrea Dykes (27), John Light (32) and Nick Moore (31).

The Angel Cabaret Bar

21 Church Street, Stratford, London E15 3HU Phone 020 8555 1148
E-mail info@angelcabaret.com Web www.angelcabaret.com
An attitude-free and friendly mixed gay bar. Surprisingly, the mix is a good fifty-fifty – men-to-women – and, even more surprisingly, they get on well together! The venue consists of a main room with an extra-large, well-used stage and dance floor and a smaller comfortable lounge bar for chilling (or arguing). As the name of the venue suggests, this is a cabaret and karaoke bar with a DJ-hosted disco each night. At the time of writing a late licence has been applied for, which should extend the opening hours 'til 0200 over the weekend. (See also the listing for their sister venue The New Angel Cabaret Bar.) **Open** Monday-Saturday 1900-2300. Sunday 1900-2230

Bar Aquda

13-14 Maiden Lane, Covent Garden, London WC2 7NE
Phone 020 7557 9891
Bar Aquda – as in Baracuda – is situated behind The Strand, off Bedford Street. This is a stylish and modern venue catering for a very mixed trendy gay and lesbian crowd. The atmosphere is relaxed and social, quite the opposite of your typical West End gay pub. A full menu is available throughout the day until 1930 and the prices are affordable, which for the location is something of a rarity. It's popular during the day with the local office crowds and it's a relaxing place to unwind after a hard day's work. In the evening the lighting and music are at just the right pitch, so you do not have to shout inanely at your friends. Formerly known as Bar Coast (which was aimed at the trendy hetero pool) it never really took off and so the brewery, Bass, gave it a name change and added it to their ever-increasing portfolio of gay bars. All in all, Bar Aquda seems to be the right place to meet up with your friends in a

delightful atmosphere and plan for the night ahead. **Open** Monday-Saturday 1200-2300. Sunday 1500-2230 **Tube** Covent Garden

Bar Fusion   45 Essex Road, Angel Islington, London N1 Phone 020 7688 2882
Extremely cruel fluorescent lights outside the venue make you look haggard and drawn, particularly if you have had a skinful. Once inside you will be glad that you have (had a skinful) for this is a drinker's bar: you visit with the intention of getting drunk – very drunk. A long, narrow bar becomes the Holy Grail and the more times you visit it the more attractive and younger that moose who has been eyeing you up becomes. The young (and the old, looking for the young) take their positions on, under and above the rickety seating desperately trying to get hammered before the bar closes at the stroke of midnight. Despite this, it is very good fun and if you want to make a fool out of yourself it doesn't really matter 'cos no one will remember it the next day... not least you. **Open** Monday-Thursday 1300-0000. Friday-Sunday 1300-0100 **Tube** Angel

Barcode   3-4 Archer Street, Soho, London W1 Phone 020 7734 3343
A busy, young bar over two large floors, filled to capacity with sexy 'blokes'. The downstairs dance area with DJ (Thursday to Saturday) plays up-to-the-minute dance tracks, whilst the quieter upstairs bar, with ample seating, gives you a chance to get your hearing back. Earlier this year Barcode was voted one of the top 25 DJ bars in London by Time Out magazine. The atmosphere is clubby and friendly with a predominantly young male crowd, although women are made more than welcome. The full range of draught beers are available in addition to a huge selection of continental and standard bottles. Barcode gets busy on Wednesday evenings when the karaoke queens belt out their fave numbers with the help of the contents from the dressing-up box – now that's just camp! **Open** Monday-Saturday 1200-0100. Sunday 1200-2230 **Price** £2-3, after 2230 **Tube** Piccadilly Circus

The Black Cap   171 Camden High Street, London NW1 Phone 020 7428 2721
Long-established cruisy cabaret bar with something going on more or less right through the week, including the all-too-familiar karaoke every Thursday. Worth popping in on a Sunday and paying a fiver for the traditional Sunday lunch in Shufflewick's. There's no admission from Monday to Thursday until 2300; after then it's £2. Fridays and Saturdays

see the admission price rise to £4. If you are in the area it's a good idea to pop in here early to see if it's worth staying. **Open** Monday-Thursday 1300-0200. Friday-Saturday 1200-0300. Sunday 1200-0000 **Price** £2-4 **Tube** Camden Town

The Black Horse

168 Mile End Road, Stepney Green, London E1 4LJ Phone 020 7790 1684
Situated opposite the Stepney Green tube, this is a cosy East End gay bar with quite a comprehensive cabaret and entertainments policy. Over the weekend the pool table gets moved to allow more room for the dancing throng. Strippers regularly take to the stage on a Tuesday and a Thursday, and there's Karaoke Showtime on a Sunday. Admission charges apply Friday and Saturday, but all other times are free. **Open** Tuesday-Thursday 2000-0100. Friday-Saturday 2000-0300. Sunday 1900-2430 **Price** £2-3 **Tube** Stepney Green

Blush

8 Cazenove Road, Stoke Newington, London N16 Phone 020 7923 9202
E-mail **enquiries@blushbar.co.uk** Web **www.blushbar.co.uk**
Around the corner from Stoke Newington railway station is Blush, the latest gay bar catering mainly for the lesbian community. There are two floors. The ground floor is light and airy, quite café-like, where original works of art adorn the walls. Downstairs is a delightful, comfortable area with a relaxed ambience, Sunday jazz, organic food and a pool table... ta daa! On Friday it's 'Lush Girls' for women only (big drink promotions before 2100). It seems strange considering the size of Greater London and since Stoke Newington already had the extremely popular Due South women's bar, that Blush chose to open up here. It may be the start of a lesbian village – which would of course put Stoke Newington on the world map, but are there enough girls to go around? Let's hope so. **Open** Monday closed. Tuesday-Sunday 1700-0000

The Box

32-34 Monmouth Street, Seven Dials, Covent Garden, London WC2 Phone 020 7240 5828
Another 'three-in-one': coffee shop, diner and bar. Café society at its best: chic, and oh-so elegant. The menu, which changes seasonally, is available daily until 1700 (1830 on Sunday) and has been devised and extensively broadened by top cookery writer Jane Pettigrew. A huge variety of teas and coffees are available along with a marvellous selection of continental ale on tap. Tables and chairs spill onto the pavement outside, giving you a good opportunity to relax, read the papers and just take it all in. That is until the evening, when the music is turned up slightly, but only to a level where you can still hear what the other person is saying. It attracts a sophisticated good-looking crowd of cosmopolitan girls and boys (this bar has been voted 'Best Bar for Women' by the Pink Paper and in addition was listed as one of the top 100 London Bars in Time Out). It is a friendly and welcoming venue for a no-attitude crowd and, because of its location, The Box is an ideal pre-club meeting place where your 'date' will not feel out of place on their own waiting for you. The free gay press, literature and flyers for most of the London clubs can be collected from here in addition to discounted tickets (Q-Jumpers) for Heaven, DTPM, etc. **Open** Monday-Saturday 1100-2300.

Sunday 1200-2230 **Tube** Covent Garden / Leicester Square

Brief Encounter   42 St Martins Lane, Soho, London WC2 4EJ Phone 020 7557 9851

This renowned cruisy bar, situated below the St Martin's Hotel has been going for simply ages and during the week still manages to pull in a few loyal, local followers. The weekend picks up a little with a younger crowd on their way to G-A-Y popping in to collect their Q-Jump tickets, but in all fairness it seems as though the days of Brief Encounter are numbered. Owned by Bass, it may, by the time this guide hits the shelves, be either sold, transferred, or have had a much-needed cash and refurbishment injection to retain and rejuvenate this 'piece' of gay history. The basement disco bar is open from 1900 all week, except Sundays, providing the darkened nooks, crannies and corners that are all-essential in a cruisy venue. **Open** Monday-Saturday 1200-2300. Sunday 1700-2230 (top bar only) **Tube** Leicester Square

The Britannia   493 High Road, Leytonstone, London E11 Phone 020 8539 6096

The Britannia is a traditional pub with a night club and, at the time of writing, this venue was undergoing a re-scheduling of their nights, prices and entertainment policy, to be finalised at some point during the summer. So check out the gay press for updated details. **Open** Wednesday-Saturday 1700-0200. Sunday 1500-2230

Bromptons   294 Old Brompton Road, Earl's Court, London SW5 9JF
Phone 020 7370 1344 E-mail info@brompton-club.com
Web www.brompton-club.com

During the week, this large cruisy bar/disco is popular with the leather, skin and uniform crowd, whilst over the weekend just about anybody and everybody joins in the no-attitude fun. The friendly, quieter upstairs bar is an area where you can actually hear what the other person is saying to you and if you are in before 2300, on Monday to Thursday, and 2230, on Friday to Sunday, you can wander between the two without paying any admission charges whatsoever. The club downstairs is a large open-plan room with the DJ box and dance floor taking up one end of the room and a sea of men everywhere else. It's always busy over the weekend with plenty of standing space to watch the new talent trip over the step dividing the dance area from the bar (always a laugh). Sunday is exceptionally busy because of their strip fest (Privates On Parade) where four strippers perform at various intervals throughout the evening. On weekdays you will be exposed to all the elements of a typical gay bar – stripper (Tuesday), karaoke (Wednesday) and cabaret (Monday and Thursday). **Open** Monday-Saturday 2000-0200. Sunday 1800-0000 **Price** £2-3 Saturday and Sunday **Tube** Earl's Court (Warwick Road exit)

The Buzz Bar   136 Battersea High Street, London SW11 3JR Phone 020 7207 3895

Traditional gay bar with a wide variety of camp goings-on including karaoke on a Sunday. The beginning of the week starts off with the quieter quiz night and bingo and things progressively get more adventurous towards the weekend. **Open** Monday-Saturday 1200-2300. Sunday 1200-2230 **Tube** Clapham Junction

Café Goya   85 Acre Lane, Brixton, London SW2 Phone 020 7274 3500
E-mail info@cafegoyabrixton.com Web www.cafegoyabrixton.com
Café Goya is not, by any means, an exclusively gay venue. Brixton itself
is quintessentially cosmopolitan, although this establishment has held
an uninterrupted gay 'lineage' since the early 1970s when it housed a
hush-hush men's 'sauna' in the basement of a greasy spoon café. Of an
evening it's not unusual to see a bit of boy-on-boy hand-holding, or girl-
on-girl kissing, alongside mum, dad, and dear old aunt Agatha on the
next table. Amazingly it all works; and that's Brixton in a nutshell! Fried
Green Tomatoes, known as 'FGT,' is an intimate women-only bar and
social club with amiable staff, a laid-back atmosphere, mood music, and
a retro feel. Board games, bar snacks and slow dancing are part of
what's happening for a mature, friendly and welcoming crowd that
meets on the first and third Wednesday of every month (from 1930 'til
late). The upstairs conservatory, lounge, and bar combine to offer a con-
vivial atmosphere with the intimacy of a shebeen. To summarise, Goya
is a warm, eccentric little place guaranteed to lift your spirits. The best
attraction is the informality; the freedom to saunter in and have a glass
of wine, a bowl of olives, read the papers and to chat with both people
you know or those that you have never set eyes on. That's something
pubs rarely provide, bars never but Goya always. Nice one. **Open**
Monday-Friday 1700-2300. Saturday 1100-2300. Sunday 1100-1700 **Price**
£10-15 dinner **Tube** Brixton

---

*We like Tower Bridge because it's camp! It's a real achievement of
Victorian engineering, and looks great, especially at night when it's well
illuminated. It's not even necessary to go inside to appreciate it – the
engines that lift the two drawbridges are a miracle. The bridge is opened
on average once a week – find out when, it's spectacular. The Tower
Bridge Experience is the award-winning attraction inside the bridge.
The animatronic spirit of Sir Horace Jones (the designer of the bridge)
and one of his builders, Harry Stoner, tell you about the bridge's history,
which spans more than 100 years. There's also four different shows,
interactive computers, full-size steam engines and working models
showing how the bridge works. If that's not enough, you can also enjoy
one of the best panoramic views of London available, from up on the
high-level walkways.*

The Candy Bar   23-24 Bateman Street, Soho, London W1 Phone 020 7437 1977
E-mail candybar@easynet.co.uk Web www.candybar.easynet.co.uk
Candy Bar opened its doors to the lesbian nation in October 1997 and
hasn't looked back since. It has instigated a revolution of social activity
and visibility to the women's gay scene including club events, festival
tents, and lesbian package holidays (this summer they are promoting a
women's week in Sitges). The Candy Bar is the undisputed girl powerhouse in the gay centre of the capital. With its unpretentious, friendly
and energetic atmosphere the venue attracts a diverse crowd of women
of all ages and their gay male friends, and has achieved a reputation in
London as the best place to find out what's going down for gay girls.

The bar is situated deep in the bosom of London's Soho, and consists of two bars – a ground floor bar and a basement dance bar. Seating is ample and is also available outside, ideal for summer schmoozing. The basement bar hosts nightly club promotions of a diverse range, each unique in its musical style and thus attracting and catering for different crowds. This is a women's bar (men alone will not be allowed in). There's an excellent music roster, hosted by some of the most well-known names on the women's DJ circuit (Princess Julia / Slamma, etc.) and putting on some of the best girly themed evenings in London. An increase in popularity has forced The Candy Bar to move into bigger premises (on the corner of Bateman Street and Greek Street), practically around the corner from their previous home on Carlisle Street. There's a couple of events taking place in other Soho venues such as the women-only strip night each Tuesday at Sunset Strip, 30 Dean Street from 2000 to 0100. This event carries an admission price of £8-10 which seems a bit steep. If this night seems interesting to you then why not pop into The Candy Bar beforehand to see who else is going and make a group night of it? Not content to rest on their laurels, The Candy Bar folk are constantly improving and adding new nights and parties to their jam-packed calendar. There's always something of interest here. (See also the listing for Candy Bar, Brighton.) **Open** Monday-Tuesday 1700-0100. Wednesday-Friday 1700-0300. Saturday 1600-0300. Sunday 1700-0000. **Price** £5, Friday-Saturday after 2100 **Tube** Tottenham Court Road

Central Station (Walthamstow) 80 Brunner Road, Walthamstow, London E17 7NW Phone 020 8520 4836 E-mail info@centralstation.co.uk Web www.centralstation.co.uk

This large-capacity venue is situated in the centre of Walthamstow, in the east of London. It's the only gay bar in the area with a late night licence during the week and has by far the latest licensing hours over the weekend. The venue is on one floor and consists of a large open-plan bar, a well-used cabaret stage, several DJs and state-of-the-art sound and lighting systems. To the rear of the building is an enormous walled garden that is planted with a riotous array of flowers of all colours and giving off a variety of scents. The garden is south-facing and makes for a very pleasant sun trap (or man trap!), with plenty of seating. Barbecues are held at weekends from time to time during the summer months. There is entertainment most nights of the week, with things getting particularly busy over the weekend. Indeed, be sure to arrive early on a Saturday night as there is often a queue. The Walthamstow arm of Central Station is not as heavy as its older sister up at Kings Cross but the same friendly attitude prevails here. **Open** Monday-Wednesday 1730-0130. Thursday 1730-0200. Friday 1730-0300. Saturday 1300-0300. Sunday 1300-0000 **Price** £1-2, weekends only **Tube** Walthamstow Central

Central Station (Kings Cross) 37 Wharfdale Road, Kings Cross, London N1 9ST Phone 020 7278 3294 E-mail info@centralstation.co.uk Web www.centralstation.co.uk

This is quite a difficult place to describe because there is almost too much going on! There are three floors: the basement, the cabaret main bar area and the upstairs sports bar and community room. The basement club, known as The Underground, is where the feature entertainments occur. It is always packed and I'm sure that there's at least one night in here that will be right up your street. So, here goes at an attempt to describe: Every Monday night The Underground hosts TCP (Tattoos, Crops and Piercings), incorporating Blacksmiths. This night is aimed at gay men only. A strict dress code ensures entry only to those dressed in leather, rubber, pervy gear, or uniform – definitely no trainers. The atmosphere is heavy and cruisy. TCP runs from 2230 to 0200 and admission will cost you £3. Every first and third Tuesday is The Beautiful Bend. Now, there are too few words in the dictionary capable of describing The Beautiful Bend. This monthly club night (devised some years ago) has been brought back by overwhelming demand. Themed nights are advertised in advance and past nights have included 'My Daughter's Wedding was a Disappointment', 'Blondes on Parole' and 'Art Exhibition'. On any Beautiful Bend night you can expect to see anything from an outrageous stripper, a pantomime cow, clothes racks full of questionable fashion (for customer's use), the chicken, the kangaroo – don't ask! – Donald, Sheila Tequila, dreadful music, uncool dancing: the list goes on. This night has it all... and more! Try it: from 2230 to 0200, with an admission price of £3. Every second and fourth Tuesday is Meatpackers: a cruisy, men-only space with no attitude. Dancing is not a major theme of this night. Cheap night, cheap men! Meatpackers runs from 2230 to 0200 with an admission price of £2. Every Wednesday, The Underground is taken over by the Bulk UK crew, for a night aimed at bigger men and their admirers, but also attended by anyone looking for a men-only cruisy night out. There's accompanying entertainment by a top stripper in the upstairs cabaret bar. This Wednesday night runs from 2200 to 0200 with an admission price of £3 (members £2). Thursday nights at The Underground are rotated: every first, third and fifth Thursday is The Locker Room; every second and fourth Thursday is The Glory Hole. The only real difference between the two is the change in DJ. The music is hard and the promoters say the men are too – there are certainly lots of them! These are nights for Kylie fans to miss! Having been around now for six years, The Glory Hole is one of London's longest-running nights promoting no attitude, no dress code and men-only in a very busy, cruisy atmosphere suited to horny guys. The Locker Room followed shortly after and adheres to these same principles. These are definitely men-only occasions, with a warm-up from a top stripper in the cabaret bar. Both Thursday nights run from 2300 to 0300, with an admission price of £4. Friday night is Strictly Handbag night, providing a slightly lighter touch to the entertainments roster. This is London's longest-running Friday handbag night! DJ Rob spins his mix, and dancing mixes with cruising to give a real fun night out. Strictly Handbag runs from 2300 to 0400 and admission is free before 2230 and is then £4 from 2230, climbing to £5 at 2330 (with doors closing at 0300). Saturday night features lots of dancing, and this DJ Lick'em-hosted night goes down a more commercial musical route with mixes of hard house, garage and other vibes. Saturday nights run from 2300 to 0400 and admission is £5 (£4 members). First, third, fourth and fifth Sundays of the month are Shoot! nights. Shoot! is a hugely popular sportswear fetish night. To gain entry you must wear at least one item of sportswear, plus trainers. It's men-only – a true feast for the eye and you'll find the place packed with guys dressed in all the latest sportsgear. There's good music to enjoy and plenty of heavy cruising (no wonder it's so popular!). Shoot! runs from 1800 to 0000 and admission will cost you £5. Remember, the dress code states that you must wear at least one item of sportswear plus trainers. That missing second Sunday of the month is reserved for Gummi, one of the longest-running and most famous fetish nights in Europe. It's incredibly busy. There's a strict dress code of rubberwear, with changing monthly themes that allow for lots of fun! Gummi is a legend amongst fetish nights: be sure to go and see what all the fuss is about. Gummi runs from 1800 to 0000 and the admission price is £5 (you can apply for membership on the night). Well, that's a list of events to exhaust even the most energetic scene queen! Central Station truly is a hive of activity. There is more though. The upstairs cabaret bar is 'a little' quieter and 'a little' more relaxed and also hosts a regular calendar of events. And at Christmas time, Central Station puts on a charity pantomime performance. Last year's starred the completely batty Dave Dale and it was the phenomenal success of this venture that led them to present a 'Camp as Tits' production about every two months thereafter. They're well worth looking out for. The December 2001 pantomime will be The Wizard of Oz and will be a guaranteed sell-out (enquire quickly or miss out). Finally, Central Station also make available their upstairs rooms to a selection of community groups (often free of charge). The groups currently using the facilities are The Gay Bridge Club (who meet every Tuesday to start play by 1900); Stepping Out (a social group for young men and women up to the age of 26, who meet every Friday at about 2000); Outrage (a political activists' campaigning group who meet every Thursday at 2000); New Beginnings (a support group who discuss and explore sexual identity, offering help to those having problems with this) and the Lesbian and Gay Policing Initiative (a liaison group who seek to encourage the reporting of homophobic crime and help the police with their empathy and sympathy towards such crimes). All in all, this is a top place – an institution no less – with top men and top events: you must visit it! **Open** Monday-Wednesday 1700-0200. Thursday 1700-0300. Friday 1700-0400. Saturday 1300-0400. Sunday 1300-0000 **Price** £3-5, Underground club only **Tube** Kings Cross

The Champion 1 Wellington Terrace, Bayswater Road, London W2 4LW
Phone 020 7423 9531
Long-running community bar serving the Notting Hill and Bayswater locals. Recently refurbished (including the toilets!) making it more of a traditional kind of venue – lots of wood. A good place to meet up with your friends before hitting the town. **Open** Monday-Saturday 1200-2300. Sunday 1200-2230 **Tube** Notting Hill

The Cock and Comfort 359 Bethnal Green Road, London E2 6LG Phone 020 7729 1476
The Cock is a large, lively, friendly and typical East End boozer (just like the one off the soap on telly, only you're unlikely to find Pauline propping up the bar, moaning). Emphasis is on booze, not the West End distractions of bopping, and the clientele is a good mix of lesbian and gay

with a smattering of gay-friendly straights that 'just love the atmosphere'. This is the only late-night bar in the area that does not incur a door charge. Accordingly, it gets quite busy over the weekend. The age range is anything from 18 years to near-dead and they all come together in a no-attitude environment. Drinks are very cheap (and so are the staff). The cabaret acts over the weekend are usually from the top names on the circuit (see the listings in the pub and gay press for advance information). The upstairs restaurant – Auntie Rachel's Kitchen – offers big portions at small prices and is packed on Sundays (1330 to 1700) and although booking is not necessary un-reserved tables may incur a wait. As for the name – it comes from a retort from the late gay cabaret artist, Mrs Shufflewick, who referred to her local as The Cock and Comfort: 'plenty of comfort but fuck-all cock'. This one has both! **Open** Monday-Thursday 1600-2300. Friday 1400-0200. Saturday 1300-0200. Sunday 1300-0000 **Tube** Bethnal Green

The Cock Tavern 340 Kennington Road, London SE11 Phone 020 7735 1013
Another pub with cock in the name! This one is a very large and traditional type of pub which caters for all ages. There are candles on the tables, wooden floors and video monitors on the walls (54 in total – I, in the excesses of my research, was sad enough to count them). It all combines to create a comfortable and pleasant atmosphere. There is a lower seating area with sofas and what-nots (that means homely things) if you require some seclusion. Over the weekend it becomes a bit more clubby – the music gets turned up and it's nose-to-nipple across every bit of available space. It's also a late-night drinking den and you don't even have to fork out an admission cost for the privilege. On Sunday you can get traditional Sunday lunch for an amazing £2 (this is always a very busy time so get here early). A very nice place, particularly during the day when you can relax with the papers. Close to The Locker Room Sauna. **Open** Monday-Saturday 1200-0100. Sunday 1200-0000 **Tube** Kennington/Oval

On the corner of Giltspur Street a fat cherub marks Pie Corner, where the Great Fire of London was extinguished. The golden statue is said to represent gluttony, manifested in the City's greed and wickedness at a time when the Great Plague of 1665 had killed almost a third of London's population.

The Coleherne 261 Old Brompton Road, Earl's Court, London SW5 9JA
Phone 020 7244 5951
This bar has a reputation for being a leather, clone bar but, in actual fact, those days have long gone, although leather – whether jackets, cockrings or chaps – is certainly in evidence. In essence, it's a cruisy macho lads' bar! There is no cabaret, karaoke or bingo to entertain and that's the way the local lads prefer it. The music – courtesy of the CD player or various visiting DJs – tends to be quite hard and gets progressively louder throughout the day. A recent re-fit included the suspended installation of 'Muscle Mary' and industrial viewing and cruising galleries which offer scope for an opportunistic passing encounter! **Open**

Monday-Saturday 1200-2300. Sunday 1200-2230 **Tube** Earl's Court

Comptons of Soho

53 Old Compton Street, Soho, London W1V
Phone 020 7479 7961 E-mail comptons@comptons-of-soho.com
Web www.comptons-of-soho.com

A bar that's popular with everyone and is usually a first stop for visitors and tourists to 'The Famous Gay Street' (just so that they can say 'I've been there'). It's always very busy. There's state-of-the-art sound and lighting systems, a DJ most nights and it's very cruisy. The music policy is on the heavier side of techno and helps to create a fun, party atmosphere. Saturday nights and Sunday afternoons tend to be very busy (considering the sheer volume of talent that passes through this street though, this is definitely not a problem!). The free gay press and flyers that offer discounted door charges into most of the major clubs can be picked up from here. Well laid out – the venue that is, not the punters – the top room is a little bit more intimate, with small tables and chairs, and is generally quieter than the ground floor. You'll find Q-Jump tickets for Crash and G-A-Y available at the bar. **Open** Monday-Saturday 1200-2300. Sunday 1200-2230 **Tube** Piccadilly / Leicester Square

The Coronet

119 The Grove, Stratford, London E15 1EN Phone 020 8522 0811

A popular gay bar that has been refurbished recently to expand the disco and stage area. There's something going on here to keep the punters entertained most evenings and it usually takes the form of some sort of quiz. Tuesday is 'Drink Like a Millionaire' with not increasing cash prizes but increasing drink prizes there for the taking (prizes range from a pint to a one-minute bar grab!). Wednesdays and Thursdays are music quizzes and disco, and Fridays and Saturdays see two cabaret shows at 2200 and 2330 interspersed with, and followed by, a disco. Sundays are for karaoke and disco and also feature regular appearances from ex boy-band member Michael Morrison (to be appearing autumn 2001 on the BBC's Star for a Night programme). Over the weekend, the upstairs chill-out bar is open and offers a welcome space to relax those old weary bones. **Open** Sunday-Thursday 1730-0000. Friday-Saturday 1730-0300 **Price** £2 after 2230, Friday and Saturday **Tube** Stratford

Drill Hall

16 Chenies Street, London WC1E 7EX Phone 020 7637 8270

The Drill Hall is an arts organisation with a national and international reputation for innovative and high quality theatre work. The bar here is normally only open at the time of a show or performance, but Monday evenings prove the exception when the women flock to this part of town for a regular weekly get-together. If you are in need of something a bit more nutritional than fermented barley and hops then pop along next door to The Greenhouse restaurant, where you will find a good selection of vegetarian food at reasonable prices. **Open** Monday 1730-2300. **Tube** Goodge Street

Due South

35 Stoke Newington High Street, London N16 8DR Phone 020 7249 7543

A bar predominantly for women (exclusively so, each and every Thursday) but also welcoming men. Being in the north of London it attracts a local crowd of different sorts: from the professional lone woman reading papers and drinking wine at the bar to the crowd of up-for-it girls knocking back the tequila slammers and getting ready for a night on the tiles! You'll see boys too – and few that look like they have just crawled out of the sewer. Presiding over this mêlée is the infamous Y'landa – club promoter of various events taking place in London at one time or another throughout the year. Her bar is fast-becoming an institution on the dyke scene where all who enter that dark blue façade know a friendly welcome and an attitude-free space awaits. The front bar consists of a pool table, ample seating and a bar similar to the one in TV's Cheers, where all the gossiping and giggling takes place. The back room is a bright, modern space and is well utilised for private parties and provides an overspill for those who require a bit of privacy. Sunday is packed as clever clogs do duel in the lighthearted quiz. Go there! **Open** Monday-Friday 1700-0000. Saturday-Sunday 1200-0000 **Tube** Rectory Road Mainline

3

The Duke of Wellington
119 Balls Pond Road, London N1 4BL Phone 020 7503 9672
A cosy, intimate and friendly venue with a mixed gay and lesbian crowd of all ages and types. The Duke is one large room with a central bar. There is also an additional games room with a pool table. Karaoke takes place on Friday, and quiz and bingo during the week. After quite a long period of being run down, with no money whatsoever to spend on refurbishment, the old proprietors have left and a new management team have moved in with promises to reverse this downward trend. It won't be an easy task and I wish them well. **Open** Monday-Saturday 1200-2300. Sunday 1200-2230 **Tube** Highbury and Islington

Dukes of Vauxhall
349 Kennington Lane, Vauxhall, London SE11 Phone 020 7793 0903
A popular men-only bar/club venue which caters for a cross-section of the community with bears/cubs and their admirers featuring quite strongly. There's usually something to keep you entertained on most nights, such as Lines and Bears on Tuesday (nothing narcotics-related, it's just line dancing). On Thursday, it's Karaoke with Jackie which is very busy and popular and includes seasons of 'Search For a Star' competitions. Friday and Saturday see cabaret and/or strippers take to the stage. Dukes is also the regular meeting place for Chunkies (big men and their admirers) and Bear Hug and more details regarding these groups can be gained by phoning the venue. **Open** Monday-Tuesday 2000-0100. Wednesday-Saturday 2100-0200. Sunday 1500-2230 **Price** £2-3 **Tube** Vauxhall

The Edge
11 Soho Square, Soho, London W1V 5DB Phone 020 7439 1313
E-mail info@edgesoho.com Web www.edgesoho.com
What was once a redundant bank is now a comfortable and friendly café-bar in Soho Square, with seating that spills out onto the pavements when the weather permits. This makes spending a Sunday, or any other afternoon or evening for that matter, a pure joy. With four floors of bars and a friendly, young clientele The Edge should be a regular drinking den on anyone's list. The top floors are available for private hire (more

information can be gained by visiting the website or calling the venue). Weekends tend to be packed, especially when the weather is dry and the street becomes the focal point of the area (so much so that actually getting a drink at the bar becomes near-impossible). Flyers and ads for entry to most of the major events in London can be obtained from the information point at the bottom of the stairs. **Open** Monday-Saturday 1200-0100. Sunday 1200-2230 **Tube** Tottenham Court Road

Escape

10a Brewer Street, London W1R Phone 020 7734 2626
E-mail info@kudos-bar.co.uk Web www.kudos-bar.co.uk/escapesoho
Escape attracts a young, energetic crowd of mainly gay men. It is open daily from 1600 to 0300, on Monday to Saturday and from 1200 to 2230, on Sunday. Busy from the early evening, it attracts an after-work crowd who, rather than go home first, meet friends in the West End for a drink. Later the crowd changes into those who are out for a night on the town and then the atmosphere really hots up! Something really special gets placed on the entertainment menu every night of the week. Thursday, as in all Kudos Group venues, is the Crush Bar where, when the featured artist appears on the video screens, it's a drunktastic two-for-one on all drinks. Saturday is the pre-Trade party night with an admission charge of £2 after 2230. You can purchase Q-Jump tickets at the bar. Alternatively, you might be one of the lucky people to receive a freebie ticket, courtesy of the handouts of the Trade Cops who tend to make an appearance at some point throughout the evening. (I, incidentally, being the cynical bitch that I am, tend to think that only friends of the Trade Cops get the tickets – so don't hold your breath.) Sunday is one for the girls: Girl Bar, 1700 to 2300. This is a good night for girls who are looking for a change of scenery (and pussy) that is different from the usual girly haunts. The Escape is nearly always busy, sitting as it does in the very heart of Soho and just a minute's mince away from 'Queen's Street'. A good bar crawl venue. **Open** Monday-Saturday 1600-0300. Sunday 1200-2230 **Price** £2, after 2230 **Tube** Leicester Square

The Fort

131 Grange Road, Bermondsey London SE1 3AL Phone 020 7237 7742
An obviously very popular (and well-known) gay men-only venue. There's a dark, cruisy atmosphere with an interesting mix of all age groups and types, including many local guys and international visitors too. No attempt whatsoever is made to disguise the fact that this place is, quite plainly, an indoor cruising ground. There's simply the added bonus that it also serves alcohol. The other bonus is that it is a safe environment with a choice selection of men, including many straight-ish lads who like to sample the delights on offer. Underwear parties (Thursday) are always busy with the stipulation that footwear and underwear must be worn (the admission charge covers the clothes check). Phone the venue for further details about this event. Wednesday is Slave Training, a new night in association with Fettered Pleasures, where masters are required to deal with the queues of slaves! Friday is the relatively new Sportswear Night, which has a strict dress code of sportswear only – this can include shorts, rugby/soccer kit, trackies, jocks or nothing (no jeans). Saturday and Sunday nights are Boots-Only

nights. The venue is on the route of several main bus services. **Open** Monday-Friday 2000-2300. Saturday 1400-1900 and 2000-2300. Sunday 1400-2230 **Price** up to £3 **Tube** Elephant and Castle

The Freedom Café Bar

60-66 Wardour Street, Soho, London W1V 3HP Phone 020 7734 0071
When this place first opened it was a popular haunt for the most fashionable and gay of people. Nowadays it has settled down to become just another bar with an above-average, but still rather pricey, food and drink menu. Most of the trend-setting gays that contributed to the reputation of this venue have now migrated to the next big thing, leaving the straights to pick at the leftovers. There's a popular hetero-predominant DJ-led dance club in the basement, which opens on Tuesday through to Saturday from 2100 to 0300. The music played is better than good – hence the listing in this guide – and during the day the café-bar itself can still be a nice place to enjoy a cappuccino and read the papers. **Open** Monday 1100-2300. Tuesday-Saturday 1100-0300. Sunday 1100-0000. **Price** £3-5 **Tube** Piccadilly

Friendly Society

79 Wardour Street, Soho, London W1 Phone 020 7434 3805
A fashionable new bar to join Soho's gay village. Free membership is available at the venue and is required if you wish to take advantage of the late-night drinking. **Open** Monday-Saturday 1300-0100. Sunday 1300-2230 **Tube** Piccadilly

George and Dragon

2 Blackheath Hill, Greenwich, London SE10 Phone 020 8691 3764
This venue bills itself as Greenwich's premier cabaret bar, although I can think of at least a couple of alternatives that would prove this statement rather unfounded. There's some sort of entertainment going on most nights throughout the week, such as the usual karaoke on Monday, the piano bar on Tuesday or the stripper on Wednesday, and so on. The weekend sees the place come to life with a disco and cabaret party, and with no admission and late drinking on offer it may be worth your while popping in – but only if you are in the area. Whilst you are here you could perhaps nip off for a quick cruise around Greenwich Park on Shooters Hill Road, where you'll find a very active cottage (see cruising listing) with abundant cover. **Open** Sunday-Thursday 1700-0000. Friday-Saturday 1700-0200

The George Music Bar

114 Twickenham Road (corner of South Street), Isleworth, London TW7 7DJ Phone 020 8560 1456 E-mail GeorgeMBar@onmail.co.uk
The George is a busy, traditional and friendly gay bar located at the junction of South Street and the Twickenham Road, Isleworth. There's free and easy parking in the evenings in the car park in South Street opposite the pub. **Open** Monday-Friday 1700-2300. Saturday 1200-2300. Sunday 1200-2230

Gladstone Arms

64 Lant Street, London SE1 1QD Phone 020 7407 3962
The Gladstone Arms is a traditional gay venue that could be described as an alternative to the West End scene. A social and friendly place where the emphasis is on conversation rather than dancing. The well-

used free jukebox and the occasional quiz night provide the entertainment for the predominantly male clientele, although lunchtime also sees the local office workers popping in for a pint and a bite to eat. Easily accessible by tube, with Borough Station on the corner of Lant Street. **Open** Monday-Friday 1100-2300. Saturday 1200-2300. Sunday 1200-2230 **Tube** Borough

---

The city of London is often referred to as the 'Square Mile' – the original area of the walled town. In AD43 the Roman General, Aulus Plautius bridged the Thames and in effect founded the town. In just a few years it had become a great trading centre. Boudicca and her warriors destroyed it in AD60, but the town was soon rebuilt. It continued to be an important centre for the next 1,000 years. Following the Norman conquest in 1066, London became the capital of England.

---

3 | **The Glass Bar** | West Lodge, 190 Euston Road, London NW1 Phone 020 7387 6184

The longest-running, indeed, the only permanent women-only bar in London (men are not even accepted as guests). Now over four years old, with a membership list in excess of 15,000 which proves just how popular this place is. Actually finding the place can be quite a frustrating experience: there must be whole scores of lesbians wandering up and down Euston Road on the lookout for this bar. Why? Well, the bar is set within a grand Grade Two-listed building that is one of two gatehouse lodges on the Euston Station concourse. The huge 30-foot doors form the entrance and the sign requests that you knock loudly for admission. Once inside, you will find The Glass Bar comfortably laid out over two floors; the downstairs is the main bar and the upstairs houses the toilets and chill-out area (soft comfortable furnishings, etc.). The venue has a homely atmosphere, one akin to walking into your own living room (that's assuming you have a nice living room). There is partly disabled access, namely to the ground floor, and help is available to carry people to the toilets upstairs. If you have not been out on the scene before or if you have just left a long-term relationship and are looking to start your social life again, then Thursdays might serve as the ideal night to start. Singles Mingles is a friendly introduction night which gives you the opportunity to meet new people in a welcoming and safe environment. All the free gay press is available, along with pertinent lesbian literature. Such is the friendliness of this venue that you are welcome to phone beforehand if you are a little bit nervous about coming in alone and someone from the bar will meet you at Euston and walk in with you; this offer is also extended to those who cannot find the entrance! Another excellent night hosted here is the Jewish Lesbian Group evening, which takes place every first Wednesday of the month. There is also a monthly 'eating out group' which is really less about sampling cuisine and fine wine and more an excuse for stuffing your face and getting pissed. This monthly get-together takes place on the last Saturday of the month. Bear in mind that there is no admission after 2330 during the week and the closing hours depend on how busy the venue is – it could stay open 'til 0500 if you are partying hard enough. **Open** Monday-Friday 1700-late. Saturday 1800-late **Price** £1-2 **Tube** Euston

| **Halfway to Heaven** | 7 Duncannon Street, London WC2 4JF Phone 020 7321 2791 |

Halfway to Heaven

7 Duncannon Street, London WC2 4JF Phone 020 7321 2791

Traditional pub, good beer, friendly crowd and an OK place to meet up with friends prior to an evening of sex and debauchery. There are also regular late-night charity evenings. **Open** Monday-Saturday 1200-2300. Sunday 1200-2230 **Tube** Charing Cross

The Havelock Arms

113 Albion Drive, London Fields, Hackney, London E8 4LT Phone 020 7241 2118

Newly re-opened as a gay boozer although this is about as far as you can get from a stereotypical gay bar – no camp singing (yet), no karaoke, and no drag cabaret. This is a drinking man's pub and it shows in the clientele that hog the bar stools. Rough (straight?) East End barrow boys chat to old and peculiar pensioners swigging down pints of Old Peculiar! This is the sister bar to Route 73 @ The Londesborough (see separate listing). **Open** Monday-Saturday 1500-2300. Sunday 1200-2230

Jack Cohen was the founder of the Tesco Supermarket chain. Jack was born in Whitechapel, the son of a Polish Jewish tailor. Shortly after the first world war, he set up a market stall in Well Street Market, Hackney, selling re-labelled tins of rejected and salvaged produce at rock-bottom prices. When he needed a name for a bulk consignment of unmarked tea he famously combined the tea supplier's initials 'TES' with the first part of his surname 'CO'. The brand name 'Tesco' was established. Over recent years the brand has reinvented itself and become Britain's most successful supermarket chain and biggest retail employer.

Jacomo's

88 Cowcross Street, Farringdon, London EC1 Phone 020 7553 7641

Jacomo's is a mixed gay and lesbian venue, formerly the home of the Her/She bar, one of the first women-only venues in London, which has now sadly finished. The venue is a bright, modern space with wooden floors and minimalist décor. The room itself is divided with sofas and comfy chairs in addition to the traditional small bar-tables and chairs. The clientele during the day is a mix of locals and suits from the nearby offices. The evenings, however, seem to cater for a younger, more trendy crowd. Entertainment comes courtesy of the CD stacker and occasional DJ-hosted party nights. Unfortunately, this venue is closed over the weekend and is usually hired out for private parties. **Open** Monday-Friday 1200-2300 **Tube** Farringdon

The Joiners Arms

116-118 Hackney Road, London E2 7QL Phone 020 7739 9854

The Joiners is a large, friendly traditional bar, open to all, irrespective of gender, and is a place with a lively and fun atmosphere. There is a good mix of all ages, although the weekends, as you would expect, see a predominantly 18 to 30-something crowd. **Open** Monday-Saturday 1800-0200. Sunday 1100-2230 **Tube** Old Street

Jonathan's

1st Floor, 16 Irving Street, Leicester Square, London WC2 Phone 020 7930 4770

Jonathan's is a small, members-only West End drinking club that is over 50 years old and is popular with locals, visitors and celebrities. The photographs on the wall show that the club has been (and still is) frequented by many gay media icons over the course of its history, from Francis Bacon to Lily Savage. Situated in the heart of the West End, the atmosphere could be likened to a gay version of TV's Cheers! – a place where people actually go just to talk to each other. It is intimate, friendly and relaxed, with light background music and subdued (not dark) lighting. Situated on the first floor, Jonathan's is not really suited to the disco bunny, it's much more for that intimate, discreet rendezvous with a certain gentleman friend.... **Open** Monday-Saturday 1700-2300. Sunday 1700-2230 **Tube** Leicester Square

The Jubilee Tavern
79 York Road, Waterloo, London SE1 Phone 020 7928 7596
Extremely gay-friendly, cosy and traditional bar that hosts regular disco and cabaret events. **Open** Monday-Saturday 1100-2300. Sunday 1100-2230 **Tube** Waterloo

Kazbar
50 Clapham High Street, London SW4 Phone 020 7622 0070
E-mail kazbar@kudos-bar.co.uk Web www.kudos-bar.co.uk
It seems that at The Kazbar (another Kudos venue) the running event throughout the week is cheap drinks – Monday is cheap drinks, Tuesday is selected two-for-ones on beers and alcopops, Wednesday is cheap lager and so the list goes on, right through the week. On Saturdays they sell tickets for Crash and Queer nation. Sunday is anything but a day of rest; it actually sees the bar at its busiest from early afternoon right through 'til closing, because they have a happy hour that lasts all day. **Open** Monday-Friday 1600-0000. Saturday 1200-0000. Sunday 1200-2330 **Tube** Clapham North

King Edward VI
25 Bromfield Street, Islington, London N1 0PZ Phone 020 7704 0745
Those are Roman numerals you fool: the King Edward VI (sixth, not vee-one) is one of North London's oldest gay bars. The Edward hosts regular charity weekends in aid of worthy organisations; these are always well attended and there's always top-of-the-range raffle prizes up for grabs. Each year over the spring bank holiday, along with other gay venues, they take part in the annual Pink Angels weekend. This is a massive HIV/AIDS charitable event, so keep an eye on the gay press or enquire at the venue for details. During the summer months, the secluded beer garden opens up, offering you the opportunity to drink and dine alfresco. This place is also popular for its value-for-money Sunday lunches. **Open** Monday-Saturday 1200-0000. Sunday 1200-2230 **Tube** Angel Islington

King William IV
77 High Street, Hampstead, London NW3 1RE Phone 020 7435 5747
An old-fashioned bar that's near to Hampstead Heath. Olde-worlde-stylee with a quiz night onWednesday at 2130. That's as much as you need to know, and to be perfectly frank that's probably about as much as you'll get. **Open** Monday-Saturday 1200-2300. Sunday 1200-2230. **Tube** Hampstead

Kings Arms 23 Poland Street, London W1V 3DD Phone 020 7734 5907
Conveniently situated close to the shops at Oxford Circus, this traditional, and very busy, English pub offers a pleasant atmosphere with
equally pleasant bar staff. Located several streets away from the Soho
scene, it still appeals to the after-work crowd though they mix fine with
the bears and clones that populate the place on most nights of the week.
Various weekly and monthly meetings have a healthy patronage, such as
Bear Hug (for big men and their admirers) who use the upstairs bar on a
Wednesday and Friday evenings (interested parties can find out more by
popping upstairs and speaking to the organiser). Lovers of real ale and
pipe smokers make the KA their London home. It is also the regular
meeting place for members and friends of The Long Yang Club each
Saturday (for more details visit the Long Yang website at
www.longyangclub.org/london where you will find complete and up-to-
date details). The KA can be pretty cruisy at times, although it is more
of a social venue than a fully-fledged cruise bar. The age range is mixed
and the clientele is predominantly male. Most importantly though the
atmosphere is friendly – very friendly. You'll also be able to pick up the
whole range of gay press, maps and flyers. **Open** Monday-Saturday
1100-2300. Sunday 1200-2230 **Tube** Oxford Circus

Krystal's 97 Stoke Newington Road, London N16 Phone 020 7254 1967
A local's fun bar with something going on more or less every night. On
Sundays, the place gets particularly busy as Miss Demeanour hosts
karaoke with a difference – not only do you get to sing, but you can join
in her hilarious games such as Scavenger Hunt, Erotic Balloon Dancing
and the much-loved Helga and Irene interpretive dancing game. **Open**
Monday-Friday 1600-2300. Saturday 1100-2300. Sunday 1100-2230 **Tube**
Old Street (but then a further ten minute bus ride)

Ku Bar 75 Charing Cross Road, London WC2H 0NE Phone 020 7437 4303
E-mail enquiries@ku-bar.co.uk Web www.ku-bar.co.uk
A large, trendy bar over two levels, catering mainly for young gay men
and women and their friends. This friendly establishment has candlelit
tables upstairs and jukebox entertainment on the lower floor. The clientele tends to be a mix of suits and trendy guys and girls preparing to take
to the town. Unfortunately, there is no draught beer or lager, only the
bottled stuff which tends to be a little bit more expensive, but hey, who
cares? We're on the pull. Situated next door to 79 CXR, this venue
makes for an ideal meeting place during the day (outdoors is nice, with
tables that spill out of the bar and onto the pavement) or evening.
Cocktail happy hours are everyday from 1200 to 1900. **Open** Monday-
Saturday 1200-2300. Sunday 1300-2230 **Tube** Leicester Square

Kudos Café Bar 10 Adelaide Street, London WC2N 4HZ Phone 020 7379 4573
E-mail kudos@kudos-bar.co.uk Web www.kudos-bar.co.uk
If it's Popcorn at Heaven then it's Butterkissed at Kudos – this is the pre-
Heaven meeting place for Mondays and other days throughout the
week. Tuesday's Velcro is a joint venture with sister bar The Escape in
Soho. This retro party begins in Kudos and ends up at The Escape 'til

0300 – you can pick up a free admission flyer to Escape from Kudos. Wednesday is again a pre-Heaven warm-up: Fruit Machine at Heaven – Tutti Fruttti at Kudos. Thursday is the infamous Crush Bar, and here, as with all Kudos venues, whenever the featured artist appears on screen all drinks are two-for-one. As for Saturday, it's Heaven at Heaven which means that pre-Heaven shenaningans start here yet again with Pure Heaven at Kudos – meet up and be sure to buy those Q-Jump tickets for later from the lower bar. **Open** Monday-Saturday 1100-2300. Sunday 1100-2230 **Tube** Charing Cross

The Little Apple 98 Kennington Lane, London SE11 Phone 020 7735 2039
Mixed gay traditional bar which attracts a large percentage of women. Every Wednesday sees the well-established and very popular Killer Pool competition with free buffet (£2 stake – cash prize). This is very much a drinker's bar and due to the friendliness of this place it is probably a good place for our girls to go out to kick-start a flagging social life. Food is served Saturday and Sunday. **Open** Monday-Saturday 1200-2300. Sunday 1200-2230 **Tube** Kennington

Manto Soho 30 Old Compton Street, Soho, London W1V 5PD Phone 020 7494 2756
E-mail enquiries@mantogroup.com Web www.mantogroup.com
After kick-starting the Manchester gay scene into what it is today (a-ha – so they're to blame are they?) the Manto concept was brought to the heart of the gay scene in London during 1999. Three floors of minimalist luxury, soft lighting and lavish leather seating make this venue a welcome retreat on any night of the week. On Saturday and Sunday, Manto has a special breakfast/brunch menu available all day: the ideal cure for the worst hangovers. Every evening from 2000, DJs take to the booth and feed you music that cannot be bettered in any bar across the country (a bold statement, but you can always try to prove me wrong). Thursdays sees Manto become the official pre-Atelier @ The End meeting place where the Atelier crew will be giving out free admission invites (only if your face fits, of course). You can also become a Manto member, free of charge, which will entitle you to a huge discount at Manto plus selected clothes shops, gyms, clubs and cinemas around London. The card will also give you discounts at Manto and Paradise Factory in Manchester. **Open** Monday-Friday 1100-2300. Saturday 0900-2300. Sunday 0900-2230 **Tube** Piccadilly / Tottenham Court Road

The New Angel Cabaret Bar 2 Markhouse Road, Walthamstow, London E17 Phone 020 8509 2177
E-mail info@newangelcabaret.com Web www.newangelcabaret.com
Sister venue to The Angel in Stratford that offers more of a clubby vibe as well as regular entertainment throughout the week that tends to attract the young guns. The Star Bar hosts the regular nights, including Angels on a Friday (a place for TVs/TSs/CDs plus their friends and admirers) and karaoke on a Monday amongst others. The Club Bar is the main dance area where you'll find regular top-notch cabaret acts. During the fine weather the beer garden opens up with a whole medley of burnt barbeque offerings to choose from (it needs the winter to set in before they get the hang of how the 'fire thingy' works). **Open** Monday-

Wednesday 1900-0000. Thursday-Saturday 1900-0100. Sunday 1900-2300 **Tube** Stockwell

The Oak Bar   79 Green Lanes, Islington, London N16 9BU Phone 020 7354 2791
E-mail info@oakbar.co.uk Web www.oakbar.co.uk
A large gay bar, formerly known as The Royal Oak in Islington, which is particularly popular with the ladies. Stylish furnishings, fantastic atmosphere, friendly helpful staff and an unpretentious air – phew! The weekends offer a staggering array of 'different' club nights. Saturday nights, for example, have four different events that rotate over the course of the month: the first Saturday is Tainted Love ('70s and '80s retro); the second Saturday is Saturday Night Beaver (oh pleeeease! that's almost as bad as Pussy Galore.); the third Saturday is Hoppa (courtesy of The Club Kali crew, featuring Greek, Turkish and Arabic sounds with dance entry admission setting you back £3-5); and the fourth Saturday is Liberty (a strictly women-only night). As for the rest of the week, the madness doesn't relent: Friday night is a good one to watch out for – Hoochy-Koochy – as it's women-only with men as guests night. Sunday is a long-running Karaoke Party night which brings with it the equally long-running tradition of the 50p tequila rush (whenever you hear 'that' tune). **Open** Monday-Thursday 1700-0000. Friday-Saturday 1700-0200. Sunday 1300-0000 **Price** £3-5, after 2200 **Tube** Manor House or Angel

The Olde Ship   17 Barnes Street, London E14 7NW Phone 020 7790 4082
A traditional East End pub: wood-panelled walls, comfy seating and a noticeable air of friendliness which makes you realise just how cold and unwelcoming some other gay places can be. Wednesday is jammed, when the popular Weakest Link takes to the floor (overseas visitors may not yet know about the God-awful Anne Robinson). Del Ria drags up as AR and comperes this piss-take quiz night. The clientele are local every-day lads and lasses; most are on first-name terms with each other and being real Eastenders they will more than likely extend this cordiality to you too. Sunday lunch and bar snacks are available at most times and there is also a separate games room with pool tables and games machines. A very nice change. **Open** Monday-Friday 1800-2300. Saturday 1900-2300. Sunday 1200-2230 **Tube** Limehouse DLR

The Penny   135 King Street, Hammersmith, London W6 9JG Phone 020 8600 0941
Farthing   A little pub that's busy in the evenings and at weekends. At the time of writing plans were being made to increase the opening hours and enter-tainment policy. Check the gay press for news of this. Sunday lunch is available at £4.99. **Open** Monday-Saturday 1200-2300. Sunday 1200-2230 **Tube** Hammersmith

The Pigeons   120 Romford Road, Stratford, London E15 4EH
Phone 020 8522 7101 E-mail stratford@hotmail.com
This used to be pretty much a straight venue, but over time it has become more and more gay. Friday and Saturday nights see this place packed as Club Bent takes over at 2100 straight through 'til 0200. On Friday the music tends to be more mainstream, charty and camp whereas on

Saturday it's a nice mix of UK garage and house. The Pigeons is a large local venue with loads going on in every corner: three pool tables, sport on large screen TVs, music videos on some 15-or-so monitors dotted throughout plus more gaming machines than Blackpool promenade. To gain cheaper admission at £3 over the weekends you'll need to cut or tear out the ad in the free gay press or pick up a flyer from the bar. And finally, you can get a good value-for-money roast Sunday lunch for the bargain price of £3.95. **Open** Monday-Thursday 1200-2300. Friday-Saturday 1200-0200. Sunday 1200-2230 **Price** £3-4, Friday-Saturday evening **Tube** Stratford

The Quebec
12 Old Quebec Street, Marble Arch, London W1H 7AF
Phone 020 7629 6159

Two floors of pure fun with a DJ-hosted disco in the basement every Thursday, Friday, and Saturday. On Sunday they host Chubbs and Chasers and, as the name suggests (ever so slightly!), it's for, but certainly not restricted to, big men and their admirers. The Quebec is a traditional venue with a cruisy lower disco bar that is a dark and intimate complement to the bright, spacious contemporary drinking den on the ground floor above. The clientele at the start of the week seem to come from the more mature end of the spectrum. Come the weekend, however, the age range plummets as a younger crowd bar-hops its way around the capital. The late-night opening hours during the latter part of the week, and the lack of any admission charges, mark this venue out as an OK place: good for surveying the local talent whilst passing through the area. **Open** Monday-Wednesday 1130-2300. Thursday 1130-0100. Friday-Saturday 1200-0200. Sunday 1200-2230 **Tube** Marble Arch

---

Saint Paul's Cathedral was built on the site of a Roman temple to the goddess Diana. This most impressive part of the London skyline was raised by Sir Christopher Wren in 1697, after the previous Norman cathedral had been destroyed in the Great Fire of London. Wren had submitted plans to demolish and rebuild that dangerous structure only six days before the blaze itself, but the commissioners had refused to have the old Norman building pulled down. The earlier Norman cathedral was even bigger than Saint Pauls and had the tallest church spire ever built.

The Queens Arms
63 Courthill Road, Lewisham, London SE13 Phone 020 8318 7305

This is south-east London's smart, up-market and friendly gay bar. Bar prices are amongst the lowest in the area with the addition of regular happy hours which means that the bar is nearly always busy, with a predominantly young crowd getting pissed for a lot less cash than their neighbours. The beer garden with barbeque opens up in the summer. **Open** Monday-Friday 1400-2300. Saturday 1200-2300. Sunday 1200-2230

The Queens Head
27 Tryon Street, Chelsea, London SW3 3LG Phone 020 7589 0262

A cosy and traditional single-floor venue with three bars. This was a gay bar before it was even legal (knock three times on the shutter and say 'I'm a friend of Quentin's'). Every month or so they organise a themed party, such as a beach party, when all the floor is covered in sand, sun loungers and pina coladas, or a garden party, where the floor is covered in turf, with more than the odd queen roaming around, cucumber sandwiches and so on (phone the venue for details of the next spectacular). Rather a mixed age range here, tipping slightly towards the more mature end of the scale perhaps, but the friendly atmosphere ensures that everyone gets along just fine. **Open** Monday-Saturday 1100-2300. Sunday 1100-2230 **Tube** Sloane Square (five minute walk)

The Ram Bar   39 Queens Head Street, Islington, London N1 8NQ Phone 020 7354 0576
The Ram Bar has been operating as a gay-only bar since 1992. The present owners have been here for five years and are gradually improving the décor and facilities. The bar's patrons are predominantly a gay male local crowd. It comprises a comfortable lounge bar that has an intimate, friendly atmosphere. In addition to this there is a second bar with darts and a pool table. Definitely not a bar for the disco dolly; much more of a traditional social drinking den. **Open** Tuesday-Sunday 1800-0000 **Tube** Angel Islington

Red Stiletto   108 Wandsworth Road, London SW8 Phone 020 7771 2165
Close to Sainsbury's on Wandsworth Road, this is a typical traditional drinker's bar, albeit one catering for our gay boys, girls and their gay-friendly straight friends. Entertainment consists of a pool table that is free on Monday and Friday. **Open** Monday-Thursday 1500-2300. Friday-Saturday 1200-2300. Sunday 1200-2230 **Tube** Vauxhall

The Retro Bar   2 George Court, Adelphi, London WC2 Phone 020 7321 2811
A young and friendly gay bar which plays the best music from the '70s and '80s, as well as loads of indie thrown in to please just about everybody. The most important night is Friday, when the Retro Bar becomes the official Pre-Popstarz piss-up bar. Cheap drinks ensure that the brilliant Popstarz night goes off with a bang (see separate listing for Popstarz). The Retro Bar is on two floors – the lower one is themed in a '70s/'80s style whereas the upper bar is more of an indie chill-out lounge. There's something going on every night of the week including retro karaoke on Wednesday, an amateur DIY DJ night on Thursday and board games on Sunday. Purchase your Popstarz Q-Jump tickets from here (it's cheaper than paying at the door). (See the listings for Wig-Out @ The Tube, Popstarz @ The Scala, Miss-Shapes @ The Liquid Lounge too.) **Open** Monday-Friday 1200-2300. Saturday 1700-2300. Sunday 1700-2230 **Tube** Charing Cross

The Roebuck &   25 Rennell Street, (off Lewisham High Street), London SE13 7HD
Voltz Nightclub   Phone 020 8852 1705
Situated close to The Lewisham Centre is this gay pub and club combination. There's late drinking every night and there's usually something off the cuff from the management to keep you entertained, such as quiz nights along the lines of Mr and Mrs, The Weakest Link and Blind Date. Warming up to the weekend things get even more musical with karaoke on a Thursday and disco over the weekend. Once Roebuck closes at 2300

Voltz Nightclub opens up and if you are not in the building by 2300 you will have to pay the nominal admission. The late weekend opening hours tend to attract some gay-friendly straights and in doing so it enhances rather than spoils the atmosphere. **Open** Monday-Thursday 1200-0200. Friday-Saturday 1200-0400. Sunday 1200-0000 **Price** £1-3, after 0230 **Tube** Lewisham DLR

Route 73 @ The Londesborough 36 Barbauld Road, Stoke Newington, London N16 0SS
Phone 020 7254 5865 E-mail sean@route73.co.uk Web www.route.co.uk
A very popular local cabaret bar in Stoke Newington with an abundant amount of goings-on throughout the week, from the bingo and quiz nights running at the beginning, to the disco and karaoke (every third Saturday) at the end. Sunday tends to get absolutely jammed when all the stops are pulled out with some of the best cabaret to be found on the circuit. This is the sister bar to The Havelock Arms in Hackney. **Open** Monday-Saturday 1100-0000. Sunday 1200-2230

The Royal Oak 73 Columbia Road, Bethnal Green, London E2 7RG Phone 020 7739 8204
A large old-fashioned pub with a lot of character(s) and history. It is the very pub that Goodnight Sweetheart (amongst others) was filmed in. The Sunday 0800 breakfast licence is that old it's probably carved in stone, and was granted for the famous flower market right outside the pub (providing ample opportunity to do your Eliza Dolittle and Mr 'iggins repertoire). Sunday mornings do see an influx of late-night clubbers popping in for a bite to eat and to chill out from their late night revelling. The Royal Oak also hosts popular once-a-month charity nights in aid of various worthy organisations and the party atmosphere ensures that the place is packed to the rafters to watch the drag acts (singers, cabaret, strippers and so on). A mixed gay bar with a majority that is certainly gay but that welcomes all. **Open** Monday-Thursday 1300-2300. Friday-Saturday 1300-late. Sunday 0800-late **Tube** Old Street (five minutes)

Five things you (do not) really need to know about The British Airways London Eye: (1) It weighs in at a hefty 1,900 tonnes. (2) It takes 30 minutes for the eye to complete one full revolution, at a speed of 0.26 miles per second. And it's not a ride – it's a flight! (3) On a clear day you can see for a distance of 25 miles. (4) The capsules were made in France, the bearings were made in Germany, the main structure was built in Holland (using British Steel) and the hub and spindle were made in The Czech Republic. The British? Well, we made the tea! (5) The Eye is said to represent 'the turning of time – celebrating London's past and looking forward to the future.' Oh pleeeze!

Royal Vauxhall Tavern 372 Kennington Lane, Vauxhall, London SE11 5QH Phone 020 7582 8212
This was one of Lily Savage's early hangouts (you can see where she gets it from now). A lively venue where there is strictly no attitude and every evening is rife with fun. Weekends tend to be packed to capacity, particularly on Saturday evening with Amy Lame's 'Duckie' (a different mad-as-a-hatter theme every week). Zest is a women-only night that comes

around every second Friday of the month, replete with women DJs and go-go dancers. This Saturday night institution may be moving later in the year to a new venue to accommodate the burgeoning crowds. Check the gay press for any changes. Note: This venue is under threat of closure by developers and there is no guarantee as to how long they will leave this national institution alone. Only time will tell. **Open** Monday 2100-0200. Friday-Saturday 2100-0300. Sunday 1200-0000. **Tube** Vauxhall

Rupert Street   50 Rupert Street / Archer Street, Soho, London W1V 7HR
Phone 020 7292 7141
Rupert Street is a large open-plan venue. It's very trendy and very 'now' – a description that extends to the clientele. It's a good place to bring someone who you are trying to impress, although you will soon be sussed when you go to pay the bar tab! **Open** Monday-Saturday 1200-2300. Sunday 1200-2230 **Tube** Piccadilly Circus

The Skinners   60 Camberwell New Road (entrance on Foxley Road), London SE5
Arms   Phone 020 8582 3397 E-mail info@skinnersarms.co.uk
Web www.skinnersarms.co.uk
Known – affectionately – as The Slappers Arms! A lively all-age crowd inhabits this friendly traditional bar and nightclub. Regular cabaret and personality DJs offer you a fun-filled night out with a list of weekly events that include karaoke on Wednesday and strippers on Thursday. Saturday is the night for TVs, TSs and cross-dressers of all persuasions, either all gowned up or not (£5 admission to this night). (See the listing for Bird of Pride in Croydon too.) **Open** Monday-Thursday 2100-0200. Friday-Saturday 2100-0300. Sunday 1900-0000 **Price** £2-5, Wednesday, Friday and Saturday **Tube** Oval (three-minute walk)

Southern Pride   82 Norwood High Street, West Norwood, London SE27
Phone 020 8761 5200 E-mail enquiries@southernpride.co.uk
Web www.southernpride.co.uk
A premier south London gay drinking den and hotspot! Loads of karaoke going on here (Tuesday, Thursday and Friday) and a rather special 'Kruz' night in the club space on Sunday. Monday is good news for the alkies amongst you since vodka is 75p all night and if that sounds good then the Friday night '123' is just as good: admission before 2300 is £1.23 and all drinks until 2300 cost an astonishing £1.23 (each, of course). After 2300 the admission escalates to £3-4 and drinks return to their normal prices. **Open** Monday-Tuesday 1900-0100. Wednesday-Thursday 1900-0200. Friday 1900-0300. Saturday 1800-0300. Sunday 1300-0000 **Price** £3-4, Friday and Saturday **Tube** West Norwood BR

The Stag   15 Bressenden Place, Victoria, London SW1E 5DD Phone 020 7828 7287
Close to the station and The Victoria Theatre this down-to-earth, friendly local bar tends to get busy with a mixed gay crowd. Office workers in suits rub shoulders with brickies and tradesmen. This is also the venue where the sports kit group, Sports and Shorts, meet every two to three months. **Open** Monday-Thursday 1200-0000. Friday 1200-0200. Saturday 1700-0200 **Price** £2-3, Friday-Saturday after 2230 **Tube** Victoria

Stonewall's   286 Lewisham High Street, London SE13 6JZ Phone 020 8690 5758

A cabaret and dance bar that opens seven nights a week featuring Slag-Tags on Friday, which is basically a no-attitude booze and cruise night. Saturday is Riot, a dance night which includes a complete mix of musical styles from house to chart. During the week they offer live jazz (Tuesday) cabaret (Wednesday) and a Weakest Link-type quiz night on Thursday. Stonewall's is a modern, trendy venue which caters for a mixed gay boy and girl clientele of all ages. **Open** Monday-Wednesday 1600-0000. Thursday 1600-0100. Friday 1600-0200. Saturday 1500-0200. Sunday 1500-0000 **Price** £4, Friday and Saturday after 2230 **Tube** Lewisham DLR

SW9   11 Dorrell Place, Brixton, London SW9 Phone 020 7738 3116

Mixed gay and straight stylish café-bar, used as a pre-club venue for the girls and boys of Brixton. **Open** Monday-Wednesday 0900-2300. Thursday-Saturday 0900-0100. Sunday 0900-2230

Ted's Place   305a North End Road, Fulham, London W14 Phone 020 7385 9359

Situated on the junction of Lillie Road, this predominantly men-only basement bar is extremely popular with TVs/TSs on Thursday evenings and with the rough trade during the week. The clientele are extremely diverse (not your average in-crowd) which adds to the flavour of your experience. Although the Seed nights (dedicated to rough-trade cruising) on Monday, Tuesday and Friday are strictly men-only, karaoke on Wednesday and TV/TS night onThursday see the doors open to all. **Open** Monday-Tuesday 1800-2300. Wednesday-Thursday 1900-2300. Friday-Saturday 1800-2300 **Tube** West Kensington

The Two Brewers   114 Clapham High Street, London SW4 7UJ Phone 020 7498 4971

After a recent million pound refurbishment a year or so ago, this well-known bar, close to the infamous Clapham Common, is now barely recognisable. It has been transformed into a modern and lively club without losing the appeal and charm of the old venue. The club bar is now similar to an industrial warehouse while the dance club has had a state-of-the-art sound and lighting system installed. The Two Brewers always had a reputation for putting out some of the best cabaret around and now it's quite possibly one of the premier gay cabaret bars in London. Weekends tend to be very busy as everyone tries to get in before the 2130 deadline to avoid paying an admission charge. If you arrive here later than that then expect to queue. There are no specialist evenings anymore although you will find a whole spectrum of the gay community in evidence. The friendly and welcoming atmosphere has been retained ensuring you an exceptional evening (particularly for newcomers to the scene). Remember Clapham Common is nearby if you do not pick up in here! **Open** Monday-Thursday 1600-0200. Friday-Saturday 1400-0300. Sunday 1400-0000. **Price** £2-4 **Tube** Clapham Common

The Union Tavern   11 Bunton Street, Woolwich, London SE18 6LS Phone 020 8855 2490

A friendly gay pub that opened only a year or so ago. Current entertainment is limited to the pool tables and drag acts that appear every

Saturday. The Union have applied for a late licence so the opening hours may well be extended and there's also a host of new entertainment planned throughout the week. **Open** Monday-Saturday 1200-2300. Sunday 1200-2230 **Tube** Woolwich Arsenal

The Vespa Lounge

The Conservatory, Centrepoint, St Giles High Street, London WC2H 8LN Phone 020 7836 8956 E-mail vespalounge@aol.com
A no-attitude lesbian lounge bar centrally located at Centrepoint Tower and serving a cross-section of the lesbian community. Loads of flyers, cheap tickets and info for the London visitor as well as something cool going on every night of the week. Tuesday is a particularly good night when the students gather and the place nearly overflows with cheap booze. Wednesday has more of a community vibe with a bisexual women's group meeting (1800-2100), but the pub is open to all after that. Friday and Saturday sees the Vespa Lounge go all dolly-disco with an atmosphere that induces you to drink loads and then go on to girly clubs. The last Sunday of the month is the women's stand-up comedy night, Laughing Cows. This is really popular and is always extremely busy. It is promoted from outside The Vespa and admission is around £6 (men are admitted as guests in the company of a female). **Open** Monday-Saturday 1800-2300. Sunday 1800-2230 **Price** £5-8 (monthly comedy nights only)

Village Soho

81 Wardour Street, Soho, London W1V 3TG Phone 020 7434 2124
A stylish and trendy establishment that was once the flagship of Soho's gay scene. But that was then. Now, it attracts the tea-time crowd of professional gents and as the evening goes on, the music gets louder and the crowd gets younger. Situated on the corner of Old Compton Street and Wardour Street with four bars on three levels, including a new, large Moroccan-style basement bar (albeit without the drugs). **Open** Monday-Saturday 1130-0100. Sunday 1130-2230 **Price** £2, after 2300, Friday and Saturday **Tube** Piccadilly

West 5

Popes Lane, South Ealing, London W5 4NB Phone 020 8579 3266
A very smart and large, exclusively gay venue situated around the corner from South Ealing Tube Station. It includes Streisand's Piano Bar (which hosts popular sing-along get-togethers for all ages and has the added bonus of an open mike). There is also the lounge bar which is comfortable, intimate and the place to go if you're after a bit of quiet. The Manhattan cabaret lounge, as its name suggests, is where all the week's activities take place; including the hugely popular disco which runs all through the week. There is also a pool and games room, which includes three pool tables, darts board and pinball machine. During the summer the garden (decking, walkways – secluded!) opens up to accommodate around 300 people, all anxious for a break from the madding crowds. The beginning of the week offers you a singles night (Tuesday) and quiz night (Wednesday) and both events are light-hearted and lots of fun. Sunday offers you lunch for just a fiver, and is very busy, so I'd recommend you get here early. West 5 may be slightly off the tourist track (15 minutes to the heart of London by tube) but, if you are in the area, this

is the place to be. **Open** Monday-Tuesday 1800-2300. Wednesday-Thursday 1800-0000. Friday-Saturday 1800-0100. Sunday 1300-2230 **Price** £2, after 2130 Friday-Saturday **Tube** South Ealing

West Central   29-30 Lisle Street, London WC2 Phone 020 7479 7981

West Central is a pub that occupies the ground and first-floor space of this building. Within, you will find bar dancing, drink promos, drunkeness and debauchery – the regular gay bar stuff. There is also a basement club which is open from Monday to Saturday and it's here where all the action goes on, though there is a door charge each and every night. Monday offers very cheap drinks with all the regular tipples priced around the £1 mark. The rest of the week is a pot-pourri of events including a sleazy pick-up night on Tuesday, which might not be to everyone's taste. One night more likely to be though, is the maddest party night in residency here: Shinky Shonky. It comes around every Friday and not only do you get free badges, JellyBelly jellybeans, mini-cheddars and mini-milks (yes, a sweet tooth definitely adds to the appeal), you also get fantastic ch-ch-ch-choons (great music) from DJs Boogaloo Stu and Newton and Ridley. Saturday carries the title theme Fairylea: a night that is not quite cheese. As for Sunday's Around The Old Camp Fire: it's just one big piss-up party. Also held here every alternate Thursday is Pink Bitch, a night of groovy garage and funky rhythm and blues which costs £2 to get in and starts at 2230 and runs until 0200 with door whores Mizz Cara and Liz sp'dick as your hosts. **Open** Monday-Thursday 1500-0200. Friday-Saturday 1500-0300. Sunday 1500-2230 **Price** £2-3, Monday-Wednesday. £4-5, Friday. £2-4, Saturday **Tube** Leicester Square

The White Hart   51-57 The Hale, Tottenham, London N17 9JZ Phone 020 8808 5049

A mixed gay and straight venue where entertainment is doled out in The Lee Paris Variety Bar. There's a quieter lounge downstairs with an adjoining pool room. DJ and cabaret from Friday tries to keep you entertained. **Open** Monday-Thursday 1200-0100. Friday-Saturday 1200-0200. Sunday 1200-0000 **Tube** Tottenham Hale

The White Swan / BJs   556 Commercial Road, London E14 7JD Phone 020 7780 9870

From the outside The White Swan looks a bit old-fashioned and sad and you could be forgiven for thinking that it's closed down (partly due to the fact that it doesn't open until 2100). Investigate further and venture through the door and you will find that The White Swan is a treasure chest of talent of all ages from all parts of the oh-so-sexy East End. The venue itself is split into two parts: a large sociable bar with plenty of seating and a larger cabaret room (BJs) with a well-used stage. Wednesday is strictly men-only (because it's the very popular amateur strip night) but at other times all are welcome, particularly on Sundays when the Joe Purvis' Tea Dance takes place. The White Swan is situated close to Sailors Sauna (572-574 Commercial Road – see separate listing), so in between pints you can pop in for a bit of... well, you know. **Open** Monday 2100-0100. Tuesday-Thursday 2100-0200. Friday-Saturday 2100-0300. Sunday 1730-0000 **Price** £3, weekends only **Tube** DLR/Limehouse

The Woolwich Infant 9 Plumstead Road, Woolwich, London SE18 7BZ Phone 020 8854 3712
Exclusively gay after 1900 (mixed prior to this), The Infant is a safe and friendly public house that provides for the needs of its clientele, whom the management prefer to call their friends. Although female-dominated (The Woolwich is run by two ladies) it does have its fair share of men vying for their turn on the much-used and abused pool table. No one is ever left on their own and all efforts are made to introduce new customers to the existing crowd, therefore making this venue a good local starting place for the newcomer to the gay scene. In the summer the garden is used to celebrate birthdays, blessings and anything else where there's an excuse for a good piss-up. Tuesdays see a relatively new night called Wigs. This is a night specifically for TVs, TSs, CDs and their friends and admirers. There is no need to come on the bus all dragged up though as there are plenty of changing room facilities and mirrors at the venue. The weekends from Friday onwards are boosted by regular cabaret acts and karaoke and despite the late-night opening hours there is no admission price on entry. **Open** Monday-Wednesday 1500-2300. Thursday-Saturday 1500-0200. Sunday 1500-0000

The Yard 57 Rupert Street, Soho, London W1V 7HN Phone 020 7437 2652
Recently relaunched and situated just one street away from its sister pub The Village. The Yard has bars on two floors with a balcony overlooking the courtyard, and when the sun shines the patio bar is filled with a stylish, professional and trendy crowd. Not the place for disco dollies, but a great place for hanging out, chilling and chatting. You'll find a large number of after-work suits reading the papers in the downstairs 'café' bar or relaxing in the comfortable top bar but keeping a discreet eye on who is entering the building. **Open** Monday-Saturday 1200-2300. Sunday 1200-2230 **Tube** Piccadilly Circus / Tottenham Court Roa

Clubs

Backstreet Wentworth Mews (off Burdett Road), London E3 Phone 020 8980 8557
E-mail info@thebackstreet.com Web www.thebackstreet.com
Backstreet is a very cruisy, men-only Tom of Finland kind of club and operates an ultra-strict dress code of leather and rubber. At least one item of rubber or leather must be worn (such as a jacket, jeans, shorts through to leather chaps and harness, one-piece rubber body suits, full motorcycle racing colours with boots and gauntlets or rubber jock and thigh-high waders!). A hanky does not count! The Backstreet has the most exacting rules in the world. It is a club for those who take pleasure in the ritual and eroticism of wearing leather and rubber. Expect to be refused entry if you do not wear appropriate clothes (denim and khaki will not get you through the door!). Changing facilities are available. Membership costs £7.50 per year and enables reduced price entry every evening. Members also receive the Backstreet newsletter and advance notification of special events and parties. Should you happen to be under 25 you are able to gain free admission at all times so long as you can supply positive proof of age. **Open** Thursday 2200-0230. Friday-Saturday 2200-0300. Sunday 2100-0100 **Price** £2-4 and members free on

Thursday **Tube** Mile End

The Block

28 Hancock Road, Bromley By Bow, London E3 3DA
Phone 0909 464 6804 (60p per min) E-mail info@the-block.co.uk
Web www.the-block.co.uk

The well-trodden roads of leather, rubber, skinhead, uniform and industrial all lead to the land of The Block. This is one of London's biggest and most established leather and fetish bars. This wonderful East End venue is constantly evolving to make sure that their members always have an interesting and safe space to cruise in. The Block is a members' club although guests will be admitted with discretion. Membership may be purchased at the club. International visitors to London should bring along their passport to gain membership. Entertainment starts on Wednesday with Underworld – a night promoted from outside The Block and hence membership does not apply. There is, however, a strict dress (or undress) code of underwear only. Underworld will cost you £3, but this includes a free bag check. Friday and Saturday admission is cheaper if you arrive before 2300 (guests will pay £1 more than members). A strict dress code of leather, rubber, skinhead, industrial and uniform applies – trainers are not acceptable under any circumstances. On the fourth Thursday of every month is Gummi's Hanky Code night which runs from 2100 to 0300 (see Central Station (Kings Cross) listing for Gummi details). Wear those colours with pride! If you want to stay in local accommodation that caters your needs then phone 020 8211 7829 (The Bear Den) for more information (you will have to mention this Gay Times Travel Guide). Finally, Pleasure in Streams (formally a night at Central Station) has recently restarted here as Streams of Pleasure, on the first Sunday of the month. The name says it all! **Open** Wednesday-Thursday 2200-0300. Friday-Saturday 2200—0600. Sunday 2200-0300 **Price** £3-4, Thursday and Sunday. £3-6, Friday-Saturday **Tube** Bromley By Bow

Club Artful

139 Southgate Road, Islington, London N1 Phone 020 7226 0841

One of the nicest things about this place – apart from the dead sexy blokes that come in here – is that you can wear (and do) what you like and no-one will give a toss, be it feathers, leathers, rubber, ballgowns or uniforms. It is an extremely busy, traditional, men-only cruise bar, although women are welcome in the front bar. The age range is like most other places: mixed, although it's predominantly a twenties and thirties crowd. The venue is well laid out over three floors. The ground floor has a main bar area with seating and a pool table and a back bar with camouflage nets and a dance floor – all dark and cruisy! Upstairs is the main cruise bar (well-known to all). Thursday is the popular Underwear Party (upstairs) which will cost you £1 for your clothes check. On Fridays and Saturdays there's a stripper flaunting himself which gives you a break from the week-in-and-out disco. Members receive a nominal discount on the doors over the weekend but it is not really necessary to become a member (£5 if you do – ask at the bar for details). Sunday sees the place open from lunchtime and it appears to be a favourite with some of the post-Trade boys – particularly those who danced the night away and had no time for any 'how's your father'! The rest of the week it's cruise, cruise and cruise. **Open** Monday-Wednesday 1800-0000. Thursday 1800-0100. Friday-Saturday 1800-0200. Sunday 1300-0100 **Price** £4-5, Friday and Saturday only **Tube** Highbury/Angel (though a good ten-minute walk away)

Crash

66 Albert Embankment, Goding Street, Vauxhall, London SE11 Phone 020 7820 1500 E-mail info@crashlondon.co.uk Web www.crashlondon.co.uk

Housed in a huge Vauxhall railway arch, 200 feet long and 30 feet high is Crash – the sexiest, raunchiest, sweatiest venue for 1,000 of London's hot-hot-hottest party boys. Saturday night's Crash is no less than a gay institution! With two rooms featuring the best underground house, four bars, go-go boys, two chill-out areas, projections and visuals, it has established itself as one of the biggest gay nights in the city to rival the success of Trade (which, incidentally, is the place to head for when Crash comes to a close at 0500). Above the raised main dance floor are two elevated sections, one overlooking the floor and the other shielded from the music to provide a necessary respite away from the music. The sea of well-defined muscle overflows from the dancefloor and cascades across every conceivable bit of floor space. High on the vibes and the energy you'll find yourself torn between cruising this wonderland of testosterone or dancing – you'll probably decide to do both. For the rest of the week the venue converts quite nicely into a smaller space, referred to as Crash 2. First and third Wednesday of the month is Red Hanky (see separate club night listing) and all other Wednesdays are Hanky Code nights, for sexy and dark men only with discounts to men displaying their coloured hankies. DJ Carlos keeps things ticking over. Thursday is Men's Room; a no dress code, no attitude, no holds barred, no nonsense cruise night with DJ Merran at the decks. On Fridays there are various club nights that rotate throughout the month (most of these are straight except for Feersum that takes place every last Friday. Feersum is a very big night of hard house that attracts a mixed crowd. To conclude, if G-A-Y is not your bag then Crash, in all certainty, will be. Trust me – I'm a right whore! **Open** Saturday 2230-0500. Wednesday-Thursday 2230-0300. Friday depending on production **Price** £8-10, Saturday. £4, Monday-Thursday **Tube** Vauxhall

David Warriors 'A' Bar

82 Great Suffolk Street, Borough, London SE1 0BE Phone 020 7928 3223 E-mail enquiries@theabar.co.uk Web www.theabar.co.uk

Situated off Southwark Street close to The Tate Modern, so you can have culture and cock on the same day! You will find the one and only, original David Warriors 'A' Bar. The 'A' stands for 'attitude' which lends its name to the underwear- or boots-only night that takes place here on Wednesday (2000-0100), Saturday (1400-2000) and Sunday (1400-2000). On Monday you are treated to Grope – a busy, busy cruise in the dark session. Tuesday is Bunkerboy for all you leather, rubber and uniform fetishists. Thursday sees something different from the norm when they host Players for those who love contact sports and athletic wear (strict dress code). Friday is the infamous Warriors night – a young, hard and up-for-it cruise session. Saturday, after Attitude, is another Warriors session. Sunday, again after Attitude, is Grope which is the same cruise session as Friday's Warriors night but under another name. In summary, the nightly names might change but the same cruisy atmosphere, fit bloke quota and 'attitude' always – and I mean always – prevails. A resounding ten-out-of-sleazy-ten! Tip: get in here early. Not only will the admission be lower (it rises after 2200) but you will also be able to get the most out of the night(!). **Open** Monday-Thursday 2000-0100. Friday 2000-late. Saturday 1400-late. Sunday 1400-0000 **Price** £3-5 **Tube** Southwark, Borough, Elephant and Castle

Heaven

Under The Arches, Villiers Street, Charing Cross, London WC2 6NG
Phone 020 7930 2020 E-mail info@heaven-london.com
Web www.heaven-london.com

Probably the most famous London gay club in the world, situated within the railway arches of Charing Cross station. Since its massive £3-million refurbishment in 1998 the venue has gone from strength to strength and from very busy to very, very busy – averaging over 7,000 customers a week! Q-Jump tickets for Saturday nights are available from The Box and Kudos, priced at around £8. You will also be able to pick up reduced admission flyers from here (alternatively you can rip the ad out of the free gay press – usually Boyz). Remember to pick up your flyer or ad first before buying your ticket. So – to the entertainments. The main event is Saturday. Saturday is – pure and simple – Heaven! It is the flagship night in Heaven's fleet of entertainments. A mish-mash of all musical styles distributed right throughout the club. The main floor plays the best in hi-nrg, commercial house, club classics, disco (aargghh) and Heaven favourites. Meanwhile the Star Bar plays the latest UK speed garage and underground vocal house (in my humble opinion, the best room on a Saturday). Saturday comes with a strict gay and lesbian door policy. If you do have trouble trying to convince the doorman that you really are a screaming poofter then just mention you saw their listing in this guide. And if you don't want to queue then get here very early or make sure you have your Q-Jumper ticket. This club though is much more than just one great night. Monday is Popcorn night and the emphasis is firmly on fun. If you are bored with heavy music (quite impossible me thinks) then get down to Heaven for a night where gays, strays, straights and girly girls make for the place where the dancefloor pumps to all your favourite disco and chart hits mixed with the trashiest '70s and '80s poptastic classics. As the night draws on the music gets a little harder with commercial house and dance thrown in. To keep the Monday party going with a swing there is a plethora of cheap drinks on offer. On to Wednesday and Fruit Machine, where three styles of music play in as many rooms. The main room is Fruit Machine proper, which offers you the very best house music around. If your bag is more garage, r'n'b or soul and swing then shift your arse up to The Star Bar. Alternatively, if you're after a little bit of camp then mince your way over to The Powder Room in The Departure Lounge and dance your tits off to Steps and other predictable sounds. It's another great night with plenty on offer. And so to Friday, and the night that kicks the weekend off proper: on this night you can shake your booty around the whole of this super club, in time to the best DJs ever, from the best clubs ever who rotate around one another all night long. It's dance music at its very best and is certainly one of the best Friday nights out in London. Note that on the nights I haven't mentioned, Heaven sometimes hires the venue out for a straight or mixed event (some of these midweek straight nights are excellent – if you are interested then phone for further details or keep an eye on the website). Heaven is a great place and will not disappoint. Try it! **Open** Monday and Wednesday 2230-0300. Friday 2230-0600. Saturday 2200-0500 **Price** £1-6, Monday and Wednesday. £5-12, Friday-Saturday **Tube** Charing Cross

The Hoist   **Railway Arch 47C, South Lambeth Road, Vauxhall Cross, London SW8 1RH** Phone 020 7735 9972
E-mail info@thehoist.co.uk Web www.thehoist.co.uk

The Hoist is an exclusively men-only club situated in an old railway arch with full air conditioning (the club that is, not the arch). Now, I say club although in reality it's more of an indoor cruising ground with beer, trancy music and a ready supply of willing cock thrown in for good measure. This place is dark and cruisy with a heavy, sexy, industrial feel that gives you a sense of heart-racing trepidation as you wander around and explore the myriad of darkened corners and cubicles. Splitting the two floors apart is a metal mezzanine level – and hoist! Every second Sunday of the month comes Whack, a CP night opening earlier than conventional Sunday hours dictate, from 1700 until 0000, with an admission of only £3. There is also Rubber Muscle which happens every last Saturday of the month and goes on late until 0400. Rubber Muscle nights carry a rather strict dress code (although the bottom line is no trainers). Leather, rubber, uniform, denim, skinhead and industrial gear and so on will get you in – Versace won't. Other events held here include SM Gays – an extra monthly social and a cruising ground for those who like it rough (every third Thursday from 2000 to 0000, costing £2.50-£3.50). Club membership is available for £25 per year and entitles you to free admission on a Sunday and free admission before 2300 on Friday and Saturday or £2.50 after. **Open** Friday-Saturday 2200-0300. Sunday 2100-0100 **Price** £3, Sunday; £5, Friday-Saturday **Tube** Vauxhall (exit 1)

The Spiral   **138 Shoreditch High Street, London E1 6JE** Phone 020 7613 1351
E-mail enquiries@spiral-london.com Web www.spiral-london.com

Just around the corner from Old Street is this shining jewel in the East End crown. It may be not be as large, or indeed as grand, as some other venues, but this, as you will find out, adds to its popularity. The Spiral is a local club with a huge, local, loyal following and you, as a stranger, will be invited into their family like a long lost friend! That's assuming you want to be of course! The club is divided into two levels. The upstairs has the bar and lounge area – a modern dark blue and metal meeting, drinking and chatting space. The downstairs is the font of all things clubby – a black and white den where enjoying yourself without poseurs and preening is all too easy. One of the best nights at The Spiral (for me anyway) is the Piano Bar with Ian Parker on a Sunday. Ian

Parker, as you may know, is a member of The Hollies and each week the bar scene metamorphoses into an East End-style (drunken) sing-along – à la Mary Poppins! Tip: if you are an East Ender that has not been out on the gay scene before – come here. You will not regret it! **Open** Wednesday-Thursday 2200-0200. Friday-Saturday 2200-0400. Sunday 2200-0300 **Price** £1-2, Wednesday-Thursday; £2.50-4, Friday-Saturday **Tube** Old Street

Substation South	Units 1-4, 9 Brighton Terrace, Brixton, London SW9 8DJ Phone 020 7737 2095

Cruisy, dark, dancey, fun – a sexy basement club which caters for a wide range of gay boys and girls. Substation South has now been going for seven years and still continues to bring you some well-hot and sleazy nights. Monday is the long-running and immensely popular men-only cock-fest which goes by the name of Y-front. Y-front has a dress code that stipulates underwear only. There's a free coat check included and changing facilities are provided. Tuesday is Sub FC, a new big night for horny sportswear lovers where London's finest get their tackle out. This is a men-only night with top DJs Martin Confusion and Rob C playing a sweaty and sexy mix of sounds that'll rock the terraces and get the kit room buzzing. There's a strict dress code – football and rugby kits to judo suits and jock-straps – and changing facilities are provided. You can get in free before midnight if you can manage to get your mitts on an advert or flyer, otherwise it's £3 to members and £4 to non-members. Wednesday is the men-only Bootcamp which also comes with a 'Sir, yes Sir' dress code – a uniform of leather, jocks and boots. The music is commercial house and disco. Thursday is Blackout which is a men-only night of dark, dirty and cruisy fun. Friday is Dirty Dishes which is a very busy mixed gay night of hard house. Saturday is Queer Nation, the legendary Patrick Lilley-hosted mixed gay night, where you'll hear a nice mix of US garage, nu-nrg and commercial house. Sunday is Marvellous. No really, it is. A night of indie, Brit-pop, new wave and punk music hosted by Joan Dairy Queen; a drunken, dirty party night which is very good fun and goes on right through 'til 0400 Monday morning. Work? Oh fuck it! **Open** Monday 2200-0230. Tuesday 2200-0200. Wednesday 2230-0300. Thursday 2230-0230. Friday2230-0500. Saturday 2230-0600. Sunday 2200-0400 **Price** £3-4, Sunday-Thursday. £5-6, Friday. £6-8, Saturday **Tube** Brixton

Club nights

Atelier @ The End	18 West Central Street, London WC1A 1JJ Phone 020 7419 9199 E-mail atelier@the-end.co.uk Web www.the-end.co.uk

Atelier is now well into its second year as a laid-back 'place to be seen'; a weekly foray into the upper echelons of gay clubbing. Featured DJs are Alan Thompson, Luigi Rosi, Femi B, Jeffery Hinton, Tom Stephan and Luke Hope who rotate around each other in the main room, plus Mark Bambach and Slamma in the Beatroute Soul Lounge. The concept behind Atelier is to provide an alternative forum, alternative to conventional bars that is, for people who work in the fashion, design, music, film and media industries to meet after work and utilise the facilities of a smart, modern London night club and enjoy groovy, laid-back house music from top DJs. Atelier is open from 2100 'til around 0400 every Thursday evening. The last guests will be admitted at midnight. Platters of delicious food prepared by AKA are available at Atelier until 2200. Food, drinks and cocktails are served in a lounge-style environment, with an accompaniment of groovy laid-back music. This relaxed space encourages conversation. As the evening progresses the music gets funkier, with more up-tempo sounds that create a slightly clubbier atmosphere. Every Thursday, Atelier's highly experienced production team transforms The End into a comfortable and stylish haven, with velvet drapes, leather sofas, catwalk shows projected onto giant screens and off-beat bespoke mannequins, fashioned and attired by Aroino, style guru and Artistic Director of Adel Rootstein. Do not expect to be admitted into the venue if you look decidedly 'naff'. Even if you do manage to blag your way in, the look of sheer horror on your face as you pay for your drinks will surely give you away. Pre-Atelier meet-ups are at Manto Soho so you can always try and pick up a 'regular' and walk in on their arm! **Open** Thursday 2100-0400 **Price** £5 **Tube** Tottenham Court Road

Benjy's 2000   562a Mile End Road, London E3 Phone 020 8980 6427
A long-running busy Sunday-night disco with occasional PAs and a youthful mix of lads. **Open** Sunday 2100-0100 **Price** £2 **Tube** Mile End

Club Kali   1 Dartmouth Park Hill, Tufnell Park, London N19 Phone 020 7272 8153
@ The Dome   E-mail clubkali@clubkali.co.uk Web www.clubkali.co.uk
Club Kali is the world's largest South Asian music-based lesbian and gay club (attracting regular crowds in excess of 600 people). DJs Ritu and Riz play a mix of Bhangra, Hindi film soundtracks and Arabic, mixed together with some Western tunes and seasoned with a touch of handbag. The atmosphere is totally attitude-free, friendly and electric; so much so that the popularity of Club Kali has enabled it to increase its stints to twice a month. Bear in mind that these two monthly events are always extremely busy, so early admission is advised unless you are willing to queue. Coach trips to Club Kali are organised from Leicester (Dover Castle), Coventry and Birmingham, details of which are available from the following PO box address below, or by phoning Sonny on 0116 254 1747 (c/o Leicester Gay Men's Health). If you are gay and Asian and wish to experience the phenomenon that is Club Kali then write to the PO Box number for further information and advice. Club Kali, PO Box 25628, London N17 6ZJ. **Open** First and third Friday 2200-0300 **Price** £4-6 **Tube** Tufnell Park

Coco Latte   143 Charing Cross Road, London WC2 Phone 020 7619 9198
@ The Velvet   E-mail info@cocolatte.net Web www.cocolatte.net
Rooms   The newly refurbished Velvet Rooms was formerly home to Sunday afternoon clubbing phenomenon Arvo. It is currently home to the much-celebrated Off The Hook on Mondays (r'n'b, hip-hop and garage from 2200 to 0300; free before 2300 and £4 after). It is also host to DJ Fabio's

Swerve on Wednesdays (drum 'n' bass) and DJs Carl Cox and Jim
Master's Ultimate Bass which blasts out hard house and techno every
Thursday. It is now the new home for the stylishly decadent, mixed gay
Coco Latte family after their moonlit flit from the swanky Chocolate
Bar in posh boys' Belgravia. Resident DJs Mark Bambach, Luigi Rosi
and Luke Hope are retained for business on the decks and they are still
spinning the funkiest and most uplifting house sounds in town. **Open**
Friday 2200-0300 **Price** £5-8 **Tube** Tottenham Court Road

DTPM @ Fabric   77a Charterhouse Street, London EC1 **Phone** 020 7439 9009
E-mail info@dtpm.net Web www.dtpm.net
DTPM is foremostly a gay club night. The emphasis, however, is on 'the
right attitude' and so it attracts a wide range of young, friendly people
(gay and straight) and in particular, people who are involved in the club
scene itself, including high profile DJs such as Danny Rampling, Pete
Wardman, Fat Tony and Boy George, with many other celebrities – too
numerous to mention. Almost the entire roster is filled with DJs who
have been DJing for at least five years; most of them can boast twice as
many years' experience. This, plus much more new talent that is coming
forward; DJs whom DTPM are encouraging and nurturing to become
tomorrow's greats (test tapes are welcomed). The club has never really
worked the way most clubs do; they do not rely on employing big name
DJs to pull in the crowds. They prefer instead to promote the night as a
whole, so the success of the night is not determined by which DJ is playing. That is not to say they do not employ top DJs. They do, but they
rarely advertise it: the DJs request to play at this club night 'for the pleasure of it' because they believe in the ethos and direction of its policy
and they like the credibility associated with the night. The music at
DTPM is uplifting but it has a deeper and harder edge: garage, deep
American house and hard house. Membership to DTPM is available for
£50 a year (renewals are £25). This may seem steep but you do get four
free tickets on your birthday and discounted entry each week. You also
get regular discounts off associated events: if you are a regular then it's
well worth the investment. Q-Jump tickets are available from The Edge,
The Box and Manto Soho. These will give you a reduction off the full
door price. All in all, DTPM is a 'unique' night in an equally unique
venue – Fabric is fast-becoming known as one of the best clubbing
venues in Europe. Their hard core of customers (known as the family)
are very loyal and return regularly to receive a warm welcome from the
staff and the promoters, who do take a genuine and personal interest in
the club. A 'family' has been created and this is a large contributing factor helping to sustain the success of DTPM. **Open** Sunday 2200-0500
Price £9-13 **Tube** Farringdon

Dysfunctional   23 Romilly Street, Soho, London W1 **Phone** 020 7737 5424
Dandy @ The   This affair is just so different, so Victorian, and so utterly, utterly camp!
Two Thirty Club   Imagine: Lady Fanshawe-Smythe-Warren throws a parlour cocktail
party and you are invited – get the idea? Your host – the chocolate lic-
quer-swilling – I mean sipping – Daniel Fitzgerald pays tribute to gay
artistes who have long since departed into immortality (or oblivion) –

the likes of dear, dear Noel or Quentin for example. This must surely be the true alternative to the homogenous commercial gay scene, where boy bands are banned, dance movements have not yet been accepted into polite society and the company is a diverse range of discerning socialites. So set sail my dear boys (and girls) on a musical voyage from the 1920s to the present day. Abandon yourself to the strains of Noel Coward, Billy Mackenzie, Sidney Lipton and his Grosvenor House Dance Orchestra, Goldfrapp, Xavier Cugat and his Waldorf Astoria Rhumba Romeos and Amanda Lear! Eclectic hey? This is what being British is all about – eccentricity at its finest. A most welcome change and a 100 per cent must for our civilised American visitors. Top hole! **Open** Every fortnight on Thursday 2000-0100 **Price** £3

Endorfiends @ Central Station (Kings Cross)　37 Wharfdale Road, Kings Cross, London N1 9SE
Phone 020 7278 3294 E-mail **endorfiends@ekno.com**
Endorfiends is a women-only afternoon session in the underground club at Central Station. Affiliated with SM Dykes, this is the UK's only 'women-only' play space. Do not expect a frenzied orgy – nor drink or drugs (both are unavailable) – it's more about interaction with one another and agreeing your own boundaries before acting out your scenarios – this can be anything from a massage to a whipping session on the cross. Pleasure and pain is very much the order of the day; and in view of this, various props and equipment are provided, along with ample supplies of gloves and lube. The atmosphere is sexual but it is still very laid-back and there is no pressure to take part. In fact, many women sit back and watch whilst talking to others. Dark basements may not be everyone's cup of tea but if you are open-minded, sexually liberated and into public displays of infliction – then Endorfiends will be right up your... street! **Open** Every fourth Sunday of every other month – August; October; December; etc.) 1300-1700　**Price** £3 **Tube** St Pancras

EVOL @ The Garage　20-22 Holloway Road, Highbury Corner, London N1
Phone 020 7607 1818
Does it stand for EVOLution or LOVE? Whichever way you look at it, rest assured that it plays the most underground and hardcore indie music that the alternative homo scene has to offer; brought to you by hosts and DJs Peter Knight, Mark Newman, Angela Martin and Farzana Fiaz. Keep an eye out for up-and-coming indie groups who will be doing their thing here at regular intervals. This event has taken over from the popular Club V @ The Garage. **Open** Every third Saturday 2200-late **Price** £4-5 **Tube** Highbury and Islington

Exilio Latino　Houghton Street (off Kingsway), Holborne, London WC2A 2AS
Phone 0956 983230 E-mail **gexilio@aol.com** Web **www.exilio.co.uk**
Exilio is London's sensational Saturday gay and lesbian Latin dance club with a regular attendance of 250 people. If you are after something completely different to do on a Saturday night this may well be it. Latinos are notoriously late for most things, so the place does not get busy until after 2300. If this is your first visit it may be a good idea to arrive early to get a feel for the place and the music. The promoters of

3

Take your pick of the...

liveliest

loudest

sexiest

biggest

smallest

trendiest

friendliest

bars in London

3

RUPERT STREET
50 Rupert Street W1
Tel: 020 7292 7141 [FCв]

COMPTONS OF SOHO
53 Old Compton Street W1
Tel: 020 7479 7961 [P]

BAR AQUDA
13-14 Maiden Lane Strand WC2
Tel: 020 7557 9891 [FCв]

HALFWAY TO HEAVEN
7 Duncannon Street WC2
Tel: 020 7321 2791 [FP]

THE RETRO BAR
2 George Court (off John Adam Street) WC2
Tel: 020 7321 2811 [P]

WEST CENTRAL
29-30 Lisle Street WC2
Tel: 020 7479 7981 [LFXP]

THE BLACK CAP
171 Camden High Street NW1
Tel: 020 7428 2721 [LFCаXP]

THE CHAMPION
1 Wellington Terrace Bayswater Road W2
Tel: 020 7243 9531 [P]

THE COLEHERNE
261 Old Brompton Road Earls Court SW5
Tel: 020 7244 5951 [P]

THE GLOUCESTER
1 King William Walk Greenwich SE10
Tel: 020 8293 6131 [FCаP]

THE TWO BREWERS
114 Clapham High Street SW1
Tel: 020 7498 4971 [LCаXP]

GUIDE TO BAR FACILITIES: L-LATE NIGHT F-FOOD
B-BAR CB-CAFE-BAR P-PUB X-CLUB CA-CABARET

this night also used to run the hugely successful Juanchito Gay – a stricter dance night (in the musical sense) and a re-launch is planned for later on in the year. There are also plans for a Mr Gay Latino competition (phwoor!). Keep your eyes peeled to the gay press for details. **Open** Saturday 2200-0300 **Price** £6 **Tube** Temple (two-minute walk)

Factor 25 @ Hanover Grand

6 Hanover Street, Mayfair, London W1
Phone 020 7405 5475 E-mail factor25@lineone.net
Factor 25's weekly Saturday evening session (now more than three years young) continues to pack in a top quality (usually muscle) crowd at the swishy three-floored Hanover Grand (rather unknown on the gay scene as a clubbing venue at present). This is a prime time Saturday party that is the talk of the town and is perfect for your main Saturday night outing into the world of gay clubbing. There's highly acclaimed fresh, uplifting, house sounds served up by the rotating resident DJs, which, together with the fabulous interior of Hanover Grand, produces an end-of-the-week atmospheric concoction, unrivalled anywhere else on the scene. Large walls of top quality digital projections provide colour and movement throughout the dance areas. The toilets are a stroke of innovation – I'm funny that way! – with movie trailers playing whilst you pee (as if we need an excuse to keep us in the toilet!). But, beware of sharing your cubicle with anyone: you might find yourself outside in the cold if the security team spy it! (Well no-one told me!) The scene's own A-list are regularly 'scene' here, along with lots of other beauties that we don't even know! There's a social, friendly ambience within the balconied and staircased grandeur of this 850-capacity club. People are here to party, to chat and to show off a bit (or a lot). There are seating areas mixed in with the dance areas and the party goes on all around you – literally. The resident DJs – Chris McKoy, Rob Sykes, Stevie P, Guy Williams (Defected Records) and Paul Harris – all rotate around one another and there are also guest DJs from time to time. The music policy is 'Factor', which means cutting-edge house tunes, from funky to up-front. Factor 25 has built its reputation on its music over the last three years and its exclusive DJs that give it that special bit extra over the rest. The music is fantastic. There is no dress code, although most people look hot and make an effort. The venue is a lot closer to Soho (just off Regent Street) than the former Rock @ Victoria and makes it one of the most central gay club nights in London. (See the Factory @ The K Bar listing also.) **Open** Saturday 2230-0500 **Price** £5-8 **Tube** Embankment

Factory @ The K Bar

84-86 Wardour Street, London W1
Phone 020 7405 5475 E-mail factor25@lineone.net
This is the bar that Prince William allegedly frequented – then, an upmarket A-List wine bar; now, a superior, 500-capacity, predominantly straight, sociable bar and dance-space, with an alluring and fresh, graded blue interior. It's likely now that somewhere else has opened with an even more expensive admission and bar list – and so the trend-setters have moved, leaving us gays with sloppy seconds – albeit only one night per week. Trying to guess where the future King of England sat is a popular pastime and only the vulgar and ill-bred would go around seat

sniffing (isn't that right Martin?). Friday nights are promoted externally, all in the capable hands of Mike Bailey (Factor 25 @ Hanover Grand). This is a space where you can dance, chat or just lounge around looking glam on one of the multitude of sofas dotted around the place. Since its launch early last November, the club has been madly popular, as much with the girls as the boys, and has received first-class reviews and praise. DJs on rotation include Jeffrey Hinton, Chris McKoy, Rob Sykes, Stevie P, Guy Williams and various guests. A brand new sound system has just been installed and is currently being abused with everything from funky house to up-front and uplifting dance sounds as the night heats up. The night attracts a good-looking and friendly gay crowd, with a generous helping of girls, who party all the way on to 0400. There is no dress code, although most people do try and make an effort. Expect a highly charged atmosphere every week with plenty of willing totty for those in the mood! Tip: get here early – well before the official opening time – not only for the lower admission charges but also to avoid queues which build up from quite an early hour. **Open** Friday 2200-0400 (last admission 0300) **Price** £5-10 **Tube** Oxford Street / Piccadilly Circus

3

**Fiction
@ The Cross**

Bagley's Yard and Studios, Kings Cross Freight Depot, London N1
Phone 020 7439 9009
Fiction @ The Cross is brought to you by those very same polysexual people who bring you DTPM (see separate listing). Fiction is one of those rare clubs that lets the music do the talking – preferring to rely on their excellent resident DJs rather than so-called 'Big Name Stars'. This approach has allowed the residents to build up a good rapport with the regular crowds. The team of residents (all of whom are well established in their own right) are Malcolm Duffy, Miguel Pellitero, Justin Ballard, Laurent Roure, Harj, Fat Tony plus guests on rotation. Fiction is located at the beautifully refurbished The Cross off Goods Way at Kings Cross Freight Depot (next to Bagley's) This gorgeous venue boasts seven arches of debauchery, four bars, two lounges and a VIP lounge which is open to all (no elitism here) So, if you feel like being surrounded by a laid-back crowd with quality music in one of London's top venues then Fiction is for you. Remember to make an effort in the frock department! **Open** 2300- **Price** £8-12 **Tube** Kings Cross

**Fist @
The Imperial
Gardens**

299 Camberwell New Road, (entrance on Medlar Street),
Camberwell, London SE5 Phone 020 7252 6000
E-mail suzie@fist.co.uk Web www.ainexus.com/fist
Suzie Kreuger's Fist is London's premier 'alternative' night club for queers and dykes. Fist is unique, attracting clubbers from all over Europe – and beyond. Ever since the first Fist in February 1993 at The Chunnell Club in Vauxhall, EJ Doubell has been the resident DJ, selecting the finest, cutting-edge Euro techno, including sub-genres: uplifting, hard rave and trance. In June 1995, Fist opened at Substation South in Brixton. Here, DJ Karim joined EJ Doubell, and formed a dynamic DJuo. Two years later, Fist upped roots again and hit the road in search of new pastures. It discovered its present, best-ever location: The Imperial Gardens. And so, the legend continues: every second Saturday

of the month you'll find EJ Doubell and Karim dictating Fist's dance-floor antics with the best in spinning, thumping, cutting-edge, nose-bleed-inducing, underground techno. Fist attracts a large, fierce crowd, all decked out in the dress code essentials of rubber, leather or pervy gear. Suzie herself keeps a watchful eye on the door and ensures that the dress code is enforced! Once inside the club you will be treated to numerous delights, including a porn cinema, a cruising gallery, a large play room and... well, that's just for starters! Tip: this is a good place for any fetish novices to start. Put on your outfit and get on down. **Open** Every second Saturday of the month 2230-0600 **Price** £13 **Tube** Oval

G-A-Y @ The　　157-165 Charing Cross Road, London WC2 Phone 020 7434 9592
London Astoria　E-mail enquiries@G-A-Y.co.uk Web www.G-A-Y.co.uk
Saturday night is G-A-Y, which equals Good As You. This wins both Gay Times' and Boyz' 'Best Club Night Of The Year' on a regular basis. It is busy, busy, busy – not surprisingly, since it is one of only a couple of major club nights in Soho. The music can be pretty mainstream but the dance floor is always packed to breaking point with a sea of muscled young flesh washing all around (a sea in which I'm rather fond of drowning). There is plenty of seating up in the galleries – ideal for chill-ing out and scanning the talent. Saturday nights take place in the cav-ernous 2,000-capacity London Astoria, when a PA by some top artist or an up-and-coming boy band will take to the stage. Remember to grab yourself a copy of Boyz from any London gay venue where you'll find a regular G-A-Y advert with the latest information on who's on as well as a discount entry voucher. Visitors to London may find the club drink prices a little steeper than those they are used to, so it may be prudent to quaff a few drinks before entering. You can get hold of Q-Jump tickets from The London Astoria foyer on Friday evenings and Saturday after-noons between 1300 and 1700. You can also pick these up from Ku Bar, Rupert Street, Brief Encounter and Comptons of Soho (remember those vouchers). Friday night at the Astoria is Camp Attack – the ultimate party night and one which will prepare you for the big one on Saturday. G-A-Y is 100 per cent camp and retro and you can bet your last dollar it will always be full. (See the separate listing for G-A-Y's Pink Pounder @ The Mean Fiddler – formerly LA2.) For up-to-date information you can call the info line on 0906 1000 160 (calls cost 15p per minute). **Open** Friday 2300-0400. Saturday 2230-0500 **Price** £3-7, Friday. £5-£10, Saturday **Tube** Leicester Square

G-A-Y Pink　　　157-165 Charing Cross Road, London WC2 Phone 020 7734 6963
Pounder @ The　 E-mail enquiries@G-A-Y.co.uk Web www.G-A-Y.co.uk
Mean Fiddler　　 Mondays give you the opportunity to get over the weekend; Thursdays, the opportunity to get ready for it. The Pink Pounder is a long-running club night which operates on both these nights and enables you to get pissed for a relatively small outlay of money. The music played at these events ranges from cheesy pop and retro in the Camp Attack Bar to '90s classics on the main floor. The clientele you'll find in here is the same as the G-A-Y, London Astoria mob – young and spirited. Just as with the London Astoria night, remember to cut out your vouchers for discount-

ed entry from the current edition of Boyz. The Mean Fiddler used to be known as LA2 (London Astoria 2). The name has changed but the night is still the same. Tip: always ask the barman what the cheap drink offer is before you order. **Open** Monday and Thursday 2230-0400 **Price** £1, with voucher from Boyz **Tube** Tottenham Court Road

Gia
@ Shillibeers

Carpenters Mews (off) North Road, Islington, London N7 9EF
Phone 020 7607 0519
Gia – thoughtfully named after the late gay supermodel Gia Carangi – is a very well-attended monthly dine-and-dance club for women. Gia comes around every third Saturday of the month. You can dine at the ridiculously low price (for London) of £14 for a two-course meal with a glass of wine and then receive free admission to the club. Alternatively, you can skip the grub and go straight into the club for £3 before 2130 or for £6 after. Girls of all types and ages populate this up-market venue and the mainstream music seems to appeal to all of the clientele. Shillibeers can accommodate around 400 women, and the two balconies overlooking the dance floor give plenty of scope to cruise or be cruised. Do women do that? Of course they do! Booking a table is advised (to be eating at 2000). Men are admitted, but only in the company of a woman. **Open** Every third Saturday 2000-0200 **Price** £3-6 **Tube** Caledonian Road

Giant

Yet to be named London venue Phone 020 7820 1500
E-mail info@giant.uk.net Web www.giant.uk.net
If size matters then Giant is for you. On Bank Holiday Sundays, the big guns of the capital's gay scene come together for one huge party. The likes of Crash, Trade, Heaven, Hoist and Barcode are all here. The re-launch night in April 2001 at the 3,000-capacity Bagley's in Kings Cross suffered from a few 'teething problems' such as extensive queues for entry and the cloak. There were also problems with the door security staff who were not used to dealing with such large gay crowds and allegedly confiscated combination therapy medication. This, promises the organisers, will all be remedied for future events. The night subsequently moved to the SE1 club (Weston Street, London Bridge) but who knows where next? Tickets are usually grabbed up well in advance. Keep an eye on the press and the website too (limited though it is). The website does provide you with the essential details and also enables you to book your tickets. **Open** 1000 – 0800 **Price** £15-18

Gummi

BM 414, London WC1N 3XX
Gummi is the foremost rubber club for gay men in the world and is now in its seventh year. The club meets monthly at a central London venue (check the listing for Central Station, Kings Cross) and attracts around 2-300 guys to each event. There is a strict rubber dress code – at least one item of rubberwear in addition to any rubber boots or gloves. The one item of rubberwear can be anything from a full one-piece rubber suit with hood and mask to a rubber jock! Gummi has a membership running into hundreds of members, who not only receive reduced admission prices to events but also get a bi-monthly newsletter – The Rubber Sheet – discounts at many major rubber suppliers in the UK and abroad,

discounts with other gay venues, and news of Gummi members-only events. There's a member's monthly free raffle, with £100 and £50 prize vouchers to spend on rubber gear at Rob (see separate listing for Rob shop). There is usually food available, as well as the bar at the events, plus changing-room facilities and coat check. Don't be overwhelmed by the large numbers of gay men who attend Gummi events – the atmosphere is friendly and talkative and this helps make newcomers to the scene feel welcome. For details about Gummi events write to the postal address.

Juanchito Gay
@ The Phoenix

37 Cavendish Square, London W1 Phone 07931 374 391
E-mail juanchitogay@aol.com
Live la vida loca every other Friday. Salsa and pachanga to Ricky Martin amongst others. This queer Latin dance fest has been known to take long breaks so you'd be wise to check it's on before setting off. **Open** Every fortnight on Fridays 1030-0300 **Price** £5

LA3 @ 333 Club

333 Old Street, London EC1
Phone 07957 137 627 E-mail info@sortedpromotions.co.uk
Web www.sortedpromotions.co.uk
A Sunday night out for gay boys and girls at this normally (very) straight, three-storey bar. For those of you with long gay memories of yore you will remember that this was the site of the old stalwart The London Apprentice – hence the club-night name, LA3. However, long gone are the Muir caps, the leather chaps and the clone moustaches – in stay the cruisy atmosphere and the friendly vibe that was 'once' prevalent at The LA (note: there is no darkroom or associated 'activity' as this will get you thrown out on your arse). What makes this weekly club night work is that it caters for a 'type' that is normally hard done by in the clubbing sector. The type who do not need to pose, the type who do not scream when Steps come on the decks (indeed, Steps and disco are not on the playlist here, the music is rough and tough – wahaay!). In short, the type who remember the days when going out clubbing was not an effort and you weren't judged on how you dressed or acted: they come here for either the music, the boozing, the cruising or the socialising but most, come for it all. Remember to hunt out those flyers or adverts that will entitle you to discounted admission – these should be in most of the bars and the free gay press. Try this place out and give work a miss the following day. **Open** Sunday 2200-0400 **Price** £3-4, before 0000 and £5-6 after **Tube** Old Street

Lifted @ Rock

Hungerford House, Victoria Embankment, London WC2
The swishy venue of Rock has become the new home for this much-missed night since its launch at Leicester Square's superclub, Home. This is a night for those who just love to dress up, for the extroverts and the show-offs. T-shirt, slacks and a sensible pair of shoes will just not cut it! Remember to get here before 2300 unless you want to pay the extortionate amount of £12. **Open** Friday 2200-0400 **Price** £8-12

**Love Muscle
@ The Fridge**

1 Town Hall Parade, Brixton, London SW2 1RJ
Phone 020 7326 5100 E-mail info@fridge.co.uk Web www.fridge.co.uk
The Fridge is a converted cinema with a total capacity for about 1,100 people. With two floors and three bars it is without doubt one of the best clubbing venues in London, and it is regularly nominated as 'club of the year' across various publications, both gay and straight. Love Muscle has changed the face of gay clubbing since its launch in 1992 and keeps on going from strength to strength. This is a hugely popular monthly gay party, with a different theme every month that you'll see well advertised in the free gay press. The music policy ranges from happy house to commercial and from Euro trash to handbag. You can pick up advance tickets from the Fridge box office, Kudos, Clone Zone or Prowler Soho. Also, try out a relatively new gay night called E-male @ The Fridge Bar, each and every Tuesday. Log on at 2100 and keep connected until 0300 on this free admission night. **Open** Every fourth Saturday 2200-0600 **Price** £11-13

**Miss-Shapes
@ The Liquid
Lounge**

257 Pentonville Road, Kings Cross, London N1 Phone 0956 549 246
E-mail info@popstarz.co.uk Web www.popstarz.co.uk
Miss-Shapes – formerly known as Mis-Shapes(!) – is the long-running night brought to you by the Popstarz crew. It is about one thing and one thing only – having fun, dancing and getting pissed (OK, it's about three things, three things only, but you get the point). Have fun, dance and get pissed: that is the simple Miss-Shapes concept and it works. It attracts a large number of girls (hence the name change). Expect to hear a mix of pop, indie and retro '80s alternative tracks, all emanating from the decks of DJ Lush – as seen and heard in The Retro Bar. **Open** Saturday 1800-0300 **Price** £3-5 **Tube** Kings Cross

**Oi! Skinhead
@ The Fringe**

330 Kennington Lane, Vauxhall, London SW11 Phone 0161 273 2074 / 07956 808 142 E-mail info@oiclub.co.uk Web www.oiclub.co.uk
Still the night that the horniest lads in the UK and Europe gravitate to. This is the original Oi! night; the one that brought a breath of fresh air to the stale, hard gay scene and it is going to do it again. At Oi! they think it is sad that the skin scene has taken on the attributes of the old leather scene where organisers and punters are more concerned with what is being worn than what the guy looks like. They quite rightly feel that the 21st-century skins and crops look dead horny in contemporary street wear be it the trainers, trackies or sports tops that your average skin/crop gay guy likes to wear. (The '80s look of boots and braces does look rather horny on some guys but I feel it is my duty to remind people that it is a fashion now that is more than a quarter of a century out of date and a large number who still fly the flag look like overgrown boy scouts! Anyway, enough!) Future 2001 dates for this excellent event have been set for August 11th, September 8th, October 20th, November 17th and December 15th – however, it's best to phone first to confirm. (See the other listings for Oi! At Manchester, Liverpool and Birmingham.) **Open** monthly – phone for exact dates **Price** £8-10

3

One Nation Under A Groove @ Turnmills

63b Clerkenwell Road, Farringdon, London EC1 Phone 07931 424 905 E-mail patrick@queernation.org Web www.queernation.org

One Nation was previously a massive monthly Friday-nighter at the 333 Club in Old Street but it moved to Turnmills earlier this year in order to go weekly. An all-star DJ line-up takes residence here, including Richard Welch, Tallulah and Martin Confusion to name but three of a cast playing authentic house straight out of New York. **Open** Sunday 2200-0400 **Price** £8-10 **Tube** Farringdon

Paradise Sound @ The Sound Club

Leicester Square, London W1 Phone 020 7494 2756 (Manto Soho) E-mail enquiries@mantogroup.com Web www.mantogroup.com

Manchester's Paradise Factory has teamed up with gorgeous The Sound Club to bring you a midweek club night that goes by the name of Paradise Sound – catchy eh? In the main room you can expect to hear happy, funky house and loads of vocals, whereas in the Noise Bar the tempo steps down a couple of grooves and you are treated to smooth r'n'b, soul and some alternative mixes. It's an ideal night for the clubbing crowd who just can't wait 'til the weekend for their dance fix. This is one of the best midweek no-nonsense club nights around, although £8 after 2230 on a Wednesday seems a little dramatic (bearing in mind that drink prices at Sound aren't exactly cheap). My tip is to go to Manto – see if you can cadge a free ticket (quite possible) and have your fill of drinks there. If you have been unable to scam a ticket get down to Sound before 2230 and pay £6 rather than the £8 after 2230. **Open** Wednesday 2200-0300 **Price** £6-8 **Tube** Leicester Square

| **Popstarz** | 275 Pentonville Road, Kings Cross (by Thameslink), London N1 |
| **@ The Scala** | Phone 07956 549 246 E-mail simon@popstarz.co.uk |

Web **www.popstarz.co.uk**

A Friday night dance club that runs from 2200 right through 'til 0500 and admission is free before 2300 (which gets my vote right from the start). Popstarz is a massive (regularly 1,400 punters) long-running London institution hosted by that very nice man Simon Hobart. A young student-type crowd cram into every corner of this venue and it is nice to note that there is a good mix of gay girls to gay boys. There's various rooms to wander through and a great music policy: this is a night that you can't go far wrong with. The Common Room will bring you the best current and classic indie plus old skool alternative. The Rubbish Room plays exactly that (when will they let '70s, '80s and retro chart stay in the past to be forgotten about?). The Love Lounge has returned and in here you can listen to Motown, r'n'b, funk and disco and there is a new addition to Popstarz in the form of the Big Beat Bar (dance). Get reduced price Q-Jump tickets from The Retro Bar (see separate listing) which is also the official pre-Popstarz venue. (See Miss-Shapes@The Liquid Lounge and Wig-Out @ The Tube listings also). **Open** Friday 2200-0500 **Price** £5-8 after 2300 **Tube** The Angel

| **Progression** | 13 Coventry Street, Piccadilly Circus, London W1V 7FE |
| **@ CC Club** | Phone 07939 628 296 E-mail progressionclub@aol.com |

Web **www.cc-club.co.uk**

In the heart of Piccadilly Circus, at the edge of Rupert Street and Wardour Street, is London's newest and swishest music venue. Not a gay venue (but, you never know, it may soon be, once the straights start putting their fags out on the carpet) but a corporate one, which sees this place hired out for receptions, parties and club nights. One such night is the brainchild of club promoter and DJ Oliver M (Amnesia, Factor 25) who is putting on Progression, a mixed gay and straight night, and attempting to fill this 1,000-capacity venue every Sunday. The music policy will be US house and decadent disco (in separate rooms, of course), similar to the style played at The Twilo (New York City) – with DJs on rotation including Oliver M, Luigi Rosi, Jon Dennis, Mark Bambach, Jo Public, Brent Nicholls and Stewart Who? At the time of going to press this weekly night had not even started so it's yet to prove itself. There are now a multitude of Sunday afternoon clubs and it is inevitable that some of them will suffer, so I wish this venture well. Check the website and gay press for details. **Open** Sunday 1800-0000 **Price** £3-5 before 1900; £8 thereafter **Tube** Piccadilly Circus / Leicester Square

| **Red Hanky @** | Albert Embankment Arch 66, Goding Street, Vauxhall, London SE11 |
| **The Crash Bar** | Phone 0709 222 7992 E-mail chrisff@hotmail.com |

Web **www.londonreds.org**

A bi-monthly night for those of you who like f-f-fun. An ultra-strict door policy means that if the door whore is uncertain of your credentials you will have to be able to 'prove' you know what this night is all about (mention the listing from this guide). The dress code is not so strict – raunchy to kinky (which means jeans, leather, rubber, skin or uniform). You can gain reduced entry (of £3) if you are wearing a red hanky or if you are a member of London Reds (who meet upstairs at Bromptons every first Wednesday of the month – although this is not fully supported by all members). The Crash Bar is the more-than-suitable venue for this gathering of raunchy goings-on. If you don't understand the red hanky code you may not want to go here! **Open** Every first and third Wednesday 2200-0300 **Price** £3-4 **Tube** Vauxhall

Rumours

64-73 The Minories, London EC3N 1DD Phone 0961 158375
E-mail info@girl-rumours.co.uk Web www.girl-rumours.co.uk
Over 500 women regularly cram into this normally straight city club venue three times every month. This night has been established for more than two years now and it caters for a women-only crowd of all types and ages. The music, supplied by three DJs, is not too heavy or too commercial, just a really nice mix that seems to please the majority of the punters. Considering there are not many Saturday club nights in London for a women-only crowd, this really is a place worth visiting. I'd advise that you get here early though, well before 2100, as the queues are already starting to build up by then. Finally, if you are celebrating a birthday or anniversary or a similar special occasion then phone or write to Linda in advance and a few extra special arrangements can be made for your loved one – aahh! **Open** Every second, third and last Saturday 2000-0200 **Price** £6 **Tube** Tower Hill (five minutes)

Salvation @ Café de Paris

3 Coventry Street, Leicester Square, London WC2
A monthly club night that sees top-name DJs mixing the best in house and techno sounds in the chandeliered main room whilst in the exclusive VIP room the unmistakable Stewart Who? spins a lighter set of loungey, soulful and cool vibes whilst you sit back, relax and sip those incredibly expensive and decadent champagne cocktails. Pick up advance tickets from Kudos, Kazbar, Escape or Manto. **Open** Every first Sunday 1700-0000 **Price** £3-8 after 1800 **Tube** Leicester Square

Sewing Circle @ The Ritzy Cinema

Brixton Oval, Coldharbour Lane, Brixton, London SW2 1JG
Phone 020 7733 2229
A 'ladies lounge' in the upstairs bar of The Ritzy Cinema. An unusual setting for an unusual monthly women's get-together. The Ritzy Bar is over two floors (one floor is non-smoking) where women of a 20-30-year-old 'arty' set get together to do – well – anything and everything. It really defies description. Console games, knitting, films with clips by up-and-coming women directors and film-makers. This is a true social occasion and visiting alone might make it hard to integrate into what may appear to be something of a clique – try to come along with a friend. The music is supplied by various women DJs and they play all sorts from old skool to unobtrusive film scores. Food is available on the premises too. **Open** Every last Thursday 1930-late **Price** £2 **Tube** Brixton

Shoot! @ Central Station

37 Wharfdale Road, Kings Cross, London N1 9ST Phone 020 7278 3294
This is just so weird! If you like sportswear (I do) then this is like a dream come true. Trainers and trackies, (lots of West Ham) football

shirts and shorts – the whole lot is here and what's even better is that this long-running Sunday funday is very busy from the moment it opens with like-minded souls. The promoter of this fab event was the brain behind PIS (Pleasure In Streams), the controversial (yellow) event that came to an untimely end because of its own success. Doors open at 1800 'til midnight and admission is £5 at all times. **Open** Sunday 1800-0000 (except second Sunday of the month) **Price** £5 **Tube** Kings Cross

Sound on Sunday @ The Sound Club
The Swiss Centre, Leicester Square, London W1 Phone 0207 437 4303 E-mail info@soundonsunday.co.uk Web www.soundonsunday.co.uk SOS for short! This weekly club session runs from 1800 until 0000, dishing out chart pop and party sounds from hosts Steve 'B' (Heaven, LTD) and (The Very Miss) Dusty 'O' (LTD, Babe). If you're planning on turning up after 1900 without a flyer or promotional advert from the gay press then you can expect to pay £7. If this seems a little steep for a Sunday shindig then turn up before 1900 and it will cost you a measly £2 (so long as you remember to pick up a flyer or advert from any of the gay bars or papers). This generally encourages all and sundry to pack into the club early. This night has been running since 1995, although formerly as The Gay Tea Dance @ The Limelight. It then moved to The Sound Club in January 2001 and re-named itself Sound on Sunday. The Sound Club is a gay-owned and -managed trendy venue which offers you a café, stunning audio-visual technology, loads of bars (bear in mind that alcohol stops being served at 2230 on Sunday), a VIP area, over 100 TV monitors and three video walls. Also at this fantastic venue is the Paradise Sound club night on Wednesday (see separate listing). **Open** Sunday 1800-0000 **Price** £2 with flyer/advert before 1900; £5 after with flyer/advert or £7 without **Tube** Leicester Square

Stormes @ Stepneys Nightclub
373 Commercial Road (rear of The George Tavern), London E1 0LA Phone 020 8788 4154
This is a night that continues on in the memory of the beautiful and gracious Ron Storme who tragically passed away on 3 October 2000 after losing his battle against cancer. Stormes is based in Stepney's Nightclub, adjacent to the rear of The George Tavern. The entrance to the club is on Aylward Street, which is off Jubilee Street. (Are you still with me?) Stormes (formerly Club Travestie) is a well-established club, and this night is now into its 20th year and is aimed at cross-dressers, TVs, TSs, their friends, admirers and their families. Having said that, the club itself is extremely popular with the mainstream gay and lesbian crowd in addition to no-attitude straights who thoroughly enjoy the relaxed, friendly, camp and fun-filled atmosphere. The dance floor is slightly reminiscent of Saturday Night Fever and the venue is as plush and comfortable as my gran's front parlour (only she doesn't have trannies wandering around adjusting their knickers in front of everyone). Tiered staging dominates the room enabling you to see the monthly on-stage cabaret as opposed to the back of someone's head. Staff are friendly and welcoming – even the lovely doormen (not bouncers), which makes a pleasant change – and are committed to ensuring your night out is enjoyable. Excellent cloakroom and changing facilities are available in

the club and taxis home can be booked at reception. For first-timers and newcomers to the scene who want to gain more information or be shown around the venue, then please phone the lovely Vickie for details. Hostess Andrea is always on the door to welcome you to the club and she will do her utmost to help and assist you. The dress code is smart and glam so, please, make a little bit of an effort. **Open** Saturday 2100-0200 **Price** £5 **Tube** Aldgate East

Suit and Tie Society
c/o The Philbeach Hotel, 30-31 Philbeach Gardens, Earl's Court, London SW5 9EB Phone 020 8374 8190
The Suit and Tie Society meets on the last Friday of the month. Membership is available at £18 for the year, although visitors and tourists are welcome to attend as guests. It is an informal meeting place, although the dress code is (obviously) suit and tie. The Suit and Tie Society is for drinks and conversation with smartly dressed men of all ages. It's an ideal way to meet like-minded people for networking and so forth. This night used to be held at The Lounge Club, Mayfair before it closed down (oops! same fate as The Townhouse). You can write for more information to PO Box 12453, London, N10 2BW. **Open** Last Friday of the month from 1930 onwards **Tube** Earl's Court

Trade @ Turnmills
63b Clerkenwell Road, Farringdon, London EC1 Phone 020 7700 5352
World-famous techno and banging house all-nighter with a brilliantly sexy atmosphere at Turnmills. Now over eleven years old, it still remains the ultimate clubbing experience. The club itself has enticed literally hundreds of thousands of people over the years into its throbbing vortex of light, people, performance, visuals and, of course, sound. Every Saturday-night-come-Sunday-morning, pop stars mix with builders, city professionals blend with models and doctors assort with actors. It is a place which quite literally unites everyone. There are two rooms: The Main Floor and The Lite Lounge. Trade also takes its club night to Birmingham, Edinburgh and Manchester – watch out for the adverts. Trade will guarantee you quality tunes, stimulating visuals and very sexy clubbers. The Lite Lounge DJs are The Sharp Boys (also known as George and Steven) who between them present their wicked brew of American house and British steel. One simple door policy: make an effort. Tracksuits and trainers will not get you in. Once inside the unofficial dress code might leave you without your shirt – optional, but often desirable! Membership to Trade is available at around £35 per year (£25 for renewals) which will, amongst other things, give you a £5 discount off door charges and priority admission – if you are a Trade regular then it's well worth signing up for. Phone for details of how to apply. **Open** Saturday night (Sunday morning really) 0400-1300 finishing at lunchtime on the Sunday afternoon! **Price** £10-15 **Tube** Farringdon

UP @ The Rhythm Factory
16-18 Whitechapel Road, London E1 Phone 020 7375 3774
E-mail davidchait@hotmail.com Web www.come.to/up-club
UP (Underground Party) at the cavernous – and normally straight – 500-capacity Rhythm Factory pulls in a bevy of beautiful people for a whole night of funky hard house sounds in the main room and deep house and

Latin in the lounge. All this, plus visuals and a full light show. This is an excellent cheap all-nighter for die-hard dance fans. Keep an eye on the gay press for the exact Saturday and for the theme that will be running. **Open** Saturday (twice-monthly) 2200-0500 **Price** £6-10 **Tube** Whitechapel or Aldgate East

The Way Out Club @ Charlies   **9 Crosswall (off Minories), London EC3 2JY** Phone **020 8363 0948** E-mail **info@thewayoutclub.com** Web **www.thewayoutclub.com** Billed as 'a celebration of diversity for boys, girls and inbetweenies', your hosts Vikki Lee and Steffan have been welcoming everyone to The Way Out Club in person for the past seven years. An extremely popular venue for TVs/TSs/CDs and their admirers, particularly those who would like to meet and get to know transgendered people (know what I'm saying?). However, having said that, the friendly and lively atmosphere makes for an assorted clientele with no attitude, all intent on enjoying this extremely good night out. The Way Out Girls are the regular cabaret, well known for their TV appearances and Spice Girls impersonations in the Spiceworld movie. This super venue is in a discreet location, with easy parking and taxis waiting at the door. This single level, air-conditioned venue has two areas – a full-on dance and cabaret room, plus a quieter room with plenty of seating. In the main room Way Out's DJs mix music and lights to suit the mood of the night, which can vary between '70s and '80s camp and the latest commercial dance music to a wild dance party – either way the dance floor is always full. Two giant video screens and three televisions provide a constant visual feast. Stephan and Vicki encourage gorgeous girls (and boys) to get up and strut their stuff on the Way Out catwalk. For people not willing to catch the number 49 bus in full drag, Charlies has ample changing facilities and the taxi service ensures you can be whizzed out of there under a blaze of cover! Doors open at 2100 and have a great deal to offer early birds. From 2100 there are tranny interest videos on all the screens and all drinks are reduced to city bar prices until 2300. There's also a mixture of mellow music or chart hits at a volume to suit, plus a newly extended menu of meals and cheaper snacks to choose from. The party pumps up from 2300 to 0400 with show time at 0130. For those of you wanting to drive here there is ample free parking available on single yellow lines and in parking bays very close to the club. Beware parking on double yellows, with your wheels on the pavement or in a designated parking space (you can still pick up a fine even at this late hour). This is a very safe and discreet area on Saturday nights. For newcomers to the scene, have a word with Vikki or Steffan, either on the door or by e-mail and they will do their utmost to welcome you to the club and, if necessary, introduce you around. **Open** Saturday 2100-0400 **Price** £5-8 'til 2300 and £5-10 at other times **Tube** Aldgate East

Wig Out @ The Tube   **5-6 Falconberg Court, London W1** Phone **0956 549 246** E-mail **info@popstarz.co.uk** Web **www.popstarz.co.uk** Wig Out is pure musical mayhem, combining all-time classic tracks from four decades including trash, disco, alternative and kitsch anthems and promoted by the boys who bring you Popstarz. This night is popular with students and disco bunnies alike, who all have one thing in common – getting pissed and partying! Wig Out is set in the 'atmospheric' venue that is The Tube, situated behind The Astoria (G-A-Y). Although it is a predominantly gay night, a small percentage of gay-friendly straights are allowed in, ensuring a good mix of clientele. It also has its fair share of cruising going on with plenty of secluded areas, nooks and crannies to use to your advantage! Dance, booze and cruise: what more do you want? Q-Jump tickets are available from The Retro Bar. (See the listings for The Retro Bar and the club nights Popstarz @ The Scala and Miss-Shapes @ The Liquid Lounge too.) **Open** Saturday 2230-0500 **Price** £5-8 **Tube** Tottenham Court Road

If you should find yourself in the Stoke Newington area of London, it's worth looking out for Cedar Court on Cazenove Road. This is where, in 1965, the infamous Kray twins took up residence. Reggie lived on the ground floor and Ronnie had the flat above. Born in 1933, the Krays were identical twins. Along with elder brother Charlie, they were raised in the East End of London. Juvenile success as amateur boxers and National Service in the Army did little to either instil discipline or control the violence which was to become a hallmark of their lives. Famous for their protection rackets and violence, both were arrested on counts of murder and both were given life sentences. Reggie outlived Ronnie by five years, finally succumbing to cancer in October 2000. In Stoke Newington, their legend lives on.

XXL and URSUS The London Bridge Arches (formerly Castle Corner), **53-55 Southwark Street, London SE1 1TE** Phone 020 7207 2980 E-mail **enquiries@fatsandsmalls.com** Web www.fatsandsmalls.com XXL: one club fits all. A night that caters for men of all ages, tastes and sizes – so if you are a man who's big, proud, hairy, hunky, muscley; or a bear, a daddy, a lean-admiring stud, a chubby or a chaser; then this place was designed with you in mind! Occupying four of London Bridge's arches and able to accommodate up to 1,000 people, there are two bars with realistically priced drinks and car parking for up to 60 cars. This all adds up to one big night. There is no dress code – you wear what you dare. Combined entry and membership is £15. The layout of XXL consists of the following: Arch One is the bar and meeting area – the entrance is a spacious arch with ample seating to the side of a large bar which is L-shaped and situated to the left as you walk in. To the right is the cloakroom with toilets to the side and, at the far end, a smaller archway leading to Arch Two. This arch is the dance arena – a true void of a dance floor, with no obstacles other than the DJ's platform to the right and the occasional areas for drinks to the left... oh yes, and a few platforms for the more adventurous dancers out there! There's also the odd bit of entertainment going on here during the night. Arch Three is the community area: a large space as big as the dancefloor but not intended for dancing, more of a social, meeting room. Arch Four is – I'm a little tired of saying this, but – big, huge, in fact – XXL! This is the second bar, selling all the same drinks at all the same prices but with one major difference – the atmosphere (and that's all I'm giving away there!). The aim of XXL was simply to put the fun and good times back into going out into the gay scene, no matter whether you are a fat guy, a small guy or anything in-between. One thing to note: though XXL have no dress code they do ask that you make an effort... 'cause the hottest and horniest guys on the night will get a free entry for the following Saturday night. So be brave with what you wear! They are up for anything. The same venue is used on a Sunday for URSUS the club night for bears and their admirers, though to be frank, it's virtually an extension of the night before, with only one thing wrong – it doesn't last as long! **Open** Saturday 2200-0400. Sunday 1500-0000 **Price** £6-8 or combined membership and entry for £15

Saunas

Chariots 2

292 Streatham High Road (rear of), Streatham, London SW16
Phone 020 8696 0929 E-mail info@gaysauna.co.uk
Web www.gaysauna.co.uk

With the entrance on Mitcham Lane, off Streatham High Road, Chariots Streatham has two delightful floors to discover. On the ground floor there is the main wet area where you will find the two Jacuzzis, one of which is large and warm and the other that is smaller, hot and very bubbly. There's also the steam room and a large sauna plus a number of rest rooms, each equipped with mattresses and dimmer switches to suit your mood. On the first floor you will find another sauna, more rest rooms and a high-powered sunbed. There's also a satellite television lounge with a complimentary refreshment bar that makes it the perfect place to relax and chill out. Every second Saturday of the month there is the Bear 2000 session for big boys and their admirers. There is also a special weekend pass that entitles you to come and go as you please from midday Friday to midnight Sunday, all for £15. (See the listings for Chariots 3 at Farringdon and the original Chariots at Shoreditch too.) **Open** Sunday-Thursday 1100-2300. Friday-Saturday 1100-0300 **Price** £8-10

Chariots 3

57 Cowcross Street, Farringdon, London EC1 Phone 020 7251 5553
E-mail enquiries@gayuk.co.uk Web www.gayuk.co.uk

Originally called Chariots VIP and located in the heart of London, this branch of the Chariots empire has become very popular with the city gents and local workers who require a comfortable and pleasant shag... erm, I mean break, during the day. The entrance is discreetly located, directly opposite Farringdon tube station in Cowcross Street. If you do pop in during the day you can ask one of the staff for a day pass which will entitle you to return the same day, all for the one entrance fee of £10. If you do not think you will be coming back then get here before 1600 and pay a reduced admission of £8. This same-day return pass is for weekdays only. Being situated in the Farringdon district means that this place sees its fair share of the after-clubbing crowd – those who failed to cop off down the back alley of said club and turn here to make sure they go home with an empty bag. And why not? The entire building is decorated in Chariots' trademark luxurious Roman style and it's fully air-conditioned and always warm and cosy. A very comfortable Sky TV

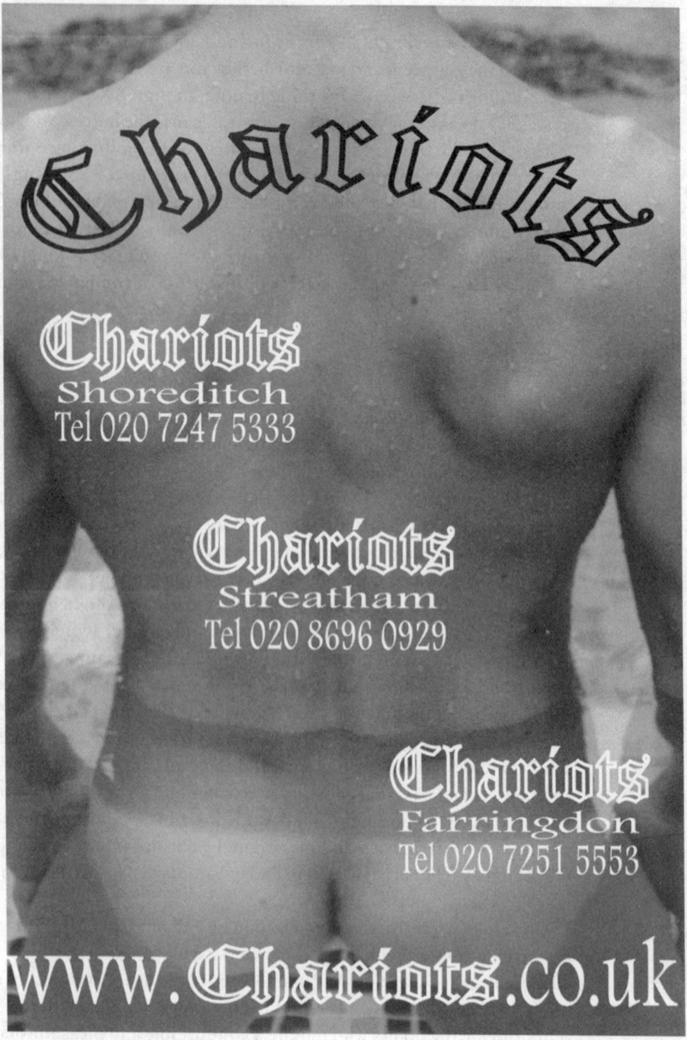
Chariots
Chariots
Shoreditch
Tel 020 7247 5333
Chariots
Streatham
Tel 020 8696 0929
Chariots
Farringdon
Tel 020 7251 5553
www.Chariots.co.uk

3

3

lounge is also available where you can enjoy complimentary tea or coffee and juices. Soft drinks and chocolate snacks are available to buy too. Usual sauna facilities of sauna, steam and willing cock can all be found here. **Open** Sunday-Thursday 1100-2300. Friday-Saturday 1100-0300 **Price** £8-10 **Tube** Farringdon (opposite)

Chariots Roman Spa

Chariots House, Fairchild Street, Shoreditch, London EC2A 3NS
Phone 020 7247 5333

This is the gay sauna that all others throughout the UK are measured by. A bold statement perhaps but on any given visit, at any given time, you will soon realise the legitimacy of this claim. A venue comprising of 20,000 square feet of 'Roman hedonistic splendour' laid out over three floors with the very best of facilities including a spacious, well-equipped gym, 20 rest rooms, a pleasantly warm swimming-pool, sauna cabins and steam rooms. On top of this there's the huge, large-screen TV room, adequate seating and relaxation areas and an excellent free refreshment bar: it all adds up to probably the best gay sauna in the UK. Visitors to London may think this glowing referral too good to be true – it's not and it is very rare to hear just criticism about Chariots. Contrary comments usually come from the more mature customers, who feel that they are, at times, passed over because of their age; favour falling with the younger punters. In reality though, the clientele in here is mostly young and, given the choice of young buck or mature gent, most will always choose the latter. (I am under no illusion that when I reach my autumn years I too will be passed over for a young stud.) Still there are young men around who plump for the more mature man; it possibly just takes that little extra bit of effort to find him. I'd advise sticking around. Highly recommended. **Open** Monday-Saturday 1200-0900 (all-nighter). Sunday 1200-0000 **Price** £10-12 **Tube** Liverpool Street

The Cruise Club

57 Camberwell Road, London SE5 Phone 020 7703 1100
E-mail **enquiries@saunaclub.co.uk** Web www.saunaclub.co.uk

The Cruise Club is 5,000 square feet of hedonistic steamy pleasure: this is a very smart, clean and comfortable gay and bi men's sauna. It's also the sister venue to The Health Club down in sexy Walthamstow, and this place retains the same customer-friendly attitude. Owners Mike and Graham have been running gay saunas for a number of years and have put all their efforts into ensuring that you are completely satisfied with your visit. If you're not then let them know so that they can do something about it. The Cruise Club near Burgess Park on the Camberwell Road has an ultra-discreet entrance (for the shy boys), with no outward sign declaring that it is a gay sauna. Look for the number 57 and enter. Once inside you'll treated to two floors of pure delight, for this is a warm, comfortable and friendly place with all the usual facilities – sauna cabin, steam room, Jacuzzi, rest rooms and more. Although this venue has not been open all that long it has already established itself as one of the best and friendliest saunas in London. (See the listing for The Health Club, Walthamstow too.) **Open** Sunday-Friday 1300-0100. Saturday 1300-0800 (all night) **Price** £8-10 **Tube** Elephant and Castle

The Health Club 800 Lea Bridge Road, Walthamstow, London E17 Phone 020 8556 8082
E-mail enquiries@cruiseclub.co.uk Web www.cruiseclub.co.uk
Is it me or does the very name Walthamstow combined with the E17 postcode sound horny? Really just me? Anyway, this East End sauna hits the jackpot. I have been here a couple of times and on both occasions have had my faith in the gay sauna scene restored by the friendliness and attitude of the staff and the punters. Try it and prove me wrong! Nothing ever seems to be any trouble: there is no brusque manner and certainly no 'I'm better than you' attitude that is so obvious at some other venues. They take the time to chat and they make you feel special. If there is anything that has marred your visit then bring it to the attention of the staff. If it can be remedied then it will be. (This excludes picking up the odd piece of trailer park trash whose performance wasn't quite up to scratch: such things cannot be remedied... although I wouldn't mind giving a second opinion!) The venue is comfortable and clean. The lounge areas are the best I have seen in any gay sauna and come complete with leather sofas for an excellent chill-out space. Refreshments can be dispensed from a vending machine, which may not be to everyone's liking but bear in mind that space is limited so something had to be forsaken. This is the sister venue to The Cruise Club over in Camberwell – read that listing and you'll note that that place also rates quite high on my sex-o-meter. In some respects The Cruise Club has an edge because it stays open all night over the weekend, which this place unfortunately doesn't. Don't let that deter you from coming here though – midnight closing simply means more choice in less time! Recommended. **Open** Monday-Sunday 1300-0000 **Price** £8-10 **Tube** Walthamstow Central

HPS 156 (Holland Park Sauna) 156 Shepherds Bush Centre, Shepherds Bush, London W12 8PP
Phone 020 8743 3264
This place is conveniently situated inside the Shepherd's Bush Concord Centre, just opposite Shepherd's Bush tube station. The entrance is rather discreet with HPS painted on both sides of the glass doors. It's popular with a local gay and bi crowd who enjoy the limited facilities of two saunas, a steam room, a small Jacuzzi, a gym, a large communal rest area, a TV lounge (smoking) and a snack bar with complimentary cakes/biscuits, but a charge against all drinks. If you happen to be 26 or under – that's real years not gay years – you will get admission for the pocket-money sum of £6 at all times after 1800 and at all times over the weekend (remember to bring some identity). **Open** Monday-Sunday 1130-2330 **Price** £12 **Tube** Shepherd's Bush

The Locker Room 8 Cleaver Street, Kennington, London SE11 Phone 020 7582 6288
Believe it or not, there used to be a laminated sign displayed in the reception area stating that '...there have been instances of older men being overcome by the heat and causing distress to the staff – therefore older people will not be admitted'. This blatant ageism was under the regime of the old management and certainly does not apply now. The present management team have been working hard to rectify the past damage. The Locker Room may not have the huge amount of space or facilities

as some other well-known London saunas but then again – as we all have come to realise – size is not everything (except, given the choice...). There's the basic facilities of a sauna cabin and steam room – both can hold approximately 18 people. The rest rooms are adequate, totalling four individual and two communal units. There's also a TV lounge (smoking) and free refreshments. Regular bus routes drop off at Kennington Road, including some night services. **Open** Monday-Thursday 1100-0000. Friday-Sunday 1100-continuous through to Sunday 2300. **Price** £6-10 **Tube** Kennington

Pacific 33

33 Hornsey Road, Holloway, London N7 Phone 020 7609 8011
Situated at the bottom of Hornsey Road, more or less opposite The University of London, is a delightful little sauna that caters for a crowd right across the board – age and type-wise. What makes this place stand out from the rest is the friendliness that pervades, even if the person you are speaking to is not your type: there is no pressure and no hidden agenda. It's just a shame that it's not bigger, which is no fault of the management. The facilities are all here – a large sauna cabin comfortably seating (kneeling!) about 16 and a larger steam room which can accommodate about 20. There is a free refreshment bar serving sandwiches, cake, fruit and hot and cold drinks and this can be found in the comfortable TV and chill-out space. There's ample rest areas in the form of two communal rooms – one subtly lit and the other completely black. Dry towels are exchanged without charge (a particular bug bear of mine is having to pay an additional charge for a dry towel). One special and unusual feature of Pacific 33 is that if you get here between 1100 (opening) and 1400 on Monday through to Thursday you will only pay £5, which is half the price of standard admission. Considering the refreshment bar is free it works out cheaper than going for lunch in a café! This being the case you will soon see that it's quite popular with the gay/bi student fraternity! Tip: students should take along their NUS identity: you may get a further discount. **Open** Monday-Thursday 1100-2300. Friday 1100 through to Sunday 2300 (continuous) **Price** £5-10 **Tube** Holloway Road (one minute)

**Pleasuredrome
Central**

125 Alaska Street, Waterloo, London SE1 8XE Phone 020 7633 9194
This place has been in operation for years and despite constant criticism concerning the cleanliness and décor it always seems to be busy. If you are in the Waterloo area and just want a quick in-and-out-no-strings-session and it doesn't (really) bother you with whom, then this is ideal. If, however, you want to kill a few hours and be more leisurely in who you choose to poke then consider going to Chariots over at Liverpool Street. Pleasuredrome is situated in the arches of Waterloo Station and every now and again you can hear the whoosh of the trains as you are servicing someone in either the steam room or adjoining dark room (it can be quite disconcerting!). Some people may be put off by the lack of privacy (it's near-impossible to find; even the 15 or so private rest areas upstairs tend to host free-for-alls and there are no doors or curtains to protect your modesty). Personally, I have had some good times here (one memorable – hi ya Irish boy!) and I usually pop in when I am in the area.

You will generally get a good cross-section of the public in here – more young than mature. There's also a regular supply of 'fresh meat' tourists. There's free self-serve refreshments and smoking is only allowed downstairs in the changing room. There used to be a sign occupying the wall by the showers that instructed you to adhere to 'British law' and 'not to suck cock' (or words to that effect). Apart from hiding a few cracks in the wall it served no purpose whatsoever.... Former sister venue Pleasuredrome North at Kings Cross is no longer with us. **Open** Daily, 24 hours **Price** £10 **Tube** Waterloo

Sailors Sauna   572-574 **Commercial Road, London E14 7JD** Phone 020 7791 2808
E-mail enquiries@sailorssauna.co.uk Web www.sailorssauna.co.uk
For the British fans of A1 this is the sauna that they did 'that' photo shoot for Attitude Magazine so you can come here and tell your friend that you were in the same hydro pool as Ben (just forget to mention that it wasn't at the same time though). The extensive facilities on offer are spread over four floors and take in three buildings on Commercial Road. Facilities include spacious changing rooms, a 12-man sauna, a 12-man steam room, 'his-and-his' showers, an 18-man hydro pool-Jacuzzi, a sun bed, a sun deck and roof garden, private rest cabins and rest rooms. There's also a video room with 55-inch cinema TV and DVD player, two lounge areas and a snack bar. In the basement there is a three-caged rest room, a peeping-tom communal rest room and a porno cinema. Sailors is a friendly and inviting place. within easy reach of the centre of London and the south-east. It's definitely well worth a visit (although I resent paying extra for additional dry towels in any sauna). **Open** Monday-Thursday 1400-2300. Friday-Saturday 1400-0600. Sunday 1400-2300 **Price** £10-12 **Tube** Bank, then two stops on DLR

The Sauna Bar   29 Endell Street, Covent Garden, London WC2H 9BA
Phone 020 7836 2236 E-mail enquiries@thesaunabar.com
Web www.thesaunabar.com
At one time this sauna had the bad reputation of not allowing any touchy-feely, sucking-and-shagging kind of action on the premises. (What? I hear you cry: this is a sauna for gay men isn't it?) That sort of thing just shouldn't be tolerated. Thankfully, the old management have had the good grace to fuck off (wondering why no-one ever returned there no doubt) and in has come someone with a far more secure grip on

reality and gay goings-on. Facilities here include a steam room, five rest rooms, a 30-man spa, a 20-man sauna, a luxurious lounge, masseurs, a licensed bar and bar food, a beautician, a hair stylist and alternative health facilities. The Sauna Bar is very well situated (more or less) in Central London and tends to attract a crowd with more tourists than locals in its make-up. **Open** Sunday-Thursday 1200-0000. Friday-Saturday 1200-0300. **Price** £10-12 **Tube** Covent Garden

Star Steam Sauna　38 Lavender Hill, Battersea, London SW11 5RL Phone 020 7924 2269

A localised, very friendly neighbourhood sauna over two levels. The first level has a reception area, a television lounge (smoking), a refreshment bar with complimentary tea and coffee, changing rooms and a high-powered solarium (£6 for 20 minutes). There is also an entrance to the garden patio which opens up during the summer months which is not overlooked (sorry exhibitionists!). The downstairs basement area is where all the fun happens. Here you'll find a massive steam room which easily holds up to 30 people (and quite often does), two sauna cabins, (one is comfortably warm whilst the second, newly installed one, is hotter – temperature-wise not activity-wise!) and two sets of communal showers with complimentary toiletries. Stay down here and you will find six lockable rest rooms and the communal video lounge. Star Steam is well placed on the gay sauna scene – the size of the venue may not be worth boasting about, but it does get exceedingly busy, particularly with the after-work crowd relieving their tensions. Incidentally, there is piped music throughout the building, even in the steam room, that can be either funny or irritating – it all depends on what you're doing! You'll find Steam Sauna on the Wandsworth Road side of Lavender Hill, conveniently close to Clapham Common (which means that if there is no one in the sauna that takes your fancy you can always take a detour on the way home.... (See Clapham Common cruising listing.) **Open** Monday-Sunday 1100-0000 **Price** £11 (£7.50 concession) **Tube** Clapham Common (10 to 15-minute walk)

Steamworks　309 New Cross Road, New Cross, London SE14 6AS Phone 020 8694 0606

Steamworks is an intimate and friendly gay men's sauna situated opposite The Town Hall in New Cross which, as you may or may not know, has rather a large student contingent (a-ha! So now you're interested !) Formerly known as Steaming @ 309 (and a few other non-complimentary adjectives besides that) it has recently been taken over by a new management team who have gone to great lengths to redress and resolve the problems and complaints about the old venue. Recently refurbished (quick-fixed) there is an on-going programme to bring the venue up to scratch and the improvements so far have been exemplary. The three so-called rest rooms of the former establishment have been demolished and in their place a large communal dark room has been installed. The upstairs lounge now has a new complimentary refreshment bar, satellite TV and ample seating space. Let's hope the improvements continue. **Open** Monday-Thursday 1100-2300. Friday 1100 non-stop through to 2300 Sunday **Price** £10 **Tube** New Cross Gate

Accommodation

Alison House Hotel   82 Ebury Street, Belgravia, London SW1W 9QD
Phone 020 7730 9529 Fax 020 7730 5494
E-mail info@alisonhousehotel.co.uk Web www.alisonhousehotel.co.uk
If you want a comfortable, convenient, clean and affordable bed and breakfast hotel in London, well placed for every attraction, then you could do a lot worse than stay here. The hotel is located just a few blocks from Victoria railway station, so all of London is just a short distance away. Even London's five airports are within easy travelling distance by road, rail and underground. All of the rooms are simple and tidy: this may not be quite the Ritz, but then you're not going to be paying £300 a night either. Their standard rooms include a TV, individually controlled heating and a washbasin. Showers and toilets are just a few steps down the hall and, as it is only a small hotel with just twelve rooms, there is rarely a wait for either of these facilities. En-suite rooms have private showers and toilets off the room. **Price** £56-75 double/twin; £85 triple en-suite **Number of rooms** 12, some en-suite **Tube** Victoria

Aster House   3 Sumner Place, South Kensington, London SW7 Phone 020 7581 5888
E-mail asterhouse@btinternet.com
Aster House is an entirely non-smoking bed and breakfast with eleven standard and three superior rooms. All of these rooms have an en-suite bathroom (shower or shower and bathtub, plus WC) and are individually decorated in an English country style. Room amenities include direct-dial phone, remote-controlled colour TV (channels include CNN International and CNBC Europe), room safe, hair dryer, fully independent air conditioning and tea/coffee-making facilities. Aster House is within easy walking distance of Kensington Palace (the late Princess Diana's London home), Kensington Gardens, Hyde Park, Albert Hall, the Science Museum, the Natural History Museum, The Victoria and Albert Museum, as well as the trendy and highly fashionable Brompton Cross and the world-famous department store Harrods. South Kensington underground station is less than three minutes' walk away and the Piccadilly Line from the station is directly connected to Heathrow Airport. There is no food and drink outlet at Aster House but Old Brompton Road and Fulham Road are a stone's throw away from the hotel and here you'll find a wide and varied selection of cafés, restaurants, and both trendy and traditional pubs. Guest rooms are located over five floors, but beware: there's no lift. Your money will get you clean, comfortable and tastefully decorated accommodation together with a healthy breakfast, and to help make you feel at home, the key to the front door is given to you at check-in so you're free to come and go as you wish. Aster House is not exclusively gay but it is extremely gay-friendly (I think I would be if I were landing £180 for every double room I booked out). **Price** £135-180 per double room **Number of rooms** 14, most en-suite **Tube** South Kensington

At Home Around the World	PO Box 19518, London SW11 6WF Phone 0171 564 3739 Fax 0171 564 3739 E-mail london@homearoundtheworld.com Web www.homearoundtheworld.com

A unique gay and lesbian home exchange agency which offers a refreshing alternative to holidaying in expensive, impersonal hotel accommodation. At Home offers a variety of individual options to suit any gay traveller, reducing, if not eliminating the cost of accommodation. Gay-owned and -run, members are part of a global network of gay and lesbian travellers: 'people like us' who value the security of dealing with a kindred spirit. They offer direct home exchanges and mutual hospitality; members provide free accommodation that is reciprocated at a later time, apartment rentals, hosting and renting a guest-room to paying guests, plus numerous other options. If the idea of having strangers at your home disturbs you, think a little harder: they only remain strangers until they become friends. The idea works because letters, e-mails, photographs and phone calls result in the building of friendships, so that by the time you are ready to make your exchange you have already established a relationship with them. The comprehensive and informative 28-page 'Guide To Successful Gay Home Exchanging', that comes as part of your membership pack, shows you how. Contact Ken on the above number for more information.

Beaver Hotel	57-59 Philbeach Gardens, London SW5 Phone 020 7373 4553 Fax 020 7373 4555 E-mail hotelbeaver@hotmail.com

An extremely popular and gay-friendly hotel in the same road as all the other major gay hotel players. The entire ground floor accommodation is non-smoking, as is the TV lounge upstairs. Facilities include lift access to all floors and complimentary tea and coffee in the basement restaurant. Car parking is available within the Beaver's own private car park for around £15 for 24 hours. **Price** £70 per double room **Number of rooms** 38 **Tube** Earl's Court

Clone Zone Holiday Apartments	64 Old Compton Street, London W1V 5TA Phone 020 7287 3530 E-mail info@clonezone.co.uk Web www.clonezone.co.uk

There are a total of four modern apartments on Old Compton Street in the very centre of the gay area in the West End. They comprise three double-bedded rooms with en-suite shower rooms and one luxury penthouse flat with a fully-fitted kitchen, en-suite with bath, shower and a spacious lounge area. You can check in at the Clone Zone shop any time after 1400 (A ten per cent discount on Clone Zone products and a discount on stays of seven nights or more are two of the included bonuses). Clone Zone staff will be happy to advise on London places of interest and, if you want to be where the action is, you can't do much better than this. **Price** £75 per room **Number of rooms** 3, 1 luxury penthouse **Tube** Piccadilly Circus

Dolphin Square Hotel

Dolphin Square, Chichester Street, London SW1V 3LX
Phone 020 7834 3800 Fax 020 7798 8735
E-mail reservations@dolphinsquarehotel.co.uk
Web www.dolphinsquarehotel.co.uk
In 1935 Sir Richard and Sir Albert Costain created Dolphin Square. Set in three and a half acres of glorious private gardens, bordered by the River Thames and surrounded by the busy streets of Westminster, the Square provided all the peace and pace of the countryside… nothing has changed. The hotel, on the north side of the square, is one of the few four-star all-suite hotels in London, with most rooms having separate kitchens and lounges. A base for business, a place for pleasure – or both. The Dolphin Square Hotel has more to offer than you could ever expect from a conventional hotel. From their gregarious head concierge (the font of all knowledge) to the support teams working behind the scenes: it all combines to make your stay as enjoyable as possible. Facilites here are practically beyond belief – squash and tennis courts, an 18-metre indoor swimming pool, health spa, hair salon, theatre ticket and travel agency, car rental, Gary Rhodes' restaurant, brasserie and bar... I could go on. It is worth noting that there are usually special offers over the weekends when you can obtain a healthily reduced tariff – always be sure to ask. This is serious style at affordable prices! **Price** £140 **Number of rooms** 148, all en-suite **Nearest tube** Pimlico

The George Hotel

58-60 Cartwright Gardens, Bloomsbury, London WC1H 9EL
Phone 020 7387 8777 Fax 020 7387 8666
E-mail reception@georgehotel.com Web www.georgehotel.com
Tucked away just north of Russell Square on the edge of Bloomsbury is a half-circle of Georgian town-houses (built circa 1807) overlooking Cartwright Gardens, once the homes of the rich but many now converted to hotels. Cartwright Gardens was named in honour of John Cartwright, a political reformer and military officer, who supported independence to the colonies (including America) and refused to fight against them. A bronze statue of Cartwright now sits in the park in the neighbourhood where he once lived. This is the perfect location for a stay in London – quiet but within walking distance of the British Museum and the West End, ideal for theatres and shopping. If you prefer to use the tube, the hotel is only two stops from Oxford Circus and Covent Garden and only three stops from Leicester Square. All bedrooms in the George have cable TV with free movie and sports channels, direct-dial phone and tea/coffee-making facilities and the prices include a traditional English breakfast that's guaranteed to fill you up. You're welcome to have another breakfast free if you're still hungry! They now

living, eating, relaxing

Situated in 3½ acres of landscaped gardens in Westminster, central London, the hotel's position and facilities make it ideal for both business and pleasure.

4 star rating • English Tourism silver award for quality • 145 one, two and three bedroom suites • brasserie • bar • conference suites • Zest! Health & Fitness Spa • swimming pool • squash and tennis courts • hotel shopping mall • car parking

Gary Rhodes, one of the country's finest chefs, is in the Square with his award-winning restaurant.

Weekend breaks and special rates available.

Call the reservations team on:
Telephone +44 (0)20 7798 8890
Fax +44 (0)20 7798 8896, **Freephone** 0800 616 607
E-mail reservations@dolphinsquarehotel.co.uk
Website www.dolphinsquarehotel.co.uk

Dolphin Square Hotel

**Dolphin Square, Chichester Street,
London SW1V 3LX. United Kingdom.**

have an e-mail facility in the lounge for guests to keep in touch with friends and family whilst travelling. The gardens are private but the hotel has a key for guest's access, which includes use of the tennis courts (they can provide racquets and tennis balls free of charge). Easy and direct access is available straight from Heathrow Airport by tube (to Russell Square station on the Piccadilly line) or by A2 Airbus (to Euston or Russell Square). Try out the relaxed and friendly atmosphere at the George on your next trip to London and be pleasantly surprised at the comparatively low cost and value for money. Over 50 per cent of their guests have stayed before or had the hotel recommended to them by previous guests. To secure a reservation let them have your credit card details (Visa, Master Card, Switch or Delta) by letter, fax, phone or e-mail and they will take a deposit equal to the cost of your first night's stay. There are no problems if your plans change and you need to cancel: your deposit will be refunded in full, provided you let them know two days before you were due to arrive. They are happy to deal with enquiries and are quick and efficient at returning correspondence. **Price** £70-90 double; £83-105 triple **Number of rooms** 40 **Tube** Russell Square

Five things to impress your friends with whilst walking around Piccadilly: (1) The name Piccadilly is derived from 'piccadil', a type of lace collar that was made by a tailor in nearby Haymarket. The tailor, on becoming rather rich had a home built which he named 'Piccadilly Hall'. (2) Piccadilly Station's circular ticket office is directly beneath the statue of Eros. (3) The statue of Eros is actually a monument to the late philanthropist Lord Shaftsbury, and was originally referred to as The Shaftsbury Memorial. The sculptor was Sir Alfred Gilbert (1854-1934). (4) The earth removed from the construction of the Piccadilly Line in 1903 was used to build up the terraces at Chelsea football ground. (5) The first flashing neon advertisement in central Piccadilly was switched on in 1932.

Grims Dyke Hotel   Old Redding, Harrow, Middlesex HA3 6SH **Phone** 020 8385 3100 **Fax** 020 8954 4560 **E-mail** enquiries@grimsdyke.com **Web** www.grimsdyke.com

The former country residence of W. S. Gilbert of Gilbert and Sullivan fame, is now an outstanding four-star hotel. It's set in 40 acres of beautiful gardens and woodlands and is only ten miles from the hustle and

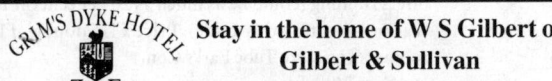

bustle of London's West End. This carefully restored country house is renowned for its special musical events (see their website), banqueting, conference and wedding facilities. The hotel has 44 rooms, 34 of which are situated in the adjacent lodge. The main house has the suites which range in price from £165-295 per night. As you might expect everything here, from the service to the food, is absolutely first class. **Price** £120 **Number of rooms 44**, all en-suite

Halifax Hotel   65 Philbeach Gardens, Earl's Court, London SW5 9EE
Phone 020 7373 4153
A predominantly gay hotel. Most rooms have a shower in the room although there are shared toilet and shower facilities on each floor. For the budget-conscious there are also standard rooms available at around £50 per double room and £30 per single. Four of the 15 rooms available to let are fully en-suite (with toilet as well as shower), at around £60 per double and £45 single. The hotel is not licensed but guests are welcome to take their own drink in. **Price** £60 per double room **Number of rooms** 15, 4 (fully) en-suite **Tube** Earl's Court

Kensington   4 Templeton Place, Earl's Court, London SW5 9LZ Phone 020 7370 4333
International   Fax 020 7244 7873 E-mail enquiries@kensington-international-hotel.co.uk
Hotel   Web www.kensington-international-hotel.co.uk
The very gay-friendly Kensington International Hotel is situated in the heart of Earl's Court, within a two-minute drive of the A4 – Cromwell Road – that leads directly to the M4 motorway and Heathrow Airport. It is also a two-minute walk from Earl's Court underground station and the Exhibition Centre. The Commonwealth Institute and Olympia Exhibition Centre are also within easy walking distance. Just over 100 years ago there used to be farming land where the Kensington now stands. In 1877 these magnificent Victorian residences were built, for the aristocrats and noblemen of the day. It was only eight years ago that the hotel was completely rebuilt and refurbished. Part of this refurbishment was to create individually-themed bedrooms and to provide up-to-date facilities and an overall unique concept in hotel styling and design. Subject to availability, guests are offered a choice of theme. All of the rooms are equipped with electronic locks, electronic safes, satellite televisions, trouser presses and hair-dryers. In addition, the hotel has a reception-come-lounge, and a bar and breakfast room-come-conservatory. Tip: always ask at the time of booking if there are any special offers running (could be as much as 20 per cent off the price outside high season – mention this guide). **Price** £115 double, £135 triple **Number of rooms** 56, en-suite **Tube** Earl's Court

London House   13 Craven Hill, Hyde Park, London W2 3EN
Hotel   Phone 020 7402 9155 Fax 020 7262 8292
E-mail londonhouse@mail.com Web www.london-house.com
London House has 35 self-contained studio apartments all equipped with en-suite shower-room and kitchenette and all with the necessary add-ons: microwave, fridge/freezer, cutlery and tea/coffee-making facilities. All rooms come with a direct-access phone, which works using a

smart calling card on very low rates. Their phone system also allows connection to the internet. The accommodation offers you a choice of single, double or triple occupancy (triple consists of one double and one single bed). London House is located within five minutes' walk from four of the main underground stations: Paddington (for mainline trains and Heathrow Express), Bayswater, Lancaster Gate and Queensway. There are many buses and tours that leave from this area too, so you can enjoy both the touristy and the quiet part of central London. In order to secure and confirm your booking they will simply require your credit card details. Any cancellation made within less than 48 hours prior to arrival will be liable for a cancellation fee charged at one night's stay. Bear in mind too that payment by credit card (not Switch or other debit cards) bears a 3.5 per cent surcharge. **Price** £86 double; £96 triple **Number of Rooms** 35 self-contained studio apartments **Tube** Lancaster Gate

---

In May 1839 Highgate Cemetery was consecrated as sacred ground by the Bishop of London. That very same week it took in its first resident – a 36-year-old single woman from Soho by the name of Elizabeth Jackson. Since then, Highgate became the 'fashionable' final residence of Victorian London's hoi polloi, including Charles Dickens and Karl Marx. Amongst the 166,000 names, inscribed on over 51,000 tombstones is that of Marguerite Radclyffe Hall. Aged 21, Marguerite inherited the entire family fortune from her father. She toured South America for a year. This was a period of self discovery. Upon returning, she realised her true sexual identity and insisted that everyone address her simply as Radclyffe from thereon. At the same time, Radclyffe took to wearing men's clothing and smoking cigars. In 1907, she came across Mabel Veronica Batten – the beautiful socialite who was to change Radclyffe Hall's life. During their nine years together, Mabel encouraged Radclyffe to publish two volumes of poetry, which sold successfully. Mabel died in 1916. Radclyffe set up home with Mabel's cousin, Una Troubridge and wrote her first novel, The Unlit Lamp. A second one followed, but it was The Well Of Loneliness, published in 1928, that ensured Radclyffe Hall's place in literary and gay history. There was a public outcry. Critics and politicians voiced their concerns, considering the book obscene. The case was brought before Bow Magistartes Court under the Obscene Publications Act of 1861, and, despite the fact that the book contained no graphic depictions of sex or profanity, it was banned from sale. In 1943, 15 years after the trial, Radclyffe Hall died of cancer. Una, who had nursed Radclyffe through her illness, arranged for her burial at Highgate, alongside her friend and lover, Mabel Batten. The Well Of Loneliness was republished in 1950. It has since sold millions of copies and been translated into several languages.

Noel Coward Hotel   111 Ebury Street, Belgravia, London SW1W 9QU
Phone 020 7730 2094 Fax 020 7730 8697
E-mail info@noelcowardhotel.com Web www.noelcowardhotel.com
This hotel was once the home of Noel Coward from 1917 to 1930. It is now a private guesthouse in the heart of Belgravia. There is also one self-catering apartment available (close to the hotel and details of this

can be gained by phoning the hotel direct). All room prices are inclusive of tax and breakfast. One night's deposit is required to reserve your room and a full 72 hours' prior notice is required for a full cancellation refund. The hotel offers many services such as currency exchange, maps, itinerary and tickets for theatres and shows. There is also the free use of the indoor swimming-pool at Queen Mother Sports Centre which is a short hop, skip and a little jump away. For those of you who just cannot be bothered to wait for a taxi at Heathrow, you can arrange to be met by a member of staff – all for a small additional charge of course! **Price** £70 per double room **Number of rooms** 15, 8 en-suite **Tube** Sloane Square

Number Seven Guesthouse

7 Josephine Avenue, Brixton, London SW2 2JU Phone 020 8674 1880 Fax 020 8671 6032 E-mail hotel@no7.com Web www.no7.com
Your hosts, Paul and John, have been serving the gay and lesbian community since 1992. Back then they decided to make No7 into a place that they themselves would be happy staying at. Their eight rooms, all with private bathrooms decorated and equipped to an exceptionally high standard, ensure that past visitors (myself included) return time and time again. Breakfast is served in the garden conservatory each morning between 0900 and 1100. Alternatively, by giving notice the previous evening, you can take breakfast in your room at a time suitable for you (although breakfast in the beautiful garden setting really sets you up for the day and is worth getting up for). Situated in a leafy Brixton suburban road, No7 is a short distance away from The Fridge and Substation South. Even Soho is not that far: a ten-minute tube ride to Piccadilly. Brixton is a fascinating melting pot of some 40-odd different cultures and is fast becoming (so succinctly put by Time Out magazine) 'the most exciting place to be'. More recently Brixton was the focus of worldwide attention when Madonna staged an 'invite-only' concert at The Brixton Academy. **Price** £60-90 per double room **Number of Rooms** 8, all en-suite **Tube** Brixton (three-minute walk)

Outlet Accommodation

32 Old Compton Street, Soho, London W1V Phone 020 7287 4244 E-mail homes@outlet4homes.com Web www.outlet4homes.com
Outlet, now firmly established as the housing resource centre for lesbian, gay and gay-friendly Londoners, has come a long way over the last six years. Their friendly central Soho office is the co-ordinating base with phone, internet and walk-in facilities for their customers.

Number Seven Guesthouse

7 Josephine Avenue, London, SW2 2JU
Best UK Gay Hotel - The Pink Paper

Tel: 020 8674 1880
Fax: 020 8671 6032
http://www.no7.com/

Comprehensive information on flat-shares, apartments and houses is provided via a unique 'matching' system that aims to take the slog out of inner-city home hunting. Most recently, heavy investment and one and a half years of development has produced a dot.com system that is unrivalled. It boasts 25 new functions for on-line customers, and will revolutionize the way in which Outlet helps people find somewhere to live. The next step is to expand into other parts of the UK, which Outlet has scheduled for late 2001. Currently, Outlet offer a matching information service which covers all areas of London; letting and management services; holiday flats; apartments and rooms in Soho; tenancy agreements; referencing and rent guarantee scheme; mobile phone rental and housing advice. Their Outlet 4 Holidays set-up will also get you sorted with essential holiday information. **Open** Monday-Friday 1000-1900. Saturday 1200-1700 **Tube** Piccadilly

Outlet 4
Holidays

32 Old Compton Street, Soho, London W1D 4TP
Phone 020 7287 4244 Fax 020 7734 7217
E-mail **enquiries@outlet.co.uk** Web **www.outlet.co.uk**

Outlet 4 Holidays offers the largest available selection of self-catering holiday accommodation and related services for lesbian and gay visitors to London's Soho area. Being the largest and most comprehensive business of its kind means that it can be extremely competitive and offer an extensive variety of accommodation, value and services. So confident are Outlet in their standing within the London lesbian and gay tourist industry that they are prepared to match any price on like-for-like accommodation and services that you can find! Anyone who knows gay London will tell you that Old Compton Street in Soho is at the hub of London's diverse lesbian and gay scene. Not only is this the street where Outlet is based, it is also where the majority of its holiday apartments are situated, with many others not more than a couple of minutes' walk away. Prices start from £54 per night for two people, based on sharing a self-catering apartment. Accommodation for two people in a private studio apartment is from £88 per night. For larger groups, there are private two-, three-, and four-bedroom apartments that sleep up to eight people. These prices range from £120 per night (four people sharing) to £180 per night (six people sharing) and £244 per night (eight people sharing). Cleanliness, good service, double- or king-sized beds, cable TV, cotton linen, towels, compact disc music systems, 24-hour emergency call-out service and an office reception within easy reach of your accommodation are standard with all of Outlet's apartments. For travellers who really want to splash out, there are luxury one- or two-bedroom apartments available. These are top of the range apartments that have had their interiors designed with furniture and fixtures by well-known designers such as Phillipe Starck. Expect top-of-the-range electrical equipment and a very high specification on décor and furnishings. The prices for these apartments start from £150 per night for two people. Outlet do not recommend or offer holiday accommodation outside of easy walking distance from Old Compton Street. The reason is quite simple – late night transport. Since so much of London's gay and lesbian scene evolves around this area it seems practical to avoid the costs and difficulties of late night taxis. Their centrally-located accommodation makes sure you don't encounter any of these hassles. Outlet's comprehensive and interactive web site has extensive descriptions of all their properties, colour photographs taken within the apartments, maps to enable you to see exactly where your apartment is located and currency converters to help you work out the cost before booking. You can even make your reservation on-line using their interactive and secure payment system. Once you are in London, whether as a guest with Outlet or not, it is worth phoning or visiting their information centre where they will be glad to assist in making your visit to London a good one. Outlet has just launched Outlet Audio Tours. These are great fun and highly recommended. Hire includes a map and itinerary (which you can keep), Walkman, batteries, headset and tape. The recording includes a step-by-step guide to Soho's gay café-bars, pubs, clubs, shops and other businesses of interest. You get lots of useful insider tips on such things as cheap tickets for theatres, night clubs, cinemas and so forth. Keep an eye on this quickly growing organization. They are expanding and by the time this book goes to print, you may have a branch in your town! New York, Amsterdam and Sydney are next on the agenda. Outlet is a big organisation and these are just a few of the other extra services they cater for: A resource centre – offering both lesbian and gay tourist advice and information; luggage storage – if you are an Outlet guest with a late departure and have to check out early, don't worry, Outlet will store your luggage for free; meet and greet – an Outlet 4 Holidays representative will meet you at the property and check you in at the apartment, which saves you going to the office when you arrive; mobile phone hire – your own mobile phone which costs you just £10 per week; mail and faxing service, where you can use their office address to have your mail forwarded or to send and receive faxes; residential housing, advice and assistance including referencing, contract packs and a rent guarantee scheme. **Open** Monday-Friday 1000-1900. Saturday 1200-1700 **Price** £54-plus **Tube** Leicester Square / Piccadilly

Oxford Hotel   13 Craven Terrace, Bayswater, London W2 3QD
Phone 020 7402 6860 E-mail **enquiries@oxfordhotellondon.co.uk**
Web **www.oxfordhotellondon.co.uk**
A gay-friendly hotel offering affordable accommodation in the centre of London. Many facilities are available here including maid service, laundry/dry cleaning, tours of London, travel arrangements, reception and security. **Price** £76 double; £86 triple **Number of Rooms** 21, all en-suite **Tube** Lancaster Gate

The Philbeach Hotel   30-31 Philbeach Gardens, Earl's Court, London SW5 9EB Phone 020 7373 1244 Fax 020 244 0149 E-mail **100756.3112@compuserve.com**
Web **www.philbeachhotel.freeserve.co.uk**
One of London's largest and friendliest gay hotels, now into its 21st year. The Wilde About Oscar Restaurant ('Probably the best gay restaurant in London' – Time Out) is open from 1900 until 2230, except Sunday and Tuesday. For reservations, call the above number. The hotel is housed in an elegant 19th-century building on a tree-lined crescent. It

is situated in the very centre of gay Earl's Court and is close to the heart of London, not far from the Soho gay scene. With the closure of their neighbour, The New York Hotel, they are now welcoming valued guests of The New York to The Philbeach. Single rooms are available from £50 with a shared bathroom, and triple rooms are available at £75, also with a shared bathroom (£100 en-suite). Car parking is extremely limited and a charge of £14 per 24 hours is made for each allotted space. If available, you can use the parking facilities at The Beaver Hotel (see separate listing) where the charge is £15 per 24 hours. In the case of cancelling a reservation, a full 48 hours' prior notice must be given for a full refund entitlement. Note also that a single Saturday night can rarely be booked – a minimum of two nights (including the Saturday) is the standard. If it's just the one night you're after though it might be worth a call to check if the hotel is not fully occupied: if not something can usually be arranged. The Philbeach also hosts The Suit and Tie Society get-together on the last Friday of every month (see separate club night listing). **Price** £90 per double room per night **Number of Rooms** 40, mixed standard and en-suite **Tube** Earl's Court

Rainbowstay   Caledonian Road, Kings Cross, London N1 0RU
E-mail rainbowstay@blueyonder.co.uk
Web www.rainbowstay.freeserve.co.uk
A small, friendly bed and breakfast that caters for gay and lesbians, in a smart and comfortable private self-contained house that is close to the gay bars, clubs, coffee bars and restaurants. The rooms have bathrooms,

TV (some have cable), video, fridge, tea/coffee-making facilities, and direct-dial phone. Collections, transport and tours can be arranged upon request. Check-in is at 1400 on the day of booking and check-out is at 1100. All bookings require a 20 per cent deposit which is refundable up to 14 days before the date of the booking (subject only to the room being re-let). They accept Visa, MasterCard, and traveller's cheques but not American Express or Diners Card. Weekends see a surcharge of £10 if only one night's stay is requested. The minimum stay at bank holiday weekends is three days. Let them know in advance if you have any particular needs and they will do their best to accommodate you, whether it be a desire for sightseeing tours, restrictions with your diet or allergies that need special provisions. **Price** Double £65-£75 **Tube** Kings Cross

Riverside Lodge Guest House

15 Brightlingsea Place, LimeHouse, London E14 8DB
Phone 020 7515 0862 E-mail enquiries@riversidelodge-london.com
Web www.riversidelodge-london.com
Riverside Lodge is a modern private gay-run guest-house, ideally suited to gay tourists seeking to explore the capital city. It's situated only a short distance from the Tower of London, St Pauls, the South Bank and Theatre land, and so is near many popular gay venues. Their aim is to provide a welcoming and relaxed stay for their exclusively gay clientele. All rooms have their own private bath or shower room and benefit from air conditioning. Accommodation is of a high standard and rates include a full English or continental breakfast. They have three double bedrooms in this newly-built townhouse, which is located just off the famous Narrow Street in the riverside area of Limehouse on the banks of the River Thames. There are ample transport links to all London airports, railway stations (including Eurostar) and road networks. London Bridge is two stops away from the nearest tube Canary Wharf, with Waterloo Station, Westminster and Buckingham Palace all relatively close too. Limehouse boasts its own bars, pubs and bistros where you can watch boats sail up and down the river with a drink in your hand. **Number of Rooms** 3, all en-suite **Tube** Canary Wharf

Russell Lodge

20-21 Little Russell Street, London WC1
Phone 020 7430 2489 Fax 020 7681 7604 E-mail russell.lodge@virgin.net
A Georgian-style guest-house close to Covent Garden and Soho. There's also a separate and luxurious private apartment available to rent on a

long- or short-term basis with two bedrooms, two bathrooms and a kitchen and near to Leicester Square tube station. For guest-house accommodation or details of the private apartment enquire at Russell Lodge. **Price** £69 per room **Tube** Tottenham Court Road / Holborn

Spencer's Hostel

Hendon Central, London NW4 Phone 020 8959 3661
E-mail spencerrolfe@aol.com Web www.geocities.com/spencerrolfe
People seeking short-term, budget accommodation in London should consider this hostel. They provide breakfast, clean bedding, washing machine, phone, kitchen and many other home comforts. Located in Hendon Central, they are only 20 minutes away from central London on the Northern Line. The night buses (N5) and (N16) stop outside the front door. So there are no restrictions for night-clubbers. Wahaaay! Phone Lee for their precise location and further info. **Price** £20 per person

Tophams Belgravia

28 Ebury Street, Belgravia, London SW1W 0LU
Phone 020 7730 8147 Fax 020 7823 5966
Tophams Belgravia has been owned by the Topham family for over 60 years and was originally known as the Ebury Court Hotel. In 1937, the hotel's founder, Diana Topham, took over a relatively nefarious drinking club from her brother and started the hotel, adding four more houses over the next few years and remaining at the helm until she and her husband, Romer, retired in 1988. Their daughter, Marianne, and her husband, Nicholas Kingsford, took over the hotel and embarked on a wide range of refurbishment whilst still retaining its character and charm. The hotel has a worldwide reputation for caring for its guests, many of whom return year after year and are welcomed by the friendly and competent staff. The hotel now occupies five adjoining houses and consists of 40 bedrooms, many having recently been refurbished and the majority enjoying en-suite bathrooms. There's also Tophams Restaurant, the Club Bar and the Garden Room (which is available for functions) to savour. Tophams has all the charm of an English Country House yet is situated in the heart of Belgravia, one of London's most sought-after residential locations. Tophams is a three-minute walk from the underground, bus and rail services of Victoria Station, and the express services to Heathrow and Gatwick make this location ideal for sight-seeing, shopping, visiting theatres and restaurants as well as getting any connections in and out of the country. Limited parking spaces are also now available (enquire when you make your reservations). Over the years, Ebury Street has seen many strange, eccentric and famous residents: Mozart (who composed his first symphony here), Lord Tennyson, Noel Coward, George Moore, George Meredith, Vita Sackville-West and Harold Nicholson to name but a few. **Price** £110-plus per double; £170 triple **Number of Rooms** 40, most en-suite **Tube** Victoria

The Town House

22 Bunning Way, Caledonian Road, Islington, London N7 9UN
Phone 020 7515 0862 E-mail sbr22@dircon.co.uk
Web www.sbr22.dircon.co.uk
A private gay-run and -managed house offering bed and breakfast. Caledonian Road is ideally situated for central London, close to both

Islington and Camden, and within easy reach of both Kings Cross and Caledonian Road tube stations. Rates for two-person occupancy include tea/coffee-making facilities as well as continental breakfast (either served in your room or in the first-floor lounge). All bookings require a 20 per cent deposit which is refundable up to seven days before the date of the booking (subject to the room being re-let). All payments must be by Visa, Access, traveller's cheques or cash. Note also that there is a £10 surcharge for a one-night only stay. The minimum stay at bank-holiday weekends is three days. **Price** £55 standard double **Number of Rooms** 3, all en-suite **Tube** Caledonian Road

Cruising grounds

Abney Park Cemetery

(High Street, Stoke Newington N16) Situated close to Stoke Newington railway station. From the station doors turn left and cross over the road. After walking for a minute or so you will see the opening into the park and almost instantly the public toilet block, which as you may have already guessed is the nucleus of the area. For those of you who may be driving, there is a free car park on the south-east corner of the park that also serves as a meeting place. The toilet block is not too far from the main road and I would strongly recommend you take your catch some-where else – not in the toilets. I should also reiterate that cruising in a cemetery is obviously far from tasteful. Please try and use another loca-tion. **Tube** Stoke Newington (mainline)

Barnes Common

(SW13) From Barnes railway station walk up Rocks Lane, about 600 metres towards the common. Cross over Mill Hill (the main road) and keep going along Rocks Lane. You will come to the common entrance, close to the public conveniences near to the tennis courts. Behind the tennis courts and bowling green there is good tree cover for privacy – it is not advisable to use the cottage. This place can get rather busy at tea-time with the after-work brigade. **Tube** Barnes (mainline)

Battersea Park

(SW8) Enter the park at the entrance that is just off Queen's Circus roundabout (off Chelsea Bridge). Walk 20 yards and take the first right. Walk down the path until you get to the nature trail and here you have it. (You should be by the bushes heading back towards Chelsea Bridge.) It can get busy during the day but it's not recommended at this time – it is after all a nature trail! However, come the evening...! The gates to the park are usually open 24 hours but it has been known for them to be closed from 0000 onwards – there seems to be no set rule. If you happen to be tramping around here in the summer, take a quick gander around the boating lake in Battersea Park – it is actively populated by gay men hanging out or picnicking with friends. **Tube** Battersea Park (mainline)

Beaulieu Heights

(Junction of A215 South Norwood Hill and A212 Church Road, Upper Norwood SE19) You want the wooded park at Upper Norwood, behind the IBA Television mast. The toilet there is open 24 hours and the adja-cent woods offer plenty of cover. This area can be quite busy at times, although you are on a much safer bet if you use the Addington Hills cruising ground situated just around the corner going towards Norwood junction. You will find a small gate on the left; go through here and walk along the footpath, down the hill and then along the footpath to the cruisy woods at the end. Lots of action day and night.

Brockwell Park (Herne Hill SW2) Close to Herne Hill railway station is Dulwich Road (A2214) and Herne Hill (A215). This location is near the main entrance to the park. Make your way to the cottage near to the basketball courts. Although the summer draws the locals out (in their closeted droves) the cooler autumn months can at times prove to be rather fruitful.

Clapham Common (Clapham SW4) Clapham Common has become infamous since a well-known politician was assaulted here some time ago. The main toilet on the A4 has since closed down but the toilet and surrounding area on Windmill Drive (by the Windmill Pub) has become busier of late. During rush hour you may also want to try the toilets out at Clapham Common railway station. It is one of those pay-as-you-go type of conveniences but 20p is a small price to pay for the chance of some takeaway local cock! The Two Brewers (see separate pub listing) is nearby as is The Star Sauna (see separate listing) on Lavender Hill (northside).

Elmhurst Gardens (Woodford E18) Elmhurst Gardens is a small piece of greenery next door to London University's halls of residence... (can you guess what I'm about to say? Students!). The park opens first thing in the morning and it will be used by a lot of people as a cut-through to various locations. The toilet is the hotspot and is busy either mornings, lunch or going-home time (1700). The park closes at around 1830 to 1900. The best access to the park is from Gordon Road and then through Latchett Road. **Tube** South Woodford

Epping Forest (Snaresbrook Road E11) Park up at the car park on Snaresbrook Road and take a wander around. There's sound action most nights. The car park is surrounded by woodland and is directly adjacent to the main road (Snaresbrook) off the A114 (the beginning of Lea Bridge Road and the start of Woodford New Road). Police do know about this area and will drive around throughout the night – so be careful! There have been a couple of corroborated stories of late-night bashings here, so be doubley careful. **Tube** Snaresbrook

Godstone Hill (A22 south-bound, Caterham) Taking the Caterham Road (A22) south, just before Junction 6 on the M25, there is a lay-by with a cottage that attracts the horny truckers and London suits looking for a bit of 'how's your father?' on their way home from work. Now, the busiest time is around tea-time (1700) although you may well strike it lucky anytime during the day (less competition). There is also another lay-by before reaching this one on the same stretch of road (although it's cottage-free it may well serve as a good place to stretch your legs!).

Greenwich Park (Shooters Hill Road, Blackheath SE10) South of Greenwich Park at the junction of Charlton Way (B210) and Shooters Hill Road (A2) is a well-

3

established cottage. It is best to take away to the abundant parkland rather than staying at the urinal. This place is very busy with passing trade which also means it could be the focus of regular police visits. Incidentally, there is a territorial army centre close by – but you wouldn't be interested in knowing more about that now, would you…?

Ham Common

(Richmond TW10) This public park is very cruisy all year round, day and night, all ages. You need to follow the footpath into the woods to find other guys. Follow the sign to Ham House (National Trust) and park beyond the football pitches. Walk into the woods on your right. Discretion is advised during the day.

Hammersmith Towpath

(Hammersmith SW6) The towpath along the river (going away from central London) between Hammersmith Bridge and Putney Bridge is quite busy after dark. Most of the cruising occurs at either the Hammersmith Bridge end, near to the old Harrods furniture depository, or at the Putney Bridge end, just past the weir, where the path is no longer paved and the road ends. Daytime cruising is practically non-existent as the area is overlooked by flats. However, late evenings, on either side, can be quite active. **Tube** Hammersmith (ten-minute walk)

Hampstead Heath

(West Heath, Hampstead NW3) Between Hampstead (Heath Street) and Golders Green (North End Road) tube stations is the exact place you want to be – North End Way on the A502 by Jack Straw's Castle, which is a straight pub (a shame really because this would make for the busiest gay pub in the world with access onto the heath!). Behind Jack Straw's car park is the entrance onto the heath (West Heath) and, to be honest, this is it – you can smell the testosterone in the air! The first part is usually for the fresh meat that might be a little hesitant to venture further into the heath. The more adventurous will probably want to carry on along the path, bearing left into the heart of the heath – this is where the action becomes heavier and busier (and darker). Like everywhere else the obligatory at-your-own-risk warnings apply (but I would say that it is very rare for major incidents to happen here). The one warning I would pass on is that, because this ground constitutes such a good thing for so many gay men, it will only take one complaint from the locals to the police for them to eventually clamp down. Do not leave condoms, tissues, beer bottles behind. During the day this side of the heath is well used by locals walking their dogs and children. Use some common sense and Hampstead Heath will continue for a few more years. Tube Hampstead Heath / Golders Green

Heston Motorway Service Station

(M4: Junction 2-3, Hounslow TW5) Between Junctions 2 and 3 of the M4, near Heathrow Airport, there's a truck stop and car parks. Here, the main toilet area is busy, both day and night. East-bound facilities close around 2200, however, the west-bound facilities are open all night. There's plenty of scope around the main doors, close to the phone boxes. This ground gets particularly busy after 2300. I wonder, do truckers have a signal to indicate that they are after a bit of cock? I have heard that they tie a ribbon or a piece of rag (any colour) to their driver-side wing mirror....

Holland Walk   (Holland Park W8) A late-night cruising ground in central-west London. The walk is a short cut between Holland Park Avenue and Kensington High Street, starting either at Holland Park tube or opposite the junction of Earl's Court Road and Kensington High Street, running along the east side of Holland Park. It is a good place to meet guys coming home from a night out in Earl's Court, but be warned they could be straight. You will find lots of cruising in the wooded areas behind the fencing – keep an eye out for man-made holes in the fence. Discretion and caution is advised (do not be too flamboyant in dress and manner). **Tube** Holland Park

Ladywell Park   (Ladywell Road, Ladywell SE13) A late-night (2200-onwards) cruising area by the river amongst the trees and bushes. No action during the day at all. **Tube** Ladywell (mainline)

Mile End Park   (Mile End E3) At present this can be rather a hit-and-miss affair as the council are redeveloping the whole park. For the moment, try the junction where Burdett Road meets Mile End Road, more or less opposite Mile End tube station. There is/was a cottage on this corner just inside the park, however, it may be demolished for the redesign. **Tube** Mile End

Russell Square   (Bloomsbury, London WC1) The tube is busy seven nights a week (very busy!), usually between 1230 and 0230. The garden area around the snack bar and the air-monitoring shack is where you should aim for. On some nights the floodlights are switched on, so caution is advised. During the summer months the council starts to cut back the shrubbery, making privacy harder to find, but it can be found. Although managed by Camden Council, Russell Square is actually on land owned by Lord and Lady Tavistock, and they and other parties have welcomed plans to close Russell Square at nights to put an end to consensual cruising. Some lobbyists, however, are insisting that the park becomes an official gay cruising ground through tradition using the equal rights / straight lovers lane argument. You'll get to know the outcome if the gates are chained up when you get there! Still, we may be down but we're certainly not out because nearby, just one block away from Bloomsbury Square (Great Russell Street and Bedford Place) there is a viable alternative. A small park above an underground car park – although quieter – is also a late evening local sex spot, catching on in popularity since all the hoo-ha about Russell Square. **Tube** Russell Square

South Ealing
Cemetery   (Occupation Lane, South Ealing W5) What is it about gay cruising grounds and cemeteries? Have you got no respect? Again, I'd recommend an alternative ground. If you do choose to come here the access will change whether it is during the day or evening. For daytime cruising use the entrance on the Popes Lane junction with Lionel Road. I have heard that the daytime shift is quite busy. At night, you will have to use the entrance on Occupation Lane which is at the opposite (south side) of the park. **Tube** South Ealing

Southwark Park (Surrey Quays, London SE16) The entrance to this evening rendezvous is on Lower Road (A200) opposite the Shell garage. Make your way to the top garden and playground area where there is adequate cover in the bushes and trees. **Tube** Surrey Quays

Streatham Common (Streatham, London SW16) By following the long footpath at the top of the common, make your way to the rookery cottage on Streatham Common South – the junction with Covington Way, adjacent to the woods. There's not much action during the day but it's heaving after dark and through to the early hours of the morning, any day of the week. There is a rumour that the cottage will be demolished but even so, it is the perimeter of the cottage that gets cruisy – so ha!

Sunbury (Sunbury Lay-by, M3: Junction 1)Located near to Kempton Park race-course: the best way to get here is from London on the A316 heading towards the M3. Just as you are getting on the motorway take the round-about to return you the way you have just come (ie. head back to London) and it is the first lay-by you come to. You will see the trucks and the cars... and the cock! By the way, this area is well known to the police and they will come sniffing around at various intervals through-out the night.

Tooting Bec Common (Bedford Hill SW16) Make your way to the area north of Bedford Hill and west of the railway cutting. This area is extremely busy late in the evening and especially during the summer months.

The Tube (All tube trains) A while ago someone posted a message on a gay website saying that people who cruise on the undergrounds should use the very last carriage on the tube – any tube. This message circulated round all the gay press and cruising guides and so to carry on this trend I repro-duce this tip here. Let me know how you fare. **Tube** Any!

West Brompton Cemetery (Earl's Court, London SW6) There's lots of outdoor cruising by the western wall where shrubbery and quite a few trees offer a degree of pri-vacy. This site is used extensively throughout the day, however, the National Park police heavily patrol the area on foot and, at times, mount a sting operation. You probably don't need me to reiterate (yet again) that this seems an entirely inappropriate ground to cruise. I'd advise you to seek an alternative ground. For those of you who won't heed a warning, the cemetery is located quite close to Brompton's (see separate listing) and practically adjoining West Brompton tube station.

Retail & Other

Ad-Hoc & Metal Morphosis 10-11 Moor Street, London W1 Phone 020 7287 0911
This place is regarded as the best seller of transvestite and alternative clothing in the country. Ad-Hoc has been associated with just about every major alternative scene of the last three decades. Not restricted to this they also sell PVC and rubber clothing, make-up, hair colourings and wigs. Metal Morphosis, the body-piercing centre, is in the shop's

basement, of which the inside-entrance to both is covered in flyers for the many alternative events and club nights happening in London at any one time. **Open** Monday-Saturday 1100-1930. Sunday 1300-1800 **Tube** Leicester Square

Adonis Art   1b Coleherne Road, Earl's Court, London SW10 9BS Phone 020 7460 3888
E-mail **stewart@adonis-art.com** Web **www.adonis-art.com**
Adonis Art specialises in fine antique and contemporary works of art that celebrate the male body in all its strength and beauty. Items on sale include oil paintings, watercolours, drawings, prints, photographs, sculptures, bronze figures and a host of other unique objects. The upstairs gallery is devoted to works of male figurative art by artists living and dead. They also stock a huge range of greeting cards, unique to Adonis Art. These cards are exclusively made of male art images that have been exhibited and sold in the gallery. The art displays are always changing as the works are bought and sold and the best part is that there is no charge to view the gallery and visitors are always welcome to browse. **Open** Monday-Saturday 1030-1830

American Retro   35 Old Compton Street, London W1 Phone 020 7734 3477
E-mail **info@americanretro.com** Web **www.americanretro.com**
From an Issey Miyake teddybear to a Trailer Trash doll. From the fabulous 'Gay Times travel guides' to 'art in the 20th century'. From .. Well, you can see for yourself as you wander round the shop with more oohs and aaahs than the firework finale at Disneyland. **Open** Monday-Friday 1030-1930. Saturday 1030-1900. Sunday closed **Tube** Piccadilly

Aveda Concept   182-184 Kensington Church Street, London W8 4DP Phone 020 7221 2266
Salon   A gay-friendly salon which offers all the usuals: facials, manicures, tanning and so forth. **Tube** Notting Hill

Clone Zone   266 Old Brompton Road, Earl's Court, London SW5 9HR
Phone 020 7373 0598
E-mail **info@clonezone.co.uk** Web **www.clonezone.co.uk**
A sex shop for gay men with outlets in most major cities throughout the UK. Clone Zone sells practically everything you could possibly need from (those kind of) magazines and books to condoms and lube. They will also be able to inform you of any events going on in the city and supply the tickets you need to gain admittance. All the free gay press and club flyers are available here and it is always worth asking the staff if there are any specialist events going on that will suit your area of interest. For example, 'Where can I go to get pissed on please?' It always works for me! **Open** Monday-Saturday 1000-2100

64 Old Compton Street, London W1V 5PA Phone 020 7287 3530
E-mail **info@clonezone.co.uk** Web **www.clonezone.co.uk**
Same as their Brompton Road store with slightly reduced weekday hours, but opening on a Sunday. **Open** Monday-Saturday 1100-2100. Sunday 1300-1900 **Tube** Piccadilly

Compton Hair   7 Old Compton Street, London W1 Phone 020 7434 0969
A hair salon that can give you a short back and sides without you so much as having to leave London's most famous gay street.

Expectations   75 Great Eastern Street, London EC2A 3HU Phone 020 7739 0292
E-mail sales@expectations.co.uk Web www.expectations.co.uk
Slaving away specialising in leather, rubber, S&M equipment and sportswear, Expectations has built up a reputation for quality crafts-manship. Their leather and rubber is handmade in their own workshop with a full repair, alteration and design service available. Alterations can be made to items bought outside the store if time permits. All items are available either from their store in London or via their secure worldwide mail-order service. **Open** Monday-Friday 1100-1900. Saturday 1100-2000. Sunday 1200-1700 **Tube** Old Street

Fettered   81-83 Pancras Road, Kings Cross, London NW1 2BQ
Pleasures   Phone 020 7713 7333 E-mail sales@fetteredpleasures.com
Web www.fetteredpleasures.com
Fettered Pleasures are specialists and stockists for Fetters, Demask, Folsom Electrical and Inner Sanctum products. They also stock and manufacture pre-19th-century irons and dungeon equipment, canes and crops, whips and floggers, suspension accessories, dildos and butt plugs. You name it. **Open** Monday 1130-1930. Wednesday by appointment only. Thursday-Saturday 1130-1930. Sunday 1130-1730 **Tube** Kings Cross

Gay's The Word   66 Marchmount Street, London WC1N 1AB Phone 020 7278 7654
E-mail sales@gaystheword.co.uk Web www.gaystheword.co.uk
Gay's The Word is probably the largest lesbian and gay bookshop in the UK. Established in 1979, they are located in the historic Bloomsbury district of London. They stock an enormous range of books from the profound to the frivolous and entertaining. Fiction ranges from prize-winning literary work through to detective, romance and erotic fiction. Non-fiction covers a wide range of issues, from how to have sex to how to tell your mother that you are gay. The free gay press, magazines, flyers and leaflets are also available and if you're just after some advice on what's happening, when and where, then all you have to do is ask the friendly and informative staff and they'll do their best to help. If you want to receive a quarterly newsletter listing the latest lesbian and gay titles then just send them your e-mail address and request. **Open** Monday-Saturday 1000-1830. Sunday 1400-1800 **Tube** Russell Square (two-minute walk)

Hard Wear   70 Essex Road, Islington, London N1 8LT Phone 020 7359 8667
A shop supplying military, sportswear, boots and industrial clothing. **Open** Monday-Saturday 1000-1800

The Host   The Arches, 45b South Lambeth Road, Vauxhall, London SW8 1RT
Phone 020 7582 2282 E-mail info@host-rubberwear.com
Web www.host-rubberwear.com
The House Of Subversive Thought (HOST) serves the community with

a wild range of in-house produced rubberwear. They stock a good amount of leather gear too for the seasoned pervert and the mildly curious (they are a dealer for Vanson, responsible for top notch biker gear if you did but know it). Brand names include Hostage, Hostile, Retarded Republic and Retro Virus and you will almost certainly find something amongst these that suits your taste. Plans for Hostess rubberwear for girls will probably come into fruition later this year. Good news, eh Suzie...? **Open** Monday-Tuesday by appointment only. Wednesday-Saturday 1200-2000 **Tube** Vauxhall

Gay's The Word, named after an Ivor Novello musical, is one of the most famous lesbian and gay bookshop in Britain. Their aim has always been to be up-front and unashamed, and to be inclusive of the diversity of lifestyle choices made by lesbians and gay men. Inspired by the emergence and growth of lesbian and gay bookstores in the States, a small group of people from Gay Icebreakers – a gay socialist group – founded the shop in 1979. Gay books weren't generally available in ordinary bookstores at this time. In their early newsletters they used to list the few bookshops in Britain where you could buy gay books. The gay movement at this period in the States was particularly vibrant and stimulated an immense amount of literature with many small publishing houses being established. Consequently, large quantities of books were imported from the States. Armistead Maupin's books were hugely popular at the shop long before his books were even being published in the UK. From the very beginning, the shop was used as a community and information resource centre. There was a coffee area and a free notice board which helped to draw people into the shop. As well as being a bookshop and a place to meet people, various community groups used the shop after hours for meetings which further helped to publicise and establish the shop. Speakers from the shop would regularly go to address different gay groups and raise the shop's profile profile. In 1984 Customs and Excise, assuming the shop to be a porn store rather than a proper bookshop, mounted a large scale raid on the shop and seized thousands of pounds' worth of books. Works by Tennessee Williams, Gore Vidal, Christopher Isherwood and Jean Genet were among the books seized. The directors were eventually charged with conspiracy to import indecent books. A campaign was set in motion and the charges were vigorously defended. Newspaper articles appeared, various MPs visited the shop and questions were asked in the House of Commons. After a long and expensive campaign the case finally collapsed. Today, Gay's The Word still remains a beacon for gay and lesbian bookselling.

It's Marvellous   5 Greens Court, London W1 Phone 020 7287 8748
It's Marvellous, in the heart of Soho, is a salon that offers a full range of styles and services from clipper cut and permanent wave through to wig dressing. They also offer a full range of complementary services, including the stress-busting massage chair, extensions and tanning systems. Appointments not always necessary. **Open** Monday-Saturday 1000-2000. Every first Sunday 1200-1600 **Price** £24 for a cut and finish **Tube** Piccadilly

3

Key Largo   19 Shelton Street, Covent Garden, London WC2 Phone 020 7240 7599
E-mail info@key-largo.co.uk Web www.key-largo.co.uk
Key Largo started life in Earl's Court during the '70s selling motorbikes
and the clothes that went with them. The most popular were the leather
jackets from the US by, the then unknown brand, Schott. The decline of
the motorbike industry forced the proprietor Alan Chapman to consider his options and with the success of Schott he was encouraged to consider general retailing. The new venue prompted a new name and Key
Largo came into existence in 1982. Then, 14 years later, when it was not
possible to pack any more labels – or customers – he moved premises
again into its present location, a spacious store on Shelton Street which
allows the classic range of Schott to be stocked in full, together with the
Levi's range and Dockers amongst other contemporary collections
(Nico Didonna, Speedo, 2x(ist), Punto Blanco, Soviet and Revenge
amongst others). **Open** Monday-Saturday 1100-1830 **Tube** Covent Garden

MOT Beauty   28 Maddox Street, London W1S 1PR Phone 020 7499 4904
Salon   E-mail info@mot-matthews.co.uk Web www.mot-matthews.co.uk
MOT is the concept of three beauty therapists: Adrienne Ashcroft,
Alicia Wong and Julie Hayden-Baker who have been treating men exclusively since 1992. MOT has now joined forces with Ian Matthews and
between them they are committed to providing excellent customer service. MOT are pioneers in the male beauty industry and offer the most
expert range of skin, hair and body treatments available to men. They
have been extremely selective in their choice of product lines, many of
which are used by the medical profession and, to ensure optimum
results, their specialised range of treatments use some of the most
advanced technology in the industry. Treatments offered include red-
vein removal, hair removal and anti-ageing treatments. This is where the
world's first shaving school originated! With over 25 years of experience
in men's grooming you can come to MOT for services including hair-
cuts, tinting, shaving and head massage, all of which are carried out in
luxurious private cubicles. Ian also has his own range of products which
include shaving creams, after-shave balms and hair and body shampoos.
Here, you can expect expert consultation, combined with many years of
hands-on experience and an unparalleled quality of treatments. MOT
are well ahead of the rest of the field. **Open** Monday-Friday 1100-2000.
Saturday 1000-1800 **Price** Various, on request **Tube** Piccadilly

Obsessions   2 Hays Galleria, London Bridge, London SE1 2HD Phone 020 7403 2374
E-mail info@obsessions.co.uk Web www.obsessions.co.uk
A gift shop that offers original and exciting gifts that look more expen-
sive than they cost. Obsessions also has shops at 90 Cowcross Street,
Faringdon, London EC1M 6BH (020 7253 0083) and at 23 Old
Brompton Road, South Kensington, London SW7 3HZ (020 7589 00711).
Open Monday-Saturday 1030-1830

Oscars Cinema   42 Northdown Street, Islington, London N1 Phone 020 7837 0188
Club   Near to Kings Cross Station and established for just over five years, this
fully-licensed 21-seat cinema is exclusively for gay men. A very friendly,

exceptionally clean little place incorporating a little lounge area where you can sit and chat in between wanks, erm, I mean films. **Open** Monday-Friday 1100-2030. Saturday 1200-2000. Sunday 1300-1900 **Price** £5 **Tube** Kings Cross

Out and Out Dining Club

72 Old Compton Street, London W1V 5PA Phone 020 8998 5674
E-mail info@outandout.co.uk Web www.outandout.co.uk

Out and Out is the UK's longest established private members' club for gay men, offering its members the opportunity to be introduced to other compatible groups of men in a relaxed and friendly atmosphere, whilst enjoying terrific events at top London venues. Over the past twelve months they have visited some 20 different restaurants on over 30 different occasions; their trips have also taken in the theatre, opera and ballet – not to mention tea at The Ritz and picnics at Glyndebourne. Most members meet up regularly between events and many have even set up home together! When you join the club you will have a long and friendly chat with one of the team and then again regularly between events. By getting to know you and maintaining personal contact they ensure that you will always be invited to the events you will most enjoy. After an interview of getting to know what your interests are, they'll make sure that you're well looked after. They're not going to sit you next to someone with opposite beliefs – or at the opposite range of the age spectrum. Nearly seven years in the business has taught them how to handle their clients with care, and with most of the evenings run by female hostesses there's less of a sexual imperative and more of an emphasis on fun and socialising. It doesn't stop at the dinner table either – they have theatre evenings and other social activities for those who wish to attend. So, if you fancy a break from clubbing, get in touch for an out-and-out evening with a difference. They also ensure that you are happy with the service that they are providing at all times. They personally host all events and strive to take care to introduce members and to ensure that everyone has a good time and is comfortable. Confidentiality is of paramount importance and details of their database are never disclosed to anyone. The club is ideal for new Londoners, couples, singles or anybody wishing to expand their social horizons and increase their circle of gay friends. For those looking for someone special there's none of the embarassment, awkwardness or uncertainty associated with lonely-hearts columns, dating agencies, blind dates or the superficiality involved in the scene. Relationships are allowed to develop in the most natural and unpressurised circumstances and by meeting like-minded men in a relaxed environment, members quickly strike up friendships. There is an annual membership fee and each dinner costs about £40. Ages range from the mid-twenties to sixty-year-olds and there's an eclectic mix of people.

Paradiso

41 Old Compton Street, London W1 Phone 020 7287 2487

Have you ever gone out and thought... 'damn, I've left my surgical steel nipple clamps at home on the coffee table?' I have, but then I know I can always get a replacement set at Paradiso for about £18. Whilst you are in here you may be tempted to buy a pair of thigh-length patent leather boots for around £125 and a riding crop to accessorise (I know I have). In fact, no matter what you forget to bring out with you in the fetish-wear department you can always get it here. Have you ever gone out and thought... 'damn, I've left my Madonna-style coned bustiere hanging up in the armoire...?' **Open** Monday-Saturday 1100-2100 **Tube** Piccadilly

Paris Gym

Arch 73 Goding Street, Vauxhall, London SE1 Phone **020 7735 8989** E-mail **info@parisgym.com** Web **www.parisgym.com**

Paris Gym is London's only exclusively gay men's gym. It was opened in May 1996 and since then the gym has become a well-established part of the London gay scene. Although there is a sauna, it is strongly recommended you look elsewhere if you are hoping for that 'other sort' of workout, as sauna-only admittance is not allowed and they certainly don't encourage any hanky-panky. The gym is run in a very informal manner, and the staff know almost every member on a first-name basis. If you have never been to the gym before you are welcome to call in at any time to look around. You do not need to make an appointment. There is also a powerful stand-up 60-tube sunbed, a hairdresser (on Fridays), a free internet station, free sweat towels to use whilst working out and free shower gel, shaving foam, hair gel and deodorant (what, no Clinique toiletries?). Shower towels can be provided for a charge of 80p. Lockers are free too. Whilst at the gym you can help yourself to a drink from the fridge and pay when you leave, or if you are a member you may prefer to run up a tab and pay at the end of the week. The gym floor is mainly machine-based. There are about 50 different stations in addition to a full range of dumb-bells from two to 50 kilos. The gym is situated in Vauxhall (south of the river) behind The Vauxhall Tavern and is a few doors away from gay club Crash. **Open** Monday-Saturday 1000-2200. Sunday 1500-2000 **Price** £7 day membership or £46 per month (by standing order per year) **Tube** Vauxhall (exit 2)

Prowler Camden

283 Camden High Street, London NW1 7BX Phone 020 7284 0537 E-mail **info@zipper.co.uk** Web **www.zipper.co.uk**

Prowler-Camden (formerly Zipperstore) is the longest-established licensed gay sex shop in the UK. They supply a mind-boggling range of videos, cards, books, magazines, leather, rubberwear and bondage gear. Their video section provides all-action stories and scenes, including smooth young lads in the Vulcan titles, tough studs in many of the R18 titles, and hot couples doing what boys like to do best! Books provide hot, one-handed fiction, cuddly love stories, non-fiction and eye-popping picture books. The CD collection includes club hits, classic covers and pumping numbers to keep you up all night. The magazine section lists many American titles full of studs, inches and rumps – something to keep you coming back for more, again and again. And their toys and accessories include all the dildos, bondage toys, lubes and condoms you could wish for. In short – if it ain't here – you don't need it! Take a look around. You're bound to find something you can play with. **Open** Monday-Saturday 1000-1830 **Tube** Camden Town

Prowler Soho

3-7 Brewer Street, London W1R 3FN Phone 020 7734 4031 E-mail **prowler@millivres.co.uk** Web **www.millivres.co.uk** In addition to the extensive mail-order catalogue and their on-line secure server, Prowler have a retail outlet that is the ultimate kind of gay shopping experience. This is Prowler's show-piece store, replete with huge windows, funky neon lighting and friendly staff who are just like you. It all adds up to a guilt-free and exciting place to shop which caters for all your needs in an environment every bit as stylish as you would find on Regent Street. The shop has at least five times more product than their nearest competitor and the enormous floor space allows them to stock the most comprehensive selection of products in each of their departments. Of course, sex is the most important part of being gay – and they have enough magazines, toys and aromas to pep up the dullest sex life. They also sell a huge amount of the latest fashion from big name designers. They also can boast that they sell more books than any other shop in the West End. In addition to all this they have an enviable selection of gifts, housewares and accessories. **Open** Monday-Saturday 1100-2200. Sunday 1200-2000 **Tube** Piccadilly

Recoil.557

The Railway Arch, Redcross Way (corner of Southwark Street), London SE1 1TA Phone 020 7378 0557 E-mail **info@dirtybastards.com** Web **www.dirtybastards.com** Recoil's workshop is based in a 1,000 square-foot railway arch. It's damp and it's dark – the ideal workspace for dirty rubber bastards. Fitted out with scaffold, rusty girders, disused metal cages and old tyres and absolutely packed with rubbergear. They also source other stuff like used boots and waders, tubing, funnels and gear that dirty pigs can enjoy. They have a unique changing room – but please don't piss in it! They also provide a full hands-on approach for their punters – they can advise on the sizing and use of their gear along with what's most popular with guys into 'certain stuff' and tips as to what you'll look most horny in. They also offer a full made-to-measure and custom service with a large percentage of their work being of an individual nature. Recoil is located on Bankside near to The Globe Theatre (an area that was once a medieval red-light district) and only 20 minutes away from Waterloo Eurostar. **Open** Monday-Wednesday 1200-1800. Thursday-Saturday 1200-2000 **Tube** Borough

Regulation

17a St Alban's Place, Islington Green, London N1 Phone 020 7226 0665
E-mail info@regulation-ltd.co.uk Web www.regulation-ltd.co.uk
Located in North London, Regulation ('the art of control') has on display over 2,000 items from full rubber suits and sleepsacks to leatherwear, in addition to a multitude of strapwork for all types of dungeon scenes. Always keen to answer the demands of their customers, they now have a range of inflatable equipment and vacuum equipment, as well as being the European distributor for Fetters bondage and restraint equipment. All of Regulation's leather and rubber gear is made in their own workshops adjoining the showroom. Tickets to most fetish venues and one-off parties (such as Fist) are available from here. There's also a comprehensive mail-order and on-line service available. Phone for further information and details on how to receive their product catalogue.
Open Monday-Saturday 1030-1830. Sunday 1200-1700 **Tube** Angel

3

Rob

24 Wells Street, London W1T 3PH Phone 020 7735 7893
E-mail roblondon@rob.nl Web www.rob.nl
Rob, established for well over ten years, is situated by the Plaza shopping centre, north of Oxford Street, and specialises in leather jackets, harnesses, rubber shirts, electro stimulation, tit wear, belts, leather hoods, whips, leather chaps, chastity belts, leather restraints, rubber suits, leather gags, rubber shorts, boots, caps, leather collars, leather posing pouches and accessories. In short: leather, rubber and twisted gear. A comprehensive mail-order service is available. Send for the catalogue which is in excess of 130 pages and costs £10 (which is refundable on any first order of £75 or more). Phone the above number for further information. You are now able to view the complete catalogue and order securely on-line. **Open** Monday-Saturday 1030-1830. Sunday 1200-1700
Tube Oxford Circus

Sh!

39 Coronet Street, London N1 6HD Phone 020 7613 5458
E-mail info@sh-womenstore.co.uk Web www.sh-womenstore.com
Sh! (pronounced shush) is for everything the modern woman could possibly want in the bedroom toy department. Displayed over two floors, you'll find everything from strap-ons to satin sheets, vibrators to videos, and everything in between. Leather-clad mistresses to suburban mums wander round this non-judgemental store sharing sex tips or mooching around wondering if there is any more room in the bedside drawer for

that delightful lickety-lick-licking-licker as featured and admired on TV's Graham Norton Show. This place is well worth a visit by all women in London – men too, but only if they are accompanied by a responsible female. **Open** Monday-Saturday 1130-1830. Thursday 'til 2000 **Tube** Old Street (two-minute walk)

Silver Moon Bookshop   64-68 Charing Cross Road, London WC2H 0BB
Phone 020 7836 7906 E-mail **smwb@silvermoonbookshop.co.uk**
Web **www.silvermoonbookshop.co.uk**
Silver Moon Bookshop was established in 1984 and is the largest women's bookshop in Europe. They are specialists in books by or about women and they offer a knowledgeable, courteous and fast service. The free gay press, flyers and leaflets to all major gay London events can be picked up from here and there is also a well-maintained notice board on the premises that is absolutely packed with women's services, events and accommodation notices. **Open** Monday-Friday 0930-1930. Saturday-Sunday 1000-1800 **Tube** Charing Cross

The Sugar Shop   35 Southwick Street, London W2 1JQ Phone 020 7402 1400
E-mail **info@sugarshop.co.uk** Web **www.sugarshop.co.uk**
This salon has been established for more than six years and is an absolute first: a shop dedicated to body hair removal and beauty treatments exclusively for men by male therapists. They offer body hair removal by the most effective and least painful method possible – the ancient art of sugaring. **Open** Monday and Wednesday 1100-2000. Tuesday and Friday 0900-2000. Thursday 0900-2100. Saturday 1030-1730 **Tube** Paddington / Lancaster Gate

Urban Life   17 Hackney Road, London E2 Phone 020 7729 0066
Urban Life offers unisex hair styling, tattoos and body piercing and they are local-authority registered. **Open** Tuesday-Friday 1100-1900. Saturday-Sunday 1100-1630

ZE Hair and Beauty   270 Fulham Road, Chelsea, London SW10 9EW Phone 020 7351 2266
A top class beauty salon for men, open seven days a week with late nights on Tuesday, Wednesday and Thursday. ZE offer a bewildering array of treatments from hairdressing (cut and finish £25), electrolysis (£22.50 per half-hour), manicures and pedicures to a full seaweed body

wrap (£45). There's pretty much everything else that you can imagine in between too. **Open** Monday 0900-1800. Tuesday-Thursday 0900-0200. Friday-Saturday 0900-1800. Sunday 1000-1600

Escorts

Bill Glen's and Adams

London Phone 020 8530 1050 E-mail enquiries@billglens.com Web www.billglens.com

A London-based top-of-the-market escort agency offering corporate entertainment, executive and personal services, and currently celebrating their 25th year in business. They offer an exclusive selection of attractive young ladies and fit young men who would be happy to meet you at the place of your choice. Whether you would like a companion for dinner or a theatre date, they can help you. **Open** Daily, 24 hours, 365 days of the year

Capital Escorts

London Phone 020 7630 7567

Capital is a small but well-established consultancy who really take the time to listen to your needs. They are friendly, professional and totally discreet. Whether you want a companion at home or abroad, for a brief meeting or a longer encounter, Capital can arrange it quickly and efficiently. That's why so many of their clients return to them again and again. You can visit them at their central London offices and view a portfolio which includes some of London's most attractive young escorts and masseurs.

Choirboyz UK Limited

London Phone 07000 794 793 E-mail enquiries@choirboyz.co.uk Web www.choirboyz.co.uk

Choirboyz interviews each escort in-depth, and only accept the few who meet their high standards of appearance, personality, interests and education. Each 'Choirboy' is a companion who will be at ease in any social setting – public or private. They also strive to match client and escort interests. Good chemistry and compatible preferences aim to ensure that both parties are happy together. **Open** Monday-Sunday 1200-0000

City Agency Escorts

London Phone 020 8888 8199 (1200 'til 2200)

E-mail theboys@thecityagency.co.uk Web www.thecityagency.co.uk

This is an escort agency that serves London and the surrounding area

3

3

and provides stunning-looking escorts for social or private engagements. Their website provides a limited choice of available escorts, although there are lads of every type available who might be without a description on the website (phone for more details).

L'Homme Male Escorts

London Phone 0802 181185 E-mail lhomme@sirens-escorts.com
Web www.sirens-escorts.com/lhomme.html

L'Homme make sure that their escorts behave in a discreet and appropriate manner. When booking a male escort of the calibre that L'Homme insists upon, you can be assured of an attractive, charming and attentive companion who will go out of his way to make sure that you enjoy yourself.

Soho is much more than the hub of London's gay scene. For a start, there's a multitude of theatres: The Shaftesbury, built in 1911, bombed and rebuilt; The Lyric, in Shaftesbury Avenue, built in 1888; The Queens, on the corner of Shaftesbury Avenue and Wardour Street, built in 1907; The Apollo, in Shaftesbury Avenue, built in 1901 and The Prince Edward, in Old Compton Street, built in 1930. Then there's the cinemas – an abundance of them; The Empire in Leicester Square perhaps the most well-known. There's also The Trocadero, in Leicester Square, which started life in 1744 as 'real tennis' courts, then went on to house a circus, billiard rooms, waxworks and theatre. Named The Argyll Rooms, it was a pick-up point for ladies of ill repute. In 1895, J. Lyons & Co. took over the building and turned it into a restaraunt. Nowadays, it houses tourist attractions. It was from the '20s onwards that Soho began to be known as a night club area. There were clubs in Gerrard Street, Coventry Street, Meard Street and Dean Street, all frequented by the rich and famous. In the '50s jazz came to Soho. The most famous remainder from those days is Ronnie Scotts, in Frith Street. There was also The Marquee, in Wardour Street, which accommodated many a famous rock group in its time. And let's not forget the world-famous Raymond's Revue Bar, in Brewer Street. But then, you wouldn't be at all interested in Soho's seedier side, would you...?

Suited and Booted

London Phone 020 7723 8788 E-mail info@suitedandbooted.com
Web www.suitedandbooted.com

Suited and Booted is committed to providing the highest possible standard in the escort business, offering a different, dynamic and quality service. They have established a disciplined approach to answering clients' needs and they strive to answer the needs of individuals and companies, whatever the service required.

Villa Gianni Escorts

London Phone 020 7244 9901 E-mail enquiries@villagianni.com
Web www.villagianni.com

This agency was founded in April 1999 and is located in sumptuous and elegant new premises with several clean and well-appointed private rooms. Only top-class masseurs and escorts work in this agency and you will definitely find one (or more) that suits you. You can choose from about 40 guys of different nationalities, from muscular to slim and

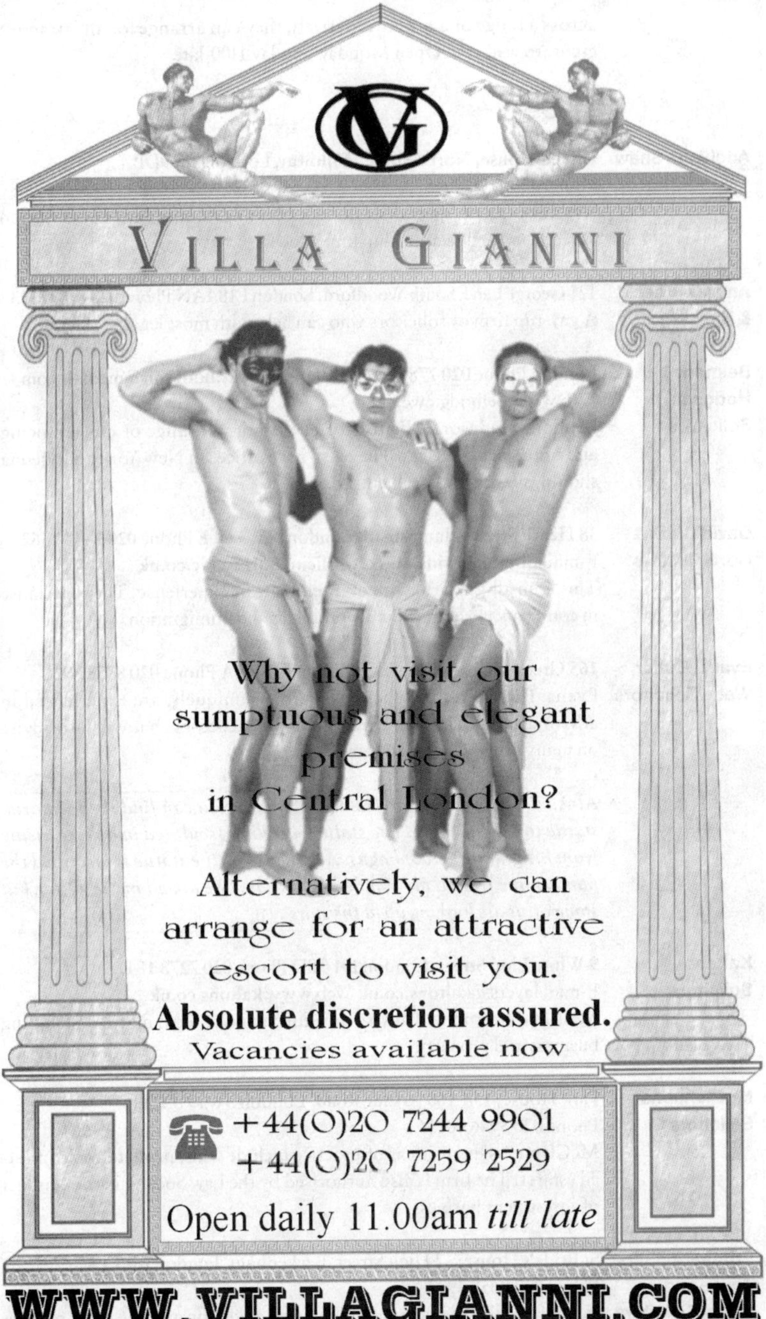
VILLA GIANNI
Why not visit our sumptuous and elegant premises in Central London?
Alternatively, we can arrange for an attractive escort to visit you.
Absolute discretion assured.
Vacancies available now
+44(0)20 7244 9901
+44(0)20 7259 2529
Open daily 11.00am till late
WWW.VILLAGIANNI.COM

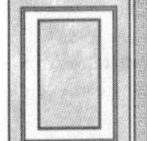

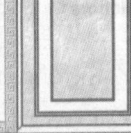

across a range of ages. Alternatively, they can arrange for an attractive escort to visit you. **Open** Monday-Sunday 1100-late

Legal

Aitchison Shaw

United House, North Road, Holloway, London N7 9DP
Phone 020 7700 0045
Aitchison Shaw specialises in children and family law, cohabitation agreements and relationship breakdowns.

Andrew Keen & Hassett

121 George Lane, South Woodford, London E18 1AN Phone 020 8989 3123
A gay-run firm of solicitors who can help with most legal problems.

Belmont Hodgson Solicitors

London Phone 020 7787 6777 E-mail belmont.hodgson@mcmail.com
Web www.belhodg.cwc.net
Belmont Hodgson Solicitors offer the normal range of conveyancing and other legal services. They also have offices in New York and Vienna should you run into problems there!

David Clark & Co. Solicitors

38 Heath Street, Hampstead, London NW3 6TE Phone 020 7433 1562
E-mail office@davidclark&cosolicitors.freeserve.co.uk
This is an all-gay firm with over ten years of experience. They specialise in conveyancing, crime, family problems and immigration.

Evans, Butler, Wade Solicitors

165 Greenwich High Road, London SE10 8JA Phone 020 8858 8926
Evans, Butler, Wade Solicitors, perhaps uniquely, are experienced in advising gay and lesbian parents and parents-to-be, but will also advise on many other gay legal matters.

At Adelaide Street, near Trafalgar Square, you can find the memorial statue to Oscar Wilde. The statue has Wilde, sculpted in bronze, rising from his granite sarcophagus. At the foot of the statue is inscribed the famous line from Lady Windermere's Fan: 'We are all in the gutter, but some of us are looking up at the stars'.

Kaltons Solicitors

9 White Lion Street, London N1 9PD Phone 020 7278 1817
E-mail layers@kaltons.co.uk Web www.kaltons.co.uk
Maitland Kalton will advise on a full range of legal matters including business and property.

McGlennons Solicitors

Park House, 158-160 Arthur Road, London SW19 8AQ
Phone 020 8946 6015
McGlennons' main areas of practice include wills, probate and contested estates. The firm is also authorised by the Law Society in the conduct of investment business.

Pritchard, Joyce and Hinds Solicitors

St Bride's House, 32 High Street, Beckenham, London BR3 1AY
Phone 020 8658 3922
A gay-friendly solicitors providing legal advice on a whole array of business and personal matters. **Open** Monday-Friday 0930-1800

Luton Pubs

Coopers Arms 55 Bute Street, Luton LU1 2EP Phone 01582 720 688
A modern and up-market gay bar that caters for a wide mix of Luton's
gay community. There's nothing really special by the way of entertainment apart from a drag act every couple of weeks on a Saturday evening.
Other than that there is only the background music to keep you entertained: more of a social venue than a dance bar. **Open** Monday-Saturday
1200-2300. Sunday 1400-2230

The Inkerman 52 Inkerman Street, Luton LU1 1JB Phone 01582 450 389
Arms E-mail info@inkerman-arms.co.uk Web www.inkerman-arms.co.uk
When Glyn and John took over the Inkerman in 2000 it had a reputation
for being an old man's boozer. Since then though, the crew have taken
the pub through a pretty radical transformation. As well as regular
cabaret, The Inkerman is home to regular strip nights and charity fun
nights (the proceeds of which go to local HIV/AIDS charity The Lodge)
Open Monday-Thursday 1500-2300. Friday 1400-2300. Saturday 1200-
2300. Sunday 1300-2230

The Temple 1 Liverpool Road, Luton LU1 1RS Phone 01582 725 491
Formerly known as Shirley's Temple this is a small, popular gay venue
catering for all ages and types. There's no entertainment during the
week as yet, although this may change throughout the summer months.
Open Monday-Friday 1600-2300. Saturday 1400-2300. Sunday 1400-2230

Saunas

Greenhouse 23 Crawley Road, Luton LU1 1HX Phone 01582 487 701
Health Club E-mail info@gay-sauna.com Web www.gay-sauna.com
Greenhouse is laid out over four floors and has a very discreet entrance
for the shy boys. On the ground floor is the reception area, adjoining
café and locker room housing 140 lockers. And yes, they are sometimes
all full! At the back of the building, next to the showers, is the rather
impressive Jacuzzi that looks like it is set in a cave, complete with stalac-
tites. In addition, two lions guard the area to discourage any unruly
behaviour. At the rear of the Jacuzzi is a rest room, complete with harness. On the first floor there are smoking and non-smoking TV lounges,
a sauna rest room and a steam room with adjoining showers. On the second floor there's more rest rooms, a video room and a communal area.
The top floor houses the hotel, which is only accessible to residents via a
lift. The rooms are £25 and you can get either a twin or a double, with
free admission into the sauna for the first guest (and half-price for the
second guest). The rooms are en-suite and breakfast is included in the
price. All in all, a great value-for-money experience). **Open** Monday-
Thursday 2300-0200. Friday 2300-0600. Saturday 1100-0800. Sunday
1200-0000 **Price** £10

Manchester

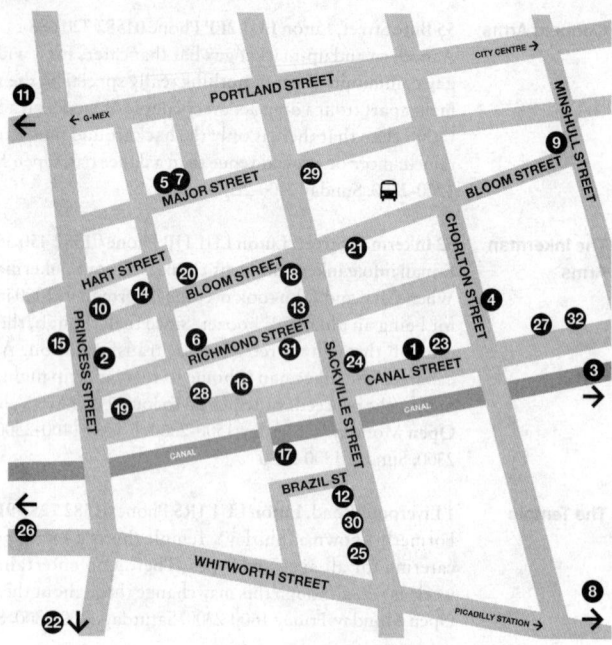

Map key

1 Bar 38	**17** Metz
2 Bar Med	**18** Napoleons
3 Basement Sauna (off)	**19** The New Union
4 Churchill's	**20** New York-New York
5 Classix / Dustys / Fussy Pussy @ Sub Cruz 101	**21** Paddy's Goose
6 Company Bar	**22** Paradise Factory (off)
7 Cruz 101	**23** Prague 5
8 DV8 (off)	**24** The Rembrandt Hotel
9 Essential	**25** The Retro Bar
10 Exodus/Poptastic @ Mutz Nutz	**26** Sin:ergy @ The Phoenix (off)
11 Fab Café (off)	**27** Slug and Lettuce
12 Gaia	**28** Spirit
13 H20 Zone	**29** The Thompsons Arms
14 Hollywood Showbar	**30** Tribeca
15 Manhattan Showbar	**31** Vanilla
16 Manto	**32** Velvet

The ancient history of Manchester can be traced as far back as AD79, when the Roman General Julius Agricola fortified several military stations, of which Mancunium was one, and a castle was built on the site of what is now called Castlefield. In 426, Mancunium reverted to the possession of its original owners, who persuaded the Saxons from Germany to assist them against the Piets. These allies, in turn, became masters, and took possession of nearly the whole of Southern Britain; and Mancunium, called Mancestre by the people, was occupied as a favourable position. In 1352, the manufacture of 'Manchester Cotton', a kind of woollen cloth, made from the fleece in an unprepared state, was introduced. At around the same time, numerous Flemish artisans settled in the town. They laid the foundation for the manufacturing of cotton to becoming (as it subsequently remained for centuries) the staple trade of the city. It was not, however, until about the year 1750, that the cotton trade really propelled the city significantly forward. In 1760, cotton goods, which until then had been made for home consumption only, found a market on the continents of Europe and America. The next 150 years saw Manchester come to prominence, at the very centre of Briatin's Industrial Revolution. Some of the first water- and steam-powered machines were invented by engineers from the Manchester area. The Victorians, keen to show their new-found wealth by building new, tall and extravagant buildings, decimated many of Manchester's most precious historical landmarks and buildings.

Today, Manchester is the major city in the north-west of England. The city's saddest moment of recent history was the morning of Saturday 15 June 1996, when a 3,500 pound IRA bomb exploded in the city centre. Prior to the blast, a 45 minute warning had ensured that the streets were cleared, saving any loss of life (although 220 people were injured). The city, though, was decimated once again, with many of its most beautiful buildings destroyed. Today, the rebuilding of Manchester is still underway and it will be some time yet before the city is completely restored.

Manchester may be short on attractions, but it is certainly not short on entertainment, particularly of the gay variety. This city has the largest gay village in the UK, all crammed into just one square mile of the city centre, starting at Chorlton Street coach station and overspilling onto Princess Street. The core of activity takes place on the world-famous Canal Street. During the glorious summer months this stretch of the city is likened to Ibiza. The music blares out of all the venues, the streets are crammed with hedonistic party animals and drag queens making glorious entrances to the whistles and shouts of an appreciative crowd and the overpowering smells of apre rasage and cannabis fills the air. It is hard to imagine that less than 15 years ago Canal Street was a dark, formiddable place with absolutely no gay venues at all except for The New Union at the bottom of the street and The Rembrandt halfway-up. Indeed, the only other gay venues in the city were on Bloom Street, with Glen Steven's New York – New York (with The Bronx night club on the first floor), Napoleons a little further up and The Number 1, up by the library on Central Street (now closed). It was only when Manto opened its doors and a new café-bar culture was introduced to the jaded scene that the village took on a new lease of life. Forward-thinking councillors took bold steps and pedestrianised Canal Street and from that point onwards, multi-national breweries invested heavily, turning delapidated buildings into award-winning establishments.

The annual bank holiday Gayfest celebrations (the last weekend in August) formerly known as Mardi Gras is the hightlight of Manchester's gay calendar. The streets around the gay village become a melting pot of gay and straight life. It all opens with a grand parade on the Saturday morning and culminates with a series of late-night parties on the Sunday evening. From 2001 the main culmination party will be held at The Printworks, the new multi-million leisure development on Withy Grove (by Victoria Station). The Gayfest event will see the venue dubbed 'The Pinkworks'. It promises to be the mother of all gay parties.

The newest club to embrace Manchester's gay scene is the fabulous Essential at the top of Bloom Street. Here, and here only, you can experience the city council's early-'90s 'dance-the-night-away' promise. Prior to this, the infamous Danceteria ran all night on a Saturday, but this was abruptly closed down by the council because of suspected drug-dealing on the premises. Essential is now your only all-night choice. Manchester is also home to the largest gay hotel in the UK – Hollywood International Hotel – and there are plans to expand this complex by another 45 rooms. When rooms here are full, the rest of the bed and breakfast accommmodation in the village starts to see more business.

Getting there

Airport   **Manchester Ringway** (0161 489 3000) is situated on the M56, about ten miles from the city centre. You can get a train from here to Piccadilly Station (four per hour, 24 hours per day) or a taxi from the concourse (it will cost approximately £12 to the gay village).

Trains   Manchester has two mainline stations. **Piccadilly Station** on London Road (about two minutes from the gay village), has routes that serve the south and east in the main. For detailed train information phone the **National Trainline** (08457 484950). **Victoria Station** on Victoria Street has routes that serve the north and west in the main.

Coaches   The landmark for the gay village is **Chorlton Street** coach station and from here you can get coaches to all parts of the United Kingdom at a reasonable price. Services are operated by **National Express** (0990 808080). The booking and information office is open Monday to Friday from 0715 to 1915 and Saturday to Sunday from 0715 to 1815.

Getting about

Metro   The fairly new Metrolink System for trams stretches across the whole of Greater Manchester from Altrincham in the south-west to Bury in the north-east, taking in about 30 stops (about ten of these lie within Manchester). Up-to-date passenger information can be gained by phoning **Metrolink Trams** (0161 205 2000).

Buses

Greater Manchester is well served with public transport. Most of the stops are based on or around Piccadilly Gardens. A couple of late-night buses apart, the services all come to a grinding halt at around 0000. Details of all routes and times can be gained by phoning **Greater Manchester Public Transport Executive** (0161 228 7811). Alternatively you can pick up a free route map and timetable from the information office in Piccadilly Gardens.

Taxis

There are two private taxi firms which serve the gay village. **Rainbow Cars (0161 236 0909) is** situated in the rear of the building that houses The Hollywood Showbar, and **Village Cabs** (0161 237 3383) is situated on Bloom Street. Friday and Saturday evenings see both ranks extremely busy and after 0200 you can expect a wait of up to one hour. The council-regulated black cabs will also be very busy, although you'll be in with a chance of flagging one of them down along Princess Street, or, alternatively you can brave the straight queues and use the rank outside Piccadilly station.

Tourist information

The **Manchester Visitor Centre** (0161 234 3169) is based within the Town Hall extension on Lloyd Street. The people here are exceptionally helpful and will be able to give you free city-centre maps and local sightseeing information. Most of the gay establishments in Manchester will be happy to help you with any enquiries too, not least Clone Zone and Funky Crop Shop.

Bureaux de change

Most travel operators throughout Manchester have their own bureau de change desks situated on the premises. The largest of these are **American Express** (0870 600 1060) along Deansgate and **Thomas Cook** (0161 251 7272) along Piccadilly.

Getting help

Police, hospital and pharmacy

Manchester Police Station (0161 872 5050) is situated on Bootle Street, opposite Manchester Central Library. This is where Steve Dodd, the gay community liaison officer is based. **Manchester Royal Infirmary** (0161 276 1234) is to be found on Oxford Street. There are no 24-hour pharmacies, although **Cameolord Pharmacy** on Oxford Street (close to the Odeon Cinema) is open daily from 0800 to 0000.

Getting in touch

Internet

Cyberia, at 12 Oxford Street, is a large and well-established café, with probably the most reasonable half-hourly rates available (£3). The largest cyber café is **Easy Everything,** on St Annes Square, by the Disney Store, with over 400 terminals. There's also a new smaller café, which has opened within **Debenhams** department store on Market Street.

GLBT Helplines   The lesbian and gay switchboard is now part of the **Lesbian and Gay Foundation** based at 15 Pritchard Street. The **GLB helpline** (0161 274 3999) is manned seven days a week from 1600 to 2000. The **TV/TS Helpline** (0161 235 8005) is manned every Wednesday and Thursday from 1900 to 2200. You can also contact the Foundation by phoning 0161 235 8000 or by visiting their website at www.lgfoundation.org.uk. There are also several groups that the Foundation can put you in touch with. **Options** is a separate service for men in a male-female relationship but who have feelings for other men. **Ice Breakers** is for men who wish to meet other men for friendship and to explore the gay scene together. **Stepping Stones** is the lesbian equivalent to Icebreakers. Face-to-face counselling is available: simply phone the number to make an appointment. **The Older Lesbians Project**, as the name suggests, offers a lifeline to lesbians who need to kickstart their social life, amongst other things. **Gay Men's Group** is for gay/bisexual men over the age of 40, with meetings every Thursday evening. There is also a weekly surgery held on the premises of LGF provided free of charge by **Monson's Solicitors** (see separate listing). Finally, **S & M Dykes** (0161 225 3709) is a new group aiming to support lesbian and bisexual S & M'ers and is in the process of setting up as this book goes to press.

Pubs

Bar 38   **10 Canal Street, Manchester M1 3EZ** Phone **0161 236 6005**
Although occupying a prime position on Canal Street, Bar 38 can at times seem to be more straight than gay. It's frequented by a mixed crowd of trendy young pre-clubbers, both girls and boys, and usually at the same time. The venue takes in two floors; the top floor opens over the weekend only. Both are open-plan and minimalist, joined together by a fabulous staircase that helps towards making that 'grand entrance' as you swish between floors. There is no karaoke or drag DJ to entertain you, only piped disco music to assault your senses. To be honest, you should come here for a look around, as it really is a nice bar, although there are more active places in the village with a higher gay percentage. **Open** Monday-Wednesday 1000-0000. Thursday 1000-0100. Friday-Saturday 1000-0200. Sunday 1200-2230

Bar Med   **109 Princess Street, Manchester M1 6JD** Phone **0161 200 1800**
Bar Med has been in the village for about three years now and despite a relatively large hiccup due to the previous management allowing entry to an 'unruly crowd' (thus alienating the gays), it is now heavily promoting it's gay-friendly status to the extent of it becoming a majority gay bar. This welcome new-found attitude is obvious even from being surreptitiously vetted by the 'new, improved' doorstaff (even a woman – Hi Tina) to the friendly and courteous bar staff. Entertainment comes to the basement club area from Wednesday (karaoke) and Thursday through to Saturday is a treat of musical 'allsorts' from the resident DJ. On a Friday they let Winnie La Freak out of her coffin to do a stint on the decks. Tip: if you have had a bad experience here before give it another try, they are getting better! **Open** Monday-Tuesday 1700-1200.

Wednesday-Thursday 1700-0200. Friday-Saturday 1200-0200 **Price** £2-3, Friday-Saturday 2230 onwards

Churchill's   37 Chorlton Street, Manchester M1 3HN Phone 0161 236 5529
Sitting on the edge of the village across from Prague 5 at the top end of Canal Street is this delightful, traditional little bar. Due to its position in the village it acts as a catchment area for gays, straights, trannies and quite a few curious. One half of the open-plan room is taken up by a raised dancefloor which also serves as an overspill space from the bar area as the room quickly fills up. There is also a mezzanine level which is never really fully used, as the access to and from is via a rickety-looking spiral staircase which becomes insurmountable after a couple of pints. Through the week, as with most places in the village, the bar is rather quiet, not coming into its own until the weekend, when the place is absolutely rammed. You'll find people meeting up ready for a night on the town and single boys downing a few pints for Dutch courage prior to searching the bars for their true love. The growing popularity of Churchill's has sparked the owners into purchasing the adjoining building, ready for a much-needed extension. **Open** Monday-Wednesday 1200-2300. Thursday-Saturday 1200-0200. Sunday 1200-2230

Company Bar   28 Richmond Street, Manchester M1 3NB Phone 0161 237 9329
E-mail info@companybar.co.uk Web www.companybar.co.uk
Richmond Street is the one that runs inbetween Canal Street and Bloom Street and is home to this intimate members-only, all-male basement bar. Dark and cruisy, it caters predominantly for the leather boys, although all male species will quite rightly be welcomed (but I cannot see it having appeal to the disco dolly). I like this bar because it has that old-fashioned 'hidden gay bar' atmosphere. People, particularly the bar staff, will actually talk to you rather than see you stand on your own – it's also a good place for the first-time leather queen to find his feet. But ultimately – the drinks are cheap! Regular monthly events include MSC (Manchester Super Chain) which comes around every first Sunday and third Friday of the month and Paws (for bears, cubs and their admirers) which runs here every third Sunday. Finally, this is a members-only club, however, membership will only cost you £1 (for life) and can easily be gained at the door. Note: the doorman is just sooo nice; you will probably want to join every time you visit just to talk to him (how sad am I?). **Open** Monday-Thursday 1600-0200. Friday 1700-0200. Saturday 1600-0200. Sunday 1700-2230-plus

Fab Café   111 Portland Street, Manchester M1 4RJ Phone 0161 236 1213 / 0161 236 2019 E-mail info@fabcafe.co.uk Web www.fabcafe.co.uk
Fab Café is a gay friendly café-bar based entirely upon the theme of cult TV. It is both famous and infamous, liked and loathed. They say that this is the nearest thing to entering another dimension! In fact, entering this place can be trickier than using the Stargate, as the absurd generalisation is made that if you're sporting Rockport-style shoes, trainers, or scally gear – whatever that is – then you are deemed to be a likely troublemaker and will be refused entry. However, change your shoes to a nice

sensible brogue or boot and you are instantly recognised as an upstanding member of the community! Yes captain, that is logical! This generalisation is also observed at their sister club Satan's Hollow, a heavily themed venue based on their version of hell – no too easy! (111 Princess Street, entrance on Silver Street behind Cruz 101). And why is Fab Café so popular then? Well, it really is a fun night out – you get to see some terrific props and ornamentation. Not only that, but the food is good and the atmosphere is lively. Make your own fun by playing the game of 'how many times can you overhear someone say 'beam me up Scotty'' or see who's pretending to be an alien by talking to people in a strange made-up language or ask the barmaid how many pints you can have for a zorb, or just enjoy it for what it is – different, and a lot of fun. That is if you can get past the door! Tip: this is a good place to bring your straight friends. **Open** (Fab) Monday-Tuesday 1745-2300. Wednesday-Thursday 1745-0200. Friday-Saturday 1200-0200. Sunday 1630-2230. (Satan's Hollow) Wednesday-Friday 2200-0230 **Price** £2-5

In Manchester's gay village, just across from The Rembrandt, is Sackville Park – the site of The Beacon of Hope, the country's first AIDS memorial. The Beacon symbolises new hope and also marks remembrance to those whom we have lost but will never be forgotten. Inside the memorial is a capsule containing the names of people who have died and each World AIDS Day on December 1st the list is updated. Around the Beacon is a timeline, representing the progress of the virus and the battles against it.

Gaia　46 Sackville Street, Manchester M1 3WF Phone **0161 228 1002**
E-mail **info@mantogroup.com** Web **www.mantogroup.com**
A luxurious lounge bar just on the edge of the gay village owned by the self-same people who own Manto and Paradise Factory. No loud music, no scallies, no cruising. In fact, you might wonder what's left to entice you into this place! Apparently, it's for the up-market gay and straight crowd, who require somewhere a bit more posher than everywhere else. It's packed with large comfy sofas, serves good food, designer drinkies and...well, that's about all I can say about it because I have been refused entry here a number of times now (given the reason that it was a members' bar / regulars only tonight sir!). I still keep trying every now and again, as you get an honest opinion from the doorman of how you are dressed; meaning if he lets you in you look smart, if he refuses you then it's because you look a bit dodgy.... Oh yeah, and the doormen are quite good looking – but now I'm being shallow. **Open** Monday-Thursday 1100-0000. Friday-Saturday 1100-0200. Sunday 1200-2430

Hollywood Showbar　100 Bloom Street, Manchester M1 6DD Phone **0161 236 6151**
E-mail **enquiries@hollywoodshowbar.com**
Web **www.hollywoodshowbar.com**
The Hollywood Showbar is owned and run by Julia Grant, Britain's most famous male-female transsexual, the subject of a long-running documentary by the BBC spanning over 25 years. The popularity of this bar/club complex (along with The Manhattan across the road) is

immense and it is probably the busiest and safest bar in the gay village: testament to how a gay venue should be run. The Hollywood is on two levels and comprises four bars and two dance floors. Downstairs, the main showbar is the heart of the venue with DJ and dancing every night of the week and top-notch cabaret from the bar's own showgirls over the weekend. From Thursday, the whole complex opens up to take in the Piano Bar, which starts off with good, relaxing intentions but quickly turns into a raucous and debauched drunken sing-along. This is the real Manchester! The Hollywood prides itself on a trouble-free and friendly atmosphere, which hits you full-on in the face as soon as you walk through the doors. This, however, has been gained by imposing a strict gay members-only policy on the door. Gay visitors to Manchester will also have to complete a lifetime membership application on the door (£2), but it is well worth every penny. This will also admit you to The Manhattan free of charge at all times. This is my 'local' and, naturally, being non-partisan prevents me from saying a lot more. Except that I rate The Hollywood 100 per cent! **Open** Monday-Saturday 1400-0200. Sunday 1400-2230/0130, alternate weeks **Price** £1 members' guests

Manhattan Showbar

54 Princess Street, Manchester M1 6HS Phone 0161 236 6151 E-mail info@manhattanshowbar.com Webwww.manhattanshowbar.com If ever there was a success story for a bar then this is it. Once upon a time, not so very long ago, this venue was a straight bar trying to gain the custom of the straight contingent visiting the gay village. The bar was open-plan, trendy and had the makings and trappings of a successful venue. On the opening night it was rammed! I imagine the owners were patting themselves on their backs and congratulating themselves on a successful venture.... Unfortunately, within weeks of opening, the only sound emanating from the place was that of a cold wind blowing through the doors. In steps Julia Grant of Hollywood Showbar fame, buys the place for peanuts, adds a stage, drag DJ, the best drag bar staff and opens the place to gays 'and' their straight friends. It is now one of the most successful venues in the village – the gays love it, the straights love it and they all get along famously. It is all held together by any one of the raucous, funny and utterly atrocious drag DJs on rotation. As the name suggests, cabaret features very strongly, in the form of Miss Felicia and her Showgirls and it is not some lame ass-tired old routine – it's performed every 30 minutes or so and it is fresh, top notch and hilariously funny, even when it's not supposed to be! What's even funnier though, is to watch the dragged-up troupe dodge the beeping traffic as they wobble across the main road on their stilettoes to do a stint at The Hollywood. Julia bills this place as The Party Capital of Manchester and in short that is exactly what it is (I would add that it is delightfully cruisy!). Whether you come in by yourself or with a group of friends, be prepared for a good old piss-up and a laugh. You should be sure to include this place on your itinerary. Highly recommended. **Open** Friday-Saturday 2100-0200. Alternate Sundays 2100-0100 **Price** £1 (£2 on Sundays); Hollywood members free, except Sunday

3

Manto

46 Canal Street, Manchester M1 3WD Phone 0161 236 2667
E-mail info@mantogroup.com Web www.mantogroup.com
Manto was the original 'trendy' bar in Manchester, setting the standard
that all the other bars were to follow and it was ultimately cited as the
bar that started the 'gay village' as we have come to know it today. It is
the official pre-Paradise venue on Friday and Saturday nights (same
owners), a night which sees the venue absolutely packed with young
party people either dancing on the spot to the loud thumping beat or
spilling out onto the street to gasp for air. Getting a drink at the bar is
very nearly impossible (but frotaging your way through the crowd can be
quite pleasurable so it's worth it). Weekdays, like other venues in the village, are a lot quieter, although from Tuesday onwards Manto provides
some good drinks offers and excellent sounds from their resident DJs.
Manto is based on two floors (the third floor is the restaurant, Sarasota).
The ground floor is totally open-plan, except for the seating in the windows which gives classic people-watching views out onto Canal Street.
Upstairs, a huge mezzanine overlooks the ground floor and offers ample
space to sit, dance or leer. The migration to Paradise on Friday and
Saturday takes place at about 2300 but the place still remains busy as bar
flys and hoppers continue to pass through the doors. These doors open
up once again on Saturday night (or technically-speaking Sunday morning) at 0230 when it becomes the Breakfast Club for the village and
Paradise crowd. Realising that 0230 is still too early to go home people
are quite willing to part with the required £5 admission (£2 if you have
been to Paradise) to carry on dancing to about four more hours of hard
beats. Bear in mind that Essential (see listing) now have their own successful Breakfast Club (Morning Worship) which opens at 0230 (£4, or
free if you are already in the club) and I'm no psychic but I can foresee a
spot of price cutting and one-upmanship on the horizon... and the winner is... us punters! **Open** Monday-Thursday 1100-0000. Friday-
Saturday 1100-0100 and 0230-0600

Metz

Amazon House, Canal Street, Manchester M1 3PJ
Phone 0161 237 9852 E-mail info@metz.co.uk Web www.metz.co.uk
A restaurant café-bar set in the centre of Manchester's gay village and
the only one on the opposite side of Canal Street (over the little bridge
across from Manto). A bohemian atmosphere prevails (that means large
wooden tables, iron fixtures, candles and more candles). Everyone and

anyone is welcome here, providing they treat other customers with the appropriate respect, regardless of their sex, age, colour or sexual preference. The extensive menu is Eastern European and is served all day from 1200, seven days a week and pre-booking is well and truly advised. Metz also gets busy with punters just coming in for a drink and as there's no thumping loud music, you can actually hear the person that you are talking to. Fun and atmospheric. **Open** Monday-Wednesday 1200-2300. Thursday 1200-0100. Friday-Saturday 1200-0200. Sunday 1200-2230

The New Union   111 Princess Street, Corner of Canal Street, Manchester M1 6JB
Phone 0161 228 1492 Web www.newunionmanchester.co.uk
Not as busy as it was in its heyday when just about everyone in gay Manchester passed through the doors at some time during the week. The Friday and Saturday night queues in have subsided due to the fact that their 'integration' policy of allowing just about anyone through the doors has meant that it now seems to be more straight than gay at times. This is evident on both Friday and Saturday nights when groups of young girls drag along their awkward-looking boyfriends through the bar to the dancefloor. Although the majority of gays are in favour of integration a balance really should be drawn. Many long-time regulars have now migrated to The Manhattan where the straight/gay quota is fiercely observed. For a bar, The Union is quite a size, four bars, a dancefloor and stage occupying the front of the bar where all sorts of cabaret and carryings-on take place. Throughout the week The Union is still fun and atmospheric, particularly on a Thursday for Roxy Hart's karaoke. If, however, you plan on openly hugging and kissing your boyfriend you can expect to be something of a sideshow for the straights. (See their entry in the accommodation listings too.) **Open** Monday-Friday 1100-0130. Saturday 1100-0200. Sunday 1100-2230 **Price** £2, weekends after 2230

New York-   98 Bloom Street, Manchester M1 3LY Phone 0161 236 6556
New York   Web www.newyorkmanchester.co.uk
This was one of Manchester's original gay bars under the reign of Glen Stevens when Bloom Street was the centre of Manchester gay life. It's divided into two sections – a quieter lower bar (formerly known as Ballans) which is first to open each day and is more of a chilling out and chatting area, and the larger main room with drag DJ Kampari playing whatever she damn well likes (and she doesn't give two hoots whether you like it or not – but you more than likely will). Fridays and Saturdays see this place packed to the rafters with one giant thronging mass of gay and gay-friendly straight bods pushed up against each other. Sunday is almost as heaving, as the entire village tries to cram into here to sample the acerbic wits and plastic tits of the dynamic duo Kampari and Roxy. It is one camp drunken party from opening time 'til around 1900 when the crowds start to go bar-hopping around the village – usually to The Hollywood where the party carries on into the late hours (Hollywood or sister bar Manhattan usually have a late night charity licence – see listing). In the olden days the club above the New York (The Bronx) was one of only a handful of places to go clubbing. Now it is used solely as a private hire venue, although the downstairs is open 'til late from

Thursday onwards. Apart from the smaller bar there is no seating at all, however, this is not the sort of place you come to sit and chat in – you come here to get drunk and party. If you are in Manchester then this should go down on your itinerary just to see where it all started. Tip: on Sundays the drinks in the smaller bar are cheaper than the main bar and the queues are a lot lighter. **Open** Monday-Wednesday 1200-2300. Thursday-Saturday 1200-0200. Sunday 1200-2230 **Price** £1.50-2, Friday and Saturday only

Paddy's Goose 29 Bloom Street, Manchester M1 3JE Phone **0161 236 1246**
Paddy's Goose is a small two-roomed venue that has been established on the scene for many, many years. It has a comfortable olde-worlde interior and it caters for a wide variety of tastes with a heavy TV/CD profile on Wednesday and Saturday evenings. Food is served throughout the day and there's an excellent value-for-money steak meal. Situated at the top end of the gay village, opposite Chorlton Street Bus Station, it is one of only a few Manchester pubs that offers complete wheelchair access. Paddy's is a traditional venue where there's scope to chat and socialise without heavy thumping music getting in the way. The age and type range is decidedly mixed although it does tend to attract the older male. **Open** Monday-Saturday 1100-2300. Sunday 1100-2230

Prague 5 40 Chorlton Street, Manchester M1 3HW Phone **0161 236 9033**
What was once an old cotton warehouse is now a modern hard-edged industrial-themed café-bar, not really coming into its own until the weekend. It is then where you will see the queues of mixed gay and straight student-like punters trying to get past the burly guards into the pub. The music is unashamedly hard which pleases the hands-in-the-air crowd who take great delight in dancing where they stand. On Thursday the bar plays host to the Cat Club (£4) which is a student gathering that runs from 2130 to 0200. If you are in the bar before this time, you will have to leave and then pay to get back in. This bar may be a little too 'straight' for some people, but is nonetheless quite popular (as the lengthy queues demonstrate). There is a dress code in operation of smart-casual – definitely no sportswear. Incidentally, Prague 5 is named after the postal district of the same name that has the highest concentration of breweries in the world – now, not a lot of people know that! **Open** Monday-Wednesday 1200-2300. Thursday-Saturday 1200-0200. Sunday 1200-2230 **Price** £4, Thursday only

The Rembrandt Hotel 33 Sackville Street, Manchester M1 3LZ Phone **0161 236 1311**
The Rembrandt has been gay-owned for more than 17 years by the same proprietors and it's a popular bar with the leather, denim and skinhead crowd, although saying that, nearly everyone pops in here on their trawl around the bars (except women – although they are not disallowed from entering). The Rem, as it's known to the locals, is deemed to be the instigator of the annual Gayfest event (formerly Mardi Gras) when, on the August Bank Holiday, they erected a tressle table outside their venue filled with bric-a-brac and donated the proceeds of the sale to the (then) Village Charity. The large open-plan downstairs bar is a general meeting

place whilst upstairs is the Bistro (with an excellent reputation for lunchtime grub, as corroborated by many good food guides). This becomes a quieter and more intimate space over the weekend when the downstairs bar is nose-to-nipple. Another good thing about The Rem, is that they never have a door charge. Oh, and the doorstaff are friendly and polite too! There is a downside – there is no branded draught lager – it's J. W. Lees which is an acquired taste, but you can always drink bottles instead. **Open** Monday-Wednesday 1100-2300. Thursday-Saturday 1100-0200. Sunday 1100-2230

The Retro Bar   78 Sackville Street, Manchester M1 3NJ Phone 0161 274 4892
The best way to describe The Retro is laid back and 'non-judgemental'. Pretty much anybody comes in here – although it does tend to attract a fair proportion of students (not that that is a bad thing). Weekends get fairly busy as some event or other gets launched or is in full swing – they don't tend to last that long so it is pretty pointless mentioning what's on, here. **Open** Monday-Thursday 1000-2430. Friday-Saturday 1100-0200. Sunday 1200-0000 **Price** £3-4, Saturday only, dependent on production

Slug and   4 Canal Street, Manchester M1 3HE Phone 0161 228 1360
Lettuce   E-mail info@sfigroup.co.uk Web www.slugandlettuce.co.uk
One of 34 Slug and Lettuce café-bars around the country – only this one happens to be in the centre of the gay village. Exceptionally modern and chic, it attracts the business suits in the daytime and the smart pre-club crowds in the evening. The surroundings are sumptuous, friendly and comfortable. I'm not keen to recommend food in any venue (as there is always the chance that I have been on a good/bad day) but here the quality of the food (and service) is always guaranteed to be good (served Sunday to Thursday, from 1200 to 2200 and Friday to Saturday, from 1200 to 2000) **Open** Monday-Thursday 1200-2300. Friday-Saturday 1200-0200. Sunday 1200-2230

Spirit   48 Canal Street, Manchester M1 3WD Phone 0161 237 9725
Spirit occupies a prominent corner on Canal Street, adjacent to the mighty Manto. This is the bar to go to when you want to chat – without shouting – to your friends. You do not come here to pick up, cruise or get pissed as a fart – it's just not the done thing! It is a smart, trendy bar on three floors, with a roof garden for a top floor (which is quite camp really). When this place opened it tried to attract an up-market smart crowd. There was even a sign outside stating these aspirations. This was subsequently removed as numbers dwindled, and a succession of managers have since tried to entice any old Tom, Dick or Harriet in, but I feel it has never really recovered and is still rather quiet, even on a Saturday night. It has become, through default, an ideal place for the older gay members of our community who enjoy the peace and quiet. **Open** Monday-Saturday 1200-2300. Sunday 1200-2230

The Thompsons   21 Sackville Street, Manchester M1 3LZ Phone 0161 228 3012
Arms   Formerly known as Central Park (the old home of the ill-fated all-nighter, Danceteria) this place has now reverted back to its original

name; The Thompsons Arms. It's been recently refurbished which has transformed the dingy old bar into a bright, modern pub/club. The clientele here tends to be mostly mixed gay and lesbian with some friendly straights that make up the numbers. There's just one open-plan room – that is not counting the club upstairs, which has a large seating area to the one side adjacent to the fishbowl windows and standing and dancing areas opposite. Over the weekend the place is consistently packed out with pre-clubbers and bar-hoppers making the most of the cheap drink offers and charty, camp music policy. **Open** Monday-Thursday 1200-0000. Friday-Saturday 1200-0200. Sunday 1200-0000

Tribeca 50 Sackville Street, Manchester M1 3WF Phone 0161 236 8300
E-mail **enquiries@tribeca-bar.co.uk** Web **www.tribeca-bar.co.uk**
A smart lounge bar where you can eat fine food and drink fine wine in a comfortable and relaxing atmosphere. The sort of place you go to impress your boss or be able to chat to your friends of an evening. **Open** Monday-Tuesday 1200-0000. Wednesday-Thursday 1200-0100. Friday-Saturday 1200-0200. Sunday 1200-2230

On the 23 June 2001 a commemorative statue of Alan Turing was unveiled in Sackville Park. It portrays the gay genius sitting on a bench, holding an apple (which signifies the cyanide-laced fruit that ended his life). He is credited as the man who, along with other scientists, created the machine that decoded the German Enigma messages during the Second World War. In 1952, Turing was arrested for homosexual crimes after police learned of his sexual relationship with a Manchester man. Always open about his sexuality, Turing made no attempt to deny the charge, seeing nothing wrong in his actions. Rather than go to prison he accepted a series of oestrogen injections intended to 'cure' his homosexuality. The Heritage Secretary, Chris Smith, said, upon unveiling the plaque, 'Alan Turing did more for his country and for the future of science than almost anyone. He was dishonourably persecuted during his life. Let us wipe that national shame clean by honouring him properly'.

Vanilla 39-40 Richmond Street, Manchester M1 3WB Phone 0161 288 2727
E-mail **steph@vanillagirls.co.uk** Web **www.vanillagirls.co.uk**
Richmond Street runs parallel to Canal Street and that makes the location of this 100 per cent lesbian bar ideal for those women who need to be a little discreet. Bright, modern and trendy, this bar is an oasis for women who now have a space to call their own (Vanilla, incidentally, is the only full-time lesbian bar outside of London). What makes this bar so successful though is the wide range of activities and events that cater for the complete spectrum of the lesbian community – monthly women-only events for the more mature woman; trance and house for the hard-assed clubbers, right through to regular nights of Disco Divas which tends to attract anyone and everyone. As you might expect, the weekend is packed to capacity with girls from all over the country passing through the doors. During the summer, Sundays tend to be one long party as the tables and chairs are transferred from the bar to the adjoining car park. From here you can either soak up the rays or join in the

swingball games. Check out the website for complete and up-to-date information on all events. (See also the listings for Fussy-Pussy, the long-running club nights in Manchester and Blackpool promoted by Vanilla.) **Open** Monday-Friday 1700-0200. Saturday 1300-0200. Sunday 1300-2230

Velvet 2 Canal Street, Manchester M1 3DE Phone 0161 236 9003
One of the more trendy and elegant mixed venues along Canal Street. A basement-style bar that has the often-referred to 'fish tank in the stairwell'. Simple and understated, it attracts the more beautiful people in the community. Sunday tends to get really busy with loads of people each trying to have a relaxing afternoon. There's minimalist décor and no loud thumping music, plus pavement seating to sit and watch the lads go by. This is another café-bar (out of only a handful in the village) where the quality of the food can be relied upon. **Open** Monday-Saturday 1200-2300. Sunday 1200-2230

Via Fossa 28-30 Canal Street, Manchester M1 3EZ Phone 0161 237 9725
Web www.viafossamanchester.co.uk
Upon entering, you may be forgiven for thinking you have walked into 'Saint Dorothy's church of the Fallen One' as the whole place is built out of salvaged and redundant architectural timber from old churches and monasteries. There is even a pulpit overlooking the central bar that gives great delight to drunken students as they bless the crowd below. During the day the main bar area serves as a meeting place for the village and the surrounding offices as gays and straights pop in for either lunch in the restaurant or a simple coffee whist they read the papers. The evenings tell a somewhat different story though as the music is turned up to an acceptable level and the four bars on all five levels open for business. From the latter part of the week the basement dance area comes to life as straights and gays mix together nicely and enjoy either disco or cutting-edge house, depending on which DJ is there for the evening. Friday and Saturday evenings see the place crammed – particularly the front bar – and getting a drink is nigh-on impossible (but work your way around the venue and you will succeed at one of the other bars). The doormen here seem a little too selective, particularly when the bar is busy, and there have been reports that gay people have been turned away with the excuse that it is for regulars only, whilst smart-looking, apparently straight people were let in. **Open** Monday-Wednesday 1100-0000. Thursday-Saturday 1100-0200. Sunday 1200-2230

Clubs

Cruz 101 101 Princess Street, Manchester M1 6DD Phone 0161 950 0101
E-mail cruz@cruz101.co.uk Web www.cruz101.co.uk
Prior to the opening of Essential during the summer of 2000, Cruz 101 was the only full-time gay club in the village that had been a success since day one. Despite the fact that it is a members club it can still boast a full house on Monday, Friday and Saturday. These days you are able to join on the night (at the manager's discretion) by completing the form at reception. If you do not 'look gay' you will be challenged at the door,

but state your case, admit you're gay (even mention this guide!) and everything should be OK. It is, after all, a gay club and they are very keen to keep it that way – so don't be offended. Mondays – a notoriously quiet night for most gay and straight venues throughout the country – sees Disco Inferno, a long-running retro night that has the club packed to the hilt. The success of this night has had its imitators but the crowds still keep on coming here – all ages and all types. Weekdays are also quite successful with cheap drinks on offer, particularly on Wednesday (Cruzing) when they offer their £1-a-drink night. It's still busy but the place does not get packed again until the weekend. Layout-wise, the top floor accommodates the main room, two bars, podiums and a packed dance floor. Downstairs is a darker, subterranean, subtle cruising, boozing dance area which opens on Mondays and Saturdays. **Open** Monday-Saturday 2230-0230 **Price** £2-5

3 **Babylon**

2-8 Whitworth Street, Manchester M1 3QW Phone 0161 236 6151 E-mail info@hollywoodshowbar.com Web www.hollywoodshowbar.com The proposed opening of Babylon (the club) and the three stand-alone bars – Wells Fargo, Rawhide and a women's lounge promises to be the shake-up Manchester's gay community has been waiting for. Occupying the former premises of Rockies, Chains and Follies, the complete building has been gutted, extended and renovated for today's gay market. The location is a half-minute's stroll out of the Canal Street area, close to Piccadilly Station, and with the straight population's increasing attendance in the village this bold move is a welcome step. Babylon will play host to well-known and established club nights such as Homoelectric and various other top monthly events (details at the time of writing have yet to be confirmed). The club will be laid out over three floors, comprising six bars and five dance floors, making it the largest capacity full-time gay club in Manchester. The separate bars will all be stand-alone, each having their own entrance, and along with the club they will be able to cater for the complete diversity of Manchester's gay scene. Wells Fargo is the planned western-style bar catering for bears and cubs. Rawhide will be a full-time leather bar. The dress code and music policy will be very much dependent on the event and admission prices will be nominal, opening the way to a more inclusive gay scene. At the time of writing the contract has yet to be signed and sealed and as such, changes to these details may well be made.

Essential

8 Minshull Street, (top of Bloom Street), Manchester M1 3EF Phone 0161 236 0077 E-mail info@nmsmanagement.co.uk Web www.nmsmanagement.co.uk After taking a while to find its feet, this gay Manchester superclub has come up with a collection of nightly events that should satisfy pretty much everyone. The club itself is on three levels: the ground floor (level two) tends to be used as the meeting space with the sounds from below piped through. Downstairs (level one) is the huge main room dance area where top name resident and guest DJs spin the sounds. The very top floor (level three) is the pop lounge where the vulgar and foul-mouthed DJs rule the roost, hurling abuse and regaling the gobsmacked crowd

with disgusting anecdotes and gossip. Music and everything else up here is unashamedly camp and pop – but if it does get too much for you, you can always nip downstairs to where the 'real' music is playing. Thursday is F@G (£2 admission and all drinks £1) when Teri Fox and Miss Melanie play pop all night. Fridays at Essential is Babylon, the latest Friday night out in the village ('til 0500; £3 admission). Saturday is quite positively the best gay night out for seasoned clubbers in the north-west – nay, outside London! Not only is the music in the main room top notch (from the likes of Thaddeus and Dino – bouncy house and trance, etc.) but also, for a measly fiver you get to club right through 'til the early hours of 0600-plus, without having to go outside! This is made possible by the breakfast club (Morning Worship), so when the club 'finishes' at 0230 the top floor becomes the chill-out room and there's no break in the music downstairs (make sure you get enough pop inside you as there is no alcohol). Those who are already in the club at this time stay in for free; those who have been elsewhere (you fools!) and want to come here 'till the early hours will have to pay £4 for the privilege, assuming you can get in of course. If the weekend seems to finish a bit too quickly for you, there is always Sunday night (Sabbath), one of the hottest spots in Manchester on this day of rest. Not only is it licensed to serve alcohol every week until 0030 and stay open until 0200 (with extra 0200-licensed bi-monthly charity nights still to be confirmed), but you are able to witness the musical talents of Thaddeus and Claire Shireff playing your old skool Sabbath faves...whilst at the same time upstairs is pop in the Pop Lounge. Essential is owned by the infamous Nigel Martin-Smith (ex-manager of Take That / Star for a Night fame) and full marks go out to him and his crew for not turning this excellent venue straight after what was an initial shaky start – it now offers the best admission, music and drink prices in the village. Even cheaper than most of the pubs! See you there! **Open** Monday 2230-0200. Thursday 2200-0200. Friday 2230-0500. Saturday 2230-0230 / 0230-0600. Sunday 2130-0300 **Price** £2-5

Napoleons   35 Bloom Street, Manchester M1 3LY Phone 0161 236 8800
E-mail **napoleons1@aol.com** Web **www.napoleons.co.uk**
Napoleons first opened its doors in December 1972 and was the first gay club to open in Manchester's now well-established gay village. Nap's is one of only two gay bars in Manchester that enforce a strict gay door policy (the other being Hollywood Showbar). The few straights that are allowed in are either regulars or friends of gays. TVs and TSs are especially welcome and this place has been a 'find-your-feet' venue for cross-dressers since time immemorial. Admission for male-to-female cross-dressers is free at all times. The ground floor is plush and comfortable and can get rather cramped, particularly over the weekends – but this adds to the atmosphere; it's certainly not a downside. Upstairs (Wednesday, Friday and Saturday only) is where you'll find the dance floor and the source of the music. Chrome and mirrors form the décor – reminiscent of an '80s disco – and the cramped interior makes you feel as though you are partying in your friend's house whilst their folks are away! A perfect opportunity to let your hair down, get drunk and do all that camp dancing that you love to do at home but are afraid to do at

any other venue but this. **Open** Monday-Saturday 2130-0200. Sunday (dependent on monthly charity night) **Price** £2-3

Oi! Bar and Hotel

Helmshore Walk, Brunswick, Manchester M13 9TH
Phone 0161 273 2074 or 07956 808 142
E-mail info@oiclub.co.uk Web www.oiclub.co.uk
A new full-time Oi! venue, The Oi! Bar and Hotel, is just about to arrive in Manchester at the former Kings Arms. The Oi! institution will be well-known to the 400-odd lads who attended Oi!'s private parties that used to be held here. Once opened, it will provide a horny and much-needed men-only space each weekend. It will boast a men's bar, a basement club area, six double en-suite hotel rooms and dormitory space for 40 people with bunk beds and shower blocks! (Rooms £40 per night and dormitory space £10 per bed and locker). Up-to-date information will be published in Gay Times as soon as it is open. Here's some quick directions: head down Princess Street (A34), go under Mancunian Way (elevated), go right into Grosvenor Street, then immediately left onto Wadeson Road. At the second right – Skerry Close – go right to the end and your night of fun begins from there! **Open** Friday-Saturday 2200-0400 **Price** £6-8 (to be confirmed)

Paradise Factory

112-116 Princess Street, Manchester M1 3WD Phone 0161 273 5422
E-mail info@mantogroup.com Web www.mantogroup.com
Paradise Factory is probably the most famous gay club outside of London. What was once the home of Factory Records, now caters for a young, 'trendy' market. During the week, the club is open for various promotions, although these are usually straight-orientated. At the moment it is only the weekends that see the club go pink. The music policy on the vast expanse of Level One provides some of the most up-front music in the land, from resident DJs Little Miss Natalie, Adrian C and Richard Cobey. Level Two overlooks the main dance floor and provides seating and chill-out space, although this is more often than not used as an unofficial overspill from downstairs with hyped-up youngsters utilising the floor space as dance floor – and why not? Level Three offers club anthems and dance classics with the tunes provided by a mix of local DJs. There's plenty of seating and opportunity to socialise at the far end by the stairs. The clientele are a good no-attitude combination of mixed gay, bisexual and straight. Everyone who enters Paradise knows it is a predominantly gay venue. There is never any trouble and everyone who is there is there for a good time. Fridays and Saturdays see Paradise packed to the rafters (literally). Either arrive early or expect to queue. Cloakroom and toilet facilities are in the basement. The long winding corridor offers the weary a quiet place to chill and/or cruise (whatever is your bent). (See the listing for sister venue Manto and details of The Breakfast Club.) At the time of writing Paradise and Essential are battling it out for the loyalty of the hard-edged clubbing crowd. When Paradise closes you have to up roots and trek to Manto for the Breakfast Club and pay an additional £2, whereas Essential is non-stop dancing all night. At the time of writing the rumour is that Paradise will incorporate their Breakfast Club into their dance night but this has not yet been

confirmed. Keep your eyes on the gay press for future developments.
Open Friday-Saturday 2230-0300 **Price** £4-8

Club nights

**Black Angel
@ The Green
Room**

54-56 Whitworth Street, Manchester M1 5WW Phone 0161 228 0585
E-mail **claud_cunningham@hotmail.com** Web **www.black-angel.co.uk**
Billed as a night for queer divas and non-believers, Black Angel has been
running strong for well over a year. It is a night for lesbians and gay men
of all ages. So, if you love r'n'b, hip-hop, UK garage and ragga, come on
down on the last Saturday of every month or ring the info line for more
details. Resident DJs Ono Eno and Isis, visual artist Tracy Gue and a
host of Manchester's freshest female MCs combine to make this club
night a useful addition to the Manchester scene. **Open** Every last
Saturday of the month 2200-0200 **Price** £3-4

**Classix @ Sub
Cruz 101**

101 Princess Street (entrance on Major Street), Manchester
Phone 0161 288 2727 E-mail **classix@vanillagirls.co.uk**
Web **www.vanillagirls.co.uk**
Another successful club night for the girls and their gay male friends of
the north-west and beyond. This night aims to take you back with the
sounds of old skool lesbian classics and it certainly does just that. The
basement of Cruz 101 with its separate entrance is once again the place
for this girl's night out (gay men welcome as guests of a female) and the
layout of the venue means that even if you come in by yourself you will
not stand out like a sore thumb. This night was launched back on May
bank holiday and proved to be such a success that it was subsequently
made into a regular monthly club night out. There are pre-club meet-
ups at Vanilla from 1730 onwards (see separate listing). **Open** Every second Friday of the month 2230-0230 **Price** £4

*Manchester is playing host to the Commonwealth Games in 2002. The
inevitable clean-up campaign has already started, with a clamp-down
on cottaging and prostitution high on the council's agenda. It is
rumoured that the police are turning a blind eye to prostitution, so long
as perpetrators ply their trade outside of the city centre. They aim to
clear the Chorlton Street district and hope that these activities will
move just outside the centre to the Cheetham Hill area. No 'blind eye' is
being turned to cottaging activities though. Notorious spots such as
Victoria Station and The Arndale are being targeted as facilities to be
watched, and arrests for lewd conduct have already been made. These
crackdowns could see a few of the city's saunas taking in a larger-than-
usual clientele.*

Club Lash

Lash, PO Box 45, Levenshulme, Manchester M19 3PU Phone 0161 225 3709
Club Lash is a fetish/SM night set up and run by four women: Mistresses
Kate and Rosie, Lady Helen and the wondrous DJ Sub Sindy. Regular
male contributions come from the likes of DJs Chaos and Midnight,
and cloakroom hustlers Paul and Bobby. It is a mix of sexualities and
genders and welcomes all polite perverts (or however you choose to

describe yourself). You can expect at least 2-300 people at each event. Club Lash is generally held on the second Saturday of the month and has been in the same venue for two and a half years. The business, however, is now up for sale and they may be moving soon. The current entrance charge is £10, but membership (£10) reduces this to £5. There is a strict dress code of leather, rubber, PVC, lingerie, cross-dressing, and character dressing (doctor, school mistress, etc.). In addition to this, there are regular themes to encourage your creative self-expression and changing rooms are available to help encourage you to make the effort. Call the infoline, allowing time prior to your visit to receive venue details, rules and safer SM sex material through the post. Bear in mind that they only return business calls; all other enquiries will be directed to your home address as requested. After your initial newcomer's pack has been sent it is only paid-up members that will continue to receive regular mailings. See the wonderful site www.submission.org.uk for more info on the BDSM scene. (See the Lash for Lasses listing also.) **Open** Every second Saturday of the month **Price** £5-10

Dusty's @ Sub Cruz 101

101 Princess Street, (entrance on Major Street), Manchester M1 6DD
Phone 0161 9500 101 (Cruz 101 number)
A long-running (8 years -plus), friendly and successful night for women only in the basement of Cruz 101. The normally cruisy subterranean room of Cruz 101 is transformed for the evening by the use of chequered tablecloths and candles (no bad taste jokes please!), which creates a welcoming space for the older and younger lesbian alike. Music is supplied by Gill and Sue and don't worry, it is not too hard or trancy, just a safe sort of disco music that you can bop along to. Lesbians wanting a younger, harder atmosphere may want to try out Classix and Fussy Pussy, which occupy this venue on the second and fourth Friday of the month respectively (see separate listing). **Open** Every first, third and fifth Friday 2230-0200 **Price** £3.50-4.50

Exodus @ Mutz Nutz

105 – 107 Princess Street, Manchester M1 6DD **Phone** 07974 117 864
E-mail info@acidtunes.co.uk **Web** www.acidtunes.com
Launched in February 2001 Exodus is an all-day outing for the clubbing masses (predominantly gay with welcome straight undertones). You'll experience the most underground hardcore house, nrg and modernistic acid trance from mixmeisters such as Little Miss Natalie

(Manto/Paradise) and Dr Findlay (Sin:ergy). If the hard house trip requires you to break for a while then there is a lighter alternative in the funk room, presided over by Lee Devious and Nat Hill who spin progressive house throughout the day. This danceathon goes on for a full eight hours on the supposed day of rest in the most perfect of venues (dark, minimalist and dingy). To be part of the vibe you will have to be dragged up in your smart clubbing togs – at least until you get inside, when you can strip off to your heart's content! **Open** Every first Sunday 1600-0000 **Price** £5

Fussy Pussy @ Sub Cruz 101
101 Princess Street (entrance on Major Street), Manchester M1 6DD Phone 0161 288 2727 E-mail fussy@vanillagirls.co.uk Web www.vanillagirls.co.uk
Manchester is the flagship of the Fussy Pussy phenomenon – the well-established club night for girls. The cavernous basement of Cruz 101 is the venue, with a separate entrance which makes it the ideal location to stage this extremely popular monthly event. Fussy Pussy is regularly packed to capacity with gorgeous women of all ages and persuasions in a space that they can call their own (although gay male friends are also welcomed). The music runs right across the board, from disco classics to chart, intermingled with uplifting and commercial house. All this is provided by popular dyke DJ Sara Furey and it seems to please most of the women (most of the time) who come down here. The girly quota is across the board, and women over 'a certain age' are not left to feel that this is a young gals' night – it's a very inclusive atmosphere and like all lesbian bars – age does not really matter. What does matter though, is that you come here to enjoy yourself – as only women can – and to meet new friends. Meet up for the pre-party at Vanilla (see separate listing) any time after 1700 and then move across to Cruz on the next block whenever you are ready. Fussy Pussy is also on once a month in Blackpool and Liverpool (see separate listings) and Steph Kay (the promoter) will be taking this well-established women's club night further afield over the course of the coming year. Tip: be there or be square! **Open** Every fourth Friday 2230-0230 **Price** £4

Lash for Lasses
Lash, PO Box 45, Levenshulme, Manchester M19 3PU Phone 0161 225 3709 Run by Mistresses Kate and Rosie and DJ Sindy, approximately twice a year – winter and summer! This is a completely non-profit-making night, subsidised by the run-away success of Club Lash (see separate listing). Previously in a lesbian-run venue which has since closed, they are now using a gay-run venue within the village which can accommodate a dance area, changing space, cloakroom, supervised dungeon-play space and often a stall or two. The current entrance charge is £6, or £4 if you're a member. The night is shaped as follows: firstly, an optional 'munch' in a local bar, where you can meet other plain-clothes bi/lesbian women and build up your confidence. Then it's on to the club ready for the doors to open at 2130. A workshop of some description starts the night off at around 2200: something like Show and Tell, Favourite Toys, Flogging for Beginners, Bondage Basics (get the idea?). This is a night for lesbian, bisexual and straight women to enjoy. No assumptions are

made, but a strict dress code is in force. If you're not trying hard enough you will be asked to remove your T-shirt! Clothing advice can be given before the event – so ring them on the number above with your queries. Expect between 50 and 100 women at each event. Confess your interest in Lasses and they will add your name to the Lasses mailing list. Doing so will ensure you receive regular info and keep abreast of forthcoming events. See the website – www.submission.org.uk – for further information, including what a 'munch' actually is! **Open** Approximately 2130-0200 – full details can be sent to you **Price** £4-6

Poptastic @ The Mutz Nutz

105-107 Princess Street, Manchester M1 6DD Phone 07074 248 247 E-mail info@poptastic.co.uk Web www.poptastic.co.uk

Manchester is the birth place of Poptastic and Poptastic is the birthplace of the infamous 'shagtags' – that little piece of paper that can mean the difference between you meeting the man (or woman) of your dreams or going home alone. You are given a numbered sticker upon arrival at the club and, after having it slapped on your brand new Blur T-Shirt, you then spend the rest of the night wondering if anyone is going to leave you a message, inviting you to spend the rest of the night with them (as if you'd be that cheap!). Alternatively, you could be the hunter and do some writing yourself. Whichever way you look at it, it's an excellent way of breaking the ice for the newcomer to the scene. The music policy is indie, hip Brit and trash disco. The venues are usually split up into two rooms: the main room for the indie and the other, always called the Kitsch Bitch Lounge, for the more cheesy side of chart and retro. Poptastic is run as a gay night. The punters are usually young with no attitude, and the simple, noble intentions of having a good night out partying. Oh, and they are more than likely to be out of their tree. Why? Drinks on both nights are only a quid; that's why! Poptastic Manchester is an incredibly popular night – they fill the club every time around and always end up having to turn over 100 or so people away. So get there early if you want to get in. Members get priority. **Open** Tuesday 2300-0230. Saturday 2300-0300 **Price** £3-4 / £5-6

Sin:ergy @ The Phoenix

Booth Street West, Oxford Road, Manchester M13 9RN Phone 07974 425 344 E-mail jeremy@clubsinergy.com Web www.clubsinergy.com

The Phoenix is hired out once a week (it used to be monthly) to the Sin:ergy crew to give the good people of Manchester an excellent hard house night out. A capacity of around 600 ensures that it is small enough to be intimate and friendly and yet big enough to have atmosphere. The door policy of 'all nations – all persuasions' ensures that the crowd are friendly and that sexuality really is not an issue – fundamentally: a friendly face and the right attitude will get you in! Once inside you will find that the venue has a kind of community vibe with an underground feel to it. Resident DJs include the young and talented Paul Glazby, who plays a hard, yet uplifting style of house (he has recently been signed up to the Tidy Trax DJ Agency and regularly plays guest spots at Storm and Peach, as well as being resident at straight hard house superclub Insomniacz). Big Brett, who has been here since the start of Sin:ergy plays a more bouncy style of hard house. The chill-out floor has a varied music policy; mainly trance and anthemic/classic house (see flyers/press and the website as to what's on). The success of this club is growing month by month and I don't think it will be too long before it will have to move to a larger venue to accommodate the burgeoning crowds. Bear in mind Sin:ergy is not strictly a gay night – it can be compared to Sundissential or Kinky Booty in Brighton (punter-wise that is) for here sexuality is not an issue – it all hangs on your love of music. Tip: if hard house and a cute mixed crowd is your bag then make sure that you check this out. **Open** Friday 2200-0400 **Price** £6-8

Saunas

**Basement
Sauna**

18 Tariff Street, Manchester M1 Phone 0161 237 9996
E-mail info@basementsauna.co.uk Web www.basementsauna.co.uk
The inevitable closure of 'The Canal' cruising ground means that this 24-hour venue will soon become the safest and best alternative for our cruising activities. It is ideally situated off Dale Street by Foo Foos Palace, out of the gay village (although still within easy walking distance of) and in the vicinity of 'The Canal'. The Basement is intentionally 'seedy' and this has drawn unwarranted criticism from some parties, yet these self-same parties object to the closure of The Canal where similar activities can leave you ankle-deep in piss and shit. If you like pristine and shiny saunas then fortunately there are venues in Manchester that can provide them. The Basement is not pristine and shiny – it is without exaggeration a seedy (but not dirty) indoor cruising ground which is safe and warm. It provides nearly 10,000 feet of cavernous floor space with a multitude of maze-like corridors, rest rooms and of course – cruising space. It is also under constant refurbishment – new toilets have been added, a new fully-tiled steam room, additional communal and individual rest rooms have been added and plans are underway to install a larger Jacuzzi and extend the premises to take in an additional 5,000 feet of floor space. The facilities also include a rest room with an open-back van and mattress (we know what it's for but how did they get a van in here?). Another room contains barrack-style dorm' beds that might not be quite to scale but they do add originality and definitely serve a purpose. The huge lounge area is due to be refurbished – at present it is dingy and uninviting but rather than close it off they keep it open to provide you with another area to wander around. The Basement is open 24 hours, which makes tracking its busiest times that little bit more difficult. It is, however, safe to say that after 0100 on Saturday nights the customer count swells to quite a number, particularly with the after-club influx of punters (both gay and straight). You can gain pass-outs (from 0700 to 0700, excluding Gayfest weekend) in case you want to visit more than once throughout the day and it's worth remembering that once the inevitable Canal closure happens this place will be the obvious choice for the Manchester cruising fraternity. To conclude – if you want a no-attitude, no-strings, horny place to meet for sex then this is it – no matter what your age. Do not listen to unsubstantiated rumours – just try it out for yourself. Finally, membership is a

condition (enforced by the sauna's insurers) that you must comply with. It will cost you £4 for the year and you needn't even sign up using your correct name and address (ideal if you are playing away from home). If you are unable to carry your membership card you can leave it at reception and you'll be issued with a username and password. If you like real, raw and seedy then I can wholeheartedly recommend that you give this place a go – if you like to preen, criticise and pose go elsewhere! **Open** Daily, 24 hours **Price** £8-10

Eurosauna 202 Hill Lane, Higher Blakeley, Manchester M9 6RG Phone 0161 740 5152
Try to read between the lines here... this place is a dump. I went in on a Wednesday afternoon and there I found myself with two older gentlemen. So, we sat there, each of us waiting (in my case praying) that someone else would walk into the place. Two hours passed before I finally gave up the ghost with the sad realisation that I could have spent my money on an eighth and had a wank. But wait, it gets better. The venue sits above a derelict launderette and is located at the front of a council estate with bored kids hanging around a patch of waste ground adding to your already wracked nerves. This is probably the oldest gay sauna in the country. This, however, is not enough of a reason to encourage you to come here. The owners will have to do something with the place really soon. I'd suggest shutting up shop and moving! **Open** Monday-Sunday 1300-2100 **Price** £7-8

H2O Zone 36-38 Sackville Street, Manchester M1 3WA Phone 0161 236 3876
E-mail **sauna@clonezone.co.uk** Web **www.clonezone.co.uk**
A clean and compact gay sauna in the heart of the gay village. Despite the size (H2O is part of the Clone Zone empire) they have managed to cram in a Jacuzzi, steam room, sauna cabin, lounge café and twelve rest rooms. For the more adventurous there is also a sling room. Regulars can reduce their admission charges by signing up as a member (not compulsory). They will then receive a £2 discount on each subsequent visit. Students and those claiming benefits can get in for £7. There are also many promotional incentives, such as the Tuesday two get in for the price of one deal (try waiting outside skulking 'til another single gent goes in and then make like you're old friends!) and Thursday when Lucky Locker Day means you can win free passes and other stuff (depending on which locker you get). H2O is located above the Clone

Zone shop on Sackville Street. The clientele is a real mixed bunch (as in all saunas), however, because of the location you do get quite a few straight types going in, probably because they know of nowhere else to go, and during the day the crowd is young in the majority. **Open** Monday-Thursday 1200-2300. Friday-Saturday 1200-0700. Sunday 1300-2200 **Price** £10-12

Heat Sauna   **Manchester House, Manchester Road (off Wilbraham Road), Chorlton-Cum-Hardy, Manchester M21** Phone **0161 860 6666** E-mail **info@heatsauna.co.uk** Web **www.heatsauna.co.uk**
Heat is set over three large floors in a discreet, secure, purpose-built private building three miles from the city centre. Facilities include a football team spa, steamroom, sauna cabin, ice-cold plunge showers, giant-screen cinema, TV lounge, shower rooms, massage rooms, leather room, jail cell, video cabins, play rooms, rest rooms, sunbeds, private car park and free refreshments. **Open** Monday-Thursday 1300-2300. Friday-Saturday 1300-0700. Sunday 1300-2300. **Price** £12, plus £1 day membership or £3 annual

Thermos Sauna   85 Rochdale Road, Manchester M4 4HY Phone **0161 839 7198**
Thermos is the latest addition to Manchester's sauna scene. You can't miss it: it's situated within walking distance of the gay village over on Rochdale Road. A former pub/hotel (The Captain's Bar) you'll notice a sign painted onto the outside wall blatantly informing you that this is a men-only spa. Thermos is another 24-hour venue (along with The Basement) offering all of the usual sauna facilities, including a bar area with pool table. The wet area is downstairs whilst upstairs – the interesting part – houses the individual rest rooms and communal area. **Open** Daily, 24 hours **Price** £10 plus £4 annual membership

The IRA bomb that had such destructive effect on Manchester's city centre on Saturday 15 June 1996 was the largest bomb to be exploded on mainland Britain since the end of the Second World War. The costs to the city were conservatively estimated at £300 million and even now the city is still in the process of repair.

Stallions Sauna   c/o The Carlton House Hotel, 153 Upper Chorlton Road, Whalley Range, Manchester M16 7SH Phone **0161 881 4635**
A sauna in the cellars of The Carlton Hotel! Convenient only if you are staying at the hotel and cannot get into town or to a better-equipped place. **Open** Monday-Friday 1200-2300. Saturday 1200-2300 / 0000-0700. Sunday 1200-2300 **Price** £10

Accommodation

The Carlton Hotel   153 Upper Chorlton Road, Whalley Range, Manchester M16 7SH Phone **0161 881 4635**
The Carlton is a gay hotel situated in Whalley Range, about two miles out of the city centre. Stallions Sauna is based beneath the hotel (see separate listing) and there's half-price entry available to residents (£5).

Price £45 **Number of rooms** 15, 4 en-suite

Gayfest Accommodation

Manchester Conference Centre, Trading Services UMIST, PO Box 88, Manchester M60 1QD Phone 0161 200 8800
E-mail mcc.reg@umist.ac.uk Web www.manchestergayfest.com
Manchester Gayfest has teamed up with Manchester Conference Centre and the city's leading hotels to offer discounted rates both during the 2001 Gayfest celebrations and throughout the year too. In addition to saving visitors money, every booking made through the scheme will generate £2.50 to the Gayfest good causes fund, money from which will be distributed after the event. Accommodation offered by the scheme ranges from luxury hotels to economy student rooms. All those participating have been judged as extremely gay-friendly by the Gayfest committee. You are able to book on-line by following the accommodation link on the Gayfest site.

Hollywood International Hotel

34 London Road, Manchester M1 2PF Phone 0161 236 1010
E-mail info@hollywoodinternationalhotel.com
Web www.hollywoodinternationalhotel.com
The Hollywood International opened in May 2001 and went on to become the biggest gay hotel complex in the UK. Not only does it offer top-class accommodation at prices you'd usually associate with a bed and breakfast, it also offers men-only 15-bed shared dormitory accommodation to save you driving home or paying extortionate taxi fares after painting the town pink. There are plans to open a women's dorm accommodation facility too. Rates are nominal (£10 midweek and £15 Friday to Saturday). There is also triple accommodation (all single bed or the family double bed and single bed option with en-suite for £50). All rooms are exceptionally clean and comfortable with room and hotel facilities including TV, tea/coffee-making facilities, 24-hour porter and a late bar open to residents. The hotel also has a comfortable guests' lounge with large-screen TV, internet room, full function and conference facilities and restaurant. A grand buffet Scandinavian-style breakfast is included in the price (0800 to 1000). Evening meals can be provided if required. Finally, you just cannot get a better location than this – situated directly opposite the railway station and only one minute's walk to the gay village. Highly recommended. **Price** £40 **Number of rooms** 50, most en-suite

Malmaison

Piccadilly, Manchester M1 3AQ Phone 0161 278 1000 Fax 0161 278 1002
E-mail enquiries@malmaison.com Web www. malmaison.com
Malmaison Manchester is a classic gay-friendly contemporary hotel with a traditional French brasserie, intimate bar, a mini-spa and high-tech gym. The bedrooms are stylish, spacious and individually designed. Malmaison is situated in the heart of the city, close to Piccadilly station. The gay village is just around the corner, about one minute's walk away. This is the very hotel that Eminem booked into until he found out how close it was to the village, and then promptly went to London. Expect to pay a supplement of £12 if you book for just the one night over the weekend. Tip: over the weekend you can try and haggle for the best

price. Be persistent. **Price** £100 Double with breakfast **Number of rooms** 112, all en-suite

The New Union Hotel

111 Princess Street (corner of Canal Street), Manchester M1 6JB
Phone 0161 228 1492
All rooms have en-suite facilities, tea and coffee welcome tray and Sky TV and all rates include a full English breakfast. Due to The New Union's location (in the heart of the gay village) the weekends do tend to be booked well in advance, so get in there early. **Price** £45 **Number of rooms** 11, all en-suite

The Palace Hotel

Oxford Road, Manchester M60 7HA Phone 0161 288 1111
Fax 0161 288 2222 E-mail enquiries@principalhotels.co.uk
Web www.principalhotels.co.uk
The Palace is a fabulous, terracotta Grade Two-listed building within the heart of Manchester's city centre. It's situated opposite The Palace Theatre and is close to Granada TV studios, the Opera House, Bridgewater Hall and the Museum of Science and Industry. Owned by Principal Hotels, this is the venue where the annual Gayfest Ball is held. The Palace takes in a high quota of business guests over the course of the week and weekday room-only rates are approximately £149 per night. Weekends, however, see many more rooms available and thus the room rate drops substantially, and the price indicated below is inclusive of dinner and bed and breakfast. The hotel is very gay-friendly and is exceptionally luxurious, but at the right price. It may be worth pointing out that Oxford Road is the main thoroughfare for students and young guns coming and going from town and because of this the road can be pretty cruisy, particularly by the late-night shops – but be very discreet! **Price** £63 **Number of rooms** 267, all en-suite

Princess Hotel

101 Portland Street, Manchester M1 6D Phone 0161 236 5122
Fax 0161 236 4468 E-mail billmoss@princesshotels.co.uk
Web www.princesshotels.co.uk
Originally one of Manchester's bustling Victorian cotton mills, the building was tastefully converted to form this elegant hotel, situated in the heart of Manchester's gay village. It is not an exclusively gay hotel although due to its perfect location on the corner of Princess Street and Portland Street it is extremely gay-friendly and accommodating to a gay clientele. Parking is readily available at surface car parks adjacent to the hotel and at the nearby Chorlton Street multi-storey car park, for which the hotel has negotiated special rates for guests. The Princess is just a ten minutes walk from the mainline railways stations and only eight miles from Manchester International Airport. All rooms have an en-suite bathroom. There's also colour TV with teletext and satellite channels, direct dial phone, tea/coffee-making facilities and a hairdryer and trouser press. You can also explore their extensive menu from the leisure of your own room by taking advantage of the 24-hour-a-day room service. **Price** £65-70 **Number of rooms** 85, all en-suite

The Rembrandt Hotel

33 Sackville Street, Manchester M1 3LZ

Phone 0161 236 1311 E-mail info@therembrandthotel.co.uk

Web www.therembrandthotel.co.uk

The Rembrandt has been serving the community for over 17 years. Overlooking Sackville Park and Canal Street it is adjacent to all the major bars and clubs in the village. There are several car parks within walking distance and there's street parking opposite the hotel (meters during the day). The Rembrandt also holds a three-diamond Tourist Board rating. The actual accommodation is above The Rembrandt pub (see separate listing) and it's worth noting that due this hotel's location, right in the centre of the gay village, the weekends are usually booked up well in advance. Tip: book early to avoid disappointment. **Price** £50 **Number of rooms** 20, 14 en-suite

Thistle Hotel

3-5 Portland Street, Manchester M1 6DP

Phone 0161 228 3400 Fax 0161 236 6847

The Thistle is situated within one minute's walking distance of the gay village and is regarded as one of Manchester's better hotels. It has an excellent reputation for being very gay-friendly (this could possibly be put down to its location). The room rate does not include breakfast; this is charged extra at around £12. The Thistle is currently undergoing complete refurbishment, so if you do require absolute peace and quiet make this known at the time of booking (work should be completed by November 2001). A spacious reception and lounge area welcomes travellers and the AA rosette-awarded restaurant, Winston's offers a brasserie menu that might well be worth trying out. The Leisure Spa, with plunge pool, Jacuzzi, sauna and solarium should put the icing on a relaxing and satisfying stay. Tip: check-out is usually at 1200, however, prior arrangement could help fix you a later time. **Price** £70-120 **Number of rooms** 205, all en-suite

Cruising grounds

The Canal

At the time of writing, 'The Canal', Manchester's notorious cruising ground, is under major development. The underground towpath has now been closed off and rumours are abound as to the future of this area. The development of the Ducie Street area will not be completed for a year or so yet, however, with the Commonwealth Games looming

on the horizon Manchester Council (and the police) are cleaning up the seedy districts hoping to create a good impression for our visitors. So where does the gay cruising take place now that it has been moved from underground? Well, the area is quite large, so here is a quick-guided tour around the main part. Start on Ducie Street, which is the road going right as you leave the approach from Piccadilly Station. This is the main (but very public) cruising area. Walking to the top of the road you will come to a couple of small gardens by the canal – cruising goes on around here. Carry on walking up Ducie Street and you will come to Ducie House on the corner. Turn left and follow the road around, always turning left. These roads are very quiet (at present) and anyone hanging around here is probably there for the same reason as you. If you carry on walking (still turning left where appropriate) you will come to The Basement Sauna (Tariff Street). Walk past here to the end of the road and you will come to Dale Street. Turn left, follow the road down and you are back where you started. There are many more side grounds around here, ones which I am hesitant to describe (popular knowledge of such could well seal their fate too) but Manchester guys are very friendly and should be able to show you where to go if you ask them. As for the future? There is no doubting this area will be cleaned up. Cruisers on the road may well be quizzed by the police and threatened with arrest for importuning (yes, that's what they'll call it!) and the police presence will be a lot stronger than it is now. I suspect that The Basement Sauna (see separate listing) will be able to provide a safe space for cruisers when the clean-up starts which, if we are honest with ourselves, may be a good thing. After all, we have had a good run for our money. Tip: if you do experience trouble from cruising or cottaging contact Monson's Solicitors (see separate listing).

Worsley Wood   This place is very popular during the summer months and is fast becoming an established site, along with Broxton (in nearby Chester; see separate listing), due to the closure of the Junction 14 picnic area on the M56. Take the turn-off (J13/M62 north) and head towards Eccles. About 30 yards to your right you will come to a car park (sign-posted) adjoining the wood. Park up here and take a stroll around. This area is also popular with straight couples, some of whom are looking for a third party to join in their fun.

Retail & Other

Clone Zone   36-38 Sackville Street, Manchester M1 3WA Phone 0161 236 1398
E-mail **info@clonezone.co.uk** Web **www.clonezone.co.uk**
Well-known stockists of gay and lesbian magazines, books, videos (R18, Amsterdam-strength) and clothing. There's also aromas, fetish gear and everything else that's associated. You can buy tickets for most party nights here (subject to a booking fee). The complete range of free gay press is also available, however, these are usually gone by the end of the weekend. Unfortunately, the Manchester Clone Zone apartments are no longer available. **Open** Monday-Thursday 1100-2200. Friday-Saturday 1100-2300. Sunday 1300-1900

3

Cornerhouse

70 Oxford Street, Manchester M1 5NH Phone 0161 200 1500
E-mail info@cornerhouse.org Web www.cornerhouse.org
Cornerhouse is Greater Manchester's international centre for contemporary visual arts and film. Located in the heart of Manchester by Oxford Street railway station, the centre has three floors of contemporary art galleries (free admission), three cinema screens, a bar, two cafés and a bookshop. Cornerhouse also operates an international publications service, distributing visual arts books and catalogues. Open since 1985, Cornerhouse has built an international reputation for excellence and innovation. Gay events which they have previously been or are currently involved with include Queer Up North, Gayfest and The London Gay and Lesbian Film Festival. They have also screened individual films such as Krampack and Second Skin. Well worth a visit if this kind of thing interests you. **Open** (Bar) Tuesday-Saturday 1200-2300. (Galleries) Daily 1100-1800. (Café) Daily 1000-2030 **Price** £3.80-4.70 (cinema)

Funky Crop Shop

37 Bloom Street, Manchester M1 3LY Phone 0161 237 1032
Do you recall, in Steel Magnolias, Dolly Parton's hairdressers? Well, that's what it is like in here. Just about anyone and everyone drops in to find out what's going on in the village, pick up the gay press, flyers and believe it or not, some even come to get their hair done. The salon is not pretentious; men and women sit gossiping side by side and the reputation that Lee has built up over many years has enabled him to open a sister venue in Birmingham. **Open** Monday-Friday 1100-1730. Saturday 1100-1700. Sunday 1300-1630 **Price** £10 dry cut

Monson's Solicitors

4th Floor Dale House, 35 Dale Street, Manchester M1 2HF
Phone 0161 237 5959 E-mail info@gaycrime.co.uk
Web www.gaycrime.co.uk
Monson's are criminal lawyers with an excellent reputation in the gay community for doing all they can to stop injustice and bigotry. They also hold a free legal surgery at The Lesbian and Gay Foundation on Pritchard Street (Thursday, 1900 to 2100). Their areas of speciality go right across the board – 24-hour police station visits, defending proceedings from sexual offences to drug trafficking and possession, from fraud to murder and all areas in between, including drink-driving offences, customs and excise investigations (including VAT), trading standards investigations, company fraud and DTI investigations. They are also one of the few lawyers in the country able to defend you in computer- and internet-based crime cases. Most of their work is covered – either entirely or in part – by Legal Aid. If Legal Aid is not an option they will provide you with a detailed estimate of the probable cost and agree in advance on a method of payment. They welcome enquiries via phone or mail. Tip: if you are resident in Manchester it is always advisable to carry one of their cards around with you (which contains a 24-hour contact number) you just never know when you may need it. **Open** Monday-Friday 0900-1700

Tyler Frazer

5 Richmond Street, Manchester M1 3HF Phone 0161 236 5554
Situated down Richmond Street opposite Company Bar is another gay
hairdressing and beauty salon. Tyler Frazer specialise in Afro's, hair
extensions and weaves. They do not do dry cuts per se, but they do offer
a full hair treatment service. They also do gents and ladies beautician
work, including hair removal. New clients receive an automatic 20 per
cent discount off the bill, second visits receive a 10 per cent discount and
thereafter it's full price. **Open** Tuesday-Wednesday 1100-1830.
Thursday-Friday 1100-2000. Saturday 1000-1730 **Price** £25

Mansfield Club nights

The Yard /
Ten Nightclub

61 Westgate, Mansfield NE18 1RU Phone 01623 622 230
Every last Monday of the month sees this exclusively lesbian, gay and
TV event come around. This shindig has been in operation for well over
eight years and is as popular as ever. You can get drinks at pub prices
and there are regular cheap drink promotions. Music-wise everyone
seems to be taken care of with commercial happy-clappy sounds
upstairs and a hard house vibe downstairs. Considering the lack of gay
space in Mansfield it will come as no surprise that this 500-odd capacity
venue can get quite busy even with visitors from nearby Nottingham
dropping in on the lookout for a change of scenery. **Open** Every last
Monday of the month 2130-0200. **Price** £1.50

Saunas

Zeus Sauna   71 Ratcliffe Gate, Mansfield NG18 2JB Phone 01623 422 257
E-mail **Zeus71@gay-mansfield.com** Web **www.gay-mansfield.com**
Zeus is a small and friendly sauna situated in a discreet commercial area
of the town. It's spread out over two floors and offers large sauna (medium heat), a smaller sauna (hot), steam room, video lounge and both
individual and communal rest rooms. There is also a relaxing coffee bar
(smoking allowed). **Open** Saturday-Thursday 1200-2300 Last entry
2130. Friday 1200-0200 (last entry 2300) **Price** £7

Margate Pubs

The New Inn   New Street, Margate CT9 1EG Phone 01843 223 799
There's not much to do in Margate at any time of the year. The gay population is poorly catered for. If you should find yourself here the only
place to go is the New Inn. Gay men and lesbians mix well in this one-room public house. **Open** Monday-Saturday 1100-2300. Sunday 1200-2230

Accommodation

Copperfields   8 Gloucester Avenue, Cliftonville, Margate CT9 3NP Phone 01843 221 220
A 1924 art-deco guest-house in the exclusive Palm Bay area on the Kent
coast. Facilities available to guests include a sauna and Jacuzzi, a
rooftop terrace and private gardens. Copperfields is very close to the
beach and has views of the sea. There is also a self-catering holiday caravan (that sleeps six) in beautiful Rye that is let at the ridiculously low
rate of around £30 per night (phone for details). Rye, as you may know,
is an antiques paradise, with lots of shops, cobbled streets and tea
shops. Aah, nice. **Price** £40 **Number of rooms** 4, all en-suite

Marlow Cruising grounds

Bisham Woods   From Juncion 4 off the M40 follow the A404 towards the M4: this
stretch is about six miles long from one motorway to the other. About

midway, there is the Bisham roundabout, which signposts you off to the A308 at Maidenhead. On the M4 side of this roundabout (on the left, if heading towards the M4) there is a slip road marked as a picnic area. Turn in, park up and wander through the woods. This area is extremely busy during the summer months.

Middlesbrough Pubs

Cassady's   **41-45 Grange Road, Middlesbrough TS1 5AU Phone 01642 221 241**
Cassady's is a large gay pub on three levels with three bars and a dance floor. It is mainly a disco-pub, frequented by the young and hopeful, but there are quiet areas accommodating the older gays and lesbians and a pool room too. As Middlesbrough is rather restricted when it comes to gay venues it will come as no surprise to learn that most of the area's gays (boys and girls) meet up in here at some time or other. The upstairs function room is hired out to an assortment of gay groups and gatherings although it is best to keep an eye on the gay press for any regular events. **Open** Monday-Wednesday 1900-2300. Thursday 1900-0000. Friday-Saturday 1900-0200. Sunday 1900-2230 **Price** £3, Saturday only

The Oak   **23 Newport Road, Middlesbrough TS1 1LE Phone 01642 219 748**
The newest café-bar in the area is both stylish and gay-owned and serves food daily from 1200 to 1500. This spacious one-level venue with ample 'dance where you stand' space offers disco on a Friday ('70s to present day) and dance music on a Saturday. Sunday is a camp all-day party, ideal as a chill-out from the night before or to just get tanked up. **Open** Monday-Saturday 1100-2300. Sunday 1200-2230

Clubs

Strings   **49a Langhorne Road, Middlesbrough TS1 5BS Phone 01642 231 353**
E-mail **info@stringsnightclub.com** Web **www.stringsnightclub.com**
Situated in the heart of the town, Strings is Middlesbrough's largest and most popular gay night club venue, situated just opposite the Cleveland Centre, above Beaverbrooks. The club is set out over two levels, each floor playing music that caters for every taste. Strings is open most nights of the week and you can guarantee that there will always be fun of one description or another waiting for you; from strippers and cabaret to regular themed party nights with drinks promotions. **Open** Thursday-Saturday 2200-0200 **Price** £2-5

Mildenhall Accommodation

Pear Tree   **Chapel Road, West Row, Mildenhall IP28 8PA Phone 01638 711 112**
House Hotel   E-mail **peartree@12stay.co.uk** Web **www.peartree.12stay.co.uk**
The Pear Tree is a 240-year-old Grade Two-listed building, formerly The Village Inn, with beautiful gardens that are open to guests. Its centrally located and is ideal for touring the unspoilt East Anglian counties of

Suffolk, Cambridgeshire and Norfolk, with first class road links to all parts of the country. From Victorian times up until 1992 the building was the Pear Tree Inn. It has been professionally restored, keeping the best of the original features and introducing new bathrooms and quality furnishings. The guests' lounge has an impressive inglenook fireplace with roaring log fires in the winter. There is a large colour TV, a selection of board games and a comprehensive range of brochures showing places of interest to visit. The Suffolk and Norfolk coasts are a pleasant drive away and Holkham Bay is a magnificent spot (the location for many film beach scene) which includes a nudist beach with a gay section. You can also find the Queen's beach hut here (though more like a large Swiss chalet in appearance) as this place is near to her Sandringham residence. Tip: an excellent base for touring the historical houses of the south (Audley End, Euston Hall, Wimpole, etc.) **Price** £42 per double room **Number of rooms 4**, all en-suite

Milton Keynes Clubs

Pink Punters   2 Watling Street, Fenny Stratford, Milton Keynes MK2 2BT
Phone 01908 377 444 E-mail info@pinkpunters.com
Web www.pinkpunters.com
The first full-time gay night club for Milton Keynes, formerly known as The Monastery, which caters for all ages and both sexes. This large two-floor venue has a main bar upstairs and a disco bar in the basement. There's always something going on here – karaoke comes around three times a week! Pink Punters has proved itself a popular and very friendly late-night drinking den for the gay and gay-friendly community. This is a members-only club (annual membership costs £10) and although you can be admitted at the manager's discretion as a guest on your first visit, membership will be required for subsequent visits. This is the best Milton Keynes has to offer in the way of gay venues and 'tis a pity that membership is required for what is ostensibly just a late-licence gay pub. **Open** Monday-Saturday 1900-0300. Sunday 1900-0100 **Price** £1, Sunday-Thursday. £4-5, Friday-Saturday

Newcastle upon Tyne

Lovers of Earl Grey tea can pay tribute to the monument that stands 80 feet tall in Monument Mall, opposite Eldon Square. It is dedicated to Charles, Earl of Grey, who mixed Bergamot into our tea. Of course, he did a lot more than just that, being a politician and all, but his name lives on for his services to the great English cuppa'. Still, there's much more to this city than just that. Newcastle-upon-Tyne is more commonly referred to, simply, as Newcastle. It is the largest city in the north-east of England, with a rich and varied past, which dates back to the Roman era, and at one time a quarter of all the world's ship-building industry was centred here. For several decades the city suffered economic decline and gained an unfortunate reputation for poverty. Recent years, though, have seen extensive restoration and rejuvenation in the city centre and Newcastle is now, surprisingly, stylish. With several new huge shopping centres, including Europe's largest, the city has become a Mecca for shopaholics all over the country. Newcastle's buzzing night life and excellent cultural scene has seen this city transform itself into one of Britain's trendiest. This is another northern city that is famous for its friendliness and the city's people – known as Geordies – will give you a warm welcome. It's definitely worth a visit.

Getting in touch

The tourist offices at **Central Station** (0191 230 0030) on Neville Street and **Central Library** (0191 261 0610) off New Bridge Street offer free street maps – essential for finding your way around the maze of streets where the names and directions change far too frequently. There is also a dedicated **Travel Line** (0191 232 5325) operating from Monday to Saturday from 0800 to 2000 and Sunday from 0900 to 2200. **Newcastle Friend** can be contacted during the evening for any information on the Newcastle gay scene (0191 261 8555). There is also an **AIDS Information Line** (0191 232 2855) which is open from Monday to Friday from 1000 to 1900 and Saturday from 1000 to 1600. **Lesbian Line** (0191 261 8555) is open Tuesday from 1900 to 2200.

Pubs

The Barking Dog
15 Marlborough Crescent, Newcastle upon Tyne NE1 4EE
Phone 0191 221 0775
This is a very popular mixed gay and straight pub with two bars. The downstairs bar is very loud. The upstairs is used as the cabaret bar. Women tend to congregate here on a Friday evening although this is not a specific women-only night. Having just undergone a major refurbishment it is now a very stylish and cosmopolitan bar. **Open** Monday-Sunday 1200-2230

Mims
3-5 Waterloo Street, Newcastle upon Tyne NE1 4DE Phone 0191 232 2014
Formerly The Frog and Nightgown, Mims is the latest addition to the Newcastle scene and is two kinds of bar in one. The ground floor is more of an intimate, traditional hangout which caters for the older gay crowd with background music, old movie clips on the monitors and comfortable seating. Upstairs is more of a stylish dance bar. The music is louder and tuned to a younger, more energetic hands-in-the-air crowd. **Open** Monday-Friday 1700-2300. Saturday 1200-2300. Sunday 1200-2230

Strings
9-11 Waterloo Street, Newcastle upon Tyne NE1 4DE
Phone 0191 261 8664
Strings is a relatively new addition to Newcastle's gay scene. It's quite young and lively downstairs with a dance floor and pumping music, whilst upstairs is quieter: a cheerful place where you can gossip and chat. There's loads of goings-on throughout the week – strippers, karaoke and, of course, the popular disco each night. **Open** Monday-

Saturday 1100-2300. Sunday 1200-2230

Any visit to Newcastle would not be complete without sampling their world-famous Newcastle Brown Ale. It would be equivalent to visiting Dublin and turning your nose up at a pint of Guinness. It was created by brew-master Jim Portet and has been brewed in Newcastle since 1927. It has become the number-one best-selling bottled beer across England and Europe. It sits inside a clear bottle with a colourful label that includes the trademark blue star and the inscription 'The One and Only'.

The Yard / 2 Scotswood Road, Newcastle upon Tyne NE4 7JB Phone 0191 232 2037
Heavens Above The Yard, formerly known as The Courtyard, is one of the oldest gay bars in Newcastle and a recent refurbishment transformed the old, traditional downstairs bar into more of a light, airy and continental-style café-bar. Upstairs, Heavens Above is a modern dance bar where louder dance music fills the air and a younger, trendy crowd of boys and girls enjoy the cheap drinks and spot-dance to their heart's content. The club opens its doors every night except Tuesday, from 2000 to 2300 and from 2000 to 0000 on Thursday through to Saturday. Wednesday nights are for TVs and crossdressers only and the hours run from 1930 to 2300 and admission will cost you £1. There is a separate entrance to Heavens Above situated on Churchill Street, around the corner from The Courtyard. **Open** Monday-Wednesday 1300-2300. Thursday-Saturday 1200-0000. Sunday 1300-2230

Clubs

Powerhouse 21-33 George Street, Newcastle upon Tyne NE1 4DE Phone 0191 272 3621
E-mail info@power-house.co.uk Web www.power-house.co.uk
This is Newcastle's only full-time gay night club. It moved from its previous location on Waterloo Street to this venue just before Christmas 2000. The new place features three rooms, four bars, and has two DJs spinning on two separate dancefloors. Monday night is Phusion which combines cabaret with mucho-cheesy choons. Tuesday is Phruit, a night for the lover of chart disco. Wednesday is the weekly Poptastic night (see separate listing) and Thursday is Phagtastic, an excellent night of new and old club anthems. Friday sees both rooms open to give you '70s to present day tunes on offer in the main room and commercial dance in the ground floor disco. Membership to Powerhouse can offer you discounted admission to most nights and this can be obtained from the reception after midnight on a Friday or Saturday evening. Bear in mind that over the weekend the admission charges increase by £1 every half-hour after 2330. **Open** Monday-Thursday 2200-0200. Friday-Saturday 2200-0300 **Price** £2-4, Monday-Thursday. £4-7, Friday-Saturday

Rockshots 78 Scotswood Road, Newcastle upon Tyne NE4 7JH Phone 0191 232 6536
Known locally as Rockies this is Newcastle's oldest and original gay club. The gay club tag is rather contentious though as it nowadays tends to be rather straight (and young). Despite this, Rockies is still a good, very gay-friendly club for those of you who like your music a little hard-

er and less camp. It's particularly gay on Wednesday and Saturday when club night Nice fills the place. **Open** Monday 2200-0200. Wednesday 2300-0200. Saturday 2200-0300 **Price** £2-8

Club nights

Poptastic @ The Powerhouse
21-33 George Street, Newcastle upon Tyne NE4 7JL Phone 07074 248 247
E-mail info@poptastic.co.uk Web www.poptastic.co.uk
The queer clubbing phenomenon has another baby, this time in Newcastle's leading gay venue, The Powerhouse. There's two rooms playing indie and alternative in the Indie Playground and '80s cheese mixed with current pop in The Kitsch Bitch Lounge. Add the ever-popular ShagTags into the mix and you'll get exactly what you expect from Poptastic – a cheap night out, some cheap beer and a cheap shag! Wahay! **Open** Wednesday 2200-0200 **Price** £3

Saunas

Blue Corner Sauna
164B Heaton Park Road, Heaton, Newcastle upon Tyne NE6 5AD
Phone 0191 240 0122
A basic little sauna that has had the stronghold on the Newcastle scene, yet without offering all that much. Upstairs is the wet area with sauna cabin and steam room. Downstairs there's the individual rest rooms, communal rest area, TV room and a soft porn video room. **Open** Monday-Saturday 1000-2200. Sunday 1200-2000 **Price** £8

Top 2 Bottom
85-89 Blandford Street, Newcastle upon Tyne NE1 3PZ
Phone 0191 230 4110
A new men-only sauna for the lads of Newcastle and its surrounding areas. Here you'll find a steam room, two TV lounges, free sun bed and a pool table, shower area and coffee shop. There's a monthly Bears Night which comes around every last Saturday. Admission is structured to ensure that the earlier you go in the less you pay (£5 before 1700; £6 between 1700 and 1900 and £7 after 1900). The membership of £10 may seem a little steep but you will more than get this back from reduced admission prices and discounts against the pool table and sunbed. It is worth noting that the £10 membership is available to the first 1,000 members only; it will then be standardised at £20 (which is steep). There

are plans to open the sauna for a full 24 hours – keep an eye on the gay press for details of opening and admission changes. **Open** Monday-Sunday 1200-0000 **Price** £5-7 and £10 for annual membership

Accommodation

Imperial Guest House

194 Station Road, Wallsend, Newcastle upon Tyne NE28 8RD Phone **0191 236 9808** Fax **0191 236 9808** E-mail **enquiries@imperialguesthouse.co.uk** Web **www.imperialguesthouse.co.uk** Behind a plain and unassuming terraced frontage lies a guest-house with a difference. The proprietors at the Imperial are committed to giving you the highest standards of service and comfort. This Victorian house has been superbly restored, not to one particular period, but in a careful blending together of various styles, to create an elegant and supremely comfortable interior. The bedrooms on offer are a choice of double and twin rooms and charges are per person – the single guest has the added comfort of a double room. Each room is tastefully decorated, with colour TV, phone, radio/alarm clock, wash-hand basin, hair dryer and razor point. Complimentary tea and coffee, together with biscuits, mints and mineral water are in plentiful supply. Little luxuries, such as a selection of toiletries, tissues and towelling bathrobe, completes their commitment to quality. Tip: check-in time is around 1600 – if you require an earlier time then ensure you make arrangements when booking. **Price** £40 **Number of rooms** 4, 1 en-suite

Cruising grounds

The Gardens

The Gardens are situated between the Quayside and Newcastle train station, next to the Castle Keep and the high-level bridge. This is a lightly wooded area. Cruising starts about lunchtime until 1500 and then from 1700 until about 2000. It starts up again at 2200 and things fizzle out around 0300. On the Gateshead side of the high-level bridge you will find much the same, except most of it goes on in cars.

Newquay Club nights

Pinkys @ Sandridge Hotel

Headland Road, Newquay TR7 1HN Phone 01637 872 089 In an area decidedly lacking any sort of gay meeting place, Pinkys takes place each weekend in the basement bar of the hotel. Don't expect a 20,000-watt sound and lighting system, nor trendy, cosmopolitan décor. What you will get though is a friendly and welcoming atmosphere; a place where you are allowed to enjoy yourself and just have fun. There is no dress code, no age limit and never ever any problems. Accommodation is available from £20 per person per night, including breakfast and free admission into the club. Phone the hotel for further details. The entrance to the 'club' is through the hotel front door, which should be well lit and signposted. **Open** Friday-Saturday 2000-late **Price** £2.50

Northampton Pubs

K2 Club

39 Sheep Street, Northampton NN1 2NE Phone 01604 622 822

Being Northampton's only gay venue it's not hard to imagine how busy this place gets most evenings and particularly over the weekend. Although the crowd is a predominantly young gay and lesbian set, there are a few of the older generation (thirty-something!) propping up the bar too. The first two floors contain the three bars and two dance floors. The third floor is a chill-out and quiet social area whilst the fourth floor contains the relaxation rooms – ooops! Sorry, I just slipped into sauna mode – I meant to say another chill-out and (very) social area. Entertainment through the week consists of practically everything – strippers every other Tuesday and karaoke on a Sunday with tons of dancing in between. Being late-licensed means that this place does get very busy, particularly over the weekend. Tip: get in free before 2200 on Fridays and Saturdays. **Open** Tuesday-Thursday 2000-0200. Friday-Saturday 2100-0300. Sunday 2000-late **Price** £4, Friday-Saturday after 2200

Cruising grounds

A43 Northampton to Kettering

There are some long lay-bys situated about halfway between these two towns. They are well screened from the A43 and things particularly hot up late at night with easy access to the nearby fields. Police do tend to sniff about, but there have been no reports of any arrests.

Becketts Park

(Bedford Road) There's activity near the town centre, by the River Nene, all along the river path in the evening. There are two cottages, one near the town, the other about halfway down the river path. Beware of occasional police activity here. The bushes near the second loo are a favourite place; and also the nature reserve over the bridge. Police cars patrol at night here, so again be careful. Further down are the meadows. The parking area should be closed at night but most of the time it isn't. Cross the bridge and wander through the area. Once again, police cars do visit this area, so watch out.

Norwich

Norwich, the largest provincial city in England three centuries ago, is still considered to be the capital of East Anglia and it remains an attractive and prosperous city. Central streets follow their medieval course, outlined by the remaining parts of the ancient city walls, which enclose a wealth of historic buildings, including the honey-coloured Norman cathedral and castle (which dominate the city) and the medieval Guildhall. There are many other historic buildings which visitors flock to, making this an interesting place to explore on foot. Norwich has, for example, more medieval churches than any other city in western Europe. The city was said at one time to have a church for every week of the year and a pub for every day. Not surprisingly, brewing was one of the chief industries here for more than two centuries.

Getting in touch

Free maps and a travel planner can be obtained from the **Tourist Information Centre** (01603 666 071) at the Guildhall in the Market Place, which is open Monday to Saturday from 0900 to 1730. The **Lesbian and Gay Switchboard** (01603 592 505) is manned each Monday from 2000 to 2200. **WOW** (01603 625 822) stands for Women on Women. They are a Norwich-based group of lesbian and bisexual women working Saturdays from 1330 to 1530 to enhance the well-being of the lesbian community.

Pubs

The Castle

1 Spittalfields (off Ketts Hill), Norwich NR1 4EY Phone 01603 768 886
An old, traditional gay venue with a louder dance area in the rear bar. Plans are afoot to modernise the barn at the back of the venue into a disco ready for the summer. **Open** Monday-Saturday 1100-2300. Sunday 1200-2230

The Lord Raglan

30 Bishop Bridge Road, Norwich NR1 4ET Phone 01603 623 304
A traditional-style, very friendly gay bar with a (mostly) male clientele, although lesbians and TVs are more than welcome. There are monthly theme nights (Rocky Horror, Construction to name but two) and a free weekly raffle (bottle of spirit for the winner). The Lord Raglan is a local's local, catering for all ages and types, but is not really for the trendy disco dolly. The beer garden opens to popular acclaim in the summer and there is also accommodation available at £45 per double room and £30 per single. **Open** Monday-Saturday 1200-1400 / 1900-2300. Sunday 1200-1500 / 1900-2230

Clubs

The Loft Nightclub

80 Rose Lane, Norwich NR1 1PT Phone 01603 623 559
This must surely be the longest running gay club in Norfolk – now into it's 20th year, although it has been renamed several times. This is a very popular spot for gays and lesbians on Thursdays, Saturdays and Sundays. The rest of the week it is hired by independent promoters including Gas Station and Marvel, who alternate every other Friday – Gas Station is a bit more retro with a live band downstairs and Marvel is more of a hip-hop / drum and bass night. Whereas both these Friday nights are straight-orientated this venue is still first and foremost a gay club and you can depend on their being a good gay quota. Back to our gay nights though: Thursday is rather a student-based night, where cheap drinks and admission draw in the crowds – can't say the handbag and cheesy chart music does though! Saturday sees the DJs on rotation every third week so, although commercial house is the backbone, the style and pace does tend to change from DJ to DJ. Sunday is just a chill-

out in the downstairs bar which helps the rehabilitation process following the night before. The Loft is an intimate, little affair with a capacity for just 200 or so. This intimacy helps the atmosphere; one that is largely laid back and entirely without attitude. Based on two floors the downstairs bar offers seating and chatting space whilst upstairs is the full-on club space. **Open** Thursday 2200-020. Saturday 2100-0300. Sunday 2000-0000-plus **Price** £2, Thursday 2200-0200. £4 before 2300 and £5 after on Saturday

Club nights

Absolution @
The Waterfront

139-141 King Street, Norwich NR1 1QH Phone 01603 632 717
The Waterfront is run by UEA's student union and is one of the biggest clubs in Norwich. For those of us who like the banging hard house and trance music style then this is the night to scribble into your diary. It takes place every other month in the upper half of the club. It's a mixed gay and straight dance night although you will find the majority of the punters are gay. The age range is between 18 and 30 and the clientele are totally without attitude. The quick sell-out of door tickets reflects the popularity of this club night and it is recommended that you purchase your tickets in advance, either from the box office (01603 508050) or HMV or from The Castle. There are, naturally, limited tickets available on the door but you will have to get there early if you want to get one of these few. **Open** Every third Friday **Price** £4-5 advance and £6 on the door

Cruising grounds

A11

This is a lay-by with a cottage, in heavy woods, on the left-hand side of the A11 dual carriageway, about ten miles out of Norwich. There's not much going on during the day, but the nights can be very busy. Police patrols are occasional. Rumour has it that an off-duty policeman walks his dog there hoping to catch someone at it... (Sad!) Note: Norwich City Council have given permission to the police to install hidden miniature surveillance cameras in notorious cottages. Several prosecutions and convictions have followed. Be aware.

Nottingham

Everyone has heard of Robin Hood, Nottinghamshire's most famous son and one of the world's favourite folk heros. His adventures have been told and retold down the generations, from medieval ballad to Hollywood movie. Tradition has it that Robin Hood was an outlaw who poached the king's deer in the royal hunting forest of Sherwood. Stories relate how travellers through the forest provided rich pickings for the gentleman robber and his band of 'Merry Men'. Nottingham offers much more than the lore of Robin Hood though. There are historic pubs, a large number of museums and a medieval castle, the bulk of which was tragically destroyed by fire, but which still houses a fine manor house and museum.

Getting in touch

Nottingham City Council has just refurbished and re-opened a large **Tourist Information Office** (0115 915 5330), adjacent to the Old Market Square at 1-4 Smithy Row. the office is open Monday to Saturday from 0830 to 1700 and Sunday from 1000 to 1600. For information and advice phone the **Lesbian and Gay Switchboard** (0115 941 1454) which is open five nights of the week, Monday to Friday from 1900 to 2200.

Pubs

AD2
74 Lower Parliament Street, Nottingham NG1 1EH Phone 0115 950 2727
Formerly The Admiral Duncan, which, as some of you may remember was an absolute dive. Now it's one of the hottest Nottingham spots available to us gay folk. There are two rooms – the first is the main bar area and the second is a smaller, quieter chill-out room. A disco is put on from Wednesday through to Saturday and a staff review is held each Sunday. Open Monday-Saturday 1300-0030. Sunday 1500-0030

The Central
Huntingdon Street, Nottingham NG1 3LH Phone 0115 958 5883
Formerly known as Gatsby's this is a two bar gay venue that caters for the entire spectrum of the gay scene. The bar is divided into two sections, the first is the traditional bar occupied by the older members of the community and the second, more lively space is for the younger disco dollies. On Thursday it becomes a meeting place for the town's trannies, who also gather here on a Saturday. On Thursday through to Saturday there is a disco in the second bar and any additional entertainment is advertised on the notice board. Plans are afoot to totally refurbish the venue later on in the year and these entail the building of an additional bar. Open Monday-Saturday 1200-0000. Sunday 1500-2230

Forester's Arms
18 St Anne's Street, Nottingham NG1 3LX Phone 0115 958 0432
A mixed gay traditional pub which is very popular with the girls. Something goes on most nights with karaoke a regular on Mondays and Thursdays and disco appearing on Tuesday, Friday and Sunday. Open Monday-Saturday 1100-2300. Sunday 1100-2230

Forester's Inn
183 Huntingdon Street, Nottingham NG1 3NL Phone 0115 941 9679
There's a mixed gay and straight clientele during the day which turns predominantly gay in the evening. This is a fair-sized venue with three bars and a pool room. There's nothing much in the form of entertainment through the week. Actually, there's just nothing, although they are planning to start up a Sunday afternoon disco for the summer (can't wait...!). In the meantime just come in here and erm... drink! Open Monday-Saturday 1200-2300. Sunday 1200-2230

Jacey's
47 Heathcote Street, Nottingham NG1 3AQ Phone 0115 941 7888
Jacey's is the largest gay bar in Nottingham with a capacity for around 400 and it's just a stone's throw away from the other gay venues. The bar

has three distinct areas, all now fully refurbished. The Dance Bar is a large open-plan space with a central service area that runs the full length with the multi-levelled dance floor looming above. The inclusion of a new sound and lighting system makes for a thumping club atmosphere, complete with visuals. The Snug Bar is a more intimate affair, with comfortable seating that provides a quieter place to sit, chat... and watch! The Café Bar, set in a further raised area, is a light, airy cosmopolitan space, open throughout the day as well as the evening. This is a haven, away from the hectic dance floor with a lower level featuring a pool table and shooter bar. Nightly events have been planned and they will include some sort of entertainment such as strippers, cabaret and game shows and they will be backed with some style of disco. Innovation and a gap in the Nottingham scene has prompted plans for a women-only night which looks set to run every fortnight on a Sunday under the name of Aurora. **Open** Monday 1200-1500 / 1900-0000. Wednesday-Thursday 1200-1500 / 1900-0230. Friday-Saturday 1200-0000. (Sunday private hire)

The Lord Roberts

24 Broad Street, Hockley, Nottingham NG1 3AN Phone 0115 941 4886
The Lord Roberts is a long-established, theatrically themed gay-friendly pub in the centre of Nottingham. There is no regular entertainment except for a pop quiz on a Thursday evening. You will have to remember that this is a gay-friendly bar and there are several rules on behaviour that are rigidly enforced, such as no snogging in the venue (gay or straight)! This is a place where they say you can bring your mother or your straight friends (or your mother's straight friends even) as a gentle introduction to the gay scene. **Open** Monday-Saturday 1200-2300. Sunday 1200-2230

The Mill

27 Woolpack Lane, Hockley, Nottingham NG1 1GA Phone 0115 964 4941
A long-established two-floored venue with a disco on the top floor, that is only open on Wednesday, Friday and Saturday, and a traditionally styled bar on the ground floor. There's loads of cheap drink offers on throughout the week, particularly on Wednesday when all drinks are either £1 or £1.50 after 2100 (hence the admission of £1 on the door if you are not in the bar before this time). The bar downstairs caters for a real mix of people, with the younger punters more in evidence on the disco nights. **Open** Monday-Saturday 1900-0000. Sunday 1900-2230 **Price** £1, Wednesday after 2100

Clubs

NG1 and Soba Bar

76-80 Lower Parliament Street, Nottingham NG1 1EH
Phone 0115 958 8440
This is Nottingham's only dedicated late-night gay venue with four bars and two dance floors and even a café. The late opening hours and absolute nominal admission charges ensure that this venue gets rammed most nights of the week and moreso over the weekend. The opening of the new bar Soba as part of the NG1 complex means that you now have a decent and trendy pre-club bar that benefits you with free admission into the club, provided you're at Soba well before 2200. After this time

you will have to pay a small admission charge. Music throughout the week is a complete mix of commercial house and chart. On Saturday, the whole complex opens up and gives you a choice of commercial chart downstairs and happy house and funky techno upstairs. On Sunday you can chill out or revel in the party atmosphere until the wee, small hours. Membership is available at the reception and will cost you £3 for the year. If you are planning to use this venue as your regular late-night dance spot (which I recommend you do) then it will be money well spent, as you will save bucket-loads on reduced admission charges and it will also passport you into the club on those tricky, busy nights. **Open** Monday-Tuesday 2000-2300 (Soba Bar only). Wednesday 2200-0300. Thursday 2200-0230. Friday 2200-0300. Saturday 2200-0400. Sunday 2200-0130 **Price** £2-3, Wednesday-Thursday; £4-6 Friday-Saturday

Club nights

Revolution @ The Palais

Greyfriar Gate, Nottingham NG1 7EF Phone 0115 950 1075

Pete Martine brings his monthly gay party to Nottingham's normally straight venue, The Palais. Here you can gawp at go-go boys and girls gyrating on their podiums. The music is right across the board and includes gay anthems, commercial house and chart hits – in fact anything that draws the blood-curdling screams from the sweaty, young crowd. This is Nottingham's flagship monthly gay night and it's not hard to figure out why – The Palais is a great night club and the drinks are very cheap – particularly before midnight. That's all you need to know! **Open** First Monday of the month 2200-0230 **Price** £3-5

Accommodation

Holiday Inn Nottingham

Castle Marina Park, Nottingham NG7 1GX Phone 0115-993 5000
Fax 0115-993 4000 E-mail enquiries@holiday-inn.com
Web www.holiday-inn.com

A very gay-friendly, corporate hotel located at Castle Marina. The Holiday Inn offers you luxury accommodation at reasonable prices – with high standard guest rooms, both spacious and comfy. The hotel is within sight of Nottingham's historic castle and the city centre is just a short walk along the canal path, where you'll pass many cosmopolitan bars and cafés on the way. **Price** £75 **Number of rooms** 128, all en-suite

Willows Private Hotel	184 Burton Road, Gedling, Nottingham NG2 4QN Phone 0115 952 4156 The Willows is a long-established gay guest-house; about a ten minute drive to the gay venues of Nottingham. There is a bus service outside the premises that can take you direct to the city centre. A large Edwardian building built in 1897 and formerly the home of Alfred Shaw (a cricketer apparently!). Although the double rooms are not en-suite there are bathroom facilities next door to each of the rooms. **Price** £40 **Number of rooms 6**, all standard

Cruising grounds

Normanshill Wood Car Park	Known locally as 'Thieves Wood'. Take the A60 from Nottingham, past Nestead Abbey. At the Larch Farm junction, turn left onto the B6020 towards Kirkby/Sutton in Ashfield. Then take the second turning on the right. This road will sweep and bend to the left and into the forest area. Normanshill Wood Car Park is up on the left. Pull into the car park and park up. It's busy here all day and late at nights as well. Plenty of travelling salesmen, local regulars and courting couples (usually evenings) frequent the area. There's ample opportunity to cruise around the area and there's plenty of trails in the wood that will lead you to the hot spots. Police activity is limited to patrolling the car park. If they are seen entering the woods, cruisers in their cars are known to beep their horn twice (don't rely on this though).

Oxford

Despite the crush of tourists, the speeding students on bicycles and a very near lack of any distinguishable gay scene, Oxford still has that magical something, that makes the city worth visiting. The centre of Oxford is dominated by the University colleges, the most famous of the 36 being Christ Church and Trinity. But most visitors orient themselves around Carfax, a crossroads in the very centre of the town. From here you can access The High to the east ('One of the world's great streets' – Nikolaus Pevsner), St Aldates to the south, leading down to the river, Cornmarket to the north and Queen Street to the west which is where you'll find the main shopping streets.

Getting in touch

Once in Oxford, call in at the **Oxford Tourist Information Centre** (01865 726 871) at Gloucester Green for details of attractions and more ideas of what to see and do in the City. The office is open Monday to Saturday from 0930 to 1700 and Sundays from 1000 to 1300 (and 1330 to 1530 during the summer months). There are also walking tours which leave the centre several times daily, throughout the year. Gay visitors to Oxford should visit the **Lesbian and Gay Community Centre** (01865 200 249) on St Michael's Street, where you can pick up plenty of free gay press, leaflets and information sheets. **OXAIDS** (01865 243 389) is a local service offering health information.

The Castle Tavern

24 Paradise Street, Oxford OX1 1LD Phone 01865 201 510

The former owners of The Royal Blenheim have taken over this venue in an effort to create a gay village in Oxford. Paradise Street is already home to The Jolly Farmers and hopefully this will be the kickstart that Oxford's gay community desperately needs. At the time of writing, this place was not up and running although the plans to promote this venue as a young, lively place will no doubt come into fruition. The opening hours are at present under review and they will probably be extended 'til 0100 over the weekend (a nominal admission charge will apply to patrons after 2230 on a Friday and Saturday). Keep an eye on the gay press for updated information. **Open** Monday-Saturday 1200-2300. Sunday 1200-2230

The Jolly Farmers

20 Paradise Street, Oxford OX1 1LD Phone 01865 793 759

The Jolly Farmers is a late 16th-century public house (close to Westgate Shopping Centre) that's full of character (and characters) and is noted as one of the oldest pubs in the city. The building consists of low-beamed ceilings, an open fireplace and snugs, with a designated no-smoking area. Warmer weather sees the opening of the enclosed beer garden. The clientele during the day is a decidedly mixed gay and straight crowd which turns predominanly gay by the evening. This is not a cruisy place, it's more of a sociable drink kind of joint. **Open** Monday-Saturday 1200-2300. Sunday 1200-2230

Club nights

Flirt @ The Old Fire Station

40 George Street, Oxford OX1 2AQ Phone 01865 249 819

Flirt is a gay club night in the normally gay-friendly but predominantly straight venue of The Old Fire Station. The main dance area is on the ground floor with café-style seating that allows you to sit and talent-spot across the dance floor. On the top floor is a quieter lounge bar which has more of a pub atmosphere: quieter and more relaxing and ideal for chatting up your new found friend. The atmosphere in this venue seems to be a lot more relaxed than in The Coven. Everyone seems to know everyone else and it seems a good place to make friends on the gay scene. **Open** Monday 2200-0200 **Price** £3

Loveshack @   Oxpens Road, Oxford OX1 1RX Phone 01865 242 770
The Coven   Loveshack is a busy gay and lesbian night happening every Friday. The
Coven is a large venue, popular with the student fraternity. Cheap drinks
can be found here week after week and there are occasional PAs, plus
cabaret once a month. The music tends to be happy handbag with classic club anthems thrown in for good measure. Meet up at either The
Castle or The Jolly Farmers on Paradise Street beforehand. **Open** Friday
2200-0300 **Price** £4

Peterborough Pubs

The Cross Keys   Oundle Road, Peterborough PE2 9QS Phone 01733 563 333
Also known as The Hatters Bar this is a sociable kind of venue with a
welcome late licence from Thursday evening onwards. Comprising two
rather large bars; one with a dance floor and the other – more of a
lounge bar – has a pool table. The punters are of all ages and types and
include TVs/TSs (Northern Concorde have their weekly meet here on
the first Tuesday of the month). There's a karoke session each Thursday
and Sunday and either cabaret or a stripper over the weekend. This is
one of Peterborough's busiest gay venues and there's little doubt that
you will be popping in here at some time during a visit. **Open** Monday-
Wednesday 1900-2300. Thursday-Saturday 1900-0200. Sunday 1900-
2230 **Price** £2.50, Thursday-Saturday after 2230

Club nights

Don't Do It @   42 Broadway, Peterborough PE1 1RS Phone 01733 352 412
Break For The   This 650-capacity BFTB-hosted night has established itself as one of the
Border   east of England's biggest gay nights. It is always packed to the rafters, so
an early admission is advised. With DJ Pete Martine (of Revolution
fame) at the decks, cheap admission for nearly five hours of clubbing
and (extremely) cheap drinks, it's one of the very best ways to spend a
Tuesday evening. BFTB occupies the splendid old library building next
to the new library and the College of Arms. Once a month theme parties are organised and in the past these have ranged from beach parties
to combat parties and white parties. Pete Martine's music isn't all that
hard but it does get a bit more solid as the night goes on. **Open** Tuesday
2130-0200 **Price** £3

Cruising grounds

Nene Valley   This place is known as Wansford lorry park. From the A1 follow the sign
Picnic Area   for the A47 (Peterborough). Almost immediately, a sign indicates 'Picnic
Area'. The entrance is easy to miss. You will come to a large car park
with spaces for lorries, vans and the like. Here there is a toilet facility
and absolutely tons of action, day and night, although, excluding lorry
cabs, privacy will be hard to find. Police patrol the area on a regular
basis and, on occasions, have been known to raid the toilet block. Care
and discretion is advised.

Plymouth

Plymouth is the biggest of Devon's towns and one of the cultural centres of England's South-West. Although quiet during the winter months, spring and summer bring thousands of tourists from all over the world. Situated on the border with Cornwall, Plymouth has unrivalled opportunities for sightseeing, sitting as it does in some of the world's most beautiful countryside, replete with thatched-roof cottages, wonderful country inns and picture-perfect fishing villages – breathtaking scenery at every turn. Not far away to the north lie the stunning, unspoilt wilds of Dartmoor. The English Riviera is close by too, boasting some of England's finest beaches. Plymouth lends its name to more than forty places across the world, including Plymouth Colony in Massachussetts, which is where the Mayflower ship, carrying the Pilgrim Fathers from England in the 17th century, docked. The place that they set sail from is known as the Mayflower Steps and it is still one of Plymouth's major tourist attractions.

Getting in touch

The **Tourist Information Centre** (01752 264 849) is at Island House, 9 The Barbican, which is situated on Sutton Harbour, south of the bus station. This building is of significant historical interest, as it said to have housed the pilgrims just before their departure on The Mayflower. Office hours are Monday to Saturday from 0900 to 1700 and Sunday from 1000 to 1600. For information of any gay referral services contact the **Gay and Lesbian Switchboard** (01209 314449) on Monday and Friday between 1930 and 2230.

Pubs

The Clarence

31 Clarence Place, Stonehouse, Plymouth PL1 3JP Phone 01752 603 827
This is a large-capacity gay-friendly pub that caters for all of the gay community. During the evening the gay to straight percentage lies somewhere around the 70/30 mark but don't expect too much. This is a traditional drinking pub as opposed to a disco clubby bar. It's ideal though if all you're after is just a relaxing night rather than a boozy cruisy evening. Discos and karaoke are held about once a month and are advertised well in advance within the venue. **Open** Monday-Saturday 1100-2300. Sunday 1100-2230

The Mechanic's Arms

31 Stonehouse Street, Plymouth PL1 3PE Phone 01752 660 176
Don't expect camp karaoke, disco or any kind of cabaret as this is purely a traditional drinking man's pub. It's not a gay pub but it is an extremely gay-friendly venue. There is a good selection of cask-conditioned ales and continental bottled beers for the connoisseur. **Open** Monday-Saturday 1130-2300. Sunday 1200-2230

The Swallow 59 Breton Side, Plymouth PL4 0BD Phone 01752 251 760
E-mail info@theswallow.net Web www.theswallow.net
This has been a watering hole since the 1920s and is now probably Plymouth's longest-established gay pub. It stands on the edge of the city's historical Barbican area and quayside with its wealth of shops, restaurants and galleries, and such attractions as the Dartington Glass Museum and the National Marine Aquarium. Plymouth's famous Hoe is about 15 minutes away. The Swallow is a traditional gay venue which welcomes all members of the community into a no-nonsense atmosphere. There's not really that much by the way of entertainment, although they do have a karaoke session every second Friday and a trivia challenge quiz night on a Wednesday. **Open** Monday-Saturday 1200-2300. Sunday 1200-2230

Clubs

Legends 142 Vauxhall Street, The Barbican, Plymouth PL4 0DF
Phone 01752 255 966
This is the newest and most exciting gay venue to hit Plymouth in ages and it's destined to be one of those clubs that will become the heart of a slowly forming 'village'. Legends is an excellent club on three floors. The main floor is themed around Hollywood legends (hence the name) and is all decked out in blue and silver, with a fab sound and light system. There are also specially-lit podiums (and poles) to accommodate the male and female dancers. Then there is the Kingfisher Bar where you can chill out and relax a while. You may wish to visit the themed 'playroom' as an alternative escape from the dance floor.... As this is a new venue it will take a while for it to find its feet. There are many plans being discussed about in which direction it will go but one thing is for certain – it will be a place for the gay community. Future events in the pipeline for regular club outings are Pussy Galore – a women-only club night – and then various ideas from uniform nights to a night for boots and braces, and much more. Each Sunday from 1600 there is cabaret and an all-round easy-to-unwind-to party atmosphere. **Open** Friday-Saturday 2200-0200. Sunday 1600-0000 **Price** £3-5

Zero's 24 Lockyear Street, Plymouth PL1 2QW Phone 01752 662 346
Zero's is the only full-time gay dance club in Plymouth. What makes this place so good is that there is usually no door charge through the week, giving you ample opportunity to drink and dance without breaking the bank. The club is set out over three floors. The basement is a bar and chill-out area and is shortly to have a new dance floor installed. The ground floor is the main dance area and stage and the first floor is the second, smaller dance area. Only Saturdays see all three floors in action. The music policy covers pretty much everything, although things never get too hard; it's usually handbag, hi-nrg and uplifting happy house. Late night drinking, free-to-cheap admission and a dance floor – you can't go wrong here. **Open** Monday-Friday 2200-0200. Saturday 2200-0400. Sunday 2200-0100 **Price** £2-4, Friday and Saturday

Club nights

Cherub
@ Le Kepi Blanc

27-31 Coburg Street, Plymouth PL1 1PS
Phone 01752 251 122 E-mail lekepiblanc@aol.com
This is a popular gay club night which comes around every fotnight at
this normally straight venue. Le Kepi Blanc has a capacity for nearly 650
and capacity is usually achieved on these gay Thursday nights. The
music is uplifting happy house, that gets progressively harder as the
night goes on. **Open** Alternate Thursdays 2100-0200 **Price** £2-3

Poole Cruising grounds

Canford Cliffs

You want to head for the toilets, near to the library. It is very small and
quiet but it has been known to happen. Look for parked cars outside
with male occupants; they are likely to be there for the same reason.
There's plenty of places to take away to (especially during the summer).

Portsmouth Pubs

Martha's
/ 1 Above

227 Commercial Road, Portsmouth PO1 4BS Phone 023 9285 2951
An exclusive gay bar and club for the community of Portsmouth.
Martha's Bar is the pub part of the venue. After pub hours you are
moved up to 1 Above, the club. The bar is one large open-plan room
which contains two pool tables and a separate dining area (with a full
menu available every day). There is also a weekly karaoke session on a
Sunday and cabaret on a Friday. The club – small but perfectly formed –
was voted runner-up for the best weekend club in the Boyz reader
awards, and quite rightly so: 1 Above is a very popular dance space for
all sorts of gay folk with a selection of camp and charty tunes to enjoy.
Open Monday-Thursday 1200-0200. Friday-Saturday 1000-0200. Sunday
1600-2230 **Price** 1.50-£3, Monday-Thursday; £4-5 Friday-Saturday

The Old Vic

104 St Paul's Road, Portsmouth PO5 4AQ Phone 02392 297 013
E-mail oldvic4u@hotmail.com Web www.oldvicpub.co.uk
The Old Vic is one of those bars that, as soon as you step through the
doors, are made to feel instantly at home. It is a community-spirited
pub and the popularity of the place is testament to this. During the day
the clientele is a mix of gay and straight, however, come the evening it is
nearly exclusively gay. Entertainment takes place on about five of the
seven nights: karaoke on a Tuesday and Thursday; disco all over the
weekend and a cabaret and camp party night on a Sunday. Later on in
the year they will be opening the upstairs as a members-only 'club'
called High Society. This will probably be a late-licence quiet space – an
alternative to the chaos downstairs. Membership details and opening
hours will be announced shortly. **Open** Monday-Saturday 1000-2300.
Sunday 1000-2230

Saunas

Tropics Sauna   2 Market Way, Portsmouth PO1 4BX Phone 02392 296 100

Tropics is a compact, friendly sauna spread out over three floors, situated in Portsmouth's city centre. Ground floor facilities include a reception area, sunbed, showers, changing room and a TV lounge, which is the only part of the venue in which smoking is allowed. The first floor accommodates two sauna cabins, a steam room, more showers and a toilet facility. The second floor houses yet more showers, yet another toilet facility and a large rest area. This subtly lit rest room is partitioned at intervals which allows you a modicum of privacy. Bathrobes are available if required. Right that's the sauna in a nutshell; now you need to get there: directions to the 'pay and display' car park are as follows. From the M27 turn on to the M275 and into Portsmouth and follow this road to the end. At the roundabout take the first left and then turn right into the small car park. From here it's a short walk. Walk down the main road (this is the road that you would have taken if you had gone straight at the roundabout). At the next roundabout turn right and Tropics is on your right in the parade of shops just around the bend. Alternatively, you can park across the road in the Office World car park, opposite the sauna (there are signs that say your car may be clamped but there is no phone number or other address for the clamping company: trust your own judgement). **Open** Monday-Saturday 1200-2200 **Price** £8.50

Reading Pubs

The Granby   120 London Road, Reading RG1 5AY Phone 01189 352 537

Wow! The Granby had a serious refurbishment last year and is now a modern gay (and straight-friendly) venue that has all the trappings of a central London hotspot. There's two floors: the downstairs is the louder, fun-filled dance and cabaret bar and the upstairs is the (just about) quieter lounge bar with balcony. For the loafer, the upstairs monitors allow you to survey the goings-on downstairs without ever having to leave your seat. There's entertainment to keep you amused throughout the week and this includes some sort of cabaret on a Wednesday and there's nearly always something not normally seen on the scene, such as a gay hypnotist or a gay ventriloquist (with a rent boy doll – honest!). Thursday is a '70s and '80s disco night. Fridays and Saturdays give way to full-on disco nights (Friday is a harder-edged sound whilst Saturday is one outrageously camp disco party). Sunday is plain old karaoke. You should aim to get here rather early over the weekends as the place does tend to get crowded. **Open** Wednesday-Saturday 2000 0200, Sunday 1900-0000 **Price** £2, Friday and Saturday after 2100

The Wynford Arms   110 Kings Road, Reading RG1 3BY Phone 0118 958 9814

The Wynford is a traditional gay, predominantly male venue. It's split into two rooms: a large, comfortable lounge with stage and a smaller bar room. A friendly relaxed atmosphere prevails here and this venue caters for both the serious drinker and (to a lesser extent) the pre-club disco bunny. **Open** Monday-Friday 1600-2300. Saturday 1200-2300. Sunday 1200-2230

Cruising grounds

Thameside Promenade

Park your car near to The Holiday Inn, in the Thameside car park. The toilet facility here can provide you with a liason but it's considered too dangerous for anything more. It is better, and safer, to take the short walk along the promenade to the point where Cow Lane meets with the prom. This can be a busy site at any time, but is especially so from 1800.

Richmond Pubs

The Richmond Arms

20 The Square, Richmond TW9 1DZ Phone 020 8940 2118
E-mail info@richmond-arms.co.uk Web www.richmond-arms.co.uk
The Richmond Arms is a local pub with customers ranging from the young and lively to a more mature gathering; they all merge against a laid-back, friendly environment. From outside it looks just like any other pub in the area – hanging baskets (summer) and benched seating. Inside, however, it becomes obviously gay – strippers on a Wednesday, karaoke on the last Thursday of the month and a DJ-hosted disco all over the weekend. **Open** Sunday-Wednesday 1200-2300. Thursday 1200-0000. Friday-Saturday 1200-0100 **Tube** Richmond

Rochester Pubs

The Ship Inn

347 High Street, Rochester ME1 1DA Phone 01634 844 264
The Ship is divided up into three rooms. Two are predominantly gay bars and one is a mixed bar. The entrance to the gay bars is on Ship Lane. It could be described as a 'traditional' venue, and even though there are discos in the latter part of the week, there is no dance floor. There's ample floor space, however, and this seems to suffice for the shuffling of the clientele's feet. Being the only gay venue in this part of Kent, the age range and clientele is right across the board and everyone seems to fit in well. This is a tourist trap during the summer with loads of students and attractions such as The Naval Dockyard Museum (sailors?!) and the cathedral to keep you busy. **Open** Monday-Saturday 1100-2300. Sunday 1200-2230

Saunas

Boadicea Sauna

206 High Street, Rochester ME1 1JA Phone 01634 819 809
A small gay sauna with sauna cabin, steam room, fast-tan cabin, rest areas and complimentary refreshments. It's situated on the corner of Star Hill, more or less opposite Rochester station by the traffic lights. Admission will cost you £7.50 before 1600, rising to £9 thereafter. **Open** Monday-Sunday 1200-2300 **Price** £7.50-9

Romford Saunas

Essex Sauna and Steam 239 High Road, Chadwell Heath, Romford Phone 020 8597 9610
Small gay sauna on the main Romford Road. Facilities include sauna cabin, steam room, TV lounge (smoking), showers on the ground floor and toilets and rest areas on the first floor. Free refreshments are available too. **Open** Sunday-Thursday 1100-2300. Friday-Saturday 1100-late **Price** £9

Rugby Cruising grounds

M1(J18) / A5 There are various locations either side of the M1. The first is a former cottage by the motorway, which used to be the best in the Midlands but gradually died down to nothing after it was closed, then later pulled down and the lay-bys ripped up for a new development. The road has now been re-opened and initial signs are that activity is starting again in new lay-bys which are much reduced in size. For the second location, continue further north for about two miles and get to the radio mast in the lay-bys. Additionally, there is the truck stop opposite and lanes leading to and from Lilbourne.

Ryton Accommodation

Hedgefield House Stella Road, Ryton NE21 4LR Phone 0191 413 7373
E-mail leewood@hedgefieldhouse.freeserve.co.uk
This is a stunning Georgian mansion which stands in four acres of fabulous wooded gardens. The house is situated on the edge of the beautiful Northumbrian countryside, yet is only ten minutes from the lively night life of Newcastle's city centre (£5 for a taxi to the city centre). Beautiful period rooms, friendly personal service, peaceful, relaxing surroundings and secure on-site parking are all part and parcel of your stay. **Price** £45

Salisbury Cruising grounds

Southampton Road (A36) A cottage and cruisy park at the A36 Southampton Road, in addition to the car park opposite Salisbury College. Be aware that the car park is under video surveillance (but the cottage and park are not).

Scarborough Accommodation

Interludes Hotel 32 Princess Street, Scarborough YO11 1QR Phone 01723 360 513
Fax 01723 368 597 E-mail interludes@ntlworld.com
Web http://homepage.ntlworld.com/interludes
Interludes is a Grade Two-listed Georgian townhouse in the heart of Scarborough's Old Town conservation area. It enjoys panoramic views

over the pan-tiled rooftops of the south bay and harbour and down the coast to Flamborough Head. Since first opening its doors in 1991 it has gone on to win a series of recommendations from Gay Times to The Sunday Times (who, in 1997 said it was the best guest-house along the north-east coast) and a mention in Which? Hotel Guide's last five annuals. The hotel, which is completely non-smoking, is elegantly furnished and well equipped. Four of the five bedrooms have en-suite facilities and sea-views. All have central heating, quality beds, TV, radio, alarm clock, hair-dryer and a tea and coffee tray. There is a guest lounge with leather Chesterfield sofas and a dining room where breakfasts and, on most nights, evening meals are served (at 1800 – this must be pre-booked). They are also the holders of a residential licence allowing alcohol to be served to guests who have reserved sleeping accommodation. Interludes is a mixed gay and straight hotel (no children allowed though) and the décor in the hotel is decidedly theatrical with a full troupe (or two!) of posters, photographs and programmes to distract you as you climb the stairs! **Price** £55 per double room **Number of rooms** 5, 4 fully en-suite

Shaftesbury Cruising grounds

Henstridge

On the A30, three miles east of Henstridge (which is about halfway between Shaftesbury and Sherborne) there is a double road lay-by on the left-hand side as you go west. Action happens in the woods behind the furthest bit of lay-by. It remains busy all afternoon and especially at going-home time.

Accommodation

Sunridge Hotel

Bleke Street, Shaftesbury SP7 8AW Phone 01747 853 130 Fax 01747 852 139
The Sunridge is a listed townhouse hotel dating from 1877 and situated in the heart of Shaftesbury, a thriving market town in the Dorset countryside. This is an absolutely beautiful, small hotel that occupies a hill-top position and has magnificent views over the Blackmore Vale. Shaftesbury also has many notable features, such as the Abbey Ruins and particularly Golds Hill – as featured in the famous Hovis TV advert – famous for it's steep cobbles and charming cottages. Shaftesbury is also the centre of Thomas Hardy's Wessex; known as Shaston, which features in books such as Jude The Obscure. Anyway, scenic beauty, conspicuous consumption and literary history aside... the rooms have en-suite facilities, either with bath or shower, TV, clock-radio, direct dial phone, hair-dryer and welcome tray. Dinner, if required, is served in their Orchid Restaurant which is elegant without being too formal. There is also a lounge bar for guests to use – a cosy room which has a pleasant and friendly atmosphere. Whilst Sunridge is not close to any thriving gay scene (with Bournemouth probably the closest, about 30 miles away) it is ideal for those who simply wish to get away from it all. **Price** £60 including breakfast; £90 including breakfast and evening meal **Number of rooms** 9, en-suite

Sheffield

Unfortunately, there is not much in Sheffield to excite the tourist, but Sheffield has been trying! In 1999 The lottery-funded National Centre for Popular Music opened its doors to the public as a showcase and museum for popular music in all its varied forms. Sheffield is most famous for its steel industry, an industry which is over 700 years old and one which was at the forefront of world steel production in the 20th century. If you have ever eaten out in England then the chances are you have been using cutlery that has its origins here. Sheffield is an industrial city and the history of these industries and the working classes of the area can be examined in the most minute detail in several of the museums and galleries dotted around the city. This is also the birthplace of the spring tape measure, the child's bouncing ball, the railway buffer, the folding umbrella and, not surprisingly, stainless steel.

Getting in touch

The **Tourist Office** (0114 273 4671) is based within The Peace Gardens on Union Street, part of the massive Town Hall annexe. The office is open Monday to Saturday from 0930 to 1715. **Sheffield Gay Switchboard** (0114 258 8199) is available for confidential information and advice from Monday to Wednesday from 2000 to 2200. There is also a dedictad **Lesbian Line** (0114 2491630) each Wednesday from 2000 to 2300 and a gay social group that meets each alternate Monday from 2000 to 2200 (phone the switchboard for details).

Sheffield is the home of Trebor Bassett, makers of the world-famous Liquorice Allsorts. The business was founded by George Bassett in 1842 and the mixture of varieties which made the firm famous was stumbled upon by accident in 1899. Apparently, a salesman knocked over the sample tray in front of a customer, and voila! History was made! Nearly half a century later, a new product was launched, to celebrate the end of World War Two – these jelly sweets were called 'Peace Babies'. They later became better-known as Jelly Babies.

Bar-Celona   387 Attercliffe Road, Sheffield S9 Phone **0114 244 1492**
Situated close to The Planet (see separate listing) and about five minutes from the town centre by taxi, Bar-Celona is a large, split-level European-style bar. It's bright and lively with a good friendly atmosphere. Boys, girls and everyone in between will be made welcome. In the latter part of the week you can catch the campest drag DJs you are ever likely to see, namely Ken and Barbie. During the summer the rooftop garden opens up adding yet another floor for you to troll around on. **Open** Monday-Saturday 2030-2300. Sunday 2030-2230

The Cossack   45 Howard Street, Sheffield S1 2LW Phone **0114 281 2654**
A traditional city centre gay bar owned by the same people who run Bar-Celona, Bronx Sauna and Planet. There are midweek goings-on with

disco most nights of the week. Wednesday is a fun quiz, Thursday is karaoke and on Saturdays The Cossack lays on its own mini bus to take you to Planet. **Open** Monday-Saturday 1200-2300. Sunday 1200-2230

Legend has is it that Nottingham's most famous son, Robin Hood, the disinherited nobleman Robin of Loxley, actually came from the village of Loxley to the north of Sheffield, and not from Nottingham at all.

Manhattan Cabaret Bar

504 Attercliffe Road, Sheffield Phone 0114 244 2772
This place re-opened back in June under this new name (it was formerly The Manhattan Dance Bar). They promise that each weekend they will have top name cabaret acts on their stage with male and female stripers alternating most weekends. This bar is a mix of gay and straight, but no fears, all are here for a good time. **Open** Monday-Thursday 1200-1400 / 1900-2300. Friday-Saturday 1200-1400 / 1900-0100. Sunday 1900-2230

Clubs

Planet

429 Effingham Road, Sheffield S9 3QD Phone 0114 244 9033
E-mail **planetangel@compuserve.com**
The Planet is a large, exclusively gay (though straight friends welcome) club that gets very busy and, at times, very hot and sweaty! Spread out over two floors, the main room is the dance area, with seating either side of the dance floor for those who can't keep up with the pace. The girls usually hang around the stage whilst the men (or blokes, well... it is Sheffield after all!) take advantage of the circuit, from downstairs to the quieter upstairs Globe Bar. The music policy is mostly mainstream house with the more camp sounds emanating from the club's chill-out lounge. This is predominantly a young person's venue – very lively and friendly, but without the suburban cliqueyness. **Open** Thursday-Friday 2230-0200. Saturday 2230-0330. Sunday 2200-0100 **Price** £3-7

Club nights

Poptastic @ NCPM

6 Paternoster Row, Sheffield S1 2QQ Phone 07074 248 247
E-mail **info@poptastic.co.uk** Web **www.poptastic.co.uk**
Poptastic moved earlier in the year from the City Hall to this new venue – The National Centre For Popular Music (yes, it is a club). This move has enabled the Poptastic crew to go weekly. There are three rooms at this new venue: The Indie Playground, which is, of course, the grungey indie main room; The Kitsch Bitch Lounge – where everything is retro and camp and The Clubber's Kitchen – which is harder round the edges and rather funky. **Open** Every Saturday 2230-0300 **Price** £4-5

Saunas

Bronx Sauna

208 Savile Street East, Sheffield S4 7UQ Phone 0114 278 0383
Occupying the premises of a former pub this sauna is a treat for men who just want to go somewhere safe for a bit of man-on-man fun. The walls are painted black, the corridors are dark and cruisy and the rest

rooms are active. All the facilities are here including the huge two-room sauna cabin (from warm to hot) and the Jacuzzi in a garden setting – plants and even a park bench! Mazes, dark rooms and cinemas give you plenty of opportunity to flaunt yourself and if you are into resting then there is plenty of seating dotted around this venue for just that. Just what Sheffield needed and very discreet for those who do not go out on the scene. **Open** Monday-Tuesday and Thursday-Sunday 1300-2300. **Price** £5-9, plus £5 membership

Accommodation

Brockett House   1 Montgomery Road, Sheffield S7 1LN Phone 0114 258 8952
Fax 0114 211 2868 E-mail brocketthouse@yahoo.com
Web www.brocketthouse.com
Brockett House is an exclusively gay and lesbian (non-smoking) guest-house situated in the leafy Victorian area of Nether Edge, one mile to the south-west of Sheffield city centre and the train station and a bit further to gay Sheffield and Meadowhall. Standard rooms are available with a shared twin shower room, or you can get a luxurious en-suite with a corner bath and shower. All of the rooms are individually designed and are spacious and elegantly decorated. The beds are either double or twin, and most are king-sized. Continental breakfast is included in the price with a choice of coffee, tea, juice, cereal, pastries, toasts and preserves on offer. There is a complimentary video library with latest titles and a varied selection to suit all tastes. A video player is provided in all the rooms. Built in 1873, the proprietors have furnished it to a very high standard, combining the elegance of antiques and colonial furniture with the freshness of present day décor and all the mod-cons. Earliest check-in time is 1700 from Monday to Friday and 1500 over Saturday and Sunday. Latest check-out time is 0900 from Monday to Friday and 1100 over Saturday and Sunday. Other times may be accommodated. Normally though, checking out later than 1400 will incur an additional full day's charge. A 50 per cent deposit by cheque is required when you book. This is refundable only if you cancel seven days before your arrival. Full payment of the balance by cash or cheque is required at arrival. **Price** £50 per double room

Southampton

Southampton sits within the county of Hampshire, on the southern coast of England. The county is overflowing with incredible landscapes, charming villages, world-famous stately homes, forests, castles and manor houses and also incorporates England's former capital – the historic and beautiful cathedral town of Winchester. Southampton is an industrial city, seaport and resort. It is the place where The Titanic sailed from on her disastrous maiden voyage on 10 April 1912. Today it is still a major UK port with container traffic and ferry links to the Isle of Wight and the Continent. It is a also a city with a wealth of character and heritage, its rich and colourful history preserved in a host of fascinating remains, monuments and buildings. Much of the Old Town walls and fortifications remain intact, including the Bargate – the impressive north entrance to the medieval town.

Getting in touch

The main **Tourist Information Office** (023 8022 1106) is on Civic Centre Road, where handy town planner maps are available free of charge. The office opens Monday to Friday from 0830 to 1730 and Saturday from 0900 to 1600. Gay information and advice realting to HIV and AIDS can be gained by contacting **Solent Lesbian and Gay Switchboard** (02380 637 363) on Monday, Thursday and Friday from 1930 to 2200.

Pubs

42 THS

42 High Street, Southampton SO14 2NS Phone 02380 638 999
This is a gay-friendly bar and brasserie (food is served Monday to Friday from 1200 to 1530; Saturday from 1200 to 1700 and Sunday from 1200 to 1800). Thursday is a cheap night out for students. Sunday sees live jazz from 1430 to 1800 and from then on it's a night of funky house music in the form of Trashed, with DJ Nick Denton. Every other Wednesday a lesbian group meets here (all are welcome to turn up). **Open** Monday-Saturday 1200-2300. Sunday 1200-2230

The Edge

Compton Walk, Southampton SO140BH Phone 02380 366 163
A busy and popular three-in-one venue – bar, restaurant and pub. The Edge is a lively open-plan venue for a mixed gay and lesbian clientele, replete with pool table, gaming machines and soft furnishings. The bar can get quite cruisy over the weekends (boys and girls!), although it's not really a cruise bar. Karaoke is staged every Tuesday and disco every night. There is also cabaret on Thursday, followed by party nights on Friday and Saturday, when all the bars open to the thronging Southampton locals. **Open** Monday-Saturday 1900-0200. Sunday 1200-1800 **Price** £2-5

The London Hotel

2 Terminus Terrace, Southampton SO14 3DT Phone 02380 710 652
E-mail info@gaylondonhotel.com Web www.gaylondonhotel.com
The London Hotel is a warm and friendly gay venue. Matt and Roger

(the proprietors) have one aim in life; that is to have fun. The London Hotel and the events it holds reflect this aim. The mixture of entertainment – cabaret (Sundays), quiz nights (Wednesdays), trips out, charity events and theme nights show their commitment to having a good time. This hardcore commitment is echoed at their sister venue, The Smuggler's. The London Hotel, despite the name, is not a hotel... yet. Upstairs conversion work is well underway to provide six rooms for bed and breakfast. Hopefully, the conversion will be complete by autumn 2001. **Open** Monday-Saturday 1200-2300. Sunday 1200-2230 (late licence applied for)

The Smuggler's Arms   114 Bernard Street, Southampton SO14 3DZ Phone 02380 399 144
E-mail rp.price@btinternet.com Web www.thesmugglers.co.uk
The Smuggler's is a large, open-plan bar room with regular discos each weekend. It's a friendly, no-attitude, welcoming pub, with a young mixed clientele of lesbian and gay. This venue seems to have some sort of party going on each night and a host of special drinks offers, so it may be wise to ask before you order. Every Thursday they put on their karaoke session and from Friday through to Sunday there's a disco that goes under different names but that each boil down to the self-same pub-disco night formula. There is also a mini-bus that leaves here each Saturday night to take you to The Edge. **Open** Monday-Thursday 1800-2300. Friday 1600-2300. Saturday 1400-2300. Sunday 1400-2230

The Victoria   51-53 Northam Road, Southampton SO14 0PD Phone 02380 333 963
E-mail victoria.inn@virgin.net Web www.gayvictoria.co.uk
Built in 1870, The Victoria Inn is an impressive Victorian building close to the city centre of Southampton and only a short walk away from the two late-night gay venues. It is the largest of the gay pubs in Southampton and has been operating as a gay venue for around twelve years. Prior to that it was known as The Glebe Hotel. It has stood under several different guises during its time as a gay pub: The Queen Vic, The Gaol House, Pinkies and more recently The New Victoria. The pub tends to be popular with 'the butch crowd' – from bears to leather and uniform – and is the regular meeting place for the southern branch of the Gay Bikers who meet here on the third Tuesday of each month. Bears tend to congregate on the first and third Saturday of each month (although most other Saturdays see a high number in the house too).

Open Monday-Friday 1830-2300. Saturday 1500-2300. Sunday 1500-2230

Voltz 188   188 Above Bar Street, Southampton SO14 7DW Phone 02380 331 604
Probably the most popular and certainy one of the newest gay venues in
Southampton. Voltz 188 is two minutes away from The Edge, so it comes
as no surprise that this place attracts all the pre-clubbers ready for a
night on the tiles. This is a modern, young and trendy place comprising
two bars on two levels – the top level cocktail bar is more of a quieter
chill-out space, which suits the older, more sedate punters, whilst the
music downstairs is more club-like. Food is served each day from 1200 to
1500. This venue does attract a lot of lesbians, though it's not a lesbian
bar – gay boys and girls mix well in what is a fabulous gay atmosphere.
Excellent! Open Monday-Saturday 1200-2300. Sunday 1200-2230

Saunas

Pink Broadway   79-80 East Street, Southampton SO14 3HQ Phone 023 8023 8804
Sauna   Taking over the former premises of Black's Camping and Leisure shop is
the Pink Broadway Sauna, the latest addition to Southampton's rapidly
expanding gay scene. The venue has a host of facilities to help relieve
you of the stresses of everyday life including two twelve-man sauna cabins, a twelve-man Turkish bath, TV lounge, sunbeds, refreshment area
and, of course, those all important rest areas. The admission charges
include same day re-entry or pass-out (ask at reception for a pass if you
intend to return on the same day). Open Monday-Thursday 1200-0000.
Friday 1200-0400. Saturday 1200-0600. Sunday 1200-1800 Price £10

Cruising grounds

Southampton   At the top of Hill Lane you should find daytime action. The toilet is now
Common: north   boarded up but there is a huge amount of action in the woods over quite
a large area. You'll find mainly young to middle age men here.

Southampton   Near the county cricket ground, Cemetery Road. There's night-time
Common: south   action and easy parking. This is a large cruising ground with plenty of
action in the woods. There are many different ways out so it is advisable
to familiarise yourself with this area before doing anything. Note: I have
been reliably informed that the police are taking more than a passing

interest in the use of the south side of the common. This is due to the careless disposal of condoms, and the fact that this south side is used by families and children. The police have received more than a tolerable amount of complaints from the public. It is in your own interest therefore, to use the north of the common for your activities, to deter 'police interest'. You should dispose of rubbish carefully and exercise caution and common sense. The lads get younger as the evening progresses (apparently).

Southend on Sea Pubs

The Cliff Hotel   48 Hamlet Road, Southend on Sea SS1 1HH Phone 01702 344 466
E-mail info@thecliff.co.uk Web www.thecliff.co.uk
The Cliff is a mixed gay and lesbian community-based venue and there is usually some sort of charity event going on here each week. It's a traditional pub – all brass and wood – with friendly and welcoming staff. On Wednesday there is a general knowledge quiz night (very popular and lots of fun) and on Thursday through to Sunday there are discos with music that ranges from funk to over-the-top camp. **Open** Monday-Saturday 1200-2300. Sunday 1200-2230

St Ives Accommodation

Barkers Hotel   11 Seaview Terrace, St Ives TR26 2DH Phone 01736 796 729
A delightful Edwardian house overlooking the harbour. A home-from-home kind of place – free and easy with minimal restrictions. Barkers is popular with Londoners after a break away from the hustle and bustle of the city and is situated close to the nudist beach. **Price** £45

Ryn Anneth   Southfield Place, St Ives TR26 1RE Phone 01736 793 247
The oldest gay bed and breakfast in St Ives, open all year and offering cable TV and a full English and/or vegetarian breakfast cooked to order as extras. Smoking is allowed in the room but not encouraged. A five-minute walk will get you to the town centre. Ryn Anneth is not far from the nudist beaches.

Stoke-on-Trent

Stoke-on-Trent is a great and unique British city made up of six separate towns – Tunstall, Burslem, Hanley (the city centre), Stoke, Fenton and Longton – affectionately known as The Potteries. It is also home to the world's greatest manufacturers of pottery, including Royal Doulton, Ainsley and Moorcroft. The city boasts visitor centres, ceramic museums and factory shops, plus excellent leisure and entertainment facilities.

Getting in touch

You can find the **Tourist Information Centre** (01782 236 000) in Hanley at The Potteries Shopping Centre on Quadrant Road. It is open Monday to Saturday from 0900 to 1730. For confidential advice or general enquiries of gay or lesbian concern contact the **Gay Switchboard** (01782 266 998) which is manned Monday, Wednesday and Friday from 2000 to 2200.

Pubs

Bar Monique   Goodson Street, Hanley, Stoke-on-Trent Phone 01782 280 354
This is a new cabaret and disco bar in the centre of Hanley. This place was due to open at the time of writing and unfortunately I do not have many details to pass on to you. No doubt there will be a heavy drag presence and bucket-loads of entertainment to keep you amused. **Open** Monday-Saturday 1900-2300. Sunday 1200-2230 (subject to change)

The Three Tuns   9 Bucknall New Road, Hanley, Stoke-on-Trent ST1 Phone 01782 769 293
Sister venue to The Club and open every night of the week. Disco and cheap drinks are available every night and there's a karaoke session on Sunday. This is a very hospitable venue. It has changed beyond belief over the past year or so – now no longer a dull and dingy meeting space but a lively, down-to-earth bar catering for all ages of the gay community. **Open** Monday-Friday 1900-2300. Saturday 1600-2300. Sunday 1400-2230

Clubs

The Club   14 Hillcrest Street (rear of Bucknall New Road), Hanley, Stoke-on-Trent ST1 2AA Phone 01782 201 829
E-mail **enquiries@theclubstoke.co.uk** Web www.theclubstoke.co.uk
The longest-running gay club in Stoke-on-Trent. Monday is hi-nrg dance mixed with the best from the '80s. Wednesday is a cheap night out regardless of whether you are a student (although students get free admission with a valid NUS card) and the music is a simple mix of chart and pop. Friday sees the male stripper swinging his bits around for your entertainment (female stripper last Friday of the month when the club stays open 'til 0300). Saturday is happy house and a good mix of dance

music and it's a night that sees the whole venue open up – four rooms and two dance floors. If you are planning to be a regular at this club it is worth becoming a member (about £2). This will entitle you to discounted admission and free tickets on your birthday. Every second Thursday of the month The Club holds a fetish night organised by the Desyre Foundation with all play equipment provided by D-Space (admission is £10 on the door or £7 for members in advance). Further information on this night can be gained by phoning 01782 285 479 or checking out the website at www.desyre-foundation.com. (See the listing for their sister venue, The Three Tuns too – it's practically next door.) **Open** Monday, Wednesday, Friday and Saturday 2200-0200 **Price** £1-4

Stourbridge Saunas

Heroes
Health Club

5 Lower High Street, Stourbridge DY8 1TE Phone 01384 442 030
E-mail info@heroeshealthclub.com Web www.heroeshealthclub.com
What was once a pub in a previous life is now Heroes Health Club in Stourbridge. Overall it is a pleasantly clean gay and bisexual men-only sauna with all the facilities you'd expect, including the steam room which they claim is the biggest in the UK (I thought it was Neros in Bury, Greater Manchester). They have also recently added a mini-cinema and chill-out room. Being well out of the Birmingham gay scene it tends to miss out on the after-club trade (there are no gay venues in Stourbridge), but it does tend to get the custom of people travelling well out of their own area. The ultra-cheap admission of £5 is certainly worth at least a trial saunter out of Birmingham. **Open** Monday-Thursday 1200-2300. Friday-Saturday 1200-0200. Sunday 1200-2300 **Price** £5

Stratford upon Avon Accommodation

Abbey House

56 Rother Street, Stratford upon Avon CV37 6LT Phone 01789 267 348
A small but comfortable Edwardian guest-house, just five minutes' walk from the theatres, river and shops. This is ideal for a stop-over if you want to escape the scene and sample some culture, yet close enough to Birmingham (a 30-minute drive) should you require a weekly scene fix. There is also a self-contained two-bedroomed suite that can sleep four, available to rent for £109 a night. **Price** £50 **Number of rooms** 3, 2 en-suite

Swindon Pubs

The Cricketer's Arms

14 Emlyn Square, Swindon SN1 5BN Phone 01793 523 780

The Cricketer's Arms, situated close to the train station, is a lively and popular bar, with an age range that goes right across the board. It's very nearly exclusively gay, with a good mix of lesbians and gays. The adjoining pool room is popular (especially with the ladies) and there are regular cheap drink promos along with happy hours between 1900 and 2100 each evening. (See the separate listing for the Cricketer's Arms' sister venue London Street.) **Open** Monday-Friday 1900-2300. Saturday 1200-1600 / 1900-2300. Sunday 1200-1600 / 1900-2230

Clubs

London Street

Unit 1 London Street, Railway Village, Swindon SN1 Phone 01793 523 780
E-mail info@londonst.co.uk Web www.londonst.co.uk

Modern, bright and vibrant. The aluminium dance floor, the stainless steel bar, the metal tables around the pillars, all in contrast to the purple and blues of the décor: this an ideal place for the trendy ones amongst you. Once-a-month bashes for the lads see the lights on the lowest setting, a male stripper cavorting around and cheap drinks to help you get in the mood. The ladies' bash is just as good (the fact that there are no men allowed in should be reason enough to turn up). This is the only gay club in Swindon and so everyone tends to swan here after meeting up in Swindon's only gay bar – The Cricketer's Arms. It may be best to ask at the bar for directions; either that or just follow the crowd. Remember, it is a members-only bar (membership is free though), so phone the above number for further details or enquire at the Cricketer's Arms. **Open** Wednesday 1900-2300. Thursday 1900-0000. Friday-Saturday 1900-0200. Sunday 1900-2300 **Price** £2-3.50, Friday and Saturday after 2100

Cruising grounds

Cotswold Water Park

The Water Park is situated just off the A419, north of Cricklade. Travel from Swindon to Cirencester on this road and follow the signs for Ashton Keynes, looking for the sign for Cotswold Water Park. Once there, hang around outside the area surrounding the toilets and you might just get a bite.

Tavistock Cruising grounds

Brentnor Woods

(Chillaton) Situated in the quaint country lanes, halfway between Tavistock and the A30. This is a late-night woodland cruising ground near to Brentnor Church. Locate the car park and park up and wait around. There's not much cover around here, nor is it the most appropriate of areas.

Torquay

Torquay's origins as a holiday resort date back to Victorian times, when it was a fashionable destination for the English aristocracy. Today, the legacy remains: beautiful gardens, elegant Victorian terraces, clean white villas and the famous seven hills – a beautiful backdrop to Torquay's popular modern facilities and busy shopping centre. The waterfront is the focus of life in the town. Here you'll find the palm-lined promenade, sea front gardens, a lively harbour and an international marina. Beautiful beaches, easily accessible by foot or road, lie within a few minutes of the town centre.

Getting in touch

There is a **Visitor Centre** at Vaughan Parade (0906 680 1268 – calls cost 25p per minute). The centre is open Monday to Saturday from 0930 to 1800. Torquay has no dedicated gay switchboard, however, you can get information and advice from the following resources: **Body Positive** (01202 297 386), **Gay Men's Health Project** (01202 848 567), **Lesbian and Gay Helpline** (01202 318 822), all of whom will be able to advise you or put you in touch with an appropriate group.

Pubs

The Clipper Inn   14 Melville Street, Torquay TQ2 5SZ Phone 01803 380 388
E-mail **david@matthewsd63.fsnet.co.uk** Web **www.theclipperinn.com**
The Clipper Inn is a small and intimate, traditional gay and lesbian bar. The bar is bedecked with ornaments, giving it a real old-fashioned feel – noticeably and refreshingly different if you are from a city that has the cloned style of every other café-bar. The staff and punters are friendly and welcoming. **Open** Monday-Saturday 1200-2300. Sunday 1200-2230

The Meadfoot Inn   7 Meadfoot Lane, Torquay TQ1 2BW Phone 01803 297 112
E-mail **petermeadfoot@aol.com**
A small and friendly gay pub, whose clientele consists mainly of gay men from Torquay and the surrounding area. Being a popular seaside resort though, they also see visitors from other parts of the country and many other places across the world. The venue has been under the same ownership for many years and is completely gay-owned and staffed. The Meadfoot is a popular bar over the weekends, with a very wide age range between 18 and 80 years. Although the crowd is made up mostly of gay men, lesbians and TVs are also made to feel extremely welcome. It's situated above the harbour and is close to all of the gay hotels and clubs. **Open** Monday-Saturday 1200-1600 / 1900-2300. Sunday 1200-1600 / 1900-2230

Rocky's   Rock Cottage, Rock Road, Torquay TQ2 5SP Phone 01803 292 279
Rocky's is a small-ish three-storey club on Rock Road. It's a members-only club, but, bizarrely, you can get membership on the door. This is a

rather busy venue, particularly during the weekends and summer months. The top floor comprises a gallery-bar which overlooks the dance floor, which in turn leads down to the dance area and disco bar. The stairs will take you down to the food bar and the quieter chill-out area (which is closed Monday through to Wednesday), and further down still to the basement, where you'll find the (surprisingly busy!) toilets and corridor. For visitors to Torquay, free admission passes (or discounted tickets) are available from most of the gay hotels in the area (see individual accommodation listings for details). For the most part, Rocky's attracts the younger end of the market, although you'll happen upon most ages in here at one time or another. **Open** Monday-Saturday 2130-0200 **Price** £2-4

Torquay is television's fictional home of the world-renowned Fawlty Towers Hotel, mis-managed by the bungling Basil Fawlty and his dragon of a wife, Sybil. Legend has it that the idea of Fawly Towers came to John Cleese, not whilst in Torquay, but in Oxford – the four-star Randolph Hotel, to be precise. The story goes that an exhausted Cleese was awakened by a phone call early one morning from the porter, announcing that the newspaper he had ordered was not available and therefore, would an alternative be acceptable. Cleese informed the porter that he did not order a paper and promptly hung up the phone. A while later, the phone rang again and Cleese stood dumbfounded as the porter announced that he was indeed correct – the newspaper wasn't for him, he had been mistaken, and he apologised for disturbing him in the first place. The rest, as they say, is history.

| **Wharfe Review Bar** | Rock Road, Torquay TQ2 5SP Phone 01803 211 523 |

Recently opened, this bar is already drawing in a lot of the younger pub-goers, away from the older bars. This is a nice, classy joint on three levels with the ground floor serving as the restaurant and bar. The middle level is the disco area and the top floor is the balcony bar. There's bucket-loads of entertainment going on throughout the week from karaoke on Sunday and Wednesday, a quiz, usually on a Thursday, and disco most other nights, culminating into a full-on house party over the weekend. Sunday lunch is also available from 1200 to 1500. **Open** Monday-Saturday 1900-2300. Sunday 1200-2230

Saunas

The Boiler Room

Ocean House Hotel, Hunsdon Road, Torquay TQ1 1QB
Phone 01803 296 538 E-mail info@oceanhouse.co.uk
Web www.oceanhouse.co.uk
The steam bath is part of this luxurious gay hotel. It is popular with the locals and residents of the hotel and it attracts the younger age group which the hotel caters for well. The facilities you'd usually associate with a custom-built sauna are limited but something is better than nothing in this beautiful part of the world. **Open** Thursday-Sunday 1800-2300 **Price** £7

Accommodation

Manderville

18 Thurlow Road, Torquay TQ1 3EE Phone 01803 313 336
E-mail manderville@eclipse.co.uk Web www.eclipse.co.uk/manderville
Manderville is a gay-owned and -run mid-19th-century villa set in an area of delightful gardens and about a three minute walk from the beach and the closest gay bar. It is a private (non-smoking) house where guests are welcomed as friends. As a guest you have many priveleges, much the same as if you were staying with friends and relatives. Rooms can be let on a room-only or bed and breakfast basis at all times. Manderville is also disabled-friendly with a stair lift, a bath hoist and tracks and ramps that offer disabled visitors complete independence. All rooms are spacious and very well furnished with quality accessories and antiques. The Manderville is a friendly and flexible place. Highly recommended. **Price** £50 **Number of rooms** 4

Ocean House Hotel

Hunsdon Road, Torquay TQ1 1QB
Phone 01803 296 538 Fax 01803 299 936
E-mail info@oceanhouse.co.uk Web www.oceanhouse.co.uk
Ocean House is one of Torquay's few remaining plantation-style houses, built over 110 years ago. The location is perfect for a gay retreat as it is in a quiet conservation area, yet the gay bars and clubs are only six minutes' walk away. The swimming pool is surrounded by sub-tropical gardens and sun decks which are south-facing. All rooms are spacious and have private en-suite bathrooms. In the lounge, large ceiling fans cool you in the summer and real log fires glow in the winter. They also have a dining room, bar and a steam room to spoil and pamper yourself. On Sunday summer afternoons they introduce their famous barbecue that is a favourite with non-residents. All guest rooms have private bathrooms or shower rooms, are light and spacious, with tea/coffee-making facilities and TVs. There is a choice of premier double, standard double, single and twin rooms. The premier rooms have a five-foot bed, the standard doubles have four and half foot beds. Twin rooms have one double and one single bed. Single rooms have a standard double bed in a slightly smaller room. (See the listing for the Boiler Room sauna too; part of this same complex.) **Price** £64 **Number of rooms** 14, all en-suite

Oscars Hotel and Restaurant	Belgrave Road, Torquay Phone 01803 293 563

E-mail reservations@oscars-hotel.com Web www.oscars-hotel.com
The price includes a full-cooked vegetarian or English breakfast with a good breakfast menu available too. All rooms have colour TVs and free tea/coffee-making facilities. An evening meal is available every day, again, with a good choice on the menu. The hotel restaurant is normally open from Wednesday to Saturday and offers a full à la carte menu. The hotel's bar is usually open every evening from 1830 where you can enjoy a drink and socialise with the other guests. Price £70

Palms Hotel   537 Babbacombe Road, Torquay TQ1 1HQ Phone 01803 293 970
This is excellent value-for-money accommodation with cheaper rates for longer stays. A very friendly and welcoming establishment. Price £40
Number of rooms 10, all en-suite

Rainbow Villa   24 Bridge Road, Torquay TQ2 5BA Phone 01803 212 886
An elegant gay-owned Victorian guest-house; centrally located and open all year. All bedrooms are non-smoking. Price £49

Cruising grounds

Petit Tor Beach   This is the naturist beach in Torbay. Take a long walk down towards the sea; take a left at the bottom and continue down. On the beach, the gay area is to the left. There's plenty of action in the bushes and also amongst the rocks at the far end.

Truro Saunas

Woodbine Villa Sauna   Fore Street, Truro, Cornwall TR2 4QB Phone 01726 882 005
A compact gay sauna (known as Viz) attached to a small, exclusively gay guest-house, yet which is also open to non-residents. Due to the location and the complete lack of localised gay facilities, this venue, though limited, offers the gay male a welcome chance to meet up in a relaxed and friendly atmosphere. The outside of the property offers no visible clue as to the nature of the building, so it may be advisable to phone beforehand for a precise location. It is open two days of the week only and is rather popular with the locals as well as the tourists to the area. The Woodbine Villa is an exclusively gay guest-house – phone the venue direct for details of accommodation. Open Wednesday and Sunday 1800-2200 Price £5

Wakefield Pubs

Bar Zeus   6 Lower Warrengate, Wakefield WF1 1SA Phone 01924 201 705
This is a large-capacity dance/cabaret pub, occupying one of the oldest public houses in Wakefield and situated on the quieter side of the city centre, at the bottom of the cathedral precinct. The door policy is extremely liberal, the widespread belief being that all people, gay and

straight, male and female, able and disabled can all come together to enjoy themselves. The atmosphere is local and communal, with a broad age range, background and taste every night of the week. You'll find leather clones, students, mature lesbian couples and everyone else in between in here at one time or another. Bar Zeus is very popular with the women of Wakefield and its surrounding areas, particularly on a Sunday. There's fun throughout the week, with a stripper on a Thursday and drag DJ entertainment, DJ Jools' disco and cabaret for the remainder of the days. **Open** Monday-Wednesday 1200-0000. Thursday 1200-0100. Friday-Saturday 1100-0100. Sunday 1200-2300

Downtown **46 Kirkgate, Wakefield WF1 1TQ** Phone 01924 380 633
This large gay venue is extremely popular with lesbians of all ages, hence the female stripper on most Friday evenings. The boys are not left out though – they can gawp at the male stripper the following day on a Saturday. From Thursday through to Saturday there is a disco. On Sunday there is cabaret. The venue consists of two bars, a dance floor and a pool table and caters for a wide selection of the gay community. **Open** Monday-Wednesday 1900-0000. Thursday-Saturday 1900-0100. Sunday 1900-2300

Cruising grounds

Clarence Park This park is very cruisy most of the day and into the evening. The usual peak periods are lunchtimes and then from 1600 to 1800. The large hill in the middle of the park, behind the bandstand in amongst the trees, is where you will find the action. You'll also find it by hanging around in close proximity to the toilet facility on the main road, where you can expect to be cruised quite easily.

Methley From Junction 30 of the M62 head towards Wakefield and take the first left and then follow the road around until it passes under the motorway. Take the next left. Alongside the motorway is a lane. It is here in the evenings that some action will be taking place. Bushes along the walkway will provide some cover. Police activity will be in the form of patrols, so care and discretion is recommended.

Walsall Pubs

The Golden Lion 41 Birchills Street, Walsall WS2 8NG Phone 01922 610 977

The Golden Lion incorporates Monroe's Bar and is the only late-night gay venue in Walsall. On warm nights (and all through the summer) the doors to the garden are opened up and because of the interesting way the fencing has been erected, a delightful little cruising area on the premises has been created. Of course, everyone is going to deny it is a cruising area, and would prefer to call it a 'patio'. This area enables you to walk from the club, through the garden, through the pub and around again without having to backtrack on yourself. This is a very popular place, not least because it is the only gay venue in the area. Sundays are particularly busy as are any of the late-night openings. **Open** Monday and Wednesday 2030-0000. Tuesday and Thursday 2030-0200. Friday 1930-0200. Saturday 1300-0200. Sunday 1300-0000. **Price** £2, Friday-Sunday after 2200

Wells next to the Sea Cruising grounds

Holkham Beach This place can be very wild on a hot sunny weekend. Park at Queen Anne's Lane and go down to the beach and turn left. Walk for miles, until you see a sign informing you that you are entering the nudist beach, and you are there. Contact can be made in the sand dunes. The nearby woods offer some privacy. A word of warning: watch out for the wardens –they will call the police and will hold you until they arrive. They are apparently easy to spot... they're the ones wearing clothes.

Winchester Cruising grounds

A31 lay-by Travel from Winchester to New Alresford on the A31. Look for a long lay-by about two miles from New Alresford. The toilets are now demolished but the area is still very busy throughout the day and quiet, but not dead, after dark. You'll find businessmen, lorry drivers and some locals here. Follow the lay-by as far as the right-hand bend, passing the private house on the left (do not park close by here!) and continue into the trees and park up. There's lots of sitting in cars and occasional forays into nearby bushes by mainly older guys. One path leads down a long track to total seclusion: it can be fun! Be warned police pay regular visits.

Wisley Cruising grounds

Wisley Woods There's some deep woodland that runs off a lay-by at the side of the A3 adjacent to the M25 junction. It's safe and is very active after dusk on most days. To find your way in, enter the woods about 15 yards south of the footbridge over the A3. Bear left and you will meet the path from the footbridge. If you face along the main path into the woods away from the bridge, you will see that there is a hill climbing to your right. It is very cruisy at the top of this hill, but to find the main activity you need to follow the path into the woods. It rounds the side of the hill and comes to a fairly obvious end. Now, swing left along the narrower path into the woods and you'll see a clump of trees under which there is usually someone hanging around. Alternatively, cross the gravel track, bearing slightly to the left and you will find an area where all sorts are going on. Police do not appear to bother with this place. Apparently, a few years ago they used to ride through on their motorbikes until someone tied a piece of rope across the path and they haven't been back since (I would strongly advise against any such actions though). This place can, in places, be very dark, so it is advisable to walk around during the daylight to familiarise yourself with the area first. Note: you cannot reach the lay-by direct from the M25 or A3 as it is on the slope road leading on to the A3. Turn on to the roundabout at the M25/A3 interchange and take the exit for Guildford (A3) keeping to the near-side lane. Keep your speed down, as finding a parking spot is tricky. Park in the lay-by immediately before, or after the footbridge. The lay-bys are busy so it may take a few attempts. Although the directions above sound complicated, once you are there you will find that they are precise rather than awkward, but well worth the hassle. It should be noted that there were some muggings reported in this area in the summer of 1998.

Wolverhampton Pubs

The Greyhound 14 Bond Street, Wolverhampton WV2 4AS Phone 01902 420 916
Wolverhampton's well-established, 170-capacity gay venue, now into its eighteenth successful year. The Greyhound is a large venue with four distinct 'areas'. It's busy most nights of the week, with a predominantly male clientele, whereas lunchtime customers seem to be more a mix of gay and straight. The Greyhound is a pre-Sky Club (see separate listing) feeder bar on Fridays and Saturdays. It cannot be described as a cruise bar, since it consists mainly of couples and friends socialising. All in all, a welcoming venue that particularly extends a welcome to leather, bear, uniform and industrial crowds. **Open** Monday-Friday 1200-1400 / 1900-2300. Saturday 1300-2300. Sunday 1200-1500 / 1900-2230

The White Hart   66 Worcester Street, Wolverhampton WV2 4LQ Phone 01902 421 701
The White Hart is a trendy, exclusively gay venue. It's very cruisy and intimate and popular with the girls as well as the boys of the town. A coach is arranged that whisks Wolverhampton folk off to Birmingham's Subway City every fortnight, with plans to extend the coach trips to other gay venues across the Midlands. A welcome late licence and loads of cheap drink offers – it can't be bad! **Open** Monday-Friday 1200-0100. Saturday 1200-0200. Sunday 1200-0000

Cruising grounds

West Park   Park Road West sees after-dark action but do stay away from the toilets.

Workington Pubs

The Steam Packet   51 Stanley Street, Workington CA14 2JG Phone 01900 621 86
The Steam Packet is the only gay bar in Cumbria and is, naturally, quite busy. The summer months particularly so, owing to the influx of tourists that make for this beautiful part of the world. The popular Saturday night disco attracts a lot of people, all trying to get in before 2130, so they have an extra £1 to spend at the bar! Even though it is a friendly and welcoming gay pub, it is extremely straight-friendly and this ensures that the mix is just right. There is a main bar area with dance floor, plus

a pool room and an additional late-night snack bar which opens on Saturday nights (you'll need it!). Bed and breakfast accommodation is also available (at very competitive rates) though this is usually fully booked during the summer, so make sure you get in there early. **Open** Monday-Saturday 1200-2300 (summer season) **Price** £1-2

York

York is an attractive city – perhaps historically England's finest – with winding medieval streets, elegant Georgian terraces and pretty rivers. Overshadowing them all though is the city's magnificent cathedral. York Minster, or the Cathedral and Metropolitan Church of St Peter, to give it its proper name. This is York's most famous tourist attraction. Several churches have existed on this site over the centuries and work began on the present cathedral in 1220, taking just over 250 years to complete. At 525 foot long, 250 foot wide and a massive 196 foot high, it is the biggest medieval cathedral in the whole of northern Europe. It dominates York's skyline. The well-preserved city walls were built by the Romans in the 1st century. The Normans then built the first stone walls around the city shortly after William the Conqueror came to the throne in 1066. Some of the Norman's work can still be seen, but most of the remains that you see today date from around the 13th century. Although parts are missing, much of the medieval City Walls have survived, and they are considered to be one of the best-preserved examples of medieval fortifications in the whole of Europe. York's city centre is bustling with things to do, with over 30 different galleries, museums and tours to gauge your interest. There is also a rich choice of shops, both in the centre and in the new designer village that has just opened up on the outskirts of the city.

Getting in touch

There are excellent tourist information centres throughout the city that can furnish you with maps and attraction guides. Start by visiting **De Grey Rooms** (01904 621 756) in Exhibition Square. There is a smaller branch at the railway station on Station Road, on the west side of the walls and also **The York Visitor and Conference Bureau** at 20 George Street, near the bus station. York has no gay scene to talk about, but, with Manchester only an hour or so away, it's not too much of an upheaval for visitors and locals to trek out of the city for their activities. **Yorkshire Lesbian and Gay Switchboard** (0845 345 2449) can give you all the information you might require. They are open Tuesday to Saturday from 1930 to 2130.

Pubs

Fusion Bar   54 Gillygate, York YO3 7EO Phone 01904 627 679
Formerly known as The Bay Horse, this bar has an entertainments policy that consists of some sort of disco each and every night throughout the week. It should come as no surprise that since this is York's only gay

venue it does get considerably busy, with a crowd of all ages and types – gay-friendly straights included. Each Wednesday they promote ITZ, an outrageous drag show disco. Wednesdays also accommodate the monthly Trans York meeting; a social night for transvestites, transexuals and cross-dressers (phone venue for exact dates). **Open** Monday-Saturday 1200-2300. Sunday 1200-2230

Scotland

4

4

Scotland is a defiantly distinct country within the United Kingdom, so culturally different from the English and Welsh worlds south of Hadrian's Wall. Its cities revel in arts, heritage and culture. Scotland has it all, from the rampant night-life of Glasgow and Edinburgh to the sleepy, slow-pace and rugged grandeur of the Highlands and the lush green river valleys of the Lowlands. Cities like Edinburgh, Glasgow, Dundee, Aberdeen and Inverness cater for the most sophisticated tastes while the countryside is never more than a few minutes away.

Scotland as a whole is little over half the size of England, but with a tenth of the population. Unlike England, Scotland possesses open spaces and natural splendour, with the Highlands containing some of the last great wildernesses in Europe. From the craggy, heather-sloped mountains and silver beaches on the west coast to the haunting mists of the Hebrides, off the mainland.

Aberdeen

The principal seaport of north-east Scotland situated between the rivers Dee (south) and Don (north). Known to the Romans as Devena, or the 'town of the two waters', it is the third largest city in Scotland – a cultural centre, a fishing port and a centre of the offshore North Sea oil industry. Today, Aberdeen is known as The Granite City, in reference to the many grey buildings scattered across its cityscape. There is a high student population here and a very small gay scene. The bars and clubs along and off the principal Union Street tend to be rather mixed, relaxed and informal.

Getting in touch

The main **Tourist Information** centre is at St Nicholas House, Broad Street in the city centre (01224 632 727). Try to pick up a free copy of What's On from the centre for a comprehensive diary of current events. For gay-specific help and advice you should phone the **Aberdeen Switchboard** on either Wednesday or Friday between 1930 and 2130 (01224 212 600). **Aberdeen Lesbian Group** meets every third Wednesday of the month in Aberdeen Women's Centre, Shoe Lane (01224 625 010) from 1930 onwards. **Ab-Fab** is Aberdeen University's only gay society. They meet every Thursday in the SRC Building on High Street. To find out more you can visit their website at www.ab-fab.org.

Pubs

Castro's

47 Netherkirkgate, Aberdeen AB10 1AU Phone **01224 639 920**
This is the only full-time gay venue in Aberdeen. If this state of affairs sounds rather drab then look on the bright side: with no other available venues, nearly all of Aberdeen's gay life is crammed into one place and is just ripe for the picking! Castro's is very well managed, there's no 'take it or leave it' attitude about this place – every effort is put into making this venue a safe and friendly gay space, and the Aberdeen community seems appreciative. The music policy throughout the week is quite commercial except for Tuesday when a harder house sound is doled out. Wednesday sees cheap drink offers to the fore which encourages the student fraternity to come out in their droves. The venue is on two floors. The downstairs club area opens each night at 2200 and the upstairs bar stays open through 'til closing time as a comfortable chill-out space. **Open** Monday-Friday 1700-0200. Saturday-Sunday 1200-0200 **Price** £3 after 2300

Dundee

Dundee became very much a regenerated city from the mid-'90s on into this new century. In the past it had a reputation for being drab and dreary; nothing special compared to Glasgow, Edinburgh and Aberdeen. Solid investment and town centre re-thinking has changed all that. Two of the most significant developments over the past five years have been the opening of Dundee Contemporary Arts Centre and Overgate Shopping Centre. These have brought a buzz to Scotland's fourth biggest city, famed also for Captain Scott's ship, Discovery, which sits proudly at its waterfront. Dundee is also the home of The Dandy and The Beano, British boys' comic books which have stood the test of time.

Getting in touch

The **Tourist Information Office** is at 21 Castle Street (01382 527 527) and you can pick up all the information and maps you will need from here Monday to Saturday from 0900 to 1800. Dundee's gay switchboard is **Diversitay** (01382 202 620) and is open for all gay-specific enquires every Monday between the hours of 1900 and 2200.

Pubs

Brooklyn's

2 St Andrews Lane, Dundee DD1 2HB Phone **01382 200 660**
Formerly Bar 'XS' and the sister venue to Liberty Club, Brooklyn's is a luxurious pre-club bar that is housed in the same building as Liberty Nightclub and is accessed via a spiral staircase. The bar first opened its doors in 1998 and has recently installed large-screen videos. Bar XS is open seven nights a week; its hours run from 2100 to 0000. Friday nights are particularly busy with their regular karaoke nights; Mondays too with the ever-popular Team Quiz nights! Discount tickets for Liberty Nightclub are available over the bar. **Open** Monday-Sunday 1700-0000.

Charlie's Bar

75-79 Seagate, Dundee DD1 2EH Phone **01382 226 840**
This is pretty much a local, predominantly male-orientated gay bar with the obligatory pool table and video jukebox. There's a large bar with a separate dance area which comes to life each Saturday when the weekly disco takes place. Karaoke is also on the calendar – the first Thursday of every month. **Open** Monday-Saturday 1100-0000. Sunday 1230-0000

Clubs

Liberty Nightclub

124 Seagate, Dundee DD1 2HB Phone **01382 200 660**
E-mail **club@liberty-nightclub.co.uk** Web **www.liberty-nightclub.co.uk**
Liberty Nightclub is the sister club to Brooklyn's. Open Wednesday to Saturday, the club has a capacity for 340 people and every Friday and Saturday night DJ 'BP' plays all of your favourite commercial and gay tunes with some house music in between. Other nights see Ally Hill on the decks and early evening on a Wednesday sees drag slut Surreal Bastille hosting the ever-popular karaoke show. Every singer has the chance to win free time behind the bar where they are entitled to help themselves to any beverage available! The venue is gay-owned and managed and provides regular PAs from people like Hazel Dean, Hannah Jones and Nicki French. **Open** (Liberty) Wednesday-Thursday 2330-0230. Friday-Saturday 2330-0230. (Brooklyn's) Monday-Sunday 1900-0000 **Price** £3, Wednesday-Thursday; £4-6, Friday-Saturday

Cruising grounds

Riverside Drive   This is a truck stop where you'll find quite a bit of night-time action, especially along the track that leads up the side of the airport. It is wise to cruise this area in your car rather than on foot. There is also some action to be found around the sports pavilion opposite.

Dunfermline Cruising grounds

Pittencrief Car Park   This area is a night-time hot spot (at times!). It is advisable to take the car rather than walk. You can find action during the day in the park but it is worth saving yourself for the evenings. Exercise caution if you are cruising in the day – there will be lots of people using the car park.

Edinburgh

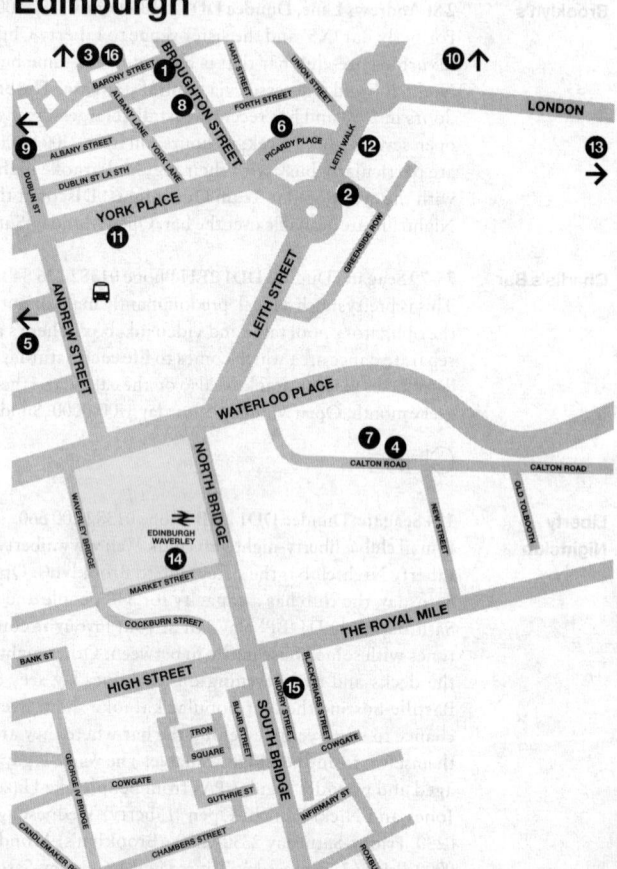

Map key

1 Blue Moon Café Bar	**9** Newtown Bar / Intense Cellar Bar
2 C C Blooms	**10** Number 18 Sauna (off)
3 The Claremont Bar (off)	**11** OOT – Out in Edinburgh
4 Divine Divas / Up @ The Venue	**12** Planet Out
5 Hot Stuff (off)	**13** Stag & Turret (off)
6 Joy / Lush @ Club Ego	**14** Tackno @ Club Mercado
7 Mingin' @ Studio 24	**15** Taste @ The Honeycomb
8 MsDemeanour @ The Phoenix	**16** Townhouse Sauna (off)

Pronounced Ed-in-Bur-ra, this is the jewel in Scotland's crown. King David I moved his capital to Edinburgh in the 12th century. International trade assured the capital's prosperity and it became the permanent capital and Royal residence in the 16th century. These days the city is internationally recognised as a thriving cultural centre: testament to this – the million or so that flock to the world-famous Edinburgh Festival every year. Tourists from all over the world gather for this showcase of new and seasoned talent. The festival's growth has meant that the main straight arts have become overshadowed by the various generic mini-festivals – dedicated to arts, music, TV, fringe theatre, literature and other niches besides, all taking place simultaneously, all under the one festival umbrella. Edinburgh's gay scene takes full advantage of this summer festival, offering pretty much everything it can in the name of art. Significantly though, it also has a diverse and integrated scene the rest of the year around and so there's nothing (bar the chill factor!) to put you off coming here either side of the Festival. Prince's Street, the main thoroughfare that runs east-west through the centre of town, is usually the first place visitors to the city start exploring. It was this street that was immortalised in the opening shots of the celebrated Scottish film Trainspotting.

Getting there

Airport

Edinburgh International Airport is situated to the west, just outside the city centre. There are frequent bus services that run between the airport and Waverley Bridge (next to the main railway station) in the city centre. Phone **Lothian Buses** (0131 555 6363) for further information.

Trains

Waverley train station, situated just behind Princess Street, provides services to all parts of the UK. **Scotrail** operates regular services to Glasgow, which can run as frequently as every 15 minutes during the day. A cheap day-return is currently only £7.50. Services also run regularly up into the highlands if you fancy a change of scenery. Services to London are provided by **GNER** which after recent problems seems to be offering many special offers.

Coaches

National Express services operate thoughout the UK and beyond. Services generally leave from St Andrew's Square bus station.

Getting about

Buses

Edinburgh doesn't yet boast any form of underground or transit system so the main choice for getting around has to be the bus. Services are frequent and generally reliable. All the local bus companies offer daily, weekly or monthly passes, though tickets between the companies are not interchangeable. Tickets for single journeys can also be bought from the driver although the exact fare is required for the purple (Lothian Regional Transport) buses. Fares are cheap, usually only 50p or 70p if you're within a couple of miles of the city centre. Phone **Lothian Buses** (0131 555 6363) for further information or First Bus (0131 663 9233) for information on their services.

Taxis

These are ranked outside all railway stations and practically on every corner around Prince's Street. Two reputable firms to call upon are **City Cabs** (0131 228 1211) or **Central Radio Taxis** (0131 229 3331).

Tourist information

Edinburgh and Scotland Information Centre, 3 Princes Street (0131 473 3800) is situated right in the centre of town next to Waverley Shopping Centre. It's open seven days a week and all year round, with extended hours during the summer. This is an extremely busy, but efficient office and they can assist you in practically anything, whether it's bus tickets or theatre tickets you're after, a bureau de change facility or simply the dishing out of info on this great city.

Bureaux de change

Apart from the sub office in the Information Bureau there is an **American Express** office on 139 Prince's Street (0131 225 7881). Most high street banks are also to be found in this area.

Getting help

Police, hospital and pharmacy

Edinburgh's main station is at 5 Fettes Avenue (0131 311 3131). For emergencies dial 999 (no coins required). Edinburgh's main hospital is the **Royal Infirmary of Edinburgh**, 1 Lauriston Place (0131 536 1000). In an emergency you can be treated free of charge within the Accident and Emergency ward of any hospital. The police hold information of late night pharmacy openings, should you require to pick up medication urgently.

Getting in touch

Internet

With a city at the forefront of so much by the way of culture and communication, internet cafés, not surprisingly, are popping up here as much as they are across the rest of Britain's city streets. **EasyEverything** (58 Rose Street) gives you 24-hour access to the net and any loved ones at the other end of a modem. **Web 13** (13 Bread Street) and **Electric Frog** (42-44 Cockburn Street) are other options to accommodate your late-hour surfing needs (open 1000 to 2200 daily).

GLBT Helplines **Edinburgh Lesbian and Gay Switchboard** (0131 556 4049) is housed in the Lesbigay Centre at 60 Broughton Street and runs nightly from 1930 to 2200. The switchboard has a specific **Lesbian Line** (0131 557 0751) which runs every Monday and Thursday from 1930 to 2200. The Lesbigay centre also houses several gay businesses including **Nexus Café**. Edinburgh is also served by **Bisexual Helpline** (0131 557 3620) which runs every Thursday night from 1930 to 2130. And if you are living with or are affected by HIV or AIDS you can contact **Solas Support Centre** (0131 661 0982).

Pubs

Blue Moon 1 Barony Street, Edinburgh EH3 6PD Phone 0131 556 2788
Café Bar A long-established café-bar serving food, coffee and drinks to a mixed gay/straight clientele in a relaxed and friendly atmosphere. In the base-ment there's the Out Of The Blue shop selling posters, cards and other stuff. Pick up your free gay press from here as well and get hold of flyers for up-to-the-minute info on all the latest club nights in Edinburgh. **Open** Monday-Friday 1100-2430. Saturday-Sunday 0930-2430

C C Blooms 23-24 Greenside Place, Edinburgh EH1 3AA Phone 0131 556 9331
Situated next to The Playhouse, C C Blooms is a large ground-floor bar and basement disco where, as they say, every night is a party night. This is probably the nearest you can get to a permanent gay club in Edinburgh with people of all ages and types coming in, and usually stay-ing in. There's free admission at all times and a late licence should ensure that the popularity of this place long continues. Through the week this venue can fill up nicely with a disco on offer each and every night and karaoke featuring on Thursday and Sunday. This is a very busy venue with a good reputation amongst the gay community. You must pop your head in here – at least once. **Open** Monday-Saturday 1830-0300. Sunday 2000-0300

The Claremont 133-135 East Claremont Street, Edinburgh EH7 4JA
Bar Phone 0131 556 5662 E-mail Robin@scifipub99.freeserve.co.uk
Web www.scifipub99.freeserve.co.uk
The Claremont is one of the strangest venues on the Edinburgh scene. They describe themselves as straight-friendly, that is to say that the mix of gay and straight does not interfere with the great, friendly atmos-phere. Wednesday night has become one of the busiest nights of the week with non-stop entertainment – a cross between the TV tom-fool-ery of Noel's House Party and It's A Knockout! As it is only one of three 'sci fi' pubs in the United Kingdom, the décor, as you may have guessed, is devoted to a massive assembly of cult TV memorabilia (Star Trek / Space 1999 / Logan's Run, etc.). Each night there is something sci-fi going on for those who may be interested. Dr Who? night is on Mondayzzzz... Sorry, must have nodded off there. Now, where was I? Ah, yes, the venue is on two floors divided by a mezzanine level which means that you can quite easily cruise around, mingle and discuss whether Tom Baker was a clown, a fuckwit or just an angst-ridden

genius. On the first and third Saturday of every month The Claremont brings you a male-only night, specialising in leather, bears, masters, rubber, skinheads, slaves and fetish (aha, now that's more like it). Worth a trip – it's quite fun. **Open** Monday-Saturday 1100-0100. Sunday 1230-0100

One of the most photographed statues in Edinburgh is Greyfriars Bobby, a dog, whose claim to fame is the immense loyalty he showed to his master, John Gray, an Edinburgh policeman in the 1850s. It is said that upon John Gray's death of tuberculosis in 1858, Bobby, a Skye Terrier, took up residence on the grave in Greyfriars Churchyard, immediately following his master's funeral. It was here he stayed until his own death, 14 years later. Bobby's devotion to his master quickly turned him into a local celebrity, but also raised the question of whether he constituted a 'stray' and thus, should he be allowed to roam the street without a licence. Fortunately, the Lord Provost of Edinburgh, Sir William Chambers, was so impressed by Bobby that he agreed to pay the license, thus sparing the little dog's life. On his death in 1872, the people of Edinburgh decided Bobby should be interred in the Kirkyard, by his master – an unparalleled move. Bobby's tombstone reads 'Greyfriars Bobby. Died 14th January 1872. Aged 15 years. Let his loyalty and devotion be a lesson to us all.' His statue was erected a year later, just outside the entrance to the yard and opposite the Traills Coffee House. The coffee house is now a pub and has been renamed Greyfriar's Bobby Inn.

Hot Stuff

87-89 Rose Street Lane North, Edinburgh EH2 3DT Phone 0131 225 7651
Formerly The French Connection, Hot Stuff is a very popular and lively one-floor venue catering for a mixed gay and straight clientele. A recent refurbishment has resulted in them losing the '70s theme and reintroduced the traditional Scottish pub atmosphere. One of only a few venues in Edinburgh that has a large TV/TS following although I'd be quick to point out that anybody and everybody will be, and are, made welcome. **Open** Monday-Saturday 1300-0100. Sunday 1400-0000

**Newtown Bar /
Intense Cellar
Bar**

26b Dublin Street, Edinburgh EH1 6NN Phone 0131 538 7775
A popular gay venue for a predominantly male crowd of all ages. The Newtown Bar is a traditionally styled venue more for the drinking and socialising sort of crowd rather than the disco dolly and karaoke crowd. Free admission and an open door policy make it an ideal place for late night drinking. The evenings see the bar extend to the basement disco (Intense). This basement bar used to have a dress code of rubber, leather and the like, however, the policy has now changed and it is open to all including gay-friendly straights. **Open** Monday-Thursday 1200-0100. Friday Saturday 1200-0200. Sunday 1230-0100

Planet Out

6 Baxter's Place, Edinburgh EH1 3AF Phone 0131 524 0061
Formerly Route 66 (a long time ago) this has to be one of Edinburgh's busiest gay bars. A smart, contemporary atmosphere prevails and the room is subtly divided into different themed areas. Ages and types go right across the board which is probably largely responsible for making this such an atmospheric venue. **Open** Monday-Friday 1600-0100.

Saturday-Sunday 1400-0100

Stag and Turret   1 Montrose Terrace, Abbeyhill, Edinburgh EH7 5DJ Phone 0131 661 6443
The Stag may be slightly off the beaten track but a visit should be well
worth it. Recent new ownership got rid of the dowdy interior and transformed this popular gay drinking hole into a bright and modern venue.
Karaoke on Wednesday, Friday and Sunday keeps the punters entertained. **Open** Monday-Saturday 1200-0100. Sunday 1230-0000

Club nights

Divine Divas   15-21 Calton Road, Edinburgh EH8 8DL Phone 0131 557 0751
@ The Venue   E-mail jean@lgls.org
This is a women-only get-together on the top floor of The Venue. All
profits go to Lesbian Line. For more information pop into the LGB cen-
tre on Broughton Street or phone the switchboard. **Open** Every second
Saturday 2200-0300

Joy @ Ego   14 Picardy Place, Edinburgh EH1 3JT Phone 0131 467 2551
E-mail joy.scotland@virgin.net
Maggie and Alan Joy are still together hosting this long-running gay
club night, albeit in another new venue (formerly at Wilkie House). The
music is good, solid house from Maggie and Alan and chart, garage,
pop and whatever else from the Cocteau Lounge downstairs, courtesy of
Trendy Wendy and Sally Findlay. Although this is advertised as a gay
club night, there is a good following of no-attitude gay-friendly
straights in evidence. This is one of the busiest gay house nights in
Edinburgh. There's no pretension and no dick-heads. **Open** Every fortnight on Saturday 2230-0300 **Price** £7-8

Lush! @   14 Picardy Place, Edinburgh EH1 3JT Phone 0131 478 7434
Club Ego   E-mail info@clublush.co.uk Web www.clublush.co.uk
Lush! is a twice-monthly mixed club night in the 700-capacity Club Ego.
It is hosted by two of Edinburgh's best-known club DJs. On the first and
third Sunday of the month Dale Wilkinson and Craig Dempster try to
re-capture some of the success that they created last summer when the
venue was known as Eden. The club is aimed at mixed gay and straight
up-for-it clubbers who like commercial dance, funky disco and cheesy
pop and house. Upstairs in the Mail Room is where you'll find Dale and
Craig spinning the handbag and funky dance, whilst downstairs in the
Cocteau Lounge you can chill out, gossip or just mingle in the comfortable candle-lit environment. The music may not be to everyone's taste
but it is a good, affordable night out on a Sunday in Edinburgh. **Open**
Every first and third Sunday 2230-0300 **Price** £3

Mingin' @   24 Calton Road, Edinburgh EH8 8DP Phone 0131 467 2551
Studio 24   E-mail its.mingin@virgin.net
Alan Joy's club 'Mingin' is an intense and intimate affair. The music
policy is dark, sexy, dirty trance and features DJs Alan Joy and Brian
Dempster. The crowd is friendly, relaxed and going for it! This is an

economy night out – only £5 for entry – and with Studio 24 having probably the cheapest bar prices in the whole of Edinburgh's club land, a night out certainly won't break the bank. The atmosphere is always electric and the people will be stripping off their togs before the night has ended. The original concept for Mingin' was to bring top-notch DJs to Edinburgh every month. It soon became clear, however, that this meant there was no consistency across the club nights from one month to the next. Following a new (and successful) strategy, local DJ Brian Dempster was brought in to play the first half of the night. His music starts out quite mellow but by the time he's finishing his set, he is racing along and has the crowd eating out of his hand. For the second half, Alan Joy takes over, playing a much darker, dirtier, sexier, trancier style than his usual sets at Joy (see separate listing). **Open** Every fortnight on Saturday 2230-0300 (variable: phone to confirm times) **Price** £5

Sean Connery is one of Edinburgh's most famous son's. His devotion to both country and family can be glimpsed if you squint closely enough at the tattoos on his right arm; one reads 'Scotland Forever' and the other, 'Mum and Dad'. He had these inked on when he was 16. A few years later he was modelling nude for the Edinburgh Art College. (I wonder if he was surrounded by Pussy Galore back then?). By the wee age of 21, Connery was already losing his hair and few people realise that he actually wore a toupee for every James Bond film he starred in.

MsDemeanor @ The Phoenix

46 Broughton Street, Edinburgh EH1 3SA Phone 0131 557 0234
E-mail msdemeanorUK@aol.com Web www.msdemeanor.co.uk
The only regular monthly club night in Edinburgh for TV/TS (and their admirers) held in the basement club of The Phoenix. The dates vary each month so you should check out the website or write for information on dates. The club is self-contained with its own entrance, own toilets and also a changing area with mirrors and dressing table. The atmosphere is sort of clubby-by-candle-light. It is not a large venue and there are a limited number of tickets available at the door – it's recommended that you purchase your tickets in advance to ensure admittance. You can do so by sending a cheque or postal order to MsDemeanor, PO Box 17176, Edinburgh EH11 1TD. Tickets are £4 if you're dressed and £5 non-dressed. You will need to enclose details of the date you wish to attend, as well as an SAE and then allow a week for processing. Tickets can also be collected at the door or sent to you direct. This is a night for everyone: straight, gay, TV/TS or anywhere in between – the night is about enjoying yourself for who you are not what you are. **Open** Once a month on varying Saturdays 2030-0100 **Price** £4-5

OOT – Out in Edinburgh

Stand Comedy Club, 5 York Place, Edinburgh EH1 3EB
Phone 0131 558 7272 E-mail admin@thestand.freeserve.co.uk
Web www.thestand.co.uk
Out On Tuesday: this is the place where it all started – the gay comedy nights that is – and so successful was this monthly venture that the formula has now been taken down to Glasgow (although that one runs on a Sunday: see separate listing). Hosted by the very funny Craig Hill, there

is usually one headliner and two supporting acts. There is also the very popular Gay Blind Date with the winners being treated to a meal in one of Edinburgh's finest chip shops – just kidding – it's a full-on restaurant bash as prize. OOT is something different for the gay scene and that can only be a good thing – so go along and crack your face. **Open** Every second Tuesday 2100-2300 **Price** £5

Tackno @ Club Mercado
36-39 Market Street, Edinburgh EH1 Phone 0131 467 2551
E-mail http://hello.to/trendywendy
DJ Trendy Wendy spins the retro sounds on this very popular gay night out. The choice of club itself is quite apt – one expanse of floor space with a camp psuedo-modern feel about it (don't worry, even I don't know what that means). There is quite often a fancy dress theme which serves as a good excuse to rummage through the local Oxfam shop and play with your make-up box. If you don't take yourself too seriously then you will enjoy this night for exactly what it is – lots of fun! **Open** Every last Sunday 2230-0300 **Price** £5-6

Edinburgh Castle is the home of the One O'Clock Gun. This is fired every day except Sunday, at precisely 1300, to provide everyone with an accurate check for their clocks and watches. It will certainly startle you if you are anywhere near the Castle at the time!

Taste @ The Honeycomb
Niddry Street, Edinburgh EH1 1LG Phone 0131 557 4656
E-mail info@taste-clubs.com Web www.taste-clubs.com
After finishing a period of their history at Wilkie House, the gay-friendly Taste crew have finally made the move to their new premises – The Honeycomb. A great deal of time and money has been spent transforming the former vaults from a damp and dirty dive into Scotland's premier underground dance venue. The Honeycomb has two dance floors with top quality sound and lighting in both, two bars, lots of comfortable seated areas, and air conditioning throughout. The main room features resident DJs Brian Fisher and Mark Price, who whip the crowd into a frenzy every week with awe-inspiring sets that build from vocal house, through tough and funky disco-tinged house to hands-in-the-air euphoric anthems. Top quality guest DJs from the UK, USA and Europe whose style complements the Taste sound join them about once a month (admission rises to £10 when guest DJs appear). The back room at Taste is a slightly more laid-back affair where residents Martin Valentine and Marco Smith (and occasional guests) spin deep, funky house and US garage all night long. But don't expect to chill out; this is a back room for bumping, grinding and shaking your ass. Pre-Tasters usually meet up from 2100 at The Gilded Saloon on Cowgate. Martin Valentine and guests play garage and deep house to warm you up for the main event (no admission charge). (See the listing for their sister club night in Glasgow, Fruitfly @ The Arches, too.) **Open** Sunday 2300-0300 **Price** £6-8-10

Up @ The Venue
15-21 Calton Road, Edinburgh EH8 8DL Phone 0131 557 3073
E-mail info@upclub.co.uk Web www.upclub.co.uk
This is the club with 'that' bouncy castle and two rooms with good-

sized dance floors. The main room plays chunky progressive US house, and the second plays progressive trance with an atmosphere. The club has a capacity for 800 and not all are gay, in fact, this is another integrated club night where sexuality is not an issue. During the summer the club usually stays open 'til about 0500 in the morning. These dates are not rigidly fixed so if you tell yourself that your night will end at 0300 – it makes for a nice surprise when you find you are able to dance for an extra couple of hours. There is a dress code of no shirts, ties or football strips – but anything else goes! Bear in mind that there is a theme for each 'Up' and it usually involves you getting dressed in one outfit or another. For those who do make the effort there are limited free admission places, usually to the first five who turn up in the appropriate theme costume. **Open** Every last Friday 2230-0300 **Price** £6

Saunas

Number 18 Sauna

18 Albert Place, Edinburgh EH7 5HN Phone 0131 553 3222
E-mail info@number18sauna.co.uk Web www.number18sauna.co.uk
Facilities include a Jacuzzi, twelve-man steam room, sauna cabin, communal and private rest rooms, TV lounge and more. **Open** Sunday-Friday 1200-2200. Saturday 1200-2300 **Price** £8

Townhouse Sauna

53 East Claremont Street, Edinburgh EH7 4HU Phone 0131 556 6116
E-mail info@townhouse-sauna.co.uk Web www.townhouse-sauna.co.uk
Townhouse Sauna occupies four floors in a grand Georgian townhouse. It must rank as one of the most luxurious gay saunas and gyms in the United Kingdom and is certainly the largest in Scotland. The basement houses two sauna cabins, a steam room and an extra-large Jacuzzi. Off this area is the all-new video lounge and darkened Kruze Zone. Upstairs you will find the smoking and non-smoking TV lounges and licensed bar area. Here, members relax and read the daily newspapers with a refreshing drink. As a member you're welcome to help yourself to complimentary tea and coffee, or you can purchase a freshly prepared meal or snack from the café. Throughout the week there are several offers available to entice you in, for example: Monday is free admission if you are between the ages of 18 and 22 (proof of identity required). Wednesday offers discounted admission of £12 per couple. On Thursday, more discounts allowing you to get in for £6 if you are here before 1600. And Friday sees beer and spirit prices slashed in half for the day. There's also a bears meeting which takes place on the first Saturday of the month and Sunday offers students the opportunity to get £1 off admission (NUS card required). **Open** Sunday-Thursday 1200-2300. Saturday-Sunday 1200-0000 **Price** £6-9, plus £2 annual membership

Accommodation

Alexander Palms Guest House

63 Brunswick Street, Edinburgh Phone 0131 556 5094
E-mail alexander@gayscotland.com Web gayscotland.com/alexander
An exclusively mixed non-smoking gay guest-house practically on the doorstep of the majority of gay venues in Edinburgh. This beautifully

restored Victorian residence features polished floors and marbled fire-places. All rooms have TV and video (a selection of videos are available for guests' use) and an extended continental buffet breakfast is available 'til midday. As a resident of the hotel you can also gain concession tickets to Townhouse Sauna (see separate listing). There is also a self-catering apartment available to let (phone for more details). Alexander Palms is the sister venue to the men-only Alva House (see separate listing). **Price** £39-59 **Number of rooms** 4, 1 en-suite

Alva House   45 Alva Place, Edinburgh EH7 5AX Phone 0131 558 1382
Fax 0131 556 8279 E-mail alvahouse@gayscotland.com
Web www.gayscotland.com/alvahouse
This men-only guest-house occupies a prime position in the Abbeyhill Colonies, itself an area of historical and architectural interest. Built in the 1860s to provide simple housing for local workers and artisans, the present owners have transformed this traditional stone-built residence into a stylish and comfortable guest-house. Alva House is just a short ten-minute walk from the bustling Broughton Street, the focal point for Edinburgh's gay community. The rainbow flag is a familiar sight in this particular neighbourhood, and is your assurance of a warm welcome in the many gay-owned shops, bars, cafés and other businesses. An expanded continental breakfast buffet is served each morning from 0800 'til midday in the kitchen. Fresh fruit and juice, cereals, croissants and muffins are on the menu, complemented by tea, coffee and hot chocolate. Breakfast, seated around the table in the kitchen, provides an ideal opportunity to exchange information with your host as well as your fellow travellers. **Price** £40-59 **Number of rooms** 5, 1 en-suite

Aries Guest   5 Upper Gilmore Place, Edinburgh EH3 9NW Phone 0131 229 4669
House   A two-star gay-friendly guest-house in the city centre, close to the gay pubs and clubs. Reasonable rates and a good location ensures that this property is pretty much always full, so book well in advance. **Price** £30-£50 **Number of rooms** 5

Children's letters to Santa Claus have a fair chance of landing up in Edinburgh! You see, Father Christmas has two addresses. Letters addressed to 'The North Pole' have to be sent to The North Pole, since, obviously, the place exists. Letters addressed to 'Toyland' or 'Snowland', however, for some reason, go to Edinburgh!

Devon House   2 Pittville Street, Portobello, Edinburgh EH15 2BY
Guesthouse   Phone 0131 669 6067 Fax 0131 669 6067
Devon House is an elegant Victorian detached villa, situated in the peaceful residential area of Portobello, adjacent to the promenade and beach. Edinburgh city centre is only 15 minutes away. Accommodation at this friendly guest-house comprises six bedrooms (four with private facilities), including single, double, twin, triple and family rooms. All are attractively decorated and have TV, tea/coffee-making facilities and are centrally heated. Portobello is situated on the A1 and is close to the city bypass. Buses to the city centre include numbers 15, 26, 85 and 86,

which run approximately every 15 minutes. After midnight there are hourly night buses. There is also a regular rail service to Glasgow which runs every 30 minutes from Waverley and Haymarket stations. **Price £36-50 Number of rooms** 6, 4 en-suite

Garlands Guest House 48 Pilrig Street, Edinburgh EH6 5AL Phone 0131 554 4205
E-mail bill@garlands.demon.co.uk Web www.garlands.demon.co.uk
Garlands is a fully non-smoking guest-house among a row of Georgian terraces. There are six well-appointed rooms – single, double and twin, with some rooms able to accommodate three or four sharing. All rooms are en-suite with shower and toilet, as well as TV and tea/coffee-making facilities (a kettle!). The house is fully centrally heated and you can control the temperature to suit your own requirements. Garlands is a realistic 15-minute walk to the centre of town and there is an excellent and frequent bus service from the end of the road. And yes, Garlands was named after Judy. It's a long story! **Price £60-70 Number of rooms** 6, all en-suite

Mansfield House 57 Dublin Street, Edinburgh EH3 6NL Phone 0131 556 7980
Fax 0131 466 1315 E-mail mansfieldhouse@cableinet.co.uk
Web www.mansfieldguesthouse.com
An exclusively gay guest-house based in the Georgian new town district of Edinburgh. The location is central to Edinburgh's gay scene and main tourist attractions, all of which are within easy walking distance. En-suite rooms have mini-fridges and all the rooms have dining tables for the self-service continental breakfast, which is available until midday. Check-out time is 1200 and rooms are generally made available from 1400. Mansfield House is almost always busy, so advance booking is advised. **Price £60-70 Number of rooms** 9, 6 en-suite

Park View Villa 254 Ferry Road, Edinburgh EH5 3AN Phone 0131 552 3456
E-mail enquiries@parkviewvilla.com Web www.parkviewvilla.com
Park View Villa is a gay-owned and gay-friendly (but not exclusively gay) guest-house located just over a mile away from the centre of Edinburgh. The property is a beautiful terraced Victorian villa which has been trading as a guest-house since the 1920s and manages to evoke the atmosphere and splendour of that period whilst providing modern home comforts in tastefully decorated and furnished rooms, all of

which have either a shower room or bathroom, colour TV and tea/coffee-making facilities. There is also a large guest lounge, which has an open fire (lovely on a winter's evening) and a large dining room serving full Scottish breakfasts that get many favourable comments in the visitor's book! Vegetarians are catered for too. Groups as many in number as 18 can be accommodated for and your hosts Stuart and Gary can provide dinner if required at an additional rate. The house enjoys spectacular views over George Heriot's rugby ground, towards all the well-known Edinburgh landmarks including Arthur's Seat, Calton Hill and Edinburgh Castle. **Price** £40-60 **Number of rooms** 7, all en-suite

Cruising grounds

Calton Hill

Night-time activity can be found here. The Regent Terrace side is the area that you are after. Avoid the actual hill, as it can be a little bit dangerous. Earlier this year newspaper reports highlighted a spate of queer-bashings in this part of Edinburgh. Be extra-careful.

Warriston Cemetery

Not the most appropriate place for cruising activities and it is hoped that a more suitable location will be used. During the hours of daylight there are people walking their dogs and, of course, everyday visitors to the cemetery, making the area unsuitable. How about trying the Townhouse or Number 18 saunas?

Retail

Bobbies Bookshop

220 Morrison Street, Edinburgh EH3 8EA Phone 0131 538 7069
This is a mixed book-shop selling a good selection of UK and imported gay magazines. **Open** Monday-Saturday 1000-1730

Fantasies

8b Drummond Street, Edinburgh EH8 9TU Phone 0131 557 9413
This is a licensed sex shop selling all manner of things that you tend to keep under your bed. On the ground floor there is a good selection of gay men's videos, toys and magazines. Upstairs, the slings, rubber and leatherwear. There is also a sister venue on Easter Road (unlicensed) where you will find the glamour wear and rubber wear items that do not need the licence. **Open** Monday-Saturday 1000-2100. Sunday 1200-2100

Leather and Lace

25 Easter Road, Edinburgh EH7 5PJ Phone 0131 623 6969

The unlicensed sister shop to Fantasies on Drummond Street. This venue sells glamour wear, rubber wear and accoutrements that do not need a sex shop licence. **Open** Monday-Saturday 1200-1800. Sunday 1200-1600

Glasgow

Map key

1 Aurall @ MAS	**9** MacSorleys Bar
2 Bennets	**10** Moda
3 Candle Bar	**11** OOT in Glasgow (off)
4 Centurion Health Club & Sauna	**12** Planet Peach
5 Court Bar	**13** The Polo Lounge
6 Delmonicas	**14** Revolver Bar
7 Fruitfly @ The Arches	**15** Sadie Frosts
8 The Lane	**16** The Waterloo

Glasgow has seen more changes in the past two decades than almost any other UK city. From a declining industrial centre with widespread pessimism about its future, Glasgow has been transformed into a forward-looking city and one of the hippest spots in Europe. In a recent survey Glasgow was voted the coolest city in Britain, not so much for the weather – more for the attitude of the people, and all it takes is one night on the town in this fine city to make you realise that this is no hyped-up claim. As Glasgow is a sprawling city there is no city centre as such although George Square is deemed to be the centre with the railway stations and coach station close by. It is also a city of cultural opportunity with free museums and galleries vying for the attention of locals as well as tourists. The city that had an ill-founded reputation of crime and commercial lacklustre is now firmly on track as a 'not to be missed' tourist location.

For visitors that tire of the city's delights, Glasgow offers easy access to some of Scotland's beautiful mountains, glens, lochs and unspoilt coastline. Loch Lomond, for instance, is only 20 miles away. The city's northern latitude means that although summer days are long and light, the weather tends to be unpredictable throughout the year and can be particularly cold and wet in winter.

Getting there

Airport

Glasgow Airport (0141 887 1111) just south-west of the city is Scotland's busiest. Paisley's **Gilmour Street** railway station is the nearest to the airport (about two miles away) with regular trains to and from **Central Station**. Alternatively, the frequent no. 905 bus service will take you directly to Glasgow's city centre with drop-off points at various locations in the city. There is also **Prestwick International Airport** (01292 511 211) which is about 30 miles south of the city. It serves flights to various UK and European destinations and many of the budget airlines operate from here. It has the distinct advantage of having its own railway station but there are also coach services direct from the city centre operated by Stagecoach bus company for the 50 minute journey to Buchannon Street.

Ferry

Travel via the Renfrew/Yoker Ferry. This ferry route is one of the oldest in Scotland and is the only remaining local ferry crossing of the River Clyde. The ferry operates from Monday to Saturday between the hours of 0630 and 2130 and on Sunday from 1000 to 1830. Christmas and New Year are the only times the service closes. For more information contact **Renfrew Ferry Enquiries** (0141 885 2123).

Trains

Trains for The Highlands and the frequent services to Edinburgh depart from **Queen Street** (and whilst you're waiting you can always pop down to Sadie Frosts which is situated just beneath – see separate pub listing). Only walking distance away is **Central Station** which is where trains to the south arrive and depart. It has two levels (as well as a tube station). The upper level is for mainline trains to London, Manchester and the like, whilst the lower level is for local and suburban services. Both **Virgin West Coast** (who are normally cheaper) and occasionally **GNER** (via the east coast) operate services to London so you can pick which one to take your chances with. Phone **National Rail Enquiries** (08457 48 49 50) for further details. **Strathclyde Passenger Transport** (0141 848 4330) will be able to answer questions about train and tube services.

Coaches

The combined bus and coach station is situated two blocks north of **Queen Street** station on North Hanover Street (0141 332 7133). The ticket office is open daily from 0630 to 2230 (except Sundays; 0700 to 2230). There is also a luggage storage facility available here daily from 0630 until 2230.

Getting about

Tube

Although Glasgow has a tube system, known locally as 'The Clockwork Orange', you couldn't really call it extensive. Still, the bright orange trains are reasonable, reliable and serve stops between the city centre and the west end on its one circular line.

Buses

Scottish Citylink will be able to give you information on bus services that operate across Glasgow (0990 505 050). The buses are plentiful and routes criss-cross the city.

Taxis

Glasgow is served by a fleet of black taxi cabs ranked outside all railway and coach stations. There is private competition though, one of which is **City Cars** (0141 434 1212).

Tourist information

The Glasgow Visitor Centre is situated on 11 George Square (0141 204 4400). This office can arrange hotel bookings (at a fee of £2 per room) and there are also bureau de change facilities here. Opening hours are Monday to Saturday from 0900 to 2000 and Sunday from 1000 to 2000.

Bureaux de change

There is an **American Express** office at 115 Hope Street (0141 221 4366). Your next-best option is the high street banks.

Getting help

Police and hospital

Glasgow Central police station is situated on Stewart Street (0141 532 2000). Glasgow has two hospitals with accident and emergency facilities: **Glasgow Royal Infirmary** 84 Castle Street (0141 211 4000) and **Western Infirmary** Dumbarton Road (0141 211 2000).

Getting in touch

Internet

You can wiggle a mouse and download your mail in Glasgow. **The Internet Café**, 569 Sauchiehall Street is open Monday to Sunday from 0900 'til as late as 2300. There's also **Java Internet Café** at 152 Park Road and the always-open **Easy Everything** at 57-61 St Vincent Street.

GLBT Helplines

Glasgow's **Lesbian and Gay Switchboard** (0141 332 8372) is accessible daily from 1900 to 2200 and can help and instruct on most gay-specific matters. There is also **Lesbian Line** (0141 354 0400) which runs every Wednesday evening from 1930 to 2200. **Glasgow GLBT Centre** at 11 Dixon Street (0141 221 7203 and www.gglc.org.uk) aims to develop into a truly inclusive space that will be seen as a beacon in the west of Scotland for all members of the LGBT community. They welcome drop in visits or phone calls. They can offer advice, support and referrals. They also rent office space to HIV prevention agencies (**Steve Retson Project**), **Stonewall Scotland**, **Phace West** (a BGL youth group) and they also have a shop and café on their premises. They are open from Monday to Sunday between the hours of 1000 and 0000.

Pubs

Candle Bar

20 Candleriggs, Glasgow G1 1LD Phone 0141 564 1285

This recently refurbished bar in the heart of the merchant city is bright, modern and trendy and is fast becoming the place to be seen. Cabaret is provided on Tuesdays and Thursdays, there's a DJ most nights and the old faithful karaoke appears on Sunday. **Open** Monday-Sunday 1200-0000

Court Bar

69 Hutcheson Street, Glasgow G1 1SH Phone 0141 552 2463

Situated in the heart of the Merchant City and close to most of the other gay bars in Glasgow, Court Bar is a small, friendly pub where you are guaranteed excellent service at all times. The music is predominantly '60s, '70s and '80s and is played at a level that allows for conversation while you are standing in the bar or seated with your friends. Court Bar has a breakfast licence, enabling you to roll in from the clubs on a week-day morning in order to get something hot inside of you. The complete gay press is available, as are discounted tickets to the local gay clubs. This place can be rather straight during the day, with the suits popping in from the nearby offices, but in the evening it gets gayer, particularly pre-Bennets (see separate club listing). **Open** Monday-Saturday 0800-0000. Sunday 1230-0000 **Tube** St Enoch Square

Delmonicas

68 Virginia Street, Glasgow G1 1TX Phone 0141 552 4803

E-mail **delmonicas@poloounge.co.uk** Web **www.pololounge.co.uk**

Young and attitude-filled boys and girls populate this large, modern bar, the sister venue to The Polo Lounge and Moda (see separate listings). The music tends to be a bit predictable each night and the bar feels rather cliquey so it's not wise to come here without your mates. Monday is perhaps one of the best nights around for skinflints as cheap drinks are on offer right throughout the day, however, don't make a special journey as the regular happy hours (which are good) are available every day (from 1200 to 1400, from 1700 to 1900 and from 2100 to 2200) where all pints and mainline spirits are only £1.30. From Friday through to Sunday you are able to get £2 passes (free on Sunday) from Delmonicas into The Polo Lounge if you buy a drink at Delmonicas after 2300. There is some sort of entertainment every night, from games and bingo on a Wednesday (is it me or is this another night to avoid?) to quiz night... yawn .. on a Thursday. The rest of the week focuses on camp classics or cheesy classics or sometimes both! Oh! and before you think it cannot be that bad – karaoke is on a Sunday... another big yawn. **Open** Monday-Sunday 1200-0000 **Tube** St Enoch Square

MacSorleys Bar

42 Jamaica Street, Glasgow G1 4QG Phone 0141 248 8581

MacSorleys is noted for being the second oldest bar in Glasgow – some 102 years old! An open-plan room with several tiers and a small balcony gives plenty of scope to mingle or just sit and chat. Live bands play regularly through the week, providing an original alternative to tired old karaoke. This is not an exclusively gay bar – on the contrary, it is a bar that welcomes everyone, irrespective of their sexuality, particularly the thirty-somethings who want to sample 'the scene' without it being too full-on and in-your-face. Not really suitable for the young disco dollies. **Open** Monday-Saturday 1200-0000. Sunday 1230-0000

Moda

58 Virginia Street, Glasgow G1 1TX Phone **0141 553 1221**
E-mail info@pololounge Web **www.pololounge.co.uk**
At the time of writing this café-bar had not even opened, however, the few details I could muster are as follows: Moda will be style-orientated and label-trendy, fitting in somewhere between Polo Lounge (posh) and Delmonicas (not as posh). Moda will be situated in the old Café Latte space – a space that is due to be totally gutted and restyled to turn it into the ideal place for the pre-Polo clubbers. There will be a door at the back of the venue that opens up at 2300 allowing free entry access into the club and if you are not in before 2300 you will have to pay the £5 admission – that is unless you have bought a drink at Dels after 2300 and gained the discounted pass from the bar. **Open** Monday-Thursday 1700-0100. Friday 1700-0300. Saturday-Sunday 1200-0300 **Price** £5, after 2300 Friday-Sunday

---

When walking through St Georges Square, take a look at the mounted Duke of Wellington to see if he is wearing his 'traffic cone hat'. It is one of the gentler demonstrations of Scottish anarchy that has near-become a national custom. It seems that every time it is removed it mysteriously returns within a short space of time – particularly on a Saturday night.

The Polo Lounge

84 Wilson Street, Glasgow G1 1UZ Phone **0141 553 1221**
E-mail info@pololounge.co.uk Web **www.pololounge.co.uk**
The Polo Lounge opened in November 1996. It comprises three bars and two dance floors and is spread over three levels. Housed in the former headquarters of the Scottish Legal Life Assurance Society, situated in the Merchant City area of Glasgow, the building took more than one year to rebuild, with complete restoration and refurbishment of all the original marblework and tiling in addition to sourcing all of the original antique furniture and fittings. The music here is pretty mainstream although Friday (Fresh) there is house and indie in the club and '80s and '90s crap being played in the Trophy Room. On Saturday nights you can get to hear some classic anthems in the club whilst camp tunes get played relentlessly in the Trophy Room. If you are at Delmonicas (their sister venue) over the weekend you can pick up a £2 admission pass if you buy a drink there after 2300. If not, and you want to have a gander at this splendid building get here well before 2300 to make sure you get in for free. **Open** Monday-Thursday 1700-0100. Friday 1700-0300. Saturday-Sunday 1200-0300 **Price** £5, after 2300 Friday-Sunday **Tube** Buchanan Street

Revolver Bar

6a John Street, Glasgow G1 1JQ Phone **0141 553 2456**
E-mail info@revolverdotbar.com Web **www.revolverdotbar.com**
The newest bar to open in Glasgow and one for the grown-ups! This is going to be catering mainly for the over-21 crowd in a space that encourages sociability and belonging. Entertainment is provided courtesy of a

free, well-stocked jukebox (3000-plus tracks) and karaoke will be a definite no-no. Plenty of seating occupies this basement bar, even bar stools, which seem to be a rarity these days – all very TV's Cheers-like. Food is available at all times and drink prices are kept to a minimum. **Open** Monday-Saturday 1100-0000. Sunday 1230-0000

Sadie Frosts 8-10 West George Street, Glasgow G2 1DR Phone 0141 332 8005
The sister venue to Bennets, this trendy and quite up-market bar seems to be attracting the straight crowds whilst disenfranchising themselves from the gay community that has served them so well over the years. If you find you want to give it a go you will find it situated under Queen Street station. **Open** Monday-Sunday 1200-0000 **Tube** Buchanan Street

The Waterloo 306 Argyle Street, Glasgow G2 8LY Phone 0141 229 5891
The oldest gay bar in Glasgow, The Waterloo has a good reputation for being a friendly and inviting watering hole. All ages bar-hop through here at some time during the evening from the very young through to the very old and a fair amount of girls can be seen propping up the bar alongside a predominantly male clientele. There's a DJ that takes to the decks from Thursday through to Sunday and a camp bingo session that releases its balls every Sunday. **Open** Monday-Saturday 1200-0000. Sunday 1230-0000

Clubs

Bennets 80-90 Glassford Street, Glasgow G1 1UR Phone 0141 552 5761
E-mail info@bennets.co.uk Web www.bennets.co.uk
Bennets is Glasgow's longest-running gay night club, having been in operation since 1981 and still thriving. The addition of a new floor to the venue in the summer of 1998 has also made Bennets the biggest. Bennets has seen an extensive list of performances from well-established acts (Wet Wet Wet, Sister Sledge and Take That – who? I hear all you non-British residents cry) and they still continue to have weekly PAs from chart acts and up-and-coming bands. There are nightly drink promotions as well as the naturally popular Sunday drinks night (where all beers and spirits are only £1.25, which, incidentally, is subject to change). All this then, in addition to probably the best DJs in Scotland, namely Karen Dunbar, Sara Martinella, John Fraser and Grant Duff. Weekends see this place absolutely packed with long queues running right down the road. **Open** Tuesday (straight night) and Wednesday-Sunday 2300-0300 **Price** £3-6 **Tube** Buchanan Street

Club nights

Aurall @ MAS 23-29 Royal Exchange Square, Glasgow G1 3AJ Phone 0131 557 4656
E-mail info@masclubbing.com Web www.masclubbing.com
From the promoters of Fruitfly and Taste comes a relatively new weekly Sunday nighter for a mixed gay and straight crowd who just cannot let go of the weekend. Despite the fantastic cheap joke mileage of its name, Aurall is a club for those that love their garage and house. There are two

rooms offering sheer musical pleasure and an extremely friendly atmosphere, where the focus is on harmonious bump and grind set against a background of quality beats. Fischer and Price (Fruitfly), Princess Julia and other top jocks (sorry, no pun intended!) will be making their presence heard on rotation each week, and the precise line-up will be advertised well in advance. **Open** Sunday 2300-0300 **Price** £5-7

Fruitfly @ The Arches

Midland Street, Glasgow G1 Phone 0141 404 1510
E-mail info@fruitfly-club.com Web www.fruitfly-club.com
Fruitfly is a sister club of Taste (see separate Edinburgh listing), with a combined membership of over 3,000 people. Fruitfly attracts well over 600 up-for-it anything-goes clubbers, attracted by the talents of residents Fisher and Price, who play everything from garage to hard, pumping house. They are joined regularly by guests of international standing whose music fits in well with the Fruitfly sound. Amongst the recent visitors have been Dimitri (Amsterdam), The Sharp Boys, Mark Moore and Rob di Stefano – all of whom have visited more than once. Meet up at (friendly, straight) pre-club venue Soba on Mirchel Lane to see who you'll be bumping into later on in the evening. Ask for reduced price passes at the bar whilst you're there. Fruitfly have created a club environment free of prejudice and bad attitudes, where members and their guests are guaranteed a hassle-free night in like-minded company. After almost two years, Fruitfly is now firmly established as the biggest and best gay-friendly house dance club night in Glasgow, with numbers increasing all the time. And all, purely, by word of mouth. **Open** Every third Saturday 2300-0400 **Price** £8-12 **Tube** St Enoch Square

OOT in Glasgow

Stand Comedy Club, 333 Woodlands Road, Glasgow G3 6NG
Phone 0870 600 6055 E-mail admin@thestand.freeserve.co.uk
Web www.thestand.co.uk
Something completely different to the usual pub and club outing. OOT (Out On Tuesday – yes, I know it's on a Sunday!) originated in Edinburgh, and so successful was that night that The Stand brought it down to Glasgow – but kept the original name – a-ha! A headline act and two supporting acts, usually up-and-coming talent, do all they can to make you laugh and all this is held neatly in place by your regular host for the evening, Craig Hill. The very popular Gay Blind Date competition has also been imported from Edinburgh with the winners being treated to a meal for two in some local salubrious eaterie – yes, in Glasgow! **Open** Every second Sunday 2030-2230 **Price** £5

Planet Peach

32-34 Queen Street, Glasgow G1 3DX Phone 0141 226 8990
Planet Peach goes gay twice a week on Monday and Tuesday with Aqueerious on a Monday (handbag and chart) and Passionality on a Tuesday (a harder club dance music style). Flyers are available from most gay bars throughout the city and they offer discounted entry on a Monday. Both nights do get rather busy, although Passionality on the Tuesday slightly has the edge there and is the better night of the two. **Open** Monday-Tuesday 2300-0200 **Price** £3

Saunas

Centurion Health Club and Sauna

19 Dixon Street, Glasgow G1 4AL Phone 0141 248 4485
E-mail centurionspa@gay.com Web www.centurionspa.co.uk
Loads of changes have happened to the Centurion this past year. New management have come in and made some sweeping changes to the venue. First off, the cum-soaked carpets, curtains and chairs have been binned and replaced by more hygienic wipe-clean materials. New showers have been installed and the dark room has been turned into a sexy construction zone. Not too much work can be instilled upon this venue though, since the whole building is due to be demolished in 2002! Fear not though; new, bigger premises will be bought in order for you to carry on your... erm... health and fitness regime. For the time being, Centurion is getting better day by day (I am aware of the previous problems, but these are being sorted out). The numbers are increasing and the age range is widening. If you have been here before and encountered a problem I'd recommend you return and give it another go. **Open** Sunday-Friday 1200-2200. Saturday 1200-0500 (all-nighter) **Price** £9.50 **Tube** St Enoch Square

The Lane

60 Robertson Lane, off Argyle Street, Glasgow G2 8HZ
Phone 0141 221 1802
Ideally situated across from The Waterloo Bar, The Lane has been completely refurbished and will no doubt be as popular as ever now. Sauna, steam room and rest rooms are probably all that you lot are interested in and that is pretty much all that you'll get. This is an affordably cheap alternative to the cruising grounds that are these days becoming rather more risky. **Open** Monday-Friday 1300-2200. Saturday-Sunday 1200-2200 **Price** £8

Accommodation

Albion Hotel

405-407 North Woodside Road, Glasgow G20 6NN Phone 0141 339 8620 Fax 0141 334 8159 E-mail albion@glasgowhotelsandapartments.co.uk
Set back from the bustling Great Western Road and tucked in a quiet cul-de-sac in the heart of Glasgow's fashionable West End is the Albion Hotel. Extremely gay-friendly, although neither gay-owned or -run, it offers a warm and friendly welcome to guests from all over. The Albion is ideally located close to Glasgow University, the Botanic Gardens, Kelvingrove Park, Western Infirmary, BBC Studios and many other visitor attractions, as well as countless restaurants, cafés, bistros and bars. It is also just one mile from the city centre and only a minute's walk from Kelvin Bridge tube station. They are close too to the access road to and from Glasgow International Airport and to Junction 17 off the M8 motorway (which runs through the centre of Glasgow from east to west). All guest rooms have en-suite facilities, courtesy tea/coffee, refrigerator, colour TV, direct dial phone, safe, iron, ironing board, trouser press and hair dryer. **Price** £54 **Number of rooms** 16, all en-suite **Tube** Kelvinbridge (one minute)

Cruising grounds

Kelvingrove Park

This park is as famous as Manchester Canal and Hampstead Heath put together. It's well known: be cautious. For outsiders, the place to be heading for is the area opposite the university tower (after dark). The punters tend to be young and adventurous. Note: Kelvin Way is a straight road that runs through the park, actually splitting it in two, and it is not rare to see the same car driving past twice, especially after it gets dark. As with similar large open grounds, it seems extremely prudent to have a walk around the area during daylight in order to become familiar with escape routes as well as the spots where the action takes place.

Queens Park

You want the Victoria Road side of the park. Use the entrance at the bottom of the road. Alternatively, enter the area via Polockshaws Road. Cruising goes on at the top of the park in the area behind the flagpole.

Retail

Clone Zone

GGLC, 11 Dixon Street, Glasgow G1 4AL Phone 0141 248 2593
E-mail info@clonezone.co.uk Web www.clonezone.co.uk
Clone Zone has its own unit situated within the Glasgow Lesbian and Gay Centre. **Open** Monday-Saturday 1100-2100. Sunday 1200-1900

Silks and Secrets

308 Argyle Street, Glasgow G2 8LY Phone 0141 572 1017
A very friendly fetish wear and lingerie shop. It caters for all markets including TV/TS. Magazines and toys are also available. **Open** Monday-Saturday 1000-1745. Sunday 1200-1700

Kirkcaldy Cruising grounds

Ravenscraig Park

Ravenscraig Park gets a lot of night-time action. It is best to park in the first car park and walk through the trees towards the sea. This area can be very dark so you must have your wits about you.

Largs Cruising grounds

A78 Sea Front

(Fairlie) The sea front toilets by the picnic area at night can be a hive of activity. It is advisable to park in the picnic area and walk along the sea front to take in some air. The toilets are open 24 hours although it is safer to cruise the front rather than the cottage.

Motherwell Cruising grounds

Strathclyde Country Park

This place can be good at times. There are lots of small car parks with plenty going on in the bushes.

Wales

5

5

The peace and tranquility of the Welsh landscape gives a somewhat false notion of its turbulent history. The Romans occupied Britain for 400 years but never succeeded in entirely conquering Wales. In Caerwent, the beautifully constructed core of the Roman town wall still fascinates archaeologists today, despite the fact that much of its facing stone has been re-used in local houses and farms. The Romans were succeeded by the Saxons, the Picts, the Vikings and the Normans. And it wasn't until parliamentary acts between the years 1536 and 1543 that Wales was finally unified with England.

Wales' history is one of struggle against invaders from within and outside of mainland Britain. It has left Wales with more castles per square mile than any other country in Western Europe. The sweet irony of these great monuments is that they contribute so much to the outstanding beauty of the Welsh landscape.

Abergele Cruising grounds

Abergele Beach   Late in the evenings straight couples meet up for a snog and a poke, whilst gay men cruise the area near to the public toilet block (who says we can't get along together?). The area gets quite active during the hot summer months and forms part of a circuit along with the goings-on at Rhyl (see separate listing). What with the lack of gay facilities on the North Wales coast and locals who aren't willing to travel the distance to Manchester or Chester, even the winter months can prove to be quite fruitful.

Anglesey Cruising grounds

Llanddwyn Beach   Access to the beach is easiest from Newborough on the west coast of Anglesey. Follow the signs to the beach and park up in the designated car park. When you get on to the beach, turn left and walk for about 15 minutes. The high dunes constitute the start of the cruising ground. This area is particularly busy during the summer months. Anglesey attracts a lot of visitors, who stay in the many caravan parks surrounding the area, so do be careful.

Cardiff

It is hard to believe that Cardiff only became the capital of Wales less than 50 years ago. It used to be just a sleepy provincial seat. The rise of the coal industry changed all that and Cardiff burst into prominence in the late 19th century when it served as the main port for Welsh coal. It has been home to the Welsh regional government since the 1997 vote for devolution. Today's Cardiff, after extensive redevelopment, is now home to a world-class opera house, superb museums, excellent sporting venues and a vibrant night-life, situated mainly around Cardiff Bay (originally known as Tiger Bay) – the recently rejuvenated docklands area. This area is about two miles south of today's city centre, but in many ways this part of the city can lay just claim to being its 'centre', since it was this area's industry that transformed Cardiff from a small village into a thriving city. The gay quarter is based on and around Charles Street, in the city centre, by Queens Arcade.

Getting there

Airport   Cardiff is served by its own international airport at **Rhoose**, a 20-minute drive from the city centre, with regular direct flights from European destinations. Intercontinental flights to Cardiff are best served via Amsterdam Airport. Those who prefer to travel via London Heathrow Airport can continue their journey to Cardiff by high-speed Inter-City train or coach.

Trains	**Central Station,** Central Square is situated south of the centre behind the bus station. **The Travel Centre** is open Monday to Saturday from 0900 to 1800 and on Sunday from 1200 to 1630.
Coaches	**National Express** on Wood Street operate a travel centre and booking office. Their opening hours run Monday to Saturday from 0700 to 1745 and Sunday from 0900 to 1745.

Getting about

Buses	**Bws Caerdydd** or Cardiff Bus (029 2039 6521) on Wood Street run an extensive network of orange buses through Cardiff and the surrounding areas. The timetable is not always as reliable as it should be, so be sure to arrive at least five minutes earlier than the departure time shown.
Taxis	**Metro Cabs** (029 2046 4646) and **Supatax** (029 2022 6644), both run 24 hours and are ranked outside the train and bus stations.
Tourist information	The main office is situated at **Central Railway Station** on Central Square (029 2022 7281). They offer free, detailed maps showing all the city-centre sights. Their hours run Monday to Saturday from 0900 to 1830 and Sunday from 1000 to 1600. Tour operators **Leisurelink** (029 2052 2202) run a one-hour bust tour, visiting about 19 or so sites (phew!) and this service leaves from the main gate at Cardiff Castle every half-hour or so. Charges are in the region of £7 with discounts available to students.
Bureaux de change	**The American Express** office is at 3 Queen Street (029 2066 8858) and is open Monday to Friday from 0900 to 1730 and Saturday from 0900 to 1700. There are also bureau de change facilites available at the main post office at 2-4 Hill's Street, off The Hayes, as well as the city centre high street banks.

Getting help

Police, hospital and pharmacy	The main police station is based at the **Civic Centre,** opposite Cathays Park. For non-emergency assistance phone 029 2022 2111. **Cardiff Royal Infirmary** is at 50 Newport Road (029 2049 2233) and a list of late-night chemists is held at the police station.

Getting in touch

Internet	Just two of a selection that are now popping up in the city centre: **Cardiff Cyber Café,** 9 Duke Street is open Monday to Sunday from 1000 to 2200 and **Grassroots Cyber Café,** 58 Charles Street is open Monday to Saturday from 1200 to 1800.
GLBT Helplines	The main gay switchboard for Cardiff is **Cardiff Friend** (029 2034 0101). You can also contact **Cardiff Lesbian Line** between 2000 and 2200 (029 2037 4051) and **Cardiff Youthline** from 2030 to 2130 (029 2034 0101).

5

Pubs

The Golden Cross

283 Hayes Bridge Road, Cardiff CF10 1GH Phone 029 2039 4556

A long-established traditional gay venue which caters for a wide spectrum of the gay community from the very young to the very old. Food is served every day and two meals can be bought for only a fiver with Sunday lunch for £4.25. Wednesday is 241 (buy one get one free). Thursday is Quiz Night with the most popular question being 'What would you like to do to Anne Robinson?' and Friday is Strip Night. Each night the music is turned up and a disco takes place with the usual cheesy, charty, camp sounds. **Open** Monday-Wednesday 1200-2300. Thursday-Saturday 1200-0100. Sunday 1200-2430

Kings Cross

Mill Lane / Caroline Street, The Hayes, Cardiff CF1 1FF
Phone 029 2064 9891

Kings Cross is the oldest establishment on Cardiff's gay scene and has been running for about 28 years. It has a rather raw and down-to-earth atmosphere and is still the choice of the younger end of the market. It is not a large venue – one floor and one bar is all you get – but there is always something going on throughout the week to keep you entertained. For example, Sunday sees the atrocious and wickedly funny Fanny Dazzle hosting the karaoke. Wednesday is a drag duo and each Thursday is Bears and Braces a no-dress-code men-only night, particularly for bears and... erm... braces! **Open** Monday-Wednesday 1100-2300. Thursday-Saturday 1100-0100. Sunday 1200-0000

Caerdydd, as Cardiff is known by those who speak the language, comes from the word 'caer' meaning fortress. Fitting then, that its most famous and perhaps beautiful landmark is its castle, to be found in the unlikely setting of its city centre. Inside and out, the Victorian additions startle and dazzle. The interiors are decorated flamboyantly (perhaps 'camply' is a more apt description), indeed, so flamboyantly that you'd be forgiven for missing the castle's medieval features. Astrological symbols, nature's creatures, the pleasures of the seasons, biblical characters dressed in gilt robes, Moorish designs and heraldic features – these are some of the themes that run rampant throughout Bute's famous castle.

Out Bar and Club

Harlech Court, Bute Terrace, Cardiff CF1 2FE Phone 029 2022 4756

This is a large pub and club venue in the building that was formerly known as Atlantica Bar and Wow nightclub. The Out Club is open from Wednesday through to Saturday only. It is a large venue with just one floor and a good up-front music policy. Wednesday is Student Night, where cheap admission and some pretty good drinks offers ensure a full house. The Out Bar has regular cabaret and drag acts, including spots from Dr Bev Ballcrusher and Miss Kitty. Resident DJs provide you with a mix of music and there are regular drinks promotions. **Open** (Bar Out) Monday-Saturday 1200-2300. Sunday 1200-2230. (Club Out) Wednesday-Saturday 2200-0200 **Price** £2-6

Clubs

Club X and The Edge

35-39 Charles Street, Cardiff Phone 029 2040 0876

Club X is the largest gay club in Wales, providing an attitude-free zone to the young serious clubbers of south Wales. Comprising two dance rooms – there's a choice of music that ranges from cheesy chart to hard house – a balcony area, three bars, pool room, chill-out area and a garden terrace. This is a straight-friendly venue and there is never any attitude or trouble. Weekly events currently stretch to a Student Night every Wednesday which includes a stripper. Thursday is regularly set aside for the women and Saturday sees a relatively new all-nighter that takes place from 2200-0600. Club X will soon be introducing a membership scheme, benefitting members reduced entrance fees, loyalty privileges and regular club news. **Open** Wednesday-Thursday 2200-0200. Friday 2200-0300. Saturday 2200-0400. Sunday 1900-0000 **Price** £1-5

Exit Bar

48 Charles Street, Cardiff CF1 4EF Phone 029 2064 0102

This is a popular gay bar and club situated on the main gay street in Cardiff. It attracts a positively young, mixed gay crowd. An extension was added last year which now accommodates the quieter, relaxing upstairs bar. Music in the basement club is a mix between mainstream chart and club classics. **Open** Monday-Saturday 1930-0200. Sunday 1900-0100 **Price** £1.50-3

Saunas

Locker Room

50 Charles Street, Cardiff CF10 2GF Phone 029 2022 0388
E-mail lockerroom@ntlworld.com
Web http://homepage.ntlworld.com/lockerroom

Locker Room is an intimate little sauna situated next to Exit Bar. The ground floor comprises a reception which leads through to the comfortable café area and changing room. Continuing through you come to the wet area with the sauna, steam room and Jacuzzi. On the first floor there is the video lounge (non-smoking) and TV lounge (smoking). The second floor is devoted to relaxation – either by yourself or communally! Locker Room is a clean and luxurious little sauna which gets extremely busy at weekends. **Open** Sunday-Friday 1300-2300. Saturday 1300-0600. **Price** £10 plus £2 membership

Accommodation

Courtfield Hotel

101 Cathedral Road, Cardiff CF11 9PH Phone 029 2022 7701
E-mail courtfield@ntlworld.com Web www.courtfieldhotel.co.uk

Over 100 years old and retaining some original features this hotel is set in a tree-lined conservation area that is within minutes of the city centre and Cardiff Castle. This is a licensed Victorian town-house which is ideally situated for getting around this lively, cosmopolitan city. All bedrooms include central heating, direct dial phone, Corby trouser press and welcome tray. **Price** £55 **Number of rooms** 11, 6 en-suite

Cruising grounds

Bute Park

Make your way to the area behind the Welsh College of Music and Drama. This is a busy, well-established 24-hour cruising ground. After 1800 the main cruising ground is at least a half-hour's walk from anything remotely resembling civilisation. The best way to get there is to find Cardiff Castle first. This bit is easy as it is in the centre of Cardiff and all the roads in south Wales seem to lead to it. If you stand facing the main gates, you need to turn left and follow the road all the way down, keeping the castle grounds on your right. You will pass a lot of 'stone creatures' on the right and the Forte Posthouse Hotel on the left. You'll come to a bridge, which crosses the River Taff. Just on the other side of the bridge, on your right, is an entrance into the castle grounds. If you walk through this entrance and start up the side of the river, the first (and in the summer, the least active) cruising area is about 200 yards down this path. You'll find a few guys leaning against the railings and this is your starting point. From here, carry on along the path for about a mile (it is impossible to get a vehicle down here, so it's walking only I'm afraid). Eventually, you will come to a footbridge and if you cross this into the main castle grounds you'll find the main action. Turning left after crossing the bridge will put you in the middle of the real heavy stuff, whilst a right turn will take you to the gentler cruising, and towards the area where the daytime cruising happens. In the daytime, of course, you can enter via the main castle gates (which will save you about 20 minutes of walking), but bear in mind that the grounds are heavily policed during the day and cruising is not a good idea.

Llandudno Club nights

Hellbent @ The Washington

East Promenade, Town Centre, Llandudno Phone 0788 147 8675
E-mail theboyz@hellbent.freeserve.co.uk
This monthly two-room event (dance room and cabaret/camp room) is another north Wales gay party run by the Boyz Behaving Badly team. The venue is very easy to find – just head for the seaside! Smart dress is appreciated by this mixed crowd but is not essential. This is also a drag and TV-friendly affair. There's safe on-street parking in abundance.
Open Every third Thursday 2000-late (no admission after 2300) **Price** £4

Newport Saunas

Greenhouse Health Club

24 Church Street, Newport NP20 2BY Phone 01633 221 172
E-mail info@gay-sauna.com Web www.gay-sauna.com
Another well-maintained Greenhouse sauna (sister venues in Barnsley, Luton and Darlaston – see separate listings) on three floors. The ground floor from reception leads you through to the changing rooms, snack bar and dining room. You'll also find a large shower facility, toilets, Jacuzzi steam room and sunbed room on this level. The first floor hous-

es the sauna cabin, more showers, more toilets and two TV rooms (one smoking, one non-smoking). The top floor is where you'll find the private and communal rest rooms. There are plenty of dark corners and passageways to explore and the rest areas are more than adequate. Phone the venue for directions if you need assistance. You should find it quite easy to get to though: exit Junction 27 off the M4 and head towards Newport town centre. **Open** Monday-Thursday 1100-2300. Friday 1100-0200. Saturday 1100-0300. Sunday 1200-2300 **Price** £10

Cruising grounds

A449

You want the A449 heading north from the M4/J24 towards Raglan and Abergavenny. About two miles along there is a lorry park, picnic area and lay-by on the right. If you have the time to drive along the dual carriageway to the opposite side you may find action there as well.

Penmaenmawr Saunas

Jack's Sauna

Beach Road, Penmaenmawr LL36 6AY Phone 01492 622 878
E-mail **info@gaypennanthall.co.uk** Web **www.gaypennanthall.co.uk**
Jack's Sauna is part of Pennant Hall hotel, an exclusively gay hotel and leisure complex on the north Wales, Llandudno to Bangor coast. Sauna guests are welcome to use both the hotel à la carte restaurant and licensed bar and can return to the sauna afterwards at no extra cost. Non-residents are welcome to use the sauna facilities at any time. The lack of gay venues in this part of north Wales means that this sauna is quite popular with the locals as well as visitors from the surrounding areas. A separate entrance leads into the sauna wherein you will find limited facilities including Jacuzzi, sauna cabin, steam room, TV room, sun room (and terrace) and individual rest rooms. **Open** 1230-2230 Monday-Sunday **Price** £9

Accommodation

Pennant Hall Hotel

Beach Road, Penmaenmawr LL34 6AY Phone 0800 074 0873
Fax 01492 622 875 E-mail **boyz@gaypennanthall.co.uk**
Web **www.gaypennanthall.co.uk**
Pennant Hall offers a warm welcome for gays of all ages. Arrive alone or with your partner: either way there's opportunity to make new friends in this comfortable hotel. This Edwardian villa is set in secluded grounds on the beautiful north Wales coast, ideally located for touring Llandudno, Chester, Anglesey and Puffin Island. Accommodation comprises eleven elegantly furnished en-suite bedrooms in singles, doubles and twins – all with TV and tea/coffee-making facilities. The reasonable rates include a full breakfast and guests have the use of a private residents' TV lounge. Well-trained pets are welcome too. The hotel organises regular commitment weekends where you are able to have your relationship blessed by a minister in a formal service. There are also Singles Weekends and Murder Mystery Weekend breaks organised (no arguing

who's going to be Jessica Fletcher!). For details of all these events, phone the venue direct. (See the separate listing for the adjoining Jack's Sauna.) **Price** £30-48 **Number of rooms** 11, all en-suite

Prestatyn Club nights

Hellbent @
Nova Ballroom

Central Beach, Prestatyn **Phone** 0788 147 8675
E-mail theboyz@hellbent.freeserve.co.uk
This is a large monthly gay event in one of the biggest ballrooms on the north Wales coast. Hellbent is usually held on the first Friday of the month (I'd advise you phone to confirm if you are travelling especially). Events are run by the Boyz Behaving Badly team (see separate Hellbent, Llandudno listing) with the event having a mixed music policy for the mixed boy/girl/young/not-so-young crowd! There's regular themed events and cabaret and the venue can be found within the Nova Centre leisure complex that is well signposted off the A55 and throughout the town. **Open** Every first Friday 2100-0200 **Price** £5

Rhyl Cruising grounds

Rhyl
Promenade

Make your way onto the promenade, just past the car park situated between the fairground and the Sun Centre. In the season (March to September) the area is buzzing with guys from all parts of the country, either holidaying or just up for the evening for a change of scenery. There will be straight couples milling around up until about midnight and after that an increase in the gays 'til at least 0300. Ages, because of the area and lack of gay pubs and clubs, will be wide-ranging. Off-season you will still be able to find action, as the locals from all the surrounding districts would otherwise have to travel to Chester for a decent night out.

Swansea

Swansea is one of Wales' most beautiful and unspoilt places. The Gower Peninsula was the first area of Britain to be designated as an 'area of outstanding natural beauty'. Swansea is a busy and bustling city but it is this wonderful, varied landscape located on a beautiful sweep of Swansea Bay that makes it such an attraction to tourists the world over. And it's just as well, 'cause there's only a handful of gay places to keep you occupied. Check out the tourist centre for alternative thumb-twiddling ideas.

Getting in touch

Swansea Tourism (01792 468 321) is the main tourist office and can be found on Singleton Street. **Swansea Gay Switchboard** (01792 301 855) runs rom 1900 until 2200 every Tuesday and offers help and advice on all matters gay, lesbian and bisexual. There is a dedicated **Lesbian Line** too (01792 651 995), operational on Wednesdays from 1900 to 2100 and an **HIV/AIDS Line** (01792 546 303) which you can call on Thursdays between 1500 and 2000.

Pubs

Champers Wine Bar   210 High Street, Swansea SA1 1PE Phone 01792 655 622
This is a very friendly mixed gay venue which caters for all of the gay community. Entertainment changes throughout the week, but usually there is karaoke on Thursday and a disco over the weekend. There are several monthly events organised (theme parties and such), so keep an eye on the board for details. Champers Wine Bar also serves as the pre-H20 meeting-up place. **Open** 1100-2300 Monday-Saturday. 1100-2230 Sunday

---

Swansea Museum is Wales' oldest museum, open since 1841. Swansea's most famous son, perhaps the 20th century's finest and most notorious poet, Dylan Thomas, described it as a 'museum which should be in a museum'.

Exchange Bar   10 The Strand, Swansea SA1 2AE Phone 01792 645 345
This is a friendly gay bar with a disco on Saturday evenings. **Open** Monday-Saturday 1200-2300. Sunday 1500-2230

The Waterside / H2O

18 Anchor Court, Victoria Quay, Maritime Quarter, Swansea SA1 3XA
Phone 01792 648 555
E-mail gaywaterside@boyznow.net Web www.gaywaterside.com

The Waterside (bar) and H2O (club) – somewhat resembling a giant greenhouse – is located behind Swansea's leisure centre and opposite The Industrial Maritime Museum. Throughout the day the stylish and very smart café-bar serves food ('til 1800), drink or whatever. Come the evening the lights dim, the music gets turned up and the bar metamorphoses into a fabulous and always packed pre-club space. Gays of all ages fill the place before either going home to a cocoa or moving on upstairs to the club. The H2O breakdown of weekly events is as follows: Monday is the '70s and '80s night; Tuesday and Wednesday is without a real theme as such, but the music is a bit more clubby; Thursday sees some stripper come in and give the guys an inadequacy complex (and you pay £3 for the privilege); Friday and Saturday means all the floors are open and you're treated to probably the best gay club nights in south Wales. And whilst the club rests for a day, Sunday sees Waterside take the limelight as local drag artiste Miss C. C. Swan entertains the troupes with her fun karaoke rendition. **Open** (Waterside) Monday-Saturday 1200-2300. Sunday 1200-2230. (H2O) Monday-Thursday 2230-0200. Friday-Saturday 2230-0400 **Price** £3-5, Friday-Saturday (H2O)

5

Ireland

6

The island of Ireland is split between the Republic of Ireland (Eire) to the south and the six counties of Northern Ireland, part of the United Kingdom, to the north. Eire, often overshadowed in people's minds by the troubles in the north, is a country of outstanding beauty; of picturesque villages, blue mountains, lakes and coastline; a country that can still provide a glimpse into the traditions of Irish song and dance. Belfast, in the north, is the flipside: a modern city of industry and animation. Both north and south share a love of traditional music and folklore as well as a rich artistic and historic tapestry and a vibrant heritage of pub culture, one which almost seems to sustain the warmth and welcome that Ireland is famous for.

These countries share pure air, clear water and unspoilt stretches of countryside, yet are still divided by a living history. The turbulent past and the present imperfect peace are part of the everyday consciousness and creativity of this island's people.

Belfast (Northern Ireland)

Belfast began life as as a collection of little forts built to protect a ford across the River Farset, which nowadays runs beneath High Street. Belfast was slow to develop as a city and its history doesn't really start until 1604, when Sir Arthur Chichester was 'planted' in the area by James I. By the 18th century, the cloth trade and ship building industry had expanded tremendously, and the city's population increased ten-fold in the space of a hundred years. Back then it was a city noted for its liberalism, but in the 19th century the sectarian divide became wider and increasingly violent. Although Partition and the creation of Northern Ireland, with Belfast as its capital, inevitably boosted the city's status, the Troubles exacerbated the industrial decline that hit most of the British Isles during the 1980s. This decade was a torrid time for the city with bombing and bloodshed savagely illustrating the widening gulf between its people. A massive programme of regeneration commenced in the 1990s as the peace process gathered momentum. This regeneration was fuelled by the billions of pounds pumped in from Britain, the European Union and the International Fund for Ireland. The hope was that political stability would ensue. It proved an attraction to businesses both new and old; the linen and ship-building industries just two of those reinvigorated. As yet, there's no sign of this bubble bursting, but it is one that is still floating precariously. Today's Belfast has a real sense of liveliness: it is no longer a city under siege.

Getting there

Airport

Belfast International Airport (02890 422 888) is based just north of the city of Aldergrove. The **Airbus** (02890 333 000) runs to **The Europa Bus Station** on Glengall Street in the city centre (Monday to Saturday, 0630 to 2130) every half-hour. On a Sunday this service is reduced to an hourly service (0700 to 2045).

Ferries

Ferries arrive at the **Belfast Sea Cat Terminal** (01345 523 523). Larne ferry terminals are easily reached by bus or train from the city centre (Buses Monday-Friday about 15 per day. Sunday about three per day).

Trains

All trains arrive into Belfast's **Central Station** on East Bridge Street (02890 899 400). Some may also stop at **Botanic Station** on Botanic Avenue, situated in the centre of the university area or **The Great Victoria Station** next to The Europa Hotel.

Getting about

Buses

There are two main stations in Belfast, which serve the east and west of Ireland. Buses travelling to and from the west and the Republic operate from **The Europa Hotel**. Buses to and from Northern Ireland's east coast operate from **Laganside Station**. Services run Monday to Saturday from 0730 to 2030 and Sunday from 0900 to 1930.

Taxis

Belfast's black cabs run set routes to west and north Belfast, picking up and dropping off passengers along the way (about £1 standard charge). Cabs heading to catholic neighbourhoods are marked with a Falls Road, Andersontown or Irish language sign. Those going to Protestant neighbourhoods have a Shankhill sign or a red poppy. Yellow-plated black cabs are official City-Hall-registered vehicles. There are also plenty of ordinary 2-hour metered cabs such as the wheelchair access-friendly **City Cabs** (02890 233 333) and **Jet Taxi** (02890 323 278).

Tourist information

The main tourist information office is in St Anne's Court on 59 North Street (02890 246 609). They can dish out information about Belfast and the surrounding areas and provide free maps, transport schedules and itineraries. They also offer an accommodation service (and advice on where to stay). Beyond these services their facilities are fairly limited.

Bureaux de change

There's an **American Express** office on Royal Avenue (02890 242 341). Additionally, post offices provide bureau de change facilities for a minimal fee. Most banks offer the service also, including Ulster Bank at 47 Donegal Place, **First Trust** at 8 Donegall Square and **Northern Bank** at Donegall Square West.

Luggage storage

Security measures are such that there is no luggage storage facility at airports, railway stations and coach stations. Your place of accommodation may be able to store your luggage for a limited period of time, if your check-out time is significantly prior to your departure time, but always be sure to check that they are able to do this (not all will).

Getting help

Police, hospital and pharmacy

Belfast's main police station is at 65 Knock Road (02890 650 222). **Belfast City Hospital**, 9 Lisburn Road (02890 329 241) and **Royal Victoria Hospital**, 12 Grosvenor Road (02890 240 503) both have accident and emergency facilities. The police hold information on all late-night chemists and out-of-hours medical care.

Getting in touch

Internet

You can find **Revelations Internet Café** at 27 Shaftsbury Square. Revelations is open Monday to Friday from 1000 until 2200, Saturday from 1000 to 2000 and Sunday from 1200 to 2200.

GLBT Helplines

Northern Ireland Rainbow Project serves the whole of Northern Ireland. Phone for help or advice (02890 319 030). There is also **Lesbian Line** (02890 238 668) open Thursday from 1930 to 2200.

Pubs

Kremlin

96 Donegall Street, Belfast BT1 2GW Phone 028 9080 9700
E-mail kremlin_online@hotmail.com Web www.kremlin-bar.com
As Northern Ireland's first gay-owned and -run pub and club complex,

the Kremlin has well and truly established itself as the core of the country's gay social scene. The venue's layout and décor reflects an image of Soviet Russia... somewhat! Opened recently, the Tsar pub bar is open from midday daily and is ideal for those that want to pop in for a quick drink, a chat with friends or just to pop a video on the new DV-jukebox – without having to enter the club itself. On arrival at the club on weekend nights prepare to be amused and shocked (but certainly welcomed) by the stars of Kremlin, namely, The Baroness Titti von Tramp and Revvlon, the club's resident drag queens. Titti, rarely out of the Irish press, brings a touch of glamour to the club with her Bond-girl-meets-Charlie's-Angels persona, whilst Revvlon is more your 'alternative' drag queen. At over seven feet tall (!) and almost as wide (!), no one gets in her way. The club is open seven nights a week, from Tag and Shag and The Weakest Pink on Tuesdays to the flagship Saturday night Revolution. Kremlin has something to suit everyone. Mince! On Fridays the club is transformed for it's weekly Boru Vodka theme nights. Every Friday is different and you could one week find yourself in the Land of Oz, surrounded by wannabe Dorothy's, whereas the week before you could have found yourself surrounded by PVC and rubber with performing angle grinders as backdrop on stage. Another couple of weeks down the line could see Abba Night or the popular Dusk 'til Dawn monthly all-nighter (that sees revellers partying to 0500). Sanctuary on Thursdays sees the hottest acts on the gay cabaret circuit performing live on stage at the club. Students get half-price admission and this night can always be banked on for a massive turnout. The Belfast crowd like to make the most of their weekends and Super Sundays keep the momentum going with a pounding camp attack, courtesy of Revvlon, which goes on until 0200 and there's free admission to boot. The music policy is geared for all tastes with an eclectic mix of resident DJs. There's Regal MC, one of Belfast's most popular DJs, known for his camp-it-up classics and his quirky mix of commercial kitsch! Regal has very much become the anchorman – and rightly so; he plays to maximum capacity with arms-in-the-air sounds. Jamesy is the latest addition to the resident team. His name is well known on the scene as a high-energy spinner, whooping crowds up with a full range of pop, dance and trance club anthems. Current renovations, when finished, will see the club almost double its capacity and Belfast's gay community can look forward to another year full of thumping club nights, exciting theme nights and a few surprises, well into 2001 and beyond. **Open** Monday and Wednesday 1200-0100. Thursday-Sunday 1200-0300 **Price** £3-8

Parliament Bar   2 - 6 Dunbar Street, Belfast Phone 028 9023 4520
E-mail **goodtimes@theparliament.co.uk** Web **www.theparliament.co.uk**
A large Tudor-style traditional gay venue with a welcome late licence most nights of the week. The Parliament is a three-storey building with Club Heat on the uppermost floor (open Friday and Saturday only). The rest of the week offers you all sorts of entertainment from quiz nights and bingo (Monday) to live music (Wednesday) and karaoke (Friday nights and Saturday from 1600). In addition to these diversions there is a disco on one of the remaining floors. The venue also has an excellent

restaurant which serves a wide and varied menu on Monday through to Friday from 1200 to 1500 and on Saturday from 1200 to 1600. **Open** Sunday-Thursday 1200-0100. Friday 1200-0300. Saturday 1200-0400 **Price** £4, Friday; £4, Saturday before 2300, £6 after 2300 and £10 after 0100

Club nights

Forbidden Fruit @ Milk

Tomb Street, Belfast Phone 028 9027 8907
E-mail jill@clubmilk.com Web www.clubmilk.com
On Mondays, Milk plays host to Forbidden Fruit, a unique gay club night which offers a wide variety of cabaret and live acts in association with Playground (Dublin, see separate listing). The music policy on this night is varied; from trashy chart to vocal house. Surprisingly, it works very well. Milk is a well-respected clubbing venue in Belfast and their ultra-strict non-discriminatory door policy ensures a better than average night out. Other nights include Play on Tuesday, which is a mix of vocal house (2100 to 0300; £3). Wednesday is T-Minus, a funky house night with bi-monthly resident Danny Rampling (2100 to 0300; £5-7). Thursday is Milk 54, based on New York's long-gone but not forgotten Studio 54 (2100 to 0300; £6). Friday is Iced, a mix of funky house and US house and garage, usually with top name guest DJs (2100 to 0330; £5-7). Saturday sees Pleasure in the main room – a sexy mix of house and garage – and Pain in the smaller dance room – a mix of r'n'b alternative (2100 to 0330; £10). Sunday is Kama Sutra which finishes the week off with a night of pure hedonistic dancing pleasure, for those who don't need to get up so early in the morning (2100 to 0200; £5). **Open** Monday 2100-0300 **Price** £5

Juice Bar @ The Duke of York

7-11 Commercial Court, Belfast BT1 2NB Phone 028 9024 1062
This is a rarity in Belfast – a women-only disco night held every second Thursday of the month. This popular and well-attended night is held in the upstairs bar of this normally straight, but entirely gay-friendly venue. **Open** Every second Thursday 2130-0100 **Price** £3

The Albert Memorial Clock on Victoria Street provides one of those photo opportunities that just begs to be taken. The historical importance of the clock is that it leans about one and a half metres off the vertical... anyway, the fun bit is, that, if you position yourself some way down the road, grab someone who can point a camera back towards you in front of the clock and you can actually make it look as though you are sitting on Belfast's most famous timepiece!

Slosh @ White's Tavern

White's Tavern, 1-4 Wine Cellar Entry, Belfast BT1 1QN
Phone 028 9024 3080 E-mail info@whitestavern.co.uk
Web www.whitestavern.co.uk
This is a weekly gay night in what is possibly the oldest tavern in Belfast (dating back to 1630). Although this night offers a welcome scene change it doesn't really offer that much in the way of something different. Nothing that you can't find in any of the more established gay venues at least. For a tourist, however, it is essential that you cram in as

many experiences as possible, and so a visit here is a must, even if it is only for the historical relevance. The rest of the week, this gay-friendly venue offers live music on a Thursday through to Saturday (usually Irish folk) that makes an amusing and interesting departure from the bars belting out Kylie and Steps. **Open** Wednesday 2100-0200 **Price** £3

One of the best ways to see the alternative sights of Belfast, including the political wall murals located on the Protestant Shankill Road and the Catholic Falls Road, is to take a special black taxi around Belfast (phone Michael, 028 9064 2264). This is a set tour with a fun and informative commentary, lasting about two hours, and costing about £10 per person for a minimum of two people. Expect to see all of the following and more: Harland and Wolf Shipyard (this is the shipyard where the Titanic was built), Napoleon's face on mountain, Crumlin Jail, Fortified Police Stations and British Army Barracks, Belfast City Hall, The Europa (the most bombed hotel in Europe), The Peace Line, Milltown Cemetery, Crumlin Road Court House, Laganside Area, The Crown Bar, Queens University, The Grand Opera House and Albert Clock.

Swank @ Thompson's Garage

3 Pattersons Place, Belfast BT1 4HW Phone 028 9032 3762

Since opening as Thompsons Garage in 1994, this excellent gay-friendly venue has been at the forefront of city centre clubbing. It's located at the heart of Belfast's city centre. Monday is when the homos come out in force and the night is widely advertised as a full-on in-your-face gay night. Musically, the evening tries to please everyone by playing vocal house, club anthems and a little bit of chart. If the Monday night is not as hard as you would like then try the place out on any of their weekly events. Thompsons can pride itself as one of the few Irish clubs to constantly promote the various genres of underground, cutting-edge dance music. Throughout the years the club has accommodated a wide variety of DJs, from Danny Rampling to Freddy Fresh, Angel Morales to the Scratch Perverts, Steve Lawler to David Holmes. Thompsons is well renowned for its up-for-it clientele, contagious atmosphere, quality tunes and booming sound system. Perhaps the once-a-week Monday gay night is not enough for you and you wish to experience a harder dance club vibe over the weekend: well, this is the place to come to. On Friday they promote Club Code (2100 to 0300; £5-7) which is a hard-hitting house night dedicated to pushing the boundaries of progressive and techno house. Code One pulls in Ireland's finest DJs to guest alongside Steve Boyd in an aural feast of tribal workouts, pounding beats, pulsating basslines, driving rhythms and sweeping breakdowns. Saturday is Congress (2100 to 0300; £10). From twisted disco to sublime gospel garage, Congress provides Belfast with possibly the finest slices of American house music this side of New York. Resident Steve Boyd is joined by top UK and international guests, laying down velvet vocals and funk-fuelled rhythms to the glammed-up faithful. Sunday is Faith (2100 until late; free before 2200 and £5 after). Old skool club classics with nostalgia-fuelled anthems are the order of the day, as a loyal congregation are treated to flashback after flashback. Residents Gleave Dobbin and Davy Cash are joined every fortnight by the cream of local talent and offer a full retrospective of house music to those wishing to extend the weekend. Thompsons is a great club and with gay nights a bit thin on the ground in these parts you could do a lot worse than spend some of your spare clubbing nights at this gay-friendly venue. **Open** Monday 2100-0300 **Price** £4

Cork (Eire)

The beautiful and historic city of Cork is rich in both culture and beauty, yet is most famous for the single block of limestone known as the Blarney Stone, set in the tower of Blarney Castle, in the village of Blarney, some five or so miles north of the city. The stone is Ireland's lucky charm and is reputed to have magical powers. Legend has it that an old woman cast a spell on a king as a reward for saving her life. Under this spell, if he kissed the stone he'd gain great powers of eloquence. Today, people travel from all over the world to County Cork to kiss the stone and gain the 'gift of the gab'.

Getting in touch

You can pick up the Cork Area City Guide (for around IR£2) from the **Tourist Office** (021 270 900) situated at Tourist House, Grand Parade. This office also runs an open-top bus tour (IR£8-10). The office opens Monday to Friday from 0900 to 1800. **Cork Gay Switchboard** (021 271 087) operates twice a week on Wednesday from 1900 to 2100 and Saturday from 1500 to 1700. There is also **Lesbian Line** on Thursday (same phone number) from 2000 to 2200.

Pubs

Bodega   46-49 Cornmarket Street, Cork Phone 021 27287
This is a popular gay-friendly bar and restaurant, particularly accommodating to women. **Open** Monday-Sunday 1200-2300

Loafers   26 Douglas Street, Cork Phone 021 311 612
This is a very friendly place with a seemingly young, student type of crowd. Women meet up in the back bar each Thursday night. **Open** Monday-Saturday 1200-2300. Sunday 1200-2230

Clubs

The Other Place   7- 8 Augustine Street, Cork Phone 021 427 8470
The Other Place is Cork's gay community centre. The Southern Gay Health Project, a gay switchboard, a bookstore, a small café and offices are all housed here. The centre has a large dance floor where the popular Friday and Saturday night discos are held. The first Friday night of the month is given over to women only. **Open** Tuesday-Sunday 1900-2300 (bar). Friday-Saturday 1900-0200 (bar and club) **Price** IR£2

Saunas

Cork Sauna   36 Lower John Street, Cork Phone 021 503 606

This is Cork's only gay sauna, occupying what were previously ware-house premises. It can be somewhat difficult to find – the entrance is in an alleyway that runs up from Christy Ring Bridge. The facilities and furnishings are all in need of refurbishment or repair, however, it is better than nothing and offers a hook-up spot for people who, for one reason or another, may not want to venture out onto the gay scene. Tip: you can purchase lube and condoms from reception if you forget yours. **Open** Monday-Thursday 1200-0100. Friday-Saturday 1200-0400 **Price** IR£10

Accommodation

Amazonia   Coast Road, Fountainstown, Cork Phone 021 483 1115
E-mail **amazonia@indigo.ie**

A women-only guest house with a very relaxed atmosphere in a beautiful, coastal location, twelve miles south-west of Cork City. Free tea and coffee are available all day and breakfast is served until noon. Guests can be collected from the airport or ferry port and camping is also available (phone for further information).

There are many legends associated with St Finbar's Cathedral, on the south side of the city; the most famous of which concerns the golden statue, perched high on one of the cathedral's pires. It is said that when the golden statue falls for the third time it will mark the end of the world. Doomsday watchers note: it has fallen twice already!

Roman House   3 St John's Terrace, Upper John Street, Cork Phone 021 450 3606
E-mail **rhbb@eircom.net** Web **www.interglobal.ie/romanhouse**

A haven in the heart of Cork city, The Roman House provides an ideal base for you to explore the city markets as well as the stunning beauty of West Cork and Kerry. It is also only a five-minute drive from Blarney Castle. All the rooms are large and bright with colour TV and complimentary tea/coffee-making facilities. Breakfast (vegetarian, continental or full grill) is served between 0800 and 1000 (1030 on weekends). **Price** IR£40 **Number of rooms 4**, none en-suite

Dublin (Eire)

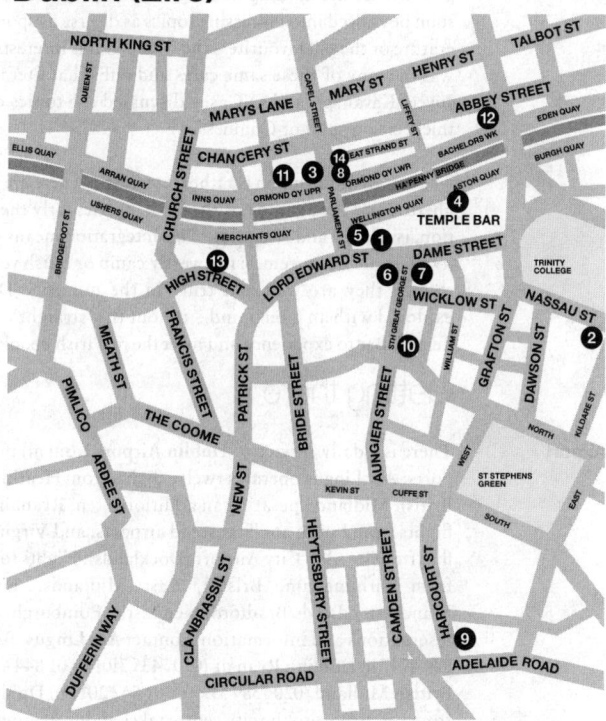

Map key	
1 The Boilerhouse	**8** Gubu
2 Disko @ Pegs (Kildare Hotel)	**9** HAM / Hilton Edwards @ POD
3 The Dock	**10** Hogan's
4 Essential @ Switch Night Club	**11** Out on the Liffey
5 Front Lounge	**12** Pravda
6 The George & The Loft	**13** Stonewallz @ Malloy's Bar
7 The Globe	**14** The Vortex

Dublin is stylish, young and energetic, which seems rather odd considering Ireland as a whole has a reputation for it's relaxed pace and rural quiet. The friendliness of the Irish people, their hospitality and their love of a good time is legendary – and you are able to find it in abundance even amidst the tourist trappings of a big city like this. Dublin sits quite comfortably on both sides of the banks of The Liffey going west to east. The more famous sights and the 'better' establishments reside on the south side whilst the down-to-earth and grittier establishments occupy the north side which has a reputation for being 'the rougher end of town'. Medieval and Georgian architecture provide a stern backdrop to the bustling and lively streets, filled with street entertainers of all kinds. The aroma of freshly brewed coffee mingles with the distinct smell of hops from the nearby Guinness brewery. Street-side cafés and pubs are always buzzing with animated conversation and visitors may soon be enticed into discussing topics as diverse as sport, politics and literature or the old favourite – the weather. It is interesting to note that it was in many of these same cafés and pubs that literary giants such as Joyce, Kavanagh and O'Casey discussed the topics of the day over a thick, creamy pint of Guinness.

The gay scene in Dublin is rather integrated. There are no gay villages or ghettos and the attitude of the Irish, particularly the younger generation, is relaxed and accepting. This integration means that in the majority there are no extremes: no overtly camp or fetish venues. Some exist, though they are well and truly in the minority. Dublin should be explored with an open mind – try out the 'straight' venues away from Temple Bar to experience and meet the real Irish people.

Getting there

Airport

There is a daily service to **Dublin Airport** from all major London airports; **Aer Lingus** operates twelve flights from Heathrow Airport, with **British Midland** operating an additional ten; **Ryanair** operates several flights from Luton and Stanstead airports, and **Virgin Atlantic Cityjet** flies from London City Airport (Docklands). Flights to Dublin also leave from Birmingham, Bristol, East Midlands, Liverpool, Luton, Manchester, Leeds/Bradford, Newcastle, Edinburgh, and Glasgow. For reservations and information, contact **Aer Lingus** (020 8899 4747 or 01 844 4747 in Dublin); Ryanair (020 7435 7101 or 01 844 4411 in Dublin), or British Midland (020 7589 5599 or 01 842 2011 in Dublin). Journey time from the airport to the city centre takes about 30 minutes, but it may be longer in heavy traffic. **Dublin Bus** operates a shuttle service between the airport and the city centre, with departures leaving from outside the arrivals gate. A single fare is around £2.50 and the service runs all day, from 0730 to 2300 at half-hourly intervals, to the main bus station in the city centre next door to Connolly Rail Station. A taxi is a quicker alternative to get from the airport to Dublin's centre. Taxis wait by the arrivals gate and a fare for the 30-minute journey to any of the main city-centre hotels will set you back about £12. It's advisable to check the price before leaving the airport though.

Ferries

All of the ferries on both of the principal routes serving the Irish Republic – Holyhead-Dublin and Fishguard/Pembroke-Rosslare – take cars. Fishguard and Pembroke are relatively easy to reach by road. The car trip to Holyhead, on the other hand, is sometimes difficult, with delays on the A55 North Wales coastal road during the summer not unusual. Two companies sail to Dublin from Holyhead on the Isle of Anglesea: **B & I** and **Stena Sealink**, whose ferries go to Dun Laoghaire, a few miles south of Dublin. Buses into Dublin meet all the ferries from the docks. The total journey time from London is around eleven hours. The cost of your trip can vary substantially, so spend time with a travel agent and compare prices carefully; flying is sometimes cheaper.

Trains

The main train stations in Dublin are **Heuston Station** (01 703 2132), just south of Victoria Quay, and **Connolly Station** (01 836 3333), centrally located on Amiens Street. The former provides train services to the south and west; the latter provides services to the north and north-west. Contact the **Irish Rail Travel Centre**, 35 Lower Abbey Street (01 836 6222) for information.

Getting about

Buses

Dublin Bus (01 842 2011) runs services across the whole city. There are many different termini within the city centre and the main station is **Busaras** at Amiens Street, next to Connolly Station (01 830 2222).

Taxis

There is a rank at the airport and in the city centre, close to the train and bus stations.

Tourist information

The main centre of tourism in the restored former church of St Andrew should be an absolute must for all tourists. During the summer months there is a hefty queue, although there is plenty to keep you occupied whilst waiting for your number to be called out (remember to get your queue ticket from the dispenser on arrival), such as the café, the Irish shop and shed-loads of free tourist literature and maps. There are other main offices at Suffolk Street, Dublin Airport, Dun Laoghaire Ferry Terminal, The Square Tallaght and Baggot Street which are open throughout the year. There are an additional fifty or so offices open throughout the summer months only.

Bureaux de change

Banks will offer you the best rates. **Bank of Ireland** or **AIB** on Lower O' Connell Street are both central. You can also change currency at the post offices or the main **Tourist Office**. The nearest **American Express** office is at 116 Grafton Street (01 677 2874).

Getting help

Police and hospital

For southside emergency medical assistance contact **Meath Hospital**, Heytesbury Street (01 453 6555 or 01 453 6000 or 453 6694). They are open 24 hours. For northside emergency medical treatment contact **Mater Misericordiae Hospital**, Eccles Street (01 830 1122). **The Dublin Dental Hospital**, 20 Lincoln Place (01 679 4311) has emergency facilities and lists of dentists offering emergency care. The main police station, **The Dublin Metropolitan Garda Headquarters**, is located on Harcourt Square, Dublin 2 (01 475 5555).

Getting in touch

Internet

A few to choose from: **Cyberia**, Temple Lane South (open Monday to Saturday from 1000 to 2300 and Sunday from 1200 to 2000); **Global Internet Café**, 8 Lower O' Connell Street (open Monday to Saturday from 1000 to 2300 and Sunday from 1200 to 2200); **Planet Cyber Café**, 23 South Great Georges Street (open Sunday to Wednesday from 1000 to

2200 and Thursday to Saturday from 1000 to 0000). You can expect to pay about IR£2 for 30 minutes of internet access.

GLBT Helplines **Dublin Switchboard** (01 872 1055) is open Sunday to Friday from 2000 to 2200 and Saturday from 1530 to 1800. **Dublin Lesbian Line** (01 872 9911) operates every Thursday from 1900 to 2100. National TV/TS Line (01 671 0939) also operates on Thursdays from 1900-2200. **LOT** (Lesbians Organising Together) is a drop-in centre at 5 Capel Street (01 872 7770). **Outhouse**, 6 South William Street (01 670 6377) is a gay community centre and café. **Dublin AIDS Alliance** (01 873 3799), **AIDS Helpline** (01 872 4277) and the **AIDS Resource Centre**, 14 Haddington Road (01 660 2149) all offer help, support and advice to those suffering or affected by AIDS.

Pubs

Baileys Duke Street, Dublin 2 Fax 01 670 9811
A re-modernised pub moving away from the traditional Irish pub image to a more continental-style café-bar. Out went the chintz and comfortable furnishings and in came the hi-tech designer-styled timber and chrome. Not a gay bar as such, but pleasantly mixed and an ideal location to chill out in pleasant company. **Open** Monday-Saturday 1130-2330. Sunday 1600-2300

Front Lounge 34 Parliament Street, Temple Bar, Dublin 2 Phone 01 670 4112
A gay and straight venue in the Temple Bar area of Dublin which means that you will be paying 'top dollar' for your drinks and you'll struggle for elbow room on one of those plush, comfy sofas. This, however, is one top-class joint and there's ample opportunity to pose with the best of them – so you really don't mind the price and squeeze. Sundays tend to be predominantly gay and Tuesdays see cabaret in the form of an 'open stage' where the well-oiled punters perform their party pieces. **Open** Monday-Saturday 1130-2330. Sunday 1600-2330

Renowned for their creativity, the everyday people of Dublin have crafted nicknames for many of the city's famous commemorative statues and sculptures. The millennium-commissioned sculpture of Anna Liffey in O'Connell Street is locally known as 'The Floozy in the Jacuzzi'; the statue of Molly Malone at the bottom of Grafton Street is known as the 'The Tart with the Cart'; the women at the Ha'Penny Bridge are 'The Hags with the Bags' and poor James Joyce is more commonly referred to as 'The Dick with the Stick'.

The George and The Loft 89 South George's Street, Dublin 2 Phone 01 478 2983
The George and The Loft is a combined pub and club space and following its recent expansion it now boasts a capacity for around 800-plus homos. This is a well-established venue and, despite the increased competition, it still manages to retain a loyal following. The George Bar is overly camp in décor – some might say tacky, what with the scarlet wallpaper and gilded portraits that adorn the walls. The club upstairs is a huge dance area, which caters for a mostly male crowd with a musical

policy of chart disco through the week which gets progressively harder over the weekend. Each Sunday in the bar they host Gay Bingo, an event that has become something of a Sunday tradition on the Dublin circuit. On Wednesday they host Space 'N' Vada, a full-on, in-your-face house and trance club night. **Open** Monday-Tuesday 1230-2330. Wednesday-Sunday 1230-0230 **Price** IR£5-8, Wednesday-Saturday after 2200

The Globe   11 South Great George's Street, Dublin 2 Phone 01 671 1220
The Globe is well known for being a mixed gay-friendly and straight bar, although being so close to Hogan's the gay quota is significantly less than the straights (boo!). By day it is a smart European-styled café-bar serving lunches, snacks and, of course, booze. By night, from 2330 to 0230, the Ri Ra Club opens up and the bar becomes part of the club-bing venue. Monday tends to be a busy night here with more gays coming in for the retro disco. At other times the musical policy has more of a harder dance vibe. **Open** Monday-Saturday 1200-0230. Sunday 1400-0230 (bar and club) **Price** IR£5-8 (club)

Gubu   7-8 Capel Street, Dublin 1 Phone 01 874 0483
This venue started life as a proposed gay venue, but over time it has become decidedly mixed. Even so, there are plenty of gay boys and girls popping in for a change from the usual scene. It is a stylish two-floored venue with the downstairs more of a relaxed chill-out and chatting area with plenty of comfortable seating. Upstairs, however, is a loud and atmospheric dance bar with stage. **Open** Monday-Wednesday 1600-2330. Thursday-Saturday 1600-2430. Sunday 1300-2330

Hogan's   35 South Great George's Street, Dublin 2 Phone 01 677 5904
A continentally styled bar and club area which attracts, as Dana herself would say, 'all kinds of everything' – men, women, gay and straight. To be fair though, it is the younger end of the gay and straight pre-clubbing market that tends to come here. From Sunday through to Wednesday the bar is used as a relaxed chilled-out drinking space. From Thursday onwards the downstairs 'club' opens up, with more of a European-styled mix of music than you are probably used to – different, but still immensely popular. The good thing about this place is that there are never any admission charges, despite the late openings, which means you can spend more of your money on getting rat-arsed. **Open** Monday-Wednesday 1230-0000. Thursday-Saturday 1230-0230. Sunday 1200-2300

Out on the   27 Ormond Quay Upper, Dublin 1 Phone 01 872 2480
Liffey   Out on the Liffey is the bar part of this combined guest-house, sauna and bar complex. Situated on Dublin's north side and facing the Liffey (obviously), it is one of only a handful of 100 per cent gay venues in this fair city. No trainers or sports shoes allowed! **Open** Sunday-Tuesday 1030-2330. Wednesday-Saturday 1200-2430

Pravda   Lower Ormond Quay and Liffey Street, Dublin 1 Phone 01 874 0076
This trendy Russian-themed gay-friendly bar is set on three levels, situated just across the Ha'penny Bridge. Disco nights from Wednesday to

Saturday play all sorts of musical styles from disco to house and everything in between. There's free entry for late-night openings. **Open** Sunday-Wednesday 1200-2330. Thursday 1200-2430. Friday-Saturday 1200-0230

Club nights

Baby 2K
@ Club Mono

Wexford Street, Dublin 2 Phone 01 475 8555

Formerly known as The Mean Fiddler. The thing that stands out in this place is the sheer size of the dance floor – and the bad-attitude doormen (may have changed, but doubt it). This is a very popular club night in an excellent clubbing venue, which incidentally is home to (Liverpool's) Cream when they 'do' Dublin. They regularly have themed nights, including Ibiza-style foam parties and these tend to draw in the predominantly young gay crowds. The music is alright – not too camp or charty, but certainly not cutting-edge – just alright! This 700-odd capacity club is situated above a plush, velvety lounge bar that is open before the club, so it may be wise to come here first as a pre-club meeting space where you can gauge the quality of the talent before parting with your 'hard-earned'. **Open** Monday 2300-0300 **Price** IR£6

Little Ship Street was originally known as Pole or Poole Street, because of the nearby pool behind the castle. This pool was the 'dubh linn', from which the city derives its name. Wellington Quay was the last of the city quays to be constructed. It was built around 1812 and was named after Arthur Wellesley, later, the Duke of Wellington.

Disko @ Pegs

Earl of Kildare Hotel, Kildare Street, Dublin 2 Phone 01 202 716352

A mixed gay and straight disco night held in the basement club (Pegs) of The Earl of Kildare Hotel. This is a fine club night if you like bopping around to disco music; the admission is low and there are often cheap drinks to be found. It would not suit those who like their music slightly harder and the club facilities are rather basic. That said, you do get what you pay for – a night of disco at Pegs! The Tuesday night was formerly known as Soapdish and Sunday's session used to go by the name of Prince. Apart from the names, the nights were exactly the same, so they combined them and they both now go under the Disko name. **Open** Tuesday, Thursday and Sunday 2300-0230 **Price** IR£5-6

Essential @
Switch Night
Club

Eustace Street, Temple Bar, Dublin 2 Phone 01 668 2504

Spread over two floors, Switch has over time become one of the better clubbing venues in Dublin. Monday's Essential is a mixed gay and straight affair which attracts a young, lively crowd of passionate clubbers who are serious about their music and know how to party in style. One of the main ingredients of this fabulous club night is the high calibre of the DJs – well-known names from England as well as Ireland. The main floor plays host to the best, funky, uplifting, dance-based club sounds, whilst upstairs in the Lipstick Lounge things get a little camp and that keeps the disco bunnies happy and contented. **Open** Monday 2230-0300 **Price** IR£4

HAM (Homo Action Movies) @ POD

Old Harcourt Street Station, Harcourt Street, Dublin 2 Phone 01 478 0225
HAM is located in a building that's as off-beat as it is historic (it used to be an old railway station) and without a single hint of conventionality within its portals. POD (Place of Dance) is an excellent clubbing venue with a serious degree of style and is equipped with almost 5,000 square feet of floor space and a 20k Turbo Sound System (I'm no anorak but that sounds to me like one big mutha of a system!). This Friday club night offers the dance-crazed gay folk a fabulous night of deep house and funky techno from two top name DJs: Shay Hannon and Hugh Scully. POD is divided into two rooms – the first main floor as described above and the second, The Chocolate Bar (check out the toilets) is a more chilled-out affair. Admission is granted to gay-friendly straights but make no mistake – this is a hard gay dance night and everyone who enters the doors know it as such. The punters are a young 'shirts off at any opportunity' crowd out for a good time, and that is exactly what they get. Each fortnight pre-HAM event Gristle (crap name!) takes place at 2100 with cabaret, starring the legendary Miss Panti, Shirley Temple Bar and Bon Veda (IR£5 before 2300). You'll need to dress accordingly to get in. Once in though you can (and probably will) strip your top off.
Open Friday 2300-0300 **Price** IR£8

Hilton Edwards @ Spy

Powerscourt, South William Street, Dublin 2
The ultra-trendy Spy club is located behind the Powerscourt Shopping Centre and occupies what was once a former gay club: Hooray Henry's. During the week they cater for a straight crowd but Sunday is just for us gays with a few friendly straights admitted for good measure. The age range seems to be over-21s (the promoters aim this night at the over 25s) and the music policy is a confusing mix of current chart and house. The night is supposed to be a laid-back, lounge-style kind of evening: it may not suit everyone's tastes. The low admission, however, and the late opening hours could round off your Sunday evening nicely. **Open** Sunday 2000-0300 **Price** IR£3-5

Q & A @ Eamonn Doran's Crown Alley

Crown Alley, Temple Bar, Dublin 2
Q & A stands for Queer and Alternative and that is exactly what this club night is all about. It has been likened to Popstarz (London) with its heavy indie influence on the music policy. Like Popstarz you will get the same wacky punters of indie boys and grungey girls out for a good piss-up (although the drinks prices are not as cheap as at Popstarz) and the opportunity to dance to The Smiths, Blur and Nirvana. There's a bit of chart thrown in for good measure too, so nearly all are satisfied. The venue is the basement club of Eamonn Doran's, which is pleasantly raw with exposed brickwork and supporting archways. Further down into a sub-basement there is the cloakroom (£1 per item) and chill-out space.
Open Every third Tuesday of the month 2300-0300 **Price** IR£6

Stonewallz @ Molloy's Bar

13 High Street, Christchurch, Dublin 8 Phone 01 677 3207
E-mail Stonewallz@clubi.ie Web www.clubi.ie/stonewallz/
A weekly women-only club night in the very gay-friendly Molloys Bar. There is also a mixed gay and lesbian night held here every Tuesday.

Open Saturday 2100-0200 **Price** IR£3-5

Saunas

The Boilerhouse   12 Crane Lane, Temple Bar, Dublin 2 Phone 01 677 3130
E-mail **enquiries@the-boilerhouse.com** Web **www.the-boilerhouse.com**
Open since March 1997 and situated in the heart of Temple Bar, The
Boilerhouse offers the best in modern equipment in luxurious surroundings. It is conveniently close to the bars and clubs. The Boilerhouse is
cited as one of Dublin's biggest saunas (along with The Vortex) and it
would be hard to disagree as the facilities are spread out well over several levels of cruisy floorspace. **Open** Monday-Thursday 1300-0500.
Friday-Sunday open 24 hours **Price** IR£10

The Dock   21 Upper Ormond Quay, Dublin 7 Phone 01 872 4172
The Dock is a small sauna located along the quays. It's part of the Inn
on the Liffey complex and of all Dublin's saunas this one is the smallest,
though many believe this is all part of its charm and it certainly serves
its purpose. There's a reduced admission price of IR£7 if you can get in
before 1900. This rises to IR£9 after. Under-25s can gain admission for
IR£5 at all times (you will require a proof of identity). Facilities include
sauna, steam room, TV lounge and rest rooms. **Open** Monday-
Thursday 1300-0500. Friday-Sunday open 24 hours (finishing Moday
morning 0500) **Price** IR£7-9

The Vortex   1 Great Strand Street, (off Capel Street Bridge), Dublin 1
Phone 01 878 0898
The Vortex is one of Dublin's newest gay and bisexual saunas for men. It
offers five floors of hedonistic entertainment with sauna, steam room,
40 individual rest rooms, fantasy dungeon, mirror room, maze and
video rooms. The Vortex is a great place to meet all sorts of men and a
great place to hang out, especially over the weekends when they provide
regular theme nights. Twice a month, on the first and third Saturdays,
they promote Club Trash (2300 to 0900), Irelands only fetish party
night, where anything goes, from leather and rubber to combats and
jocks. The Vortex is located three minutes from O'Connell Bridge, just
off Capel Street, on Great Strand Street. To get there from O'Connell
Bridge, just walk towards the Ha'penny Bridge, turn right up Capel
Street and then take the first right. **Open** Monday-Thursday 1300-0500.
Friday-Sunday 24 hours (finishing Monday morning at 0500). **Price** IR£10

Accommodation

Fairfield Lodge   Monkstown Avenue, Monkstown, Dublin
Phone 01 280 3912 Fax 01 280 3912 E-mail **jsb@indigo.ie**
Web **http://indigo.ie/~jsb/webpage/studio.htm**
Fairfield Lodge is a self-contained luxury studio apartment attached to
the proprietor's 18th-century home, situated approximately three and a
half miles from the city centre in Monkstown, on the south side. The
apartment is furnished to the highest standard, has a king-size bed, TV,

trouser press, phone, radio-alarm, a fully-equipped kitchen and shower room. If you are more into city life and clubbing 'til all hours then this place may be a little far out, considering that the taxi service in Dublin may not be that reliable. **Price** IR£60 / IR£250 per week

Frankie's Guesthouse

8 Camden Place, (off Camden Street), Dublin 2 Phone 01 478 3087 Fax 01 475 2182 E-mail frankiesdublin@hotmail.com Web **www.frankiesguesthouse.com**

Established in 1989, Frankie's offers accommodation all year round exclusively for lesbians and gays. The property itself is a charming Georgian mews-style building, is over one hundred and fifty years old and is situated between Camden Street and Harcourt Street. All of their rooms are tastefully decorated and have a colour TV with Cablelink, tea/coffee-making facilities and full central heating. En-suite rooms are also available. A full Irish breakfast is served in the morning to start your day. **Price** IR£60 **Number of rooms** 12, 5 en-suite

Horse and Carriage Hotel

15 Aungier Street, Dublin 2 Phone 01 478 3537 Fax 01 478 4010 E-mail liamtony@indigo.ie or liamledwidge@eircom.net Web **http://aoife.indigo.ie/~liamtony/h&c.html**

The Horse and Carriage is situated in Aungier Street, two minutes away from South Great Georges Street and minutes away from Dublin's famous Grafton Street and St Stephens Green. These two opulent landmarks in Dublin are where you can shop, eat or drink in many of the nation's most famous pubs, restaurants and cafeterias. Alternatively, there is the beautiful St Stephens Green where you can stroll at your leisure or just relax and watch the day go by. The Carriage rooms are very large and spacious with queen-size beds. Carriage room number nine has one large double bed and one single bed. All Carriage rooms are en-suite and all other rooms have access to bathrooms outside their rooms on each floor. Room rates include continental breakfast served between 0900 and 1000. **Price** IR£55 **Number of rooms** 5, triple rooms are en-suite

A stay in Ireland would not be complete without a visit to the Guinness Storehouse, along St James Gate, where you can witness the industry and history behind Ireland's most famous tipple. After a tour of the brewery and museum you're invited to ascend to the Gravity Bar, at the top of the building, where you can imbibe both your complimentary pint of the black stuff and perhaps the most breathtaking panoramic views of Dublin's skyline available.

Inn on the Liffey 21 Ormond Quay Upper, Dublin 1 Phone 01 677 0828 Fax 01 872 4165

Inn On The Liffey guest-house is Dublin's most central gay guest-house and boasts more facilities than any other gay guest-house in the city. All but two of their guestrooms are en-suite and most have spectacular views of the Liffey and the Dublin skyline. Situated in the heart of the city and about seven minutes' walk to the majority of Dublin's gay venues, the guest-house is ideally located for the visitor who wishes to experience the life, the sounds and the 'craic' of gay Dublin first-hand.

Male customers of the guest-house have free admission to their sauna (The Dock – see separate listing). **Price** IR£75

Cruising grounds

Phoenix Park   This is a huge park that incorporates Dublin Zoo. It is also one of the most popular cruising areas in Dublin with the main gay location in the park moving from time to time. This switch in meeting places will require you to ask the locals as to where the current hook-up spot is.

Retail

Basic Instincts   56 South William Street, Dublin 2 Phone 01 671 2223
E-mail info@basic-instincts.com Web www.basic-instincts.com
Basic Instincts is Ireland's premier supplier of leatherwear, rubberwear, lingerie and footwear for men and women. They stock a huge range of adult toys, videos, magazines and an exclusive selection of fantasy lingerie for a wide range of discerning tastes. They are also stockists of a wide selection of 100 per cent legal herbal highs and hallucinogenics.
Open Monday-Saturday 1030-2030. Sunday 1200-1800

Books Upstairs   36 College Green, Dublin 2
A good selection of gay and lesbian books and magazines can be found on the second floor of this bookshop. They also carry Gay Community News and have a well-stocked message board of gay-related issues.
Open Monday-Saturday 1000-1900. Sunday 1300-1800

Galway (Eire)

The historic and lively city of Galway – thought to be Europe's fasting growing metropolis – lies south of Lough Corrib. It dates back to the Middle Ages, and although the old city walls have all but disappeared, the famous medieval 'Spanish Arch' remains. Galway has a reputation for being Ireland's cultural capital and lovers of the arts can enjoy fringe theatre, live comedy and several annual festivals, including the Galway Arts Festival, and the Film Fleadh. The city has two universities, and this together with the steady stream of backpackers, tourists and travellers, combines to make this small Irish city a haven for the young and adventurous. The gay scene – it must be said – is small, but relaxed and friendly. Many of the straight bars, particularly the studenty ones, are mixed.

Getting in touch

The main **Tourist Information Office** (091 563 081) is situated at Victoria Place, near to the train station and is open from 0830 to 1945. (These hours are reduced between October and April.) **Galway Gay Switchboard** (091 566 134) offers general gay-specific information or confidential advice on all gay matters. It is open Tuesday to Thursday from 2000 to 2200. **Galway Lesbian Line** (091 564 611) is the very busy sister helpline that operates once a week from 2000 to 2200 on a Wednesday. You should persist if you find the line busy – you will eventually get through.

Pubs

Stranos

William Street West (off Dominque St), Galway
Stranos is a three-storey venue that has a very trendy, continental café-bar feel to it. The main bar is on the ground floor. Upstairs on the first floor there is a comfortable chill-out lounge with huge sofas that never seem to be available, no matter what time you get in. OK, I may be stretching it a little bit there but once you get on to these sofas you won't feel like moving! The top floor houses the pool room (two tables) and offers opportunity for a quiet chat or private argument. The venue is now female-owned so, naturally, there will be a large female presence but all in all, being Galway, and Ireland, the vibe throughout the place is friendly and welcoming. **Open** Monday-Saturday 1200-2330 Sunday 1200-2230

Lynching originated with Galwayman Colonel Charles Lynch, who, during the American War of Independence (1775-1783), hanged without trial any British redcoats unfortunate enough to fall into his hands. Galway is also the birthplace of the grandmother of the famous Cuban revolutionary, Che Guevara.

Zulu's

Raven's Terrace, (off Dominic Street), Galway Phone **091 581 204**
Zulu's caters for a wide-ranging male and (a large) lesbian crowd of all ages. It is a friendly traditional bar with a vague African theme. Its small (150 in capacity) and dark and it can get rather smokey. Music is provided courtesy of a jukebox that is constantly set at 'play'. Meet up here prior to Studio 52 @ Liquid. **Open** Monday-Wednesday 1200-2330. Thursday-Saturday 1200-2430. Sunday 1400-2300

Club nights

**Studio 52
@ Liquid**

152 Upper Salthill, Galway Phone **091 527 155**
This is a popular gay club night that comes around three times a week at this infamous (normally straight) dance club. It may be referred to as either Studio 52 @ Liquid or The Attic @ Liquid: both names are correct as these gay club nights are held right up on the top floor of the venue (separate entrance). The music policy on these nights tends to be rather safe with chart and disco ruling the roost. Depending on the DJ though, you may be treated to some house and trance. One word of warning: admission is for over-21s only. If you do look under this age (like me [oh, how this copy-editor laughed]) then you'd be well advised to take along some proof of identity (or borrow someone else's!). Meanwhile, downstairs, although straight, is very gay-friendly and if you like your music then you will not be disappointed. **Open** Friday-Sunday 2200-0230 **Price** IR£6-10

Accommodation

Side by Side   96 Portacarron, Knocknacarra, Salthill, Galway
Phone 087 274 2202 E-mail **sidebysidewobandb@eircom.net**
Side by Side is a women-only guest-house situated in the west of Galway.
Price IR£40 **Number of rooms** 6, 4 en-suite